The Substance of Language
Volume III
Phonology-Syntax Analogies

The Substance of Language
John M. Anderson

These three self-contained books collectively overhaul linguistic theory from phonology to semantics and syntax to pragmatics. At the same time they revive and renew traditional insights into how the form/function relationship works in language. Each volume explores the consequences for the investigation of language of a conviction that all aspects of linguistic structure are grounded in the non-linguistic mental faculties on which language imposes its own structure. The first and third look at how syntax and phonology are fed by a lexical component that includes morphology and which unites representations in the two planes. The second examines the way morphology is embedded in the lexicon as part of the expression of the lexicon-internal relationships of words to segments.

Volume I
The Domain of Syntax

Volume II
Morphology, Paradigms, and Periphrases

Volume III
Phonology-Syntax Analogies

Phonology-Syntax Analogies

JOHN M. ANDERSON

OXFORD
UNIVERSITY PRESS

OXFORD
UNIVERSITY PRESS

Great Clarendon Street, Oxford OX2 6DP
Oxford University Press is a department of the University of Oxford.
It furthers the University's objective of excellence in research, scholarship,
and education by publishing worldwide in

Oxford New York

Auckland Cape Town Dar es Salaam Hong Kong Karachi
Kuala Lumpur Madrid Melbourne Mexico City Nairobi
New Delhi Shanghai Taipei Toronto

With offices in

Argentina Austria Brazil Chile Czech Republic France Greece
Guatemala Hungary Italy Japan Poland Portugal Singapore
South Korea Switzerland Thailand Turkey Ukraine Vietnam

Oxford is a registered trade mark of Oxford University Press
in the UK and in certain other countries

Published in the United States
by Oxford University Press Inc., New York

© John M. Anderson 2011

The moral rights of the author have been asserted
Database right Oxford University Press (maker)

First published 2011

All rights reserved. No part of this publication may be reproduced,
stored in a retrieval system, or transmitted, in any form or by any means,
without the prior permission in writing of Oxford University Press,
or as expressly permitted by law, or under terms agreed with the appropriate
reprographics rights organization. Enquiries concerning reproduction
outside the scope of the above should be sent to the Rights Department,
Oxford University Press, at the address above

You must not circulate this book in any other binding or cover
and you must impose the same condition on any acquirer

British Library Cataloguing in Publication Data
Data available

Library of Congress Cataloging in Publication Data
Data available

Typeset by SPI Publisher Services, Pondicherry, India
Printed in Great Britain
on acid-free paper by
MPG Books Group, Bodmin and King's Lynn

ISBN 978–0–19–960833–1

1 3 5 7 9 10 8 6 4 2

Contents

Preface ix
Conventions xi

Prologue 1

Part I Introduction

1. Some implications of structural analogy 19
   1.1 Introduction 19
   1.2 Structural analogy 20
   1.3 Structural analogy and 'universal grammar' 23
       1.3.1 Neglect of analogy 24
       1.3.2 Anti-analogy 31
       1.3.3 Anti-anti-analogy 34
   1.4 Levels, planes, and analogy 36
   1.5 The X-bar fallacy and the limits of analogy 42
   1.6 Conclusion 49
   1.7 Prospect: Head-based analogies 52

Part II Analogies

2. Phonology and dependency 71
   2.1 Contrastivity and neutralization 73
   2.2 The limits of linearity, I: Sonority, markedness, and beyond 79
   2.3 The limits of linearity, II: Transitivity and adjunction 83
       2.3.1 The limitations of sonority 85
       2.3.2 Complements, adjuncts, and 'appendices' 88
       2.3.3 Onsets: Status and structure 93
   2.4 Transitivity, weight, and aperture 104
       2.4.1 Transitivity and weight in English 104
       2.4.2 Transitivity and aperture in Midi French 107
       2.4.3 Measuring sonority 111
   2.5 Dependency and timing 116
       2.5.1 Dependency and secondary phonological features 117
       2.5.2 Non-dependency and Winnebago 'fast sequences' 122

2.5.3 Timing and syntax	131
2.5.4 Transitivity and ambidependency	133
2.6 Conclusion	137
3. The structure of the basic unit	141
3.1 Sonority and 'nouniness'	142
3.2 The complexity of syntactic categorization	152
3.3 Markedness and natural classes	156
3.4 Conclusion	161
4. Syntax and non-linearity	165
4.1 Introduction	165
4.2 Extrasegmentals, I: Harmony, underspecification, and opacity	166
4.2.1 Vowel harmony in Finnish	166
4.2.2 Opacity in Turkish vowel harmony	173
4.2.3 Sequence of tense as harmony	178
4.3 Extrasegmentals, II: Monosegmental realization	192
4.3.1 Extrasegmental [h] and existential *there* in English	193
4.3.2 Negative placement and stød	199
4.4 Extrasegmentals, III: Umlaut and agreement	203
4.4.1 *I*-umlaut in Old English	204
4.4.2 Agreement, in various shapes and languages	210
4.5 Underspecification and polysystemicity	218
4.5.1 Underspecification and aspect in Greek and English	219
4.5.2 Polysystemicity, aspect, and vowel systems	222
4.5.3 Coda on contrast	227
4.6 Grammaticalization	228
4.6.1 Old English umlauted vowels	229
4.6.2 Grammatical relations and concord	231
4.6.3 Morphological grammaticalization	234
4.7 Conclusion	235

Part III Why Syntax is Different

5. Categorization	241
5.1 Functional categories	244
5.1.1 The need for functors	246
5.1.2 The role of functional categories	255
5.1.3 Conclusion	262

5.2	Excursus on specifiers and intensification	263
5.3	Reduced transitivity in phonology, and minimal syllables: Kabardian	268
5.4	Reduction in lexical categories in syntax	274
5.5	Conclusion	276
6.	Structure	281
	6.1 Lexical derivation	281
	6.1.1 Affixation, mutation, and conversion	282
	6.1.2 Compounding	290
	6.2 Recursion	294
	6.2.1 Direct recursion, or why phonology is different	294
	6.2.2 Indirect recursion	306
	6.2.3 Excursus on complementizers	312
	6.2.4 Conclusion	318
	6.3 Ambidependency, projectivity, and ectopicity	319
	6.3.1 Raising and subjects	320
	6.3.2 Free absolutives and thematic structure	328
	6.3.3 Conclusion	340
7.	Analogy, dis-analogy, and secondary categories	343
	7.1 The complexity of secondary features in syntax	343
	7.2 Minimalizing the alphabet of phonology	354
	7.3 Conclusion: Configuration vs. alphabet proliferation	362
Conclusion		365
General Epilogue		371
References		379
Index of Authors Cited		397
Subject Index		401

Preface

This is one in a series of books that attempts to pull together various different strands in my research over the last few years, much of it with even earlier roots. The division into three distinct volumes might immediately seem to call into question the success of the overall 'pulling together'. This division reflects three different foci within the trilogy as a whole, foci which each demand a particular kind of detailed analyses. But the three essays are grouped together as a series precisely because of the complementary lights they shed on a central idea, that of the substantiveness of language and of its modularity. The latter involves the motivation of components of the grammar, their relative autonomy, the analogies among them, their interaction.

As a general conclusion I give in this third study my own estimate of the success in the 'pulling together' alluded to initially. Meanwhile, the motivations for the structuring of the series and for the present book are elaborated in a little more detail in the Prologue that follows the preface. This prologue is repeated in each of these books, with adaptations suited to the particular content of each volume. But before that it is a pleasure to complete this preface with some important and grateful acknowledgements that must be observed.

The formation of (parts or all of) what follows here and in the other parts of the trilogy has benefited from comments, in speech or writing, by Roger Böhm, Phil Carr, Jacques Durand, and Graeme Trousdale. Special thanks, as ever, to Fran Colman, for the benefits derived from many discussions of much of what is presented here, and from her reading of drafts of the book, as well as, more generally, for the inspiration of her own scholarship.

I am particularly grateful to Phil Carr for providing the stimulus for this third study (and not just via the curries), as well as for forcing me, by his comments on Anderson (2006a) and by his paper in the same *Lingua* volume (Carr 2006), to try to clarify my ideas about the topics discussed here, and also in the first study. It's good to have people around who often see a lot more clearly than I do the (undesirable as well as desirable) implications of the ideas that I entertain. Helpful too to the evolution of the ideas that I discuss in the third study, which stretches back to the work reported on in Anderson (1992), was the opportunity to present one aspect of them at the conference 'Des représentations aux contraintes' at the University of Toulouse-le Mirail (July 2003); a more extended version of that presentation appears in *Studia Linguistica* as Anderson (2004a), which derived further benefit from associated anonymous reviewing. None of the preceding commentators and discussants is at all responsible—at least with respect to persisting inadequacies in what follows. Finally, again my heartfelt thanks go to John Davey for all his help. The production of all three of these volumes was in the expert hands of Jenny Lunsford, Elmandi du Toit, Jess Smith, and Lesley Rhodes.

John M. Anderson
Methoni Messinias
Greece

Conventions

Footnote and example numbers run through each study in the trilogy to which this volume belongs, and begin anew for each study. Sections of course run through each chapter. In each study, 'fn. 3' etc. refer to footnotes to that study, and '(17b)' etc. to examples in that volume. In references to sections the number of the section is preceded by the chapter number, as '§2.1'. Reference to chapters, sections, and examples in other volumes are accompanied by I, II, or III, to indicate which other volume is intended.

'[ ]' enclose phonological transcriptions, unless their contrastivity is significant for the discussion at that point, in which case '/ /' are used. '( )' enclose units, sequential or not; '< >' enclose optional elements; '{ }' enclose the features of categorial representations; and '{ }' within '{ }', i.e. '{ { }}', enclose secondary rather than primary categories.

The first significant occurrence or reintroduction of important terms in each volume is emboldened, as are the (simplex) features when a feature and not the category is under discussion—as in 'C is the dominant feature in the category {C;V}'. Word forms cited in the text are italicized. The practice recommended by the Leipzig glossing rules is followed where appropriate. The rules are available at: <http://www.eva.mpg.de/lingua/files/morpheme.html>. Further such conventions are explained in the text.

Prologue

This volume is the third of three largely independent studies which collectively explore the consequences of a particular attitude to the investigation of language. This attitude is based on a conviction that in order to understand linguistic phenomena it is necessary to recognize that all aspects of linguistic structure are grounded in non-linguistic mental 'substance'. I refer to this as 'substance', even though non-linguistic mental domains are, like language, structured. This is because, from one point of view, language treats them as a substance on which it imposes its own structure; it represents them in a particular way; it grammaticalizes them. By 'grammaticalize' I simply mean 'give a specifically linguistic structure to'. Thus, syntactic categories such as noun and verb impose a certain structure on the cognitive phenomena they represent, and phonological categories such as consonant and vowel structure the perception of sound. And these categories interact to form the complex representations we call syntax and prosody.

However, as grounded representations, the form of syntactic categories and structures reflects the non-linguistic domain they represent: they preserve some extralinguistic structure. Language does not grammaticalize simple 'substance'. So that the relative distribution of nouns and verbs and other categories—the syntactic structures that the categories project—reflect aspects of the substance that each category grammaticalizes. Thus nouns, grammaticalizing what are perceived as entities, are less 'relational' than verbs, which grammaticalize 'events'.

Given this it would be more appropriate to refer to these categories by a term parallel to 'phonological categories', such as, say, 'semeiological categories': just as the former grammaticalize perception of sounds, so syntactic, or semeiological, categories grammaticalize our conceptualizations and the different perceptions they are based on. However, well aware of the rebarbative effect of insistent neologism (given the testimony of, for instance, presentations of 'glossematics'), I persist in these volumes with the traditional terminology. There are, no doubt, enough terminological innovations elsewhere in this trilogy.

These three volumes explore to what extent such an assumption of groundedness can be said to be relevant and indeed necessary to the characterization of different linguistic domains. It is not just the basic categories that are assumed to be grounded. Syntactic and phonological structure also involve the grammaticalization of extralinguistic dimensions. Syntax involves hierarchized groupings of elements (constituency) and groups are headed (dependency); and these constituents and dependencies respectively express conceptual groupings and cognitive salience. Syntax also involves linearization, which is a grammaticalization of our perception of time as well as reflecting more abstract precedences such as discourse relations, to do for instance with what is taken to be given and new. The same grammaticalizations of cognitive adjacency and salience and of perception of time also characterize the prosodic representations of phonology.

These different grammaticalizations of extralinguistic mental domains characterize what I shall refer to as different modules in the overall representation of language. The use of this term acknowledges that modularity in language is a familiar notion. But I associate it here with a particular substantive view of what modularity involves: a module is defined by its introduction into linguistic representations of grammaticalization of a particular mental substance. And one can recognize modules within the major modules of phonology and syntax—submodules, each grammaticalizing a specific non-linguistic mental dimension.

At this point it may be useful to introduce some simple definitions of basic terms deployed in these volumes, some of which have already been invoked. Let us say that:

Linguistic form is a linguistic structuring particular to a language, and **a language** is a mental artefact in which the following definitions apply:

To represent is to give to elements of some mental dimension a linguistic form that preserves essential properties of what is represented; such a linguistic form is said to be **grounded** in the substance; the mental dimension is said to be **grammaticalized** as the form.

A module is a set of representations grounded in the same mental dimension; modules can be ranked according to their placement on a scale of dimensions going from conceptualization to perception (of sound).

To re-represent is to add to a representation a new representation closer to perception or conceptualization; a re-representation closer to perception is said to **express** the representation it re-represents, and one closer to conceptualization is said to **interpret** this representation.

Exponence is re-representation (expression) by phonological categories and structures, and **projection** is re-representation (expression) of a set of categories as a structure.

An interface is the relationship between a representation and its re-representation.

There are common-language senses of most of these terms. I therefore trust that my use of these will not lead to confusion.

Conceptualization and perception are crude labels for the mental areas respectively grammaticalized by syntax and phonology. In what follows I shall usually talk about re-representation from the point of view of 'movement' from conceptualization to auditory perception—that is, from the speaker's point of view, as it were. But, either way, re-representations are cumulative, moving the complex of representations closer to one pole or the other. This does not involve the claim that all interfacing between particular modules is simultaneous, in real or abstract timing: re-representations of particular partial representations within a module can take place independently. That is, there can be a parallel processing of re-representations between different modules.

One major module, or **plane**, of language is associated with the representation of ontological distinctions such as entity vs. event, as noun and verb; this is the **content** plane. And there is another plane, that of **expression**, that grammaticalizes, as with consonant and vowel, distinctions in the perception of sound. The projection of these categorizations respectively define the modules of syntax and phonology, and the individual categorizations are themselves associated in the lexicon as the poles of minimal signs. Projection is a form of re-representation whereby sets of categories from the lexicon are hierarchized and linearized. Projection thus involves various submodules.

The poles of the sign are also related by re-representation, the variety of re-representation that has been called exponence: phonological categorizations expound a syntactic category and its subcategories. (Re-)representations are iconic to varying extents. Exponence is a 'severe' form of re-representation. In the absence of onomatopoeia, or 'size iconicity' (common words are shorter), or the like, the re-representation does not reflect the nature of what is represented. In preserving little indication of the substantive representation being re-represented the sign relation is minimally representational. Within the syntactic and phonological modules, submodules can be differentiated by the substantive domain they introduce—hierarchization, linearization, for instance. Hierarchization is added to the lexical categorizations associated with the individual words in sentences. And linearization is added on the basis of the categorizations and the hierarchizations they project. The re-representation relation between successive submodules is less 'severe'; a re-representation may reflect something of what it re-represents, as when linearization reflects hierarchization—as with word order regularities.

The trilogy is concerned, then, with the implementation of this substantive view of linguistic structure, and the modularity associated with it. The three volumes thus also share an interest in modularity. They have a common concern with motivations for and limitations on modularity in language. For though representations typically do not affect what they re-represent, we shall find that there are also counter-modular forces at work, where the result of re-representation may be seen to facilitate re-representation, particularly to enable the interface between the re-represented and the re-representation to maximize expressivity. But this is a major concern of, in particular, Volume II.

The three volumes are intended to supplement one another, on the basis of these and other themes in common. The present prologue is concerned with making more precise and concrete the preceding rather general statements about the common themes and the relationship between the individual volumes. Let me start by spelling out a bit more, at the risk of repetition, how the approach I have outlined might be implemented and how it relates to other, hopefully familiar, views of linguistic structure. This closer look will also involve the further marking by emboldening of important terms as they are introduced and where they are particularly relevant.

I, like others, take the attribution of modularity to our linguistic knowledge to encompass the hypothesis that our specifically linguistic capacities involve the interaction of coherent subcomponents that each obey distinct principles of organization. Adoption of some such notion is uncontroversial. But the work reported on in these volumes suggests not just that modularization is substance-based, but also that in consequence linguistic knowledge is much less modular than is commonly supposed.

As indicated in the above definitions, this work leads to the proposition that modular differences are necessary only when we have to do with different extralinguistic substances, cognitive or perceptual. Modularity reduces to the idea that a **linguistic module** is a set of principles of construction that apply to representations that are characterized by possession of a distinctive substantive alphabet. By **alphabet** I mean the basic elements out of which representations are constructed, and by saying they are **substantive** I mean that the members of the alphabet have content based on extralinguistic properties of mind (as discussed briefly above, and, in more detail, in e.g. Anderson 1997a, 2006b, 2007). These properties correspond to Hjelmslev's (e.g. 1953: §13) 'content-substance' or 'expression-substance'.

I have indicated that such an idea of modularity establishes, in the first place, the status as modules of the individual **planes** of language, where planes, roughly understood in Hjelmslev's (1953) sense, are the largest groupings of linguistic representations that are based on sharing a particular basic inventory, or basic alphabet (see again the other references given above). Each of the basic linguistic units that form part of the alphabet grammaticalizes an aspect of a particular kind of extralinguistic substance. There is, as we have seen, a planar module of phonology containing representations constructed out of phonetically interpretable elements, and roughly corresponding to Hjelmslev's (1953: §13) 'expression-form'. And there is a plane-sized module of syntax with its own alphabet of basic cognitively derived elements ('content-form'). Morphology has a negative status as a plane, in lacking a distinct substantive alphabet; it makes overt aspects of the 'content-form' of a word as aspects of 'expression-form'. It is an 'inter-planar' module, according to Anderson (1997a). These modules, in other words, are roughly of the dimension of what many more recent linguists have called 'components' of the grammar.

I thus take as my starting point for the whole enterprise the idea that the grammatical modules of language are the planes of syntax and phonology, and the 'inter-plane' of morphology, which is distinguished by lacking an alphabet of its own, beyond bracketing into units of formation, or **formatives**, while showing distinct principles of organization. Syntax and phonology are fed by a lexical component that includes morphology. The lexicon unites as lexical items representations in the different alphabets of the two planes; it is the repository of the **signs** of the language and derivational relations among them. And morphology is embedded in the lexicon as part of the expression of the lexicon-internal relationships among minimal lexical signs, or words.

It is in the lexicon that we can locate the major connection among modules, embodied in the linguistic sign; and it is where the information associated with the two poles of the sign (notional-syntactic and phonological) is directed to particular modules. As lexical 'processes', operations of morphology are part of this 'filtering' of information to the planes (as is discussed and exemplified in Volume II). That volume also explores the role of the lexicon as the major **linguistic interface**, or rather, complex of interfaces, in an effort to clarify the notion of interface in a framework of substance-motivated modularity. This introduces questions to do with directionality and 'separation'. This is part of the question of what sort of system language is. In these books I develop the notion that languages are expressive systems; they are indeed a set of re-representations of cognitive categories that facilitates ultimate expression in perceptually accessible media. And intralinguistic re-representations are largely 'one-way'; in this case the re-representation does not affect the representation being re-expressed or reinterpreted. And re-representation is cumulative.

Let me approach making all this rather more concrete by explaining in a little more detail how the trilogy that constitutes *The Substance of Language* divides up aspects of substantivity, including modularity and its compromises. The volumes are entitled:

I. The Domain of Syntax
II. Morphology, Paradigms, and Periphrases
III. Phonology-Syntax Analogies

Given their individual titles, the matters treated in the three essays might be seen as promising to overlap only slightly. Also, this third one necessarily has to be wide-ranging in pursuing the consequences of a general assumption concerning linguistic structure as manifested on the different planes, namely the assumed recurrence of the same structural properties on these planes, while the other two are more focused.

These latter deal, on the one hand, in Volume I, with what is included within syntax, and specifically with the relationship between grammatical structure and semantics, which latter relates syntax and lexicon to an extralinguistic (cognitive) domain. Volume I develops a syntax based on projection of notionally based syntactic categories supplied from items in the lexicon. Words in the lexicon can be seen as conjunctions of bundles of phonetically interpretable and of semantically interpreted categories; these are minimal lexical signs. And the syntactic, morphological, and phonological structures associated with the signs are determined by these categories.

What is of particular interest for the concerns of Volume I is the limitations on what counts as syntactic in terms of the substance-based approach adopted here. Crucial in delimiting the domain is insistence on this notional basis, which determines what is distributionally and in other respects most relevant to the formulation of syntactic generalizations. Specifically, one can distinguish prototypical members of each category that conform straightforwardly to particular semantic concepts: crudely, nouns are entity-based, verbs event-based. And the behaviour, including distribution, of semantically prototypical members—say, *girl* as a noun, or *run* as a verb—is criterial for the syntax of the category, and can identify and distinguish the non-prototypical.

To begin to turn to 'the other hand' anticipated at the beginning of the previous paragraph, i.e. the contents of Volume II: while syntax is characterized by a distinct alphabet of semantically grounded categories, morphological structures do not introduce a distinct alphabet, but relate syntactic to phonological categories. Words may be categorically complex, incorporating basic and derived categories. Morphological structures make overt the lexical structures of some such words, which may involve, for instance, nouns based on other primary categories such as verbs. It may also make secondary syntactic categories (such as tense and gender) overt. **Primary categories**, such as, say, noun/verb or plosive/vowel, determine the basic distribution of units and the secondary categories they attract. **Secondary categories**, such as aspect/gender, or rounded/uvular, offer further contrastive possibilities with respect to units of a particular primary category. Such syntactic distinctions are largely manifested paradigmatically, but also by the 'fine-tuning' of the distribution of words—or, in the phonology, of segments. Other secondary syntactic categories, such as 'concrete'/'Aktionsart', are primarily associated with derivational relationships.

Other derivational relationships involve the conversion of one primary category into another—say, by deverbal nominalization. This kind of derivation is limited to syntactic categories. Phonology does not involve the conversion of one primary category into another. This is one of the dis-analogies between phonology and syntax that the present volume attempts to account for (in Part III), against a background of pervasive analogy of structure between the two planes.

Volume II is concerned particularly with the relationships of syntax and phonology to the expression of morphological structure. This thus involves two rather particular domains. Within the first domain, the syntax/morphology interface, it looks at the role of grammatical periphrases and their relation to inflectional morphology; and within the second domain, the phonology/morphology interface, it looks at paradigmatic (conjugation/declensional) class, and its role in facilitating phonological representation of syntactic categories. These two areas illustrate the overt 'bridges' morphology provides between syntax and the lexicon and phonology and the lexicon. The former phenomenon involves the cooperation of syntax ('analytic' expression) and morphology ('synthetic' expression) in the representation of secondary syntactic categories (such as aspect and passive). The latter phenomenon involves the 'repackaging' of combinations of such syntactic categories to facilitate their morphophonological expression. Both periphrastic expression and 'repackaging' remedy limitations in the morphological paradigms available in the languages concerned. Both phenomena are counter-modular, in the sense that they compensate for the strict separation of exponence: syntax and syntactic categories are adapted to the needs of morphophonology, counter to the exponence relation.

As anticipated, the theme of this third volume is the degree to which the two planes of syntax and phonology are structured in the same way—that is, the degree to which they conform to an assumption of structural analogy between the planes. But it is also occupied with elucidating the degree to which breakdowns in analogy can be attributed to differences in the nature and extent of their alphabets and the substantive (semantic and phonetic) properties that the alphabets grammaticalize. Perceived similarities between how the two extralinguistic domains can be represented, as well as dependence of the planes on the same logical apparatus for the linguistic structuring of these domains, foster analogies in structure between them, just as perceived differences frustrate analogy. Both factors fostering analogy underlie the major structural analogy between the planes, namely the desirable restriction whereby within a module representations are constructed non-mutatively and without recourse to 'empty' elements (non-signs). And they also relate to the parallel distinction made in the two planes between primary and secondary categories. More fundamentally, perhaps the ultimate motivation for anticipating that there will be analogy is the recognition that both syntax and phonology are representational subsystems within the overall system of re-representations, or re-expressions, that constitutes language.

And this last is manifested in the analogous submodular architecture of the two planes, as presented in Figure 1 from the prologue to Volume 1 of this series.

```
                    LEXICON
   syntactic categories ─────────▶ phonological categories
                    exponence
```

```
   syntactic categories              phonological categories
```

```
   syntactic categories              phonological categories
          +                                  +
     dependencies                       dependencies
```

```
   syntactic categories              phonological categories
          +                                  +
     dependencies                       dependencies
          +                                  +
     linearizations                     linearizations
```

```
   syntactic categories              phonological categories
          +                                  +
     dependencies                       dependencies
          +                                  +
     linearizations                     linearizations
          +                                  +
     intonations ─────────────────────▶ prosody
```

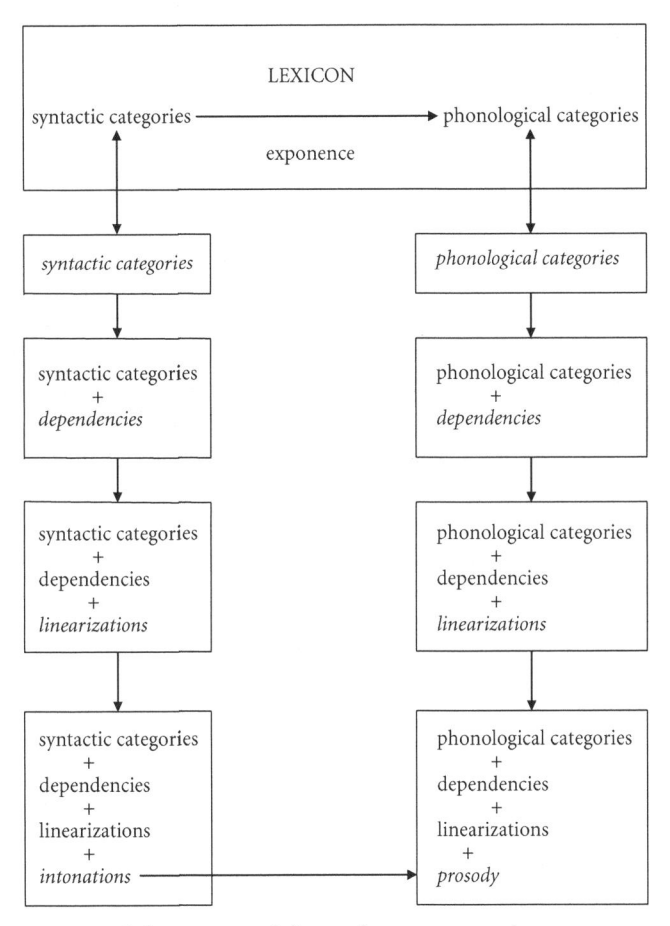

FIGURE I.1 Substance, modules, and re-representation

That prologue comments on this figure as follows:

Each single-headed arrow there is a re-representation. The topmost box contains the lexicon module, which is characterized by lacking an alphabet of its own. The categorial boxes immediately below the lexicon contain the substantively based alphabets that characterize syntax (on the left) and phonology (on the right). Their relation to the lexicon is not one of re-representation, but one of containment as parts of lexical entries. The boxes below show the adding of the substantively based dimensions that characterize the submodules of the two planes that are defined by the alphabets of the categorial boxes. The defining dimension of each (sub)module is italicized. The diagram recognizes a syntactic submodule that provides phonological, particularly intonational, expression. The medium of expression, of course, remains phonological, based on perception of sound, but it directly expresses syntactic categorization. As indicated at the bottom of the figure, both syntax and the lexical phonology contribute to prosody, or utterance representations.

This shared modular structure is the basis for many of the analogies that are discussed in what follows in this book.

Despite the various differences I have noted, the books are united in their concern with the relationships contracted by different sets of representations, including, in principle, sets of extralinguistic representations or operations, in the case of semantics and phonetics, and the limitations thereby imposed on strict modularity, or encapsulation. Within this general framework, each volume focuses on some aspect of the contents of planes or the relationship between linguistic modules, sets of linguistic representations differentiated by the substantive alphabets that the representations are constructed out of—or by the lack of a distinct one.

We can sum up the basic assumptions concerning the substance of linguistic categorization made in the books thus:

(a) the categories of phonology are phonetically grounded;
(b) the categories of syntax are semantically grounded;
(c) morphology lacks a distinctive alphabet, but unites syntactic and phonological categories.

Justification of the second assumption is the burden of the first book: the syntactic plane is not autonomous, and its categories are cognitively grounded. Assumption (c) is the basis of the second study. Investigation in the present volume of the structural parallels between phonology and syntax and the limits on these depends in part on the first two assumptions, involving groundedness: perceived similarities and differences in substance underlie the analogies in structure.

Certainly, the essays concern themselves with very different aspects of the relationships between planes. However, certain further concerns recur in the three discussions, in particular relating to the nature of categorization, and especially the motivations for making a distinction between functional and lexical categories, and one between primary and secondary categories, as well as concern with the evidence for there being a substantive basis for these distinctions.

Thus, Volume I involves the denial of a linguistically internal planar division between semantics and syntax: syntactic categories are meaningful, and this content is available for processing by general cognitive systems. Much of this study is concerned with showing that syntactic structures based on notional categorization need not be 'mutative' (e.g. transformational): 'movement' and 're-structuring' are not characteristic of syntax. Syntactic structure is built up by cumulatively projecting notional categories on expressions couched in the different substantive dimensions associated with the **submodules of syntax**—our perception of time, sound, salience. The expression of syntactic structure is limited to such substantive dimensions, and does not have recourse to substance-less categories or abstract manipulations of linearity and attachment.

The second volume in the trilogy focuses on two areas that illustrate something of the complexity of the exponence relation as manifested in morphological structure, and the complexity of the relationship between modules, which accommodates both this basic relation of exponence and particular relations that run counter to it. Both these studies introduce limitations on the independence of the linguistic planes, as indeed does the third.

The present volume in the trilogy, Volume III, accepts the modularity of syntax and phonology, as is required by their distinct substantive basic alphabets, related respectively to the extralinguistic capacities involved in cognition and perceptual implementation, but argues that nevertheless the phonological and syntactic modules show analogies in how they are structured. As observed, these analogies are fostered by perceived similarities between the two substances of syntax and phonology, and by the application of the same logical processes to the construction of representations on both planes. The major modules not only interact intimately, but they also show the same structural properties, to the extent that this is permitted, in the case of syntax and phonology, by the 'demands' of their different alphabets, which, for reasons I shall attempt to make explicit, necessitate distinctive kinds of organization.

That the substantive alphabets make 'demands' is another compromising factor in the integrity of modules. Alphabets incorporate expectations and restrictions from outside the linguistic system, both associated with the role of language in presenting our cognition, on the one hand, and with its perceptually accessed incarnation, on the other. These demands on the two planes overlap, but they also by their differences contribute to the individuality of the linguistic modules vis-à-vis each other. The different substantive bases for the alphabets restrict the kinds of similarities in structure that we can associate with the different planes. The conflict between such extralinguistically instigated restriction on analogy between the planes and the factors favouring analogy is a major theme of this volume.

For if the first great substantive, rather than structural, analogy between syntax and phonology is their both having a non-linguistic basis, it is the different natures of these respective non-linguistic substances that is perhaps the most important factor in frustrating analogies. Both substances have their own structures partly independent of the linguistic representation of them, and these are not necessarily always amenable to the same kind of linguistic representation. The perceptual dimensions of phonetics may not need or permit the structuring that is appropriate for the immediate linguistic representation of cognition. And, though phonetic substance limits the kinds of structure that phonology can deploy, cognition continually pushes the resources of language, and encourages creativity—largely by analogy, in this case by analogizing one conceptual domain with another (most obviously, the abstract with the concrete). This capacity is facilitated by the flexibility provided by the 'double articulation' of language. Phonology re-represents syntax and lexicon in two steps, once as the gestalts we call signifiers and also as a bundle of minimal contrastive units that make up the signifier. And this flexibility is another important factor in limiting analogy between the planes.

But the difference between the planes in magnitude of the extralinguistic domains that are interpreted—as well as their relative accessibility—is also a practical problem in comparing the two domains. There is a great discrepancy in our precise understanding of their contents. The acoustic differences we hear and the articulatory movements that produce the sounds we perceive can be represented with some precision independently of language—though, certainly, such representations themselves are not directly of our perception. And our understanding of perception itself is now substantial. But the vast domain of cognition is very unevenly mappable without recourse to language. Awareness of this is a factor, I would think, in the 'retreat from meaning' in twentieth-century linguistics that is discussed in Chapter 1 of Volume I.

Basic to the description of the domain of syntax in that study is the hypothesis that syntactic structure is constructed out of **dependency**—head-dependent—relations. We shall find in what follows that the centrality of the dependency relation is a prominent analogy between the two planes. Not only that but it is also appropriate to differentiate on both planes between complements and adjuncts. Together, these properties form another great analogy, again one that is substantively based, despite the apparent formality of its structural manifestation. Dependency is a simple grammaticalization of cognitive salience, which may also be conferred by categorial properties. Specifically, headhood represents relational dominance. In anticipation, let me recall here the introduction to such dependency structures given in Volume I.

The difference between complement and adjunct is shown schematically in (38) from Chapter 3 of Volume I:

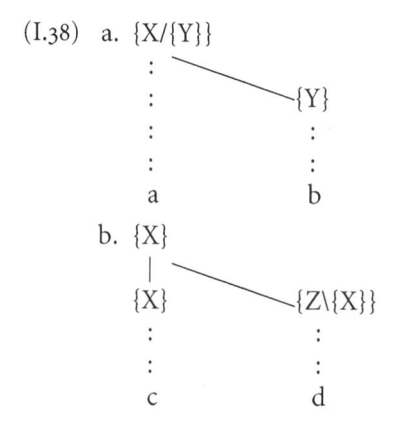

(I.38) a. {X/{Y}}

```
    ⋮ ╲
    ⋮    ╲{Y}
    ⋮      ⋮
    ⋮      ⋮
    a      b
```

b. {X}
```
    |  ╲
   {X}   ╲{Z\{X}}
    ⋮      ⋮
    ⋮      ⋮
    c      d
```

The braces, '{ }', enclose categorial representations; 'X' might be that for a verb, for instance. The upper categorial representation in (I.38a) says that this instance of the category {X} takes category {Y} as a complement, as in, say,... *met Bob*; the complement relation is indicated by the slash (solidus), with the head to the left, complement to the right. These categorial representations are part of the lexical entry of the items concerned. In forming a syntactic construction a {Y} is made dependent on an {X} category that is marked as taking such a complement, giving the substructure in (I.38a). Here a lexical item 'a' (identified by its content, including syntactic categorization) is **associated** with (indicated by a dotted line) a category {X/{Y}}, which has dependent on it (at the lower end of the solid line) a '{Y}' associated with item 'b'. In this way the syntactic representation is built on the information given in the lexicon.

This 'building' includes also the imposition of word order, largely on the basis of such dependency relations: the use of 'left' and 'right' above and the left-to-right placement in (I.38) are arbitrary until position is assigned by the principles of linearization proper to the particular language, some of which are unmarked, defaults. Typically in a language, dependents overwhelmingly either follow or precede their heads. In English they largely follow.

In (I.38b) the member of the {X} category is not represented as taking a complement. Rather, it is accompanied by a member, 'd', of category {Z}, which is marked in the lexicon as seeking to modify (indicated by the backslash, '\') an item of category {X}. This might be appropriate for... *disappeared yesterday.* Some modifiers are dedicated modifiers (such as *soon*), but often they can also be complements; and in the latter case the lexicon allows for both possibilities (largely by redundancy rule applying to items of particular categories). As a result of this lexical marking involving the backslash, in the syntax a duplicate of category {X} is projected above the {X} taken from the lexicon, and the modifier is made dependent on this duplicate. The vertical line in (I.38b) is again a dependency arc (or directed line), with head at the top and dependent at the bottom. But in this case the categories joined by the dependency arc are associated with the same item, in this instance 'c'; they do not occupy positions in the representation that are potentially linearly distinct; they are not subject to principles of linearization. The two instances of the {X} category in (I.38b) thus involve a relation of **subjunction** rather than of **adjunction** (as with the other dependency lines in these representations). But again the syntax is projected on the basis of the lexical categorizations.

Given that item 'd' in (I.38), of category {Z}, takes as a head any item of category '{X}', items 'a', 'b', and 'd' might be combined as in (I.39a):

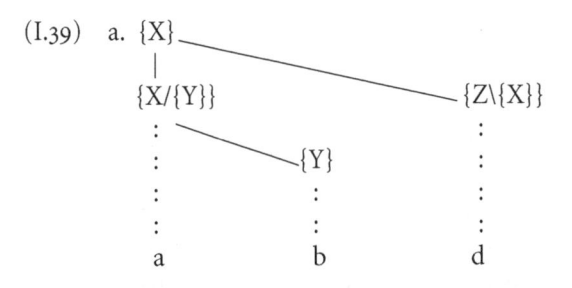

(I.39) a.
```
        {X}
         |                                  
       {X/{Y}}                  {Z\{X}}
         :        \                 :
         :         {Y}              :
         :          :               :
         :          :               :
         a          b               d
```

(I.39a) would fit the sequence ... *met Bob yesterday*. Such relationships as these constitute fundamental analogies between syntax and phonology: as we shall see, phonological structure too is based on dependency, and it involves complements and adjuncts.

All three books have a primary concern with the ways in which even the degree of modularization envisaged initially here, as necessarily substantively based, is compromised. Recent concentration, in the interest of isolating for each module a core 'computational device', on the (assumed) limited interaction of modules at 'interfaces' (as in e.g. Reiss 2007) has the drawback of drawing attention away from the interpenetration of modules, whose internal generalizations make reference to properties of other modules and properties shared among them. This is a major focus of Volume II. Volume I is primarily concerned with the notional basis in syntax for its own basic alphabet as an expression of cognitive distinctions, but it also illustrates that an adequate account of the expression of syntactic categories must invoke phonology, particularly intonation. The linguistic modules are not independent 'automata'; they are independent neither of each other nor of the extralinguistic dimensions they grammaticalize. The interesting question is where and how interpenetration is restricted. This is again related to the expressive function of language and its 'directionality', and specifically to the relationship between the different kinds of re-representation embodied in exponence.

In different ways, the three volumes focus on what unites different planes: in the case of the first and third, it is substantive and structural properties that are in common between phonology and syntax that make the link; in the case of the second, it is the phenomena of periphrasis and conjugation themselves that unite morphology with syntax and phonology respectively. The trilogy also provides different routes into the same complex of issues centring on the nature of categorization and the expressive relationship between structure and category, both of which aspects are substantively based.

It is also my intention, however, that though the studies comprising the trilogy should be mutually supportive in various ways, they can be read independently, i.e. without essential reference to each other, for the sake of the reader with a specific interest in view. To some extent, the exception here is Chapter 3 in the first book, which should repay reading as an introduction to the general framework used in all the volumes, though the other two depend on it in different ways and to different extents. However, I have endeavoured to give a relatively self-contained account in each volume of the concepts and notations most pertinent to that volume. The intended relative 'autonomy' of the three books thus means that there will be for the reader who persists with all of them some repetition in expositions of relevant aspects of the general framework assumed. But, in my experience, this might not be a bad thing—though I ask the indulgence of those who find it irksome.

Part I
Introduction

1

Some implications of structural analogy

My concern in this volume is with the status of parallelisms between the modules of phonology and syntax in particular, and with the implication of these parallels for other assumptions about the structure of language. In this chapter I attempt to provide some background to the development of the **structural analogy assumption**, which contends that these parallels are not merely not gratuitous, but central to our understanding of how linguistic structure is constructed. Much of what follows in the chapter is closely based on parts of Anderson (2006a), since what is discussed there seems to me to form the basis for an introduction to the aims of the present study, which explores more fully than previously, as far as I am aware, something of the extent of analogy and the nature of limitations on its implementation.

1.1 Introduction

As Anderson (2006a: §1) points out, there seem to have been debates in the grammatical literature about the role of 'analogy' vs. 'anomaly' in linguistic structure for about as long as those surrounding 'nature' vs. 'nurture'. And the two issues are of course related, though not in a simple way. However, while both debates are ancient in origin, being initially associated with the development of early Greek and of Roman theorizing, the former, which at that period essentially concerned how regular and uniform, vs. irregular and diverse, the grammar of a language was, has subsequently received rather less acknowledged attention than the latter. But it can be argued that the attitudes underlying the 'analogy'-'anomaly' debate remain as substrates to more recent divergences in views concerning the nature of linguistic structure. Indeed, these attitudes, though often unacknowledged as such, are often intertwined with considerations pertaining to more recent versions of the other debate, concerning the richness or poverty of the specifically linguistic genetic endowment to be attributed to 'homo loquens'.

This will be evident in what follows, where I shall discuss the status, as an instance of a particular 'analogist' assumption, of a view of analogies in structure that is related to but has a rather different focus from the 'analogy' of the ancient debate. This is the idea that extensive structural parallelism is to be found between syntax and phonology, in particular, and that this is to be expected. I shall specifically present here the particular version of this idea that I have called the structural analogy assumption. I shall be concerned with the viability of this assumption and with the implications that follow, if it is so, for other aspects of structure, and particularly its relationship to assumptions concerning 'universal grammar', in the 'innate' sense discussed in Volume I.[1]

Such a view of 'universal grammar' can be said to be 'anomalist', at least in terms of the most 'austere form' of it that excludes phonology from 'universal grammar'. This discrepancy in status of the planes of linguistic structure might be taken to imply a lack of expectation of extensive analogy between them. Whereas, if the planes are both constructed by learners without benefit of innate universal principles of language structure, but using the same general cognitive capacities applied to evidence presented to them of culturally preserved individual languages, analogy is to be expected. This correlation in recent times between the two ancient debates is one of the consequences of confronting the evidence for analogy between the planes that has attracted the attention of a range of scholars of different outlooks (some of whose work is discussed in Anderson 1987b).

1.2 Structural analogy

Anderson (2006a) is occupied with only one manifestation of the 'analogist' attitude, which, on its widest understanding, posits regularity and homogeneity as essential to language. Clearly, such a position cannot be maintained globally, as the ancient 'anomalists' demonstrated even in relation to the more specific claims of 'analogists' such as Aristarchus, who were primarily concerned with the regularity with which particular grammatical categories were expressed. There are manifest irregularities in this and in other respects in any natural language, irregularities whose appropriate repository is the lexicon. But some, more specific but generally applicable, 'analogist' assumptions about structure can be seen to limit the potentiality for anomaly in various ways.

---

[1] Here and elsewhere I use the term 'universal grammar' in this restricted sense. When necessary, I shall prefer to talk about 'general grammar' or 'universal properties' when we are concerned with properties that are found generally in language, without these necessarily being attributed to anything like a 'universal grammar' in the sense discussed in the main text.

There have been various suggestions from diverse quarters in linguistics that representations in phonology and syntax, in particular, possess shared structural properties. As I have noted, Anderson (1987b) points to some of these 'structural-analogist' proposals of the twentieth century, without (given the dimensions of the work) that account being in any way exhaustive (see too e.g. Bauer 1994). Proposed analogies have ranged from relatively local ones, some of which nevertheless eventually generalized themselves over different kinds of representations (such as the 'etic'/'emic' distinction), through more global ones (such as the attribution by Halliday to both syntax (1961, 1966) and phonology (1967) of analogous 'systemic organizations' and hierarchies such as a 'scale of categories', or Pike's (1967) suggested parallelism among grammatical, phonological, and lexical 'hierarchies'), to Hjelmslev's assertion of 'structural homology' between the planes of content form and expression form (e.g. 1953: 101):

It turns out that the two sides (the planes) of language have completely analogous categorical structure, a discovery that seems to us of far-reaching significance for an understanding of the structural principle of a language or in general the 'essence' of a semiotic.

On this see particularly Siertsema's (1965: 207–11) tentative attempt to spell out the consequences for his structural proposals of Hjelmslev's various discussions of this 'discovery' (notably 1937, 1938, 1939).[2]

---

[2] See too for an earlier, sceptical discussion Kuryłowicz (1949). Martinet (1957) registers a reservation with respect to the proposed 'isomorphism' which is equivalent to the clause in the formulation of mine given just below in the text, which recognizes that there may exist differences due to the relationship between the levels. As Martinet puts it (1957: 105): 'on parle pour être compris, et l'expression est au service du contenu' (though Jacques Durand has drawn my attention to the complexities of the relationship between Hjelmslev and Martinet as discussed in Arrivé and Driss (2000), and how this affected Martinet's published evaluations of the 'isomorphy' hypothesis). And Bazell (1949a: 86) adopts a perhaps even more cautious position: 'though it has now become axiomatic that either plane must be judged with reference to the other, a real equality of treatment remains an ideal still far from fulfilment', while elsewhere (1952: §IX) he is even more critical of glossematic theory and practice. A recent alternative implementation of the notion of 'isomorphy' is provided by Mulder (2000).

It is possible to cite a range of 'analogists' (of varying committedness). But I mention a few here only as familiar exemplars of an (implicit or explicit) attitude, not necessarily to endorse the proposed analogies. Indeed, the spread of (for instance) the '-eme' notion in application to different levels of linguistic representation has had in my view something of the same scale of undesirable effects on the study of language as the adoption of the universal grammar hypothesis considered in what follows here. Something of this emerges, as concerns the former notion, from the series of -eme articles by Bazell (e.g.1949b, 1954, 1956). If the -eme has been pursued to implausible ends, this is not merely the case also with the pursuit of the universal grammar hypothesis; it is argued in §2.4 of Volume I that a strict version of the universal grammar assumption renders plausible analogies between syntax and phonology apparently inexplicable, as well as, like the –eme terminology, lending credence to false analogies.

As anticipated, the implementations of structural analogy I shall mainly be concerned with here recognize the considerable restrictions on analogy imposed (directly or indirectly) by non-linguistic capacities in particular. These restrictions include the discrepancy in the 'richness' of the respective domains that are grammaticalized by the two planes. Also a limiting factor is the exponence relation between syntactically categorized representations and phonological. However, within these limits, analogy is the unmarked assumption: this results from the application of the same cognitive apparatus in structuring domains that, in addition, are perceived as sharing some substantive properties drawn from the respective extralinguistic domains with which they interface. What needs to be accounted for, on this view, is why it doesn't hold in particular cases. Is the particular non-analogy understandable in terms of differences in the substances grammaticalized by the planes or in terms of the relationship between them? If not, the non-analogy is likely to be spurious.

Analogy is of interest in the context of the present series of studies in the limitations it imposes on the distinctiveness of the linguistic modules, despite their basis in different substances. This is a different kind of restriction on the separateness of modules from that which follows from the permeability of the syntactic module to semantic and phonological properties argued for in Volume I. But both limitations on the distinctiveness of modules derive from outside language, from their substantive bases and from the nature of general cognitive capacities. Analogy and its limitations are closely bound up with extralinguistic constraints on language.

From the mid 1980s several researchers have explicitly deployed such an implementation of the analogy assumption in a number of works concerned with various aspects of linguistic structure: see particularly Anderson (1985, 1986a, 1992), Anderson and Durand (1986), Anderson and Ewen (1987: §8.1), Durand (1990: §8.2, 1995: §6), Staun (1996), Carr (2005). And such a view is already implicit in Anderson and Jones (1974). The assumption is formulated as an injunction on linguistic structure by Anderson (1992: 2):

Minimise (more strongly, eliminate) differences between levels that do not follow from a difference in alphabet or from the nature of the relationship between the levels concerned

Much of what follows are attempts to render the consequences of this injunction more precise; and to explain why the stronger form cannot be realized. Let me firstly comment on some of the terms used in this formulation.

The levels of representation that have been attributed to language vary considerably (depending particularly on the degree of derivationality attributed to phonology and syntax), but almost all recent approaches have recognized a distinction between syntactic and phonological representations. From the notionalist viewpoint outlined in Volume I, these two (sets of) levels differ in their 'alphabets', based on the character of the substance in which their categories are grounded. That both levels are substance-based is a basic analogy and the basis for many more. But, as just observed, differences in substance may also limit the application of particular analogies, and the identification of these differences is a major concern of this study.

Also, as indicated initially in this chapter, the attribution of substance itself interacts with other assumptions about language, particularly those to do with the existence and (depending on this) the nature of 'universal grammar'. And here it should be apparent that the discussion of Volume I is highly relevant. Before looking at the evidence for the pervasiveness of inter-planar analogies, let us therefore look at the issues involved in the interaction between analogy and 'universal grammar', which are fundamental to our understanding of language, and of different views of what is essential to language.

1.3 Structural analogy and 'universal grammar'

Various other structural proposals made since the mid-twentieth century illustrate rather well the pertinence of analogy assumptions to other assumptions concerning the structure of language. And I thus want now to spend a little more time outlining some of these and their interest for our present concerns, as a short prelude to the central concern of this section.

Let us recall, to begin with, that a number of developments in the 1960s in theories of syntactic representation and of the organization of the syntax were apparently inspired by perceived analogies based on concepts familiar from phonology. A rather more recently proposed analogy of this kind is Jackendoff's (1990) exportation of the notion of 'tier' from the phonology to lexical structure. Also here belongs the application of ideas of 'violability' and 'optimality' to all of phonology, morphology, and syntax, with application to the last lagging somewhat behind the first (but already documented in Archangeli and Langendoen 1997, for instance).

Earlier, in terms of organization, the principle of the cycle, in particular, already well established with respect to the phonology (Chomsky, Halle, and Lukoff 1956), was then introduced as an organizing principle for the application of syntactic (transformational) rules.[3] And, in terms of representation,

---

[3] Indeed, the beginning of Pullum (1992: 209) moves from talking about the origin of 'the cyclic principle' in phonology (Chomsky, Halle, and Lukoff 1956) to a consideration of what he calls 'the

the notion feature was extended to the syntax from the phonology, where it had been familiar for some time. Its pervasiveness in the study of phonology was enhanced by its adoption into early 'generative phonology', from the work of Roman Jakobson and developments thereof—see e.g. Jakobson and Halle 1956). The extension of features to the syntax involved a recognition that the basic sequential units in both domains could be analysed into componential elements which played a systematic role in the formulation of linguistic regularities. Both of these innovations in the syntax (cyclicity and featurization) were embedded in the grammatical framework expounded in Chomsky (1965).

1.3.1 Neglect of analogy

It has been argued (by e.g. Anderson 2004b: §1) that, despite what has just been said, the representational innovation of feature notation has had a rather small impact on syntactic descriptions, compared with the centrality of its role in the phonology, particularly perhaps in the case of those features that are used to characterize the primary categories. Primary categories are those classifications in terms of which we can express the basic distribution of elements: they are what identify the 'word classes' of syntax and the 'major classes' of phonology. But the featural characterization of the primary syntactic categories remained vestigial indeed (e.g. in Chomsky 1965: ch. 2, §2) until its elaboration in Chomsky (1970) and (particularly) Jackendoff (1977a,b); and even since then the role of the cross-classificatory capacity (and other capacities) afforded by featural representation of the primary categories of the syntax has not been presented as particularly important in the description of languages.

To be sure, over the last several decades some treatments of syntax have attempted to justify the use of such a notation by illustrating its cross-classificatory capacity, typically in relation to the primary categories, as does e.g. Radford (1988: 146–8), in arguing for the by-then-familiar featural representations in (1):

(1) *Chomskyan primary categories*
    Verb = [+V,−N]   Adjective = [+V,+N]
    Noun = [−V,+N]   Preposition = [−V,−N]

analogous principle in syntax', without (to be sure) making much of the use of this adjective in this context. However, this reflects a willingness within this 'transformational' tradition at the period under discussion to expect and indeed look for such analogies between syntax and phonology, and to expect ideas from the two planes to interact—with e.g. work in syntax in turn serving as the basis for the development of the strict cycle condition in phonology (cf. Mascaró 1976).

Radford points out that we can represent the 'supercategory' which includes verbs and prepositions as [−N], and that this 'supercategory' is invoked by a generalization concerning complementation in English, namely that only members of the [−N] 'supercategory' can take NP complements, as illustrated by the grammaticalities in (2)—where the asterisks indicate that the bracketed material cannot be omitted:

(2) a. John loves Mary
    b. John brought a present for Mary
    c. John's admiration *(for) Mary
    d. John is fond *(of) Mary

And he also cites the categorial distribution of gender in Italian, for instance, which is limited to nouns and adjectives (among the categories under discussion), as motivating in this case the 'supercategory' [+N].[4]

Such arguments run parallel to those for 'natural classes' in the phonology: cf. e.g. '...a set of speech sounds forms a *natural class* if fewer features are required to designate the class than to designate any individual sound in the class' (Halle 1964: 328). Thus far, the syntax/phonology analogy is exact: features are a shared structural property whereby classes and cross-classes are identified componentially. But the exploitation of featurization in syntax has been rather limited; and this, I suggest, arises in large part from assumed differences between the featural alphabets of the two modules.

Thus, Radford's arguments differ from discussions of 'natural classes' in phonology, in so far as there is no appeal in them to an equivalent, with respect to the syntax, of the common phonetic substance presumed to be shared by members of a phonetic 'natural class' or 'supercategory'. Thus, in a typical vowel system with the categories [i, e, a, o, u], the 'supercategory' represented in binary features as [+high], which includes [+high, −back] [i] and [+high, +back] [u], is associated with a particular phonetic character, such as is implied by the label [+high]. As a textbook of the 1960s puts it (in its most bland form),

---

[4] Radford (1997: 63–5) adds a couple more illustrations of the appropriateness of the syntactic 'supercategories' which can be defined in terms of (1) to those that are invoked in Radford (1988); and, following on from then more recent work, he adds to those in (1) the feature [±F], where 'F' = 'functional'. Other recent-ish textbooks, such as Haegeman and Guéron (1999), however, scarcely mention the cross-classificatory properties of the primary categories. And this kind of cross-classification (or 'supercategorization') of primary categories plays little role in even the presentation of English syntax offered by Radford (1988, 1997) himself, except perhaps in the case of the innovated feature [±F] of Radford (1997), to which there is attributed at least some cross-linguistic properties (whatever one makes of the 'functional categories' proposed there—Radford 1997: §§2.9-10). In terms of the notional framework outlined in Chapter 3 of Volume I, such a feature is unnecessary—though the functional/lexical distinction itself is fundamental to syntax.

'the features shared by the class members should be limited to those which have a certain degree of phonetic plausibility' (Harms 1968: 26).

This discrepancy between phonology and syntax reflects the autonomist view of syntax espoused by the tradition adhered to in Radford (1988). What substantive content one might attribute to these syntactic features typically is ignored, and is presumably to be assumed to be null, or at least syntactically irrelevant. Such content receives at best such cursory comments as Chomsky and Lasnik's isolated and inconsequential footnote (1977: 430, fn. 16): 'in more or less traditional terms, we may think of [+N] as "substantive" and [+V] as "predicable"'. In this formulation it even remains unclear what conceptual domain these labels might inhabit. Do they have any content other than being different?

This is where notions of structural analogy impinge on the discussion of Volume I. In that discussion, there is opposed to an autonomist view the idea that the syntactic features that differentiate syntactic classes are notionally grounded, and it was argued that syntax and phonology are analogous in manifesting substance-based categories. The formal properties of categories and differences therein follow from their (differences in) substance—though in both domains the categories may also, of course, exhibit further grammaticalization, or de-naturalization. I say 'further grammaticalization' here because all of grammar is a grammaticalization of cognitive material, and its distance from that material, with respect to a natural relation between linguistic behaviour and substance, may increase over time.

On this notionalist view, with respect to syntax one can substitute 'semantics' for 'phonetic shapes' in the following quotation from Chomsky and Halle (1968: 295):

> ... if we represented lexical items by means of an arbitrary feature notation, we would be effectively prevented from expressing in the grammar the crucial fact that items which have similar *phonetic shapes* [my italics—JMA] are subject to many of the same rules.

The categories of the syntax are semantically grounded, just as phonological categories are phonetically grounded. On this view, the substance of the two modules is different (otherwise, they'd be the same module), but they are both substantive, phonetic or notional. And the correlation between possession of a shared substantively based feature and exhibition of a distribution in common that is embodied in the notion of 'naturalness' holds in both.

§2.4 of Volume I looks, in an informal way, at how the ignoring of grounding has led syntacticians to put forward false claims concerning the syntax of nouns and verbs on the basis of the 'parallelism' assumption of

'X-bar syntax'. Verbs and nouns do not project analogous syntactic structures; indeed, arguably, nouns don't project anything at all beyond a noun node. Apparent 'complements' and 'adjuncts' are due to the presence of a verbal that the noun is based on: they are associated with derived nouns. To take such as typical is misleading. What determines the syntax of word classes is the behaviour of the semantically prototypical members of the class, not that of just any member. And in this respect there is a lack of parallelism between verbs and nouns. The failure to recognize the notional basis of syntactic categories leads to such false assumptions of parallelism, and also to a neglect of categorial componentiality, when compared with work on phonology.

Certainly, nouns and verbs share the property of being associated with a specific functional category (noun—determiner, verb—operative). And, to be sure, some of the same general notional distinctions, such as 'enumeration', are relevant to the classification and detailed syntax of both nouns and verbs—a sharing that is argued to be extensive by Rijkhoff (2002). A number of the notions, such as enumeration, expressed by the concomitants of both nouns and verbs are shared, and may be reflected in shared linearity generalizations, for instance. But these properties cannot be articulated syntactically in the same way, since nouns prototypically lack both complements and adjuncts. And this syntactic difference from verbs follows from the different basic substantive properties of the two categories.

The situation in the autonomist textbooks I have referred to, namely the lack of prominence given to the componentiality of primary syntactic categories, does not seem to misrepresent the degree of interest shown in this area in the syntactic literature within the frameworks to which these works serve as introductions. Certainly, we can register the occurrence of sporadic experiments with the system of features, such as proposals for 'cross-linguistic neutralizations' of categories (e.g. Stowell 1982—see Anderson 1997a: 68), and Chomsky's (1981: 51, 55, §2.7) invocation of derived 'neutralizations' of such, and van Riemsdijk's (1998) 'feature magnetism'. But little consistent appeal has otherwise been made to the notion 'natural class' (or 'supercategory') in the syntactic literature. In some recent work, feature bundles representing secondary (or 'subcategorial') categories (number, case, etc.) are invoked in agreement and 'checking' processes, and some syntactic features are conceded to be semantically interpretable; and this is again reflected in such textbooks as Radford (1997: particularly chs. 5 and 10). But 'natural classes' of primary syntactic categories, in particular, do not figure largely in the formulation of syntactic regularities. And this contrasts, as indicated, with the situation in the phonological literature in the same general ('generative') tradition, wherein such 'major class' features as [±consonantal] and [±sonorant], for instance, are pervasive in formulations of a variety of phenomena, as will be apparent from inspection of any recent-ish comparable phonology textbook.

I have been using the testimony of familiar textbooks here as a convenient way of illustrating what seems to me to be a striking discrepancy in the importance of the role which has apparently been thought to be appropriate to syntactic and phonological (primary) category features. Another indication of this is the fact that in the 'minimalist program' (as envisaged by Chomsky 1995), despite '[±N]' being noted as a 'formal feature' (p. 230), the primary category features have apparently no significant role to play in syntax (cf. too in this respect e.g. Lasnik 1999). And this, as anticipated above, raises interesting questions. Particularly: does this discrepancy between the 'components', if I have correctly identified a discrepancy, reflect presumed fundamental perceived differences between phonology and syntax on the part of researchers (as in the work of Burton-Roberts 2000, to which we return below)? Or does it in the case of other current researchers embody merely atrophification of the prevalent ways of looking at syntax? Perhaps a combination of the two is involved. However that may be, we have a correlation between the difference in the extent to which primary features are appealed to in work on phonology and syntax and a rather general failure to recognize, or indeed denial of, the substantive basis for the analogies in the formal representation of phonological and syntactic structure.

For the notionalist, the existence of these structural analogies depends on similarities in substance (in that both planes are substance-based, and there are perceived similarities in the substances) as well as on the structures being due to a shared structuring capacity. A stumbling block for the autonomist, apparently, is antipathy between recognition of the groundedness analogy between the modules and the postulation of 'universal grammar'. Groundedness of syntax is incompatible with (i.e. for the notionalist, renders unnecessary) an innate set of abstract autonomous principles determining the form of language. Thus, recognizing the groundedness of phonology but not of syntax, Burton-Roberts (2000) expels the former from the core of language defined by 'universal grammar'. And Hale and Reiss (2000a: 181), on the other hand, 'rescue' phonology by rejecting its groundedness as well as that of syntax: '...we propose leaching all substance out of phonology in order better to observe the abstract computational system'. I have already indicated in these volumes that I do not consider that to attribute to language—or mind in general—the properties of current computational technology can contribute much, if anything, to our understanding of its nature.

On the assumptions of Hale and Reiss (2000b), analogies between the modules might be said to follow from 'universal grammar'. But, given the inappropriateness of the kinds of predictions made by the syntactic embodiment of autonomous principles (such as the structural parallelism predicted by 'X-bar' theory), the extension of these to phonology is scarcely to be welcomed. Substance-free phonology can then certainly admit the kind of abstractness, involving 'empty categories' (as in 'government phonology'— e.g. Kaye 1990, 1995—and its descendants), that makes the principles of syntax allegedly unlearnable, and so necessarily specified by 'universal grammar'. But positing such abstractness is even less plausible in the case of phonology, and at least equally unnecessary.

Moreover, the analogies to be suggested in the chapters that follow do not appeal to capacities other than the general cognitive. Nor do the non-analogies involve a specifically linguistic capacity manifested in the one plane rather than the other. They are associated with the asymmetrical relation of the planes, which need not be part of a 'universal grammar' and the relative complexity of the structures in the two planes, and particularly of their lexical categorizations. If, on these grounds, analogy is, alternatively, relegated in status to a phenomenon associated with Chomskyan 'E-language', it is difficult to imagine what might be the content of 'I-language'. Analogy involves the basic principles and properties of structure in both the planes, the principles and properties that define the cultural artefact we call language.

As should be clear from Volume I, the apparent discrepancy between the linguistic modules with respect to the assumed content of features and of the extent of their employment (which are related) does not seem to me to reflect a genuine difference between syntax and phonology. They are both substantively based. Indeed, appeal to substance enables the syntactician to maximize the role of an otherwise underemployed feature notation: distribution in both modules reflects the substance of the category involved, and this substance is represented linguistically by the speaker in the form of features. As suggested above, there are analogies between phonology and syntax precisely because they both grammaticalize extralinguistic domains (with perceived similarities), using a common cognitive apparatus that lends itself to analogous formal implementation.

However, recently the discrepancy between the assumed categorial structures of phonology and syntax has become even more marked in the work of many practitioners. Let us observe finally in this subsection how, in the generative tradition, there have developed further asymmetries between the respective treatments of (categories in) syntax and phonology, in contrast with 'grounded' approaches.

Much work on phonology in the 70s and 80s in particular was devoted to the elaboration of the expressive potential of phonological notations, both in relation to suprasegmental phenomena (in the representation of accent and intonation—as reflected, for instance, in the work reported on in the chapters in Goldsmith (1995) by Kager, Halle and Idsardi, Odden, Yip and Selkirk) and segmental structure (one variant of which is presented by Clements and Hume in the same volume), another in the work of van der Hulst discussed in §7.2 below. I am concerned at this point with the latter area, and the discrepancy between the richly articulated internal structure for segments envisaged by (for instance) the just-cited Clements and Hume (1995) and a range of phonologists in the 'autosegmental' tradition, on the one hand, and the rather poorly endowed internal syntactic structure commonly attributed to the basic unit of the syntax, on the other.

'Feature geometry', for instance, has, to my (certainly fallible) knowledge, not been a term recurrent in the syntactic literature. And Jackendoff's (1990: §7.1) adoption of the 'tier' notion of autosegmental phonology, for instance, does not seem to me to be applied appropriately. For instance, most of the Jackendoffian 'tiers' are not autonomously syntactic, while 'tiers' in phonology are all both phonological and phonetically based (see further Anderson 2006b: §9.1). And more characteristic of recent work in syntax has been the dissolution of categories into abstract syntactic structures surreptitious 'lexical decomposition' (as in e.g. Hale and Keyser 2002). The prevalent ideas of the categorial structure of word vs. segment have moved even further apart as a result of the kinds of attention paid to representation in the phonology of the 70s and 80s and of such recent developments in syntax.

In contrast with this situation there is outlined in §3.3 of Volume I a view of word structure as categorially and relationally complex, not merely primitively componential by virtue of simple featurization. Words may be represented lexically by dependency structures wherein one category is said to be subjoined to (dependent on but not linearly distinct from) another, as we shall examine more explicitly below. These subjunction paths of categories are not linearized syntactic structures; they are lexical structures attributed to a single item, say with a verb subjoined to a noun in a derived noun item; and the component categories occupy the same single position in syntax.

On this view, it is also important to recognize (as argued in Anderson 2006b: §10.1) that the internal syntactic structure of words, whether, as commonly is the case, represented by bundles of features specifying (primary and secondary) categoriality, or represented by any more complex 'geometry', need not be reflected in the morphology, which (depending on the language) can be relatively impoverished. Syntax is not driven by morphological considerations but by notional-categorial, which categorization need not be implemented morphologically, though it may be so expressed. The complex categorization is primarily manifested in distributional behaviour. As in the phonology, distributional behaviour reflects (particularly primary) categorization. But in the syntax there may be a path of primary categories affecting aspects of distribution, as with the derived nouns discussed in Volume I—though the head of the path is decisive overall.

Our understanding of the basis for the categorial differences which underlie such behaviour in expression (both morphological and syntactic) is impeded by inadequate articulation of categorial structure. In this respect, as I have been indicating, widely accepted ideas of syntactic structure—particularly the categorial structure of the word—are primitive compared with notions of segment structure in phonology, whereas the words of syntax invite potentially more complex structuring than the phonological segment. Despite this poverty of articulation, the categorial structure of words, such as it is, generally receives only a vague delineation: the typology of features outlined in Chomsky (1995: §4.5.1), for instance, remains undercharacterized and apparently open-ended.

1.3.2 *Anti-analogy*

By the usual strange conjunction, the most overt 'analogists' in developments associated with 'transformational-generative' grammar emerge in recent work within the 'government-phonology' framework (Kaye et al. 1985, 1990) and its descendants, and in the tradition leading to 'radical CV' and 'head-driven' phonology (van der Hulst 1989, 1994, 1995, 2000; van der Hulst and Ritter 1999), at the point when elsewhere in that tradition ideas on syntax and phonology are drifting ever further apart (as described above). Increasingly more typical of the central tradition has been the apparently 'anti-analogist', or 'anomalist', attitude defended by Bromberger and Halle (1989), who announce that 'a major result of the work of the last twenty years' is 'that syntax and phonology are essentially different' (1989: 69). They claim, in support, that 'syntax is concerned with the relations among representations that encode different types of notation', whereas 'phonology is concerned with the relationship between representations that encode the same type of information'.

It seems to me, on the contrary, that a major result of the work of the last how many years is that both these characterizations are very controversial. Within the core transformational-generative tradition, syntactic categories are uniformly autonomous, as far as the syntax is concerned, so that it is unclear what would differentiate 'different types of notation'. And the second characterization, that of phonology, fails to confront issues to do with the relationship between phonology and phonetics, as well as 'competence' and 'performance' (cf. Harris and Lindsey 1995: §3.1). Even in terms of a view that Bromberger and Halle espouse elsewhere (2000: 30), a phonological derivation is conceived of as involving 'a kind of transubstantiation... through which mnemonic elements were converted into articulatory ones'—mystical as this view is.

And the other main support for their contention that 'syntax and phonology are essentially different' depends on the assertion that only phonological rules apply in an arbitrarily stipulated order. But the analyses in §§2 and 3 of their paper that are intended to illustrate this are not well supported: see e.g. Anderson (1992: 8–10), Coleman (1995: §6), Durand (1995: §§4–5), and Kaye (1995: §3.1). More generally, there is much agreement that arbitrary rule ordering is not a necessary part of the description of phonological structure.

Perhaps what is mainly of interest here, however, is the relationship that can be seen between the claim 'that syntax and phonology are essentially different' and the development of the 'radically internal' 'universal grammar' hypothesis, which is a major concern of Carr (2000: §4.3). He disputes the appropriateness of the analogies proposed in the work in 'government phonology'. In some cases they are allegedly simply trivial ('syntactic and phonological objects both possess arboreal structure'—Carr 2000: 92), and thus (2000: 90) 'of no particular scientific interest'. But even arboreality characterizes only certain classes of phenomena (and the arboreality of linguistic structure is indeed a matter of dispute—see e.g. recently Matthews 2007). Moreover, Carr points out, the phonological interpretation of the analogies invokes perceptual characteristics not relevant to syntax. And Carr argues further that the formal characters of the proposed analogical properties are indeed not analogous at the two levels.

The 'strongly innate' conception of 'universal grammar' that is argued for by Burton-Roberts (2000), Carr (2000), and others necessarily excludes phonology, which (in what has been the 'major tradition') is substance-dependent, so not 'internal'. Such a view is unfavourable, it would appear, to the positing of fundamental analogies of structure between the syntax and the phonology. Carr (2000: §4.3) accordingly dismisses in general 'putative syntax-phonology parallels': the perceptually based structural relations of phonology cannot be analogical to the 'strictly linguistic' relations that are attributed to the syntax, which are '"austere" in the sense intended by Chomsky (1993)' (Carr 2000: 90). However, in drawing this distinction between syntax and phonology, Carr (2000) fails to specify what the fundamental principles of 'universal grammar' on which it is founded might be; and he certainly doesn't motivate on any such basis the schema of categories and relations that has often been attributed to it (which for the notionalist are cognitively but extralinguistically based).[5]

Hauser et al. (2002) and Fitch et al. (2005) arrive at a very constricted view of 'the language faculty in a narrow sense' whose distinctive fundamental property is 'recursion', the capacity for which there is no reason to associate uniquely with the 'language faculty'. It is indeed hard to believe that, for instance, various recursive musical figures or the conception of 'Russian dolls' (matryoshka dolls), where recursion is limited only physically, depends specifically on the language faculty. However, discussion of 'recursion' is vitiated by lack of clarity about exactly what the overfamiliar concept involves, how it is manifested in different formal frameworks (phrase-structure-based, dependency-based, etc.), and how it relates to proposed mechanisms of structure-building, such as 'Merge' in recent generative approaches. This serves to confuse the unpleasant debate on Pirahã and universality chronicled in Everett (2010). What does emerge is the lack of a transparent characterization of 'recursion' whereby it is necessarily either universal in or unique to human language. And some similar uncertainties afflict the debate between Jackendoff and Pinker (2005) and Fitch et al. (2005).

However all that may be, recursion does not seem to be a very plausible candidate for exemplification of the unique interest of the human linguistic capacity. More significant in the characterization of language is recognition of the roles of the 'double articulation' of linguistic representations and the linguistic embodiment of paradigmaticity and syntagmaticity. But, though possession of the capacity for 'double articulation', for instance, and indeed acquisition in general, may be subtended by physiological, perceptual, and cognitive capacities, including of course some which may be innate (though not all necessarily uniquely human), these structural properties—double articulation, paradigmaticity, and syntagmaticity—as embodied in language, are largely cultural products that can be learned.

---

[5] I do not consider here, for example, the weaker position whereby principles of universal grammar might be seen as genetic 'residues' of general cognitive principles, perhaps along the lines adumbrated by Newmeyer (1990: 220, 1991)—though I would argue that such a universal grammar is also unnecessary, though it might be easier to reconcile with manifestations of the structural analogy assumption. But it is unnecessary for explaining analogies. Moreover, if phonology is excluded from universal grammar, the perceived analogies between the two planes would depend on the one case on genetic transmission, on the other on learning. On the assumption that neither plane is based on a universal grammar, the analogies are recognized and reconstructed with respect to both planes from the outputs with which language learners are confronted.

I also do not address here the position advocated by Bermúdez-Otero and Börjars (2006), who claim (not very precisely) that 'both phonological and syntactic knowledge...is *self-contained* but partially *nonarbitrary*' (p. 2), and who stress the role in acquisition of 'performance self-monitoring'. But in their case too I would question the need to invoke a range of specifically linguistic universal (rather than general) categories.

Moreover, what is more fundamental to the identification of the essence of our humanity is the flexibility and imagination with which these cultural artefacts are deployed—though I do not underestimate the difficulties in attempting to characterize the manifestations of these creative capacities. Such considerations suggest to me that it's time for 'universal grammarians' to 'minimalize' things just a little further and thereby confront the illusory and obfuscatory character of what they have been pursuing in the search for what ensures autonomy.

1.3.3 *Anti-anti-analogy*

In response to the alleged incompatibility of structural analogy and 'universal grammar', Anderson (2006a) contends that the kinds of arguments for such a view of 'universal grammar' adduced from acquisitional considerations (notably arguments from 'poverty of stimulus') are inconclusive, and illustrates this by an examination of what he took to be a typical discussion of evidence for the unlearnability of the fundamental principles of syntax, viz. that in Lightfoot (1999: ch. 3). There, as elsewhere, the argument depends on the positing of 'empty categories'. These are allegedly a property of 'universal grammar'. However, given their 'emptiness', they are necessarily unlearnable: the prediction of the unlearnability of these properties is self-confirmatory. Just as the autonomy assumption is not an empirical hypothesis but rather at best defines a research programme, so arguments for 'universal grammar' lack any empirical basis as long as they are based on such inherently unlearnable abstractions. It is incumbent upon the defender of 'universal grammar' to show that the acquisitional phenomena involved cannot be accounted for without the invocation of such unlearnables. In the case discussed by Anderson (2006a), this duty had not been fulfilled, and the argument necessarily fails.

A more general threat to 'poverty-of-stimulus' arguments comes from such work as that reported in Lappin (2005) and Lappin and Shieber (2007). This work offers support for the notion that language acquisition can be achieved via general machine-learning methods on the basis of minimal settings for a few linguistic categories and relationships. To the extent that even these settings can be derived from expectations with a notional basis, there is no need to attribute categorial and structural properties to 'universal grammar'. For related discussion see Sampson (1997).

Anderson (2006a) argues that the structural relations exhibited by the syntax are cognitively based, just as the phonological are perceptual. The notion 'head', for instance, discussed by Carr (2000: 90–1), is dismissed by him as a potential 'parallel' pertaining to both domains. He argues that such notions as 'head' or 'government' in syntax are 'strictly linguistic', unlike the alleged manifestations of these in the phonology. But 'head' can be given an analogical cognitive basis in both syntax and phonology; it is associated with 'cognitive salience', as acknowledged in Carr (2005: particularly §3), who argues in support of this analogy (see too Carr 2006).

In the present work (following Anderson 2006a), it is maintained that syntactic and phonological 'heads' share not just a cognitive basis but detailed formal similarities. These formal similarities result from the construction of both syntax and phonology using the same mental capacities in relation to phenomena that are perceived as analogous. The similarities involved are introduced in a preliminary way in §5 of this chapter, which outlines why the similarities involving headhood are among the fundamental attributes of the phonology. In doing so, it offers a more detailed account of the kinds of headed structures that underlie the recent history of the debate on heads and analogy outlined in this subsection.

It is then the concern of Chapter 2 to illustrate in more detail something of the extent of this analogy in relation to a range of phenomena, and not just involving headhood itself but also properties associated with the concept 'head', such as 'complement', 'adjunct', and even 'specifier'. These analogies are difficult to account for on the basis of Carr's 'innate, radically internal, encapsulated' conception of 'universal grammar' (2000: 89), which excludes phonology. The existence of such analogies, and of the range of further kinds of analogy surveyed in Chapters 3 and 4, which are not just head-based, is a challenge to the positing of an abstract 'universal grammar', given their ultimately substantive basis.

Anderson (2006a) also shows, along the lines of §2.4 of Volume I, how recognition of the cognitive basis for syntactic categories, which is denied by 'radically internal' 'universal grammar', could have avoided the development of an influential false analogy, in this case the intra-syntactic one mentioned above, namely the theory of X-bar syntax, which proposes detailed parallelism in the structures projected by different syntactic categories. Both Anderson (2006a) and §2.4 of Volume I argue that the syntax of particularly verbs and nouns is fundamentally different, and point out that this can be predicted from their semantic character. It is, indeed, in the spirit of the structural analogy assumption to recognize that differences in substance are likely to frustrate putative parallelisms even plane-internally. I shall return to this below.

The consequences of differences in substance is pursued across planes and in more detail in Part III of the present volume, which is concerned with the limits set on analogy spanning the planes of syntax and phonology by the demands of the extralinguistic domains with which the syntax and phonology respectively interface, as well as by the character of the overall relationship between syntax and phonology and between each of them and the lexicon. At this point, some further consideration of the fundamental notions level and plane is in order, and particularly their relation to substance: this occupies the next section, which provides some background to the view of modularity proposed in the Prologue.

1.4 Levels, planes, and analogy

In this section I shall try to elucidate further what I see as the motivations for the rather bald injunction involved in the cited formulation of the structural analogy assumption, as well as the notion of 'level' invoked therein. Recall Anderson (1992: 2):

> Minimise (more strongly, eliminate) differences between levels that do not follow from a difference in alphabet or from the nature of the relationship between the levels concerned

This will necessarily involve us, for clarity's sake, in some of the history of the development of ideas concerning levels of representation, as well as concerning the extent to which analogies between different levels should be recognized. One thing that emerges from this is the often unacknowledged persistence of certain ideas concerning the architecture of grammars. This is particularly striking where these ideas come to be embedded in different theoretical approaches that are usually viewed as fundamentally opposed in their aims and methodologies.

The recognition of 'levels', as in the above formulation of the structural analogy assumption, is in itself 'counter-analogical', since a major motivation for recognizing different structural **levels** of representation has been on the basis of differences in the principles which govern the construction of the putative levels—i.e. modularity. In this sense of 'level', stratification into levels arises from the modularization of certain principles of construction. The basic architecture of grammars is embodied in the structure of stratification invoked that is necessitated by the modularization of structural principles.

Thus, for example, Chomsky (1957: 107) summarizes a central part of his discussion of the content of a transformational-generative grammar with the following:

> We consequently view grammars as having a tripartite structure. A grammar has a sequence of rules from which phrase structure can be reconstructed and a sequence of morphophonemic rules that convert strings of morphemes into strings of phonemes.

Connecting these sequences, there is a sequence of transformational rules that carry strings with phrase structure into new strings to which the morphophonemic rules can apply. The phrase structure and morphophonemic rules are elementary in a sense in which the transformational rules are not. To apply a transformation to a string, we must know some of the history of derivation of this string; but to apply non-transformational rules, it is sufficient to know the shape of the string to which the rule applies.

The phrase-structure rules and the transformational define different levels.

The phrase-structure and the morphophonemic rules, however, though both non-transformational, can be said to determine distinct levels not just because different types of rule seem to be involved, but also on the grounds, in their case, that the categorial alphabet of morphophonemics is at least partly distinct (in being phonetically based, phonemic) from that manipulated by the phrase-structure rules. Indeed, we can say that phonological and (both pre- and post-transformational) syntactic representations manifest a difference in **plane**, on such an account. This constitutes a particular kind of difference in level: a plane is a (set of) level(s) constructed out of a distinctive kind of 'alphabet' of categories; distinctiveness of alphabet necessitates a difference in level. For the notionalist the alphabets of both the syntactic and the (morpho)phonological planes are distinctive by virtue of their differing extralinguistically based substance.

Apart from in difference in the principles of construction themselves, i.e. simple modularity, there are two places in which we can look for motivations for structural differences, i.e. lack of analogy, between two planes. And these differences account indeed for the essential differences in principles of construction. Some planar differences are intrinsic to the different alphabets—e.g. simply the relative sizes of their membership, as well as the nature of their substance. Such differences have to do with the respective extralinguistic domains with which they interface. There are also discrepancies occasioned by the relationship between two levels or planes—e.g. an interpretive role of one vis-à-vis the other.

In such terms, Chomsky's phrase-structure and morphophonemic levels belong to two different planes: they have distinct basic alphabets, and they differ in number of basic elements. And the two planes are related asymmetrically: the morphophonemic level interprets the phrase structure, via the transformations, i.e. it interprets the output to the syntactic plane, which includes the results of the application of the transformations. It is such planar differences that will be held to account for the limitations on analogy addressed in Part III. The transformational rules posited by Chomsky, however, apparently do not introduce a difference in plane with respect to the objects determined by the phrase-structure rules, in that they manipulate objects constructed out of the same basic alphabet. They are at most different levels belonging to a single plane. Given the formal differences between transformational and phrase-structure rules described by Chomsky, the transformational rules do appear to construct a different level, governed by different structural principles and related asymmetrically to the phrase-structure level. But there are lacking motivations for recognizing a planar difference in this case.

In the terms introduced here, transformational-generative grammars should be viewed as having not a tripartite structure, as suggested by Chomsky (1957), but a basic bipartite structure, with the levels determined by the phrase-structure and transformational rules constituting a plane distinct from the level constructed by the morphophonemic rules. The former plane in turn shows a bipartition into levels respectively determined by the phrase-structure rules and by the transformational rules. The basic modules are syntax and phonology, and syntax is further modularized in such a transformational grammar.

The appropriateness of this kind of articulation of what is proposed in Chomsky (1957) is confirmed in Chomsky (1965), wherein the 'base' (roughly corresponding, leaving aside different treatments of 'subcategorization', to the 'phrase-structure rules') and 'transformational subcomponent' are grouped together as the 'syntactic component'. There, too, the levels determined by the two subcomponents are distinguished as 'deep structure' and 'surface structure'. Let us pursue, continuing to follow the course of Anderson (2006a), some of the ways in which this line of thinking developed, as it will lead us back into our main theme, as well as, hopefully, being of some historiographic interest.

Much work in the transformational tradition subsequent to Chomsky (1965)—central here is perhaps Emonds (1976)—conspired to suggest that the objects created by 'phrase-structure' and 'transformational' rules were after all very similar, and not just in alphabet invoked: 'surface structure' was governed, to an overwhelming extent, by the same principles as hold at 'deep structure', despite the asymmetrical relation between the two levels. 'Transformations' are a set of rules which maps one level onto another one composed of the same kinds of object governed by the same, or minimally different, principles. Whatever differences there might be between the two levels—differences which could indeed be taken to motivate the recognition of them as distinct levels—can be attributed to this asymmetrical relationship between them, mediated by the transformational rules.

Moreover, say syntactic representations are supplemented by 'tracking devices' to accommodate cross-reference and discontinuities arising from differences between the successive sublevels that constitute transformational derivations, and that these sublevels are seen as not successive but alternatives obeying the same principles. Then one direction in which such a recognition of principles in common between 'deep' and 'surface' could lead would be to the collapse of the 'deep'/'surface' distinction and the positing of a single syntactic level governed by a single set of ('phrase-structure') principles. This is familiar from e.g. the tradition(s) associated with Gazdar et al. (1985) and Pollard and Sag (1994). But, in this case, the recognition of only one level of representation for the syntax depended on the importation into phrase structures of what I have called 'tracking devices' that can be argued to have much the same function as the 'empty categories' of the continuing transformational tradition, and, as non-signs, the same undesirable properties. Neither set of developments described in these two paragraphs provided a satisfactory solution to the problems (associated with excessive power) arising from the introduction of the transformational level.

In the traditions that continued through the 80s to draw a distinction between 'deep' and 'surface' structure—or (terminological or substantive) modifications thereof ('D-structure', 'S-structure', as in e.g. Chomsky 1981)—there eventually developed a recognition that attempts to motivate well-defined levels of 'D(eep)-structure' and 'S(urface)-structure' are misguided. Chomsky has alleged that 'the empirical justification' for the recognition of a level of 'D-structure' and the 'evidence' for 'S-structure' are in both instances 'substantial' (1995: 187, 192). But he nevertheless goes on to argue that the postulated role of 'D-structure' as an interface between lexicon and grammar is problematical, and that the principles of grammar that allegedly apply thereat 'are dubious on conceptual grounds' (Chomsky 1995: 187); and that it seems to be unnecessary to propose that there are conditions that apply at the hypothesized level of 'S-structure' (Chomsky 1995: §3.4). It is thus conceded that it is undesirable to postulate such 'internal' levels in addition to the 'external interface levels' of 'logical form' and 'phonological form'.

As far as the distinguishing of levels is concerned, we arrive, on the basis of this development, at a conception very reminiscent of proposals made much earlier in the twentieth century, when there was recognized a basic planar distinction between 'content form' and 'expression form'—see e.g. Hjelmslev (1954), as well as other post-Saussurean developments. And this characterizes the position adopted by the tradition underlying Anderson (2006a) and maintained here. As far as this post-Saussurean tradition is concerned, the main difference in this area from recent 'transformational-generative' work has come to be the insistence in the latter on the 'autonomy of syntax'. As argued in the first volume of this trilogy (and see again Anderson 2005a), this is an anti-Saussurean development: signs are identified by a conjunction of two substances, and the categorizations of the two planes are distributionally identifiable classifications of substance.

I have said that structural analogy is the unmarked assumption. This is because the two powerful determinants of linguistic structure lead one to expect it. In the first place both planes are grammaticalizations, including categorizations, of mental domains associated with perception, though one is specifically based on a particular medium of perception, and the other involves more general capacities of conceptualization. Secondly, the structuring of the two planes utilizes the same cognitive capabilities of conceptualization and representation; thus they are both 'representational', in something like Burton-Roberts's (2000) terms. The first determinant encourages analogies based on substantive similarities, the second analogies in 'formal' properties; though in particular instances both may be involved. As we shall see, the analogy of headhood relies mainly on the substantive property of cognitive salience, manifested (in different media) in both syntax and phonology, while that of transitivity is more obviously 'formal'. These reflect the predominance of one or the other of the sources of analogy.

On present knowledge at least, we should not insist, however, on a firm distinction between 'formal' and 'substantive', given that the means of expression in each plane are ultimately substance-derived, in involving salience, linearity, presence vs. absence. As discussed in relation to the submodules of syntax in Volume I, even 'formal' analogies have some kind of substantive corollary, even if only indirectly. We shall find, for instance, that even 'transitivity' can be related to 'quantity' or 'weight' on both planes. And substance underlies one of the most fundamental 'formal' analogies between the two planes, namely the non-mutative character of their principles of construction. Moreover, 'formal' analogies are usually those that depend least upon the particular character of the substance being grammaticalized. Particular substantive demands lead to dis-analogy.

Thus, the syntactic structures projected from lexical categorizations are non-derivational, in so far as their erection does not appeal to (extrinsic) ordering of individual projections. So too with lexically derived phonological representations. We encounter here a fundamental analogy: the structural elaboration of lexical content in both planar modules is non-mutative, structure-building. This is made feasible by reference to substance, so that in syntax, for instance, it is semanticity that permits long-distance connections to be made and incomplete structures correctly interpreted. And mutation in phonology is incompatible with direct phonetic interpretation.

This non-mutational character of the planes may be obscured by further modularization. In so far as the implementation, with respect to both planes, of discourse demands can involve different principles from those involved in projection from the lexicon, we can recognize plane-internal modules: we can differentiate between levels of lexically determined syntax and phonology, on the one hand, and levels of utterance determined by discourse considerations, **lexical levels** vs. **utterance levels**. The distinction has a rather different status with respect to the two planes, however, and this has to do with their asymmetrical (sign) relationship, though parallelisms persist.

Syntactically, utterances differ from predications in involving contextually determined omissions and the like, as with many answers; they may not be fully-formed predications. But discourse requirements may be manifested predicationally, via a lexical category (such as 'topic'), as well as in utterance structure (by ellipsis, for instance). Phonologically realized utterances differ from the phonological words derived from the lexicon in accommodating sequences of these to predicational demands, as with phonological marking of questions in English, or to the demands of the utterance structures resulting from the interaction of predication and discourse. Utterances in both planes are underdetermined by lexical and predicational structure.

I shall not be further concerned here with utterances as such, or with the internal principles that relate predications to utterances. It is important to observe, though, that these distinctions in lexically based vs. utterance based representation have a substantive motivation in contextuality; they do not involve arbitrary derivational ordering. They instantiate another relation between levels, a re-representation. And their structural differences reflect the substantive difference between lexical and utterance motivations.

I have already recognized other submodules within the planes. I assume in this series of volumes the strict requirement that all differences in level of representation, and thus in (sub)module, are substantively motivated; there are no purely abstract modular distinctions. This restricts the kind of interface phenomena that can be expected within language: they occur only as mediation between the substantive media associated with different levels, as discussed in Volume II. This constitutes another limitation on modularity: it must be substantively motivated. Thus, the submodules of syntax introduce, alongside the basic categorial vocabulary, relations of salience (formally, dependency), time (concatenation), and sound (exponence). Analogical submodularization is to be found in the phonology. But the most significant substantive difference is between the substantive bases for the plane-particular alphabets of syntax and phonology.

What we seem to be able to conclude is that, other things being equal, the structural analogy assumption would expect inter-planar application of analogies to be limited only by differences between the alphabets of the two planes of content form (syntax, including the syntactic categorizations in the lexicon) and expression form (phonology, including the phonological representations in the lexicon) and by the character of the relationship between the planes. The proposed reasons for the limitations should of course be transparent if they are to be explanatory.

And, further, the particular members of each alphabet make different structural demands because of their different content. Each plane is thus not necessarily structurally homogeneous. I cite again the observation that discrepancy in the substance of categories is the basis for the lack in analogy of structure between nouns and verbs discussed in §2.4 of Volume I; and this is the reason for the failure of the X-bar theory of syntax. This is another manifestation of the dependence of structural differences on differences in substance. Let us, in the context of analogy now, look again at the significance of this discrepancy in the behaviour of syntactic categories.

1.5 The X-bar fallacy and the limits of analogy

Anderson (2006a: §5) observes that, once one moves away from the apparently relatively safe territory of verbs, the applicability of the distinction between complement and adjunct is either unclear or clearly rather different from what seems to be involved with verbs. It is not obvious, for instance, how and how far the complement/adjunct distinction is relevant to English adjectives and prepositions.

In terms of the system of categories discussed in Volume I, the verb is {P;N}, where the predicability feature **P** predominates over the referentiality one **N**, and the adjective is {P;N} and {N;P}, i.e. {P:N}, where the two features are mutually preponderant. The adjective, unsurprisingly, given the semantic property of high predicativity it shares with the verb, is a less problematical category, in terms of the complement/adjunct distinction, than the preposition, which is the null combination of the two features.

Certainly, on most occurrences, most simplex adjectives are either 'intransitive' (*old, red*) or they take an optional but semantically complement-like dependent (*proud (of his achievements), happy (with the results)*). The former (basically 'intransitive') set take only lexicalized complement-like dependents (*red in tooth and claw, red in the face*). And omissibility of the equivalent of complements with adjectives is much more general than in the case of verbal semantic complements: compare the pair in (3a-b):

(3) a. She resembles *(her mother)
    b. She is similar (to her mother)
    c. She is like *(her mother)
    d. She is alike

The untypical non-prepositional complement of *like* in (3c) is like that in (3a) in normally requiring an overt complement; of *like*-forms, only (3d) provides an analogue to the short form of (3b). And some adjectives with prepositional complements are quite strongly 'transitive' (*fond of praise, desirous of praise*).

Anderson (2006a) thus concedes that perhaps one could make a case for distinguishing between the two prepositional phrases in (4) as respectively 'complement' vs. 'adjunct':

(4) They were aware of their mistakes to some extent

But there is certainly with adjectives nothing like the rich array of complement types and adjunct types that we can associate with verbs. The most verb-like in this respect are deverbals like *pleased, worried* etc., as we expect, given their verbal base.

Adjective constructions do provide what has often been seen as the paradigm case of the characteristic pre-modifier often referred to as a 'specifier': *very*, etc. (though see further §4.2), but this does not render it any more verb-like in the structures it projects. What is to count as the 'specifier' of the verb is not at all obvious.

Prepositions take a dependent that is either obligatory (*It was at the window*) or apparently optional (*It flew in (the window)*), and they show a limited capacity for apparent nesting of the head (*It flew in at the window*), as well as plausible instances of 'specification' (*It flew right in the window*). Including the traditional 'subordinating conjunctions' (*when, while,* etc.) in the class of prepositions extends the complement types that we can associate with the class. And we can perhaps treat some 'adverbs', such as *away,* as prepositions that are obligatorily 'intransitive'—though only apparently, in terms of the lexical-incorporation analysis of Volume I, whereby the 'adverbial preposition' has a lexically converted complement. Unlike prototypical prepositions such as *at*, these adverbs typically incorporate some point or space of reference, as do 'prepositions' like *in*, which, if apparently 'intransitive', are normally interpreted as elliptical. In all of these cases the element, whether traditionally regarded as 'preposition' or 'adverb' or 'conjunction' can be analysed as transitive, with linearly distinct or subjoined complement.

As Anderson (2006a) points out, the evidence for the predicted complement/adjunct distinction for prepositions that is assembled by Radford (1988: §5.4) is rather tenuous, depending as it does on a highly questionable analysis of *completely* in *He was (so) completely in the wrong* as a prepositional 'adjunct' and on the behaviour of the idiom *at odds with*. None of this relates very easily to the very generally applicable verbal complement/adjunct distinction. And there is again, of course, nothing parallel to the rich system of verbal complement types and adjunct types. And the insistent presence of particular kinds of complementation associated with prepositions is associated with their status as a 'functional category', the category that I call 'functor'. Functional categories are characteristically transitive (cf. Volume I, §3.4).

Also, though it appears that the adjective and the preposition may each be associated with a fairly obvious distinctive lexical class of 'specifiers', in the case of verbs, as observed above, the same can scarcely be said; the identity of their 'specifier(s)' has remained contentious. Moreover, §5.2 argues that lexical categories (including adjectives) do not take 'specifiers'. This is another structural projection that is not general throughout the primary categories of syntax. It is not merely the complement/adjunct distinction that is a problem.

As we have seen, nouns introduce yet other problems for X-bar theory, even apart from the difficulties in motivating a 'specifier' for nouns, on the assumption that determiners are disqualified as such, but are indeed a functional category complemented by the noun (an assumption argued for in e.g. Anderson 1976a: ch. 4, 1986c, 1997a: §3.7, and adopted here). There seems to be a small set of 'relational' nouns that normally require a complement: *mother, side*, etc.; in the absence of an overt dependent, they are interpreted as elliptical. And nouns which are (overtly or covertly) derivative of verbs can manifest the pattern of dependents associated with the corresponding verb, though in their case the equivalents of the verbal complements, including the equivalent of the subject, are generally omissible. Compare (5a) with (b):

(5) a. (His) desire (for unlimited pleasure) [overcame him]
    b. He desires unlimited pleasure

And (6a) also illustrates that the argument dependent of the agentive noun may be absent even when the base verb, in this case *murder*, is insistently transitive, as illustrated by (6b):[6]

---

[6] This is despite, or perhaps, rather, manipulated by, literary uses such as the following:

Besides, what could he, a stranger, say to Miss Pantil, Mr Newey and young Maude to convince them that in fact it was one of their friends who had murdered?

(Graham Greene, *The Ministry of Fear*, ch. 4).

(6) a. [He is] a murderer (of little children)
    b. He murders *(little children)

And, again shown in Volume I, a deverbal noun also allows for an additional distinction compared with the corresponding verb, involving a dependent which is not the equivalent of either a verbal complement or adjunct. We return to it in a moment; first, more on 'complement' vs. 'adjunct'.

(7a) shows nominal dependents equivalent to the post-verbal complement and adjunct in (7b), and the respective statuses of the two dependents in (7a) is arguably manifested in the anomaly of (7c):

(7) a. [He is in love with] a student of physics at Glasgow
    b. S/he studies physics at Glasgow
    c. *[He is in love with] a student at Glasgow of physics

In English the complement equivalent must normally be nearer to the head than the adjunct equivalent.

However, as anticipated, the noun in (7) allows for other apparent dependents that are not available to the verb:

(8) a. [He is in love with] a student of physics at Glasgow from Surrey
    b. *S/he studies physics at Glasgow from Surrey

The only way I can make any sense of (8b) is if the student is construed as pursuing a distance-learning course at Glasgow University while resident in Surrey, which is not the obvious sense to be attributed to (8a). Volume I distinguishes the distinctive kind of dependency manifested in (8a) by the traditional term **attributive**, which is apparently a relation available to nominal dependents that is distinct from both complement (equivalent) and adjunct (equivalent).

The attributive is awkward at best in English if placed closer to the head than the other dependents:

(9) a. *[He is in love with] a student from Surrey of physics at Glasgow
    b. ?*[He is in love with] a student of physics from Surrey at Glasgow

The attributive may also be used with non-verb-based nouns, whether they are 'relational' (10a) or are the prototypical 'non-relational' nouns exemplified in (10b):

(10) a. [He is in love with] a mother of 10 from Surrey
     b. [He is in love with] a girl from Surrey

But it is not clear that even a relational noun can take an adjunct, as distinct from an attributive. And prototypical non-'relational', non-verb-based nouns lack the equivalents of both kinds of verbal dependents, and complements, in particular.

The preposed 'dependents' of the verb-based noun in (11) are ambiguous between an adjunct(-equivalent) reading and an attributive one:

(11) a. [He is in love with] a Glasgow student of physics
b. [He is in love with] a Surrey student of physics

The lovee is understood to be either a student at Glasgow or Surrey University or to come from Glasgow or Surrey.

Likewise, we can associate the ambiguity in (12a) with whether the adjective is an adjunct equivalent (cf. *Bobbie dances beautifully*) or an attributive:

(12) a. Bobbie is a beautiful dancer
b. Bobbie is a former dancer

On the attributive interpretation Bobbie is beautiful irrespective of his/her dancing, whereas on the reading associated with the adjunct equivalent the beauty resides in Bobbie's dancing.[7] 'Tensed' adjectives that cannot be predicative, such as that in (12b), allow only the adjunct-equivalent reading: cf. *Bobbie formerly danced/Bobbie was formerly a nun*. This is so even with nouns that are not obviously verb-based, as in *She is a former nun*. The 'tensing' and the restriction to an adjunct reading (cf. *She was formerly a dancer*), however, is again (after all) suggestive of some sort of predicative base for these constructions in general, despite the absence with such as *former* of any overt marking of such a lexically derived status (as argued in the discussion of *pilgrim* and *pilgrimage* in §2.4 of Volume I).

Thus, to sum up, the equivalents with nouns of verbal complements and adjuncts behave rather differently from the corresponding verbal elements, and they are limited to non-prototypical, typically deverbal nouns; and nouns in general are associated with a distinct class of 'dependents' traditionally called attributives. Even these 'dependents' Anderson (2007: §2.3.3) regards as heads: as we have already assumed, prototypical nouns have no dependents whatever.

---

[7] Cf. the discussions of this distinction by e.g. Bolinger (1967), Kamp (1975), and Siegel (1980), for instance. Anderson (1997a: §3.7.2) offers a rather different analysis from that suggested here, which latter is based on the proposals made in Anderson (2006b). Given the syntactic consequences of the distinction, it is in retrospect ironic that Selkirk (1977: 286–7) should cite the alleged asyntacticity of this semantic distinction as a motivation for 'the thesis of the autonomy of syntax'—if this refers to 'strong autonomy' in Langacker's (2003: 41–2) sense.

Van Roey (1969) discusses further complications with nouns, involving 'post-nominal modifiers'. But notice too that there is nothing parallel with verbs to the complex word-order conditions associated specifically with pre-nominal dependents/attributives in English. There are particular pragmatic circumstances for preferring a particular order of the adjuncts in (13):

(13) (with Mary)
  Bill left (on Tuesday)
   (by bus)

But the conditions associated with the ordering of **pre-nominal attributives** in English are of quite another order.

A phrase like that in (14), which, I think, instantiates the 'unmarked' pre-nominal sequence, illustrates something of this:

(14) [the] same crass retired English provincial high-court judge

The conditions on these sequences are examined by, among others, Chatman (1960), Goyvaerts (1968), Vendler (1968), Juul (1975), Bache (1978), and Rijkhoff (2002).[8] Whatever conditions are involved here seem to be specific in English to pre-nominal attributives. Whatever is perhaps generalizable to other phenomena in English and other languages invokes cognitive/semantic distinctions, to do e.g. with 'description' vs. 'classification'. These partly specifically English conditions on sequencing are overall poor candidates for 'universal grammar'. They are patently learnable.

According to Chomsky (1973: 275), this phenomenon is 'inexpressible in any natural way in a transformational grammar'. But it seems that the only way to discount such phenomena (which are in some form not unique to English) as evidence for the nature of syntactic categories, if we discount 'universal grammar', is the familiar, but nonetheless reprehensible, stratagem of arbitrarily excluding them from the domain of syntax.

We see again that devotion to the X-bar analogy, in particular to the uniformity assumption it embodies, distorts our understanding of the syntax of the categories. Though they certainly share some properties, the syntax of nouns and verbs in particular is radically different; the representations of the structures in which they occur will diverge considerably. This difference

---

[8] Bache, who offers the most comprehensive study, makes preliminary distinctions (1978: §0.3) between orders that are reversible and those that are not, between reversible orders where the variation is semantically distinctive and those where it is not, and between non-distinctive reversible orders where one possibility is preferred and those where there is no preference. And he goes on to elaborate a rich and detailed analysis of the order possibilities. Compare here too the relevant parts of Halliday's discussion of what he calls the 'experiential structure of the nominal group' (1994: §6.2).

and this divergence follow from their semantics, as argued in §2.4 of Volume I. As the heads of categories they manifest different kinds of substantive salience. The prototypical verb, as a label for an event type, is relational and dynamic: the verb is the prototypical predicator, it is eminently predicable. As relational, it entails participants of different types, reflected in its subcategorization: it has the cognitive salience of pre-eminent capacity for headhood. And, as dynamic, it attracts optional, or elective, secondary features such as tense and aspect (S. R. Anderson 1985: §2.2.1). The prototypical noun, as a label for an entity type, is discrete and stable: it is the prototypical descriptor of a potential referential, it promotes referential identification by its stability and discreteness. As discrete, it is not subcategorized for arguments, but, as stable and discrete, it permits further subclassification of its denotation by attributivization, and it attracts inherent secondary features such as those to do with non-transient, basic classifications (gender). Thus the semantic distinction between them informs the respective morphosyntaxes of verbs and nouns.

The point in recalling here this situation, described in Volume I, is its consistency with the structural analogy assumption, which is our concern in the present volume. It is not that the respective representations of nouns and verbs involve different kinds of alphabets, as with distinct planes; but rather that the substance of their respective representations in the alphabet of syntax is so divergent (in that in nouns the referentiable feature is dominant whereas with verbs it is the predicable) that the scope for analogy of projected structure, which on the assumptions of notional grammar reflects the semantically based substance attributed to the features, is very limited. The actual discrepancy between verbs and nouns is obscured if we pay attention only to distribution. The major point to be made is that it is not just that the dys-analogy of X-bar theory makes incorrect predictions, but that it would be purely accidental if it happened to make correct ones.[9]

---

[9] Anderson (2006a) points out that it follows from the characterizations of phonology and syntax suggested there and in work in the same tradition that (*pace* e.g. van der Hulst 2000) we should not expect X-bar theory to be applicable to phonology either. However, a comment by an anonymous reviewer prompted Anderson to stress that the major theme of his discussion of 'X-bar syntax' is not intended as an argument for analogy between syntax and phonology (in the reviewer's words: 'X-bar syntax doesn't work that well in syntax, so the fact that it doesn't work that well in phonology either is actually evidence that the two are similar'). Rather, it argues against an intra-syntactic analogy, one which would not be available in a cognitively based syntax, i.e. a syntax that does not invoke a 'universal grammar' hypothesis that embraces arbitrary principles like 'X-bar' parallelism in the projections of syntactic categories.

In this section I have presented arguments based on the discussion in Anderson (2006a) that supplement the revisiting of material presented in §2.4 of Volume I in illustrating the kind of limits placed on intra-planar analogy. These limits are imposed by different interface requirements associated with the different cognitive bases for nouns and verbs, in particular. In Part III we look in some detail at the restrictions on inter-planar (syntax-phonology) analogies deriving from difference in the demands made by their respective interfaces, on the one hand representational needs associated with the semanticity of syntax, on the other the severe limitations imposed by phoneticity.

1.6 Conclusion

This chapter is intended as a preparation for the chapters to follow, in introducing the structural analogy assumption, as a systematic descendant of all those attempts in the history of linguistics to deploy analogous structural ideas in different planes or levels. Let us firstly look back at that assumption before proceeding to illustrate the kind of issues we shall be concerned with in the rest of this volume, via a further consideration of some of the discussion that has preceded it elsewhere.

Largely following the arguments of Anderson (2006a), I have proposed that phenomena, suggestive of analogy, if correctly observed, are most readily understood on the basis of the assumption that the planes, or linguistic modules, are both grounded. The sharing of groundedness facilitates analogies based on perceived similarities (such as 'cognitive salience') in the admittedly distinct substances whose representation determines the structures of phonology and syntax. Further analogies, however, may depend, instead or as well, on these representations of the substances being allowed by the same ('logical') mental apparatus in both cases. This is what might be predominantly involved in the attribution of 'transitivity', in what immediately follows, to both phonology and syntax.

On the other hand, such analogies are difficult to square with a view of linguistic structure whereby only phonology is grounded, and is thereby excluded from 'universal grammar'. This alleged discrepancy between the planes of language led Anderson (2006a), as described in §1.3, to question the viability of arguments for 'universal grammar' based on 'poverty of stimulus'. And he concludes, admittedly on the basis of attending, as illustration, to only one well-known instance of such arguments, but against a background of similar questioning, that these depend on the positing of the autonomy of syntax, including 'empty categories'. This necessarily renders 'universal grammar' unlearnable, confirming circularly the predictions made by the definition of 'universal grammar'. However, learnability can be said to depend on, among other things, including memorability, the natural correlation between syntax, particularly syntactic categories, and semantic or functional content, i.e. extralinguistic substance. 'Empty categories' are excluded by this correlation, thus calling into question the need for 'universal grammar'. The learnability of syntax becomes that much more plausible.

Further, lack of recognition of the cognitive basis for syntactic structures (categories and relations), a lack which is a necessary property of a 'universal grammar' hypothesis based on the autonomy of syntax, has encouraged, or at least by this lack has failed to prevent, the elaboration of a false analogy, the cross-categorial symmetry predicted by the X-bar theory of syntactic structure (§1.5). This already illustrates the constraints on analogy imposed by interface considerations, which, as indicated, is the major topic of Part III, though mainly involving there a comparison of the two planes rather than divergent structural properties within the single plane of syntax, such as those that undermine the symmetry predicted by X-bar syntax.

Different syntactic domains, such as 'VP', 'NP', 'S', are not as homogeneously structured as is supposed in terms of the inappropriate intra-planar analogy embraced by X-bar theory of syntactic structure—inappropriate, at least, if applied in a wholesale fashion. I stress here that what is inappropriate is the uniformity assumption that is the major innovation of X-bar theory—not, for instance, the postulation of headedness of constructions, a notion anticipated, more radically, by dependency syntax and some other formal grammars. The reasons for the lack of symmetry among projections of different classes are also problematical for the 'austere' notion of 'universal grammar', in so far as they can be seen to involve the cognitive basis of syntactic categories. On the other hand, it is also compatible with, indeed a concomitant of, the structural analogy assumption that cognitively based differences should frustrate analogy, as well as manifesting it, a topic that (as indicated) will occupy us more fully in Part III.

Analogies depend on groundedness, as well as the deployment of common cognitive capacities. And groundedness is associated not just globally with the categories and structures of the linguistic modules of syntax and phonology, but also with the differentiation of different levels within the planes. §1.4 differentiated levels that are devoted to discourse considerations beyond what is provided by the lexicon (utterance levels). The lexicon itself is not a plane, but the major interface between the lexical categories of syntax and phonology. The inter-plane of morphology, if present in a language, makes overt some of the lexical relations that constitute the basis for the interfacing (some of which were relevant to the concerns of Volume II). The lexicon is the major locus among the permitted interfaces, these being restricted to the 'collision' of substantively differentiated levels. Other such interfaces relate e.g. the submodules of syntax, differentiated by their respective introduction of dependency, linearity, and phonology, in turn differentiated by their respective substantive bases. This restriction on interfaces—as mediating the 'collision' of different substances—not only limits the proliferation of putative interfaces, but also reflects the limitation on modularization: modules and submodules must be substantively differentiated.

In the chapters which follow, constituting Part II of the volume, we shall explore in some detail proposed analogies of structure between the syntax and the phonology. In Chapter 2 I shall be concentrating on establishing more firmly some fundamental properties of the phonology, particularly those 'formal' ones associated with the notion of 'head', such as 'transitivity'; these do not seem to be as directly related to simple particularized demands by an extralinguistic interface as linearity and headhood itself, and thus are most likely to reveal analogical behaviour. A range of further analogies is investigated in Chapters 3 and 4. In Chapter 5, again as indicated, we then return to concentration on the limits of analogy and their basis in differing interface requirements.

These requirements, and the resulting limitations on analogy, are the basis for perhaps the major difference between the view of structural analogy assumed here and the 'remarkable isomorphism' (Kuryłowicz 1949: 48) attributed by Hjelmslev to the two planes. For Hjelmslev, the language system is in principle autonomous (though this is not always obvious from his practice—see §1.2 in Volume I of the present series): there can be no extralinguistic interface requirements injected into the representation of language system; and the categorial alphabets of the plane are contentless. Hjelmslev propounds rigorous application of the structuralist assumption that a language is 'an object of autonomous study' (Matthews 2001: 152), a view which came to dominate twentieth-century linguistics (though, of course, the development of structuralism is more complex than this—see e.g. Anderson 2005a for one view of some of the complexities). In this respect, what I am advocating can be seen as a return, in this respect, to pre-structural (non-autonomous) linguistics.[10]

---

[10] Fischer-Jørgensen (1952: 8) alludes to the kind of problems that arise if no reference is made to 'substance' in, for instance, the identification of phonemes, and concludes: 'without recourse to substance, one identification will be as good as another, and it will be impossible to proceed further'. And she goes on to reveal (1952: 8–9) that though 'in his writings, Hjelmslev seems to deny

Further, the 'formal' analogies displayed by the two planes need not be seen as evidence for an autonomous faculty that includes such properties. In the absence of evidence for the restriction of such structural properties as are involved to language, the preferable hypothesis is that these analogies reveal the operation of general cognitive capacities whose working is evident in other cognitive domains. Rejection of 'universal grammar' does not entail the rejection of the idea of universal properties of mind, as envisaged by many earlier 'philosophical grammarians'. Pre-twentieth-century ideas on universal grammar did not involve autonomy. 'Pre-structuralist' also means 'pre-universal grammar' in the modern sense—though 'universal grammar' is not a necessary consequence of structuralism, of course. The insistence on the autonomy of syntax, and on 'universal grammar', depends, is indeed a 'hangover' from (a strict interpretation of) the structuralist assumption of autonomy referred to in the preceding paragraph, the assertion of the autonomy of language. However, the autonomy associated with 'universal grammar' is applied to the assumed universal basis of any natural language system, rather than to the differing systems of individual languages, as in 'pre-universal grammar' structuralism. The autonomy of early structuralism introduces obvious learnability problems, but it is an admission of defeat to resolve these by invoking an autonomous 'universal grammar'. It is time to go back to the future, whatever.

1.7 Prospect: Head-based analogies

As an illustrative prelude to the chapters that follow, let us look at the debate about the headhood analogy that Anderson (2006a) reflects. As we have seen, Carr (2000) objects to the postulation of the dependency relation as a transplanar analogy. Headhood in the phonology is reflected in 'perceptual salience' (Anderson and Ewen 1987). But, according to Carr (2000: 91), 'the notion "head" in syntax is quite different from this: it does not make any reference to salience, let alone *perceptual* salience'. He does concede (ibid), as pursued in Carr (2005), that headhood in syntax could be associated with 'semantic prominence', and this could be subsumed with 'perceptual prominence' as manifestations of 'cognitive salience', for him an undesirable move, given its incompatibility with the 'universal grammar' hypothesis. But (as

---

this', 'in oral discussions he has recently admitted that the elements are set up by considering the interplay between form and substance'. See further, as well as Anderson (2005a), Chapter 1 of Volume I in the present trilogy.

Anderson 2006a attempts to show) arguments for the analogy are based not just on this alleged shared substantive (cognitive) property but also, despite Carr's claims, and his insistence on the plausibility of only substantive analogies, on shared formal characteristics. These arise from application of the same formalizing capacities to perceived similarities in the substance-based planes.

On this joint basis, the notion of head, though indeed it cannot be a part of an 'austere' version of 'universal grammar', as this is envisaged by Carr (a position he has since abandoned), is a trans-planar analogy. This analogical status seems to be acknowledged not merely within the traditions cited by Carr (government phonology, dependency phonology, strict CV phonology, etc.) but also (despite Bromberger and Halle 1989—cited above in §1.3) by Halle and Vergnaud (1987: 6–7), for instance: '... sequences of linguistic elements are composed of one or more constituents, in which one element is specially marked—made the *head*—and the rest are said to constitute the *domain*. This is true both in phonology and in syntax.' This invites the question: 'why is this true of both syntax and phonology?' And this is what we are trying to begin to answer here.

In both syntax and phonology the head of a construction is the essential identifying component of the construction: verb phrases are identified by the presence of a verb, rhymes by the presence of a rhymal peak. In syntax, a head may also be associated with a **complement/adjunct distinction**. Adjuncts are optional extensions of a headed construction. Complements are semantically integral parts of the basic construction; their apparent absence is usually interpreted as elliptical, perhaps signalling the indefiniteness of that complement. Thus, in (15a) the transitive verb is accompanied by a complement, which satisfies its 'subcategorization' requirements, whereas the adjunct in (15b) is not demanded by the intransitive verb of that sentence:

(15) a. Flossie visited her aunt
 b. Flossie left today
 c. Flossie visited her aunt today
 d. *Flossie visited today her aunt

(15c) contains both a complement and an adjunct, in that order, as the unmarked possibility in English—cf. the at best awkward serialization of (15d), with the order reversed.

As in Volume I, and as anticipated in the Prologue to the present volume, we can represent the appropriate structures for (15) by the dependency trees in (16):

(16) a.

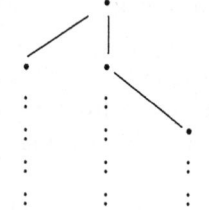

Flossie visited Doris

b.

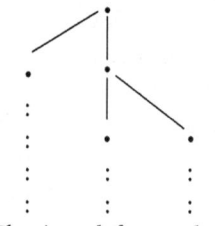

Flossie left today

c.

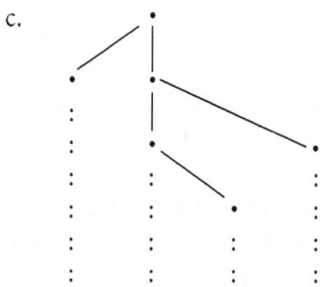

Flossie visited Doris today

d.

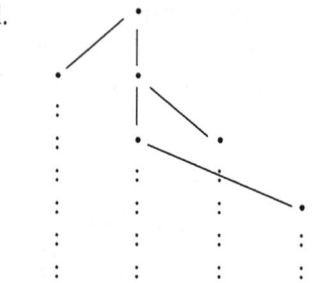

Flossie visited today Doris

These particular representations suppress categorial specifications in the interest of displaying more transparently the structural relations involved. The representations include some pairs of nodes linked by dependency relations, those represented by the vertical lines, which do not correspond to linearity differences, i.e. they are subjunctions. In this way a single item, here the verbals, may be simultaneously head of more and less inclusive constructions. The complement in (16a/c) attaches to the lowest node associated with the verb; the adjunct in (16b/c) is represented as attaching to a non-terminal node. Thus the latter representations involve an 'inner' and an 'outer' verb phrase, or 'VP', displaying recursion (under subjunction) of the verb node. (16d) would involve (in this instance) unmotivated 'tangling'.

I leave aside here the status of the subject: it is a complement that is nevertheless associated in (16) with a higher node, that which characterizes the 'sentence', usually distinguished as a quite different construction type from 'VP'. As a complement it should be attached to the lowest verbal, and positioned to its right. The factors that disturb these expectations involve considerations beyond the simple, unalloyed distinction between 'complement' and 'adjunct' that is in focus here. These factors are introduced below (and recall the discussion of subject formation of §3.7 of Volume I).

Carr claims that 'the adjunct/complement distinction, widely attested in syntactic organization, is simply absent in phonological organization' (2000: 92). Anderson (2006a) argues that, in the first place, this 'attestation in syntactic organization' is far from being as wide or as uncontroversial as Carr implies, particularly if framed in purely distributional terms. The application of the distinction is far from straightforward. It certainly cannot be reduced to: 'complements of verbs are said to be obligatorily present' (Carr 2000: 91). Consistently with notionalist assumptions, in the syntax the distinction can usefully be drawn only in semantic terms, i.e. in terms of semantic complements vs. semantic adjuncts, and adjuncthood is in some sense gradient: adjuncts may be more or less tightly bound to the core predication (see e.g. Anderson 2006b: §9.2). This appears to be recognized in general terms by e.g. Jackendoff (1977a: 264): 'complements [= dependents, in the terminology used here—*JMA*] can in fact be divided up on essentially semantic grounds, corroborated in part by syntactic evidence'. Nevertheless, there are formal consequences of the distinction whose manifestation may be partly language-particular (as we shall see).

On the other hand, to return to the alleged absence of such notions from the phonology, Anderson (2006a) points out that there is, despite Carr's claim to the contrary, a clear analogue to the syntactic set in (15) apparent in the phonological phenomena represented in the orthographic forms in (17):

(17) a. pack, pat
 b. peak, peat
 c. pact
 d. *patc

The accented **checked** rhymal peak in (17a) requires a complement to constitute part of a full monosyllabic lexical item: *[pa] is not a monosyllabic item of English. Whereas the **free** peak of (17b) does not, as shown by (18):

(18) pea

The vowels differ in **transitivity**. The final consonant in (17b) is distributionally an adjunct, in this respect. Complement and adjunct are combined in (17c), necessarily in that order—cf. (17d), which, like (15d), would involve 'tangling'.

Of course, just as in the syntax, some of the same categories may be complement or adjunct. Compare with the forms in (17) the sentences of (19), where *five miles* is respectively a complement and an adjunct in (19a) and (b):

(19) a. He covered five miles
 b. He drove his car (five miles)
 c. *He drove five miles his car

This functional overlap is more obvious in the phonology, given the limited alphabet available. (19c) shows the abnormal adjunct-before-complement order. Used without overt complement, *covered* and *drive* are elliptical.

Now, there is a distinct perceptual basis for the differentiation of checked and free vowels that is apparently absent with transitive vs. intransitive verbs (which seem to be distinguished purely by their semantic-complement requirements): the free peaks are perceptually 'heavier' (moraically, or however one measures it). But this is unsurprising: the alphabet of phonology is perceptually based; that of syntax is not. The latter alphabet is semantically based, and the transitive vs. intransitive distinction certainly has a substantive basis in syntax as well. But this seems at first glance to be a rather different kind of distinction from phonological 'weight', which is relevant to the phonetic implementation, as well as the constructional requirements.

And it is this kind of difference that can serve to limit the precise equivalence of any substantive analogy, as anticipated by the structural analogy assumption, and as will be illustrated more fully, as I have indicated, in Part III. At this point we can already observe that syntax permits ditransitives as well as monotransitives among valency types, whereas this further distinction does not seem to be replicated in the phonology. However, to pursue the 'weight' analogy, a case might be made for intransitive verbs as being predicators that can constitute the 'weight' of the entire predication. We are, of course, in the realms of metaphor here, but metaphors involve recognition of substantive similarities. But also complements in both planes serve by virtue of their 'weight' to complete the construction. It is thus perhaps premature even in this case to simply dismiss the possibility of the analogy being based on groundedness, rather than merely distributional properties.

Similarly, ellipsis of complements traditionally has also been seen as limited to syntax. The capacity of language users to deal with ellipsis is based on the semanticity of syntax, in many cases again on awareness of the valency of the verb, which makes recoverable at least the type of the missing complement. In such circumstances as are illustrated by *Have you eaten?* a transitive verb is apparently intransitive. But again, might there not be a phonological analogy in the relevant aspect of 'weak' or 'reduced' vowels, where a lexical item can contain a normally transitive vowel that is unchecked under low stress, as in [ʃɪ] for *she* (for exemplification and discussion see Obendorfer 1998). Can this analogy be carried further substantively? All such cases require careful scrutiny.

However that may be, and however the (metaphorical) 'weight' of intransitives is to be characterized (see e.g. Anderson 1986b: §7), it seems that exactly analogous representations to those in (16) are arguably appropriate in the relevant aspects of the phonology of English:

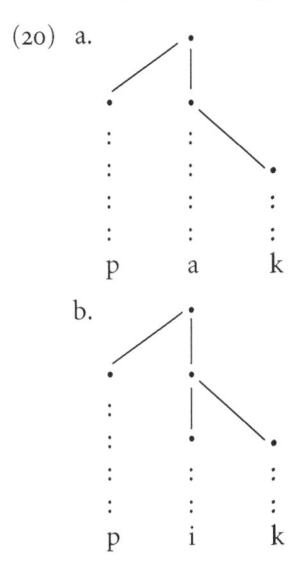

(20) a.

p   a   k

b.

p   i   k

c.

```
         •
       ╱ │
     ╱   │
    •    │
    ┆    │╲
    ┆    • ╲
    ┆    │╲ ╲
    ┆    ┆ •╲
    ┆    ┆ ┆ ╲
    ┆    ┆ ┆  •
    ┆    ┆ ┆  ┆
    p    a k  t
```

d.

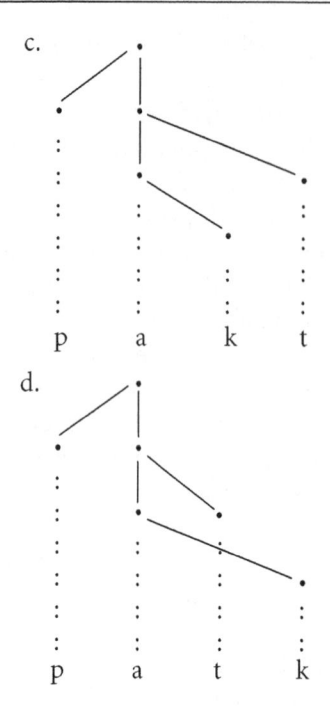

```
         •
       ╱ │
     ╱   │
    •    │
    ┆    │╲
    ┆    • ╲
    ┆    │╲ ╲
    ┆    ┆ •╲
    ┆    ┆ ┆ ╲
    ┆    ┆ ┆  •
    ┆    ┆ ┆  ┆
    p    a t  k
```

(16) and (20) involve respectively syntactic and phonological manifestations of the trans-planar cognitively based relation of dependency, which indicates relative cognitive salience, and of the associated notions complement and adjunct, which reflect the semantic or phonological requirement of the 'peak'. The implied onset/subject parallel introduces further considerations that will be taken up below. However, at this point we can at least acknowledge familiar motivations for excluding them from rhyme and VP, respectively.

Of course, it is already clear that various structural properties are elaborated further in the syntax than in the phonology. This is again unsurprising, given the difference in the size of vocabulary which is available as realizations of the respective alphabets of categories and the range of possible combinations, and in general, and most basically, the complexity of the domain to be represented by the syntax. It is also unsurprising given the relationship between the planes, such that, to repeat the words of Martinet (1957: 105), 'on parle pour être compris, et l'expression est au service du contenu'. All of this is associated with the semanticity of syntax. This difference in domain and the range of structures needed to represent it also accounts for limitations in phonological transitivity. It does not follow that 'if the putatively formal relationship between a checked vowel in English and its coda is parallel to the formal relationship between a transitive verb and its complement, then one should also expect to find a formal phonological analogue, in English, or elsewhere, to verbs which require two complements' (Carr 2005: 22). This claim is based on assuming isomorphy, which is not implied by structural analogy. On similar grounds, structural analogy does not require that this phonological analogy be found in all languages.

Note further in relation to the complement/adjunct distinction, that, as Carr (2006) points out (and as is well attested), there are syntaxes in which the 'tangling' of (16d) is indeed tolerated; and the projectivity-observing linear manifestation of the complement/adjunct distinction is apparently sacrificed (cf. e.g. van Riemsdijk 1992). This is also true of English given certain considerations of 'weight' (on a slightly different understanding of the word): *He met in Vienna the object of all his dreams*. But the configurational and overall distributional parallelism remains even in such cases.

Moreover, in Chapter 5 of Volume I, motivations were offered for analysing at least some such languages (viz. those which apparently allow 'tangling', represented by (20d)) as showing, in the case of such apparently 'displaced complements', another adjunct instead, in apposition to a lexically incorporated complement. I allude to examples such as (136b) from Volume I, compared with the anomalous 'equivalent' from English:

(I.136)   a. *John kisses often Mary
        b. Jean embrasse souvent Marie

Here (what are on the analysis of Volume I) the two adjuncts of (I.136), where the second is in apposition with a lexically incorporated 'complement', do not necessarily involve 'tangling'. This is another illustration of the problems with interpreting 'brute distribution'. The sequence in (I.136b) does not exhibit equivalent complement and adjunct assignments to those in *John kisses Mary often*, where tangling is avoided; it contains two adjuncts. Such observations immediately undermine the application to this case of Carr's (2005: 22–3) assertion that 'if there are genuine syntax/phonology parallels they must be universal in nature': this holds only ceteris paribus—which is not the case, in this instance, in French.

Yet further, notice that (I.136b), by virtue of incorporating an argument (to which *Marie* is apposed), can be thought of as acquiring extra 'weight', sufficient 'weight' to enable it to function as the whole basic verb phrase. Is this 'weight' an even more 'tangible' substantive analogy (than with 'inherent' intransitives) to the perceptual 'weight' of 'free' vowels like that in (18)? To be sure, we are here in the realm of metaphor again—but such figurativeness can be argued to be the basis for most of syntax (as embodied, for example, in the localist hypothesis discussed in Volume I, §3.5), not just for an understanding of transitivity.

In (I.136) we have but a minor illustration of the fact that the basic syntactic structures of languages are much more diverse than is commonly supposed, particularly given the different complex lexical structures that may be adopted in the lexicon. Syntax (and lexicon) is a medium of representation that may be diversely structured whatever universals may appertain to our perception of the world. Thus, alternative conceptual figures may be adopted in the representation of the cognitive domain, and such conceptual representations largely determine syntactic structures. And, together with our interpretation of what language we are exposed to, our capacities for figurativeness guide our acquisition of that language.

Tallerman (2006: §4) objects to the complement/adjunct analogy that 'in syntax, adjuncts are typically, and crucially, of a different syntactic category than complements'. But this cannot be 'crucial', and it too cannot be part of 'universal grammar', given not merely its non-universality in English (as illustrated in (19b)) but also the existence of languages, like Japanese or Lake Miwok or Lak, in which both complements and adjuncts (as well as 'subjects') are typically marked uniformly by presence of a 'particle' which is a postposition or 'enclitic' or inflection, depending on the language. (Her other objections rest on the semanticity of syntax and phonology's lack of such, which is not as such in dispute.) Moreover, as argued in Volume I, there are reasons for regarding the heads of 'noun phrases' and 'adpositional phrases' as belonging to the same category, what I call 'functor', as far as their function in the predication is concerned: they both realize functor phrases.

Anderson (2006a) suggests that a cross-modular analogical view of linguistic structures would also be consistent with the view that syntactic structures are ontologically analogical elaborations of properties establishable in relation to the phonology. If 'the syllable-shaped mental representations which emerge during child development are rooted in babble-based vocal motor schemes which link production and perception' (Carr 2005: §1), it is possible that the development of much of syntactic structure involves a planar reallocation of the syllable-characterizing structural properties that emerge in this way. The substantive differences and the asymmetrical relationship between the planes frustrate Hjelmslevian 'isomorphism', of course; syntactic structure is not the same as phonological. Such an ontological suggestion that phonology may be the major source of analogies, however, introduces an extensive debate that

Anderson (2006a) wisely eschews, particularly given our lack of understanding of the range of inter planar analogies to be found in language.[11]

We can perhaps say, at the very least, that such syntax-phonology parallels reveal the operation of the same mental processes in different situations which nevertheless are perceived as having a suggestive similarity in crucial respect(s). In the present case, this mechanism is particularly transparent in relation to the syllable analogy if we regard what it is in syntax that resembles the phonological onset as not the 'subject' (as has sometimes been suggested) but the 'topic' (which the 'subject' is a further grammaticalization of). Both onset and topic (though in adult language only typically in the case of the latter) are initial, and they are very commonly present; and they are not fully integrated into the structure that follows. This gives them respectively a phonetic and a semantic salience. Topics may show no syntactic connexion with the following predication; and onsets do not interact strongly with the syllable peak, as does the coda, nor do they participate in rhyming (except as part of a so-called 'feminine rhyme'). But they do participate alone in alliteration. Subjecthood is then a syntax-particular phenomenon, associated with presence of functional categories in syntax but not in phonology (see again § 3.7 of Volume I), and with further grammaticalization.

Even when we recognize the limits of analogy, there is nevertheless also a need for caution in dismissing from phonology properties alleged to be characteristically syntactic, as well as vice versa. Carr, in an aside (2000: 90), claims that 'recursion' is absent from phonological structures. But, as noted in §1.2, phenomena associated with cyclicity, however they are to be treated, have been associated by different investigators with both the syntax and the phonology (cf. e.g. the contributions to Denton et al. 1992); and various researchers (cf. e.g. Crystal 1969: §5.10.2; Ladd 1986, 1990; Anderson 1986b) have argued for nesting of tone units within one another. Consider too e.g. the recursive account of lexical tone advocated by Clements (1981), as well as the recursive subjunctions in (20b-c), parallel to those in (16b-c).

Certainly, physical limitations impose an obvious constraint on the elaboration of phonological nestings in a way that they do not as directly impinge on potential nestings in the syntax. We cannot attribute **indefinite recursion** to phonology. But this again is a reflection of the relationship between the

---

[11] Anderson (2006a) does suggest, however that the fact that syntax is structurally more elaborated than phonology is not in itself a problem for Carstairs-McCarthy's (1999) rather different view that syntactic organization has its evolutionary source in phonology, given a shared 'core' of properties, any more than the citing of alleged discrepancies between syntax and phonology (e.g. Bauer 1994) is in itself problematical for the structural analogy assumption. However, see Bickerton (2000), Newmeyer (2000), and Tallerman (2006) for more negative views of Carstairs-McCarthy's proposal.

planes and, in particular, of the more circumscribed and specifically perceptual cognitive domain inhabited by phonology, as is argued more fully in Chapter 5. And this domain is immediately responsible to the demands of physical implementation. This underlines what I have urged, namely that it is important to recognize that we are still in a poor position to fully evaluate the extent of syntax/phonology analogy. Thus, Anderson (2006a) insists that it is unsafe to assume without thorough investigation that any particular allegedly syntactic property necessarily lacks a phonological analogue.

To illustrate this, Anderson (2006a) chooses the (rather controversial) notion 'specifier'—despite uncertainty as to whether, as deployed in various syntactic analyses, this is a coherent notion. This uncertainty is even more the case with it than with 'complement' or 'government'. There is not a lot of agreed clarity or detail in common in proposed characterizations I am aware of, beyond a shared association with the first-dependent place in (the equivalents of) a representation such as (21), i.e. that associated with the element represented there as a, where the uppermost node is the maximal projection of the head category b:

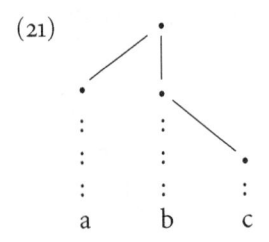

(21)

a b c

Apart from, for many (but not all) scholars, the 'specifier' being 'non-recursive', not much more seems to be agreed on, and the identification of the 'specifiers' of different head categories has been very variable. For Jackendoff (1977a: 256), 'the distinction between specifier and complement is to be regarded here as only a convenience'. For Bresnan (2000: 335, note 3) '...here the attribute SPEC refers generally to the most prominent argument of verbal and nominal categories (the subject and possessor, respectively)'. Some have associated the 'specifier' with determination of agreement on its head (see e.g. Haegeman and Guéron 1999: §3.7.4 for a textbook account); but it is difficult to see how this can be plausibly generalized without extensive appeals to the covert. Elsewhere, 'adjuncts' have been reinterpreted as 'specifiers'. Some of this diversity, in some recent manifestations, pervades Adger et al. (1999). It is thus unclear what content, if any, to give to the notion 'specifier' in general.[12]

---

[12] Emonds (1987: 36) associates nominal specifiers with the expression of 'quantification and ostension', verbal with expression of 'time and aspect', adjectival with expression of 'degree',

However, if we consider what seem to have been relatively uncontroversial cases like the monolexical 'specifiers' of adjectives and prepositions in English (*very aware of the problem*, *right at the back*), Anderson (2006a) suggests that we can say that lexically the **archetypical specifier** also belongs to a small class that is particular to the category of head it 'specifies' (though it is possible that certain putative specifiers depend on more than one category of head). I shall continue to use scare quotes around the word to indicate the uncertainty concerning the status of 'specifier' in syntax. It is not intended to throw doubt on the potential analogy eventually suggested below, apart from that arising this syntactic uncertainty.

Say we can motivate some such notion for the syntax. It is not obvious that there is an analogue to 'specifier' in the phonology. And there should, indeed, not be a phonological analogue if 'specifier' is part of 'universal grammar' and 'universal grammar' does not include phonology. But it may be that this particular property has simply not been elaborated in the phonology, or some phonologies, without this being evidence that 'specifier' is part of 'universal grammar'. Certainly, in the absence of serious consideration of the question of possible analogues we should suspend judgment. Let us briefly contemplate here, however, in a preliminary way, again following Anderson (2006a), the character of a potential analogue.

Now, we have already met with a configuration such as (21) applied to certain phonological sequences, viz. those in (20). And we might say that the onset of the syllable is a kind of 'specifier' analogous to the 'subjects' in (16), though the status of 'subjects' as 'specifiers' is itself controversial (see e.g. Pollard and Sag 1994: §9.4), and we might rather, as suggested above, prefer topics as an analogue. And in neither case do we have 'archetypical specifiers',

---

adpositional with serving as 'an intensifier'. The introduction of 'functional categories' has complicated and compromised these assumptions, however.

Curiously, as far as the identification of particular specifiers is concerned, the 'specifier' of VP, which is identified as being instantiated in English by *all* in *The detectives have all read the letters in the garden shed after lunch* in the textbook treatments by Haegeman (1991: 83, 1994: 91-2), following Sportiche (1988), and which is the instance of 'specification' used to first introduce the notion in these books, is not mentioned, as far as I am aware, in the textbook of English grammar of Haegeman and Guéron (1999), though a number of other instances of 'specification' are elaborated upon.—We should perhaps recognize as a possible explanation, however, that it may be that this reflects different pedagogical aims.

In another textbook, Radford (1997: 90) abandons any attempt to offer a characterization of 'specifier' beyond illustrating 'some of the ways in which the term is used in the contemporary linguistic literature', and the glossary to the book offers only the following vaguenesses: 'the grammatical function fulfilled by certain types of constituent which (in English) precede the head of their containing phrase' (1997: 528). And uncertainty over specification is well illustrated by the contributions to Adger et al. (1999).

as characterized above. What would be more interesting in the present context than the (fairly simple) analogy between 'topic/subject' and 'onset', whether or not we associate it with 'specification', would be the identification of a phonological analogue to the more specific notion of archetypical specifier.

Anderson (2006a) suggests that a possible analogue might be the structure that Anderson (1986b: §7) proposes for such syllable onsets as that in (22), which represents English *spree*, where 'S' is the unspecified segment realized in these circumstances as [s], and 'P' is the neutralization class of plosives (lacking the contrasts [p]≠[b] etc.):

(22)

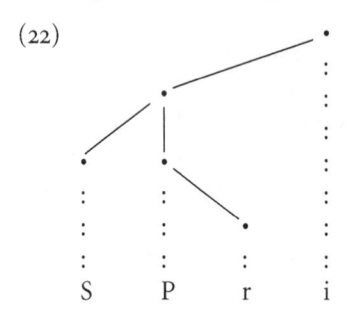

S   P   r   i

Dependency within consonant clusters is argued by Anderson (1986b)—contrary to the tradition underlying Anderson and Ewen (1987)—to be anti-sonority: the optimal consonant, and thus the head of the cluster, is the one that contrasts most, in substance, with the vowel; it is, by contrast, most salient.

This depends on the assumption that salience in phonology cannot, any more than in syntax, necessarily be associated with just one particular substantive property, such as 'most sonorous'. The immediate transition from one pole of the sonority to the opposite, as with voiceless plosive-to-vowel, can render both segments salient by contrast (cf. for more detailed discussion Ohala and Kawasaki 1984: §3, for example). 'Perceptual salience', as well as 'cognitive salience', may be manifested in different aspects of substance. The relation between grammaticalized form and particular substance is context-dependent.

This is perhaps an appropriate point at which to recall that the relationship between form and substance is also more complex in another respect. Carr comments on the proposed transitivity analogy: 'to the extent that Anderson's analogies concern the grounded notion of constituency in syntax and phonology, they seem valid; to the extent that they are taken to be formal analogies, they seem to me less persuasive' (2005: 22). But does 'transitivity' involve purely 'formal' analogy? From a notionalist point of view, transitivity is not merely grounded in so far as its attribution to both phonology and syntax reflects the operation of the same mental apparatus in the grammaticalization of two substantively different domains; it is also associated with a substantive property in common between vowels and verbals, their relationality, which enables them to serve as heads to complements and not merely (like consonants and nouns) as at most 'modified' heads. Both syllables and predications can be seen as articulated around the verbal/vocalic and nominal/consonantal poles, with the former as the centres, the latter as peripherals—though this is complicated in the syntax by the presence of functional categories, with apparently no phonological analogue (another instance of the further elaboration of syntax compared with phonology—again, see further Chapters 5 and 7). Identifying what is purely 'formal' is hazardous.

But let us now look, in the light of all this, at the internal structure of the onset in (22). If we look only at the relation between the head and a following consonantal segment, we can perhaps say that the relation between [P], representing the neutralization of [p] and [b], and [r] is at least head-adjunct-like. Various classes of head may be extended by the adjunct, and some heads even impose further, complement-like, restrictions: [pr, pl, br, bl, fr, fl, θr, *θl] etc.—though the idiosyncratic character of these suggests a selectional rather than a complementing relation is involved. So, [P] takes adjuncts not complements, as we expect of a consonant (and, traditionally, a noun)—in this case to the right, as an onset consonant, in accord with sonority.

But are there any grounds for considering the pre-head [S] to be a specifier? Well, as occupant of this position, [S] doesn't just belong to a small class, it is unique in English in this position—as signalled by the capitalization in (22). And, like an archetypical syntactic specifier, it identifies the following head as belonging to a particular class, here the plosive-neutralization class, with the neutralization again signalled by a capital, which also here abbreviates (without suggesting neutralization) the place contrast. And the specifier makes overt that the cluster belongs to the class of cluster which has such a head. And the 'formal' analogy may again have a substantive, or at least functional, basis, in (in this case) a common function of identification, rather than merely of modification.

Carr (2005: 23) observes concerning the specifier analogy that in English:

/s/ may appear in several other syllabic slots: it may be the sole segment in onset position and in coda position (complement position for Anderson), and this is the case for syntactic specifiers (*very*, for instance, can appear within NPs, as in *the very idea*), but it cannot appear as the complement of a transitive verb, whereas /s/ can appear as the 'complement' of a lax vowel or as the 'adjunct' to a free vowel.

He concludes (ibid): '<i>t seems to me that that the sub-division of non-heads in phonology into specifier, complement and adjunct is more tenuous than the general head/non-head distinction....'.

However, I suggest that Carr's argument concerning [S] as a specifier is derailed by his adoption of phonemics. A consequence of recognizing neutralizations, in accordance with contrastivity, is that not all instances of [s] are categorized in the same way—as I have tried to indicate, as a short-hand, by use of the 'S' symbol. Unitary categorization, as I discuss elsewhere (e.g. in §2.1 below), is an unwelcome figment of phonemics. Similarly, *very* in *very difficult problems* does not belong to the same category as it does in *the very idea* (whatever the relationship between the two *very*s might be). The argument for specifier status for [S] is based on the analogous distribution and function and small-class status of the category abbreviated as [S], not just any category that is realized as [s].

This may, nevertheless, turn out to be an inappropriate analogy. But rejection of the possibility of a phonological analogue to specifier, if indeed that notion is relevant to the syntax, would seem to be premature, given the present state of our understanding.[13]

---

[13] Carr objects (2005: 23) that '/s/ may appear in several other syllabic slots', whereas the distribution of *very* is largely limited (if we ignore such as *the very man*) to that of 'specifier' of gradable adjectives. He is perhaps misled here by the use in Anderson (2006a) of the notation '/s/' for the first segment in (10), a notation which many associate with phonemic status. Rather than my using this unhelpful notation to indicate simply a segment that is locally contrastive, it would perhaps have been less misleading to put here '[S]', with capitalization as a (crude) 'flag' of its distinctive status. This [S] is a unique category in English, just as [P] is distinct from all other stops found in other positions; and though the former may share its realization with a category or categories labelled [s], its place in the system is quite different.

The substance of Carr's objection, as suggested, is an artefact of 'phonemics', and what has been called its 'biuniqueness requirement'. The latter is formulated by Sommerstein (1977: 63) as:

No two utterances which contrast at the phonetic level may be analysed as phonologically identical, and no two utterances which are phonetically identical, or are in free variation, may be analysed as phonologically distinct.

Carr appears to be appealing to the second part of this 'requirement', which is a stipulation that has no phonological motivation—though it has no doubt been useful in devising orthographic systems. The 'emic'/'etic' distinction, in so far as it is a manifestation of type vs. token, is unproblematical, but the importation of alphabet-based criteria is inappropriate. It then goes without saying that since 'emic'/'etic' distinction is irrelevant to phonological representation, the pursuit of analogies in the other plane (and the inter plane) is misguided. What is analogical is the application of the distinction between contrastive and redundant.

It is not clear either that the limited presence of specifiers in the phonology—a straightforward specifier for vowels in English is not readily identifiable—is so very different from the situation in syntax. Here too the identification of specifiers is at best uncertain. It may indeed be that they are much more restricted in their distribution throughout construction types than is predicted by wholesale application of the X-bar apparatus: see further §4.2.

We turn now to further analogies, initially involving, in Chapter 2, elaboration of the head-based analogies outlined in this section. Our discussion in Part II of a diversity of analogies, including further elaboration of the proposed analogies already encountered, provides some motivation for supposing phonology to be grounded. This is particularly striking in what emerges in Chapter 2. In that chapter in particular phonology will be shown to share with syntax, partly on the basis of this groundedness, structural properties traditionally most closely associated with the latter. This discussion thus, in this respect, complements the discussion of the groundedness in syntax of Volume I. Most analogies can be given some substantive or common functional basis, and thus presuppose groundedness. The establishment of various analogies depends on perceptions of parallels between structure based on substantive properties, such as salience and linearity. This depends on the groundedness of both syntax and phonology. And this is confirmed by the further analogies pursued in Part II, particularly Chapters 3 and 4, involving properties many of them traditionally viewed as purely phonological or syntactic.

Part II
Analogies

2

Phonology and dependency

This chapter sets out to provide further evidence that the dependency relation is a fundamental element in phonological structure, as it is in syntax, and at the same time to flesh out the structural descriptions provided in the preceding discussion, as a preparation for the elaboration of this (i.e. dependency-based) and other analogies in the present and the succeeding chapter. Dependency is a 'formal' property that is associated with both syntax and phonology. But the notion 'head' can be given a substantive interpretation, in terms of 'cognitive salience', appropriate to both planes. Headhood grammaticalizes this substantive property. Moreover, as already maintained, the interpretation of linguistic structures as networks of dependency relations also reveals the operation of the same logical processes throughout language, in the implementation of the same 'formal' properties. In whatever context, heads identify the substructures they head; they are the characteristic element of a construction type, as well as headhood being manifested more substantively in terms of salience (which obviously is not unrelated to the head's role as characterizer of its construction).

In this chapter I shall concentrate on phonology, attempting to show its possession of a subset of the properties of dependency structures that have been attributed to syntax. In part this is because, as far as I am aware, the attribution of headhood to syntactic structures pre-dates and has been much more fully studied than headhood in phonology. Comparisons here with syntax will thus largely rely on reference to work published elsewhere, as well as (particularly) to Volume I in this series, in justifying the syntactic implementations of dependency in syntax. Parts of the material and discussion in this and subsequent chapters in the present study were given a preliminary airing in Anderson (2004a).

§§2.3 and 2.4 in particular argue that notions connected with headhood can have a contrastive/lexical status—though not all of them have such in all languages. §2.3 builds on the discussion of §1.7 to suggest that dependency and the distinctions complement/adjunct/specifier have a role in determining the range of possible sequences of phonological segments. That is, these more 'formal', or (at least) less obviously interface-based, properties play a part in projecting the linearity required by the interface to phonetics. Before that, §2.2 provides a general introduction to the status of linearity, and in particular to the role of other substantive interface properties, crucially associated with sonority, in determining sequencing within the syllable. This is a prelude to the elaboration of the contribution of the concepts associated with dependency in §2.3. In §2.4 the role of vocalic transitivity in determining (some instances of) vocalic weight and aperture differences is illustrated, again suggesting that this reflection of dependency is among the basic properties of the phonology. And §5 in this chapter suggests that dependency, and lack of it, have a crucial role to play in the determination of another interface property, that of timing.

A subsidiary theme throughout these sections is the overwhelmingly non-contrastive status of linearity, including timing within segments. This is not to deny the overwhelming linearity of the representations that grammaticalize our perception of speech, whether this is characterized segmentally or prosodically. It is just that from the point of view of expressional re-representation much of this linearization is predictable, no matter what might be its importance in interpretation. Recognition of redundancy should not be confused with the abstractness introduced by mutative derivationality, which is eschewed. Recognition of contrast and redundancy involves the removal of properties (such as many linear relations) from contrastive representations; mutation involves changing the contrastive relations in the course of a derivation. If the former is to be described as involving 'abstractness' (as suggested by a reader), it is, to my mind, not offensively so—and certainly not to the extent of mutation.

Even the more 'formal' properties associated with dependency relate to interface demands. Nevertheless, it is the 'formality' of these properties that means that it is particularly among them that we can expect to find syntax-phonology analogies such as those that are explored in the present chapter. And it is largely those properties closer to the interface and to substance that limit the kinds of phonological analogies to the syntax that do occur, as we shall find in Part III of this volume. And, clearly, the more particular, substantively, to one interface a property is, the less likely are we to find close analogy. Chapters 3 and 4 survey a number of further analogies based on a combination of consistent 'formal' interpretation and substantive or functional motivation.

In the discussion of major examples of important points in the argument of the chapters that follow, I aim to provide a sufficiently complete, or delicate, analysis for evaluation of the point (relevant to analogy) being made. In some places, this involves aspects of the analysis which go beyond simple illustration of this point; and indeed might seem to sidetrack the reader from the major themes of the book. However, my intention is to try to ensure that there is not lurking in some unconsidered related phenomenon evidence that might call into question, however indirectly, the status of the particular argument being offered. And I trust that the analyses proposed are of interest in their own right.

The discussion of timing in §2.5, for instance, which is based on the operation of Dorsey's Law in Winnebago, dwells at some length on accent placement in general in the language. This is justified in the terms I have just announced, in my view—as well as offering an alternative analysis of the accent phenomena which (it seems to me) merits some attention for its own sake. And I hope that this is also true of other discussions in what follows that might seem to involve as much or even more of an excursus. Overall, though, I shall endeavour to keep the general goals of the discussion in focus, particularly substantiveness and its role in analogy and dis-analogy.

2.1 Contrastivity and neutralization

Much of the history of phonological studies is, unfortunately, characterized by failures to follow through the consequences of the assumptions made in the studies themselves. The fossilization that we can associate with 'structuralist phonemics' is one instance of this. The crucial recognition of the notion of contrast at this point in the development of phonological ideas did not lead to any thorough investigation of **contrastivity** by the major proponents of 'phoneme theory'—at least outside the Praguian tradition and some neglected discussions such as Twaddell's (1935) introduction of the 'microphoneme'. I pursue this particular 'failure to follow through' at this point in that it involves a notion that is itself a major source of analogies and because it is associated with further dependency-based analogies.

The pursuit of contrastivity was sidetracked by, for instance, the application of principles which are not phonologically motivated but which reflect procedural (rather than theoretical) demands and extra phonological concerns to do with the requirements of alphabetic writing systems (encouraged by the use of representational systems like the International Phonetic Alphabet). Consider the **neutralizations** (discussed in relation to (22) in §1.7) evidenced in the onset of *ski* in English, compared with, say, *see* and *key*, particularly the uniqueness of [s] in initial position in a form like *ski*; it contrasts only with its absence. Such neutralizations are typically obscured by phonemic representations that are dictated by symbol economy, typified by Bloch (1941).

Recall from note 13 Sommerstein's (1977: 63) formulation of the 'biuniqueness requirement':

> No two utterances which contrast at the phonetic level may be analysed as phonologically identical, and no two utterances which are phonetically identical, or are in free variation, may be analysed as phonologically distinct.

This eliminates the need, which is present if neutralization is acknowledged, for different contrastive symbols or representations for the [s] segments in *sea* and *ski*, for instance. If 'biuniqueness' is applied generally, the number of contrastive units (and alphabetic units) can be considerably reduced.

As acknowledged in the subtitle to Pike's *Phonemics* (1947)—*A Technique for Reducing Languages to Writing*—such concerns as symbol economy reflect in large part non-phonological aims. Compare Firth (1948: 134) on such theories as being built on the 'phonetic hypostatization of roman letters' (also more recently e.g. Aronoff 1992). Trying to fulfil these aims restricts the identification of where contrastivity lies and does not lie. One of the virtues of the 'Firthian' tradition has been to highlight this failure to appropriately locate contrastivity by 'phonemic' representations which were determined by principles distorted by the prism of alphabetic orthography. In this respect 'phonemics' failed to fully implement the principle of contrastivity; nor did it provide phonological (as opposed to procedural) motivations for not doing so. The phoneme is not a relevant concept in any phonology that seeks to fully express what is contrastive and what not.[14]

Significantly, Schane's (1971) reconsideration of the 'phoneme' was in effect a defence of 'surface contrasts', not of the 'structuralist phoneme'. He identifies what we might call 'phonological' contrast, as opposed to 'linguistic contrast':

---

[14] Lyons (1962) is, in my view, too generous in according to 'phoneme theory' one end of a typological continuum (the 'cardinally phonemic' end) with 'prosodic analysis' at the other extreme (the 'cardinally prosodic' end): '...it may be suggested that the goodness of fit of one model of analysis rather than the other should be made a criterion in the typological classification of the phonology of languages' (1962: 132). 'Phoneme theory' would be appropriate only to languages with no 'prosodic' (trans-segmental) phenomena whatsoever (apart perhaps from things to do with accent and intonation) and offering no evidence of polysystemicity; whereas all other languages would have to be accommodated by 'prosodic analysis', in which tradition it was never claimed, as far as I am aware, that a language could consist entirely of 'prosodies'—or even that there couldn't be a language without such. It seems to me that Lyons is proposing here an interesting typological dimension, but it has to do with the relative 'prosodicness' of languages (what range of features is prosodicized in each), not with a distinction between 'phoneme theory' and 'prosodic analysis'.

Another consequence of the alphabetic interference manifested in classical phonemics is oversegmentation (Faber 1992). This may be true of even, for example, the representation of long vowels as two successive 'timing slots' or 'X-positions' or the like (see e.g. Giegerich 1992: §6.7): the 'slot' metaphor has no phonetic basis: a long vowel is not divisible in this way.

contrast that ignores non-phonological neutralizations of the contrast. Sapir's discussion of 'the psychological reality of phonemes' (1933/1963) is likewise not quite to the point: it avoids the problem of neutralization, and his evidence consists of how native (and other) speakers write or otherwise discriminate what to them sounds same or different. One of his examples (pp. 48–52 in the English translation) involves, uncontroversially, classical allophony and the unwillingness of a native speaker to write the allophones distinctively: the distinction is non-contrastive. Two others (pp. 52–5) involve alleged morphophonemes. On the first, involving a native speaker's apparent wish to discriminate in sound two homonyms in his language, see Silverman (2006: 19–22). The second concerns the use by a literate speaker of symbols which have no phonetic content but which are motivated by morphological considerations, by alternation. A fourth example (pp. 55–8) involves a native speaker's recognition of the parallel phonetic content (in this case glottalization) of different classes of segments (obstruents vs. sonorants), although they had been traditionally transcribed (by non-natives) in such a way as to obscure this. Sapir's final example (pp. 58–60) involves the influence of English syllable structure on transcriptions made by English-speakers. None of this supports the 'psychological reality' of the 'classical phoneme' (cf. Twaddell 1935: §II), or undermines the contention that analyses based on 'phonemics' failed to reflect contrastivity.

Such has been apparent for some time, I think. But there are yet other aspects of phonological structure that are non-contrastive, but which most frameworks of phonological representation fail to recognize as such. As Anderson (1987a, 1994) argues, much of linearity is not contrastive but predictable from other properties, and this is not represented as such in most accounts of phonology—even, ironically, in so-called 'non-linear' approaches, which (as has often been pointed out) are more appropriately to be referred to as 'multi-linear'. Typically, the latter provide parallel linearizations connected by principles of association between elements in the respective sequences. Of course, some sequencings are irreducible, contrastive, such as noticeably the sequence of syllables. But in many other cases linearization is derived from other phonological properties that may or may not have a contrastive role.

Contrastivity and neutralization—where the latter is the absence in some subsystem of a contrast found elsewhere in the system—are subject to redundancies that feed the interface phenomena that mediate between the grammaticalizations of language and perceptible substances, including linearity (in time or space). We can also distinguish between paradigmatic and syntagmatic contrastivity. In phonology, the traditional 'minimal pairs test' is intended to elicit paradigmatic contrasts: minimal sound distinctions in segments that distinguish between the linguistic representations that the segments are part of. The sequence of syllables, on the other hand, shows syntagmatic contrastivity.

In syntax, members of the same word class are in paradigmatic contrast; they encode cognitive distinctions. And syntagmatic contrastivity is exhibited in e.g. (23):

(23) a. She will leave
b. Will she leave?

Contrastivity is in common between syntax and phonology, though syntax involves distinct notional categories related to different phonological shapes (the phonological poles of the minimal sign) or linear positions (in a syntactic sign), and phonology involves distinct phonological categories and linear positions belonging to the semantically distinct phonological shape (phonological pole) of which they constitute a part.

Similarly, beside the phonological neutralizations shown in (22) of §1.7, neutralization of cognitive distinctions is exhibited not merely in the lexicon (as homonymy—e.g. *bank* 'margin of river' vs. 'monetary establishment') but also in the syntax, as with ambiguity of speech act (*That open window is draughty*—simple statement vs. request—recall §6.1 of Volume I of this trilogy). A kind of lexical neutralization is also associated with morphological expression of syntactic categories, so that for the most part the traditional 'preterite' form in English can signal either past time reference or irrealis status (recall here §§6.5, 6.7 in the first of these studies and Chapter 4 of the second).

So too 'inverse neutralizations', or **diversifications**, are manifested phonologically, in the form of traditional allophony or 'free variation', for instance, and, in syntax, as in (82) and (84) from Volume I:

(I.82) Did Bert leave on Tuesday?
(I.84) Bert left on Tuesday?

This is apart from the lexical diversification shown in (24), which includes diversification of word class:

(24) a. Mary is like her mother
b. Mary is similar to her mother
c. Mary resembles her mother

This is not to ignore the instability of such syntactic and lexical diversifications, whose members tend to specialize in some way (as again discussed in Volume I of the trilogy).

This instability in the content plane reflects the conflicting demands of the substances grammaticalized by the two planes. In syntax, distinctions in expression, whether expressed syntagmatically or paradigmatically, are utilized to carry the burden of semanticity. In phonology, allophonic distinctions, for instance, reflect the demands of phonetic context, though 'free variants' can become contrastive, in the service of semanticity. Nevertheless, these relations of neutralization and diversification are, as expected in terms of the structural analogy assumption, characteristic of both planes and their lexical interface, the lexicon.

In summary, I offer below a speculative tabulation of where 'contrast effects' arise. The table attempts to provide a crude roadmap of the interfaces on the chain of expression from cognition to sound at which 'contrast effects' are to be found.

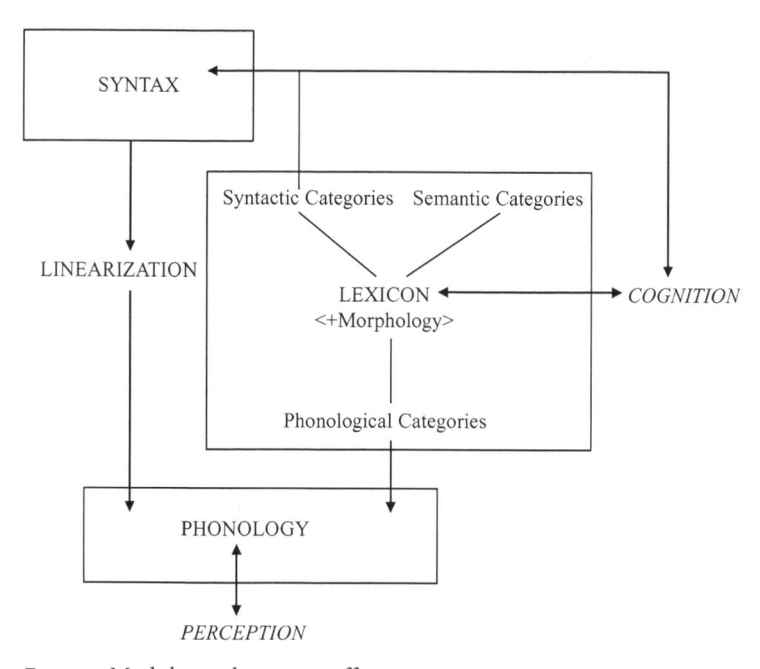

FIGURE 1 Modules and contrast effects

The italicized capitals represent non-linguistic modules; roman capitalization represents linguistic (sub)modules, including the two planes of syntax and phonology and their internal interface, the lexicon, with its optional overt inter-plane of morphology. The arrows indicate major unilateral or bilateral directions of influence or constraint. Each arrow indicates a locus of 'contrast effects', mappings involving contrast or neutralization.

As indicated, in this chapter I shall look at the phonological role of linearity and other aspects of representation. Partly, this is in order to establish the contrastive status of various phonological properties; but also I want to use their role in relation to contrastivity to establish at least a partial set of properties that are in this respect fundamental to phonology. Of particular interest is where these properties are not directly promoted by interface properties, viz. are not properties, like sequencing, that correlate directly with exponence, in this case, in time, and derive their motivation for fundamental status (also) from this. Overall, Chapter 2 thus seeks to establish some of the (contrastively) fundamental properties of phonology and their role both in contrast and in further analogies. This discussion leads on to Chapters 3 and 4, which, as already anticipated, consider further to what extent phonological properties, more and less substantively based, are replicated in the syntax, and try to identify in a preliminary way structural discrepancies between phonology and syntax. These discrepancies and their motivation are taken up more systematically in Chapters 5 and 6.

The concerns of the present chapter rest on the desirability of such a radical attitude to contrastivity as I have adopted here. But is it desirable to view phonological representations—or linguistic representations in general—in this way? i.e. as fundamentally organized in terms of the contrastive vs. the redundant? Such an approach is called into question by, for instance, Steriade's (1995: 166) doubts concerning the principle of 'lexical minimality': the requirement that 'underlying representations must reduce to some minimum the phonological information needed to distinguish lexical items' (1995: 114). However, she misleadingly associates the principle with 'derivationality'. And, on the one hand, her own allegedly 'nonderivational' discussion of Guaraní alludes, for instance, to whether or not (1995: 158) 'nasality... is allowed to associate *underlyingly* to Guaraní continuants' (my italics—JMA); while, on the other, the underspecified accounts invoked in what follows here involve 'derivations' only in the sense that some aspects of structure are predictable from others, with the former being 'derived' only in this sense—i.e. redundant.

Moreover, if the contents of lexical entries do not maximize contrastivity, it is necessary to ask how else their minimal content is determined. To be sure, we can also store items as gestalts, and this is no doubt true of many familiar items. Our minds store much that is redundant, and, among other things, this is of benefit in the presence of 'noise' and in general in economizing in processing time. But this does not invalidate the reality of the redundancies permitted by the assumption of contrastivity. And these redundancies are important in, for instance, the assimilation of new items, say loanwords, to the phonology of the language concerned.

I shall, however, make no further attempt here to address this issue—the desirability of taking contrastivity as basic in the construction of linguistic representations—directly, since the motivation for total abandonment of contrastivity is unclear, and any 'intermediate abandonments' would require justification in relation to a simple maximum-contrastivity requirement. Let me rather begin the present discussion, on the basis of the contrastivity (or 'lexical minimality') assumption, by recalling the main point of Anderson (1987a, 1994), the redundancy of many stipulations of linearity. This will lead us into a consideration of other aspects of phonological representation and their contrastive status. In §2.2 we thus look in this light at linearity, in particular, before returning, in §2.3, to dependency and analogies with syntax. It will be clear that the interest or otherwise of this discussion depends to a large extent on the appropriateness of the contrastivity-maximization assumption.

2.2 The limits of linearity, I: Sonority, markedness, and beyond

It is apparent that many, indeed most, of the linearity relations within syllables are not contrastive. This follows from the familiar fact that typically placement of segments is in accord with relative **sonority**, perceived inherent salience. Typically, salience within syllables declines from the **centre** towards the margins, with the centre being characterized by the presence of the most sonorous segment type, prototypically a vowel (cf. e.g. Blevins 1995: §2). In this way, once we know whether a consonantal segment precedes or follows the centre, we know what position it typically will occupy relative to other (non-vocalic) segments. In the unmarked case, relative sonority determines placement relative to the syllable centre, as illustrated by the English monosyllable in (25):

(25) clamp

Linear placement in (25) is in accordance with some such partial hierarchy as is given in (26):

(26) *partial sonority hierarchy 1*
    a. *class:*
       vowel > sonorant consonant > obstruent
    b. *representation:*
       {V}   {V,C}   {C}
   '>' here indicates 'is more sonorous than'

(26b) embodies the kind of representation advocated in Anderson and Ewen (1987), which I shall take as my starting point throughout this discussion:

V and C are **simplex features** characterized by Anderson and Ewen (1987: 151) as respectively 'relatively periodic' and involving 'periodic energy reduction'. Here I would emphasize that these are acoustic correlates of the features, which are perceptual. Combinations of these features distinguish the 'major classes', or **primary categories**, those categories that determine the basic syntax of segments. Thus vowels in (26b), for instance, are characterized as 'having only V', while consonants involve the presence of C. In the representation for sonorants in (26b) ';' means 'simple combination', so that sonorant consonants contain an equal proportion of C and V; unlike obstruents, they contain a proportion of V. Each categorial representation is enclosed within curly brackets, as in representations of syntactic categories.

The proportion of V vs. C present reflects relative sonority. I come back below (in §4) to spell out a possible sonority metric more precisely: in (26) it is rather transparent, given that, in this rather undifferentiated hierarchy, no other segment type than sonorant contains both V and C. The categorial representations given at this point are provisional, awaiting elaborations and differentiations that will arise as we look at further aspects of syllable structure, and thus a more extended system. The sequencing in (25), as expected, is based on primary categories; directly or indirectly, serialization in both syntax and phonology is primarily determined by primary categorization. And, in this unmarked case in the phonology, sequencing simply reflects relative sonority, relative preponderance of V, plus orientation towards the centre. Let me try to spell this out a little more explicitly before extending the hierarchy in response to further phenomena.[15]

Firstly, however, it is important to emphasize that the contrastive representations proposed here are **system-dependent**: the representations reflect the dimensionality of the system. Representations for one system that are minimal in embodying only what is contrastive in that system will not suffice for a system with more oppositions. This means that sounds in different systems that are phonetically similar may have different representations in these different systems of contrast. And this is why the system of (26) is provisional in relation to English, whence I have drawn my examples. Even in a single language, the 'same sound' also may have different contrastive representations in different circumstances, given that, in the interests of maximizing the expression of contrastivity, the description is **polysystemic**, or 'sub-system-dependent'. This will become apparent as we proceed.

---

[15] Initially for expository reasons, I have not adopted here the suggestion (see e.g. Anderson 1994) that vowels are contrastively unspecified as to primary category, or 'major class'; but there are reasons for thinking that such a suggestion may be undesirable anyway. See further below, particularly Ch. 3.

The sequencing stipulations that have to be attributed in the lexicon to the segments in (25) reduce at most to those in (27b); only they are contrastive:

(27) a. a, k, l
     b. a + m, a + p

'+' indicates 'precedes', not necessarily strictly (immediately). The centre of the syllable is identified as the most sonorous element, [a]. If we assume that C(onsonant) + V(owel) is the unmarked sequence, we need to stipulate lexically only the marked sequencings, as in (27b). The linearity relationships between [a] and [k] and [l]—i.e. those in (27a)—follow from the redundancy in (28):

(28) *unmarked syllable structure*
     C + {V}

where unbracketed 'C' is any consonant, any segment whose representation contains C, thus including sonorants. So, from invocation of (28) we get the progressive linearizations in (29a):

(29) a. k + a, l + a
     b. k + l (+ a), (a +) m + p
     c. k + l + a + m + p

The markedness assumption (28) and stipulation as having coda status (post-{V}) thus determine the basic sequence in syllables. The linearization relative to each other of the consonants in both pre- and post-centre position is given by sonority: the less sonorous segment is further from the centre; we get both sets of orderings in (29b) from sonority sequencing, in accordance with (26). (29c) expresses the overall linearity relations, most of which are derivative of unmarked syllable structure and sonority: cf. here (27).

Such an approach to intrasyllabic linearity as I have outlined is discussed in Anderson (1994: §2). Let us refer to it as the **partial non-sequencing** approach to intrasyllabic lexical content. Anderson (1987a: 212–18), however, suggests a still more radical approach to such cases of intrasyllabic linearity (see too Anderson et al. 1985: 213–14), which eliminates it entirely from contrastive status. There it is suggested that syllables are represented lexically as bundles of unlinearized elements, with an interior bundle corresponding to the contents of what will be the rhyme, which belongs, along with the contents of what will be the onset, within a more inclusive bundle corresponding to the contents of the syllable as a whole: we thus have an inner and an outer domain within the bundle constituting the contents of the syllable (a similar suggestion is made by Gil and Radzinsky 1984). Linearization follows from the subsetting relation between the bundles, the relative closeness of association of the consonants with the syllable centre. The proposed relative closeness of vowel and coda can be related to a number of phenomena, from the tradition of rhyming verse to the important role of rhymes in determining syllable weight. It is also reflected in the structural relations discussed in the following two sections. I shall refer to this approach to the linearization of the segments in syllables as a proposal for **total non-sequencing,** at the lexical level, of the elements of the syllable.

We can express this (total non-sequencing) proposal as in (30) and (31), where (30) gives the lexical representation for *clamp* (where I have arbitrarily ordered the elements external to and internal to the inner bundle in terms of increasing relative sonority), and where (31) gives the rule deriving linearity:

(30)   k,l(p,m,a)

(31)   *linearization with respect to the syllable centre*
     a. C({V} ⇒ C + ({V}
     b. C,{V} ⇒ {V} + C

(31a) gives the linearizations provided by invocation of (28) on the previous account, i.e. those in (29a); and (31b) linearizes with respect to the centre the elements whose sequencing had to be stipulated on that account, i.e. those in (27b).

(30) thus substitutes in the lexical entry the less specific, or less complex, subsetting relation, involving relative closeness of association, for linearization stipulations, and permits us to drop reference to (28). If something like what is embodied in (31) is appropriate, then contrastive linearity in lexical phonology is in principle restricted to the sequencing of syllable bundles. Mention of sequencing of syllables should also remind us that we must indeed give some consideration to what happens at syllable margins, when syllables 'collide'. But I delay consideration of this until later chapters, where are considered some limitations on syntax/phonology analogies; and in the course of that, as well as in the discussion in the following subsection, we shall find other roles for (28).

In the previous chapter I suggested that a syntactic analogy for the C({V} bundling of (31a) might come from the topic/comment distinction, roughly represented here, accordingly, as in (32):

(32)   top({P}

Linearization in this instance, however, has a marked and unmarked option, as presented in (33):

(33) a. *marked* top({P} ⇒ {P}) + top
    b. *default* top({P} ⇒ top + ({P})

And linearization within the construction headed by {P} is more complex than the phonological equivalent. We take up the reasons, to do with demands of the different substances with which the planes interface, for these discrepancies between syntax and phonology in Part III.

What emerges from the present section is that the directly substance-based property of linearity is often not contrastive in phonology. This is true whether one conceives of sequence as unilinear or multilinear, as will emerge in the latter case from what follows. Thus, for instance, most of the 'event structure' that Bird and Klein (1990) attribute to phonological representations is redundant as such, it is non-contrastive; it facilitates phonetic mapping.

As we have seen, linearity within the syllable frequently follows in particular from relative sonority, involving contrastive primary categories. Sonority involves perceived inherent salience, and it is thus itself in principle another interface-determined property, though there is some controversy over its phonetic exponence (recall again e.g. Ohala and Kawasaki 1984). Let us here, however, pursue our concern with contrastivity in relation to some notion of sonority and to linearity. For, despite the fundamental role of sonority in determining intra syllabic sequencing, there are indications even in English (and more strikingly in some other languages, such as Polish) that this direct mapping from relative sonority (plus orientation towards the centre) to linearization is insufficient as an account of syllable structure. Further structural properties are involved, further properties that partially determine linearity, and are not obviously direct interface-determined properties. And these may be language-particular. Let us now consider these.

2.3 The limits of linearity, II: Transitivity and adjunction

We can recall firstly that the centre of the syllable qualifies as **head** of the syntagm, in so far as it is both necessary to and distinctive of—i.e. characteristic of—the syllable as a construction: no centre, no syllable. Headhood, in this case, correlates with the sonority peak: the centre of the syllable is associated with both properties, headhood and sonority maximum. Headhood itself is a 'formal' property; but here this 'formal' property correlates with a substantive property, the sonority peak. The centre nevertheless shows further properties we can associate with headhood rather than sonority as such—i.e. with the 'formal' rather than that particular interface aspect of the syllable centre.

Thus, as observed in the preceding chapter, some centres in English require to be **complemented**; there are no lexical monosyllabic items in English of the character of (34a):

(34) a. *[ba], *[bɛ]
 b. bad, bet
 c. [bi] 'bee', [bei] 'bay'
 d. neon, chaos = [ni-], [kei-], not [nɛ-], [ka-]

Compare the well-formed (34b), where the centres are complemented by a consonant, and the centres illustrated by (34c) which do not require a complement. In (34d) the vowels of (c) are in pre-hiatus position; there are no words showing the vowels of (34b) in accented pre-hiatus position. We can distinguish, then, between transitive centres and intransitive, within the major (accented) vowel system, and we can represent this structural characteristic of the former as in (35a):ɔ

(35) a. [a], [ɛ] = {V/C}
 b. [i],[ei] = {V}

As in syntax, '/' indicates 'is complemented by'. This is further behaviour we would expect of a head: potentially to be subcategorized for a complement. In syntax this is associated particularly with verbals; like vowels, they are inherently salient. The phonological analogue to the head of the predication is the syllable centre, prototypically a vowel.

And the head and its complement can be interpreted as instantiating a dependency relation, whose orientation here correlates with relative sonority. We can represent this structural relationship in graph form, as in (36):

(36) {V/C}
           ＼
       :   {C}
       :   :
       :   :
       :   :
       ɛ + t

Thus, in the phonology the head of the syllable is perceptually salient; in the syntax the head of the predicator, a verbal, is cognitively salient, as the relational centre of the predication. The headhood analogy has both 'formal' and substantive (interface-based) motivations.

Linearity in (36) correlates with both relative sonority and dependency. However, we do not seem to need to invoke dependency in relation to the determination of sequencing as such here, given that the latter follows from relative sonority anyway, and sonority is apparently relevant elsewhere—as in the specifying of sequence between the members of consonant clusters. Thus, in phonology, while complementation necessarily invokes headhood/dependency, with the complement to the right of the head, linearity otherwise can be seen as following from sonority (plus orientation with respect to the centre, or subsetting in terms of total non-sequencing)—at least as far as concerns the limited set of examples from English that we have considered so far.

In syntax, however, unmarked linearity typically follows directly from dependency—though dependency itself is determined by categorization of the elements involved. Thus many languages are head-final languages ('XV'), others head-initial ('VX'—with its variant 'SVX')—though there are often apparently deviant sequences in particular languages. In phonology, complements appear on the right of the centre; there is no such variation in language type (or within a language). Phonological adjuncts, as we shall see, may precede or follow the centre (though there are coda-less languages—i.e. where there are no post-centre dependents), just as in particular languages syntactic adjuncts may precede or follow the verb; but there is no way in which it can be said that phonological adjuncts can intervene between centre and complement, as may be the case in the syntax of some languages. In phonology the complement/adjunct distinction is scarcely categorially dependent, except that assignment of the distinction depends on the sonority hierarchy and sequencing.

These differences in variability in linearization between syntax and phonology reflect the greater variety of complementation and adjunctive types in syntax, on the one hand, and, on the other, the limitations imposed on phonological structure by its direct instantiation in phonic substance, including time and sonority. Such observations undermine the parallelism between syntax and phonology in hierarchization of the submodules that is implied in Figure I.1 reproduced in the Prologue. We are already encountering the kind of limitations on analogy imposed by the different demands of their extralinguistic interfaces. But other considerations are more directly relevant at this point to our exploration of sonority and linearity.

2.3.1 *The limitations of sonority*

We now have to acknowledge that there are, of course, apparent anomalies in an account of syllable sequencing based on sonority alone. I am not alluding here to instances of what one can regard as 'fine-tuning' of what is allowed by relative sonority. With respect to any language there are very many possibilities of consonant combinations which conform to the requirements of sonority sequencing but which are non-occurrent in that language. This is illustrated, by the familiar present-day English restrictions, or combinatory gaps, in (37):

(37) *[kn-], *[pf-], *[-mb], *[-fp]

Many such restrictions reflect failure by the combination to achieve a minimum sonority distance requirement (cf. Steriade 1982), based on a preference within clusters for steep rises/falls in sonority. Such general or particular stipulations supplement but do not violate sonority sequencing requirements; they add further constraining factors, based on such clusters being disfavoured perceptually. Real anomalies do arise, however, in a couple of areas in English, for example.

As is again familiar, some pre-centre s-initial clusters, including some we have already encountered, cannot be reconciled with sonority sequencing requirements, as illustrated in (38a):

(38) a. sport, strip, squeeze
 b. slow, snow
 c. cusp, disk, pest
 d. chasm, prism

The clusters in (38b) are in conformity with sonority sequencing, as are the post-centre clusters in (38c); whereas that in (38d), /-zm/, isn't. The initial two elements in (38a) are both obstruents, therefore remain unsequenced by hierarchy 1 in (26). If we extend (26) as in (39), sonority-based sequencing can be seen to be in accord with what we find in all the clusters in (38b-c) but not those in (38a/d):

(39) *partial sonority hierarchy 2*
 a. *class:*
  vowel > sonorant > fricative > plosive
 b. *representation:*
  {V}   {V;C}   {C;V}   {C}

(39b) differentiates the specification for plosives, with C alone as a primary feature, and that for fricatives, which involves a dependency contrasting with sonorant consonants in the direction of dependency, {C;V} vs. {V;C}.[16]

---

[16] The interpretation of fricatives given here departs from that offered by Anderson and Ewen (1987: ch. 4), which invokes mutual dependency. What follows should make clear that this is in accord with our goals of identifying the locus of contrast and the character of primary (as opposed to secondary) features, as well as enhancing conceptual simplicity, which underlie the revised interpretation of

All the clusters we have considered so far are compatible with (39) except for those in (38a/d). (38d) may simply constitute an isolated exception. And there is indeed a tendency to syllabify the sonorant, when of course any anomaly with respect to sonority sequencing disappears, and the configuration coincides with one rendering of such as *prison*. But (38a) represent a well-integrated part of the phonology of English—and a number of other languages.

A second familiar area of discrepancy with respect to the requirements of sonority sequencing is illustrated in (40):

(40) a. sex, apse, bits
 b. seeks, creeps, beats
 c. logs, jobs, adze
 d. leagues, vibes, weeds
 e. act, apt
 f. creaked, steeped
 g. dragged, bobbed
 h. plagued, daubed
 i. width, depth

In the first four sets in (40) the final fricative is preceded by a plosive, contrary to application of hierarchy (39). In the next four—(e) to (h)—the final cluster consists of two plosives, which cannot be sequenced by (39). The final set again involve another (voiceless) fricative further from the centre than a plosive, which latter can be either voiced or voiceless. Every second set in (40) involves an intransitive vowel; but there is no such set corresponding to the transitive (40i). (40i) is morphologically complex, and the source of the base contains an intransitive vowel. The forms in (40) with an intransitive vowel are almost always also morphologically complex. This also applies to voiced final clusters: (40c) and (d), and (40g) and (h). So too the examples with sometimes mixed voicing in (40i). Here sonority requirements are overridden by morphological structure. The possibilities involving items with transitive vowel and final voiceless cluster—i.e. those exemplified by

---

voicing suggested in the text below. We shall find similar reasons to modify the interpretation of nasal consonants as well as voiced obstruents suggested by Anderson and Ewen.

Anderson and Ewen (1987) interpret relative prominence as a further (intra segmental) manifestation of the dependency, or head-modifier, relation (and we return to this in §4 of this chapter). The widespread unfolding formal analogy with the representation of syntactic categories involving the pervasiveness of dependency (as developed in relation to the syntax in Volume I of this trilogy, particularly Ch. 3) will be apparent. That this should be the case is the unmarked assumption, of course.

(40a) and (40e)—thus seem to be the most fully integrated into the phonology of English, in this respect

Let's start a fuller investigation by looking at the phonological structures involved with the kinds of items illustrated in (40), before returning to the problematical onsets of (38a). The final segments in (40), which are all **coronal obstruents**, are often described as '**appendices**' or 'extra-metrical'. They extend our usual expectations concerning the dimensions of the syllable in English, as well as violating sonority hierarchy (39): they do this not merely by allowing a final segment which violates the requirements of sonority sequencing but also in some cases by allowing more segments than are normally associated with the post-centre cluster.[17]

In the following subsection I (re)introduce representations for adjuncts and 'appendices' alongside that for complements, in more detail, before we take up again the anomalous onsets of (38a). Complements, adjuncts, and 'appendices' involve the same structural distinctions as have already been made in the syntax in Volume I. And this begins to illustrate something more of the extent of the dependency-and-head-based analogy that is the major concern of this chapter.

2.3.2 *Complements, adjuncts, and 'appendices'*

Normally, an intransitive centre in English is followed by only one segment, and so is a transitive centre together with its complement. Thus we do not find the possibilities in (41a) and (b):

(41) a. *helmp, *creelmp
 b. *creelm, *creamp, *creelp
 c. helm, help, hemp
 d. creel, cream, creep
 e. text(s)
 f. field, fiend

The acceptable forms in (41), except (e), all conform to the requirements of sonority sequencing, though the first form in (41c) requires an extension to the current formulation that we return to in a moment. The vowels in (41a), transitive and intransitive, reject the two-element-adjunct coda, though the coda conforms to the sonority hierarchy (if again we include in it the upcoming extension). The examples in (41c) with transitive vowels contain

---

[17] Also showing an 'extra coda segment'—as well as some of (40)—are such as *strange* and *lounge*, involving [n] and the voiced affricate following an intransitive vowel, either [eɪ] or [aʊ]. Affricates are often associated with exceptional distributional properties. See further note 21.

the post-verbal sequences in (41b), which have intransitive vowels; and (41d) show permissible post-intransitive monosegmental sequences. Again, the coronal-obstruent-final codas in (41e) and (f) seem to escape the restriction exemplified in (41a–b). The coronal-obstruent 'appendices' may occur as second or (in some cases) further adjuncts. And all of this also illustrates the equivalence of intransitive syllable centre and transitive centre plus complement.

As indicated, the first example in (41c) requires an extension to the hierarchy as given so far, an extension which might be incorporated as in (42):

(42) *partial sonority hierarchy 3*
    a. *class:*
        vowel > liquid > nasal consonant > fricative > plosive
    b. *representation:*
        {V}   {V;C}   {V:C}   {C;V}   {C}

The nasal consonant is represented here by mutual dependency (like the adjective), indicated by ':' (again a departure from Anderson and Ewen 1987, whose system was our starting point). That is, it combines V;C and C;V. However, we reconsider this categorization for nasals below in the light of fresh considerations (which move us further still from the system envisaged by Anderson and Ewen 1987).

Before returning to the coronal obstruents 'appendix', I want to consider how we are to capture explicitly the restriction on the dimensions of post-centre clusters which do not include such an 'appendix', i.e. the restriction that the latter apparently violates. The final consonants in (41b) and (c) are extensions to the core of the syllable represented by the centre (± its complement). We can formulate this in abbreviated form as in (43):

(43) *consonant adjunction*
    C ⇒ \{V}

Simple 'C' again indicates any consonant, any representation containing C, whereas {C} is a voiceless stop. (43) states that there is available to consonants the possibility of modifying the maximal obligatory construction headed by a vowel (so both transitive and intransitive projections in this case). To the right of the backward slash in (43) is specified the category that the consonant seeks to modify, as in syntactic representations of modification.

The adjunct adjoined by (43) attaches it to the maximal available construction headed by {V}, so including complemented {V}s. Maximality is guaranteed by the head convention, a notion familiar from studies on dependency grammar:

head convention (Anderson 1986a: 70):
A regularity that mentions the head of a construction is interpreted as invoking the construction as a whole unless a subordinate of the head is mentioned by the same instance of that regularity

This means that we can attribute to the relevant segments in *help* the structure in (44a) which differentiates in a familiar way between complement and adjunct, while (44b) illustrates the structure for an intransitive centre with an adjunct, as in *keep*:

(44) a.
```
        {V}
         |    \
      {V/C}    {C\{V}}
       :  \      :
       :   {V;C} :
       :    :    :
       :    :    :
       ε +  l +  p
```
b.
```
      {V}
       |   \
      {V}   {C\{V}}
       :      :
       :      :
       i  +   p
```

[p] instantiates an adjunct rather than a complement in both cases.

As in the syntax, a redundancy like (43) introduces a node of the same category as specified to the left of '\' in its representation, above the original node. In this way we recognize that the head determines the basic syntax of the construction; it is another property of heads to accept adjuncts (as well as to require complements, and to characterize the construction). Syllables containing such adjuncts are referred to by Hall (2001) as 'superheavy syllables', with a distribution that is more restricted than that associated with adjunct-free syllables (provided one syllabifies medial clusters onset-maximally).

These clusters of course are regulated also by sonority sequencing, and this limits the possible combinations. Thus a complement [p] cannot be followed in the coda by a [m], for instance. In addition, [ŋ] is an exception to (43), as formulated in (45), and fails to occur as an adjunct, as illustrated by (47):

(45) [ŋ] ⇒ ~ (43)

[ŋ] occurs as a complement in (46):

(46) transitive V + [ŋ]: sing, sink

But it cannot occupy the adjunct positions in (47):

(47) a. transitive V + C + [ŋ]: *silng
      b. intransitive V + [ŋ]: *seeng

[ŋ] is always a complement in English. Thus the distribution of [ŋ] reflects the complement/adjunct distinction, which is apparently a 'formal' rather than an interface-sensitive property.

Let us return to the 'appendices' illustrated by (40). These are not sequenced in accordance with sonority. But they seem to represent a higher-level adjunct that belongs to a rather specific category, namely 'coronal obstruent'. They introduce the extra structure in (48), compared with (44):

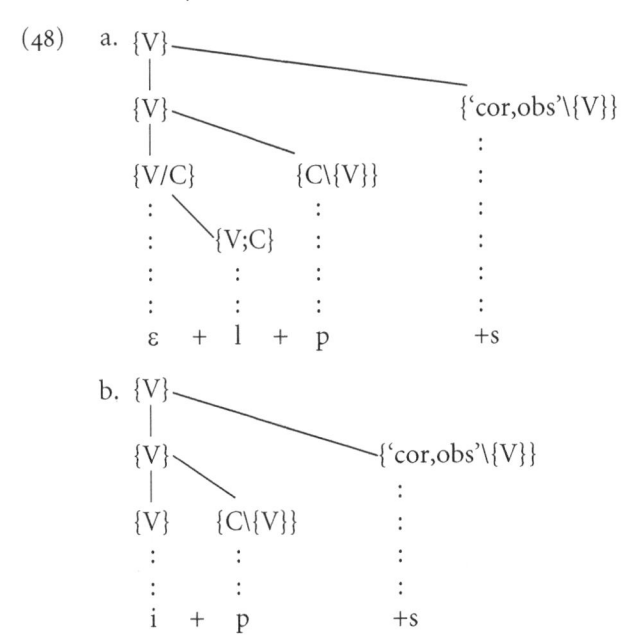

(48) a. {V}
          |
         {V}   {'cor,obs'\{V}}
          | :
         {V/C}   {C\{V}}   :
          :   \   :   :
          :   {V;C} :   :
          :   :   :   :
          :   :   :   :
          ε + l + p   +s

      b. {V}
          |
         {V}   {'cor,obs'\{V}}
          | :
         {V}   {C\{V}}   :
          :   :   :
          :   :   :
          i   +   p   +s

There is a case for regarding coronal as the unmarked 'articulation'—see, for instance, contributions to Paradis and Prunet (1991). But I am not concerned here with the characterization of 'coronal obstruent', which labelling here has simply the status of a cover term (though we shall return below to the characterization of the relevant secondary phonological category, to supplement the representation of obstruent).

What is relevant at this point, however, is that the 'appendix' is sequenced by relative sonority only with respect to the vowel, as in the lexical representation for *clamps* in (49), involving partial non-sequencing (recall (27)):

(49) a. a, k, l
      b. a + m, a + p, a + s

or as in (50), with total non-sequencing (recall (30)):

(50) k, l (p, s, m, a)

The 'appendix' is always lexically part of the rhyme. Linearization of the 'appendix' with respect to the other consonants of the rhyme must apparently be part of the specification of the adjunction itself, as given, in a provisional form, in (51):

(51) {'cor,obs'} ⇒ +{ \{V}}*, in environment C

This is what the '+s' notation in (48) is intended to express. We should note finally here that the asterisk in (51) indicates that (51) is recursive, allowing for examples like (41e) and the others in (52):

(52) a. acts, widths, sixth, text
      b. sixths, texts

Recursion seems to be restricted to adjunction of the voiceless coronal obstruents, a restriction I have not built in. But I am principally interested in this context in the characterization in principle of such 'extrametricality'. Though the present regularity is limited to a rather specific phonological class, we have again here a 'formal' determination of sequence, involving the relationship of adjunction.

At this point, I want to reconsider the linearity stipulation built into (51). Say we assume that the more specific adjunction of (51) applies after consonant adjunction (43), resulting because of this in representations like those in (48). I am suggesting that the order of adjunction of elements within a domain, and therefore their closeness to the head, is determined by the relative simplicity of the primary categorization of the adjoined element, with the simpler taking precedence over the less so. The ordering of application is thus substantively motivated. And this relative simplicity does seem to correlate with the relative integration of the element in the construction (as revealed in e.g. the relative significance of morphological boundaries).[18]

---

[18] This ordering of application involves what the elderly and/or literate reader (and/or anyone who has read Volume II) might see as a curious reversal of the rule-ordering principle known as 'Proper

Phonology and dependency　93

Now, if order of application and relative closeness to the centre are determined in this way, it is unnecessary, after all, to include linearization as part of (51), since it follows from projectivity ('no-tangling') requirements. Recall that 'tangling' involves the crossing of lines (dependency arcs or association lines) in the graph. Projectivity is preserved in the present case only if the coronal obstruent, which is attached last, also comes in final position, as can be verified by inverting any of the non-vocalic elements in (48), along the lines of (16d) in §1.7. The order of application determines the sequencing, which need not be stipulated, so that we can substitute (51)* for (51), dropping the serialization and environment specifications:

(51)*　{'cor,obs'} ⇒ { \{V}}*

Thus far we have ignored in this section the assignment of structure to onsets, and thereby various questions remain unanswered, including particularly those relating to the anti-sonority initial clusters of (38a). The next subsection attempts to remedy this.

2.3.3 *Onsets: Status and structure*

A return to the sonority sequencing discrepancy illustrated by (38a), repeated here as a reminder, brings us to a sharp confrontation with the possibilities at the pre-centre position:

(38)　a.　sport, strip, squeeze
　　　b.　slow, snow

Let us look first, however, at initial clusters that do not present a problem with respect to sonority sequencing requirements.

In accordance with the account suggested by Anderson (1994), involving lexical partial non-sequencing within the syllable, a consonant in a monosyllable whose sequencing with regard to the vowel is not lexically stipulated will be sequenced before that vowel. Again, in English, such a consonant is clearly an adjunct to the vowel; it seeks a vowel to modify, as represented in (43):

(43)　*consonant adjunction*
　　　C ⇒ { \{V}}

Inclusion Precedence' (see e.g. Koutsoudas et al. 1974, and contributions to Koutsoudas 1975). However, we are not concerned here with mutations or with rules of exponence, but with simple structure-building by adjunction. Moreover, from a 'top-down' perspective, 'Proper Inclusion Precedence' of a sort is indeed ensured.

If, in terms of (53), with partial non-sequencing, segments lexically linearized with respect to the centre are adjoined before the lexically unlinearized, this will give us structures like (54), for *camps*:

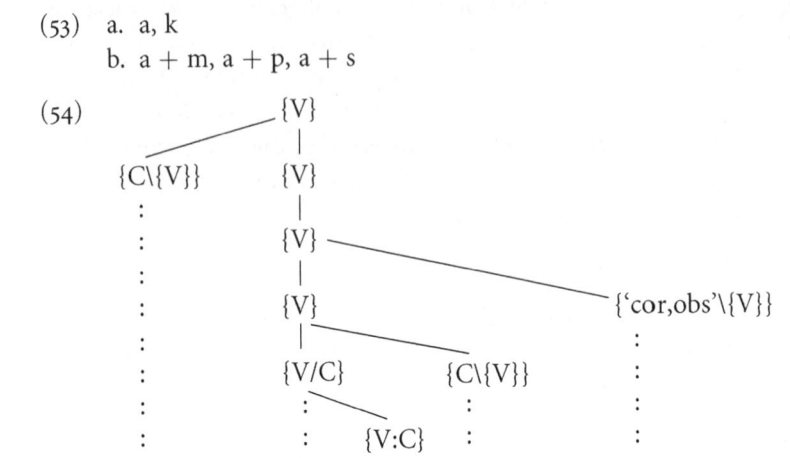

(53) a. a, k
      b. a + m, a + p, a + s

(54)

```
                    {V}
                     |
   {C\{V}}          {V}
     :              |
     :             {V}
     :              |
     :             {V}                    {'cor,obs'\{V}}
     :              |
     :            {V/C}     {C\{V}}
     :              :         :
     :              :  {V:C}  :
     :              :    :    :
     :              :    :    :           :
     k    +    a  +  m  +  p      +      s
```

We can say that the onset is the highest adjunct of the centre, {V}; the rhyme is everything else subordinate to a {V}.

[ŋ] is exceptional with regard to both applications of (43), with respect to both the coda and the onset. We can generalize over the two exceptions as in (45), or simply (55):

(45) [ŋ] ⇒ ~ (43)

(55) [ŋ] ≠ {C\{V}}

[ŋ] is never an adjunct. For [h], on the other hand, (43) is obligatory, and, moreover, its serialization is never stipulated lexically (Anderson 1986b, 2001a), so that it is limited to onsets, as formulated in (56), assuming partial non-sequencing:

(56) [h] does not occur in the lexical environment V+

The first of these exceptional constraints on linearization thus reflects a 'formal' property, the complement/adjunct distinction, while the second invokes the onset/coda distinction (but see §3.3), which has a substantive basis, in sequencing.

If we adopt the more 'radical' approach to sequencing proposed by Anderson (1987a), i.e. total non-sequencing, then the order of the applications of (43) follows from the closeness of association between the consonant and the centre, as reflected in representations such as (56):

(57) k(p,m,a)

The most closely associated consonants, co-members of the inner subset, the inner domain, i.e. those in the rhyme, are adjoined first. This is consistent with the notion that order of adjunction reflects degree of integration of the dependent with the head.

Consider now sonority-respecting two-consonant onsets. Much work on dependencies in phonology has assumed that dependency follows sonority (cf. e.g. Anderson and Ewen 1987): that is, of two elements joined by a dependency arc, the more sonorous will be the governor. This is embodied in (43), for instance, in the dependency relations that hold between the centre of the syllable and consonantal elements. Anderson (1986a: §6) argues, however, that consonant-to-consonant dependencies reverse this relationship: in the case of two consonants linked by a dependency arc, the less sonorous governs the more. Just as the optimal position for a consonant is before the vocalic centre, so the optimal consonant is the one furthest in sonority from the vowel: the optimal syllable contains a plosive, and specifically voiceless, onset (cf. e.g. Cairns and Feinstein 1982). Perceptual salience here is provided by maximal syntagmatic contrast with the centre.

The dependence of headedhood on sonority and syntagmatic contrast, both contributing to perceptual salience, raises another question. It can be argued that headhood is based on substantive analogies in syntax and phonology, alternative manifestations of 'cognitive salience'. But is there a more precise syntactic analogue to the sonority hierarchy? Well, maximum strength in **V** does favour vowels as the 'ultimate heads' in syllables, and **P** (finiteness) is associated with the 'ultimate heads' of predications. Are we dealing with parallel dimensions of syllabic prominence and predicational prominence? Syllabic prominence correlates with sonority, whereas it is perhaps less obvious what the semantic substance of predicational prominence would be. However, we might think of the notional hierarchy corresponding to sonority as involving degree of 'dynamism', with {P}s involving maximum 'dynamism' as embodiments (in main clauses) of the act of speech itself, and of its contextual coordinates and modulations. Also, verbal predicators are certainly the most 'powerful' relators in syntax, providing the predicational skeleton, just as syllable peaks provide the contour on the margins of which non-syllabics are articulated, while they, like verbals, occupy the centre. As concerns syntagmatic contrast, name and pronoun arguments provide the maximal contrast to verbals in terms of reference to 'particular entity' vs. denotation of an 'event type' and its relation to the act of speech.

To return to cluster structure, I adopt the above suggestion concerning inter-consonantal dependencies here: namely, that it is based on **anti-sonority**. The maximally unmarked syllable structure should thus be expressed as specifically (28)* rather than simply (28), i.e. as involving a voiceless stop rather than any consonant:

(28)   unmarked syllable structure
       C + {V}

(28)*   maximally unmarked syllable structure
       {C} + {V}

It should be pointed out that, in terms of (28), the head in this case satisfies the formal criteria for headhood only rather weakly: any consonant, not just voiceless plosives, can constitute an onset; we are merely claiming that non-plosives are onsets *faute de mieux*, as it were. The prototypical onset is a voiceless plosive, and so the consonant closest to a voiceless plosive in sonority is head in an onset cluster. It is only in this weak sense that the less sonorous consonant can be said to be characteristic of the onset. But nouns are if anything even 'weaker' heads, to the extent that they too are almost all non-complement-taking, minimally relational, and they require to be subordinate to {N} to serve as arguments.

I thus interpret the second consonant in *clamps* as an adjunct to the first, and [m] as an adjunct to [p], with a structure as shown in (58):

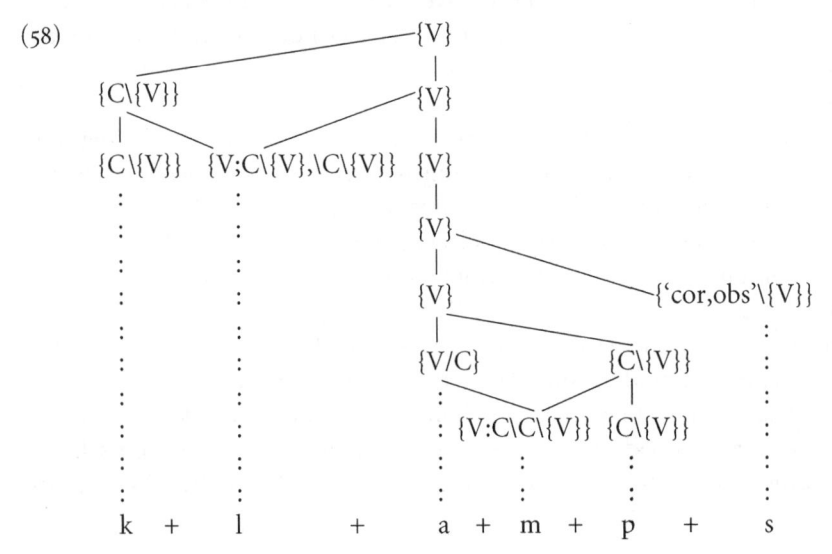

(58)

```
                              {V}
                               |
      {C\{V}}                 {V}
        |                      |
   {C\{V}}  {V;C\{V},\C\{V}}  {V}
     :         :               |
     :         :              {V}
     :         :               |
     :         :              {V}                  {'cor,obs'\{V}}
     :         :               |                     :
     :         :             {V/C}      {C\{V}}      :
     :         :               :          |          :
     :         :          : {V:C\C\{V}} {C\{V}}      :
     :         :               :    :      :         :
     :         :               :    :      :         :
     k   +     l      +        a +  m  +   p    +    s
```

The appropriate subconfiguration is allowed for by (59):

(59) *cluster headship*
 $C_i \Rightarrow \backslash C_j$, iff $C_j < C_i$, where C_i and C_j are adjacent,
 and '<' = 'lower in sonority than'

(59) applies to the [m] in (58), which, as shown there, is thereby adjoined to the [p] as well as to the [a], whose complementation requirements the [m] satisfies. And consonant adjunction will attach [l] to the centre, as well as its being adjoined to [k] by (59). In both these cases we have double-motherhood, or **bidependency**, again also a 'formal' property of syntactic representations (see §3.8 of Volume I). The dependency created between [m] and [p] is the vehicle for the agreement in articulation between these two elements, which is a property of the construction that together they constitute.[19]

The effect of consonant adjunction to the centre and cluster headship among consonants is to maximize dependency relations among the segments in a syllable; consonant adjunction and cluster headship are freely available to consonants, and are blocked only by sonority requirements, and by 'extrametrical' adjunctions, as with the coronal obstruent in (58), which does not participate in cluster headship (59). We shall see in §2.5 that **dependency maximization** has interesting consequences for the interpretation of timing among elements of the syllable. I shall be suggesting there that some apparent timing 'aberrations' are a consequence of the result of a loss of dependency between the elements involved. Maximization of dependency ensures timing relations among the segments. The timing of the final consonant in (58), however, is ensured by its morphological status.

We can now finally proceed to a consideration of the sonority sequencing discrepancies illustrated by (38a), which are not restricted to English, but recur in different forms in sundry languages—frequently involving an [s]-type consonant:

---

[19] (59) will also apply to the medial clusters in *winter* and *whimper*, and *thunder* and *lumber*, where again the dependency relation is the channel for agreement in articulation. See further §2.5.

 Agreement in voicing between [p] and [s] in (58), on the other hand, is a requirement on any adjacent obstruents, whether or not directly linked by dependency; and such agreement can indeed be violated, as in *width* of (40i). The lesser degree of structural integration of [s] that is apparent in the representation in (58), by virtue of its failing to undergo (59), might be taken as a formal characterization of 'extrametrical' or appendix status (in such cases, at least) and the possibility of violation of obstruent-cluster voicing, as in (40i). In this respect we lack the maximization of dependency that I associate with guarantee of timing relations (see further §2.5). In general this will be guaranteed by the morphological structure, however.

(38) a. sport, strip, squeeze

The last two examples in (38a) also show an extra segment to the left of the centre compared with what we have considered so far, which have all involved two-member onsets. The [s] that occurs uniquely among consonants in this position and the equivalent in the first example does not satisfy sonority sequencing requirements and cannot be serialized thereby. Moreover, as observed in §1.7, not only is the [s] the only segment type that can occur in this position, as the realization of [S], but also the set of obstruents that can occur in the position following it is restricted to the minimal obstruents, representing neutralizations of [p] ≠ [b] etc.—if we leave aside here the [sf] sequence found in loan words like *sphere* and *sphincter*.

I suggested in §1.7 that [S] is another adjunct, but of a specific type. This emerges from the formulation in (60), which assumes that [S] is lexically empty, and presents a special case of cluster headship:

(60) unspecified segment adjunction
{ } ⇒ \{C₁\{V}}}, where C₁ = [P,T,K]

Lexically, i.e. remotely, in terms of relative emptiness of specification, from the phonetic interface, the segment realized as [s] in such an environment is empty, and is filled out by redundancy.[20]

The {C} and {V;C} segments in such clusters as *str* are sequenced in accordance with relative sonority. The sequencing of [S] follows from the fact that the very specific adjunction of (60) will apply after (43) and (59), which respectively adjoin [P, T, K] and [l,r] to the vowel and adjoin [l,r] to [P, T, K]. The adjunction which applies to only a subset of potential heads, as par excellence in (60), is attached last. To preserve projectivity, [S] must be sequenced in front of the plosives. This allows for the relevant parts of the representation in (61a):

---

[20] Notice that, if we assume, with e.g. Anderson (1994), that vowels are contrastively unspecified (recall note 15), then the 'empty' segment of (60) would have to be differentiated in some way.

Before laterals, [s] is in contrast with [f]: *slow, flow*. But only [f] and [θ] occur before [r]: *free, three*. In all of these cases the initial clusters conform to sonority. [s] does not contrast with anything before nasals. We can perhaps associate this with the minimal 'stop' secondary feature ({c}) in nasals that is suggested in the revised representation proposed below, viz. {V;C{c}}, so that a specifier-like status, as far as association with neutralization is concerned, is spread from the [P,T,K] situation to these other stop contexts.

Phonology and dependency

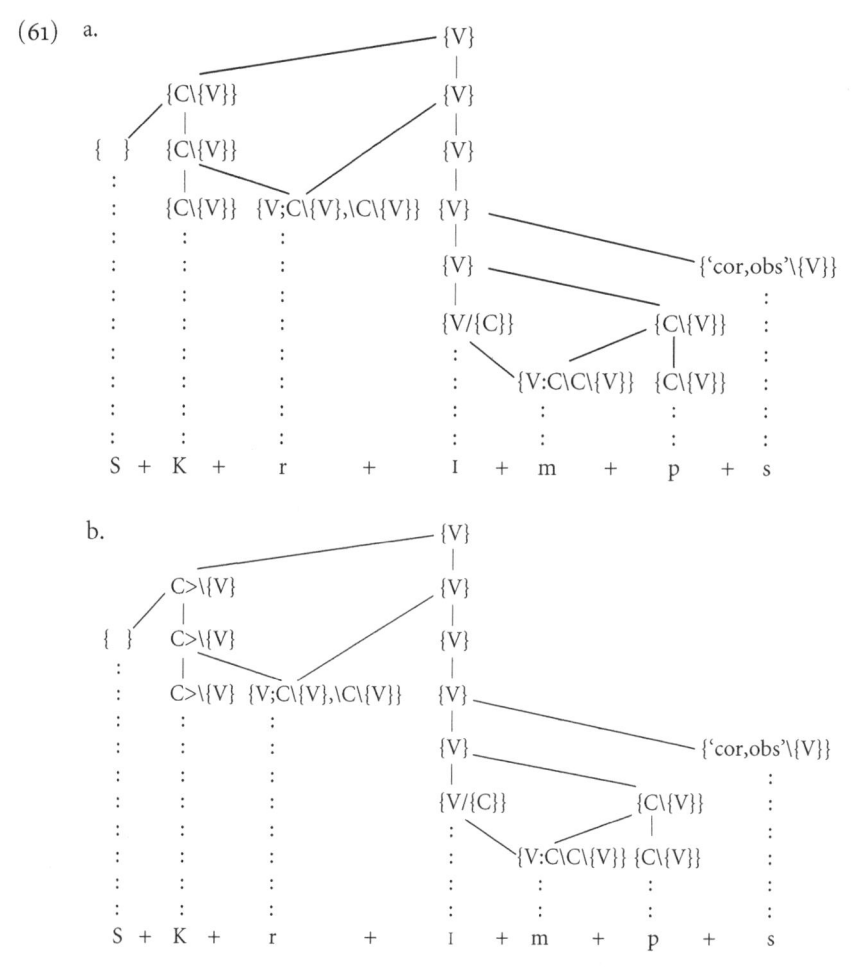

(61) a.
```
                              ─── {V}
         {C\{V}}               │
         │                    {V}
    { }  {C\{V}}               │
         │                    {V}
         {C\{V}} {V;C\{V},\C\{V}} {V} ─────────
          :       :       :    │               ─── {'cor,obs'\{V}}
          :       :       :   {V} ──────                :
          :       :       :    │        {C\{V}}         :
          :       :       :   {V/{C}}    │              :
          :       :       :    :         │              :
          :       :       :    :  {V:C\C\{V}} {C\{V}}   :
          :       :       :    :    :        :          :
          :       :       :    :    :        :          :
          S  +  K  +   r    +    I  +  m  +  p  +  s
```

b.
```
                              ─── {V}
         C>\{V}                │
         │                    {V}
    { }  C>\{V}                │
         │                    {V}
         C>\{V} {V;C\{V},\C\{V}} {V} ─────────
          :       :       :    │               ─── {'cor,obs'\{V}}
          :       :       :   {V} ──────                :
          :       :       :    │        {C\{V}}         :
          :       :       :   {V/{C}}    │              :
          :       :       :    :         │              :
          :       :       :    :  {V:C\C\{V}} {C\{V}}   :
          :       :       :    :    :        :          :
          :       :       :    :    :        :          :
          S  +  K  +   r    +    I  +  m  +  p  +  s
```

The initial lexically empty category realized as [s] identifies a following plosive as a minimal plosive, one that neutralizes the distinction between [p] and [b], [t] and [d], [k] and [g]. Indeed, if we regard the few forms like *sphere* (with [s] + fricative) as marked as exceptional, then the place after initial [s] neutralizes all distinctions among obstruents, except those of place. The representation in (61b) is then more appropriate, where 'C>' is any consonant where C is preponderant. In the context in (61), 'C>' is realized as a minimal stop, with neither aspiration nor voicing.

As in Chapter 1, I shall refer to the kind of adjunct illustrated by [s] in (61) as a specifier, in this case the minimal-plosive specifier. This seems to be another fundamental 'formal' type—though the recurrence of [s]-type segments in this kind of sonority violation may reflect a substantive characteristic, i.e. follow from the particular characteristics of [s]-sounds, perhaps their particular noisiness. Compare the adjectival and prepositional specifiers discussed in Chapter 1, which have in common the notional property of 'intensification' (cf. *very beautiful* and *right beside*). I thus reiterate that the label 'specifier', as with 'complement' and 'adjunct' is chosen advisedly, as discussed in §1.7, and elaborated on here. These are analogues of the constructional relations in the syntax that are labelled in the same way.

It may be objected to the analysis of English [S] as a specifier that, unlike *very*, which is an optional accompaniment to gradient adjectives, [S] is a necessary accompaniment to [P/T/K]. What is important here, however, is that [S] specifies a neutralization. The same is true of syntactic specifiers. Archetypical specifiers like *very* and *right* behave in a similar way: *very* selects gradient adjectives (*very small*—*very wooden* is figurative), and *right* locational functors (*She was seated right by John* vs. agentive **She was kissed right by* (≠ *beside*) *John*). The specifier of {P} *that* (see further §§6.2.3 on this categorization) selects subordinate {P}s, not any {P}.[21] Specifiers belong to

---

[21] This redundancy of linearity may involve further cases where we apparently have contrastive linearization, as with the pair of Greek words in (i):

(i) a. skílo 'dog'
    b. ksílo 'wood'

(where mis-linearization, as may easily be perpetrated by non-native speakers of Greek, may result, for instance, in such foreigners insisting that they want the doors and windows in their new house to be made of 'dog'—rather than, say, aluminium). We also have such pairs as (ii):

(ii) a. spátha 'sabre'
     b. psátha 'straw hat'

However, it can be argued that initially in (ib) and (iib) we have affricates, as reflected in the traditional spellings, involving a single letter, respectively ξ and ψ, while the clusters are spelled with two, σκ and σπ. Traditionally, these single graphs are called 'double letters', along with ζ, representing [z]. It is tempting to regard 'double letters' as graphs devised for representing affricates, given that typically the sound signified by Modern Greek ζ derives from an affricate (Lehmann 1955: ch. 10). The putative Modern Greek affricate in (iiib), however, is represented by a sequence of Greek letters, τσ; and it is in contrast not just with the cluster of (iiia), spelled στ, but also with the Modern Greek (putative) voiced affricate of (iiic), spelled τζ:

(iii) a. stíros 'barren'
      b. tsíros 'dried mackerel'
      c. dzíros 'turnover'

Clusters do not occur word-finally in Greek, and these are avoided even in loanwords. In native words single final consonants are generally limited to those represented by ζ (transliterated as *s*) and ν (transliterated as *n*), and ρ (transliterated as *r*). But we do find a final ξ, representing an affricate, in the archaic survival of (iv):

(iv) άπαξ 'once'

Those mentioned exhaust the set of affricates, which do not cluster with other consonants initially;

both phonology and syntax. And we can include a specifier category as a variant of those phonological categorizations that render many linearity stipulations redundant.

The obligatory association between [S] and minimal obstruents, in contrast with the optional status of syntactic specifiers, has to do with substantive factors. Syntactic specifiers disambiguate the subclass of the specifiee, where the subclass is independent of the presence of the specifier. And the specifier can be used to signal an unusual, figurative categorization, as in *a very wooden greeting* or *a very English gesture*. These functions depend, then, on semanticity, which is not as such a property of phonology. Instead, a phonological relation of specification creates a neutralization of contrast. And it is this that differentiates the specification relation from simple co-occurrence of contrastive segments.

However, there are types of specifier-like elements in syntax that, like [S], necessarily accompany a neutralization. I think that a consideration of these will help to clarify the status of phonological specifiers.

The grammatical phenomenon I have in mind is illustrated by the interpretation of SOV clauses in German offered in §7.3 in Volume I. According to this, the *daß* in (I.199a) is a specifier-like accompaniment of the subordinate clause that is necessarily accompanied by SOV order in that clause, and vice versa. And this order neutralizes the variations in word order associated with the grammaticalizations of mood-marking and information structure that contrast in such main clauses as (I.199b):

while the clusters of the (a) examples in (i)-(iii) may be extended as in (va) and also form part of the larger set of [s]-initial clusters given in (b):

(v) a. spl-, spr-, str-, skl-, skr-, skn-
     b. sf-, sθ-, sx-, sfr-

(For exemplification see Holton et al. 1997: 10–12.) In Greek onsets, the fricative [s] seems to be a specifier of voiceless obstruents in general rather than just plosives.

However, the fricative element of affricates, as well as, like the elements of clusters, being unsequenced lexically, is also marked, unlike members of clusters, lexically as exceptions to both sonority sequencing and (the Greek version of) unspecified segment adjunction (60), in being fixed as always following the stop element. The elements of the affricate thus do not cluster with other onset consonants; and the sequencing relative to each other is not part of the system that forms intrasyllabic syllable linearization. It is invariant, and may be anti-sonority, as in (iv), [-Vks], and more commonly in other languages. However, the component elements of the affricate are, I assume, susceptible to cluster headship (59).

(I.199) a. Er sagte, daß er ihn gesehen hätte
He said that he him/it seen had.SUBJ

b. Ich hatte den Hut vergessen/Den Hut hatte ich vergessen
I had the hat forgotten/the hat had I forgotten

c. Er sagte, er hätte ihn gesehen
He said he had.SUBJ him/it seen

The subordinate clause in (I.199c) lacks SOV order, in the absence of the complementizer; we have 'V-2', as is unmarked in main clauses, though there we also find 'verb-initial' as a possibility.

According to Volume I (I.199a) is marked as non-finite by its word order. In the shape of *daß* we have an obligatory 'complementizer' of a verbal that is overall non-finite but is derived lexically from a finite verb. The word order marks non-finite subordinate, and the 'complementizer' marks the presence of a finite base (with an unmarked subject) for the verb of the subordinate. *That* in English has the same function, but *daß* in addition indicates, by its presence, together with the word order, that the subordinate is demoted to overall non-finite status. And its presence is obligatory with such a demoted finite.

Volume I therefore distinguishes structurally between *that* as a simple specifier and *daß* as an expletive complement of the subordinate non-finite configuration in (I.200):

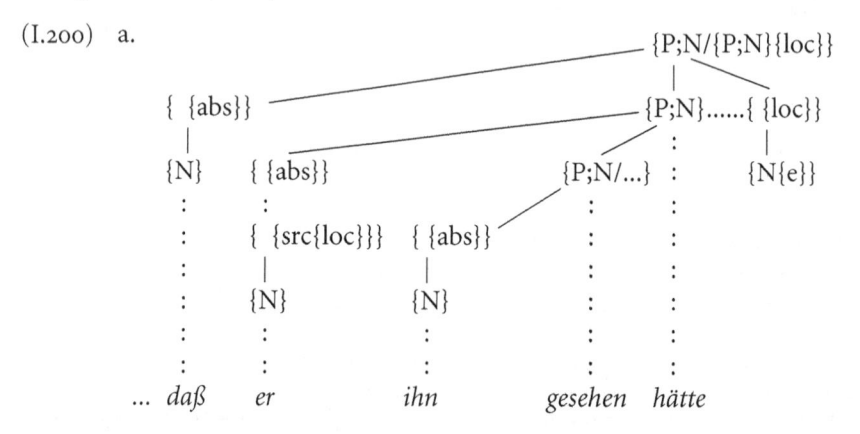

(I.200) a.

```
                                                    {P;N/{P;N}{loc}}
                                                    |         ╲
    { {abs}}                                      {P;N}......{ {loc}}
    |                                               :         |
    {N}      { {abs}}                 {P;N/...}     :        {N{e}}
    :         :                         :           :
    :      { {src{loc}}}  { {abs}}      :           :
    :         |            |            :           :
    :        {N}          {N}           :           :
    :         :            :            :           :
    :         :            :            :           :
    ... daß    er          ihn        gesehen     hätte
```

The details of (I.200a) are unimportant here: the important thing is the status of *daß* as a complement of the upper {P;N}. Compare this with the representation of the syntactic specifier *that* in (I.198):

(I.198) a.

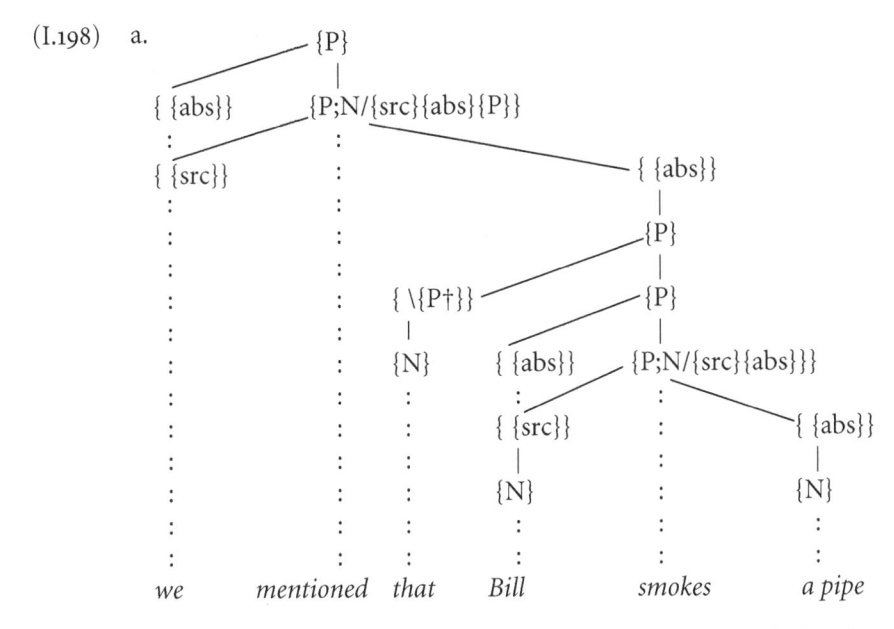

```
                    ─ {P}
                      │
  { {abs}}        {P;N/{src}{abs}{P}}
     :                :
  { {src}}            :                    ─ { {abs}}
     :                :                       │
     :                :                      {P}
     :                :                       │
     :              { \{P†}}                 {P}
     :                │                       │
     :               {N}    { {abs}}    {P;N/{src}{abs}}}
     :                :        :                 :        ─{ {abs}}
     :                :      { {src}}            :           │
     :                :        │                 :          {N}
     :                :       {N}                :           :
     :                :        :                 :           :
     :                :        :                 :           :
    we           mentioned   that    Bill     smokes      a pipe
```

That is an optional modifier of a subordinate {P}, where marking of subordination is associated with the dagger in the categorization of the specifier.

The *daß* of (I.200) has the obligatory status that is also associated with [S]. However, in phonology a consonant does not complement another consonant; consonants can complement only a vowel. Inter-consonantal dependencies necessarily have adjunct status. Such a construction is forbidden to [S]. Instead it is structurally a specifier whose function is different from syntactic specifiers for the substantive reasons presented above. What I have called the 'phonological specifier' construction thus 'neutralizes' the distinction between the two syntactic constructions we have linked it with. It is a modifier, like syntactic specifiers, and that, again like them, indicates neutralization. But its presence is nevertheless obligatory like that of *daß*, which also indicates a neutralization, in this case of word order. But it is structurally closer to the specifier. This is another indication of the greater differentiation available to the notionally based plane.

This section has tried to establish as fundamental to the phonology, in determining sequencing in particular, such 'formal' distinctions as are embodied in the terms complement, adjunct, and specifier. With respect to phonological structure, we must add these more 'formal' notions to the fundamental interface properties already discussed in §§2.2–3, linearity and sonority. And the derivative status of linearity illustrates the extent to which phonology—as well as syntax—is basically non-concatenative: the substance-based property of sequence is largely expressive of other, linguistically more basic, structural relationships. We have also begun to encounter various neutralizations. Others have been ignored in what precedes—such as those associated with the 'appendices' to the syllable—which in some cases introduce morphophonological considerations. However, it has not been my intention to confront all the possible neutralizations to be found in the phonology of English; rather, simply those associated with the alleged specifier analogy. There is, however, some further discussion of contrast and neutralization in §4.5.

2.4 Transitivity, weight, and aperture

Let us turn now to the character of the syllable centre and to linearization therein. This introduces another property whose contrastive status must be examined, namely syllabic **weight**. In many languages this interacts with transitivity. And, though weight is ultimately an interface property, it is derivative of transitivity in some cases, at least. Let us return, to begin with, to transitivity and weight in English.

2.4.1 *Transitivity and weight in English*

I have distinguished between transitive and intransitive syllable centres, corresponding to the traditional distinction between 'checked' and 'free' vowels. Intransitive, or 'free', centres in English typically have more **weight** than the corresponding transitive; they are in particular longer than a transitive of the same 'height' or sonority, in the same environment. In the case of vowels of the same weight, relative sonority correlates with vowel height as in (62):

(62) vowel   sonority
      LOW > MID > HIGH

But, in the same environments, [i] in English is longer than [ɪ], despite being higher. We have here another interface property, weight, associated in English with transitivity. Some of the intransitives in English are also clearly complex: they constitute diphthongs. In the case of both monophthongs and diphthongs I represent the weight relative to transitive vowels by a doubling of the **V** element, and the complexity of diphthongs by the presence of two secondary (articulatory) categories, as in (63), where the secondary categories are enclosed in inner braces:

(63) a. [i] = {V,V{i}}
      b. [aɪ] = {V,V{a,i}}

The elements within the inner brackets in (63) again represent secondary categories, in this case associated with placement on the vowel dimensions: the acute feature **i** is high and front (in articulatory terms) relative to the compact feature **a**. Sequence of the two elements of the diphthong need not be stipulated lexically; it follows from relative sonority, with the more sonorous **a** element (compactness) coming first, before the acuteness element **i** as in (64):

(64) {V,V{a + i}}

Only exceptions to this need be marked lexically.

It is doubtful that one needs to attribute, even redundantly, more structure, such as dependency relations, to monophthongal syllable centres and to some diphthongs: see Lass (1987). But there are motivations for suggesting that in prototypical diphthongs the more sonorous vowel governs (Anderson and Ewen 1987: §3.6.2), as in (65):

(65) {V,V{a;i}}

It would again be a rather 'weak' head, in simply reflecting relative sonority, except in so far as we can say that the more sonorous the vowel the more prototypical. We return below to the characterization of the sonority of **a**, and to the implications of the proposed characterization for the theory of primary and secondary features.

In the most familiar varieties of English, light vowels map onto transitive, or 'checked', structures, and heavy vowels map onto intransitive (as in (63)), as represented overall in (66):

(66)   weight   transitivity
    a. {V,V}   ⇔   {V}
    b. {V}   ⇔   {V/C}

Intransitivity seems to be unmarked; thus, many languages lack transitive vowels. So we can formulate a redundancy such as (67) applying to rhymes in English, which, taking transitivity rather than weight as primary, makes all but transitive vowels also heavy:

(67) *transitivity and weight in English*
      {V} ⇒ {V,V}, except in environment /C

However, this simple correlation is not universal in varieties of English, and the difference in the systems involved confirms that transitivity is indeed primary, i.e. lexical, contrastive, and that weight is derived, and thus that the directionality of redundancy (67) is appropriate, rather than one taking vowel weight as basic.

In Scottish English and Scots the weight of an intransitive vowel depends in a rather drastic way on environment: weight is assigned only if the vowel appears finally or before a tautosyllabic [r] or before a tautosyllabic voiced fricative; elsewhere, that is before stops (plosive or nasal), voiceless fricatives, and the lateral, intransitive, 'free' vowels have the kind of weight associated with transitive, 'checked' vowels:

(68)   *Scottish vowel length*
   a. FREE/HEAVY: tie, tyre, rise, live (*adj.*)
   b. FREE/LIGHT: tile, rice, life, ride, write
   c. CHECKED (so LIGHT): pit, pet, putt, live (*verb*), fir

The vowels exemplified by (68a-b) have been described as 'vowels of variable quantity' (Wettstein 1942; Zai 1942). Thus, whereas (68c) is generally the case in English, that lightness is associated with transitivity, as in (69a), and so all intransitive vowels are heavy (as in (69c)), in these Scottish and some other varieties we also find the additional requirement of (69b), which attributes lightness to intransitives in a certain environment, as outlined above:

(69)   '*the Scottish vowel-length rule*'
   a. $\{V/C\} \Rightarrow \{V\}$
   b. $\{V\} \Rightarrow \{V\}$ in env.$\{C_x\}$,
      where '$\{C_x\}$' is the environment that blocks weight
   c. $\{V\} \Rightarrow \{V,V\}$

A variable set of intransitives, but usually including [ɔ], do not participate in (69).

(69) is a further grammaticalization of the length variation before different consonants to be found in other varieties of English. Weight is rendered uniformly non-contrastive in either case. But in the Scottish varieties transitivity cannot be derived simply from the weight of a vowel: thus the vowels in both *ride* and *rid* are light, but the former is intransitive (as witnessed by *rye*), the latter transitive (no monosyllabic word [rɪ], etc.). But one cannot predict whether a light vowel preceding [-d] will be transitive or intransitive. If something like an analysis involving (69) is appropriate, then it illustrates the fundamental status of transitivity in the phonology of English, and the derivative status of weight.[22]

---

[22] I do not want here to get into extensive discussion of the identity of the victims and of the environment for what's come to be known as 'Aitken's Law' (Lass 1974; Taylor 1974) (which label has usually been applied to the historical process(es)) or its synchronic reflection, the 'Scottish vowel-length rule' (Aitken 1981), partly because the details of this are not directly relevant and partly because there not variation among speakers in this regard; and much research is still to be done on this variation (as shown by e.g. Scobbie et al. 2001).

2.4.2 Transitivity and aperture in Midi French

We find a slightly different, and perhaps more striking, illustration of the fundamental character of phonological transitivity in Midi French. In terms of distribution, the non-nasalized vowel system of Midi French (excluding schwa) falls into three sets. There is a set of vowels that is transitive (70a), another that is intransitive (b) and a set which can be either (c):

(70) a. {V}   [e] *inqui<u>et</u>, tourn<u>ée</u>, tourn<u>ait</u>, p<u>ê</u>cheur, p<u>ê</u>cheur* = {i;a}
              [ø] *j<u>eux</u>, j<u>eu</u>net, cr<u>eux</u>* = {(i,u);a}
              [o] *<u>au</u>, b<u>eau</u>té, b<u>o</u>tté, rhinoceros* = {u;a}

     b. {V/C} [ɛ] *col<u>è</u>re, inf<u>e</u>ct, prefecture* = {a;i}
              [œ] *j<u>eu</u>ne, j<u>eû</u>ne, cr<u>eu</u>se* = {a;(i,u)}
              [ɔ] *r<u>o</u>c, r<u>au</u>que, rhinoceros* = {a;u}

     c. {V</C>} [i], [y], [u], [a] = {i}, {i,u}, {u}, {a}

(examples from Aurnague et al. 2004: §3; see too Durand 1976, 1990: particularly §6.1.9). These respective vowel types are categorized (as to primary feature) as shown initially in each part of (70); and each vowel is given its secondary categorization on the right of (70), in terms of (combinations of) the acuteness, gravity, and compactness features—**i**, **u** and **a**—of Anderson and Ewen (1987). (a) and (b) differ in the preponderance of the vowel colours **i** or **u** or the **i,u** combination relative to the **a** feature.

The formulation given below in the text (§2.4.3) assumes a fairly restrictive view of the possible victims, whereby the vowels /i/, /u/, and /ai/ (with the last illustrated here) rather generally show the alternation, and /I/, /ʌ/, and /ɛ/ do not, since the latter occur only in closed syllables. However, I should acknowledge that for some speakers the distinction between the two variants of the [ai] diphthong illustrated in (68a-b), at least, seems to be marginally contrastive (Noske et al. 1982, Wells 1982: §5.2.4). As concerns the environment, the 'finally' in the formulation given in the text remains rather vague, but it includes syllable-finally (the first vowel in *bias* is heavy) and formative-finally (so that *sighed*, unlike *side*, has a heavy vowel). On the environment see further Ewen (1977) and Anderson (1988a,b, 1993, 1994); and I return briefly to the topic below.

I also do not enter here into the controversies surrounding the prevalence of the 'Scottish vowel-length rule' (among Scottish speakers, as well as among potential victim vowels), or its Scottishness, that were initiated in particular by Lodge (1984: ch. 4) and Agutter (1988a,b). But see further e.g. McMahon (1989, 1991) and Scobbie et al. (2001). See also Anderson (1988a) for a discussion of one of the apparent anomalies, the failure of intransitive /ɔ/ to show a light variant, and Carr (1992) and Anderson (1994: §5) for a discussion of the status of other such vowels.

The formulation of the vowel-length rule given in (69) involves a reinterpretation of the distinction drawn by Anderson (1993, 1994) between what he calls 'inherent length', or 'tenseness', and 'prosodic length' as one involving (in)transitivity vs. length/weight. The formulation in (69) makes it even clearer that synchronically the 'Scottish vowel-length rule' involves neither lengthening nor shortening (cf. Carr 1992)—unsurprisingly, given that length is not taken to be contrastive. The 'moraic' approach of Montreuil (2004) comes up with a not dissimilar analysis but by virtue of rendering 'weight' abstract in terms of 'moraic theory'.

In terms of their primary categorization these vowels are thus the respective phonological analogues of such verbs as *die* (intransitive), *kill* (transitive), and *starve* (either). And the association of 'high-mid' realization with intransitivity ('free' vowels) vs. 'low-mid' with transitivity ('checked') is not uncommon, and often described in terms of 'advanced tongue root'.

We also find the transitive vowels before a consonant or obstruent-sonorant cluster, plus the minor-system vowel schwa (Durand 1976):

(71) a. [ε] *guerre,* [œ] *pleure,* [ɔ] *rose*
     b. [ε] *mettre,* [œ] *neutre,* [ɔ] *socle*

This makes sense if the schwa, belonging to the same foot as the preceding vowel and dependent on that vowel, shares the consonant following that vowel with its governor, as suggested by the bracketing in [(gε[r]ə)], for instance (see Durand 1990: §6.1.9); so that the first vowel is transitive. Again the 'low-mid' variant is transitive. In French, vowels other than schwa do not form a foot with a preceding syllable; otherwise, the foot and syllable coincide. We return to such ambisyllabicity as has just been suggested within a more general context in Chapter 5.[23]

These phenomena instantiate another respect in which 'phoneme theory' fails with respect to contrastivity. Aurnague and Durand (2003: §3), observing in Midi French the lack of 'oppositions d'aperture moyenne /e/ ~ /ε/' etc., which seem to be established in Standard French, argue appropriately that in Midi French 'le système ne comporte donc que sept phonèmes vocaliques' (apart from schwa). The secondary feature distinctions given on the right of (70) are overdifferentiated: the occurrence of {i;a} vs. {a;i} is predictable. But take into account now the ambivalence of the 'extreme' vowels, [i], [y], [u], [a], as to transitivity, whereas the other groups of vowels in some sense contrast in this. This should lead us to register that the contrastivity in the system lies elsewhere: the 'environment' is contrastive; we have syntagmatic contrast. Contrastivity lies not merely in substantive oppositions but also in the phonotactics of phonological units—in this instance their (in)transitivity.

---

[23] In Standard French all vowels can be 'transitive' or 'intransitive'; they are thus indifferent to transitivity, and so perhaps interpretable as simply adjunct-taking. Transitivity ('la loi de position'), however, has a morphological role, as illustrated by pairs such as those in (i), with alternating transitive and intransitive vowels in related forms:

(i) a. [e] *céder* (intransitive) vs. [ε] *cède* (transitive), *léger* (intran) vs. *légère* (trans)
    b. [ø] *peut* (intrans) vs. [œ] *peuvent* (trans), *veut* vs. *veulent, oeufs* vs. *oeuf*
    c. [o] *galop* (intrans) vs. [ɔ] *galope, sot* vs. *sotte, idiot* vs. *idiote*

(Aurnague et al. 2004: §3).

Phonology and dependency 109

The vocalic system of Midi French illustrates this rather transparently. Consider it now more carefully.

From a contrastive point of view, simple combinations of just **i** and **u**, i.e. the combinations {i}, {i,u}, and {u}, are the only substantive elements in the major vowel system of Midi French, as is evident in the individual lexical representations given in (72), where I have retained the major divisions of (70) but interpreted them as specifically involving a set of necessarily intransitive vowels ('*/C'—(a)), a set of necessarily transitive vowels ('/C'—(b)) and a set of transitivity-indifferent vowels (c):

(72) a. [e] tourn*ée*, tourn*ait*, p*é*cheur, p*ê*cheur = {V{i}*/C}
      [ø] j*eux*, j*eu*net, cr*eux* = {V{i,u}*/C}
      [o] *au*, be*au*té, b*o*tté, rhin*o*ceros = {V{u}*/C}
  b. [ɛ] col*è*re, inf*e*ct, pref*e*cture = {V{i}/C}
      [œ] j*eu*ne, j*eû*ne, cr*eu*se = {V{i,u}/C}
      [ɔ] r*o*c, r*au*que, rhin*o*ceros = {V{u}/C}
  c. [i] , [y], [u], [a] = {V{i}}, {V{i,u}}, {V{u}}, {V{ }}

Within each set in (72) we have the same substantive oppositions (shown on the right), except that (72c) has an unspecified member, by redundancy {a}. There are no asymmetrical combinations of features, and **a** is not contrastive, but is a default value for the contrastively empty vowel.

That is, to change the orientation of (72), there is a set of {i} vowels, a set of {i,u} vowels, and a set of {u} vowels, together with an unspecified vowel, that in (72c). Within each of the specified three-member sets of vowels with the same substantive specification, there are two transitivity-sensitive members: one is necessarily intransitive, the other is necessarily transitive; and there is one member in each set that may be either—that is transitivity-indifferent. To illustrate, with **i**-vowels:

(73)   in common contrastive realization
    a. [e] = {V{i}}   */C   {V{i;a}}
    b. [ɛ] = {V{i}}   /C   {V{a;i}}
    c. [i] = {V{i}}   </C>   {V{i}}

The substantive specifications are filled out by the redundancies in (74), which respectively add a dominated unspecified element to necessarily intransitive vowels (a), add a dominant unspecified element to necessarily transitive vowels (b), and specify any empty element as **a** (c):

(74) a. {V*/C} ⇒ {V{; }*/C}
    b. {V/C} ⇒ {V{ ;}/C}
    c. {V{ }} ⇒ {V{a}}

These, together with the lexical specification of substance in (72), give the secondary-categorial representations on the right of (70).[24]

Transitivity may be contrastive, then. And this may be reflected in systems where it is possible to correlate the membership of the two subsystems relatively transparently, as in Midi French, or even in systems where such pairings of members from the different subsystems is not so obvious (except perhaps on morphophonological grounds), as in English. Thus, transitivity can be basic, and, as well as linearity, the more obviously substance-based properties of weight and 'aperture' may be secondary to it, as in respectively English and Midi French. On the other hand, it seems clear that in other systems or subsystems weight (as well as 'aperture', of course) has a contrastive status. So weight is, like aperture, another substantive property that may be phonologically fundamental, but need not be contrastive in a particular language.

Consider as an instance of the phonological basicness of weight the Winnebago forms reproduced in (75) from Miner (1979: 28–9):

(75) a. waarúč 'table', mąącáire 'they cut a piece off'
    b. hipirák 'belt', haračábra 'the taste'

The syllable centre(s) in a pre-accentual sequence in what Miner calls 'regular words' in Winnebago (the significance of which we shall return to in the section that follows) consists maximally of a heavy vowel, as in (75a), or a sequence of two lights, as in (75b). In this context, occurrence of heavy or light is independently contrastive: there is a contrast between the metrically equivalent one heavy and two light. Similarly, in Finnish, for instance, and as is familiar, weight is contrastive independently of transitivity.

We have seen, however, that the formulation in (69), appropriate for Scottish English, prescribes a derivative status for weight in this case, determined by either transitivity or segmental context. Weight, an interface-dependent property, can be determined by transitivity, as can some instances of 'vowel-height'.

---

[24] From an alternative polysystemic point of view, we essentially have, apart from [ə], two subsystems of vowels—an intransitive and a transitive—which differ only in the realization of a subset of their members:

(i) a. i y u   b. i y u
       e ø o   ɛ œ ɔ
          a   a

Just as we need to recognize that accentual differences may correlate with differences in vowel system, and that accent placement may be lexically determined, so transitivity, itself a lexical property, can lead to such systemic differentiation.

My account of the Midi French vowel system ignores some descriptive problems and much variation. See, for instance, Eychenne (2006) and Durand (2009) and the references therein.

2.4.3 Measuring sonority

Finally in this section I return to the environments in (69), relating to the 'Scottish vowel-length rule', whose characterization requires that we fill out a bit more of the English consonant system—with interesting consequences for feature theory:

(69) 'the Scottish vowel-length rule'
    a. {V/C} ⇒ {V}
    b. {V} ⇒ {V} in env.{C$_x$},
        where '{C$_x$}' is the environment that blocks weight
    c. {V} ⇒ {V,V}

Recall that '{C$_x$}' is 'stops (plosive or nasal), voiceless fricatives, and the lateral' (though in the last case not for all speakers whose speech otherwise conforms to the general pattern being described). I want to determine whether the distinction between '{C$_x$}' and the environment that allows weight to be assigned to an intransitive vowel may relate to the measurement of relative sonority or if it demands some other distinction. This will occupy our attention here, and the concepts introduced in what immediately follows will be relevant to the concerns of the following section, specifically those to do with timing.

Let me begin by formulating a simple relative sonority metric (based on Anderson (1990, 1991, 1992: ch. 6, 1993), as in (76):

(76) sonority metric
    a. {X} = 4X:0Y
    b. {X;Y} = 3X:1Y
    c. {X:Y} = 2X:2Y
    where X,Y range over V,C and combinations thereof

Applying the equivalences in (76) to the representations in (42) we get the measures in (77):

(77)   a. vowels   {V} = 4V:0C
      b. liquids   {V;C} = 3V:1C
      c. nasals   {V:C} = 2V:2C = 1V:1C
      d. fricatives {C;V} = 1V:3C
      e. plosives   {C} = 0V:4C

This merely makes a little more explicit the notion of preponderance: the greater the proportion of **V** the more sonorous the segment. The relevance of the metric perhaps becomes more apparent when we consider categorizations involving more complex combinations than those in (77), as in the works referred to immediately above. But the metric does no more than spell out (one aspect of) the contents of the notation in terms of a simple, or indeed simplistic, proportion. However, this immediately highlights some problems in relation to the Scottish vowel-length rule.

One of the liquids, [l], high in sonority by the metric, commonly blocks weight, even though blocking is mostly associated with low-sonority segments. This is one problem. Nasal consonants come, in terms of the metric, between liquids, distinguished as simple {V;C}, and fricatives, {C;V}, in terms of relative sonority. And this seems to be appropriate to a blocker. But we have still to characterize voiced fricatives, which are associated with heaviness, and which contrast in this respect with the voiceless. However this is done, it is undesirable, on general distributional grounds that voiced fricatives should emerge as more sonorous than nasals. So it may be that the environment for the vowel-length rule does not indeed involve simply sonority, but rather that the heavy variant invokes a grouping, among adjuncts, of voiced fricatives and rhotics, as envisaged by Anderson and Ewen (1987: §4.1.3), for instance. What then do the members of this grouping have in common, however?

Let us look firstly at the rhotic/lateral distinction. The former seem to be the more sonorous: thus we find the coda sequences as represented in *girl*, *pearl* in 'rhotic' varieties of English, i.e. those in which [r] is not restricted to pre-vocalic position. But this sonority ranking does not account for the grouping of rhotics with voiced fricatives as non-blockers. Relevant here perhaps is the observation that the rhotic/lateral distinction is only marginally relevant to basic distribution in the syllable, so that such forms as *girl* or *pearl* often emerge as disyllabic, or the rhotic is absent as such in various ('non-rhotic') varieties of English. Voicing is also distributionally marginal as far as sonority is concerned. In obstruent clusters voicing participates in agreement rather than determining distribution—so we find, for example, [-xt] rather than [-xd] or [-γt]. And, as we shall see, secondary features in general can 'spread'. Say then, that the extra vocalicness of rhotics (over laterals) and voiced obstruents (over voiceless) involves **V** as a secondary feature rather than a primary. That is, **V** can occur both as a primary and a secondary feature.

This would involve another analogy. In Volume I, §3.6, it was proposed that the source feature could be either a secondary or a tertiary ('second-order secondary') feature, corresponding to 'source of the action' vs. 'locative source':

Functors III: Potential Representations
absolutive absolutive{goal} locative locative{goal} locative{source} source

Similarly, we might imagine phonological representations such as those in (78), in which **V** appears as both primary and secondary, where, for clarity, I have distinguished these statuses by capitalization and its lack:

(78) a. {V;C{v}}   [r]   {V;C}   [l]
     b. {C;V{v}}   [v]   {C;V}   [f]
     c. {C{v}}   [d]   {C}   [t]
     d. {V{v}}   [a]   {V{i/u/ }}   [i],[u],[ə]

I have included (78d) to complete the picture: what I have been labelling {a} is interpreted as a secondary {v}. As we have seen, this is the most sonorous vowel. The secondary {v} retains a role in determining basic distribution, and this role is the stronger the more **V** there is among the primary features of a segment. Schwa lacks a secondary feature.

As concerns the Scottish vowel-length rule, we can say on the basis of the representations in (78) that those consonants that do not block vowel weight are those that contain both a primary and a secondary V, [r] and voiced fricatives. Instead of (69) we have (69)*:

(69) 'the Scottish vowel-length rule'
    a. {V/C} ⇒ {V}
    b. {V} ⇒ {V}/{C$_x$}, where '{C$_x$}' is the environment that blocks weight
    c. {V} ⇒ {V,V}

(69)* 'the Scottish vowel-length rule'
    a. {V/C} ⇒ {V}
    b. {V} ⇒ {V}/C ≠ {C,V{v}}
    c. {V} ⇒ {V,V}

Blocking occurs before consonants that do not conform to the pattern {C,V{v}}. This same property may underlie the possibility in the sequencing of (38d), found alongside *farm* and *film*—though again the final consonant may be syllabic:

(38) d. chasm, prism

The secondary {v} of the voiced fricative compensates for its lack of sonority vis-à-vis nasals. And it is perhaps worth observing that this again involves a sibilant, though not the [s] of eccentric behaviour elsewhere.

The representations for rhotics and voiced fricatives also share the property of involving three features, in a two-level representation. I suggest this reflects their perceptual and articulatory complexity: voiced fricatives involve two different sound sources—a harmonic and a (dominant) noisy one. Rhotics, unlike laterals, have no oral stopping, but offer instead a minor secondary sound source to the (dominant) one associated with voicing.

I left aside nasal consonants in the discussion of the use as a secondary feature of a feature that I initially introduced as primary. But nasals too are complex: they involve two resonators coupled in parallel, one of them (the oral) stopped, with resultant spectral complications. We have allowed for this complexity in a different way in the preceding, in terms of mutual dependency. But we must wonder whether the representation '{V:C}' is appropriate to characterizing the presence of a stop element together with a harmonic source with an extra unstopped resonator. {V:C} combines {V;C} and {C;V}: {V;C} seems appropriate, in grouping the nasals with the liquids, but {C;V} is the representation for fricatives.

I suggest that nasal consonants can be characterized more adequately in terms of the presence of a secondary feature, {c}, analogous to {v}, combined with the primary representation we have associated with liquids—now the representation of sonorant consonants in general, as shown in (79a-c):

(79)   a. {V;C{c}}   b. {V;C}   c. {V;C{v}}
       nasal   lateral   rhotic

These representations preserve the desired sonority-hierarchical relationship in terms of the secondary features.[25]

One consequence of this interpretation of nasals is the apparent non-utilization of mutual dependency among the primary features of the phonology, compared with the syntax. The set of sonorants can be characterized as in (79). Is this already an indication of the lesser richness of categorization of phonology that is looked at at length in Part III? Moreover, what has been proposed attributes a role—though a minor one—in 'sonority', and thus basic distribution, to those secondary features that can also be primary, rather than attempting to restrict such a role to primary categories. We shall find that dual status for the features **V** and **C** has other motivations than offered here. In §2.5, for instance, I return to the internal complexities of various sorts in the representation of certain kinds of phonological segments that we have

---

[25] In Anderson (1994: 12 (29)) /l/ is distinguished from the other sonorant consonants by the secondary (articulatory) feature of laterality. This seems to me an aberration, given, on the one hand, the limited currency of this feature and, on the other, the basic role of the primary categorial specification otherwise in determining sequence in the syllable. Likewise, the categorization for nasals given here obviates appeal to nasality as such.

introduced here. There they will assume some significance in the discussion of timing phenomena.

A consequence of the proposed dual status of some phonological features is that the categorial analogy with syntax may be even closer, to the extent that some of the subcategories of syntactic primary categories may involve the deployment of otherwise primary features. For instance, it would seem to be appropriate to characterize 'relational' nouns and adjectives, such as *side (of)* and *aware (of)* respectively, as in (80a-b), in recognition of their more verb-like character, in taking complements—parallel to the use of secondary V:

(80) a. {N;P{p}}
      b. {P:N{p}}
      c. {P{p}}
      d. {N{n}}
      e. {P;N{n}}

That is, they are subcategorized for a secondary P, the feature favouring 'relationality'. Thus, as in the phonology, the use as a secondary of a feature, such as P, that can be primary continues to be reflected in distribution. And recognition of the prototypicality of declaratives among finites (recall Volume I, §6.2) might be given by the representation in (80c). Declaratives are the prime instantiation of the licensing of syntactic independence for a construction.

Moreover, what has just been proposed in relation to nasal consonants raises the question of whether there might be still further inter planar parallelism between the features that may be primary or secondary. I suggested that P, like V, may be either primary or secondary: {V} and {v} are paralleled by {P} and {p}. It has also been suggested that C too can be primary {C} or secondary {c}. Do we also have motivations for recognizing {N} and {n}? Definites could be recognized as the prime referential, just as declaratives are the prime finite, in terms of the representation in (80d). Compare the representation for declarative in (80c). Likewise, the {n} feature enables us to characterize stative (non-dynamic) verbs as in (80e). I do not pursue this line of inquiry further here, however.

Controversy continues to surround the sonority hierarchy (and indeed the Scottish vowel-length rule). But some such perceptually based notion seems to be relevant to the distribution of elements in syllables. The introduction of the secondary-feature use of V and C complicates any computation of sonority but does not detract from the appropriateness, in this respect, of the representations proposed. We shall be looking in §3.1 at syntactic analogues to the hierarchy (such as what has been described as relative 'nouniness'). It is perhaps worth acknowledging finally that the above discussion of primary features with secondary congeners is far from comprehensive, given its concentration on the system of English. For instance, there is omitted any consideration of the secondary use of C with obstruents in distinguishing different glottal mechanisms. But comprehensiveness is not our present concern.

2.5 Dependency and timing

Another substantive property characteristic of phonological representations is **timing** (cf. e.g. Browman and Goldstein 1986, 1992; Bird and Klein 1990)—of segments and segmental components relative to each other, as well as of extrasegmental, or prosodic, components relative to each other and the segments. Thus far, we have been dealing with simple unilinear timing, linearity of segments. This property, the sequencing of basic units, is in common between phonology and syntax. But the phoneticity of phonology permits variation on this not appropriate to syntax: we look at this in §§2.5.2–3. But I am also going to look now at relative timing, or coordination, of subsegmental elements (components, features, gestures, or whatever) which may not be unilinear. Again, such coordination is clearly a property that is a reflection of the phonetic interface. Syntax has more primitive timing requirements, and it does not permit or require the multilinearity associated with the expression of the timing of different phonological features that we shall encounter at various points in this book.

It is proposed here that relative timing is guaranteed by dependency relations in the phonology. Thus, while continuing to invoke dependency, I am now focusing on a property, coordination of timing, that belongs intimately to the demands of the phonetic interface. I am not here aiming to extend to phonology a further aspect of syntactic structure (such as transitivity) but to show that even such a particularly phonetic property as relative timing of the components of segments is associated in the phonology with dependency—or, in the evolution of some diachronic processes, with the lack of it.

Firstly, we look at manifestations of the weakness of intrasegmental dependency relations in maintaining timing in the phonology, compared with syntax. Specifically, this weakness involves a tendency to substitute adjunction for subjunction. We can take the relationship between primary and secondary features to be another instance of the dependency relation, in particular subjunction: the primary feature, as head, determines the basic distribution of the segment. Similarly, in syntax it determines the position of the word. But in phonology, developments in pronunciation can lead to secondary features that are perceived as not coterminous with the primary features on which they have depended. They may extend or even change their allegiance. An account of these developments also invokes the existence of phonological features that can be both primary and secondary (as argued for in the immediately preceding section). But crucial here is the capacity of secondary features to spread, that is, their 'mobility', as in vowel harmony—discussed in Chapter 4.

At this point, however, I merely provide some phonological illustration of this 'mobility' in the form of some developments of not uncommon types that reflect the temporal weakness of a dependency link between primary and secondary phonological features, together with the primary/secondary ambivalence of certain features. §2.5.2 then looks at the consequences of the loss of dependency between whole segments, the loss of a facet of the dependency maximization I've associated with sequences of phonological segments. The result of loss reveals, I am suggesting, the importance of dependency in maintaining timing relations. And the weakness of the subjunction relation that maintains coincidence reflects the independence of the gestures that implement primary and secondary features.

2.5.1 *Dependency and secondary phonological features*

Consider here, for instance, the not uncommon kind of historical development suggested by the successive spellings in (81) from the history of English:

(81)   a. emetig(e) ⇒ emti ⇒ empty
        b. demester ⇒ demster ⇒ dempster 'judge'/name

I am not concerned here with the loss of the unstressed medial vowel suggested in each case by comparison of the first two successive spellings (though that and its relationship to accent would form part of the 'whole story'). What concerns us is that the final Modern English phonological form represented here results from what has been described as 'Middle English epenthesis' of a plosive between a nasal and a following obstruent. This, I suggest, is facilitated by weakness of the segment-internal dependency relation in ensuring timing, specifically maintenance of subjunction. And in this case we lose full coordination in timing, between the primary and secondary components of the representation of the nasal—so that the sonorant/nasal-cavity component {V;C} can terminate before the oral closure {c}, and the latter part of the closure emerges as the homorganic minimal plosive.

We can represent the development, after loss of the medial vowel, in terms of the successive stages in (82), where **u** is the gravity component of [m] (and higher structure, beyond the syllable, is not shown):

(82) a.
```
    {V}                      {V}
     |                       /
    {V/C}                  {C}
      \
      {V;C
        |
       {c,u}}
    ε      m              t      i
```

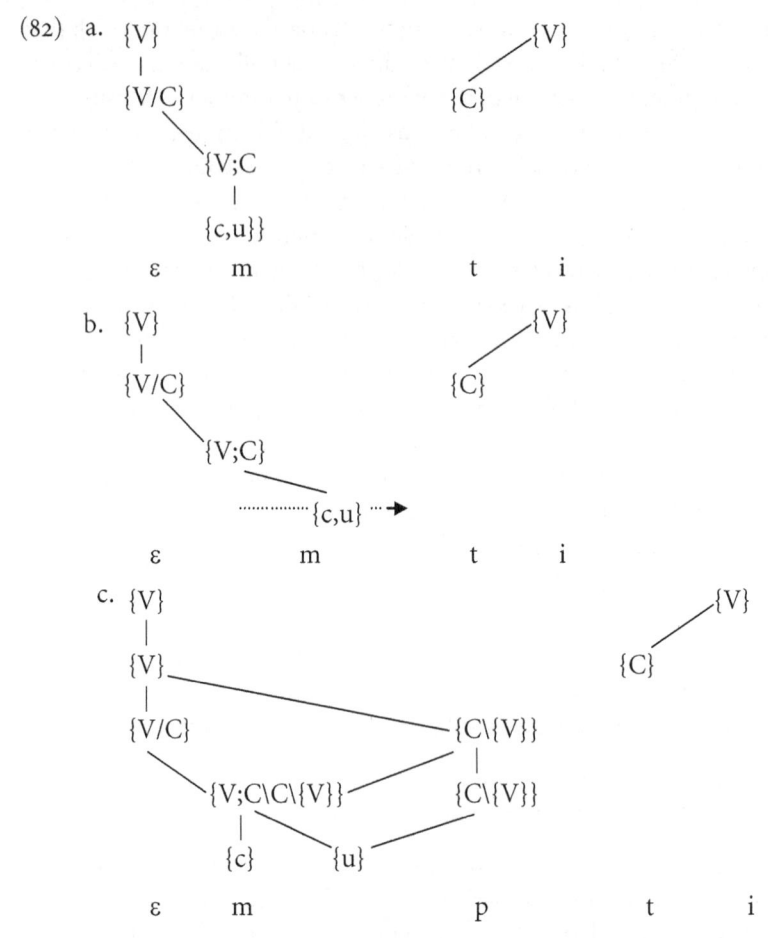

b.
```
    {V}                      {V}
     |                       /
    {V/C}                  {C}
      \
      {V;C}
         \
          ········{c,u}·····►
    ε      m              t      i
```

c.
```
    {V}                                    {V}
     |                                     /
    {V}_                                 {C}
     |   \
    {V/C}  \              {C\{V}}
      \     \                |
       {V;C\C\{V}}         {C\{V}}
          |   \
         {c}  {u}
    ε      m            p        t      i
```

(82a) represents the situation after the loss of the medial vowel, where /m/ is a complement of the first vowel. (82b) represents an intermediate stage after the de-coordination of the sonorant and grave stop components, whose timing is disturbed (as allowed by the weakness of the subjunctional relation). This is indicated there by the association of the secondary features {c,u} with both the sonorant and a position without primary category. That is, the stopping is perceived as persisting after the closure of the nasal passage. (82c) differs in showing segmental separation of the fully nasal and the stop-only extension created in (82b), and regularization of the latter by promoting the secondary {c} to primary categorization {C}. This is marked by oral stopping but no nasal opening. (82c) also involves the application of (59), cluster headship, establishing a dependency relation between the nasal and the non-nasal, thus restoring coordination in timing:

(59) *cluster headship*
    $C_i \Rightarrow \backslash C_j$, iff $C_j < C_i$, where '<' = 'lower in sonority than'

I offer the representation in (82c), with retention of a bisegmental {u}, with a double dependency, as a refinement of the representation of nasal plus plosive clusters in (58)—as, in the spirit of the Firthian enterprise, identifying the locale of contrast, which is not a single segment.

We also find attested the reverse development. This is exemplified by the Scots (and other dialect) pronunciations of *handle, candle*, etc., without a medial plosive. I suggest that the first stage in such developments is the loss of the dependency relation between the nasal and obstruent—equivalent to that in (82c)—that guarantees coordination. Nasality is perceived as persisting into the original oral stop phase. And the oral stop loses its primary status and is absorbed into the nasal. It is re-timed to coincide with the nasal opening and identified with the {c} of the nasal consonant. The complexity of nasals and the weak connection in timing underlie the instability of these sequences.

A full account of these phenomena would have to recognize other factors that are involved, such as the presence of a following syllable-initial obstruent in the case of (81) or a syllabic liquid in the case of such as *handle*. However, the attribution of de-synchronization partly to the complexity of nasals, as involving, in terms of articulation, potentially independent gestures, has some plausibility. I am associating de-synchronization with this and with the temporal weakness of the dependency relation between the primary and secondary components of the nasal. The role in timing that I am attributing to dependency is speculative, of course. But it too derives some plausibility from the range of phenomena that is exemplified in this section that is amenable to explication in these terms.

Thus Peng (1985), for instance, reconstructs an analogous but slightly different development from the preceding for the early history of Japanese. He suggests the etymologies in (83) involving nasal plus plosive clusters (where '*' indicates 'reconstructed'):

(83) a. ntama ⇒ tama 'ball'
    b. *ndori ⇒ tori 'bird'
    c. *-mbu ⇒ -bu 'sheet'
    d. *tambi ⇒ tabi 'every time'
    e. *tombi ⇒ tobi 'jumping, flying'
    f. *toŋgaru ⇒ togaru 'to taper'

Here the nasal rather than the plosive is lost (cf. *handle*, mentioned above, which involves a different environment). The plosive emerges as voiceless initially and voiced between voiced sounds. However, some dialects apparently show nasality of a vowel preceding the obstruents (Peng cites Ogura 1932: 27). This would make a plausible intermediate stage in the development in medial position in (83), and one that we might associate, once more, with the weakness of the subjunctional relation guaranteeing contemporaneousness of the primary and secondary features, as in (82b).

In this case, the primary specification {V;C} drifts off towards the vowel and the secondary {c} is absorbed by the following plosive. The original configuration is as shown in (84a) (where I have represented both consonants as adjuncts of the first vowel, for convenience, and ignored any relationship with the second syllable):

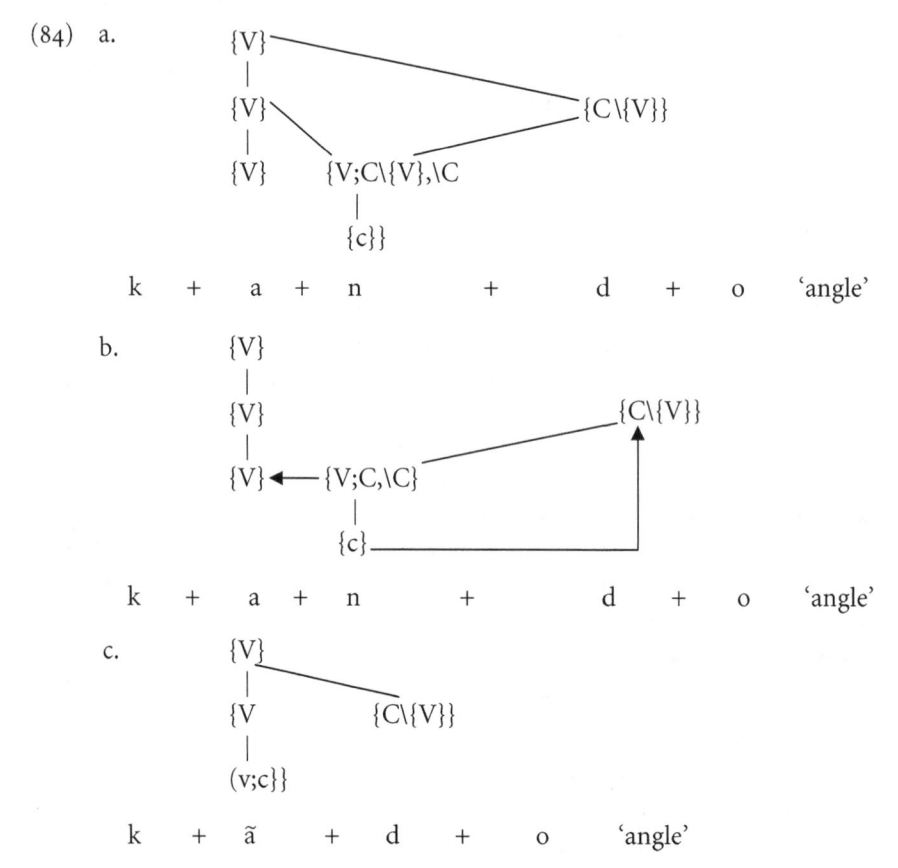

(84) a.
```
         {V}
          |
         {V}                         {C\{V}}
          |
         {V}    {V;C\{V},\C
                    |
                   {c}}

   k  +   a   +   n           +   d   +   o    'angle'
```

b.
```
              {V}
               |
              {V}                          {C\{V}}
               |
              {V} ← {V;C,\C}
                       |
                      {c}

   k  +   a   +   n           +   d   +   o    'angle'
```

c.
```
              {V}
               |
              {V           {C\{V}}
               |
             (v;c}}

   k  +   ã       +   d   +   o    'angle'
```

The 'drifting apart' is represented in (84b). What triggers it in this scenario is the loss of the dependency relation between the nasal and the vowel, in recognition of the tendency to overlap, given the temporal weakness of the dependency relation within the nasal. The supplementary resonator component of the nasal consonant is incorporated into the vowel as a secondary category, as in (84c). A nasal vowel is a vowel, {V}, with a secondary resonator, the latter represented {v;c}. The dependency on 'C' is now associated solely with the oral closure feature, which is absorbed by this following stop.

All the preceding examples relate to the complex character of nasal stops and in particular the weakness of the subjunctional relation between the primary and secondary components of their representation. And they attest to the appropriateness of considering their complexity to lie in presence of a secondary {c}, with the mobility of such features, given the weak relation between primary and secondary categories, rather than attributing the complexity to the combining of {V;C} and {C;V} as {V:C}. The developments involved in the history *handle* and those characterized in (84) introduce a new factor, the possible loss of dependency between segments, with merging of properties. In the subsection that immediately follows we look at an even more striking instance of the consequences of loss of dependency. I conclude this one with a brief look at some developments involving secondary features, particularly those that have primary congeners.

The 'mobility' of the secondary {v} with voiced obstruents is associated with the normal agreement in voicing within obstruent clusters, as in the coda of *ends* vs. *texts*: the {v} is shared between obstruents joined by a dependency. Exceptional is *width*, but it is derivationally complex. The normal sharing again reflects the temporal weakness of dependency relation between the primary and secondary categories involved. There is a partial analogy with the syntax in this case in the form of agreement or concord in syntactic secondary categories—and we return to this in §3.4. But we can already observe at this point that, whereas cluster voicing involves continuity of voicing through the cluster, as represented in (82c), syntactic agreement is manifested discontinuously, as in the Latin of (85):

(85) hīc   vir   sapiēns
     this.NOM.MASC.SG man.NOM.MASC.SG wise.NOM.MASC.SG

This difference arises from the immediacy of the implementation of the phonology as physiological timing of independent articulations, in contrast with syntactic timing, whereby agreement can be expressed only by repetition. The directness in the case of the phonology of the interfacing with phonetic timing, and its absence in the case of syntax, again limits the possibilities for exactness of analogy. The similarity in the phenomena in the different planes—involving 'shared' features—is disguised by their different relations to the realizing substance.

The complexity of [r] over [l]—{V;C{v}} vs. {V;C}—is reflected perhaps in the development of *r*-coloured vowels from vowel plus rhotic in American varieties of English, as in [bɚd] (rather than [bɪrd] or [bɪrd]). Here the vowel and rhotic have merged as {V{v;c}}, with the *r*-colouring replacing the secondary features of the vowel, resulting in neutralization. In non-rhotic varieties, even such colouring is lost in such items, which typically involve transitive vowels.

Consider too analyses (such as that in Giegerich 1999: ch. 7) of those items in 'non-rhotic' varieties of English wherein [r] and a vowel alternate as realizations of the same contrastive unit. Indeed, the intermediate stage we find in many 'rhotic' varieties, represented by (b) in (86), patently involves a change in timing compared with (86a):

(86) a. [ber]   b.   [beər]   c.   [bɛə]   'bear/bare'
     'rhotic'   'rhotic diphthongal'   'non-rhotic'

Here, in (86b), the {v} of the rhotic has extended into the preceding non-consonant space. And in (86c) the rhotic element is lost contextually, resulting in alternation in the realization of such items between a rhotic and bare schwa depending on whether a vowel follows. Again, the development is very closely tied to the physical immediacy of the realization of timing of phonological elements and the presence or absence of a dependency relation.

2.5.2 Non-dependency and Winnebago 'fast sequences'

We can perhaps associate loss of dependency and thus of guarantee of relative timing, with yet another variety of phenomenon, not involving the weakness of subjunction within segments but loss of it between them, and illustrated by the operation of Dorsey's Law in Winnebago. Dorsey's Law consists basically in the observation that a number of CVCV sequences in some Siouan languages correspond to CCV sequences in other, closely related ones. Much discussion has focused on Winnebago (vs. particularly Chiwere) in this respect (e.g. Miner 1979; Hale and White Eagle 1980; Halle and Vergnaud 1987: 31–4; Steriade 1990; Hind 1997: §5.2); and it is on the former language that I shall be concentrating here, where it has been claimed that equivalents of the correspondences described by Dorsey's Law have synchronic status. I shall argue however, that this status is rather different from that proposed by Hale and White Eagle (1980) and Halle and Vergnaud (1987).

In illustration of Dorsey's Law, Miner (1979: 27) cites such cognate pairs as those in (87a-b), as well as correspondences elicited from Robinson (1972) such as those that are shown in the remainder of (87):

(87)   Winnebago   Chiwere
   a. hoikéwe   ugwé
   b. pàrás   bláθge, bláhge
   c. -kere-   -gle-
   d. -kiri-   -gli-
   e. -sų́ nų́ -   -θlų́ -
   f. -pąną-   -blą-

And Miner comments: 'Dorsey's Law clearly represents a "vowel copy" process which broke up obstruent-sonorant clusters in Winnebago' (1979: 27).

Miner calls these sequences in Winnebago 'fast sequences', and attributes to them the properties in (88):

(88) Winnebago 'fast sequences'
   Using the formula '$C_1V_1C_2V_2$' for the 'fast sequences':
   a. C_1 is a voiceless obstruent (/p k č s š x/);
   b. C_2 is a sonorant (/m n r w y/);
   c. $V_1 = V_2$;
   d. the sequences are spoken (and apparently sung) faster than other CVCV sequences;
   e. the sequences may be reduplicated just as CV sequences may, and are the only CVCV sequences which may reduplicate.

Properties (88d) and (e) suggest that these sequences are monosyllabic, or at least equivalent to monosyllables, despite the apparent presence of two non-adjacent vowel segments; and that (88c) is the case also suggests there may in some sense be only one vowel present.

Miner points to other phenomena that appear to point in the same direction, and to support a synchronic status for an equivalent of Dorsey's Law. Thus, instead of the stem-final -e in (89a) we have in (b) an -a before the suffix -ire:

(89) a. mąąčé 'he cut a piece off'
     b. mąąčáire 'they cut a piece off'
     c. kèré 'he departed returning'
     d. kàráire 'they departed returning'

A stem-final 'fast sequence' behaves like a single vowel with respect to this alternation, as shown in (89c-d). I return shortly to the question of accent placement, marked by the acutes and graves in (89). What is most pertinent at this point is that the conjunction of properties in (88) and (89) has led to analyses seeking to account for Dorsey's Law in terms of timing.

Thus, in Steriade's (1990: 391) formulation: 'from an input syllable beginning with two consonantal gestures overlapping in duration with each other, a delay in the onset of the liquid can create a sequence in which the vowel gesture begins to "show" between the consonant gestures'. This is illustrated in (90) (her (12)):

(90)   Tiers   Gestures

        tongue body   [-]

                                r
        tongue tip   [- - - -] →

                                p
        lips   [- - - - - -]

She goes on, however, to conclude that 'since Dorsey's Law creates a sequence in which a consonant gesture has come to be nonperipherally superimposed on a vowel gesture, it automatically turns a monosyllable into a disyllable' (Steriade 1990: 391). This conclusion is difficult to reconcile with the properties, both morphological and phonetic, that we have just looked at, which suggest that monosyllabicity is retained under Dorsey's Law. The assignment of disyllabicity need not be assumed to be an automatic consequence (historically or synchronically) of rightward drift of the sonorant articulation to reveal part of the vowel gesture.

Nevertheless, in other respects, an account in terms of timing has considerable plausibility. And I shall try here to formulate the basis for the change in timing (without necessarily acquisition of disyllabicity) in terms of the framework I have been presenting in what precedes. My starting point is a suggestion of Hind's (1997: 295–6) that in turn takes its starting point in Steriade's discussion—though he, indeed, fails to recognize his account as being incompatible with Steriade's assumption of automatic assignment of disyllabicity.[26]

In terms of a framework that unites 'articulatory phonology' with aspects of 'government phonology', Hind associates the loss of coordination between the two consonants in the clusters manifested in 'fast sequences' with 'failure of indirect government' of them by the syllable centre (1997: 296). In terms of the structures assumed here, I interpret this as involving failure of consonant

---

[26] Hind indeed interprets Steriade's account as leading to the conclusion that 'fast sequences are in fact monosyllables' (1997: 297); and he comments that 'the fact that fast sequences are accented more like monosyllables than like bisyllables is not surprising if Steriade's interpretation is correct, nor is the shorter duration of fast sequences compared to ordinary CVCV sequences' (Hind 1997: 293). As indicated, I return shortly to the question of accent.

Phonology and dependency 125

adjunction (43) to apply to the second consonant in 'fast sequences'. (43) is repeated here for convenience of reference:

(43) *consonant adjunction*
 C ⇒ \{V}

Failure of (43) in the case of the second consonant in a 'fast-sequence' form like *k(e)re* 'return' reduces the onset dependencies to those in (91):

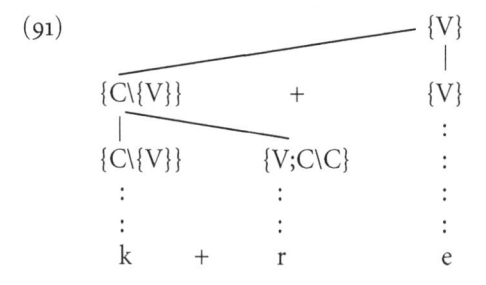

(91)
```
                              ─── {V}
                                   |
   {C\{V}}          +              {V}
     |                              :
   {C\{V}}        {V;C\C}           :
     :              :               :
     :              :               :
     k      +       r               e
```

The non-availability in Winnebago of consonant adjunction to sonorants dependent on the onset head means that they lack the dependency relation to the vowel on which their timing relative to the vowel is dependent. In (91) I have indicated the lack of a timing constraint between the sonorant and the vowel by the absence of a '+' between the relevant segments.

Compare with (90/91) the initial cluster in the English form in (58) (where the original categorial notation is maintained):

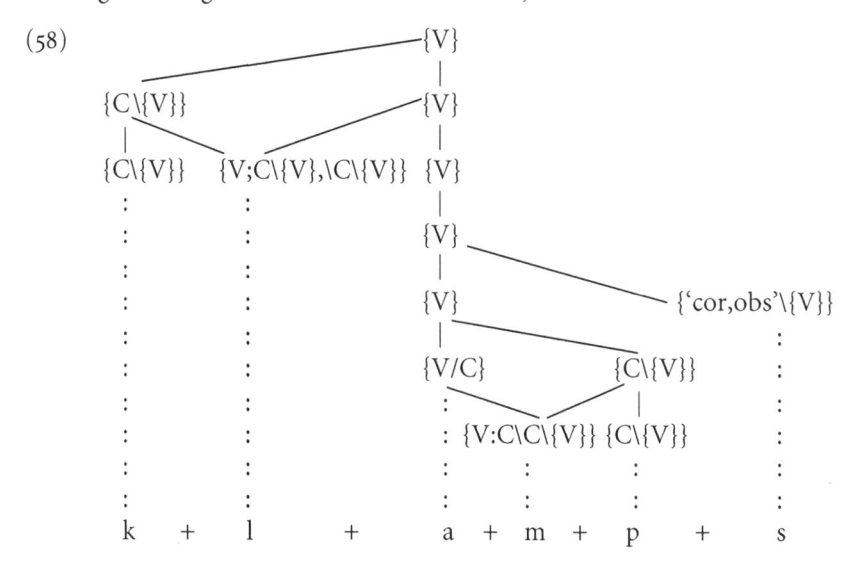

(58)
```
                                  ─{V}
                                    |
   {C\{V}}                         {V}
     |                              |
   {C\{V}}  {V;C\{V},\C\{V}}  {V}
     :         :                    |
     :         :                   {V}
     :         :                    |
     :         :                   {V}          ─ {'cor,obs'\{V}}
     :         :                    |                :
     :         :                  {V/C}      {C\{V}}  :
     :         :                    :          |      :
     :         :                  : {V:C\C\{V}} {C\{V}} :
     :         :                    :    :      :    :
     :         :                    :    :      :    :
     k    +    l    +    a    +    m    +    p    +    s
```

(58) shows the 'maximization' of dependencies resulting from unrestrained formation of complements and adjuncts. Thus both [k] and [l] are dependent on the vowel and timed appropriately with respect to it. I am now saying that this maximization, which is brought about, in this way, by unrestricted application of the rules building structure on the basis of their categorizations, is what ensures coordination of segments. A segment which loses its dependence on another becomes mobile with respect to that other.

In (91) the second consonant is dependent on the first and coordinated with it, so that, as is usual, the major portion of the sonorant articulation can be perceived after the plosive has been released. But the sonorant is not dependent on the centre of the syllable (though it is subordinate to it, via the obstruent), so its sequencing is not coordinated with it, as it is in, say, (58); but it is free to 'slide rightwards', so that we have (92a):

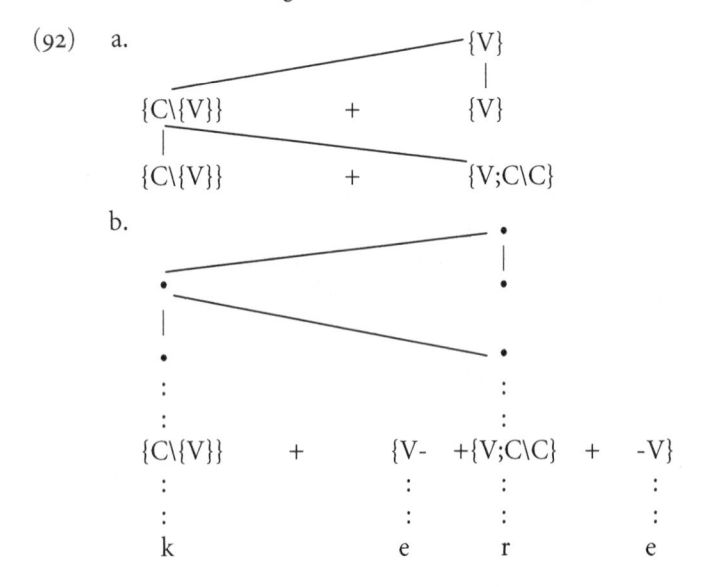

(92) a.
```
                              ┌─ {V}
                              │
    {C\{V}}        +         {V}
      │
    {C\{V}}        +         {V;C\C}
```
b.
```
          •                    •
          │                    │
          •                    •
          :                    :                :              :
        {C\{V}}    +        {V-    +{V;C\C}  +    -V}
          :                    :        :              :
          :                    :        :              :
          k                    e        r              e
```

The articulatory exponence of the centre, which, given the status of the centre as head of the syllable, is co-terminous with the syllable (cf. e.g. Coleman 1992: §6), is heard on both sides of the sonorant, reflected in the perceived sequencing of (92b). In (92b) I revert to a notation (cf. Anderson 1986a) which separates the categorial specifications, which are lexical, from the derived dependency tree, thus clarifying graphically their relations to each other and to the sequencing. It is easy to see how this could lead to disyllabicity, i.e. reinterpretation of each of the two perceptible realizations of V as a distinct centre. But the observations embodied in (88) and (89) seem to support a monosyllabic analysis of the 'fast sequences' of Winnebago, along the lines of

(92). In the absence of an undesirable abstract analysis invoking something like synchronic re-syllabification, a two-syllable interpretation of 'fast sequences' is unacceptable.

I thus interpret Dorsey's Law synchronically not as some kind of (undesirable) structure-changing rule that leads to restructuring of the forms in which it is applicable (as in Hale and White Eagle 1980 and Halle and Vergnaud 1987), but rather as the timing that results from the absence in Winnebago of the potential for undergoing (43) of onset sonorants preceded by a voiceless obstruent of the set given in (88a). The structure in (92) does indeed interact in an intricate way with the rules for accent placement in Winnebago, but not so as to call into question the monosyllabic status of these sequences. Rather, at most the singular/plural ambivalence of the V of 'fast sequences' (a single vowel with apparently two disjoint manifestations) becomes evident in this interaction. However, in confirmation of this, let us look at the operation of the accent rules. This means that we must consider firstly forms lacking 'fast sequences', what Miner calls 'regular words' (1979: 28).

Placement of the word, or primary, accent is formulated by Miner (1979: 28) essentially as in (93)—though I paraphrase his account in terms compatible with our ongoing discussion:

(93)　*Winnebago word accent*
　　　Accent the syllable containing the third **V** from the left;
　　　If the form contains fewer than three **V**s, accent the syllable containing the second **V** from the left

(94) gives some examples, again from Miner (1979: 28-9), wherein location of the word accent is indicated by the acute.

(94)　a.　hipirák 'belt'
　　　b.　haračábra 'the taste'
　　　c.　waarúč 'table'
　　　d.　mąąčáire 'they cut a piece off'
　　　e.　wasgé 'dish, plate'
　　　f.　xée 'dig, hill'

(94a-d) illustrate application of the first clause in the accent rule: the accent on (94a) and (b) is on the third syllable, which contains the third **V**; that in (94c) and (d) is on the second syllable, containing the third **V**, since the first syllable contains two **V**s. (94e) illustrates placement on the second syllable, containing the second and last **V**; and in (94f) the accent is on the first (and only) syllable, which contains the second **V**.[27]

It has seemed to me unnecessary, given the present focus of our interests, to express the representation of accent in Winnebago any more formally than in (94). And in any case the derivational machinery invoked by Hale and White Eagle (1980) and Halle and Vergnaud (1987) seems to be quite unnecessary. I turn now to secondary accents, where again the regularities will be presented informally. Firstly, I want to focus on the accentual behaviour of 'fast sequences' in the left margin, before the word stress, of which Hale and White Eagle (1980) offer no account. What follows immediately, then, relies entirely on Miner (1979).

In the pre-word-accent zone, according to the marking of accents in Miner's examples (1979: 30), 'fast sequences' can be said to behave as follows:

(95)   pre-accentual 'fast sequences' in Winnebago
These count as two successive **V**s, as illustrated by (96a), unless they are preceded by a vowel, in which case they count as one **V**, as in (96b), so that the word accent falls on the third vowel from the left, unless the sequence is final in a disyllable or monosyllable, and so must bear the word accent, in which case it behaves as two **V**s, as in (96c); in short, count so as to maximize the pre-accentual domain, consistent with (93) and its limitation to two **V**s maximum.

(96)   a. *kèrekéreš* 'colourful'
          kèrejų́ sep 'Black Hawk'
       b. hi*kòrohó* 'prepare'
          wi*kìripáras* 'cockroach'
       c. ho*kèwé* 'enter'
       d. *pàrás* 'flat'

In all these cases Miner marks the first occurrence of the **V** in the 'fast sequence', which are italicized in the forms in (96), as bearing a secondary accent; and this he does even when the 'fast sequence' constitutes the only **V** component of the word, as in (96d). These phenomena seem to me to

---

[27] The accent in diphthongs is realized on the more sonorous element, whether initial or final; thus (i) (from Miner 1979: 29):

(i)   a. hakeweákšąną̀ 'he is entering'
      b. hit'et'éire 'they speak'

This does not directly concern us here, however.

illustrate rather forcibly the ambivalence of the 'fast sequence'—one or two Vs? On this assumption of rule-governed ambivalence, accentuation in the forms in (96) is much more regular than in their presentation by Miner, who apparently abandons any attempt at a synchronic formulation (1979: 30): 'I will leave to the interested reader the tedious proof that no ordering of the rules discussed... will yield all of the correct forms... It turns out that we need a further historical assumption'.

There is some disagreement in the literature on the subject of the placement of accents following the primary assigned by (93). Miner suggests (1979: 28) that further accents are added to longer forms by iteration of (his equivalent of) (93) to the right from the end of the accented syllable. These further accents show downstepping from the primary one, and I shall follow Hale and White Eagle (1980), and depart from Miner's practice, in again marking them as secondary accents, with a grave (rather than a further acute). Miner's account would assign accents as in (97a-c)—i.e. on the third vowel following the primary accent, if there is one, otherwise on the second if there is one:

(97) a. hiižúgokirùsge 'double-barrelled shotgun'
 b. wiirágų̀ šgerà 'the stars'
 c. waipérasgà 'linen'
 d. haakítujìkšąną 'I pull it taut (declarative)'

And this is how he marks these forms (apart from my substitution of the grave for acute). According to Hale and White Eagle (1980), however, the post-primary accent pattern is alternating: accent occurs on every second V, as they are marked in the form in (97d), which they invoke as an example of 'regular' stress (though we might note that it does end in a 'fast sequence').[28] Hale and White Eagle (1980: 117, fn. 3) disagree with Miner on the placing of the accent in (97b), which they hear as having a penultimate secondary (in accordance with their expectations). And they analyse (97a) as a compound with two word accents. (97c) is neutral between the two accounts.

---

[28] As an example of further apparent discrepancies, note the contradictory accents (whatever else) respectively assigned in (i), a form with two 'sequences':

(i) a. wikìripáras 'cockroach' (Miner)
 b. wakiríparàs 'flat bug' (Halle and Vergnaud)

The discrepancy seems to relate to whether the first 'fast sequence' is counted as one V (in conformity with (95)) or two for accent placement. Some other discrepancies are acknowledged by Hale and White Eagle (1980: 117, fn. 3); and on the same page they concede 'our analysis must be taken as highly tentative, since there are residual problems'. What I say here is thus 'tentative' to a yet higher degree. The debate continues: for some earlier references see e.g. Halle and Idsardi (1995).

In what follows I shall adopt Hale and White Eagle's (1980) view that (in the terms adopted here) every second **V** after the word accent bears a secondary. As concerns word accent and post-primary accent, 'fast sequences' behave as follows:

(98)　*post-accentual 'fast sequences' in Winnebago*
　　　Fast sequences count as one **V** unless final or accented

(99) provides some examples:

(99)　a.　hara*kíšurují*ìk*šąną̀* 'you are sick'
　　　b.　hira*kóro*hò 'he gets ready'
　　　c.　wa*kiripóropòro* 'spherical bug'
　　　d.　hirat'át'a*šąnąšąną̀* 'you are talking'

The unaccented medial 'fast sequence' in (99a) counts as one **V** if it is to conform to Hale and White Eagle's (1980) alternating stress rule, but the final 'fast sequence' therein counts as two and receives secondary accent on the second part, as would a separate **V**. The accented 'fast sequence' in (99b) behaves like two **V**s, permitting the final secondary in accordance with alternating stress. The accented 'fast sequences' in (99c) also behave like two **V**s. Seemingly problematical is (99d), where one would expect a secondary accent on the first 'fast sequence' as well as the second—unless the preceding apparent reduplication *t'át'a* offers a clue that this is also what underlies the 'fast sequences' (i.e. one of the successive 'sequences' is a reduplicate), and reduplication does not count for secondary-accent determination.

However that may be, I think that the present account leaves fewer loose ends than Miner's or Hale and White Eagle's. And, overall, we have further evidence of the rule-governed segmental ambivalence of 'fast sequences' in Winnebago. Accent placement in Winnebago exploits the possibility of acknowledging either the number of manifestations of the vowel in 'fast sequences' or its unity. We certainly don't seem to have evidence of 'automatic' disyllabification. I suggest that an account involving a dislocation in timing (without disyllabification) fits best with the evidence in (88), in particular. And, in particular, I am proposing here that this reflects loss of the dependency relation that guarantees coordination of timing.

This almost ends for the moment my discussion of the role of dependency in coordinating the timing of elements in the representation of phonology. This role I have illustrated by both segmental representations, especially the internal structure of nasal consonants, and suprasegmental, specifically the representation of 'fast sequences'. Both kinds of phenomena discussed are not uncommon. As Steriade (1990: §27.2.6) observes, phenomena of the character of Dorsey's Law are not limited to Winnebago. Miner (1979: §1.1) notes that in Winnebago one can also observe the intervention 'of a slight schwa (or more precisely, a barely audible intrusive vowel having more or less the quality of a short version of the following full vowel)' between an obstruent and sonorant at morphological boundaries. He is careful to differentiate between this phenomenon (also found in other Mississippi Valley Siouan languages) and the behaviour of 'fast sequences'; but it is clearly a minor instantiation of dislocation in coordination.[29]

Complete dislocation occurs in a language when the sonorant overlaps only the final portion of the centre, and we have metathesis, involving a different kind of (diachronic) restructuring from that involved with the development of disyllabicity. What is being suggested here is that it may be that dislocation of timing in general follows from lack of regulation by the dependency relation, whereas coordination of two segments follows from the existence of a dependency relation between them. If this is so, then relative timing of segments is a directly interface-dependent property that is in itself not contrastive. However, it does have a role in accent placement in Winnebago, in providing for the ambivalence of the vowel (two or one) in 'fast sequences'.

2.5.3 *Timing and syntax*

My discussion in the preceding subsection has focused on the role of dependency in coordinating timing in phonology. And in concentrating on phenomena

---

[29] Hind (1997: §5.3), basing his account largely on some observations of Borgstrøm (1940) and Oftedal (1956), suggests that at least in some dialects of Scottish Gaelic we find similar phenomena, but exhibited by non-initial clusters, as in (i):

(i) a. borb 'savage' [bɔrɔb]
    b. arm 'army' [aram]
    c. dorcha 'dark' [dɔrɔxə]
    d. fearg 'anger' [fɛrag]

Often, the 'second, epenthetic vowel' is simply a 'copy' of the other, as in (ia-c), and even when not, as in (d), such a 'vowel' is not restricted to the small set associated with unaccented vowels (like the last in (c)) in these dialects. Moreover, the tonal structure of such 'epenthetic' forms is unlike that of disyllabic items.

Jones (1989: §3.4.6) presents a range of Middle English spellings such as those in (ii) suggestive of similar developments:

(ii) a. þuruh, þoruȝ 'through' (Old English þurh)
    b. arum, arome 'arm'
    c. nyhyt 'night'

In the case of *through* and some other forms this results ultimately in 'metathesis'. Jones (1989: §4.3.1) points to the continuation of such developments into the modern period.

associated with the implementation of phonological representation, we are in an area in relation to which we can expect analogies in the syntax to be less obvious. Given the different relationships of syntax and phonology to timing and its physical manifestation, there can be no exact analogy to the phenomena described just above. But syntax does show a correlation between dependency and timing, in so far as word order is often largely determined by the dependency relations between words. Variation in timing otherwise seems to amount to subjunction and adjunction. And there are diachronic developments that exhibit the substitution of subjunction for adjunction, thus of lexical, particularly morphological, status for syntactic.

I have in mind here the morphologization of relations between functional and lexical categories. Thus, an argument of a predicator may be historically incorporated, as has often been argued for a range of concord systems, the formatives realizing which are etymologically pronouns. Or a functional category may be absorbed historically into a dependent lexical category, as in, for instance, the development of the French future exemplified in *il ira* 'he will go'.

There is not, however, the possibility for the range of variations in timing made potentially available by the maximization of dependency that I have associated with phonology. I have related maximization to the variety of timing relationships that is a reflection of the 'concreteness' of phonology. Lapses in dependency maximization underlie the phonological developments we looked at in the preceding subsection. Of course, these lapses also involve other factors such as a complexity of certain segment types that is such as to favour separation in time of the components.

Nevertheless, despite the poverty of circumstances for any closer analogy than I have just mentioned, there is perhaps one area where there can be found closer analogy to what we have observed concerning phonology—though, obviously, any analogy is restricted by the syntactic independence of the word. Given that syntax also involves relative timing (linearity), we might expect at an analogy in variation in placement, where this is not dependency-driven.

Such variation may be what is involved in the differences among (100):

(100)   a. He replied (that) he would come tomorrow morning
           b. He replied, he would come tomorrow morning
           c. He would come, he replied, tomorrow morning
           d. He would come tomorrow morning, he replied

In (100a) we have hypotaxis, optionally marked by *that*; the second finite verbal depends on the first. In (100b) we have parataxis. And in the absence of a dependent relation, the first clause is free to 'drift' through the second, as in

(100c) and, most drastically, as in (100d). Both this phenomenon and the phonological material we have looked at involve lack of dependency, and so lack of a fixed control on timing.

2.5.4 *Transitivity and ambidependency*

Timing is also related, not just to dependency, but in particular, less directly, to phenomena associated with transitivity, and thus to a further analogy with syntax. This will require us to spell out more explicitly these syntactic structures and the categories on which they are based. The syntactic framework that begins to emerge here, along the lines of Chapter 3 of Volume I, will be invoked quite widely in the chapters that follow, and will be elaborated there. At this point a little more syntactic detail will enable us to make more precise this further transitivity analogy.

Much of the discussion in this chapter has depended on the presence in the syntax of familiar analogues to the head-based concepts—complement, adjunct, specifier—that have been deployed here in relation to the phonology. The partial structures in (101) illustrate the relevant concepts as applied to the syntax, in terms of representations which begin to introduce specifications of the categorial structure of the syntax (as developed in Volume I of this series):

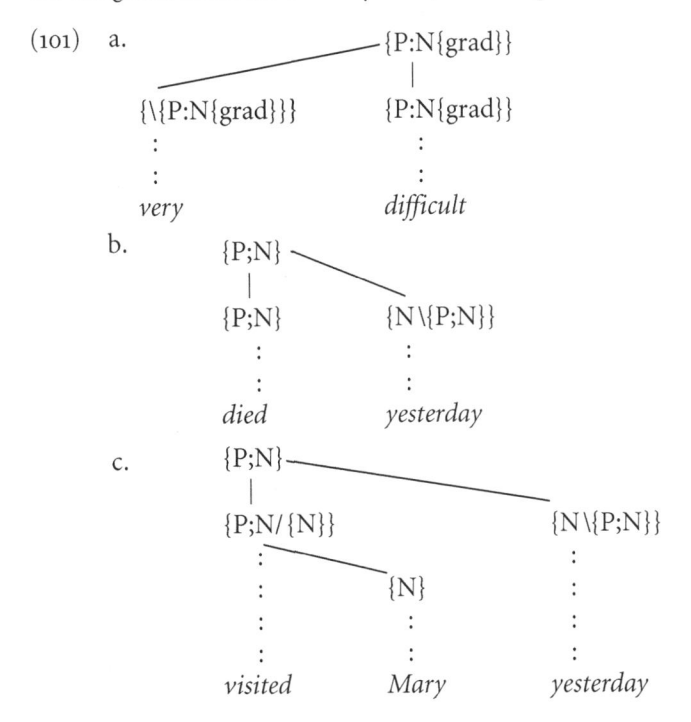

(101) a.
                              {P:N{grad}}
                                  |
        {\{P:N{grad}}}   {P:N{grad}}
            :   :
            :   :
          very   difficult

       b.   {P;N}
              |
             {P;N}   {N\{P;N}}
              :   :
              :   :
            died   yesterday

       c.   {P;N}
              |
           {P;N/{N}}   {N\{P;N}}
              :   {N}   :
              :   :   :
              :   :   :
           visited   Mary   yesterday

(101a) contains a 'traditional' specifier, (b) an adjunct, and (c) a complement and adjunct—all of them, rather uncontroversially, simply claimed here to be such (but see further §4.2). Recall that, in the primary-categorial representations given here, **P** is a notional feature of 'predicability', **N** of naming or 'referentiability'. Names (and pronouns) are non-predicable but can be arguments (so that *James* in *That is James* is equative not predicative); and as arguments they are characterized by **N** alone. The lexical verb has a preponderance of **P**, and with the adjective we have mutual preponderance of **P** and **N**, indicated by ':', (common) nouns being {N;P}. *Very* in (101a) is specified as selecting the grad(able) secondary category of adjective.

What I am illustrating in more detail at this point is that the structures in (101) involve the same structural relations and categorization types as we found relevant to our discussion of phonological representation. Recall in this regard the representation for the syllable in (61b)* (updated):

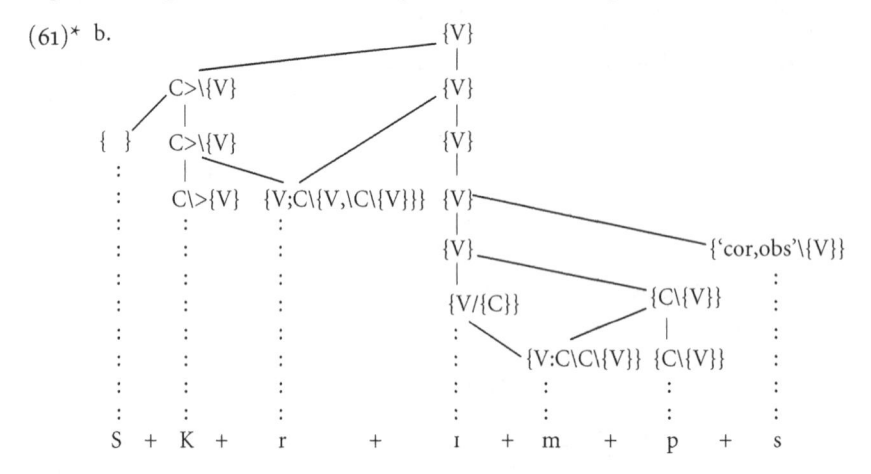

(61)* b.

```
                                            {V}
                                             |
           C>\{V}                            {V}
             |                                |
   { }     C>\{V}                            {V}
    :        |                                |
    :      C\>{V}  {V;C\{V,\C\{V}}}   {V}
    :        :           :              |
    :        :           :             {V}                    {'cor,obs'\{V}}
    :        :           :              |                          :
    :        :           :            {V/{C}}          {C\{V}}     :
    :        :           :              :                 |        :
    :        :           :              {V:C\C\{V}}  {C\{V}}       :
    :        :           :              :                 :        :
    :        :           :              :                 :        :
    S   +    K   +       r        +     I    +    m   +   p   +    s
```

[I] in (61b)* shows the complement and adjunct relations associated with *visited* in (101c), whereas *died* in (101b) is intransitive, like a vowel such as [i]. The specifier *very* in (101a) is paralleled by the [S] in (61)*.

As already acknowledged, the specifier involves perhaps the most contentious trans-planar identification, but I have suggested this may be largely due to the lack of clarity on what constitutes a specifier in syntax. However, well-established and lexically categorized syntactic specifiers like that preceding the adjective in (101a)—what I called in §1.7 archetypical specifiers—share various properties with what I have designated a phonological specifier, pre-obstruent onset [S]. It belongs to a small class, as does [S], in the latter case a class of one; *very* selects the particular class that it is adjoined to, in that it occurs only with gradable adjectives, just as [S] selects the minimal plosives, the neutralizations of [p] ≠ [b] etc. and indeed of obstruents in general. As a result of this, the specifier is an indicator of that class. And it could be more fully specified by redundancy as '{ \C>}', rather than as in (61b)*.[30]

What we are mainly concerned with here, however, is that (61b)* also shows double motherhood, or reentrancy (Shieber 1986), or bidependency, as with [r] and [m]. Particularly relevant, however, is the phenomenon of **ambisyllabicity**, such as we can associate with the medial plosives in *petrol* and *upper*. The head of the first, accented syllable is a transitive, so that the following plosive is required to satisfy its valency; but it also forms part of the following syllable, in accordance with the maximization of onsets—associated with the markedness characteristics of syllable structure, formulated above and repeated here:

(28)   unmarked syllable structure
       C + {V}
(28)* maximally unmarked syllable structure
       {C} + {V}

By (28)* plosives are the preferred onsets. The medial plosives are thus shared, as in (102a) for *upper*:

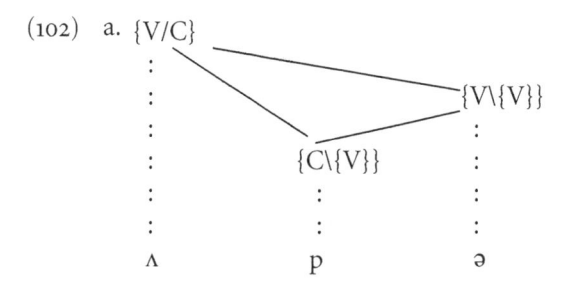

(102) a. {V/C}
                                    {V\{V}}
                  {C\{V}}
         ʌ   p   ə

---

[30] For comparison, as a manifestation of the archetypal specifier there are also perhaps such pre-prepositionals as *right* in *right to the end*. It too conforms to the requirements presented in the text: it belongs to a small class characteristic of the category that it selects to adjoin to. *Right* specifies locative functors, such as (i):

(i) a. right from the start, right to the door
    b. right in the middle, right on the hour, right at the door

Right seems to reject certain point-locations, such as clock or calendar temporals, as illustrated by (ii):

(ii) *right at 5 (o'clock)

And there are other restrictions that need not concern us, except as again illustrating the greater complexity of syntax.

b. {P;N/{P;N}}

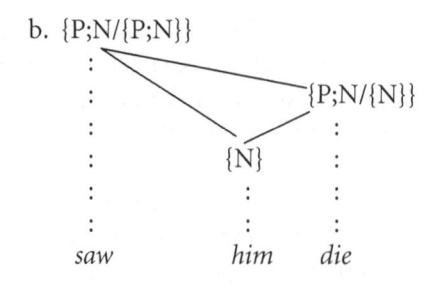

```
                        {P;N/{N}}
            {N}
  saw       him      die
```

As anticipated in Volume I, §3.8, there are motivations for recognizing this as appropriate in the syntax also, as in a (very partial) structure such as (102b). In (102b), *die* selects for a particular kind of {N}, which is thus part of the *die*-predication; but the morphology of the {N} in (102) reveals that this ('subjective') complement is also a dependent of *saw*, with the verbal configuration imposing objective case, even though *saw* is not subcategorized for *him*, but rather in this case simply for a verbal construction. The same dependencies are appropriate, even though the pattern of valency in (102a) and (b) is rather different. However, in so far as the [p] of the second syllable is 'attracted' into the first as well by the valency of the vowel of the first, there is perhaps some analogy with the syntax, as we shall see.

However, a fuller explication of the syntax involved here (including e.g. some explicit account of the treatment of the {N} as a complement of *die* and a dependent of *saw*), requires some further elaboration of the content of syntactic structure, some of which elaboration goes beyond what needs to be attributed to the phonology. Chapter 5 argues that these syntax-particular 'elaborations' are motivated by the (more extensive and varied) character of the representations required at the syntax interface. At this point I merely want to record in a preliminary fashion that double motherhood is not necessarily limited to phonology.

I shall indeed be arguing that double motherhood is common in syntactic structure, but for rather different reasons (in part at least) than, and less all-pervasively than, the bidependency associated with the phonology, where dependency guarantees coordination of segments in time (timing), an external-interface property not as obviously applicable as such to the syntax. It is this need of the interface that underlies the maximization of dependency relations resulting from complementation and unrestricted application of adjunction of consonants. But what does unite the two planes is obviously the role of bidependency in integrating the particular sequence involved. Integration drives the analogy. The integration of the foot is paralleled by that of the independent predication: feet are successive disjoint rhythmic units, as the utterances manifesting predications are disjoint discourse units; it is therefore unsurprising that ambisyllabicity is foot-internal (*pace* Jensen 2000).

Timing is relevant to syntax only in the extreme, absolute forms of succession and coincidence, unilinearity. And even the paratactic sentences in (100b-d) do not involve interruption of the basic unit, the word, there is no gradience of the linearity relation:

(100) a. He replied (that) he would come tomorrow morning
b. He replied, he would come tomorrow morning
c. He would come, he replied, tomorrow morning
d. He would come tomorrow morning, he replied

Succession and coincidence are properties syntax shares with phonology, so that in both planes a dependent may succeed or follow another (normal linearity) or coincide with it (bidependency), as in (103). But only in the phonology is dependency necessarily maximized, in order, normally, to permit implementation that is determinate in timing of segments. And it is only in the plane whose substance is directly manifested in time that we find the intermediate degrees of timing—involving overlapping of basic units—we looked at in the previous section. Such formations as *abso-bloody-lutely* are very exceptional and stylistically marked. The 'intermediate degrees' in syntax represented by (100) respect the integrity of the basic unit. And they are not in any way exceptional.

2.6 Conclusion

The preceding forms a fitting conclusion to this chapter as a whole, in which I have argued for the fundamental status in phonological representations of the dependency relation and related structural properties, crucially the differentiation of the 'formal' relations, complement, adjunct, and specifier. I have not belaboured here manifestations of obvious 'formal' properties such as the crucial part played not just by the dependency relation itself but by this relation's being deployed as part of (directed connected) trees in both planes—although I did point in the immediately preceding subsection of §2.5 to the sharing by syntax and phonology of the availability of double motherhood. These properties are manifestations, however, of general cognitive properties, relatively untrammelled by particularities of the individual substances grammaticalized by phonology and syntax. Here common cognitive capacities, confronted with sufficient perceived similarities between the two planes, can erect analogical representations for them.

Another object of the chapter is to try to establish, mainly in relation to English, to what extent different analogical and non-analogical properties, more and less 'formal', are appealed to in making contrasts. Properties that are largely contrastive or at least presupposed by other properties are described here as 'fundamental', without it being intended to undervalue the role of less 'fundamental' properties in interpretation, particularly those properties that are more directly implemented phonetically. We cannot draw any general conclusions from what we have looked at here—largely aspects of English. But it perhaps gives us a picture of one configuration of what is relatively fundamental, some of whose components may be generalizable—not unexpectedly in some cases.

For instance, a large burden of contrastivity is obviously carried by certain combinations of primary and secondary features, while, on the other hand, many other combinations are redundant. But English is also a language in which the more 'formal' property of transitivity may be fundamental, with less 'formal' properties like weight or vowel distinctions derivable from it. On the other hand, dependency presupposes sonority. But linearity is at least largely redundant. Fundamental is the grouping into onset vs. coda, whether this is expressed in linear terms or not. And the sequence of syllables is contrastive. Other manifestations of timing are not fundamental in the sense adopted—even though, as conceded, they may contribute to parsing.

Some of the analogies I have invoked thus involve aspects of structure that are relatively independent of the substance of the respective categorial alphabets and of the substantive properties of the structures they project—though headhood itself does grammaticalize cognitive salience. These analogies only indirectly involve properties that are purely interface-dependent, though the 'formal' distinctions have consequences for the latter, at least. There are languages in which phonological manifestations of these 'formal' distinctions have a lexical status, and in which they determine the distribution of other properties, such as linearity, vocalic weight and aperture differences, that are more sensitive to the interface.

Even the central substantive property of timing may reflect the role of dependency, and the lack of it, in the representation of the elements to be coordinated; and even transitivity is relevant, as in ambidependency. Timing may indeed be in general a substantive property that, unlike the others we have considered, figures only marginally as an independent (i.e. contrastive) property on either plane. It is typically determined by linguistic representations that lack the property.

In so far as linearity correlates with 'concrete' substance, ultimately time, it is perhaps exceptional here in pervading as such both phonology and syntax. However, the presence of timing is more obviously felt in the phonology, which more directly interfaces with the implementation of linguistic structure in time. As we have observed, however, linearity is only marginally contrastive in the phonology; and with respect to the syntax it is not a lexical property, but is derivative of other aspects of syntax (argument structure, weight, pragmatic considerations such as empathy, textual considerations such as focus, etc.). Though linearity and timing in general are crucial to expression and perception, their independence of other aspects of language structure is very limited. In the phonology timing is associated with maximization of dependency. Such maximization is plane-specific, given its intimate correlation with placement in time. And linearity in phonology is itself heavily dependent on sonority rather than dependency relations, unlike in the syntax. As we shall see, this is not necessarily to deny the possibility of a syntactic analogy to sonority. However, we do lack in phonology the strong motivations we find in syntax for proposing the ordering of implementations of the submodules implied by Figure 1 of the Prologue, from Volume I, such that linearization presupposes dependency assignment.

In this way, we are already encountering, in relation to linearity and timing, the kind of limitations on analogy imposed by the demands of the non-linguistic interfaces. Timing in phonology is determined and enabled by the immediate demands of real-time physiological properties, in ways from which syntactic timing is relatively remote, so that the latter is limited to succession or coincidence. I have spent some time on the Winnebago 'fast sequences' phenomenon largely to illustrate this immediacy of real-time properties, in the case of phonology; this militates against any obvious syntactic analogy. As I have already announced, we return to such limitations on analogy in Part III, on the basis of the mostly more 'pro-analogical' discussions of this and the following two chapters.

In the chapter that follows now we therefore continue to survey analogies between the planes, ones less obviously associated with heads and transitivity. There we also introduce further 'elaborations' of particularly categorial structure, especially in relation to the syntax. And we are again involved with both more 'formal' and more obviously substance-based analogies, to the extent that these can indeed be extricated one from the other.

3

The structure of the basic unit

I have used throughout the discussion in the previous chapters of this study, and particularly in Chapter 2, whose major focus was phonology, some terms which are generally more familiar from the syntax rather than phonology, namely the head-based terms complement and transitivity, adjunct, and specifier. This usage seems to me to be appropriate; and I have alluded to and tried to motivate the underlying analogies on which their use in relation to both planes is based. As well as the simple configurational parallelism with the equivalents in syntax which we can associate with the preceding phonological representations, these terms have the same categorial interpretation in both domains: a transitive element is a head that takes a substantively obligatory complement as dependent; an adjunct is an optional dependent of a head; a specifier is a member of a restricted class that identifies the sub class of the head it modifies; and these categorizations are distributionally appropriate in both planes. Moreover, more substantively, transitivity may reflect the common relationality and configurational salience of vowels and verbs.

In what precedes, the appropriateness of these concepts to both syntax and phonology was regarded as an illustration of the viability of something like the structural analogy assumption, which Anderson (1992: vii) formulates initially as 'the same structural properties recur (*ceteris paribus*) on different planes and levels'. He goes on (1992: 2) to spell this out a little more as:

Minimize (more strongly, eliminate) differences between levels that do not follow from a difference in alphabet or from the nature of the relationship between the levels concerned

It is the aim of this and the following chapter to provide more of structure and substance to the implementation of this still informal assumption, in the form of exploring a variety of other analogies, on the basis of more explicitly articulated representations of both syntactic and phonological structure, particularly categorization. Much of what follows is concerned with primary and secondary features and the relationship between them, i.e. the internal geometry of the basic unit, but also with the relationship of these units with the structures which they project and attach to.

In the terminology adopted here, phonology and syntax are different (sets of) levels of representation: this is ensured merely by the difference in basic substantive alphabet, where this alphabet is the basic set of categories out of which representations are constructed. Levels differing in basic alphabet can be said to belong to different planes. And the planes of syntax and phonology are related in a particular way, to each other and to the lexicon. Typically, phonology is seen as interpretative of syntax. Golston formulates the relationship as 'syntax outranks phonology' (1995: title). This holds with respect to both lexical and 'discourse' phonology, which are analogous to the aspects of syntax determined lexically and in discourse. As anticipated, what I want eventually to go on and examine, in Chapter 5 and its successor, is some of the ways in which the different characters of the alphabets and their asymmetrical relationship limit the scope for analogy. We have already been finding that closeness or otherwise of analogy between syntax and phonology tends to reflect relative distance of a property from a purely interface orientation.

In this and the following chapter, however, as also indicated, we look at further, more varied analogies, and here we shall be looking at structural properties that are commonly associated with phonology, rather than, or more than, syntax—unlike the transitivity analogy of Chapter 2. We shall see that these properties too are manifested in both planes. The analogies can be seen as clustering around the relationship between different kinds of categories and between them and linearity. They specifically involve the variety of relationships that features can bear to each other and the contrastive status of both the features and these relationships. In this chapter we look at the organization of the internal structure of the basic unit of each plane, word, or segment, in terms of (relationships between) features.

3.1 Sonority and 'nouniness'

At this point, let us begin to prepare the way for further, more precise, elaborations of categorial structure, particularly in the syntax, by focusing on the analogy between the sonority hierarchy in phonology and the predicability hierarchy (or, conversely, scale of 'nouniness') in syntax that began to emerge in Chapter 2. I shall flesh out the hierarchies in terms of detail of formulation and the nature of motivations for the representations of some suggested illustrations of the hierarchies.

The structure of the basic unit 143

The word classes, or rather primary categories, of syntax, distinguished by combinations of the substantive features **P** and **N**, are analogous to the major classes, or primary categories, of the phonology, distinguished by combinations of **V** and **C**: (combination of) these categories determine, among other things, the basic linear order of elements in both cases. The secondary categories, involving e.g. (in traditional terms) place of articulation in phonology, and, say, gender in syntax, provide only 'fine-tuning' of the basic distributional possibilities (particularly by those secondary features that can also be primary). The primary/secondary distinction among categories, and the partially shared membership of the sets of primary and secondary categories, are further inter planar analogies. But what is in focus at present are the consequences of the analogy whereby the primary categories are in each case distinguished in terms of varying preponderances of the substantive features. This analogy can be formally expressed, but is evidently substantively based.

Again the analogy is limited by the need for extensive structural elaboration of the lexically distinguished categories projected in the syntax, specifically more intricate combinations of features, and the absence of this in phonology. This elaboration in the syntax is once more required by the nature of the interface and thus the requirements placed on the alphabet of the plane directly associated with this interface, whose members involve semanticity rather than being simply perceptually based. And again we pursue this more systematically in Chapter 5.

We can, however, observe the similarity of basic pattern between (77), mostly repeated here from Chapter 2 in the form of (77)* but with nothing now corresponding to (c), for phonology, and (103), for syntax:

(77)* a. vowels $\{V\} = 4V{:}0C$
       b. sonorant consonants $\{V;C\} = 3V{:}1C$
       c. $\{V{:}C\} = 2V{:}2C = 1V{:}1C$
       d. fricatives $\{C;V\} = 1V{:}3C$
       e. plosives $\{C\} = 0V{:}4C$

(103) a. finites $\{P\} = 4P{:}0N$
       b. non-finite verbs $\{P;N\} = 3P{:}1N$
       c. adjectives $\{P{:}N\} = 2P{:}2N = 1P{:}1N$
       d. nouns $\{N;P\} = 1P{:}3N$
       e. names $\{N\} = 0P{:}4N$

Both the categorizations allow for the determination of hierarchical relationships among the categories, as indicated by the proportionalities (given at the end of each line); these are provided by a simple metric. It is the interpretation of nasals as {V;C{c}}, i.e. as sonorant consonants with a secondary {c} rather than as {V:C}, that renders the (c) slot in (77)* apparently empty in phonological categorization.

The proposed metric was originally introduced in relation to the phonological categories, including the representation of nasals as {V:C}. Thus it took the form shown in (76):

(76)   sonority metric
    a. {X} = 4X:0Y
    b. {X;Y} = 3X:1Y
    c. {X:Y} = 2X:2Y
    where X,Y range over V,C and combinations thereof

We can now generalize this metric as (76)*, implemented in both (77) and (103), though (c) is apparently not relevant, after all, in the phonology:

(76)*   feature preponderance metric
    a. {X} = 4X:0Y
    b. {X;Y} = 3X:1Y
    c. {X:Y} = 2X:2Y
    where X,Y range over V,C or P,N and combinations thereof

Adjectives do implement (76c)*, unnecessary in the phonology—though, no doubt associated with this complexity, they are not universal in language.

The removal of ':' from the phonological hierarchy may in itself be significant, as an indication of the less complex substantive domain whose demands underlie the more limited categorial differentiation of the phonology. But it does not undermine the principle of linguistic hierarchies based on proportionality in the presence of features. The measures in (77) define the core of the sonority hierarchy, reflected in sonority sequencing and in processes of fortition and lenition. Syntax displays a similar but more extended hierarchy characterized by the parallel measures in (103).

Some phenomena that can be interpreted as manifestations of the syntactic hierarchy have been described by Ross (1973), for instance, in terms of a dimension of 'nouniness'. Increasingly/decreasingly 'nouny' constructions are respectively less or more accessible to certain syntactic phenomena, and thus increasingly/decreasingly acceptable in certain constructions. Accommodation of this dimension further extends, beyond the illustrations in (103), the categorial differentiation necessary for syntax.

Ross's work has not received much attention as such, despite evidence of recent interest in 'gradience' in acceptability (as e.g. in Fanselow et al. 2006). But its characterization follows quite naturally from the extension of the hierarchy and implementation of the metric. In pursuing this material here, I obviously implicitly reject the notion that native-speaker judgments of acceptability do not constitute legitimate evidence for linguistic structure, while I discount the validity of their opinions on grammar (cf. Sampson 2002).

The increasing unacceptability of the sentences in (104), for instance, drawn from Ross (1973: 163), can be associated with the increasing preponderance of the **N** feature in the representation of the predicational centre of the complex subject, i.e. with increasing 'nouniness':

(104) a. That he does not prepare dinner is good for her health
       b. For him not to prepare dinner is good for her health
       c. Him not preparing dinner is good for her health
       d. ?His not preparing dinner is good for her health
       e. *His not preparing of dinner is good for her health
       f. **His not preparation of dinner is good for her health

The 'acceptability' symbols that initiate each of (104d-f) indicate successive growths, on the part of Ross, in the 'wince factor', an increase in unacceptability. In this case it relates to the relative incompatibility of 'nouny' constructions with predicational negation: the more 'nouny' the construction, as we progress from (104a-c) to (f), the stronger the rejection.

(104) illustrates only part of the scale; and (104a-c) are not differentiated in acceptability. Ross motivates the scale implied by (104) and an even more extensive scale, on the basis of a range of different phenomena varyingly tolerant of 'nouniness'. Different phenomena appeal to different points on the scale as where unacceptability increases. Ross records (1973: 161) the unacceptability judgments in (105), for instance, involving another negative construction, and again a progressive decrease in acceptability associated with 'nouniness':

(105) a. That not everyone will refuse our offer is expected
       b. ?For not everyone to refuse our offer is expected
       c. ??Not everyone refusing our offer is expected
       d. ?*Not everyone's refusing our offer is expected
       e. **Not everyone's refusing of our offer is expected
       f. **Not everyone's refusal of our offer is expected

146   Phonology-Syntax Analogies

Obviously, too, different speakers may disagree in particular cases on the location on the scale of these points of transition in relative unacceptability. And Ross recognizes that other factors may interact with 'nouniness' in determining acceptability judgments: for instance, different negators themselves, as well as constructions, are varyingly tolerant of 'nouniness' (1973: 162). Nevertheless, we seem to have here genuinely hierarchical phenomena, correlating with the relative prominence of 'nouniness'. And degree of 'nouniness' can be made quite precise in our system of categorization.

The increasing nominality of the subjects in (104), for instance, is computable from the subrepresentations on the left of (106):

(106) a. {P}
      :   {P;N} = 3(4P:0N):1(3P:1N) = 12(12P:0N):4(3P:1N) =15P:1N
      :   :
      does   prepare

b. {P;N}   = 3P:1N
   :
   :
   prepare

c. {{P;N};((N;P);(P;N))} = 3(3P:1N):1(3(1P:3N);1(3P:1N))
   :   = 3(3P:1N):1(12(3P:9N):4(3P:1N))
   :   = 3(3P:1N):1(6P:10N)
   :   = 48(36P:12N):16(6P:10N)
   :   = (1728P:576N):(96P:160N) = 1824P:736N
   :   = 56P:23N
   :
   :
   preparing

d. {{P;N}:((N;P);(P;N))} = 2(3P:1N):2(3(1P:3N);1(3P:1N))
   :   = 2(3P:1N):2(12(3P:9N):4(3P:1N))
   :   = 2(3P:1N):2(6P:10N)
   :   = 16(12P:4N):16(6P:10N)
   :   = (156P:64N):(96P:160N) = 252P:224N
   :   = 9P:8N
   :
   :
   preparing

The structure of the basic unit 147

e. {({N;P};{P;N});(P;N)}= 3(3(1P:3N):1(3P:1N));1(3P:1N)
: = 3(12(3P:9N):4(3P:1N)):(3P:1N)
: = 3(6P:10N):1(3P:1N)
: = 12(6P:10N):4(3P:1N)
: = (72P:120N):(12P:4N) = 84P:124N
: = 21P:31N
:
:
:
preparing

f. {(N;P);(P;N)} = 3(1P:3N);1(3P:1N) = 12(3P:9N):4(3P:1N) = 6P:10N
: = 3P:5N
:
:
preparation

And these also apply in the case of (105), of course. The representations in (106c-f) involve lexical derivation, which otherwise in recent work on notional grammar have been represented 'vertically', so that a noun-based verb will have a basic skeleton in which a noun categorization terminates a subjunctional arc which is initiated by a verb categorization. I have presented these relationships here in linear form in order to help comparison with the statements of proportionality that they are associated with. It is hoped that this might help with the negotiating of the sometimes lengthy (despite their local simplicity) computations in (106).

The calculations in (106) are based on generalization of the sonority metric of (76), as implemented in (77), but in some cases involving 'nested' combinations. (106a) illustrates how the metric works with nested bracketings: the inner values are multiplied by outer ones, while proportionality in the outer values is preserved:

(106) a. {P}
: {P;N} = 3(4P:0N):1(3P:1N) = 12(12P:0N):4(3P:1N) =15P:1N
: :
does prepare

This is illustrated by the conversion of the '1C' on the right of the upper unbracketed proportion to '4C', in response to the total within the inner bracket on the left counting as 12, as a result of the 4 inside the bracket being multiplied by the 3 outside, in order to be comparable with the contents of the right bracketing. This gives the proportion 12:4; the overall 3:1 ratio between left and right is preserved as 12:4. A simple count of the instances of **P** and **N** present shows a massive preponderance of the former. Let us see how this extends to the other, sometimes considerably more complex, representations in (106).

Let us note firstly, though, that the analytic verbal expression in (104a) is equivalent to the simple finite in *That he prepares dinner is good for her health*, as shown in (107):

(107) {P;(P;N)} = 3(4P:0N):1(3P:1N) = 12(12P:0N):4(3P:1N) = 15P:1N
       :
       prepare

Here again the overall governing {P} is worth three times (= 12) the total of the inner bracket (= 4), the **N** component of which is worth only 1. The finite verb is, as a result, very low in 'nouniness'. The non-finite verb in (104b) has more, as shown in (106b), but not enough to interfere with the negation in this construction:

(106) b. {P;N}   = 3P:1N
          :
          :
          prepare

However, this increase in 'nouniness' does register in terms of acceptability in (105b). The proportion comes out the same if we include *to* in the calculation, if it is itself represented as {P;N}.

The derivative status of the noun in (106f) is perhaps more clearly presented in the alternative notation in (108) deploying the graphic arc for dependency, alongside the semi-colon:

(106) f. {(N;P);(P;N)} = 3(1P:3N);1(3P:1N) = 12(3P:9N):4(3P:1N) = 6P:10N
                                                                = 3P:5N
          :
          :
          :
          preparation

(108) {N;P}
         |
       {P;N}

The derived noun of (106f) is highest in nouniness. Simple nouns, of course, are even higher, showing the inverse of the non-finite verb:

(109) {N;P}   = 1P:3N
          :
          :
          wine

The structure of the basic unit 149

Also missing from (106) is a simple derived verb such as that in (110), here with a non-finite categorization:

(110) $\{(P;N);(N;P)\} = 3(3P:1N);1(1P:3N) = 12(9P:3N):4(1P:3N) = 10P:6N$
$\qquad \vdots \qquad\qquad\qquad\qquad\qquad\qquad\qquad\qquad\qquad\qquad\qquad = 5P:3N$
$\qquad \vdots$
$\qquad \vdots$
$\qquad$ dine/wine

The forms in (106c-e) introduce further complexities.

They all involve the derived noun configuration of (106f), but in the first case dependent on a verb categorization, in the last governing it; they contrast exactly in the direction of the dependency:

(106) c. $\{\{P;N\};((N;P);(P;N))\} = 3(3P:1N):1(3(1P:3N);1(3P:1N))$
$\qquad \vdots \qquad\qquad\qquad\qquad\quad = 3(3P:1N):1(12(3P:9N):4(3P:1N))$
$\qquad \vdots \qquad\qquad\qquad\qquad\quad = 3(3P:1N):1(6P:10N)$
$\qquad \vdots \qquad\qquad\qquad\qquad\quad = 48(36P:12N):16(6P:10N)$
$\qquad \vdots \qquad\qquad\qquad\qquad\quad = (1728P:576N):(96P:160N) = 1824P:736N$
$\qquad \vdots \qquad\qquad\qquad\qquad\quad = 56P:23N$
$\qquad \vdots$
$\qquad \vdots$
$\qquad$ *preparing*

d. $\{\{P;N\}:((N;P);(P;N))\} = 2(3P:1N):2(3(1P:3N);1(3P:1N))$
$\qquad \vdots \qquad\qquad\qquad\qquad\quad = 2(3P:1N):2(12(3P:9N):4(3P:1N))$
$\qquad \vdots \qquad\qquad\qquad\qquad\quad = 2(3P:1N):2(6P:10N)$
$\qquad \vdots \qquad\qquad\qquad\qquad\quad = 16(12P:4N):16(6P:10N)$
$\qquad \vdots \qquad\qquad\qquad\qquad\quad = (156P:64N):(96P:160N) = 252P:224N$
$\qquad \vdots \qquad\qquad\qquad\qquad\quad = 9P:8N$
$\qquad \vdots$
$\qquad \vdots$
$\qquad$ *preparing*

e. $\{(\{N;P\};\{P;N\});(P;N)\} = 3(3(1P:3N):1(3P:1N));1(3P:1N)$
$\qquad \vdots \qquad\qquad\qquad\qquad\quad = 3(12(3P:9N):4(3P:1N)):(3P:1N)$
$\qquad \vdots \qquad\qquad\qquad\qquad\quad = 3(6P:10N):1(3P:1N)$
$\qquad \vdots \qquad\qquad\qquad\qquad\quad = 12(6P:10N):4(3P:1N)$
$\qquad \vdots \qquad\qquad\qquad\qquad\quad = (72P:120N):(12P:4N) = 84P:124N$
$\qquad \vdots \qquad\qquad\qquad\qquad\quad = 21P:31N$
$\qquad \vdots$
$\qquad \vdots$
$\qquad$ *preparing*

In (106d) the verbal and the derived noun configurations are mutually dependent. These representations lead, by applying the metric, to results whereby (106c) is preponderantly **P** (by more than 2-to-1) and (106e) preponderantly **N**, though the 'nouniness' of (106e) does not match that of (106f), let alone that of (109). (106d) is marginally preponderantly **P**. As before, in applying the metric, the inner brackets are calculated first, with proportionality being preserved at each stage. In the fourth stage of (106d), however, it is the inner figures that have to be adjusted to maintain proportion. The only purpose of these calculations is to show that any simple intuitive metrical interpretation of the notation, such as that in (76)*, gives some measure of place on a gradient—whatever the status of the detailed calculations. The notation embodies hierarchization.

The ambiguity of *preparing* and the rather marginal result (106d) is perhaps associated with the enduring uncertainty over the status of such forms—and, indeed gerunds in general. For English this is well documented by Poutsma (1926: ch. LVI). It has three different statuses—even ignoring the progressive and adjectival and nominal *-ing* of the type of (106f)—and one of them is almost evenly balanced between verbal and nominal.

Let us look at how the results of the calculations in (106)—or, more importantly, the hierarchization it measures—match overt indicators of 'nouniness'. The analytic finite construction in (106a), involving a non-finite dependent on a finite, is highly verbal, with a vast preponderance of **P**, as is the finite verb in (107). They show variable verbal morphology, 'bare objects', 'unmarked subjects', etc. The non-finite in (106b) still has a clear preponderance of **P**; the diminution is signalled by the absence of an unmarked subject and morphology. The non-finite in (106c), with a chain of categories governed by a verbal element ({P;N}), is also preponderantly **P**, though this is reduced in its case by its governing a derived noun configuration, which is reflected in the use of the marked 'subject', as well as in the invariant suffix. It is, in a sense, a verbal form—part of the verbal paradigm—which has been, as it were, 're-captured' from a verbal noun: this seems to be the historical scenario, and it is reflected in the synchronic categorization. The form in (106d) has equal proportions of derived nominality and of verbality; its categorial status is ambivalent, though it has marginally more **P** in terms of the metric. The increase in nominality (over (106c)) is marked by the possessive inflexion.

The constructions in (106e) and (f) have a need for *of* with the complement, associated with nominal predicators, as shown in (111a):

(111)   a. Her murder(ing) of her brother is regrettable
         b. *Her having murder(ing) of her brother is regrettable

Both of these constructions requiring *of*, derived noun, and *-ing*, also reject verb-governing 'periphrases' like (111b). Contrast (112b):

(112) a. Her murdering her brother is regrettable
b. Her having murdered her brother is regrettable

The forms in (111a) are not forms of the verb. The nominal element is clearly preponderant. This correlates with the categorizations in (106). The difference in categorization between (106e) and (f) correlates with the fact that the form in (105e) is less happy than (f) with quantifications and other nominal properties.

(113) a. ?*Some of these murderings could have been prevented
b. Some of these murders could have been prevented

The extra verbality of (113a) inhibits full utilization as a noun.[31]

Though there is an analogy here between phonology and syntax in the need for and the capacity of segmental representations to define hierarchies, the manifestations of the hierarchies in respectively syntax and phonology are rather different. The phonological hierarchy is less extended. And this is accentuated in the version of phonological representation given here compared with earlier accounts (such as that in Anderson and Ewen 1987) that include voicing and nasality in the hierarchy of primary features, rather than relegating these distinctions to secondary feature status. And this discrepancy in extension can be associated with the substantive domains of the respective alphabets. In phonology we are concerned with relative inherent perceptual prominence and the restrictions this and articulatory constraints impose on syllable structure, including its linearization. In syntax we are involved with relative access to the semantic capacity to head a fully formed predication, predications which have to be able to represent a wide range of cognitive 'scenes', with components of different kinds.

As we have seen, nouns, with low predication-forming capacity (associated with predominance of the **N** feature), are prototypically not complement-taking, and prototypically do not constitute the head of an independent

---

[31] The present account of 'nouniness' differs somewhat from the treatment of (105) and the like proposed in Anderson (1997a: §2.6.3), and it doesn't accommodate the full hierarchy suggested by Ross (1973). But it is perhaps sufficiently full to render plausible the proposed analogy. We return to such derived forms, and their significance for the syntax, in Ch. 6, as well as immediately below.

According to e.g. Anderson and Ewen (1987: ch. 6), the secondary categories in the phonology are also associated with varying preponderances of a set of (secondary) features. And Böhm (1993: §5.4, 1994) argues that the secondary features of at least the functor category in the syntax (which category, realized as adpositions or inflectionally, for example, is again discussed in Ch. 6 below) can combine in such a way, i.e. asymmetrically. See the discussion in §3.5 of Volume I of the trilogy.

predication. More adjectives than nouns are complemented (not just deverbal ones: *aware of, close to, near (to), like*, etc.), though perhaps not prototypical ones (*small, old*, etc.), and in many languages adjectives share either 'verbal' or 'nominal' properties, or both. Verbs show a fully fledged system of complementation, but only finite ones can head an unmarked independent predication. The substances of the hierarchies differ, but verbs and vowels emerge as the central syntagm-creating elements, reflected in their respective roles in syllable and clause structure. Their relationality is based on a perceived substantive analogy: vowels form the contour on which the syllable is formed, and verbs create the 'scene' in which other elements participate.

3.2 The complexity of syntactic categorization

A further analogy has emerged from these last remarks on the distinctive characteristics of the different syntactic categories when we compare them with the discussion of phonological transitivity and adjunction in Chapter 2. Analogous in phonology and syntax is the unevenness of the distribution of complementation, adjunction, and specification through the set of primary categories. Just as only vowels in English take complements, so there is no complementation of prototypical nouns, with 'nominal' complements being restricted to deverbal nouns (such as *disappearance, destruction, student*, etc.) and a small number of 'inherently relational' nouns (such as *mother, side*, etc.).

I thus argued in §1.5, in relation to the syntax, that the high degree of parallelism attributed by X-bar theory to the expansions of the primary categories is fallacious. X-bar theory is a dys-analogy. By virtue of their cognitive content nouns and verbs, for instance, enter into different kinds of relationships within the expansions of the basic category: nouns allow attributives (*blonde men, men from Iceland*, etc.), which permit further classification and identification of a referent (but only via a determiner), while verbs, as prototypically relational, require complements, and permit circumstantial adjuncts (*sang beautifully, sang at the Met*, etc.) that provide a matrix for the 'scene' being represented. Prototypically, verbs are relational, and also dynamic; nouns are minimally relational, and stable. Similarly, the structure of the syllable is governed by different principles than that of onsets and codas: vowels, the prototypical syllable heads, are maximally sonorous, the heads of consonant clusters are minimally sonorous. And, just as with the sonority hierarchy, the categorial structures of the syntax enable us to represent, in terms of different preponderances of notional features, the substantive basis for these differential aspects of behaviour.

The complexes of syntactic categories we have just been looking at allow us to make more explicit the relationship between the behaviour of derived nouns discussed in §3.3 of Volume I in this series and the characterization of the internal structure of these. And some further illustration of this, as well as completing that earlier discussion, will also highlight the extent of the discrepancy in internal structure between the basic elements of phonology and syntax.

Both attributive and circumstantial 'modifiers', as well as complements, can occur with deverbal nouns, but, as observed in Volume I, §2.4, normally in English in a certain order, as illustrated here by (114):

(114) a. students of physics at Cambridge from Iceland
      b. *students of physics from Iceland at Cambridge
      c. *students at Cambridge of physics from Iceland
      d. *students from Iceland of physics at Cambridge

(114a) shows, in that order, a post-nominal complement, an attributive, and a circumstantial. The attributive does not normally precede the circumstantial, as in (114b), nor can either of them precede the complement, as shown by (114c-d).

If we associate complements and circumstantial modifiers with verbals and attributive modifiers with prototypical nouns, then we can allow for the occurrence of all of these with deverbal nouns in terms of the complex internal structure of such nouns. I take *student* to be a concrete agent noun that, like the action noun in (104f)/(105f)/(106f) is based on a verb, which relationship I shall represent as in (108):

(108)   {N;P}
          |
        {P;N}

The structure of (114) is built around this. In the representation in (115) I ignore the role of determiners in attributivization, as well as the categorial identification of the prepositions, since these omissions do not detract from the main point to be illustrated, that concerning the relationship between an item's internal lexical structure and the nature and interactions of its dependents:[32]

---

[32] Anderson (2007) argues that attributives are dependents of determiners rather than of nouns themselves, the prototypical members of which category do not take dependents at all, complements or modifiers. I do not pursue this refinement at this point. But see further §6.2.2. See too elsewhere in the trilogy, as detailed below.

(115) {N;P}
          |
        {N;P}   { \{N;P}}
          | :
        {P;N}   :
          | :
        {P;N/{ }}   { \{P;N}}   :
          :   { }   :   :
          :   :   :   :
          :   :   :   :
        students of physics at Cambridge from Iceland

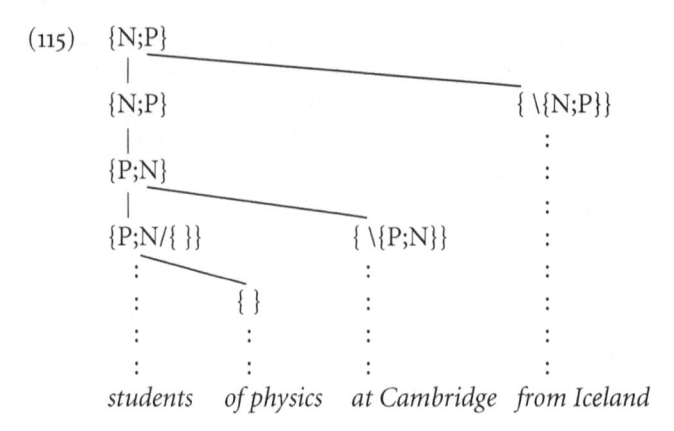

The attributive *from Iceland* is associated with the (lower) {N;P}, and introduces a like node above it; and the lower, circumstantial modifier seeks a {P;N} as head, and again introduces a higher node. The lower, basic {P;N} has a complement. (115) thus fleshes out the representations in §3.3 of Volume I, particularly (I.40), in the light of a more comprehensive set of categorizations and of the hierarchy we have discussed. It thus makes evident the dependence of syntax on the complex lexical structure of the heads of constructions. For a still fuller account of attributives—one that suggests indeed that they are not modifiers—see e.g. §7.2 in Volume I and §§5.2, 6.4, and 6.8 in Volume II.

The unmarked linear order in English is in conformity with height in the tree and is thus projectivity-preserving: there is no interruption of constructions by elements from outside the construction. Compare e.g. (116):

(116) {N;P}
          |
        {N;P}   { \N;P}
          | :
        {P;N}   :
          | :
        {P;N/{ }}   :   { \{P;N}}
          :   :   :   { }
          :   :   :   :
          :   :   :   :
        *students   from Iceland at Cambridge   of physics

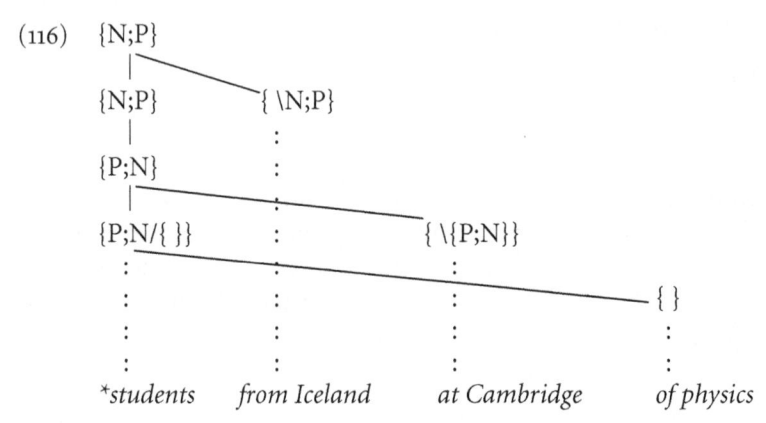

The height of the component categories of the complex item is determined by lexical derivation, and it is unnecessary to impose the order of the adjunctions arbitrarily.

As acknowledged, I have suppressed most of the less relevant category information in (115) and (116) (as well as the internal structure of the postnominal phrases). We shall, however, be looking at some of these categorial elaborations in the later chapters on aspects of syntax that are possibly non-analogous with phonology.

It is worth recalling at this point that deverbal nouns may be associated with an ambiguous modifier:

(117) a beautiful singer

The two meanings correlate with structural differences that follow from distinctions in the internal categorization of the noun. The pre-nominal modifier in (117) may be either a circumstantial (cf. the verbal circumstantial in *She dances beautifully*) or attributive (where the beauty is independent of the singing). This ambiguity depends on the presence of some such internal structure as we find in (115).[33]

Such complex categorizations are a crucial mechanism in the elaboration of syntactic structures that is not matched in the phonology. In phonology such complexity of primary categorization is limited to a few limited cases of extension beyond the kind of simple categorization presented in (77)*:

(77)* a. vowels   {V} = 4V:0C
       b. sonorant consonants {V;C} = 3V:1C
       c.   {V:C} = 2V:2C = 1V:1C
       d. fricatives   {C;V} = 1V:3C
       e. plosives   {C} = 0V:4C

Only a few segment types, such as affricates, including stops with contrastive aspiration (as in Korean), seem to require a double categorization. This discrepancy between the planes correlates with the different relations that syntax and phonology bear to the lexicon and to their respective extralinguistic interfaces. The phonology-phonetics interface is complex but highly specialized and unified. The structure, in terms of syntactic categories, that is associated with lexical items is a response to multifarious interface requirements.

---

[33] The distinction that I am terming 'attributive' versus 'circumstantial' has been discussed in a number of places under various guises. My treatment of it here has necessarily been rather brief (given the scope of the present discussion), and various relevant dimensions are ignored (see e.g. Anderson 1997a: §2.3.1, 2007: §2.3.3), including the fact that the same distinction can be attributed to predicative adjectives as well as those which are nominal 'modifiers'.

Such potentially quite complex lexical configurations of syntactic categories are projected as syntactic constructions. This lexical structure may or may not overtly feed the morphology (if we have, say, affixation rather than conversion). And this possibly morphologically complex re-representation contains a set of phonological elements that must be represented in such a way as to be processable phonetically. We have a 'double articulation' on the way from conception to articulation, and vice versa. In this way the complex substantively based lexical categorization from which syntactic structures are projected can be associated with a compact perceptually realizable phonological expression.

Nevertheless, the syntactic structures that are erected on the basis of complex categories involve the basic distinction between complement and adjunct that is potentially shared by the two planes. So we come back to the dependency-based analogies of Chapter 2. Let us now proceed with the exploration of analogies of other kinds.

3.3 Markedness and natural classes

Returning now to other syntax/phonology analogies involving the basic unit, we can observe that representations such as those in (77) and (103) also provide an inherent measure of **markedness** (as well as sonority/'nouniness'). Markedness correlates with the relative simplicity of the basic categorizations. And this applies in both planes (Anderson and Ewen 1987: §1.3.2; Anderson 1997a: §2.4). Thus, for instance, as anticipated above, within the lexical categories of the syntax, adjectives emerge as rather complex, in involving two features in a double dependency, a relation of mutual preponderance. And this correlates with evidence of markedness, of being less accessible. Accessibility is measured in terms of degree of attestation in different languages and relative acquisitional priority.

Anderson (1997a: 62) suggests the markedness metric in (118), based on complexity of feature combination:

(118)   *markedness metric*

$$\begin{aligned} &\quad 0 \\ , &= 1 \\ ; &= 2 \\ : &= 4 \end{aligned}$$

However, the upper, lesser-valued part of the hierarchy defined by (118)—involving simple combination (';') and no combination—is 'interfered with' by the functional/lexical distinction in the syntax, which introduces other considerations, and which again we shall return to in Chapter 5.

But, as far as adjectives are concerned, they are given a score of '4' by (118). Complexity in terms of (118) correlates straightforwardly here with markedness. Marked status seems to be in accord with the non-universality of adjectives and with late acquisition as a distinct class (Anderson 2000: 176). Their particular complexity—{P:N} = {P;N},{N;P} – also correlates well with the fact that in adjective-less languages items that would, on notional grounds, tend to be adjectives in other languages are either verbs—{P;N}— or nouns—{N;P} (Dixon 1982: ch. 1). In some languages (such as Cherokee— Lindsey and Scancarelli 1985) all adjectives are clearly derived from either verbs or nouns.

It has been variously argued that there are languages that lack a distinction in lexical class between noun and verb and have simply a class of 'contentives', represented in the present notation as {P,N} (and discussed in Volume I, §2.4, and more fully in Anderson 2006b: §10.2.2). This is compatible with the notionalist association between markedness and complexity of categorization: the more complex the categorization the more likely there are to be systems that lack it. In this case, it suggests that distinctions in lexical categorization are more marked than in functional categorization. Syntactic structure is non-viable without functional categories. {P}, { }, and {N} make possible predication, argument structure, and reference/deixis, and are ontologically prior (see e.g. Anderson 2007: §9.3). This means that though there may be lacking a lexical distinction between noun and verb, the language is still able to distinguish predication from argument, verbal from nominal.

We find a similar situation in the phonology, though with (again) a less extended hierarchy, a language may lack fricatives (= 2, by (118)) but not oral stops (= 0) and a language is unlikely to have fewer stops than fricatives. Although, as e.g. Menn and Stoel-Gammon (1995: 348) and Heijkoop (1998) observe, there is much individual variation in order of acquisition of categories, the primacy of stops clearly emerges in studies of phonological acquisition and loss (cf. e.g. Menn and Stoel-Gammon 1995: 348; Dinnsen et al. 1990). A reviewer suggests that this may be associated with the fact that fricatives require more fine-grained motor control—a basis for complexity.

Also relevant to markedness are the secondary features, again particularly those that may also be primary, and particularly where the dominant primary feature is contradicted by the secondary feature. Thus voiced plosives combine {C} and {v}. If we add such combinations to the hierarchy, as say '1.5', this correlates with the observation that a language is unlikely to have fewer voiceless stops than voiced (see e.g. Nartey 1979). In such terms, voiced fricatives and nasal consonants emerge as relatively marked, in combining respectively {C;V} and {v} and {V;C} and {c}. Likewise the presence of a secondary version of **P** ({p}) with relational nouns and adjectives can be correlated with their markedness. Perhaps we can rate a combination such as {N;P{p}} at '3.5', and thus highly marked in terms of our measure.

In acquisition, factors other than simple markedness are again involved, though. In, for instance, the data studied by Heijkoop (1998: part II, §3), a nasal stop, which typically in typical adult speech has a specification involving combination of a primary sonorant and a secondary stop specification, {V;C{c}}, is often the first realization in acquisition to combine a vowel representation with a consonantal, i.e. **V** with **C**. Such a nasal is thus apparently at this stage in acquisition perceived as {V,C} (cf. too again Dinnsen et al. 1990), in the absence of asymmetrical dependencies between **V** and **C**. This suggestion again exploits the system-dependent character of representations in this notation, which allows segment types to have an evolving categorization, as contrasts develop. However, this does not account for the transition from {V,C} to {V;C{c}}, and particularly the adoption of nasals as {V,C} in the first place. Why are nasals so interpreted at an early stage in acquisition?

Notice too that in other cases a fricative occupies this early acquisitional position. Fricatives, in adult language typically {C;V}, make a plausible subsequent consonantal elaboration of a first combination of **V** and **C** as {V,C}. The representation {C;V} develops in opposition to sonorants ({V;C}). Nasals, however, are not the simplest of categories in most adult languages: as we have seen, {V;C{c}} is not untypical as the appropriate representation, and this represents a considerable elaboration upon {V,C}. Why, then, we must ask again, can they also be early in acquisition?

Developmentally, nasals may represent the simplest way in terms of early performance capabilities to combine a consonantal and a more vowel-like articulation, involving voicing combined with lowered velum. This is a notion consistent with their frequency (particularly that of [m]—Locke 1983) in babbling. Again extralinguistic capacities interfere with the internal metric. The structural complexity of nasals revealed in the discussion of timing phenomena in §2.5 yields to the performance practicalities of early stages in the development of speech. Performance facility underlies the early appearance of nasals in the acquisitional transition {V,C} ⇒ {V;C} ⇒ {V;C{c}}, with the final representation involving recognition of their perceptual complexity. It has also been observed by a reviewer that in early production nasals and laterals are often substituted one for the other, perhaps reflecting a failure to perceive distinctions among liquids. For an attempt to formulate a hierarchy of oppositions in relation to acquisition that would accommodate this and other aspects of categorial representation see Anderson (1997b).

In like manner, identification with respect to speech-act participation, by deictic elements (such as *this* etc.) is in the adult system linguistically more complex than reference: the latter embodies simply the speaker's assumption that the interlocutor can identify the referent(s) of a definite expression, whereas deixis incorporates this assumption and the indication that the identification depends on the immediate speech situation. However, the visual support (pointing etc.) that can accompany linguistic expression of deixis (*this* etc.) enables its early acquisition, and indeed the development of definiteness itself (cf. e.g. Lyons 1975). Nevertheless, we can again associate acquisitional priorities with complexity of syntactic categorization. It is argued in Anderson (2000), for instance, that, contrary to what has often been claimed, it is the functional categories that are acquired first. Prominent here are names, the basic entitative { }, with a vocative function, and a relational category { /}, with an imperative function.

In the two planes, markedness clearly relates to interface properties to do with maximization of perceptual and cognitive differentiation, so that verb and noun and vowel and consonant, respectively, are maximally opposed. And the external-interface-based distinction permits in both cases the same kind of formal characterization, based on the same logic, and the same metric, as embodied, in this case, in (118). However, such close-to-interface analogy is in both planes particularly subject to other interface considerations, particularly in the early stages of acquisition of a first language, when physiological development and perceptual inheritance are important—though attenuated by exposure to the language of acquisition.

Evidence has grown over a number of years, for instance, that particular perceptual endowments interact with exposure to particular languages. Notable has been the work on voice onset time in stops showing that primates in general may inherit a capacity to discriminate short-lag vs. long-lag onset (Kuhl and Miller 1975). But exposure to a particular language eliminates over time some of the inherited discriminatory capacity for consonant types in favour of those that signal a contrast in the language concerned (Eimas et al. 1971). Part of the interest of this here is the emergence of an analogy with the development of semantic discrimination in spatial relations in the work of Levinson (2003a,b). We have, apparently, a developmental analogy.

His experiments with English-learning and Korean-learning infants support the notion, as quoted by Carr (2005: 26) that:

nine-month old infants have equal facility to make, e.g. English vs. Korean spatial distinctions, while by eighteen months they are tuned into the local language specific distinctions.

Carr (2005: 267) formulates the analogy as follows:

The idea is that, just as adult English speakers will have difficulty, say, with the three-way contrast among voiceless stops found in Korean, so they will have difficulty with Korean spatial distinctions: ...

As he points out, Levinson's conclusions, based on this evidence, 'rest on the claim that both nature and culture play a role in linguistic knowledge' (2005: 26). The 'nature' component, however, is not specifically linguistic.

Carr (2005: 29–30) points to another developmental analogy, formulated by Croft (2001). I interpret this as involving a holistic phase in acquisition such that word-length 'templates' are acquired prior to the development of categories such as syllable and segment and, analogously, constructional 'templates' are acquired prior to the development of syntactic categories. The analogy dissolves subsequently, however, due to the divergent substances accessed by the two planes. While the phonological structure of many lexical items may be stored holistically in the lexicon, only idioms and routine phrases are so stored among constructions. There is no necessity for the storing of constructions in general, which are compositional products of their component categories, and particularly of the head. Though the properties associated with constructions no doubt play a role in interpretation, constructions as such are non-contrastive, at best.

There is another aspect of the notation adopted here that is worth commenting on, distinct from its role in markedness. It is shown in §3.5 of Volume I that in relation to the syntax the notation adopted here enables us to identify various cross-classes in terms of a shared feature. The class is both 'natural' in the sense of substantively based but also in so far as the representation of the cross-class is simpler than that of the members of the class, which are differentiated from each other by features they do not share. These cross-classes are manifested in shared distributional properties of the members of the class. Thus categories containing **P** can be **predicators**; while categories with a predominance of **P** have a distribution that distinguishes them as **verbal**. The latter are 'clause-central' in various ways. The functional category that contains only **P** is the ultimate predicator and, in being finite, relates a predication to its speech-act coordinates. And categories containing **N** may participate in anaphoric relations; those having the distribution characteristic of having a predominance of **N** are **nominal**. They are the typical members of the arguments that **functors**, with no primary feature, enable to fulfil the requirements of predicators, particularly verbals. The functional category containing only **N** is fully referential and possibly deictic, not merely anaphoric.

Likewise, segments containing **C** are **consonants**, those containing **V** are **continuants**. Segments with a preponderance of **C** are **obstruents**, and with a preponderance of **V sonorants**. The linear consequences of the sonority hierarchy is perhaps the most obvious manifestation of the relative distributions of these various types. Obstruents typically occur in the syllable on the outside of non-obstruents. And non-continuants occur outside continuants. There is an asymmetry, however, in the phonology that is not reflected in the syntax, where the functional/lexical distinction gets in the way of it. Functional categories contain at most only one primary feature. But in phonology, whereas the sole presence of **V** characterizes vowels, that of **C** is associated with merely a subtype of consonant, albeit the least marked type, the **plosive**. This asymmetry reflects the dominance of the vowel, as the typical syllable head, and thus as the shape upon which the non-vowels are overlaid. A {P} element is similarly relationally central, but only via other relational elements, not in terms of substantive instantiation—even though the {P} category establishes the coordinates of the 'scene' into which other elements fit. We can perhaps say that the substantive instantiation of the inclusiveness of {P} is in interpretation. The discrepancy between the two planes again reflects the different demands made on them by their respective substantive interfaces.

3.4 Conclusion

I have tried in what precedes to illustrate in brief some of the detailed formal analogies in categorization that have been attributed to the two planes of syntax and phonology. These categorizations, based on the same formal combinatorial principles, are in both cases motivated by behaviour in the two planes that is analogous. They exhibit, for instance, the same kinds of hierarchizations: in one instance the dimension involved relates to markedness or accessibility, represented categorially in terms of relative complexity of the categorization; in the other the dimension correlates with the relative proportion of one or the other feature, **C** vs. **V**, **N** vs. **P**.

The basic segmental units of syntax and phonology also belong to more general cross-classes. This is also represented componentially, in terms of the features that are shared by the members of the cross-class, and the relative simplicity in the representation of these cross-classes compared with that of individual categories is again reflected in the shared notation type suggested here for both phonology and syntax. These cross-classes are 'natural classes': they are characterized by the presence in the representation for the members of the cross-class of a shared substantive feature or combination, and the representation of the cross-class is simpler than the representations of the individual members.

These analogies involving basic units hold in general despite the different interface demands imposed on the planes, and are no doubt supported by perceived similarities between e.g. the relational roles of vowels and verbs. Similarities between the two planes manifest classes of units of different relative complexity, and parallel similarities reflect different super-classes of units within each plane. However, we are already witnessing discrepancies between the two planes in the implementation of the hierarchies and cross-classes, discrepancies that reflect the different extralinguistic demands made upon them. We can add these to those we have encountered in the preceding chapter. Recall, for instance the discrepancies in the role of timing in the two planes, including the susceptibility in the phonology of the subjunctional dependency between primary and secondary features to breakdowns associated with phonetic implementation.

And we can add discrepancies encountered in other volumes of this trilogy. Recall, for instance, the characterizations for non-primary features of the functor in syntax, where functor is the functional category that is subcategorized by semantic features expressing the relationship between a predicator and its argument. These involve not just secondary features but tertiary, as in the representations in §3.5 of Volume I:

> Functors V: Combinations based on the Asymmetry Assumption
> a. absolutive{source} absolutive{locative} absolutive{goal}
> b. source{absolutive} source{locative}
> c. locative{absolutive} locative{source} locative{goal}

Here we have both a secondary feature and a tertiary (enclosed by the inner braces) associated with the primary categorization as functor. The role of some of these combinations is illustrated in (I.50):

(I.50) a. *They* sell well   {abs{src}}
      b. *Fido* barks a lot   {src{abs}}
      c. *Bob* believes that   {src{loc}}
      d. The water dripped *from there* {loc{src}}
      e. *The basement* flooded   {loc{abs}}
      f. *The fence* got a lick of paint {abs{loc}}

Here (I.50a) and (b), for instance, involving respectively a 'middle' verb and an intransitive agentive, contrast in whether the absolutive or the source is secondary. We can even envisage the necessity for recognizing quaternary features, such as the {source} in the representation for the 'recipient' that emerges as the subject in *Florence received a lovely present from her grandfather.* { {src{loc{goal}}}}. It is an 'experiencer' ({src{loc}}) that is also a goal ({loc{goal}}). It is not obvious that such an extension to categorization is necessary in phonological representations, even if we take into account, say, the phonologizations associated with ejectives and ingressives.

Let's leave the structure of the basic units at this point, however. I turn now, in the chapter that follows, to feature-based analogies that pertain beyond the basic unit in various ways, before we confront more directly and in more detail such discrepancies between the planes as we have been noting.

4

Syntax and non-linearity

4.1 Introduction

In this chapter we pursue analogies whose more familiar manifestation lies in the phonology rather than the syntax. These take us beyond the confines of the segment and beyond the basic dependency relations involved in complementation and modification. What we confront are **extrasegmental** elements of different kinds, elements that are not contrastively part of a basic unit or subject to the normal regularities of linearization. These are familiar from phonological phenomena such as harmony. And in §4.2 I formulate how harmony systems may be accommodated within the present framework and describe syntactic analogues to phonological harmony, as well as some of the limitations on them. The two sections that follow that one are concerned with other manifestations of extrasegmentality, including umlaut, and, once more, their analogues in syntax. Harmony and umlaut involve extrasegmental secondary features. But in §4.3 we encounter whole segments that appear to be properties of the lexical item, and whose serialization is particular to them, as well as a possible syntactic analogy.

In the course of the discussions in these sections we find that optimal systems of extrasegmentals, as well as of segments and the relationship between the two, make appeal to underspecification and polysystemicity. And we confront the issues these raise in §4.5, as well as the extent to which these notions are also appropriate in the description of syntactic categories. The chapter—and the survey in this and the preceding chapters of different kinds of evidence for analogy—is concluded with an acknowledgment of a more general analogy pervading the discussion, the phenomenon of 'grammaticalization' that characterizes both syntactic and phonological structure and their development. The representations in both planes are grammaticalized to varying extents, in the sense that their connection to the interface is varyingly weakened.

4.2 Extrasegmentals, I: Harmony, underspecification, and opacity

Both phonology and syntax are manifested linearly, given perceptual and productive interface requirements. The linearity analogy, however, can be argued to extend, perhaps more interestingly, to the 'multilinearity' associated with many late-twentieth-century approaches to phonology. Syntax too is, if you like, 'autosegmental', and in both planes 'autosegmentality'—or what I am terming 'extrasegmentality'—is associated with secondary features, and, indeed, some basic units, segments and words. But again—as we found with the regular serialization of the basic units—much of the linearity that has been associated with so-called 'non-linear' representations is redundant, non-contrastive: this is the point of the Firthian analysis of 'harmony' phenomena etc. Anchoring to the segment is frequently redundant or inappropriate. Some elements in the phonology are properties of the lexical (including morphological) item, or of the utterance. And I am going to suggest that some syntactic elements are, in a sense, properties of the clause. Pursuit of this brings us eventually to the contemplation of perhaps less obvious analogies, less obvious because of their manifestation in aspects of their respective substances that are most different from each other—i.e. because of the closer connection of the phenomena involved with the individuality of their respective extralinguistic interfaces, their substantive bases.

4.2.1 *Vowel harmony in Finnish*

Consider, in outline, the way in which many systems of **vowel harmony** might be said to operate. Let us focus, for present purposes, on so-called 'stem-controlled' harmony. On the one hand, in terms of this, all the vowels within a lexical formative are required to share lexically (in terms of simplex features) the presence or absence of some secondary property. This is thus a property associated contrastively with the lexical item rather than with individual vowels (in the absence of some clear motivation for selecting a specific vowel as the source of the harmony). Moreover, on the other hand, the property in question spreads to at least some affixes.

This can be illustrated from the well-known Finnish system. I do not pursue here some of the less relevant complexities of the system (see e.g. Skousen 1973; L. B. Anderson 1975, 1980; Ringen 1975; and much later work); the following examples are drawn from van der Hulst and van de Weijer (1995). Finnish is generally analysed as showing 'palatal harmony' or 'backness harmony': lexical items are either 'front words' or 'back words', as respectively illustrated by (119a) and (b):

(119) a. pöytä 'table', käyrä 'curve', tyhmä 'stupid'
 b. pouta 'fine weather', kaura 'oats', tuhma 'naughty'
 c. värttinä 'spinning-wheel', kesy 'tame'
 d. palttina 'linen cloth', verho 'curtain'

There are two **neutral** vowels, spelled *i* and *e*, as in (119), which, though themselves categorizable in traditional terms as 'front', can appear in either type of item, 'front' or 'back', as illustrated in (119c) and (d) respectively. Let us consider how this might be represented phonologically, particularly on the basis of a concern for (the location of) contrastivity.

Firstly let me spell out appropriate representations for the vowels, without reference to the 'harmony' phenomena, and, to begin with, not maximizing contrastivity. Such a 'fully specified' vowel system of Finnish is patently asymmetrical, as shown in (120):

(120) *the fully specified Finnish vowel system*

acute	acute + grave	grave
{i} 'i'	{i,u} 'y'	{u} 'u'
{i;v} 'e'		
	{i,u,v} 'ö'	{u,v} 'o'
{v;i} 'ä'		
	non-acute non-grave	
	{v} 'a'	

(120), of course, gives only the specification of the secondary categories; the segments are all vowels. {v}, {u}, and {i} are the vowels containing respectively only the compactness/lowness, grave/round, and acute/palatal feature (Anderson and Ewen 1987: §6.1—but I have reinterpreted their {a} as {v}). The others show combinations of these, with only one such pair introducing a difference in preponderance—of **i** and **v**. Recall that the features are not binary, but combinatory, so, for instance, 'grave', when combined with 'acute', corresponds to Jakobsonian 'flat'.

However, contrastivity again demands that we reject as lexical representations such overspecified conjunctions of secondary features as we find in (120). Moreover, if we follow Anderson and Durand (1988a,b, 1993) in associating such **asymmetry** as we see here with the presence of **non-specification**, we can posit a lexical system which is less redundant, which is symmetrical, and which makes transparent the nature of the harmony and of 'neutrality' to it. Recognition of non-specification is provided if we propose for Finnish the system of (121)—which, however, still ignores harmony:

(121)   *the underspecified Finnish vowel system*
　　　　acute　　　　　　　non-acute
　　　　{u,i} 'y'　　　　　　{u} 'u'
　　　　{u,v,i} 'ö'　　　　　{u,v} 'o'
　　　　{v,i} 'ä'　　　　　　{v} 'a'
　　　　　　　underspecified
　　　　　　　{ } 'i'
　　　　　　　{ , } 'e'

(121) contains two vowels with no substantive specification, one simplex, corresponding to *i*, the other complex, indicated by the comma in the representation, corresponding to *e*. They are realized as specified in (122), which are statements of redundancies applicable to the vowels of Finnish:

(122)　a.　{V{, }} = {V{,v}}
　　　　b.　{V{ }} = {V{i}}

Application of (122b) to the representation for 'i' gives {V{i}}. By virtue of application of both of (122a) and (b), { , } 'e' comes to be {v,i}. This is the same representation as for 'ä'. How, then, is what is spelled *e* to be distinguished from what is spelled *ä* (cf. (121))? The answer to this lies in the characterization of harmony.

Before we proceed to that, let us note again that the 'abstractness' of underspecification, if that is an appropriate term to apply to it (as some have), is very different from that of 'abstract' categories such as 'Pro' or 'traces'. With the latter there is no realization. With the former, the segmental realization is merely redundant: the underspecified, and even unspecified, segment is realized; there is no violation of substantiveness.

In terms of (121), the formatives in (119a,c) and (119b,d) are respectively 'acute' vs. 'non-acute' items, i.e. items associated with presence vs. absence of the extrasegmental acuteness/palatality feature **i**. The 'neutral' vowels, which are contrastively neither 'acute' nor 'non-acute', can appear in both 'acute' and 'non-acute' words, as in (119c-d). We can represent the relevant secondary features of 'acute' and 'non-acute' words respectively as in (123):

(123)　a.　{i}((*p*,{u,v},{u}) + (*t*,{v})) = *pöytä*
　　　　b.　((*p*,{u,v},{u}) + (*t*,{v})) = *pouta*

I have not given representations for the consonants or the syllable-internal structure, which are not pertinent here. The items respectively contain a non-local and, of course, non-linearized, or extrasegmental, {i}, indicated in (123a) by placement outside the sequence of syllables (which are all included within

Syntax and non-linearity 169

the outer round brackets), or they lack it, as in (123b). That is, the {i} is outside the segmental representation. Lexically, there seem to be no motivations for assigning a linear position to this {i}, or attributing to it an association beyond being a property of the lexical item.

The extrasegmental element, in terms of manifestation, is perhaps derivatively associated with the vowels as in (124a), where the single-headed arrows indicate the derived associations of the extrasegmental {i}:

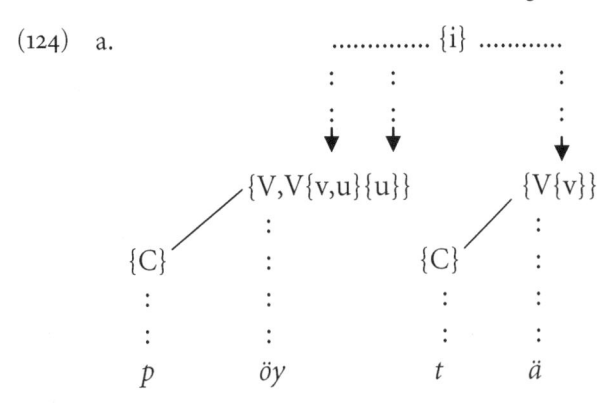

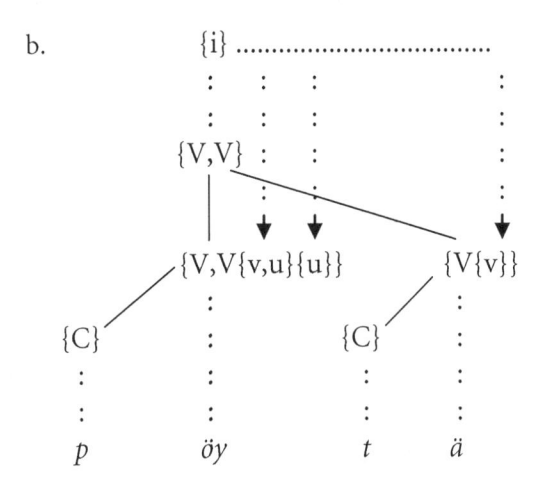

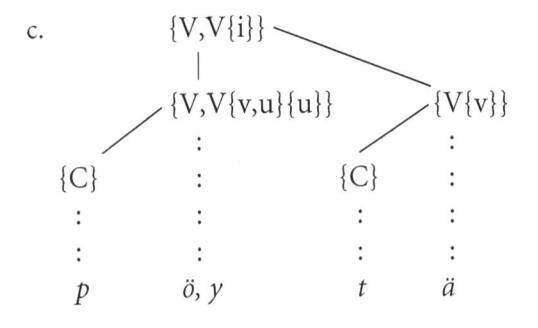

(124) a.

```
                ............. {i} ............
                  :   :              :
                  ▼   ▼              ▼
          ╱{V,V{v,u}{u}}        {V{v}}
     {C}'    :       {C}'   :
      :      :        :     :
      :      :        :     :
      p      öy       t     ä
```

b.

```
               {i} ..............................
                :   :   :                    :
               {V,V} :  :                    :
                │    :  :                    :
                ▼    ▼  ▼                    ▼
          ╱{V,V{v,u}{u}}         ╱{V{v}}
     {C}'    :       {C}'   :
      :      :        :     :
      :      :        :     :
      p      öy       t     ä
```

c.

```
           {V,V{i}}
              │       ╲
          ╱{V,V{v,u}{u}}      ╱{V{v}}
     {C}     :       {C}    :
      :      :        :     :
      :      :        :     :
      p     ö, y      t     ä
```

The representations in (124) also include primary categorizations, {C}, {V} (short), and {V,V} (long).

Anderson (1987a: §1), however, suggests that, instead of what is implied by (124a), the extrasegmental comes, as an intermediate stage, to be associated with the accented vowel, specifically with the accent node in the suprasegmental representation of the lexical item, as in (124b), where {V,V}, as phonological head of the item, governs the final {V{v}}. (124b) spells out how the extrasegmental is manifested by any eligible segment (in this case, any specified vowel) within its domain, where the domain is defined in terms of (124b) by the construction subordinate to the accent. However, given the convention—that the secondary features of a projected superjoined node are manifested within the domain of that node—we can represent the appropriate structure simply as in (124c). Of course, there needs to be a specification for each language of those segment types in which the extrasegmental is perceptually salient, or manifested (so-called 'rules of association' between extrasegmental, or 'autosegment', and segments).

The neutral vowels are apparently indifferent to the presence/absence of the extrasegmental element. This is because presence or absence of the extrasegmental {i} does not affect their realization, but merely ensures surface contrast between *e* and *ä*, as shown by comparison of the representations in (125), which shows the results of (122), where applicable, and the presence or absence of the extrasegmental of (124c):

(125) a. *i* = <{i}→>{i}
      b. *e* = <{i}→>{i,v}
      c. *ä* = {i}→{v}

The specification of the (optional) governing element (at the tail of the dependency arrow) in (125) is the extrasegmental. *i* and *e* are optionally dependent on a harmonic {i} (represented by the arrow in angles in (125a-b)); they can appear in a 'front' or a 'back' item. But this need have no effect on their manifestation. *ä*, on the other hand is always associated with harmonic {i}: cf. (125c). *e* and *ä* are thus in contrast only in 'acute' or 'front words'; and the former segment type contains a higher proportion of **i** than the latter, in combining inherent (though redundant) **i** and extrasegmental **i**. The two vowels are thus perceived as differing locally as respectively {i;v} vs. {v;i}, as in (120).

We thus might say that the contrastive segmental vowel system of Finnish is as in (126), given that a set of 'segmental' vowels—{u,i}, {u,v,i}, and {i;v} (in contrast with {v;i})—are products of harmony, in this case the presence of the extrasegmental {i} of the item in which they occur:

(126) the lexical vowel system of Finnish
    segmental   extrasegmental
        specified   {i}
        {u}
        {u,v}
        {v}
        unspecified
        { } 'i'
        { , } 'e'

We have a 'linear' specified segmental system, rather than a triangular system, for instance, as far as substantively specified segments are concerned.

But the system in (126) is still overspecified; **minimal specification** gives (127):

(127) the minimally specified lexical vowel system of Finnish
    {v}   {u}
                {u, }
    { , }   { }

That is, only the upper row in (127) is not marked as underspecified, given that *o* is conceived as spelling an underspecified vowel, represented {u, } rather than the 'fully specified' {u,v}. The full specification of *o* again results from application of (122a). In 'acute' words, the corresponding vowel, spelled *ö*, is specified as {i}→{u, }, with the **v** again being added by (122a).

The proposal of a minimally specified system is motivated by the pursuit of contrastivity: the fully specified system of (120) preserves redundancies eliminated in (121)—and (126) and, most thoroughly, (127). The adoption of minimal specification is a consequence of radical application of contrastivity to substantive representations as well as to the other aspects of phonological structure already considered, such as linearity. But, also, the underspecified system also provides the most simply characterized input to the harmony.

Suffixes in Finnish agree with their base/stem in presence versus absence of extrasegmental {i}. Thus, the suffix roughly characterized as in (128a) is manifested as in either (b) or (c):

(128)   a. *-st*{v} *illative*
          b. tyhmä-stä 'stupid' *illative*
          c. tuhma-sta 'naughty' *illative*

The extrasegmental thus 'spreads' to suffixes. This of course is not affected by whether or not the base/stem or an intervening affix contains an underspecified vowel, as in (129a); and, of course, these latter have no acuteness to 'spread' in the absence of the extrasegmental, as in (129b):

(129) a. lyö-dä-kse-ni-kö 'for me to hit'
      b. tuoli-lla 'on the chair', luo-da-kse-ni-ko 'for me to create'

Thus, if we assume base configurations like (123), further suffixes, as further dependents of the accented {V}, simply come within the domain of the extrasegmental associated with the accent, and it is unnecessary to think of this as properly 'spreading'; the 'spreading' in (130) is simply a consequence of the suffix vowel being included in the **accentual domain**, as spelled out in (130):

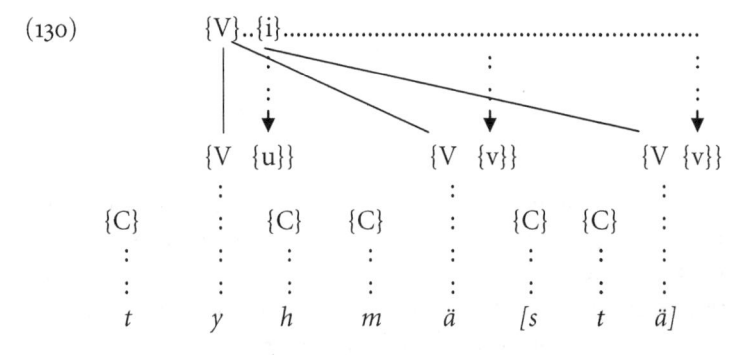

(130)

$$\{V\}..\{i\}$$

$$\{V\ \{u\}\} \qquad \{V\ \{v\}\} \qquad \{V\ \{v\}\}$$

$$\{C\} \quad \{C\} \quad \{C\} \quad \{C\} \quad \{C\}$$

t   y   h   m   ä   [s   t   ä]

This, of course, greatly oversimplifies the treatment of Finnish accent placement; (130) also omits the dependencies involving consonants, which are not our concern here.

This 'spreading' of an extrasegmental element to affixes is not something demanded directly by interface considerations, despite its substantive manifestation, except in terms of inertia, or perseveration. It is therefore to be expected that there are syntactic analogies to such phenomena, unless they are inhibited by properties of the syntactic-semantic interface. In both planes such persistences could be seen as serving to integrate the constructions involved—in the case of (lexical) phonology, the word. Before turning to consider the possible syntactic manifestations of this putative analogy, however, I need to comment on another aspect of harmony. This can be illustrated by the role of {v} segments in Turkish vowel harmony, in particular, their role in blocking 'roundness harmony'. And we now turn to this phenomenon. We shall find that 'blocking' is also a feature of the syntactic analogue to such phonological harmony systems.

4.2.2 Opacity in Turkish vowel harmony

(131) gives a fully specified representation of the Turkish vowel system, involving the dimensions acute (palatal), grave (rounded), and compact (low), with conventional spellings ('ı' is high-back-unrounded):

(131) *the fully specified Turkish vowel system*

palatal/acute	acute + round/grave	grave	—	
{i} 'i'	{i,u} 'y'	{u} 'u'	{ } 'ı'	—
{i,v} 'e'	{i,v,u} 'ö'	{u,v} 'o'	{v} 'a'	low/compact

Again we have evidence of harmony. In the first place, presence/absence of roundness, or gravity, is exhibited in each eligible vowel in the same simplex form in Turkish, as illustrated in (132a-b):

(132) a. demir 'anchor'
b. somun 'loaf'
c. kız-ın 'girl' *gen.*
d. gül-ü 'rose' *gen.*
e. havruz 'pot'
f. son-un 'end' *gen.*
g. kurd-lar 'worm' *pl.*
h. son-lar-ın 'end' *pl. gen.*

Eligible for harmony in gravity are vowels in initial syllables and non-compact vowels in subsequent syllables. The suffixes in (132c-d) also show such harmony.

Again the treatment I shall present here neglects phenomena not seen as directly relevant to the aspect under investigation, which involve in this instance opacity in harmony systems, as introduced immediately below. See e.g. S. R. Anderson 1980; Goldsmith 1990; van der Hulst and van de Weijer 1990; and Carr 1993: §10.2, for further exemplification, discussion and references relating to what continues to be yet another much investigated harmony phenomenon, that found in Turkish.

Gravity harmony presupposes a system such as (133), with again a division into segmentals and extrasegmentals:

(133) *the {u}-harmonic Turkish vowel system*

segmental			extrasegmental
palatal/acute	—		{u}
{i}	{ }	—	
{i,v}	{v}	low/compact	

The specified non-extrasegmental system is again not triangular but 'linear': {i}—{i,v}—{v}.

In initial syllables we have a contrast between [a] and [o], however, in forms that both seem to show the {u} extrasegmental elsewhere in the form, as illustrated in (132e) vs. (132f). There seems to be in initial syllables a {v} that harmonizes and one that does not. The interpretation of this situation has been controversial (see e.g. S. R. Anderson 1980; Clements and Sezer 1982). But let us take the {v} that does not harmonize, as in (132e), what I shall represent {v*}, vs. simple (harmonizing) {v}, as in (132f) or (132b), to be so marked as non-harmonic in the lexicon. A compact vowel in affixed forms such as the plural in (132g), compared with the first genitive in (f), not only does not accept the grave extrasegmental, but, as shown in the genitive plural in (132h), such a compact segment also blocks the further rightward 'spread' of the extrasegmental: in affixes it is **opaque**, rather than neutral. (132c) shows a corresponding 'non-grave' word with the same genitive. Such opacity as we find in (133h) is what I mainly want to illustrate here. In what follows I shall, for convenience, mark 'opaque {v}' as {v**}—though the opacity is a redundant property of non-initial {v}.

However, we should note at this point that Turkish also exhibits acuteness (front) harmony, which I shall now outline, to fill out the picture a little. It again 'moves' rightwards from the root, as illustrated by the possessed forms in (134a) and the plurals in (134b), compared with the possessed forms in (135c) and the plurals in (134d), which (latter) lack the acuteness extrasegmental:

(134) a. iz-i 'his footprint', demir-i 'his anchor', gül-ü 'his rose', čöl-i 'his desert'
 b. iz-ler 'footprints', gül-ler 'roses'
 c. baš-ı 'his head', kıč-ı 'his rump', kurd-u 'his worm'
 d. baš-lar 'heads', kıč-lar 'rumps', kurd-lar 'worms'
 e. gel-ijor-um 'I am coming'

There are also affixes in which acuteness harmony is blocked from rightward 'spread', as well as their introducing an extrasegmental grave: see (134e). But I shall not pursue these complications here.[34]

---

[34] Thus, as acknowledged, this brief account of an analysis of Turkish vowel harmony omits of course some important details. (i) provides some further examples of the progressive in (134e), the second syllable of which introduces a new roundness/gravity domain:

(i) a. isin-ijor-um 'I am warming'
 b. sor-ujor-um 'I am asking'
 c. gel-ijor-um 'I am coming'
 d. gyl-yjor-um 'I am laughing'

What is particularly relevant to our ongoing concerns, however, is the introduction by the first suffix in (134e) of a new **domain** for roundness harmony, within the (non-grave) domain established by the root. This notion of triggers for new domains will also assume some importance in our look at an analogy for harmony in the syntax. Now let us return, however, to the Turkish phonological system, to complete our schematic picture of harmony there.

The presence of the second harmony means that the basic set of non-extrasegmental lexical segmental vowels is even smaller than shown in (133). Indeed, it is limited to that in (135a), whose members combine with the extrasegmentals in (135b) to give other possibilities:

(135)   a. *the harmonic segmental lexical vowel system of Turkish*
          {v}   { }
     b. *extrasegmentals*
          {i}   {u}

As indicated in (134c-d), {v} is manifested as [a] and (with the acuteness extrasegmental of (134b)) as [e]; and (with the gravity extrasegmental, as in

In (ia) the base does not show gravity; it is a property of the first affix, whose second vowel is, segmentally, {v}; as the first vowel in a domain, it does not reject the gravity extrasegmental. In (ib) both the base and the affixes show gravity, but presumably independently. (ic-d) show that this first affix blocks further 'spread' of the acuteness extrasegmental of the base; they differ in that the base in (d) is grave, while that in (c) is not. This affix thus introduces, in different ways, a new domain as far as both extrasegmentals are concerned.

Another substantial omission from the account given in the text is acknowledgment of the existence of 'stable disharmonic roots' (Clements and Sezer 1982). The Turkish harmony system seems to be in comparative decline, and there is a substantial set of roots well established in the language that are disharmonic in particular ways. These roots all lack the vowels [y, ø, i]. This and various other properties of this set of roots can be characterized as in (ii):

(ii)   principle I: only one extrasegmental is allowed to attach to any one segment
      principle II: the { } segment cannot remain empty
      principle III: an extrasegmental need not attach to {v}

These generalizations underlie the forms in (iii):

(iii)   a. muzip 'mischievous', billur 'crystal'
      b. cesur 'brave', bobbin 'news, message'
      c. fiat 'price', haber 'spool'

The examples in (iiia) illustrate forms conforming to principle I in (ii), where the segmental vowels are all { }, but all filled in some way, in conformity with principle II; and the second vowel in each of (iiib) is also segmentally empty, but again filled, variously. The first vowels in each of (iiib) and the second in example two in (iiic) have segmental {v}. But the first vowel in that example and the second in the other show an unharmonic {v}, allowed for by principle III.

As indicated, I do not go further into the analysis of Turkish vowels here, however. My main object has been to give some substance to the notion of blocking of extrasegmental 'spreading'.

176   *Phonology-Syntax Analogies*

(133e) as [o]; and as [ø] (with both, as in (134a)). We have perceived realizations {v} [a], {v,i} [e], {v,u} [o], and {v,i,u} [ø]. {} is correspondingly manifested as { } [i], {i} [i], {u} [u], and {i,u} [y].

Since the accent in Turkish is generally specifically word-final (Poser 1984: 128, cited in Halle and Vergnaud 1987: 53), the domain for the 'spread' of the {u} and {i} features is presumably morphologically rather than accentually determined, as 'moving' rightwards through the affixes in a word, where this is not blocked by an opaque vowel. I thus interpret {u} and {i} as extrasegmental features that come to be associated with the morphological root, but are manifested throughout the word form, as shown in (136a):

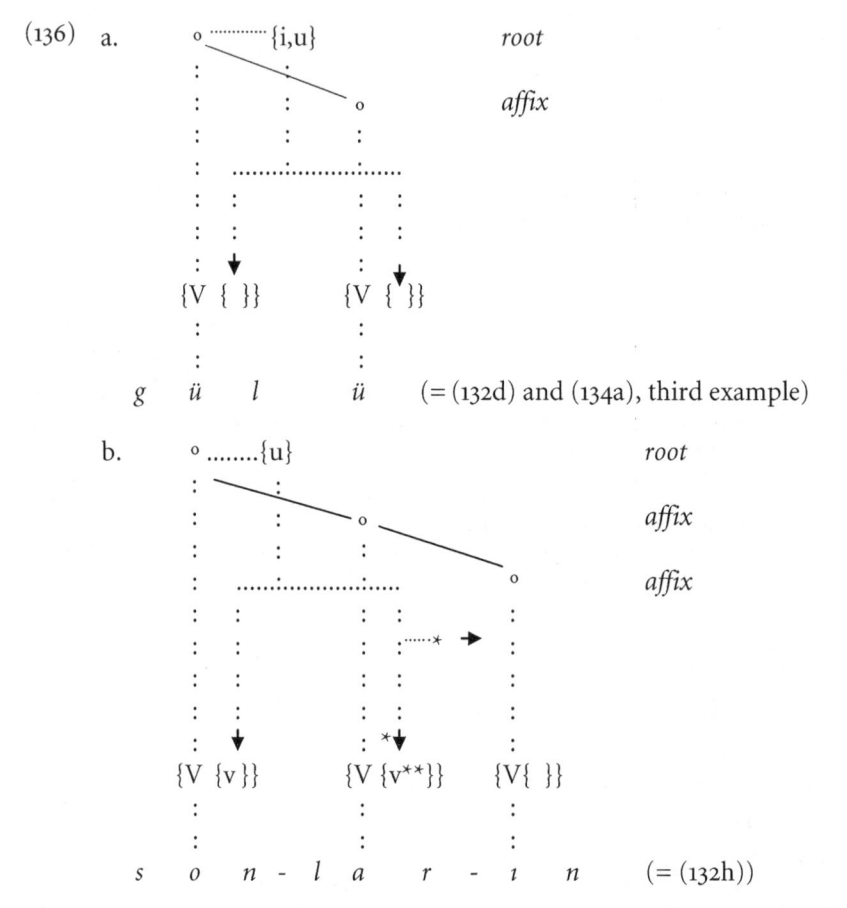

(136) a.   o ········· {i,u}   root
                                  o   affix

                       {V { }}   {V { }}

                  g   ü   l   ü   (= (132d) and (134a), third example)

       b.   o ········{u}   root
                                  o   affix
                                             o   affix

                       {V {v}}   {V {v**}}   {V{ }}

                  s   o   n - l   a   r - ı   n   (= (132h))

c. o .... {i}   root

                      o   affix

                              o   affix
                         ....{u}

                         *i̯

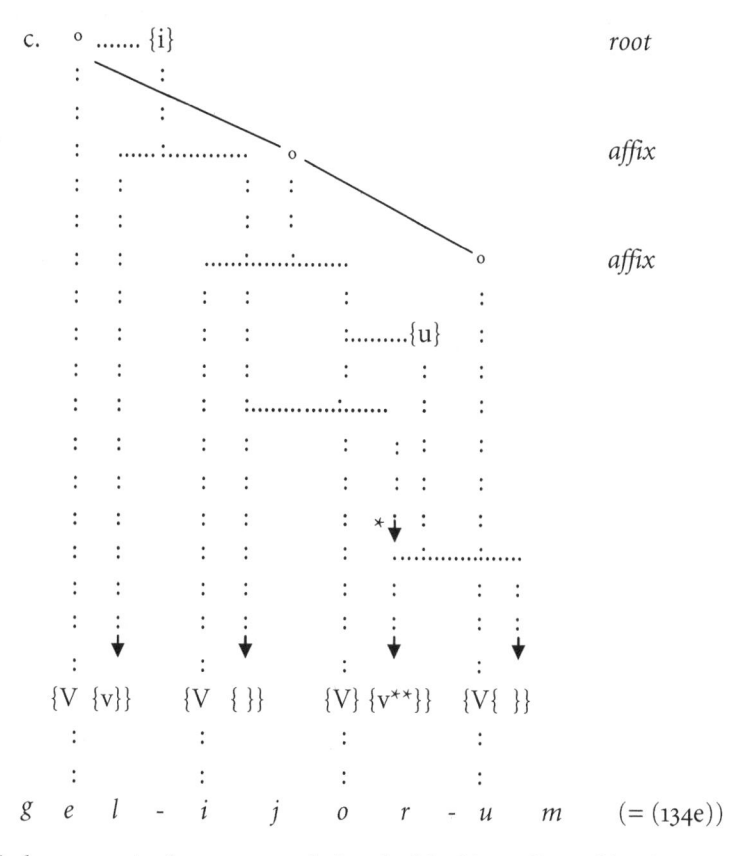

    {V {v}} {V { }} {V} {v**}} {V{ }}

    g e l - i   j o   r - u   m   (= (134e))

(136b) shows gravity harmony, and also the blocking effect of {v**}. The {v**} in (136c) blocks the 'spread' of acuteness, and is also associated as part of the second suffix with a roundness/gravity suprasegmental that establishes a new domain.

The arcs in these representations in (136) are morphological. Recall that morphological structures do not introduce, as labels for the nodes, an alphabet distinct from those of phonology and syntax; the representations are 'bare trees' (the labels on the right of (136) are expository only). I take the root, the obligatory component of any word, to be the head, rather than any affix, even if the affix signals the word class of the word (as in *kind-ness*—see e.g. Anderson 1992: §2.3): signalling a change in word class (a change in syntactic category) does not warrant the attribution of morphological headhood to that signal.

The combinations of segmental and extrasegmentals are spelled out more explicitly than above, and exemplified, in (137):

(137) Turkish extrasegmental associations and realizations

segment	extra	realization	example
o = {v}←{u}		{u,v}	son 'end'
u = { }←{u}		{u}	kurd 'worm'
e = {v}←{i}		{i,v}	sebep 'reason'
i = { }←{i}		{i}	is 'footprint'
ø = {v}←{i,u}		{i,u,v}	čöl 'desert'
y = { }←{i,u}		{i,u}	gül 'rose'
a = {v}		{v}	baš 'head'
ɨ = { }		{ }	kɨč 'rump'

The 'non-high' vowels are all based on the specified vowel {v}. And the unspecified vowel { } is manifested as the rest of the possibilities—[ɨ] (without extrasegmental), [i] (with acuteness only), [u] (with gravity only), and [y] (with both).

Only the colourless vowel [ɨ], with no associated extrasegmental, emerges as incomplete, as intrinsically a neutral vowel, whose realization interprets the absence of any positive secondary feature as neutrality with respect to the perceptual dimensions associated with the features. Correlating with this, [ɨ] is also the epenthesis vowel which breaks up clusters in loanwords in the absence in the word of rounding and frontness, as in [kɨravat].

Turkish harmony provides evidence for both left-right directionality of the 'spreading' of (some) extrasegmentals and for the possibility of there being 'blocking' segment types, as with {v**}, illustrated in (136b-c). We have also seen the possibility of the introduction of a new subdomain of a harmony, as in (136c). In the next subsection we turn to a syntactic analogue of harmony in phonology that displays detailed similarities to the phenomena we have been looking at in Finnish and Turkish.

4.2.3 Sequence of tense as harmony

The word-sized phonological phenomena we have been looking at seem to be paralleled by 'sentence-sized' properties in syntax. I suggest in particular that we find an analogy to the 'spreading' of a phonological secondary category, exemplified by (130), in syntactic phenomena like 'sequence of tenses' (as described by e.g. Chung and Timberlake 1985: 212–13):

Syntax and non-linearity 179

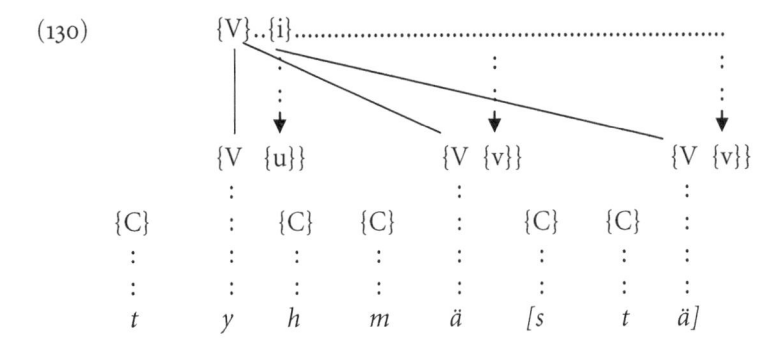

(130)

```
            {V}..{i}...............................................
             |       ⋮                ⋮              ⋮
             ↓       ⋮                ↓              ↓
           {V {u}}                 {V {v}}        {V {v}}
             ⋮                        ⋮              ⋮
   {C}   ⋮   {C}     {C}    ⋮       {C}    {C}    ⋮
    ⋮    ⋮    ⋮       ⋮     ⋮        ⋮      ⋮     ⋮
    ⋮    ⋮    ⋮       ⋮     ⋮        ⋮      ⋮     ⋮
    t    y    h       m     ä        [s     t     ä]
```

Declerck (e.g. 1988) argues persuasively against the traditional 'formal', or purely morphosyntactic view of 'sequence of tenses' adopted by Comrie (1986), and also shows that such phenomena are not limited to classic 'sequence of tenses' circumstances.

The trans-planar analogy is quite detailed, in, for instance, extending into a syntactic equivalent to the 'blocking' effect of opaque segments, as just illustrated in relation to the phonology of Turkish. In the first instance, however, compare with the representation of Finnish harmonic 'spreading' in (130) the (in many respects much simplified) representation in (138a) showing 'sequence of tense' in English:

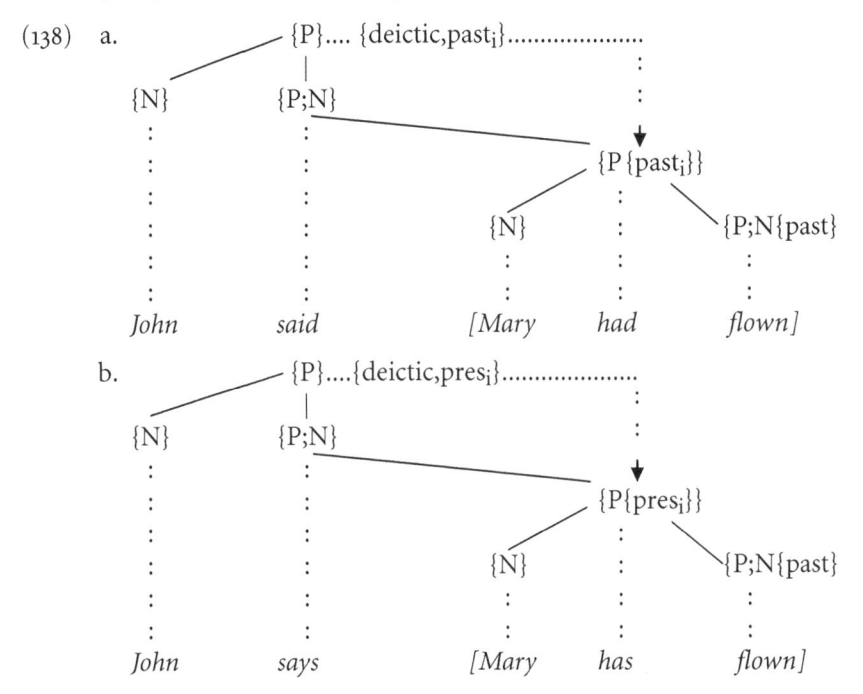

(138) a.

```
              ╱─ {P}....{deictic,past_i}......................
             ╱     |                              ⋮
         {N}    {P;N}                             ⋮
          ⋮      ⋮  ╲                             ⋮
          ⋮      ⋮   ╲                          ↓
          ⋮      ⋮    ╲                      {P {past_i}}
          ⋮      ⋮     ╲         ⋮          ╱      ╲
          ⋮      ⋮      ╲      {N}   ⋮    ╱        ╲{P;N{past}
          ⋮      ⋮       ╲      ⋮    ⋮             ⋮
          ⋮      ⋮        ╲     ⋮    ⋮             ⋮
          ⋮      ⋮               ⋮                 ⋮
         John   said          [Mary    had       flown]
```

b.

```
              ╱─ {P}....{deictic,pres_i}......................
             ╱     |                              ⋮
         {N}    {P;N}                             ⋮
          ⋮      ⋮  ╲                             ⋮
          ⋮      ⋮   ╲                          ↓
          ⋮      ⋮    ╲                      {P{pres_i}}
          ⋮      ⋮     ╲         ⋮          ╱      ╲
          ⋮      ⋮      ╲      {N}   ⋮    ╱        ╲{P;N{past}
          ⋮      ⋮       ╲      ⋮    ⋮             ⋮
          ⋮      ⋮        ╲     ⋮    ⋮             ⋮
          ⋮      ⋮               ⋮                 ⋮
         John   says           [Mary   has       flown]
```

Normally, the 'verb of saying' that is past and has a particular time reference, indicated by the subscript variable on 'past', requires that a subordinate {P} be past and have the time reference associated with the 'verb of saying'. The {past$_i$} in (138a) is a deictic past, past with respect to the moment of speaking. {pres} in (138b) has a similar status. Such a notation presupposes that generics lack both features, as was assumed in the discussion of tense in Volume II.

The harmony is expressed in a more complex fashion than in the phonology. Some differences between (130) and (138) arise from the fact that *said/say* in (138) realizes a complex category, with the specification for a lexical verb subjoined to the finiteness category, and realized as a single word form. But {past} is a secondary category of the finiteness element expounded (along with other elements) as *said*, and reflected in its morphology, just as {i} is associated with the accent in (130) and reflected in the segmental vowel. These are both secondary features that can 'spread' from heads (phonological, morphological, or syntactic) through the domain subordinate to the head, and are manifested in eligible elements within that domain. This was illustrated for phonological harmony in (130). And in (138), for instance, the dependent finite is within the domain of the **sentential past**, which is thus 'spread' to that dependent, if, as here, the {past} feature is attached initially to an appropriate predicator, such as a 'verb of saying'.

But there are major differences between (130) and (138) that mainly have to do with the different relation of the two planes to the lexicon and the semanticity of the categories of syntax, including in some cases, as here, referentiality. Phonological extrasegmentals are associated with lexical elements (roots and affixes) that are realized by the segments that will manifest the effect of the extrasegmental transmitted via the head of that lexical element. They are typically a property of whole lexical units, the expressional unity of whose forms they enhance. In the syntax the 'spreading' feature is also associated from the start only with a particular primary category, not a whole sentence, which is not a category—even though in a sense the feature 'spreads' through this sentence, again enhancing its unity. But the mechanism of 'spreading' is a form of 'agreement' and co-indexing. {past} is an independent property of the lower {P} in (138a), it is interpreted as co-referential with the {past} of the upper {P}, and co-indexed accordingly. In this respect the diagramming in (138) is rather misleading: there is 'feature-spreading' only in a rather special sense.

This asymmetry between phonology and syntax is a consequence of the restrictive assumption that, unlike lexical items, sentences or sub-sentential constructions (unless idioms—i.e. complex lexical items) are not listed in the lexicon; they are projections of the categorial information associated with the words in the lexicon that come to head the clause or other constructions. The lexicon provides lexical elements, it does not provide sentences or sentence structures or sentential templates. Words are the default maximal lexical unit; multi-word idioms are marked as exceptional. Neither sentences nor the schematizations that describe regular constructions are lexical units; regular constructions are the product of syntactic rules, specifically projections of lexical items, particularly of the head of the construction.

This difference between syntactic and phonological harmony is dictated ultimately by the different manners in which the syntax and phonology interface with the lexicon; and this difference involves ultimately the 'double articulation' associated with the linguistic sign. Both extrasegmental phonological and syntactic sentential features are associated with lexical elements, often (always in the case of the syntax) the morphologically maximal element, the word; but the potentially (morphologically and phonologically) linearized internal structure of the word is not accessible to the syntax, only the syntactic categorization (as discussed in Volume II of this trilogy). And, in accordance with inalterability (see again Anderson 2006b: §3.1.2), syntactic elements do not 'move around': 'spreading' is necessarily by agreement and co-indexing. The phonological extrasegmental, on the other hand, is a property of the whole phonological pole of the lexical item—though its salience throughout the pole is variable with respect to particular segment types.

Nevertheless, though it is associated in the lexicon with some particular lexical item, the domain of a sentential feature (trivially) lies outside the word. And this, reflecting its capacity to 'spread', correlates with a further property noted above: the $\{past_i\}$ of the sentential head in (138a) is deictic, it locates the scene described with reference to the situation, and particularly the time, of utterance. Capacity for deixis, or more generally extralinguistic reference, is a property of functional categories. The functional categories enable dependent lexical categories to fulfil certain syntactic functions: {P} confers finiteness on a construction; {N}, determiner, makes a dependent noun into a potential argument. But they can also introduce referential features that are relevant to the interpretation of the construction as a whole; and these features may be signalled at different points in the construction. The $\{past_i\}$ of the verb of 'saying' requires a subordinate {P} that shows sequence of tenses to agree in pastness and to acquire the time reference of the verb of 'saying'. The pastness as such does not spread in this case, it is a lexical property of the verb form; it is the time reference that is the 'spreading' property.[35]

---

[35] Ultimately, it is appropriate to restrict the capacity to introduce extralinguistic reference to just {N}. In the present instance, of tense, this would depend on analysis of this verbal category as being itself categorially complex, with an {N} component that tense is attached to as a secondary category. I take this up below; and see further particularly §7.1.

It may clarify what is involved if we deconstruct the reference of tense features in such a way that the functioning of the variable index is made more explicit. I suggest, as a starting point, the following:

the structure of tense reference
Let T_S be the time of speaking, and let T_i be the time referred to.
Then deictic $\{past_i\} = T_i <$ (precedes) T_S, and $\{pres_i\} = T_i \supset$ (includes) T_S.

This now interprets more explicitly the referential indexing and orientation of a feature system involving past and its absence, where past is '$T_i < T$'. Past and its absence are expressed by particular forms of the verb; present is replaced in this account by absence of past; present is the default, and we no longer need to allow for generics as having neither {past} nor {pres}, as envisaged in e.g. the description of Latin verbals in §II.3.3.1. Generics are unrestricted presents in terms of the above deconstruction—an unrestricted T_i that includes T_S. Sequence of tenses involves agreement in the form of the verb (past vs. non-past} and 'spreading' of the tense-referential specification.

We can then represent sequence of tense more adequately if instead of (138) we have (138)*, involving the complex secondary features suggested above:

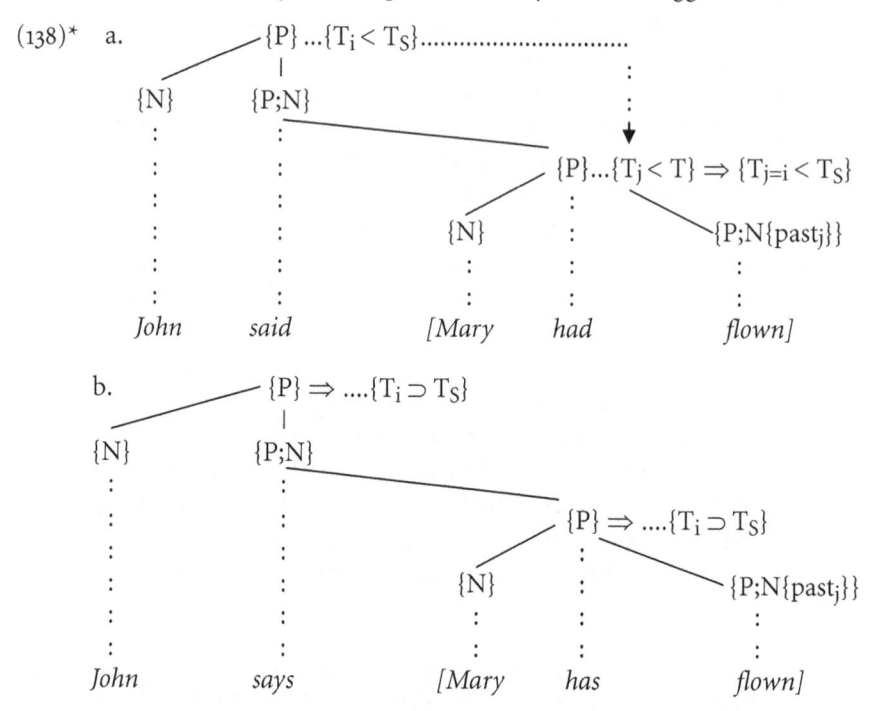

(138)* a.

$\{P\}...\{T_i < T_S\}$

{N}   {P;N}

$\{P\}...\{T_j < T\} \Rightarrow \{T_{j=i} < T_S\}$

{N}

$\{P;N\{past_j\}\}$

John   said   [Mary   had   flown]

b.

$\{P\} \Rightarrow ....\{T_i \supset T_S\}$

{N}   {P;N}

$\{P\} \Rightarrow ....\{T_i \supset T_S\}$

{N}

$\{P;N\{past_j\}\}$

John   says   [Mary   has   flown]

I ignore the past associated with *left* for the moment. What is 'spread' in (138a)*, for instance, is the identity of T_S and the equation of i and j. In the absence of a positive selection of past, the default present is introduced—as indicated by the double-shafted arrow in (138b)*. And in this case there is no harmony.

The tense feature associated with *said* is deictic, then—its specified tense reference is directly oriented with respect to T_S. It thus constitutes an **absolute tense**. For the tense feature to 'spread', any {P} within its domain that is to be susceptible to it must not be deictic, i.e. it must not have its tense reference specified relative to T_S. *Had* in (138a)* has an oriented time reference but what it is oriented toward is not specified. This is introduced by harmony with the upper {P}. Or, rather, the lower {P}, agrees with the upper in tense reference.

Even though the lower {P;N} in both of (138) bears a past feature, it is not oriented in direct relation to the moment of speech. In (138a) it is past with respect to the deictic past of the main verb: it is a **relative tense**. Similarly, in (138b) it is past relative to the reference of the governing {P}, this is $T_i \supset T_S$ by default. The past of the {P;N} does not directly involve extralinguistic reference. We can represent its tense reference as '$\{T_j < T_i\}$', where in $\{T_i\}$ is the reference of the {P} that governs the past {P;N}, whether it is $\{T_S\}$ or a 'spread' $\{T_i\}$. We can incorporate this in our description of the structure of tense reference as:

the structure of tense reference*
Let T_S be the time of speaking, and let T_i be the time referred to.
Then deictic $\{past_i\} = T_i < T_S$, and $\{pres_i\} = T_i \supset T_S$.
Relative $\{past_j\} = T_j < T_i$, where $T_i \rightarrow T_j$.

Recall that the single-shafted arrow indicates government, so that in this formulation T_j is dependent on T_i. Here the relative past is oriented as prior to a governing tense reference, whatever it is.

The representation for the perfect in (138) is thus an interpretation of various proposals that central instances of the 'perfect *have*' construction involve an 'embedded past' (see e.g. Poutsma 1926: 209; Jespersen 1931: §4.1; Huddleston 1969: §4; McCawley 1971; Anderson 1972: §XVI, 1973b, 1976b, and much other work). One variant of such a proposal is embodied in (138). The verbal sequence in (138a) governed by the lower {P} is doubly past, but neither involves independent deixis: the sequence contains a harmonizing past and a past relative to it. And this is reflected in the morphology of the finite verb and the presence of the '*have*-periphrasis'. The important observation is that neither of the pasts in (138a)—associated with the lower {P} or {P;N}—is distinctly deictic, or absolute, in the sense introduced above.

Similarly, the predicator of the lower clause in (139a), on the relevant interpretation, bears no independent past feature itself, merely the 'spread' one, and so is oriented as non-past with respect to the past tense of the main verb—to which it is identical in reference.

(139) a. John said (that) Mary flew

     b. $\{P\{T_i < T_S\}\}$ $\{P\{T_i < T_S\}\}$
            | |
        $\{P;N\}$ $\{P;N\}$

     c. $\{T_i < T_S\}$ $\{P\{T_i < T_S\}\}$
                              |
                         $\{P;N\{T_j < T_i\}\}$

The basis for this interpretation is represented in (138b). Unlike the subordinate verbals in (138a), it is not 'doubly past' in form: it marks—on the relevant interpretation, where the time reference of the two verbs is not disjoint—only the 'spread' pastness of the main clause verb. There is, of course, another interpretation of (139a), where the time reference of the two verbs is disjoint, whereby the lower verb involves a new relative tense, past relative to the tense reference of *said*.

This second interpretation of (139a) is made more unambiguously by use of the *have* periphrasis, as in (138a)*. Note, too, that the internal structure of the verbs in (139) has $\{P;N\}$ governed by $\{P\}$. Say, then, that as in the lower clause in (138)*, the $\{P;N\}$ component of the lower verb of the (139a) is, on this second interpretation, as expressed in (139c), i.e. the $\{P;N\}$ is again associated with a relative past, and harmony has occurred in this case too. That is, after all, there is harmony in both cases, and the two interpretations of (139a) differ in the absence vs. the presence of a relative tense. Non-deictic pasts of verbs may or may not have a relative past as their $\{P;N\}$ component. Recall that initial-syllable $\{v^*\}$ in Turkish was distinctive in not participating in harmony. Initial $\{v\}$ in Turkish, which may harmonize or not, is illustrated by (132b,f) vs. (132e):

(132) b. somun 'loaf'
        e. havruz 'pot'
        f. son-un 'end' *gen.*

The non-harmonic 'a' in (132e) was lexically marked as '$\{v^*\}$'. The initial deictic verb in (138)* and (139) is distinctive in that its subjoined $\{P;N\}$ cannot be a relative past.

Consider now the sentence in (140a), with successive 'saying/thinking' verbs:

(140) a. John said (that) Bill thinks (that) Mary flew
 b. $\{T_i < T_S\}$ $<\{T_j \supset T_S\}>$ $\{T_k < T_i\}$
 c. $\{T_i < T_S\}$ $<\{T_j \supset T_S\}>$ $\{T_i \supset T_S\}$

In (140a) a non-past intervenes between the two pasts, and rejects harmony; it is the equivalent of the unspecified **neutral** vowels 'i' and 'e' in Finnish, illustrated by (119c-d):

(119) a. pöytä 'table', käyrä 'curve', tyhmä 'stupid'
 b. pouta 'fine weather', kaura 'oats', tuhma 'naughty'
 c. värttinä 'spinning-wheel', kesy 'tame'
 d. palttina 'linen cloth', verho 'curtain'

And, as in Finnish, the neutral verb with default tense doesn't prevent 'spread' of the harmony. *Flew* in (140) shows the same two possibilities as in (130). The flying is either coeval with the saying—as, say, a habitual activity—or it is relative to it, as it would be in *John said (that) Bill thinks (that) Mary had flown*.

In (141a), however, the intervening verb construction is in tense a deictic future:

(141) a. John said (that) Bill will think (that) Mary flew
 b. $\{T_i < T_S\}$ $\{T_j \geq T_S\}$ $\{T_k < T_j\}$

We can interpret a future-referring {P}, of which *will* is the unmarked exemplar, as in the addition to the structure of tense reference in:

the structure of tense reference*

Let T_S be the time of speaking, and let T_i be the time referred to.
Then deictic $\{past_i\} = T_i < T_S$, and $\{pres_i\} = T_i \supset T_S$, and $\{future_i\} = T_i \geq T_S$.
Relative $\{past_j\} = T_j < T_i$, where $T_i \rightarrow T_j$.

The '$\geq$' relation allows for items like *will* to refer to the present, when they are being purely predictive about a present situation (*That'll be the postman*), as well as future-referring. This specification is attached to *will think* in (141a), as indicated in (141b). This deictic tense blocks the spread of pastness harmony, and introduces a new domain. As shown in (141b) the past of *flew* is interpreted as relative to the tense of *will think*.

Compare here the role of Turkish {v**} in (136c):

(136) c.

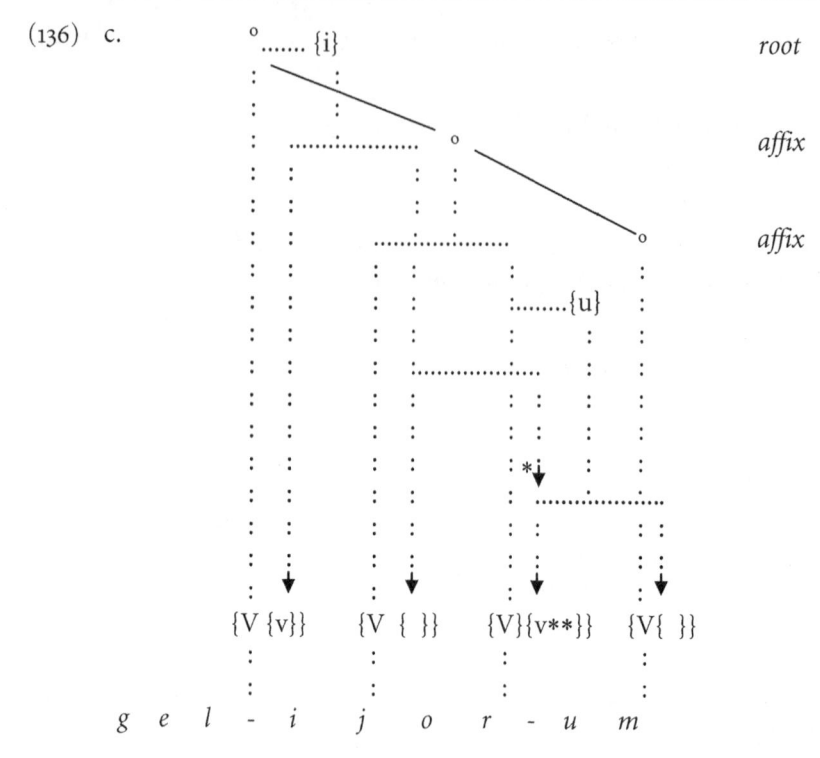

```
         o........{i}                                    root
          \
           \
            ........:.......o                            affix
                            \
                             \
                              ........:.......o         affix
                                     :......{u}
                                        *↓
              ↓           ↓           ↓           ↓
           {V {v}}     {V { }}    {V}{v**}}    {V{ }}
              :          :          :           :
              :          :          :           :
            g  e    -   i      j    o    r  -  u    m
```

{v**} blocks the frontness harmony and initiates roundness harmony.

The syntactic harmonies we have looked at are all inter-clausal, analogous with harmony into affixes. Evidence for an intra-clausal role for sentential tense, perhaps analogous to the operation of vowel harmony within roots as well as into affixes, derives from its interpretative manifestation throughout the clause. What is relevant here is not merely that inherently tensed temporal circumstantials such as that in (142a) must agree with the clause's tense, and indeed they may make its reference more precise by identifying the reference 'spread' from the verb with (a point within) some calendrical index—with the verb and adverbial thus complementing each other:

(142) a. She left last Tuesday
    b. She left on Tuesday
    c. Last Tuesday will live in my memory
    d. My souvenir will be last Tuesday
    e. She had left the previous Tuesday
    f. He knows/knew her daughter by a previous marriage
    g. She will leave on Tuesday
    h. She leaves on Tuesday

More important still is that other temporals not specified for tense are interpreted in accordance with the sentential element, as in (142b). *Tuesday* in (142b) must agree with the tense of the verb and share its reference by harmony, and, indeed, again localize it more precisely, as happens in appositions such as *the idea that he wanted it* (recall §5.3 in Volume I). *Last*, on the other hand, is independently deictic, just like absolute verbal tense, as is evident when there is no agreement with a verbal tense, as in (142c-d). Thus, in the case of the circumstantials in (142a-b) we have referential harmony in (142b), but merely referential compatibility in (141a). But the participants in (142c-d) reject harmony. On agreement in tensing between verbal and existential complements see Anderson (1973a,b, 1976b).

The *previous* of (142e-f) is relative past, on the other hand. But it is at least anchored as a relative to the T_i of the verbal, whether it is present, past, or doubly past. The referentiality of the verbal is once more available interpretatively throughout the clause. (142g), on the other hand, again illustrates simple harmony: *Tuesday* assumes the future reference of the operative, and makes it more exact. But in (142h) it is also future in reference; as a circumstantial it is either future-referring or past-referring—whereas, of course, *Tomorrow* is future-referring and *Yesterday* past-referring. The present reference—'$T_i \supset T_S$'—of the verbal in (142h), however, is compatible with specification of a future point—'$T_j > T_S$' in this case—within what is envisaged as the present, no matter how great the envisaged extent of it. The verbal present introduces a connection of the future event with the present that may be interpreted in various ways—as involving planning, or compulsion, for instance. Moreover, this reference to the present selects future rather than past as the interpretation of *Tuesday*.

Despite such complications, discussed here rather informally, the analogy with phonological harmony seems clear. In the case of (142b,g,h), in particular, the tense-referential content of the verbal has been 'spread' throughout the clause, just as an extrasegmental phonological feature is manifested at various points throughout the root. In the phonology, vowels within a harmonic item manifest the extrasegmental element; but temporal elements throughout the clause are interpreted in accordance with the clausal tense element, whether deictic or 'spread'. (142b) illustrates that the harmony need not be expressed; it is a matter of interpretation. This is intimately associated with the substance of the two planes, the plane of expression and the plane of content. The harmony in each case involves the characteristic substance, sound-perceptual vs. conceptual.

This striking difference between harmony in the two planes follows from the observation that the tensing of *Tuesday* in (142b) is not reflected in the morphology. Thus, the substance of syntax—say 'pastness'—may not be signalled at all eligible points in a domain, but the manifestation of phonology directly reflects the distribution of phonological categories. This difference has to do with the relationship between the planes determined by the 'double articulation' and with the nature of the two substances at the respective interfaces, which, among other things, require of phonology direct temporality and articulatory continuity, and, on the other hand, require of syntax a more richly endowed geometry of categories whose semantic content, or interpretation, may not all be overtly expressed. However, the agreement has interpretative reality, and this discrepancy, which is in accord with the architecture of language, does not obscure the basis for the harmonic analogy.

A consideration of intra-clausal tense harmony reveals, of course, that some manifestations of tense harmony are apparently associated with agreement between different syntactic categories (verb vs. adverb, for instance), while before we were concerned with specifically 'vowel harmony' (rather than, say, harmony between consonants—which of course is also attested). But also, typically, susceptible intervening consonants will manifest the vowel-harmonic feature to varying extents, given the role of vowel articulation as the background on which the syllable structure is built (as discussed in §3.3); the 'spreading' is more continuously perceived than the representations deployed in the preceding would suggest. Thus the signalling of the same feature by different categories is not limited to the syntax.

However, there are also reasons for thinking that the structure of verbal tense may have more in common with the expression of tense as a circumstantial locative than I have allowed for here (as is indeed proposed in §3.4 of Volume II, and pursued in Chapter 6 below). There it is suggested that pastness is not associated directly with {P} but with a locative {N} incorporated in {P}, in the same way as person-number agreement involves lexical incorporation into the verbal of functor and {N} (cf. Anderson 1976a: §3.2.4). Thus, in (142a-b), past reference would be associated in both the verbal and the circumstantial with an {N}: we would have a configuration we can abbreviate as '{loc} → {N{T_i < T}}'. In terms of our deconstruction of tense reference the 'T' of 'T_S' and 'T_i' is a feature of {N}. If this is the case, at least sequence of tense and person-number agreement both involve not just secondary features of a functional category but specifically of determiner—as is appropriate to their referential character.

And notice finally that there are possibly further analogies. Parallel to {i}, which is extrasegmental in Finnish, though in other systems it is segmental, the secondary category past, as well as being sentential, can also occur 'non-sententially', the equivalent of 'intra-segmentally'; i.e. there is also, as we have observed, a {P;N}-anchored relative past, manifested as the past participle.

For instance, the sentences in (138) were interpreted in such terms. Thus both 'sentential' and verb-anchored past occur in English. Is there a phonological analogy? The plausibility of establishing the coexistence in a single language of an extrasegmental and segmental occurrence of the same feature in the phonology partly depends on the choice of (secondary) features. It is much more evident in terms of perceptually based systems of features—such as those (in varying respects 'perceptually based') of Jakobson, Fant, and Halle (1952), Anderson and Ewen (1987), or van der Hulst (1994), wherein the contents of vowels and consonants have more in common than traditional articulatory-based systems.

And, indeed, we associated 'i' in Finnish with both the extrasegmental and the segmental system, as expressed in (126):

(126) the lexical vowel system of Finnish
      segmental   extrasegmental
         specified   {i}
         {u}
         {u,v}
         {v}
         unspecified
         { } 'i'
         { , } 'e'

{i} occurs both as an unspecified filler and as an extrasegmental.

Let us now look more carefully at the two pasts of the subordinate verbal sequence of (138a). Similarly, (143a), on the unmarked interpretation, involves both a sentential (deictic) past and a verb-anchored, and relative, past, whereas has/have + 'past participle' in (143b), as in (138b), contains only a relative one:

(143) a. She had left
       b. She has left (*last/on Tuesday)
       c. She had left the day before
       d. She may have left (last/on Tuesday)
       e. She seems to have left (on Tuesday)
       f. She seems to leave on Tuesday(s)

A finite like that in (143b) is interpreted as having clausal non-past reference in the absence of signalling of the sentential {past} feature; hence (143b) has 'present relevance' (as it is sometimes put). It also has non-specific past time reference for the 'leaving' event itself relative to the tense of the finite. Within the domain established by the deictic present tense of the finite the relative tense of the participle is incompatible with definite past time reference, as illustrated by the bracketed, and unacceptable, continuations in (143b). An event wholly preceding the time of utterance cannot be reconciled with the characterization of present as '$\{T_j \supset T_S\}$'. Introduction of a definite past reference such as is associated with *last Tuesday* is incompatible with the present reference of the clause; its effect would be to convert the perfect into a past—as has indeed happened in the history of various languages—though dual possible interpretations of a 'perfect' may persist. Non-definite reference within a period extending to the present is, of course, unproblematical, as in *I have met her on several occasions (in the past)*.

The verbal construction of (143a) is capable of definite past reference relative to another past time reference, as illustrated by (143c). Moreover, the non-finite *have*-construction in (143d) is compatible with definite past time reference, as indicated by the acceptability of the bracketed temporals. In the case of (143a/c) subordination to a past {P} removes the restriction on definite past reference. This is unsurprising, of course, since the relative past is now outside the domain of the present. In (146d) the *have* itself is subordinate and non-finite, and untensed. Compare (146e) that also allows definite past time reference. The presence of the non-finite 'blocks' any affects of presentness: the past {P;N} is no longer directly dependent on the present {P}. The past participle introduces a surrogate deictic past, and contrasts with the present of (146f), which as such is interpreted as imperfective (see further §4.5), given the characterization as '$\{T_i \supset T_S\}$'. The identity of the governor of the past participle determines whether it behaves as a perfect (when dependent on present {P}) or not.

If the deictic past of these participles is again interpreted as attached to an incorporated locative {N}, as with the clausal past, then again 'spreading' involves the functional category determiner.

Even the relative verb-anchored past of the 'perfect *have*' construction may also 'spread' 'extra-clausally', or rather into a subordinate clause, in some circumstances. So it can establish a new domain if the past is again associated with a 'verb of saying or thinking', as illustrated by (144a), where, on a salient interpretation, the form *was* reflects the inherent past of the participle in the *has* construction (cf. again Declerck 1988):

(144) a. John has never said that Mary was stupid
      b. John has never said that Mary is stupid

A form of the verb *say*, even if non-finite, has the power to establish a new tense domain. In (144b), on the other hand, the present *is* lacks the effects of spreading. Naturally only the past form can be a host for the 'spreading' tense reference. There is also another interpretation of (144a) where *was* introduces a distinct, relative past tense, whose reference is to a period earlier than the time of saying of the main clause.

Perhaps the 'spreading' from the non-finite form in (144a) is again analogous to 'spreading' from affixes; the 'past participle', like other subordinates, is in this respect equivalent to an affix. Or is it that, in so far as there is in the phonology 'spreading' of initially segmental features, it is this that would constitute an analogy to the 'spreading' of the relative past of English *have* + 'past participle' construction? This would be a kind of 'umlaut'. However, the present 'spreading' is rather unlike the umlaut discussed in §4.4.[36]

It is time to leave this tentative venture into the complex area of tensing and its harmonic character. The basic analogies are clear, I think. But I leave much unexplored, particularly the interaction of tense interpretation with Aktionsarten. However, I must at least acknowledge some of the further neglected phenomena that are probably relevant.

Other (non-verbal) items in English with relative past time reference are *former* and *last* and *ex-*. Still other items involve an inherent past-time existential, as *late* in *late President* and the like (though for some speakers *late* is ambiguous between these two interpretations). In some languages nouns can be marked as involving past existence of something or possession by someone, as in Kwakw'ala (145a) vs. (b):

(145) a. x̌ən x̌ʷakʷənxda 'my past canoe'
       b. x̌ən x̌ʷakʷ'əna 'my canoe'

(S. R. Anderson 1985: 179).

---

[36] A different manifestation of tense harmony and blocking (though not overtly discussed in these terms) is examined in Anderson (1973a,b, 1976b). Also, we should perhaps treat the {contra (factive)} discussed in Volume II as a clausal feature too. As such, it would be attached to the node associated with the propositional head of a conditional like (128a) in Volume II, and be manifested wherever there is a possible host within the domain of that head, including the head of the adjoined protasis:

(II.128) a. If it rained, she would rejoice

The {contra} clausal feature is manifested morphologically in the protasis and periphrastically in the apodosis. In this example the domain of the clausal feature is quite restricted. But Jespersen (for example) gives some examples of more extended domains for irrealis, such as the sentence I present here as (i) (involving a covert protasis):

(i) It would be no pleasure to a London tradesman to sell anything which was what he pretended it was (1931: §9.3(3)).

These, of course, all involve indefinite relative past rather than deictic {past}, and they are all also interpretable as containing a locative {N} substructure.

I'm suggesting, then, that the 'sequence of tense' phenomenon provides a rather striking analogy to harmony processes in phonology, an analogy that is manifested in some detail. Of course, the detailed mechanisms differ in the two planes, and the syntax has added complexities related to semanticity. But this is not such as to obscure the pertinence in both cases of concepts such as 'spreading', 'neutrality', 'blocking'. The 'spreading' is in referential interpretation in the syntax, and may not be expressed morphosyntactically; and also agreement in secondary tense feature (past or future) is involved. But this is natural given the basic substances of the planes. It thus seems to me that this is an analogy which (despite even much recent interest in 'interaction at interfaces') only the separateness of the too-infrequently-interacting traditions of syntactic and phonological investigations has rendered opaque. I expect that further work in an analogist perspective will render the analogy, and its limitations, yet more transparent (pun deliberate).

4.3 Extrasegmentals, II: Monosegmental realization

In terms of manifestation, different extrasegmental elements are localized with varying specificity, and varyingly perceived as localized. Thus, extrasegmental vowel elements such as those we have been looking at are generally extensively invasive (as alluded to above), given the extended manifestation of vowels and the structural cohesiveness introduced by extended manifestation of secondary vowel features. This is highlighted in a range of discussions by proponents of Firthian phonology (see e.g. those collected in Palmer 1970) and of articulatory phonology (such as Browman and Goldstein 1986, 1988, 1992). And the extended manifestation of vowels is recognized in, for instance, Steriade's (1990) diagram of the shift in timing associated with Dorsey's Law, given in (89) in §2.5.2 above and repeated here:

(89) Tiers   Gestures

   tongue body   [-]

                                    r
   tongue tip   [- - - -]   →

                                    p
   lips   [- - - - - -]

Syntax and non-linearity 193

We should note too comments such as Rialland and Djamouri's (1984: §2) concerning the {i} extrasegmental in Khalkha Mongolian that its effects can be perceived in intervening consonants in words with which the harmonic element is associated.

However, other extrasegmentals, usually non-vocalic, are manifested rather more locally. Here, in §4.3.1, I shall look at a case where an element that comes itself to occupy a segmental position is nevertheless not linearized by any of the regular rules for phonological sequencing of the kinds that we have considered. Contrastively, it is associated only with the lexical item as a whole, or some systematic part of it. This takes us back again to the status of [h] in English (and a number of other languages), briefly discussed in §2.3.3. Now I consider it as that seemingly paradoxical entity, a segmentally localized extrasegmental. And I shall again argue that there are syntactic analogues of such localized extrasegmentals. We then proceed to examine extrasegmentals that have a subsegmental realization, as in harmony, but, as with [h], strictly localized.

4.3.1 *Extrasegmental [h] and existential* there *in English*

As we saw in §2.3.3, [h] in English is limited to onsets, formulated there as (56):

(56) [h] does not occur in the lexical environment V+

But [h] is further restricted to simple (non-cluster) onsets in many kinds of English. Both of these restrictions are allowed for if [h] is simply extrasyllabic. In general its position in the syllable is derived by a redundancy that fills with [h] the onset position in a syllable that would otherwise be onset-less. A related phenomenon is the 'intrusive' [h] characteristic (in melisma, for instance) of many styles of singing, from performance of medieval chant to renderings of modern popular music. In some varieties of English (those which contrast *weather* and *whether*, for instance), it can also be the head of onsets containing vowels, i.e. semi-vowels. Its position in the syllable remains, however, determinate and unique, even in this case.

Anderson (1986b, 2001a) argues further that [h] in English is lexically extrasegmental, rather than merely extrasyllabic, in that its location in the word, as well as the syllable, can be predicted from the rest of the structure of the formative concerned. Thus, lexically in simplex words like *hiatus* or *Ahab*, [h] lies outside the whole syllabic sequence, as represented in (146) (which representation appeals to the conventions of (123), but for convenience utilizes spelling forms), and its linear position is determined by rule:

(146) a. h ((i) + (a) + (t(us)))
       b. h ((a) + (ab))

Recall (123):

(123) a. {i}((p,{u,v},{u}) + (t,{v})) = *pöytä*
      b. (p,{u,v},{u}) + (t,{v}) = *pouta*

Just as in (123a) the extrasegmental {i} of Finnish lies outside the whole syllable sequence within the outer brackets, English [h] (whatever its categorization) is analogously represented as (fully) extrasegmental. As with Finnish {i}, English [h] contrasts with its absence (as with *helm* vs. *elm*), though 'minimal pairs' showing such a contrast in the other positions it can occur in are hard to find (and this may be related to the element's diachronic and dialectal 'instability'). It differs from Finnish {i} in being a potential segment rather than merely a secondary feature. And this correlates with its occurring in a particular location in any word rather than potentially having multiple manifestations.

Anderson (2001a: 205) provides an outline of the regularity that gives the position of [h] in English:

> *h-sequencing in English*
> Serialize /h/ in an empty onset in accordance with the hierarchy:
> a) in a syllable bearing secondary stress (*hiatus, Ahab*)
> b) in an accented syllable (*Hyams, ahoy, jojoba*)
> c) in a word-initial syllable (*hysteria, jojoba*)

The example in common between (b) and (c) here illustrates that more than one instance of the extrasegmental may be associated with a single formative. The chosen onsets are all salient in some way, by virtue of accent and/or word-initial position

A fuller account would give explicit recognition to morphological considerations. But the point of the present observations is simply to illustrate an extrasegmental that comes, by rule, to occupy and be manifested at a specific single linear position in a word, as roughly diagrammed in (147):

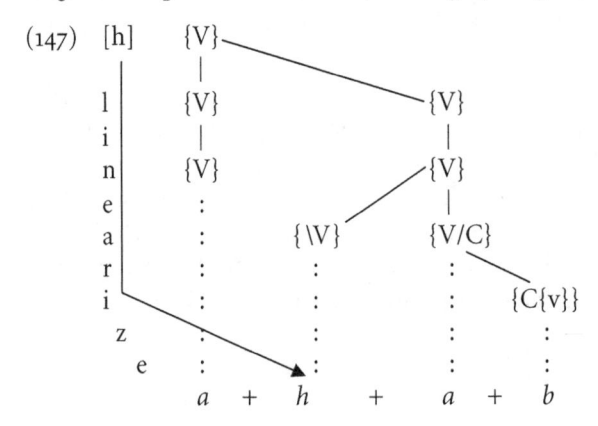

(147) [h]   {V}
        | |
        l   {V}   {V}
        i | |
        n   {V}   {V}
        e   : |
        a   :   {\V}   {V/C}
        r   :   :   :
        i   :   :   :   {C{v}}
        z   :   :   :   :
           e   :   :   :   :
               a + h   +   a + b

The configuration and positioning associated with [h] are predictable; in (147) it is located in accordance with condition (a) on *h*-sequencing, which has priority over the other options. Application of (147) means that the syllable concerned is unmarked in terms of (28):

(28) *unmarked syllable structure*
      C + {V}

In the absence of [h], languages often resort to a non-contrastive glottal stop to ensure unmarked status.[37]

Once again, it is not immediately apparent that the details of the positioning of [h] are driven directly by particular interface considerations, though, as I've implied, a preference for onset position may be natural. Positioning of [h] is driven by a mixture of rhythmic and morphological considerations. It is plausible, then, in terms of the structural analogy assumption, to expect a syntactic analogy. And such there seems to be.

Consider the alternative constructions in (148) and (149), for instance:

(148) a. Someone is in that cupboard
      b. Is someone in that cupboard?
      c. Lots of rats are in the cupboard

(149) a. There is someone in that cupboard
      b. Is there someone in that cupboard?
      c. There are lots of rats in that cupboard

In (148a) *someone* is both the 'syntactic subject'—it 'inverts', as in (148b)—and also what one might call the 'morphosyntactic subject'—in controlling concord, as shown in (148c) vs. (148a-b). (149a) involves the much-discussed so-called 'existential' construction (Jenkins 1975, etc.), with 'expletive' 'syntactic subject' *there*, which, as subject, may be 'inverted', as in (149b), whereas, at least in formal English, the post-nominal 'morphosyntactic subject' controls concord, as shown by (149c) vs. (149a-b). In relation to such as (149), Anderson (1986c: 113, 1988c: §5, 1992: 101–2, 1997a: 119), for example, argues that regular syntactic subject formation, which selects an argument of the predicator on the basis of its semantic relation (as discussed in §§3.6, 3.8 of

---

[37] As acknowledged, the discussion of *h*-sequencing here simplifies the situation somewhat: see again Anderson (1986a, 2001a) for a consideration of morphological and other complications ignored here. Also of some relevance, however, is perhaps the observation that loss of secondary stress leads to loss of [h] in a non-initial syllable (hiatus), as reflected in pronunciations of *Meehan*. Incidentally, in my speech, *Meehan* with an [h] forms a close-to-minimal pair with *paean*.

Volume I) and places it in subject position (to which we return below), has failed to apply in these cases, compared with (148).

For reasons discussed by Anderson (1997a: §§3.3.2, 3.7.2), existentials commonly lack assignment of a grammatical relation such as 'subject'. Note for instance the absence of the so-called 'topic/focus' marker in the Tagalog existential in (150a) vs. its presence in the 'non-existential' (b) (where T/F = 'topic/focus'):

(150) a. May   aksidente Kagabi
           there-was accident last-night

      b. Dadalhin ni Rosa   ang pera   kay Juan
          Will-take by Rosa   T/F money to John

The 'topic/focus' is another variety of grammatical relation based on grammaticalization of 'topic', and normally one of the arguments in a predication in Tagalog is selected as such. Basically, existentials are 'comment-only' in structure, and in (150a) 'topic/focus' formation fails. In English, the comparable failure to assign a grammatical relation is optional and partial, given (148) alongside (149); and the failure is resolved by presence of an 'expletive' in subject position.

'Existential' *there* is a competitor for the 'normal' syntactic subject *someone* of (148), which otherwise under subject formation would share its argument with the free absolutive. Consider representations of this sharing such as (54b) in Volume I, §3.6:

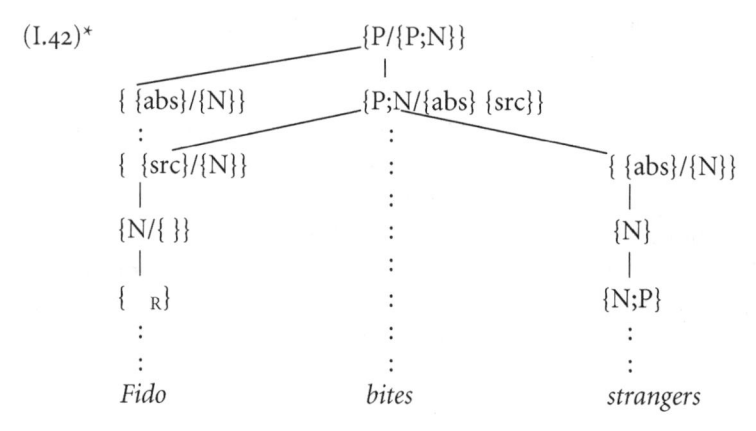

(I.42)*

```
                          _{P/{P;N}}
                           |
    { {abs}/{N}}         _{P;N/{abs} {src}}
       :                   :
    { {src}/{N}}           :              { {abs}/{N}}
       |                   :                 |
    {N/{ }}                :                {N}
       |                   :                 |
    {   R}                 :                {N;P}
       :                   :                 :
       :                   :                 :
     Fido               bites            strangers
```

In the present instance, the structure assigned to (148a) would be (151):

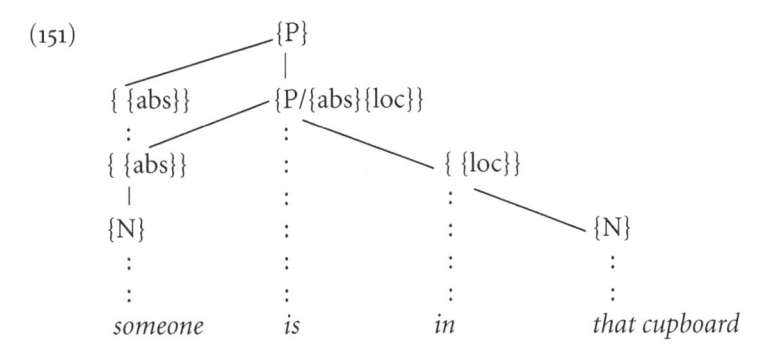

(151)
```
                    {P}
                     |
      {{abs}}      {P/{abs}{loc}}
        :          /        \
      {{abs}}     :          {{loc}}
        |         :          /    \
       {N}        :         :      {N}
        :         :         :       :
        :         :         :       :
     someone      is        in    that cupboard
```

The representation in (151) assumes that *be* undergoes finiteness formation (otherwise restricted to {P;N}, as illustrated in (I.48)) when it takes arguments other than simply a predicator. The absolutive functor associated with the upper {P} is a **free absolutive**: it is not part of the valency of this {P}, but is introduced at the lexicon-syntax interface in obedience to the requirement that every predicator must have an absolutive dependent. This absolutive lacks an {N} to complement it, and accordingly shares with the functor highest on the subject-selection hierarchy the {N} dependent on the latter, as indicated by the association between the free absolutive and the (agentive) source in (1.54b) and between the two absolutives in (151). This is the 'mechanism' for 'raising' described in Volume I, and subject formation represents a subtype of 'raising'. Our discussion here anticipates concepts to be examined in more detail in §6.3 on ectopicity and free absolutives.

The suggestion I make here concerning (149) is that 'existential' *there* in English is the equivalent of an extrasegmental element: associated with the clause, but not part of the argument structure of the clause nor, indeed, even a circumstantial in it, and thus not sequenced by any of the regular rules determining dependencies and word order in the clause. In clauses like (149), in which regular syntactic subject formation has failed, what I shall refer to as the **clausal element** *there* of (149a) comes to occupy the empty subject position. In (148a) normal subject formation has applied and any insertion of a *there* is blocked.

This *there* is categorized in the lexicon as shown in (152a): it is a locative-nominal complex which seeks to be associated with ('... → { {abs}}') the free absolutive of the functional category {P}, with dependency indicated by '←'; as in (151), the {P} in turn has (lexically) subjoined to it a {P} subcategorized for absolutive and locative, i.e. a {P/{abs}{loc}}:

(152) a. { {loc}} ┈┈▶ { {abs}} ← {P}
           | |
          {N}   {P/{abs}{loc}}
           ⋮
           ⋮
         there

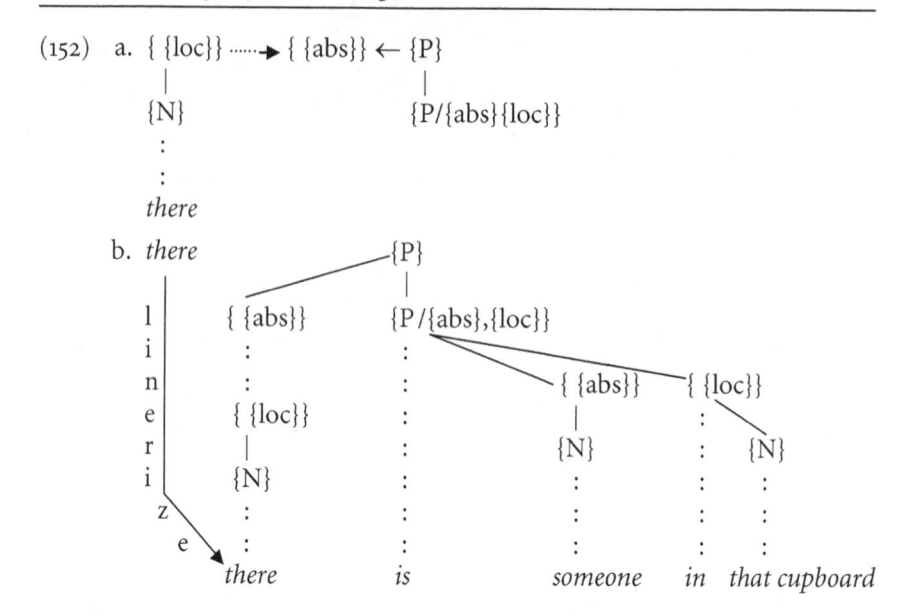

b. there   _____{P}
    l | |
    i | { {abs}}   {P/{abs},{loc}}
    n | ⋮   ⋮
    e | ↘ { {abs}} ·{ {loc}}
    r | { {loc}} | ⋮
    i | | {N}   : {N}
    z | {N}   ⋮   ⋮   ⋮
    e ↙ | ⋮   ⋮   ⋮   ⋮
        | ⋮   ⋮   ⋮   ⋮
           there   is   someone   in that cupboard

This leads to the attachments shown in the predicational structure shown in (152b), where lack of regular subject formation has left the free absolutive of the upper {P} free to host the clausal element *there*, and satisfy the requirements of (152a).

Even in (149) *someone* remains the morphosyntactic subject, by virtue of the lower {P} governing the {abs} of its valency, in accordance with the subject selection hierarchy. However, though *someone* is syntactically 'normal' as subject, in conforming to the subject-selection hierarchy, as an indefinite it is disfavoured as syntactic subject by discourse considerations. If indeed the predication is genuinely simply 'existential', as in *There are (no) unicorns*, the variant with normal subject formation, *(No) unicorns are*, is anomalous, though the positive at least can perhaps be saved by accentuating the copula.

Such an analysis for this 'expletive' *there* does not, of course, commit us to the view that *there* is necessarily contentless, i.e. a 'true expletive' (see further §5.3), though, like [h], it may be light on substance. And it may be that this 'lightness' is part of the analogy. However that may be, we can formulate the nature of the analogy in the statement that 'existential' *there*, like [h], is a lexical element that is represented lexically as outside the normal linearization regularities: it has its position in structures specified by a rule regulating lexical-to-syntax interfacing, rather than conforming to the normal principles of structure projection. We return to such *there*-sentences, and the structure in (152) in §6.3.2.

We witness in the present subsection a further analogy, involving extrasegmental/clausal elements that are realized as a segment or word in a particular position. Interestingly, in one respect at least, the syntax is less complex than the phonology. Thus, whereas the position of the segment [h] is variable, in line with the above formulation of '*h*-sequencing in English', in the syntax the extraclausal word takes up a particular position, variable only in accordance with other generalizations, such as 'inversion' in questions.

4.3.2 *Negative placement and stød*

Also 'clausal' are standard instances of negation. This is particularly transparent in systems with 'spreading' or 'multiple' or 'double' negation (cf. e.g. Jespersen 1917; Austin 1984). Consider the well-known example from the Alfredian translation of (the Orpheus and Euridice episode in) Boethius's *De consolatione philosophiae* in (153):

(153) Nan heort ne onscunode nænne leon ne nan hara nænne hund,
       no   hart not feared   no   lion nor no hare no   hound,
       ne nan neat   nyste   nænne andan ne nænne ege to oðrum
       nor no animal not-knew no malice nor no   fear to other
       ('No hart was afraid of any lion nor any hare of any hound, nor did any animal know any malice or any fear for another')

The clausal negation feature is manifested as *ne* in Old English procliticized to the verb of the clause, but it may also be manifested in other eligible places, such as in noun phrases which are neither definite nor indefinite but are 'existentially uncommitted' (e.g. *nænne* = *ne*+*ænne*), and (as in Modern English) in the alternative-signalling coordinator (also *ne*), as shown extensively in (153).

This shows a harmony system. What I am now concerned with, however, are systems of negation where a single semantic negation is expressed only in one place, but this place is variable. Again we seem to have a clausal feature, like tense, or 'spreading' negation; and lexically let us take it to be, as tense was interpreted above, a lexical feature of {P}. Here I ignore the kinds of complexities in the distribution of 'verbal negation' discussed in Chapters 5 and 6 of Volume I; and the interaction with 'existentially uncommitted' *any* and (other) quantifiers is clearly more complex than acknowledged here (as recognized in Anderson 1997a: §3.7.2). For present purposes of pointing to a structural analogy that does not depend on the precise content of what the feature abbreviates, I shall simplify by treating negation as a secondary feature, however. We are dealing with phenomena at sub-primary-category level.

In this section I begin by considering a syntactic phenomenon, and then suggesting a phonological analogue. The relevant observation is that this secondary feature may be realized as (part of) a verbal, or in an argument of the clause, but only in one of these in any one clause. The phenomenon is also distinguished by virtue of its involving an alternatively located feature, rather than a segment/word, as with [h] and 'existential' *there* in §3.3.1. Let us look briefly at such a system.

Even in systems which reject 'spreading' negation, the presence of the negative may still license the occurrence of 'existentially uncommitted' determiners such as the repeated *any* in the parenthesized gloss to (153). And such determiners may act as alternative hosts for the manifestation of the clausal negative feature, as illustrated by (154b) vs. the verbal manifestation in (a):

(154) a. Fred didn't see anyone
 b. Fred saw no-one
 c. No-one saw Fred (= *Anyone didn't see Fred)
 d. Fred did not see anyone

There is indeed for (154c) no alternative manifestation with verbal attachment equivalent to (154a). There is also the possibility of manifestation on a separate non-finite verb (on the analysis of this *not* suggested in Chapters 5 and 6 of Volume I), as in (154d). The interest of this phenomenon of alternative loci for the manifestation of a predicational feature is again that it has an analogue in the phonology, once more involving local manifestation of a constructional property. Lexically it is associated with {p}, but may be marked only by agreement on a nominal.

In phonology, consider, for example, the distribution of the Danish 'stød'. Stød is a property of certain words in Danish which is manifested as creaky voice. The location of stød is always within the rhyme of a stressed syllable, but its location in the rhyme depends on the structure of the rhyme. Thus it seems to be extrasegmental, associated derivatively with the accentual head, but realized within some segment within its rhyme. This is again a simplification, ignoring a number of important issues (see e.g. Basbøll 2005: §§2.9, 13.8, chs.14–16), but I don't think it is misleading.

We find the possibilities for location shown in (155), where '*' marks the location of the stød feature:

(155) a. lys 'light', kø 'queue'
           *   *

 b. damp 'steam'
         *

 c. deg 'day'
         *

In words whose stressed vowel is intransitive, heavy, the stød coincides with that vowel, as in (155a); with transitive stressed vowels stød coincides with the complement, which must be sonorant (have a preponderance of **V**) if it is to support stød, as in (155b).

So that we can say that stød coincides with either an intransitive vowel or, with a transitive, a dependent sonorant: either of these conditions on the rhyme provides the 'amount of sonority' that forms what is referred to as the 'stød-basis', the licence for the presence of stød. These two conditions are variant manifestations of a characterization of 'stød-basis' in terms of sonority. Intransitive vowels are heavy, redundantly {V,V}; sonorant consonants are {V;C}. The 'stød-basis' is provided by a rhyme that contains at least two instances of predominant **V**. This suggests that heaviness may be primary in this case in Danish rather than transitivity: the distribution of stød throughout the lexicon depends on sonority rather than simply transitivity. And the primary status of weight may be general in the language.

With diphthongs both conditions can be said to be fulfilled, in a sense. This is shown in the representation of (155c) given in (156c), with (156a) and (b) illustrating the rhyme structures of the other example forms in (155):

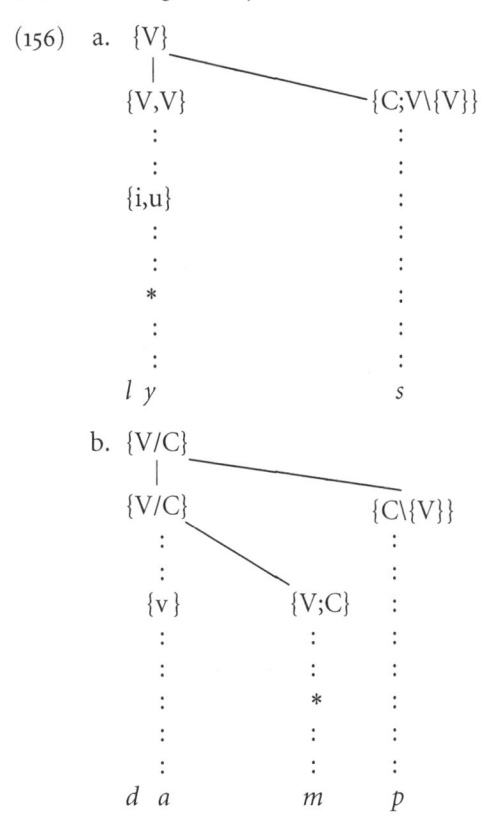

(156) a. {V}
            |
          {V,V}   {C;V\{V}}
            :   :
            :   :
          {i,u}   :
            :   :
            :   :
            *   :
            :   :
            :   :
           l y   s

       b. {V/C}
            |
          {V/C}   {C\{V}}
            :   :
            :   :
           {v}   {V;C}   :
            :   :   :
            :   :   :
            :   *   :
            :   :   :
            :   :   :
            :   :   :
           d a   m   p

c.   {V,V}

{v
       \
         i}

         *

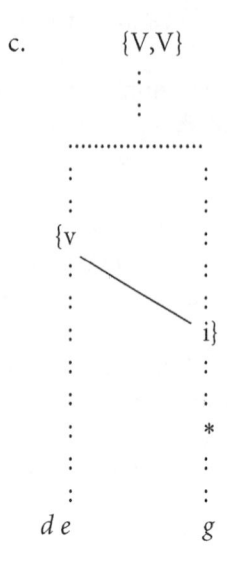

d e   g

'*' again indicates the location of the stød (however the latter is to be represented), which is lexically an extrasegmental feature. The diphthong in (156c) is intransitive, so the rhyme has two preponderant **V**s, and stød is associated with a less sonorous dependent element. This is the secondary feature which, as less sonorant than **v**, is a dependent of the **v** element: recall § 2.4.1 above.

However, some speakers also show variation with words where the rhyme consists of two sonorant consonants, such as *jarl* 'earl'; such words have a 'super-basis' for stød. In such conditions the stød may be associated with either sonorant, the complement or the adjunct. This confirms that stød may be said to be associated not just with a complement but any sonorant rhymal dependent (and not necessarily the first or last one) of the stressed transitive vowel, adjunct or complement, but only with one of them in any rhyme.[38]

---

[38] I do not attempt here to provide a categorial characterization for stød, which is not germane to our present purposes. For more details on this and other aspects, see Staun (1987) and particularly Basbøll (2005: ch. 10), who also provide reviews of other accounts, including (of most relevance here) those in Clements and Keyser (1983), Anderson et al. (1985: §3), and Anderson (1987a: §3). I differ from Staun's account (and follow Anderson 1987a) in not associating stød lexically with particular segments (constituents of the 'stød-basis'): this local association is not contrastive, but reflects a phonological redundancy, and so should not be incorporated in the lexicon into individual contrastive segmental representations.

In general, in the case of stød, we have, as with distribution of the negative feature in (154), alternative loci for an extrasegmental/clausal feature:

(154) a. Fred didn't see anyone
b. Fred saw no-one
c. No-one saw Fred (= *Anyone didn't see Fred)
d. Fred did not see anyone

Sometimes two alternatives are available, as with *jarl* and the negatives in (154a/b) or (154a/d). In other circumstances one alternative is preferred, so that with heavy vowels the vowel is preferred to any following consonant for stød location (and vice versa with light vowels), just as in (154c) the preverbal nominal is preferred to the verbal. There is clearly not complete coincidence of possibilities, and I have grossly oversimplified here the syntax of negation. But we seem to have here yet another subtype of analogy between extrasegmentals and clausal elements.

4.4 Extrasegmentals, III: Umlaut and agreement

We find that traditional **umlaut** processes in phonology also have a plausible syntactic analogy. In the past such processes were perhaps principally discussed in relation to the Germanic languages and their history. What is centrally involved in this case is the historical influence of a suffixal {i} or {u} on the vowel of the stem. Thus, despite the increase in speculation necessitated by the use of reconstructed forms, I have chosen to illustrate umlaut from the prehistory of Old English, mainly also because the historical phenomena involved will lead on rather directly to a final remark (in §4.6) on analogies and grammaticalization. But it is also an area with which I am relatively familiar. However, similar phenomena are discussed, for instance, by van der Hulst and Smith (1985) in relation to Djingili, using data from Chadwick (1975). Indeed, what follows is partly based on suggestions made there, particularly in their §4, where they suggest that umlaut in Djingili involves the spread of a feature associated lexically with a suffix: we have an affix-determined harmony.

In Djingili, an **i** feature associated with a suffix 'spreads' leftwards to vowel positions which are lexically unspecified (with some exceptions noted by van der Hulst and Smith (1985: 279–80), as well as being realized in the suffix itself, as in (157b), contrasted with (157a), which lacks the suffix:

(157)   a. galal 'branch' sg

{C}{V}{C}{V}{C}

b. galal 'branch'   +   stative sg ji ⇒ gilili

{C} {V} {C} {V} {C} – {V{i}}

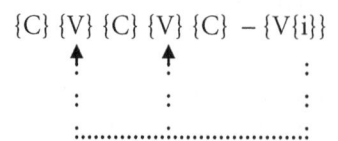

c. gara 'eel'

d. giriili(gi)ṇi 'eel' stative plural

The diagram in (157b) shows (schematically) the effect of adding the stative singular suffix to the (unspecified) stem which otherwise (in the absence of a 'spread' {i}) appears as *galal*, the suffixless singular, as in (157a). In the stative in (157d), with simple form (157c), the influence of -*ji* has 'spread' across three other affixes (according to van der Hulst and Smith's (1985) analysis) to reach the stem. Umlaut thus seems to proceed from right to left, starting with the final vowel, and morphologically contra-dependency. Vowels that are not filled in, in this way, by an extrasegmental, undergo the default (158):

(158)   {V{ }} ⇒ {V{v}}

This applies in the case of *galal*. What 'spreads' is the only secondary feature of the vowel.

With *i*-umlaut in Germanic, 'spreading' again proceeds from suffix to stem. But not all the vowels umlauted in this way are unspecified. In the latter respect the pre-Old-English process is more like canonical harmony (as described above in §3.2). However, the 'spreading' vowel, as in Djingili, is associated lexically with an affix. The Germanic system thus differs also from the advanced-tongue-root (ATR) harmony systems associated with languages like Kalenjin (Halle and Vergnaud 1981), where an (ATR) feature in either a root or an affix 'spreads' to non-ATR elements in both.

4.4.1 I-*umlaut in Old English*

We can illustrate the effects of the *i*-umlaut of pre-Old English in the second of the historical (recorded) forms in each of (159) compared with the first:[39]

---

[39] The examples in (159), which include only 'short' monophthongal vowels, are from Lass and Anderson (1975: ch. IV, §2) and Hogg (1992: ch. 5, §VI). For more traditional accounts of *i*-umlaut see Brunner (1965: 95–107), Campbell (1959: 190–204); for a succinct overview see Lass (1994: §3.8). I return

(159) a. burg 'city' – byrig 'city' *dative sg*
b. ofost 'haste' – efstan 'hasten'
c. cwæl 'died' – cwellan 'to kill'
d. faran 'go' – færþ 'goes'

All of the second forms are reconstructed as having had a suffix containing the secondary feature {i} which 'triggered' the umlaut reflected in these spellings. The {i} is 'spread' to the root, which Anderson (2005c) takes to involve (as in Finnish harmony, though in this case the 'spreading' feature originates in a suffix) the derived association of the 'spreading' vowel with the accented (and in these particular cases, transitive) vowel, as in (160):

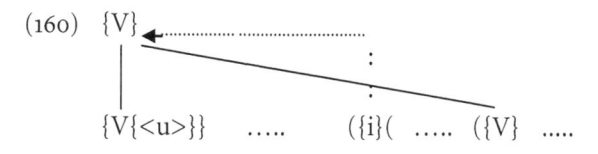

(160)   {V}
         |
        {V{<u>}}   .....   ({i}(.....   ({V}   .....

I return below to the substantive aspects of (160). Concerning the historical 'process', observe that the 'spreading' could also be formulated in morphological terms (as in Turkish, though again reversing the directionality of the 'spreading'), from morphological subordinate (suffix) to morphological head (root). But this is not directly relevant here.

Within the suffix, I interpret the {i} as extrasegmental; the extrasegmentality is again indicated by its placement outside the syllabic brackets in (160). Derivatively, it appears that the suffixal {i} is primarily associated within the suffix itself with either an unspecified vowel position, as in e.g. (159a), or with the onset, as in e.g. the reconstructed source of (159d), *[kwæl-jan]. The 'effect' of (160) itself is to attach the extrasegmental {i} of the suffix to the accentual head, so that it is manifested in any base/stem vowel (any vowel within the accentual domain) that contains either **u** or is substantively unspecified (as again indicated by the angles of optionality around the **u**

---

to some questions raised by the 'long' monophthongs in note 40, as well as, in §4.5, giving some attention to the pre-nasal short-vowel system.

Forms like *gædeling* 'companion' that are reconstructed as having had a back rounded vowel in the unstressed syllable preceding the i-bearing suffix (cf. Old Saxon *gaduling*) are usually interpreted as having undergone 'double umlaut' (e.g. Campbell 1959: §203), though the apparently reduced second vowel comes to be spelled *e* in historical Old English. Their inclusion in the historical process follows from the formulation in (160): the vowel in question falls within the accentual domain, and thus will manifest (if eligible) the extrasegmental {i}.

and the absence of any other feature). This characterization applies to all of the vowels to the left in (159).

The 'process' leads to a structure such as might be represented as in (161), where {i} is perceived as combined with a root vowel {u}, giving in this instance (in traditional terms) a high front rounded vowel, [y]:

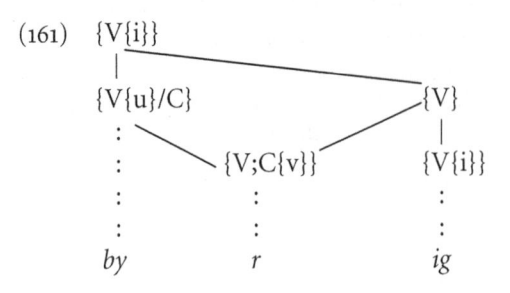

(161)   {V{i}}
         |
    {V{u}/C}   {V}
      :   \ |
      :   \ {V;C{v}}   {V{i}}
      :   :   :
      :   :   :
      by   r   ig

Combination of the extrasegmental with segmental vowels in the root is manifested, again in traditional terms, either by 'fronting' (159a-c) or 'raising' (159d) of the affected vowel one step closer, within the parameters established by the system, towards {i}. The affected vowels in (159a-b) contain {u}; those in (159c-d) are unspecified (see below). These are the two inputs allowed for by (160). Let us now look at how these proposed characterizations relate to the recorded spellings, before looking at the motivations for non-specification of one kind of input vowel. The 'front rounded' vowels (combining **i** and **u**) that result from *i*-umlaut in the history of the forms on the right in (159a-b) unrounded subsequently, rather early in the case of (159b), as reflected in the typical spelling; this apparently occurred rather later in the case of (159a), where *y* spellings persist through much of Old English. There do occur early spellings for the umlaut of the vowel of (159b) with *oi* or *oe* (*Oidilualdo* (name), *doehter* 'daughter' *dative sg*, for instance—see Campbell 1959: §196; Hogg 1992: §5.77), as well as *ui* for the high vowel (Campbell 1959: §199; Hogg 1992: §2.18). These spellings are usually interpreted (see particularly Hogg 1992: §2.18) as evidence for the postulated original outputs of *i*-umlaut, i.e. respectively 'mid and high front rounded vowels', with a 'decompositional' orthographic representation for these 'front rounded' umlauted vowels.[40]

---

[40] The system is also asymmetrical with respect to the corresponding long/intransitive system which lacks a congener of short {v}, as argued in Colman (2005). Colman presents detailed analyses of *i*-umlaut as it affects the various vowel subsystems in Old English (long/short/pre-nasal, diphthongal). There the West Saxon 'long' vowel spelled *a* in historical Old English is analysed as having been a diphthong at the time of i-umlaut.

How does (160) affect the vowel system? This system can be argued to involve non-specification. The asymmetrical fully specified system for the pre-umlaut stage is given as (162):

(162) *fully specified pre-umlaut pre-OE system of short monophthongs*
  {i} 'i' *fisc* 'fish'   {u} 'u' *full* 'full'
  {i;v} 'e' *cweþan* 'to say'   {u,v} 'o' *god* 'god'
  {v;i} 'æ' *sæt* 'sat'
          {v} 'a' *sadol* 'saddle'

Umlaut of the 'long' vowels differs from that with the 'short' in that the 'long' vowel which when unumlauted is spelled *æ* in West Saxon does not undergo it: West Saxon *dæd* 'deed', *mære* 'famous' with pre-historic *i*-suffix. This vowel seems to be absent from the inventory of the Anglian dialects, where West Saxon *dæd*, for instance, is spelled *ded*; the Anglian vowel contains {i, } contrastively, and also fails to undergo *i*-umlaut as a consequence of this (in not meeting the input conditions). The anomaly in West Saxon can be resolved if we adopt Colman's (2005) suggestion concerning the differences between the 'long' and 'short' vowel systems.

As anticipated above, she argues that the 'long' low vowel equivalent to 'short' {v} has not developed as such at this point, but remains diphthongal (its ancestor is Germanic [ai]). In this case, the West Saxon 'long' monophthong system is different from the 'short' one of (162/163), in lacking a low vowel, as shown in (ia) (underspecified) and (b) (fully specified):

(i)   *pre-OE 'long' vowel system (after Colman 2005)*
   a. *underspecified*
      {i} 'i'   {u} 'u'
      {i, } 'e'   {u, } 'o'
              { , } 'æ'
   b. *fully specified*
      {i} 'i'   {u} 'u'
      {i;v} 'e'   {u,v} 'o'
              {v;i} 'æ'

The fully specified system in (ia) lacks a vowel with **v**.

We can therefore, for the 'long' system, simplify the requirements of *i*-umlaut, compared with the formulation in (160), as given schematically in (ii):

(ii) *pre-OE i-umlaut: Long monophthongs*

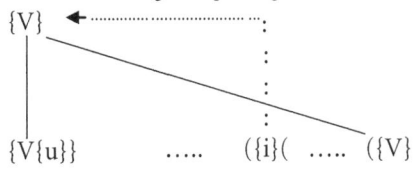

```
    {V} ◄·························⋮
     |                              ⋮
     |                              ⋮
     |           _____⋮
     |          /
  {V{u}}    ····· ({i}(  ·····  ({V}
```

That is, we can restrict *i*-umlaut to affecting just vowels with **u**; (160), on the other hand, can apply even to a simple {v}, i.e. a lexically unspecified vowel. In this way the 'long' vowel in West Saxon *dæd* etc. will not be affected by *i*-umlaut, but (ii) will apply only to 'long' {u} and {u,v}. Otherwise, *i*-umlaut and the defaults in (164) apply as with the 'short' system.

The asymmetry of (162) is evident from inspection of the short-vowel system itself: crucially, there is no grave partner to {v;i}, given that realizationally {u,v} pairs with {i;v}—the former is redundantly {u;v}. This pairing as 'high-mid' vowels is attested by later developments.

Taking again this asymmetry as a clue, I reconstruct the (underspecified) pre-i-umlaut pre-OE vowel system as in (163), which also indicates the usual spellings of un-umlauted descendants of the vowels in the system:

(163) underspecified pre-umlaut pre-OE system of short monophthongs
      {i} 'i'   {u} 'u'
      {i, } 'e'   {u, } 'o'
                 { , } 'æ'
                 { } 'a'

This less asymmetrical system emerges if we again follow Anderson and Durand (1988a,b, 1993) in associating the asymmetries in the fully specified system with lexical non-specification, in this case of two ('short') vowels, one simplex the other involving a combination. The contrast between the unspecified (compound and simplex) vowels, represented by 'æ'/ 'a', is marginal, being based on loss in a few items of the environment (associated with the traditional 'sound-change' of 'first fronting') that otherwise conditions their relative distribution (Colman 1983). Nevertheless, the vowel that is spelled *æ* when un-umlauted is usually reconstructed as providing a distinct input to *i*-umlaut in forms like (159c) (Hogg 1992: §5.80).

The underspecified representations of (163) are filled out by the redundancies of (164):

(164)   a. {V{i/u, }} ⇒ {V{i/u; }}
           b. {V{ , }} ⇒ {V{ ;i}}
           c. {V{ }} ⇒ {V{v}}

Application of (164), with sub-parts intrinsically ordered in terms of increasing generality/simplicity, so that (164c) fills in any underspecification left by (164a-b), gives us the specifications in (165):

(165)   a. {i, } ⇒ {i; } ⇒ {i;a} 'e'
           b. {u, } ⇒ {u;} ⇒ {u;a} 'o'
           c. { , } ⇒ { ;i} ⇒ {a;i} 'æ'
           d. { } ⇒ {a} 'a'

This fills out all the values for the pre-umlaut system of (162).

Historical addition and application of (160) *i*-umlaut gives (166) as representations, showing the extrasegmental on the left, at the tail of the dependency arrow:

(166) a. {i}→{u}, spelled 'y'
 b. {i}→{u,a}, 'oe''e'
 c. {i}→{a}, 'æ'
 d. {i}→{a;i}, 'e'

Interpretation and manifestation of (166a-b) are straightforward, conventionally representable as [y] and [ø] respectively: {i,u} and {i,u,a}. Compare e.g. the Finnish grave + acute vowels in (120):

(120) *the fully specified Finnish vowel system*

acute	acute + grave	grave
{i} 'i'	{i,u} 'y'	{u} 'u'
{i;v} 'e'		
	{i,u,v} 'ö'	{u,v} 'o'
{a;i} 'ä'		
	non-acute non-grave	
	{a} 'a'	

(166d) has somewhat more **i** than does (c), so that, in terms of proportions of **i** and **a**, we can differentiate them in the same way as are the 'front mid' vowels in (162). Thus, (166d) is equivalent, in segmental terms, to {i;a} and (166c) to {a;i}; and the former is spelled *e*, and the latter is spelled *æ*, as in the non-umlauted system of (162):

(167) a. cwellan 'to kill' (umlauted); cweþan 'to say' (unumlauted)
 b. færþ 'goes' (umlauted); sæt 'sat' (unumlauted)

Indeed, we have in terms of 'segmental manifestation' a system like the Finnish of (120) from §4.2, repeated in the preceding.

Such would be an interpretation of the usual assumptions about the short-monophthong inputs and outputs to (pre)historical *i*-umlaut in English. I have ignored various complexities of interpretation, however, even as regards the 'short' vowel system (for some discussion and references see Anderson 2005c). But the general shape of this is not unfamiliar in phonology. What emerges is a 'spreading' of a secondary feature from morphological or phonological (accentual) subordinate to morphological or phonological governor. The underlying mechanism here seems to be anticipatory, whereas (left-to-right) harmony involves persistence. The effect in both instances is unificatory.

4.4.2 Agreement, in various shapes and languages

Analogous phenomena in syntax are not difficult to find. The same pattern seems to characterize **agreement** phenomena. A simple but realizationally interesting instance of this is provided by Hungarian agreement in 'specificity' or 'definiteness'. The conjugational system of Hungarian shows the common phenomenon of subject-verbal concord. But the 'definiteness' of the 'direct object' is also reflected in the shape of the verb, as exemplified by (168):

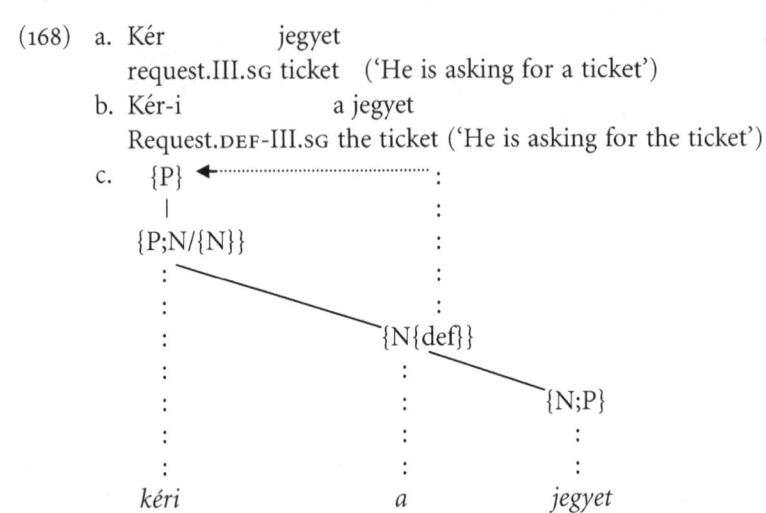

(168) a. Kér   jegyet
      request.III.SG ticket   ('He is asking for a ticket')
   b. Kér-i   a jegyet
      Request.DEF-III.SG the ticket ('He is asking for the ticket')

   c.
$$\begin{array}{ccc} \{P\} \leftarrow \cdots \cdots \cdots \cdots & & \vdots \\ | & & \vdots \\ \{P;N/\{N\}\} & & \vdots \\ & \{N\{def\}\} & \\ & & \{N;P\} \\ \vdots & \vdots & \vdots \\ \textit{kéri} & \textit{a} & \textit{jegyet} \end{array}$$

The verb form in (168b) agrees with the 'definiteness' of the complement, and this is reflected in its conjugational forms, specifically in the presence of a distinctive suffix of subject concord rather than its showing the same subject-concord form as in (168a). In (168a) 'III.SG' is marked by absence of a suffix. Definiteness agreement can be represented informally as in (168c), which presents a much simplified syntactic structure: {def} therein is an {N}-phrasal feature associated with the head of the phrase, a determiner.

This referential feature is again associated with a functional category (recall the discussion of tense in §3.2.2), and specifically {N}, before 'spreading' also to {P}, as reflected in the form of subject concord. By virtue of (168c) it apparently comes to be associated with the verb head. As with umlaut, we have 'spreading' from subordinate to head. But again, with the syntactic phenomenon, we have agreement between {N}s, as with 'sequence of tenses' rather than literal spreading. Here an incorporated {N} of the verb is in agreement with the definite {N} of the determiner phrase.

The harmony and tense-agreement of §4.2 seem to differ from umlaut and agreement illustrated here in their dependency orientation: the former 'spread downwards', the latter are oriented 'upwards' in the cases we have looked at. But the mechanism of 'spreading' is agreement in both syntactic instances. However, the agreement we have just looked at is marked overtly in some way; it is morphosyntactic, while tense 'spreading' can be merely a question of interpretation.

Of course, many agreement systems involve more dimensions than this (person, number, gender, etc.—see again S.R. Anderson 1985: §2.2.3), but the same kind of configuration is involved in the 'spreading'. Moreover, some such systems 'spread' the agreement feature to eligible positions throughout the domain, as when, in French, for instance, a gender feature apparently originating with a noun ({N;P}) is manifested throughout a determiner phrase (as discussed more fully in Chapter 6 of Volume II). In the (again) much-simplified representation in (169), the agreeing feature comes to be associated with the head of the determiner phrase:

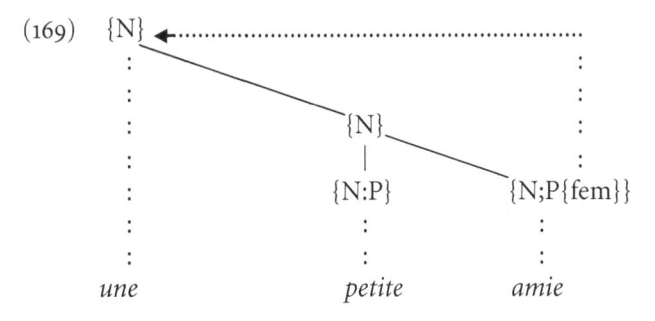

(169) {N} ◄···

                            {N}
                             |
              {N:P}   {N;P{fem}}
               :   :
               :   :
      une   petite   amie

At least in written French all three elements here, the overt determiner, the attributive (i.e. determinerized—see again Anderson in 2007: §2.3.3) adjective, and the noun itself, overtly signal feminine gender; all are in the domain of the host element, the upper {N}, and the secondary feature which is only derivatively associated with {N} is signalled in all eligible places within the domain of the latter. Here we have agreement and thus 'spreading' within a domain, as with tense.[41]

---

[41] A reviewer comments on representations such as (169), with {N} as governor of phrases terminating in nouns: '<i>f Determiner is to be taken to be the head of an NP, doesn't that run counter to the notionally based approach? Doesn't the latter suggest that an N should be the head of an NP?' If we put aside the prejudicial effect of use of the label 'NP', it seems to me that this comment, perhaps having in mind the Croftian definition of 'head' (Croft 2001: 259), confuses semantic density or distinctiveness with syntactic and thus cognitive relational salience—headedness being a relational notion. It is functional categories that articulate syntactic structure. They enable predications to express moods as complete sentences ({P}), arguments to participate in predications ({ }), and

The gender feature is apparently inherent in {N;P} and not itself lexically phrasal (or clausal) in not being associated with a functional category, or even a head; and it is not deictic or definite. Its host, however, is functional. This is characteristic of 'syntactic umlaut' (agreement) in nominal constructions. However, elsewhere the sources of agreement features are functional, as in our Hungarian example, and as we shall now see illustrated further, as we confront more complex systems of agreement. This underlines the distinctiveness of agreement within nominals noted in Chapter 6 of Volume II. However, there it is argued that gender agreement is rather more complex than this. What 'spreads' is **grammatical gender**, not the **natural gender** of the noun; and grammatical gender involves a functional category.

In II.6.4.1 it is suggested that something like (169) involves two different kinds of agreement. The natural gender of the noun, feminine, requires a feminine grammatical gender in agreement with it to be marked on a governing {N} within its maximal projection, and it is this grammatical gender that is manifested through the determiner phrase. In illustration, I repeat here (186) from Volume II, §6.4:

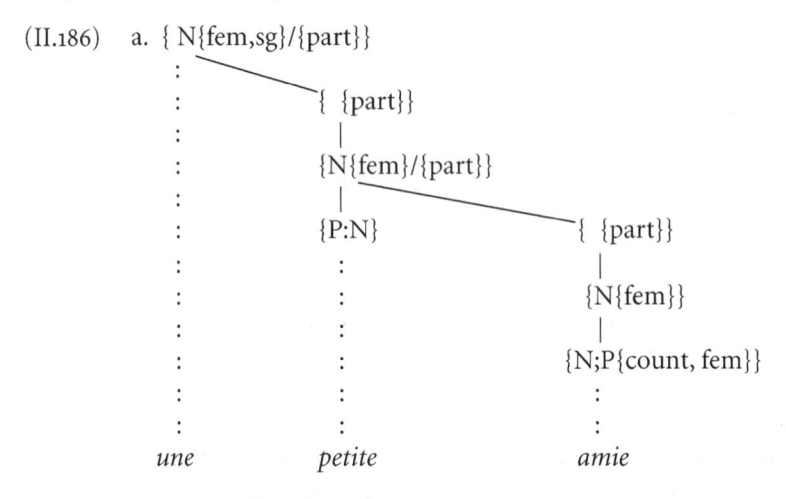

(II.186)   a. { N{fem,sg}/{part}}

```
              { {part}}
                 |
              {N{fem}/{part}}
                 |
              {P:N}            { {part}}
                                  |
                               {N{fem}}
                                  |
                               {N;P{count, fem}}
                                  :
                                  :
              une      petite    amie
```

nouns, names, and pronouns (entitatives) to constitute arguments ({N}). A root {P}is the ultimate head, and it is scarcely 'semantically dense'. It has a licensing role rather than a syntactic role in external distribution. But the distribution of subordinate clauses and phrases is determined by their heads, the category which meets the demands of the categories that the phrases complement or modify. And, as I have indicated, the most pervasive heads are functional categories. Nouns, in particular, are singularly inert syntactically. Such a confusion concerning the implications of notionalism is unfortunately endemic.

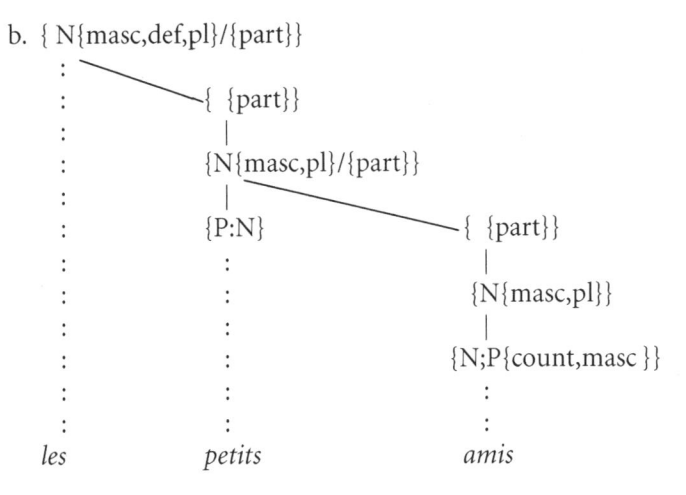

b. { N{masc,def,pl}/{part}}
    ⋮   { {part}}
    ⋮ |
    ⋮   {N{masc,pl}/{part}}
    ⋮ |
    ⋮   {P:N}   { {part}}
    ⋮   ⋮ |
    ⋮   ⋮   {N{masc,pl}}
    ⋮   ⋮ |
    ⋮   ⋮   {N;P{count,masc}}
    ⋮   ⋮   ⋮
    ⋮   ⋮   ⋮
    les   petits   amis

This displays the distribution of grammatical and natural gender within the two determiner phrases. Natural gender is a feature of nouns; grammatical gender a feature of {N}, including the {N} to which the {NP} in (II.186) is subjoined. It is grammatical gender that 'spreads'; agreement is agreement in grammatical gender. This considerably simplifies the account given in Volume II, which acknowledges among other things interaction between reference and lexical gender. (II.186) also shows number agreement, again involving {N}, and the 'spreading' of plurality. I shall return to it below. Often, too, the source of the agreement may not be marked for it morphologically.

Notice now, in the first place, that of course natural and grammatical gender may not agree. So French *table* is grammatically feminine but not naturally feminine. The relationship between natural and grammatical gender is not one-to-one. In the second place, what in Volume II is called **referential gender** can emerge in upper {N}s in determiner phrases. This is illustrated by the Greek *i kali iatros* 'the good doctor', where the noun has masculine grammatical gender, as indicated by the declension of the noun, and its natural gender is simply 'human', but the inflection of the determiner and adjective mark it as referentially feminine. But the important point in the immediate context is that the source and hosts of the 'spreading' feature is {N}. As with harmony the carrier is a functional category.

Both of the agreement systems ('umlauts') we have looked at exhibit the property of 'spreading' counter to dependency, unlike sequence of tense ('harmony'). And this seems to be true, as an instance of agreement, of verb concord in English, limited as it is. The verbal agrees with the person-number of the subject {N}, and the host is an incorporated {N} of the verbal. But a look at more complex verb-concord systems introduces further complications. First, however, let us observe a phenomenon that English shares with many of these more complex systems.

I formulated (168c) as attaching the 'spread' definiteness to (an {N} subjoined to), the ultimate governing {P} node. However, since I have assumed that the finite verb in (168c) has a categorial structure in which the {P;N} is subjoined to {P}, the feature would still be manifested in the same place whether attached to {P} or {P;N}. But when we are dealing with a separate, overt {P}, the category to which a 'spread' secondary feature is attached will be apparent from its position. So in the gloss to (168a), 'He is asking for a ticket', the features of the subject argument of *ask* are shown by concord on the operative and not on the verb which is subcategorized for that argument, i.e. *ask*. Now in this case since the subject shares its argument with the free absolutive of the operative, this is perhaps unremarkable. But it does show a preference for these features to be manifested on a functional category. And this preference becomes rather more striking when we consider more complex verb-concord systems.

Thus, the Basque case-person-number markers in (174) from Volume I of the trilogy can be seen to be attached to the operative:

(I.149c) Paulok untzia aurdiki   du
          Paul   vase.the throw.PST.PTCP NPST.(III.SG.ABS)(III.SG.ERG)
          ('Paul threw the vase')

Here the secondary features of the two functors and their dependent determiners, again features of functional categories, are signalled on the operative, even though these features 'belong to' arguments of the non-finite. This is not unusual, and not surprising, given the central role of functional categories in agreement. But it is not universal, so it is typologically interesting.

There appear to be languages where the concord is with an adjoined {P;N}. In §6.5.1 in Volume I, I presented Anderson's (2001a) suggestion that the initial future-marking 'particle' in the Greek of (I.210a) is a {P} and the conjugated form following is a {P;N} whose presence in a finite clause is dependent on the presence of such a preceding finite 'particle':

(I.210) a. Θa plirosi   o   astinomikos
             FUT pay.AORIST.III.SG. the policeman ('The policeman will pay')

In that case the {P;N} bears the concord with the subject, and the finite element does not bear any, despite subject concord's traditional status as a marker of finiteness.[42]

These alternative possibilities for signalling of concord arise from the greater complexity of categorial structure in the syntax, particularly involving the distinction between functional and lexical categories. This greater complexity also underlies another aspect of agreement, one that seems to call into question the idea that verb concord is exercised on the predicator by an argument, i.e. the assumption that the direction of determination is counter-dependency, as in umlaut. For in some languages there may be structures showing what elsewhere is apparently agreement but where in these structures there is no overt 'trigger' for the agreement.

Compare with (I.210a) the Greek example in (170):

(170)   Θa pliroso
        FUT pay.AORIST.I.SG. ('I shall pay')

This latter phenomenon, under the label of 'Pro-drop', has been the focus of considerable debate; much of Ackema et al.'s recent (2006) collection of papers on 'Arguments and Agreement', for instance, is devoted to the consequences of the 'Pro-drop' vs. 'non-Pro-drop' distinction. It will be already clear that any mechanism posited here will not entail appeal to an 'empty category' such as 'Pro'; and indeed §5.3.2 of Volume I looks at 'Pro-drop' as involving a type of incorporation.

That subsection contains a discussion of languages like Selayarese (and Basque), where quite complex 'concord' features on the verb need not be matched by any distinct argument that agrees with them:

(I.148) a. máŋŋaŋ-i   hásaŋ aló-nni
            tired-III.ABS Hasan day-this ('Hasan is tired today')

         b. la-   pállu-i   berasá-ñjo i- hásaŋ
            III.ERG-cook-III.ABS rice-   the Mr-Hasan
            ('Hasan cooked the rice')

(ABS = absolutive, ERG = ergative). All of the non-verbal material in the Selayarese sentences in (I.148) may be omitted. In Volume I it is suggested that the apparent complements in these sentences are apposed to incorporated

---

[42] This discrepancy led Anderson (2001b, 2001c) to make a distinction between syntactic finiteness and morphological finiteness, where the latter is simply the availability with a form of many of the distinctions normally associated with prototypical syntactic finiteness. This is discussed too in the first of the present trilogy of studies, Ch. 6. However, this need not concern us at this point.

{N}s; it is these {N}s and their associated functors that are reflected in the verb morphology. There is no source for the 'agreement'. Rather, it is the apposed determiner phrases that are required to agree with them.

This is difficult to reconcile with the view of agreement as counter-dependency that I have been entertaining. However, it should be observed that verb concord via apposition involves co-indexing. As in sequence of tenses, we are involved with spread of reference as well as agreement between features. And I suggest that it is harmony that is operative in appositional agreement. But in non-'pro-drop' languages—and in Hungarian definiteness agreement—there is simply agreement in feature, not spread of referentiality. But now let us consider what seems like an even more striking anomaly.

This takes us back to the number agreement of (II.186b)—the forms dependent on the topmost determiner in (II.186a) are unmarked for number:

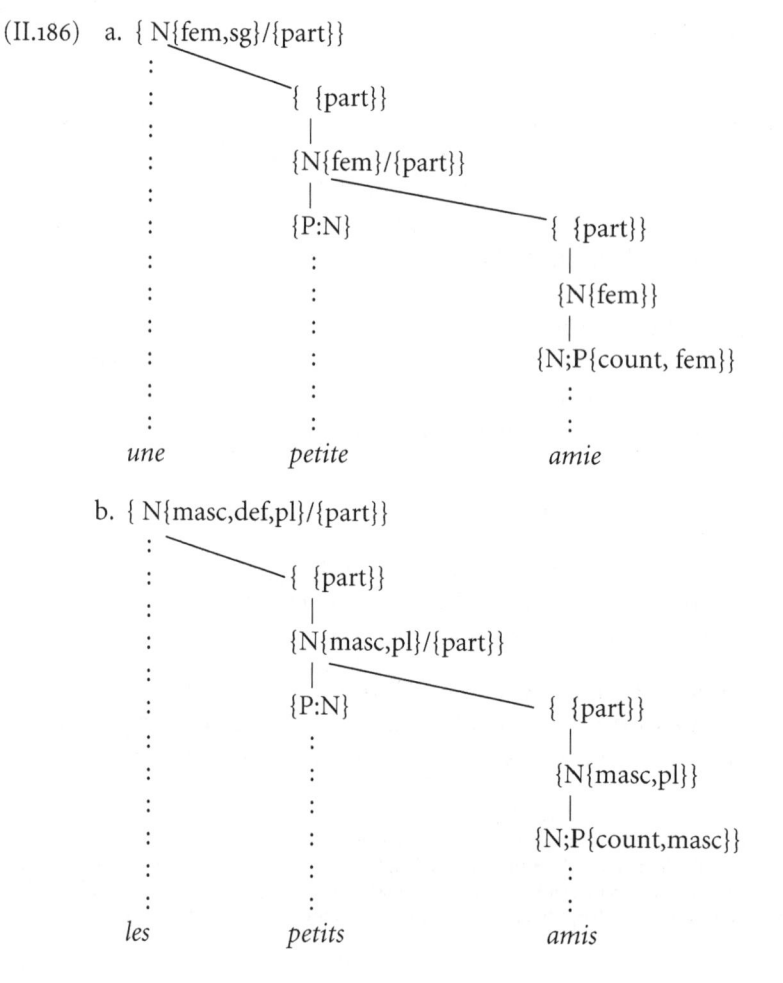

(II.186) a. { N{fem,sg}/{part}}

```
              { {part}}
                 |
              {N{fem}/{part}}
                 |
              {P:N}        { {part}}
               :              |
               :           {N{fem}}
               :              |
               :           {N;P{count, fem}}
               :              :
   une       petite          amie
```

b. { N{masc,def,pl}/{part}}

```
              { {part}}
                 |
              {N{masc,pl}/{part}}
                 |
              {P:N}        { {part}}
               :              |
               :           {N{masc,pl}}
               :              |
               :           {N;P{count,masc}}
               :              :
   les        petits          amis
```

So we are dealing with plural agreement.

Number is a category of {N}; it is applied to the referent of the determiner phrase. Nevertheless, number, like person, in participating in verb concord, is 'spread' counter-dependency, as in other instances of agreement. But in (II.186b) {pl} apparently 'spreads' within the dependency phrase in accordance with dependency, as in harmony and sequence of tenses. Could it be that, as just suggested, conventional verb concord involves only agreement in features, so applies in counter-dependency, while number agreement in the determiner phrase 'spreads' a referential index throughout the phrase, it is an instance of harmony?

However, there is evidence that plural in determiner phrases 'spreads' counter-dependency. Sometimes plurality is a lexical feature demanded by certain nouns; we have pluralia tantum, familiar from a range of languages. Often these represent objects with two parts, so that in languages which have dual number, we may find dual for the non-plural of such nouns and a regular plural, while other nouns are pluralia tantum (Corbett 2000: §5.8.2), as illustrated by the Yup'ik noun in (171a), with plural concord with the 'object':

(171) a. niicugni-ssuut-   et nipe- s-   k
         listen-   INST.NOMINALIZER-PL go.out- CAUS-OPTATIVE.II.SG/III.PL
         ('Turn off the radio')

   b. these scissors
   c. {N{pl}/{prt}} ←············ .
         :   :
         :   : ── { {prt}}
         :   : |
         :   ···········{N{pl}}
         : |
         :   {N;P{count}}
         :   :
         :   :
       these   scissors

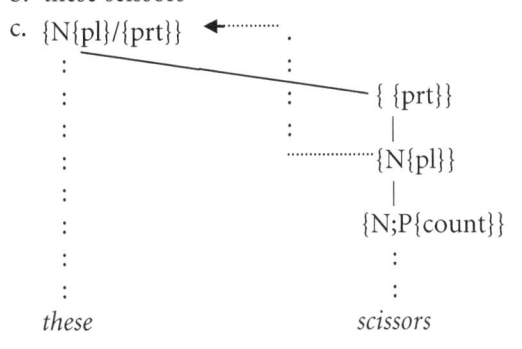

The noun in (171b) is the classic English plurale tantum, which requires the demonstrative determiner to agree with it. I suggest this operates as in (171c). Plural is the unmarked value for count nouns, as assumed in (II.186); only in the absence of plural is a singular determiner acceptable. Only the topmost determiner in (171c) and (II.186) is referential, and corresponds with properties of the referent. And this referentiality does not 'spread' downwards. What we have in (171c) is classic agreement/umlaut.

The phenomena of (171) contrast with collective nouns such as *committee* or *herd*, where the {N;P} itself is inherently plural: '{N;P{count,pl}}'. Since the plural feature is not secondary to {N} but to {N;P} it does not participate in regular agreement. But it emerges via referential agreement on the part of, exceptionally, a verbal, as in *The committee are debating the issue at the moment*. I do not pursue this here, nor the distinction between distributive and non-distributive readings of plural.

Even without such extensions, the above account of number agreement remains very speculative. However, the analogy between umlaut and gender agreement and conventional verb concord has a clear foundation—and plural agreement may belong with them. The synchronic analogy involves agreement in properties where the natural locus of the properties is with the dependent in a construction, affix (umlaut) or argument (agreement). Strictly, 'spreading' can be applied only to the phonological mechanism, which ultimately involves physical realization. Also, the situation of agreement in syntax is complicated, in the first place, by interaction between the two systems of gender, and, secondly, by the existence of languages like Selayarese, where the agreement associated with verb concord involves apposition, so that the distinct argument may not be present. Perhaps there is an analogy here with those language states where an umlaut trigger has disappeared and the vowel alternation associated with it is morphologized (*foot/feet, food/feed*). On this development in English, see §4.6.1. However, this is a diachronic development, rather than the synchronic absence or presence of a source of agreement.

4.5 Underspecification and polysystemicity

Let us look now at a consequence of the kind of analyses presented in the preceding sections of this chapter. For the notion of underspecification invoked in many of the preceding phonological illustrations and elsewhere may be seen itself to introduce another set of analogies. We have appealed to **subsystem-dependent underspecification** with respect to the representation of both primary and secondary categories, so that, for instance, complex s-onsets in English is unspecified in both respects, in primary and secondary category (recall §2.3.3). And this is system-dependent: at that point in structure, [s] is the only positive possibility. I have also appealed to the underspecifications, and indeed non-specifications, that apply to the system as a whole. [v] in Djingili (following van der Hulst and Smith 1985) was regarded as unspecified in §3.4. And there seems to be great variation—though not necessarily arbitrary—in the character of the non-specification to be attributed to different vowel systems and subsystems.

It may be too that there are **system-independent non-specifications** of secondary categories, though the identification of these is controversial. It has been suggested, for instance, that non-specification of coronal among consonants may be general (see e.g. the contributions to Paradis and Prunet 1991).[43] On the other hand, it has been argued elsewhere (e.g. in Lass 1976: ch. 6, 1984: §8.3.1) that glottal consonants may be generally unspecified as to (in our terms) secondary category, and this has some basis in the character of their exponence, with absence of stricture in the vocal cavity itself. Glottals may be an example of substantive, or irreducible, non-specification, whereas coronals, though lexically unspecified, as unmarked, are filled by redundancy and so phonetically specified. There remain many unresolved issues in this area. Nevertheless, it is possible that the secondary categories of the phonology manifest both system-dependent and general non-specification.

4.5.1 *Underspecification and aspect in Greek and English*

We find parallels to both variants of non-specification in the representation of secondary syntactic categories, both system-dependent and system-independent, the latter reflecting markedness. There is some discussion of this non-specification of syntactic features in relation to Latin verbal forms in §3.3.1 of Volume II of this series. But I shall now make these parallelisms more explicit via a comparison of (the interpretation of) the Greek sentences in (172) with their English glosses, where we are concerned in particular with the representation of **aspectual** distinctions, particularly as expressed by the underlined verb forms:

(172) a. Otan imun stin Aθina evlepa sixna tin Eleni
 when I-was in-the Athens I-saw often the Eleni
 b. Milusa sto Niko otan akuse to kuδuni na xtipai
 I-was-speaking to-the Nick when he-heard the door-bell that it-rings
 c. Iδa to Giorgo ke tu milisa ya sena
 I-saw the George and to-him I-talked about you

---

[43] The status of this particular proposed general non-specification remains doubtful, however. For instance, the longitudinal data from early acquirers of Dutch which is discussed by Heijkoop (1997) suggest that, in their case, at least, first acquisition of 'consonant place' is not based on coronal underspecification. However, other factors than simplicity of categorial representation may be involved here, as elsewhere in acquisitional phenomena.

(examples from Holton et al. 1997: 224–5). Let us look first of all at the English glosses (not simply out of perversity).

When the English past is used habitually, as in the gloss to the underlined form in (172a), 'saw', it is not necessarily specified as such, though it may be differentiated by the 'periphrasis' *used to* or, indirectly, by an adverbial (as here). However, apparently, the unmarked interpretation of the simple past is universally for notional reasons (system-independently) **perfective**, as exemplified here by the most obvious interpretation of the gloss to the second underlined form in (172b), 'he-heard'; **imperfective** is marked in the past. But in English the **habitual** variety of imperfective is not specified morphologically. The **progressive**, the other variety of imperfective, is specified in English, distinguished overtly, as in the case of the gloss of the first verb in (172b). Let us spell this out more explicitly.

We have in English the privatively expressed aspectual contrast illustrated in (173a) vs. (b):

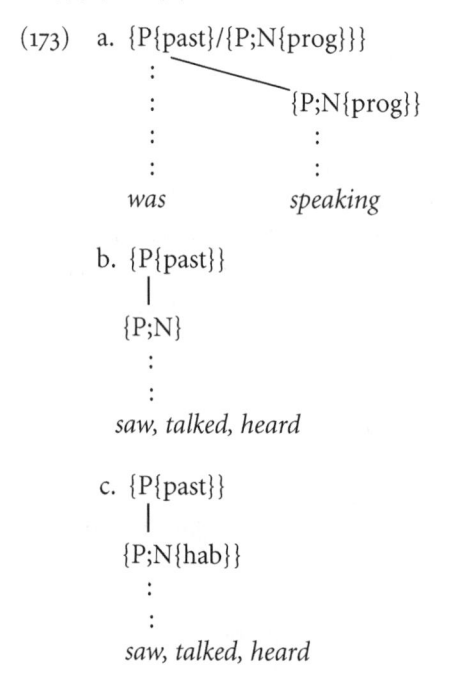

(173) a. {P{past}/{P;N{prog}}}

　　　　　　　　　　{P;N{prog}}
　　　　　　　　　　　:
　　　　　　　　　　　:
　　　　　　was　　speaking

　　b. {P{past}}
　　　　|
　　　{P;N}
　　　　:
　　　　:
　　　saw, talked, heard

　　c. {P{past}}
　　　　|
　　　{P;N{hab}}
　　　　:
　　　　:
　　　saw, talked, heard

Be in this case is subcategorized for a progressive verb form, thereby allowing the latter to occur in finite contexts (as discussed in §3.3.2 of Volume II). Only this periphrastic representation is lexically specified for aspect in finite clauses. Whether the verb in (173b) is interpreted as habitual or not is determined by the context. *Often* in the gloss to (172a) triggers the habitual represented in (173c); in the absence of such a trigger, the normal interpretation is perfective. A combination of habitual with progressive is also possible, particularly if forced by the context, as in *I was reading lots of novels at the time*.

The unmarked interpretation for prototypical (dynamic, non-durative) past verbs, viz. perfective, is cognitively natural. Thus, in languages that lack tense markers a perfective verb is interpreted as having past-time reference, unless this is overridden by the context (cf. e.g. Comrie 1976: 82–3). In English, expression of progressive and non-expression of habitual are system-dependent; non-expression of perfective in the past with prototypical verbs is unmarked.

All the corresponding Greek expressions in (172) involve morphologically expressed (rather than periphrastically marked) aspect. But what is more relevant to our present concern is that it is not progressive that is expressed overtly but **imperfective**, a more inclusive category which comprises both progressive and habitual. The underlined form in (172a), *evlepa*, is imperfective; so is the first underlined verb in (172b), *milusa*. But the first of these may be distinguished by the context as habitual, and the second as progressive. These imperfectives are typically based on the stem associated with the present in Greek; this stem is a dedicated imperfective marker. The non-imperfectives in (172b) and (c), respectively *akuse*, and *iδa* and *milisa*, have the universally unmarked perfective interpretation for pasts; their morphology expresses the unmarked aspect for pasts.

We might thus represent these various Greek forms as in (174):

(174) a. {P{past}}
  |
  {P;N{impf}}
  :
  :
  milusa, evlepa

 b. {P}
  |
  {P;N}
  :
  :
  akuse, iδa, milisa

We thus have system-dependent non-specification of progressive vs. habitual, while, of course, the unmarked status of perfective with prototypical past verbs is general.

It seems likely, then, that secondary categories in both phonology and syntax show both system-dependent and system-independent non-specification. A preliminary investigation of systems of primary categories, however, suggests that in the case of the phonology we find only system-dependent non-specification, as with the s-onsets of English discussed in §2.3.3, whereas in syntax the distribution of non-specification among primary categories is a matter of general grammar. I shall suggest at the beginning of Chapter 5 that this particular apparent discrepancy is motivated by external-interface factors. Nevertheless, presence of both system-dependent and system-independent non-specification, found in the systems of secondary categories, seems to be another syntax-phonology analogy.

4.5.2 *Polysystemicity, aspect, and vowel systems*

However, we have not quite finished with the area of aspect, which, it will perhaps already be apparent, yields another kind of analogy to familiar phonological phenomena. Typically, system-dependent non-specification in phonology is associated with polysystemicity. And in general we can attribute to a language different subsystems of phonological categories associated with different structural contexts. This also seems to be a property of syntactic categories, as again illustrated by aspect systems. These also share with the phonology polysystemic interaction with general markedness relations.

With non-past verbs (in contrast with simple pasts) imperfective, and particularly habitual, seems to be unmarked. Thus, in languages without tense markers, just as a perfective verb is normally interpreted as past (unless overridden by the context), so an imperfective verb is interpreted as non-past. The following Yoruba examples from Welmers (1973) are cited by Comrie (1976: 83):

(175) a. ó ń ṣiṣẹ́
 he IPFV work ('He is working, he works continuously')
 b. ó wá
 he came

In English non-pasts, progressive is again specified; and the non-progressive form is interpreted as perfective only in specific well-known environments— as in sports commentaries (*He passes the ball to Smyth*) or newspaper headlines (*President Shrub resigns*), though the simple non-past may also represent some kind of 'historic present' (of which headlines may be a variation, indeed). Habitual is the unmarked interpretation for non-pasts in English— as indeed is implied by the characterization of non-pasts in §4.3.3. In Greek simple non-pasts, nothing is specified; and habitual, progressive, and perfective interpretations depend on context, though the former two, collectively the imperfective, are unmarked, with the perfective again being limited to very specific environments (see e.g. Anderson 2001c: §3.2). In the past tense, the roles of the perfective and imperfective are distinguished in the way we have seen. Overall, Greek consistently avoids the morphological indication of markedness, unless the morphological affinity of the past imperfective with the undifferentiated present is taken to be some sort of indication of this.

These aspectual asymmetries in Greek in particular illustrate **polysystemicity**. For, as we have seen, the Greek simple non-past, unlike the past, does not show a formal contrast between imperfective and perfective in unmarked declarative sentences, and its range of interpretations (habitual/progressive/perfective) is greater than those of the (past) imperfect, for instance, which cannot normally be interpreted perfectively. There is an overt contrast between perfective and imperfective only in the past (and irrealis) forms.[44]

There is in this area, as observed above, an asymmetry in markedness in language in general: past favours perfective, non-past imperfective. But imperfective actions in the past are not as marked as perfective is in the non-past. And this may underlie the Greek polysystemicity: signalling a perfective/imperfective distinction in the past is more to be expected, since neither is unusual, as are present perfectives. The perfective past is unmarked, but in general imperfectivity in the past is in no way exceptional.

---

[44] There is a form of non-pasts in Greek that are subordinate to predicators of volition/intention and have imposed on them a future, or at least non-actual, interpretation, which is unmarkedly perfective, as with pasts. In this context, as with pasts, in English the progressive is overtly specified (*I want to be sitting on the beach*). In Greek it is arguably again an imperfective that is marked (as with pasts), as in (ia), which can be interpreted as habitual or progressive, while (ib) is interpreted as (the unmarked) punctual:

(i) a. θelo   na   kaθome   stin   paralia
       I.want that I.sit.IPFV on.the   beach

    b. θelo   na   kaθiso/katso stin   paralia
       I.want that I.sit.PFV   on.the   beach

We find the same contrast in Greek when the non-past verb is combined with the marker of futurity, θa.

If one adopts the proposal of Anderson (2001c) that so-called 'particles' such as θa are manifestations of a {P}, and that the inflected verbs following θa, as well as the inflected subordinates in (i), are syntactically non-finite, we can make the following generalization: in non-past finite clauses in Greek there is no marking of aspect. Recall here the discussion in §3.4.2.

The brief treatment of English and Greek given here ignores, of course, various further aspectual distinctions found in these and other languages (as is evident from such surveys as Comrie 1976, Dahl 1985, Chung and Timberlake 1985: §2, and much later work). But the apparatus deployed here seems to be generally applicable to shared subparts of these different systems.

This past/non-past asymmetry is motivated by substantive considerations to do with (the limitations of) our (capacity to provide a uniform) conceptualization of the relation between tense and aspect, which ultimately has to do with our perception of time. Particularly problematical is the association of deictic present tense with perfective aspect: this combination is thus highly marked. Markedness of this sort favours tense systems that are aspectually polysystemic, with different aspectual distinctions being distinguished at each tense. Such substance-based polysystemicity is analogous to what we often find with vowel systems, where different subsystems of contrast are associated with different contexts. In particular, under low stress or in nasal environments—in the presence of 'noise'—the system may be much reduced compared with the 'major' system. Thus English, for instance, has different vowel systems depending on the presence of accent. Extensive redundancies hold between polysystemicity and accent placement. And in low-accent syllables not only is the system reduced but also transitivity disappears as an option, so that the vowel introducing an accented syllable never shares its onset with the preceding (unaccented) syllable. As we shall see in the chapter that follows, ambisyllabicity is foot-internal. In this way, in both planes some polysystemicity arises from substantive problems of interfacing with the respective extralinguistic domain.

We can again illustrate this phonological polysystemicity in more detail from Old English, on the basis of our previous look at the major system with short vowels. Anderson (2005c) observes that in the pre-umlaut short-vowel system there are contrasts before nasals only among three vowels, {i}, {u}, and {a}—whatever variation there may have been in the realization of these vowels. This reduction in contrast is largely illustrated by a comparison of the paradigms for the strong verbs *bindan* 'bind' and *helpan* 'help'. These belong to the same historical conjugational class but differ in respectively containing and lacking a coda nasal in the root:

(176) a. *bindan* 'bind'   b. *helpan* 'help'   INF
       bint 's/he/it binds'   *hilpþ* 's/he/it helps'   III.SG
       band 'bound'   *healp* 'helped'   I/III.SG.PST
       bundon 'bound'   *hulpon* 'helped'   PL.PST
       -*bunden* 'bound'   -*holpen* 'helped'   PST.PTCP

In comparison with the 'regular' *helpan*, *bindan* lacks the 'mid' vowels [e] and [o] in the appropriate places; and it lacks the [æ] historically underlying the vowel spelled *ea* in *healp*. The paradigm of *helpan* lacks the 'equivalent' of the vowel spelled <a> that we find, instead of spellings for [æ] and its descendants, in *band*. The absence of an [a] vowel here, however, does not reflect a consistent phonologically conditioned reduction in the major system; it is merely absent from the 'regular' members of this conjugational class. We find an [a], however, in the (class VI) strong verb *faran* 'go'. This distribution is morphologically determined. Not so with the reduction in the vowel system before nasals, where the absence of [æ] and the presence of [a] is conditioned by the following nasal.

We have before nasals in Old English the basic triangular system of (177) (Lass and Anderson 1975: ch. II, §5; Anderson 1988d: §§2–3):

(177) pre-umlaut pre-OE system of short monophthongs before nasals
    {i} *bindan*   {u} *bunden*
                    {v} *band*

Moreover, there are difficulties in straightforwardly identifying these with members of the 'major' system—at least in the case of the vowel I have represented '{v}'. Recall (162):

(162) *fully specified pre-umlaut pre-OE system of short monophthongs*
    {i} 'i' *fisc* 'fish'   {u} 'u' *full* 'full'
    {i;v} 'e' *cweþan* 'to say'   {u,v} 'o' *god* 'god'
    {v;i} 'æ' *sæt* 'sat'
              {v} 'a' *sadol* 'saddle'

The effect of *i*-umlaut on the compact vowel {v} in (177) will illustrate something of the difficulties in matching it with the full system.

Thus, early spellings of the umlaut of the {v} vowel of the pre-nasal system show *æ*, as we might expect, in forms with historical [a] + nasal associated with an *i*-umlaut environment such as those in (178a):

(178) a. aenid 'duck', cændæ 'he begot'
       b. ened 'duck', fremman 'do/perform'

This corresponds to the behaviour under umlaut of the {v} of the full system. Cf. (159d):

(159) a. burg 'city'—byrig 'city' *dative sg*
       b. ofost 'haste'—efstan 'hasten'
       c. cwæl 'died'—cwellan 'to kill'
       d. faran 'go'—færþ 'goes'

However, though these spellings persist in some texts, overwhelmingly the umlauted form of this etymological class is spelled *e*, as in (178b).

Æ in (178a) represents the normal full-system umlaut of [a]; *e* in (178b), however, if it reflects simply the effects of umlaut, suggests a reinterpretation of [a] as [o], i.e. what would be represented {u,v} in terms of the full system of (162), the umlaut of which is in general spelled this way, after unrounding, as in (159b). Such a historical reinterpretation would not be unnatural, given the emphasis on the lower end of the spectrum (gravity) projected by nasals; in this context the vowel may indeed have been nasalized. But the umlaut spelling with *e* represents a late stage in the development of this vowel, and even the *æ*-spellings are not immediate evidence of the original value of the umlaut of pre-nasal {v}.

Notice too that, for the most part, pre-nasal {v} does not fall together with full-system [o], to judge from subsequent developments. The realization of the pre-nasal vowel was probably distinct in quality from both the {u,v}/[o] and the {v}/[a] of the full system (cf. e.g. Hogg 1992: §5.8). Of course, the ambivalence suggested by the persistent alternation between *a* and *o* spellings, exemplified in (179), may reflect possibly coexisting alternative specifications ({v} or {u,v}) of the vowel, but it may be associated with difficulties in recognizing orthographically the realizational distinctiveness of the pre-nasal vowel:

(179)   nama/noma 'name', mann/monn 'man'

The pre-nasal system may not be a simple subset of the 'major' one. It contains a vowel that is different from both the {v} and the {v,u} of the main system, and is perhaps realizationally intermediate between them (?[ɔ]). And this is not unusual: the neutralization of two or more contrasting segments may resemble none of them.

To sum up: polysystemicity seems to be a characteristic of both phonology and syntax—or at least, in terms of the evidence we have looked at, morpho-syntax. In the phonology its prevalence has once again been obscured by (explicit or implicit) adoption of the principles of 'phoneme theory', with its typical insistence on monosystemicity. And Anderson (2005c) argues that the prevalence of monosystemic viewpoints in historical phonology has distorted the kinds of reconstructions that have been attributed to earlier stages such as we have looked at here. Such viewpoints have been encouraged by the evidence for earlier stages of languages—where it is not preserved in syllabaries and less transparent systems of representation—being recorded in alphabetic writing systems, which tend to be monosystemic, for reasons of symbol economy. As historical linguists we need to take more account of the distortions of our orthographic lenses. To insist on polysystematicity is not to reject the principle of contrast, but only to insist that, despite the distortion of orthographic systems, it is locally, monosystemically determined—indeed it is to impose the principle more rigorously.

4.5.3 Coda on contrast

Both underspecification and polysystematicity are driven by the maximization of contrastivity. Contrastivity is a lexical and a distributional property. Phonologically, contrast in substance is what differentiates lexical items, including intonation contours that realize distinctions in syntactic category. Primary phonological categories, however, have contrastive distributions (primarily {V} vs. C), rather than contrasting paradigmatically, and their members share substantive properties. Syntactic contrastivity is similar, though more complex, as we might expect. In substance, lexical items contrast paradigmatically with members of the same word class, or contrastive primary category. We have seen that different word classes can be defined syntagmatically, as syntactic categories whose prototypical members have a shared substance, and collectively a distinct distribution from that of members of other word classes. Prototypical verbs and nouns do not share their distribution; so too prototypical adjectives are distinct in distribution, but, in being a combination of noun and verb categorially, the distribution of non-prototypical adjectives overlaps with that of both of them. Neither nouns nor adjectives in English can be finite but both can be attributive; and verbs, though having non-finite forms, are only marginally attributive, and only if this is morphologically signalled, as in *the falling rain*. Members of the verb and adjective classes can be subcategorized for a variety of complement types, so that 'stative' predicators may be either verbs or adjectives, with the appropriate valencies.

Both syntax and phonology show 'positional variants', involving syntagmatic non-contrast. In phonology these are commonly called 'allophones', in syntax 'word forms' (inflectional variants). These 'carve up' the distribution of the element which they are variants of. Thus, alongside the familiar [p^h, t^h, k^h] variants of the {C} segments in English, with their distinct distribution from other variants of simple {C}, we can place the *-ing* variant of verbs, which has unique environments in which it occurs, such as as a complement to the operative in (173a), repeated here:

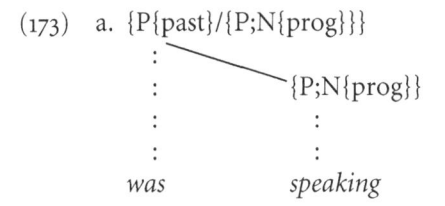

(173) a. {P{past}/{P;N{prog}}}

           :
           :   {P;N{prog}}
           :   :
           :   :
         was   speaking

However, though this *-ing* form may be distributionally determinate, it has semantic content, whereas an 'allophone' does not as such make a semantic distinction. We are again confronted with the pervasive semanticity of syntax.

This semanticity, however, is less obvious—indeed, is non-distinctive in cases of paradigmatic non-contrast. Paradigmatic non-contrast in phonology is often referred to as 'free variation', and tends to be 'triggered' by extralinguistic (social, communicative) factors. We find a similar variation in syntax in, for instance, the alternation in *They demand that Bill leave(s)*: morphological subjunctive vs. non-subjunctive.

As has already been envisaged, things are complicated in syntax by various differences from phonology in its relationship to the interfaces and the content of the interfacee. These sources of complication include a particular feature of the complex interface between syntax and the phonology that we call the lexicon, viz. derivationality, overtly marked or not. Lexical derivationality permits 'change' of category. An item of a certain word class, with the appropriate class meaning, may 'take on' another class and class meaning, giving a derived item that retains the original class and class meaning in a subordinate role, as in *kill* (verb) and *killer*, or *run* (verb) and *run* (noun). We have contrasts within contrasts. Such categorial complexity is incompatible with the phonetic demands put on phonological categories; all phonological contrasts are reflected in phonetic substance.

Moreover description of the basic distribution of syntactic elements, as well as their categorization, is complicated by the intervention of functional categories, whereas the functional/lexical distinction is not relevant to the phonology. Chapter 5 looks at, among other things, the motivations for this distinction, and the resulting dis-analogies between the planes.

Nevertheless, the basic patterning of paradigmatic and syntagmatic contrast and variation is a further analogy in the structure of phonology and syntax. And this patterning, along with the 'double articulation' provided by the lexicon, is a response, in pursuit of the communicative function of language, to the demands of the extralinguistic interfaces and the reconciliation of these, via re-representation. We have a set of sequences of re-representations that seek to reconcile semanticity of function with phoneticity of expression.

4.6 Grammaticalization

It is time that I turned from illustrating these various analogies to exemplifying more systematically the limits on analogy imposed by interfacing of different kinds, limits which, as just illustrated, I have constantly had to anticipate in the discussion so far. As indicated, this will be our concern in Part III of this volume.

Let us note finally here, however, a pervasive analogy I have neglected up till now, one that is basic to the function(s) of language. Both syntax and phonology are subject to **grammaticalization**, in the sense of the loosening of interface associations between the respective extralinguistic domain and the linguistic structure that gives it linguistic expression. We should perhaps more correctly talk about 'further grammaticalization': linguistic structure, though based on them, is not determined simply by the nature of the cognitive and perceptual domains that it relates and gives structure to (cf. more fully on this Carr 1990). Linguistic structure is also determined by the 'inter-interface', or internal, requirements of a communication system capable of expressing and signalling a complex message in a particular medium amid much noise. This is of course not to endorse the 'strongly innate' view of universal grammar argued against in the Prologue and Part II. I assume that the requirements of the inter-interface—or substance-to-substance—link that is the domain of grammar are resolved by the application of general cognitive principles, and that they are (re)acquired on the basis of these and learning strategies based on recognition of a language as a representational system.

However that may be, given the diversity of ways in which the term 'grammaticalization' has been used and (what seems to me) the vagueness of attempts to characterize it (cf. e.g. Hopper and Traugott 1993: ch. 1), it behoves me to spell out a little more what I have in mind here. In the first place grammaticalization does not in my view necessarily include semantic 'bleaching'—though the latter may have syntactic consequences, such as the development of a functional category from a lexical. Under grammaticalization I include, for present purposes, two interrelated ways in which regularities can be relatively disassociated from the interface: firstly, a regularity can become intrinsically **denaturalized**, in that the substantive basis (in phonetic exponence and semantico-pragmatic interpretation) of the regularity is less transparent; secondly, more drastically, a regularity may in addition be **displaced** from direct connection with the substance that it gave structure to. Both of these may be illustrated for the phonology from the subsequent history of *i*-umlaut in Old English.

4.6.1 *Old English umlauted vowels*

The unrounding of the front rounded vowels resulting from *i*-umlaut, spelled initially *y* or *ui*, as in (159a) *byrig*, and *oe* or *oi*, as in *doehter*, mentioned in §3.4.1, results in some denaturalization. The 'results' of *i*-umlaut are no longer a transparent outcome of 'spreading' of {i}: **u** is also suppressed relative to the vowels which are the historical sources of these umlaut vowels, and, as we saw, they collapse with other vowels spelled respectively *i* and *e*. Now, this collapse may have a functional motivation, or at least may lack counter-motivation, if, say, the contrasts involved are marginal. But there is still denaturalization.

Denaturalization can be associated also with the loss of the extrasegmental {i} in many cases, as in most of the examples on the right in (159), repeated here:

(159) a. burg 'city'—byrig 'city' *dative sg*
b. ofost 'haste'—efstan 'hasten'
c. cwæl 'died'—cwellan 'to kill'
d. faran 'go'—færþ 'goes'

But, more strikingly, this also typically results in displacement, redeployment of the alternation as morphologically determined rather than phonetically.

Synchronically in historical Old English, *i*-umlaut can be interpreted as morphophonological: it is no longer a general phonological regularity such as can be reconstructed for pre-Old English, but is a set of alternations triggered by various morphological factors. I list the alternations in (180):

(180) a. {u} ~ {i}
b. {u,v} ~ {i;v}
c. {v;i} ~ {i;v}
d. {v} ~ {v;i}
e. {v} ~ {i;v}

(180a-d) are illustrated by the respective forms in (159); (180e) occurs before nasals, such as that in *mann/menn*, involving complications I have just gone into, in §3.5.2. In these alternations only the general trajectory—'movement' towards {i} as we go from column one to column two—is preserved of the natural assimilatory process of *i*-umlaut.

Grammaticalizations are not uncommon in the phonology, with displacement often serving to feed the morphophonology, as just described. They can also lead to lexical differentiation, as illustrated by the familiar history of *staff* and *stave* in English, which originate as members of a single paradigm: the difference in root vowel arises ultimately from a natural phonological alternation involving Old English [æ] and [a] *stæf ~ stafas*, and later also a distinction between transitive (checked) vs. intransitive (free), manifested as the length of the root vowel of *stafas*, which is thereby eligible for the Great Vowel Shift, giving (in this case) something like the present quality. These two forms are also differentiated by developments affecting the non-sibilant fricative, with voicing originally being associated with intervocalic position.

But such grammaticalizations do not constitute the core of phonology, which shows natural relationships. And it is such natural relationships that are the source, often synchronically recoverable, of the denaturalizations and displacements, and which account for the residues of naturalness (as in *i*-umlaut) that persist. Moreover, the grammaticalizations are typically not 'autonomous' developments. Denaturalizations, in particular, are based on 'attritions' in performance of phonological transparency. And displacements often are interpreted as serving a functional role. They can, for instance, provide more compact marking of contrasts, or indeed preserve marking (after the loss of affixes) in morphological paradigms, for instance, as in Modern English *man/men* or *mouse/mice*, or in the expression of derivational relations, as in *full/fill*—all of which are based on the results of *i*-umlaut.

4.6.2 *Grammatical relations and concord*

We find similar denaturalizations in syntax. Thus, the so-called 'topic/focus' (TOP/FOC) marker of Tagalog illustrated in (181) as associated with *pera* ('money') does not necessarily mark an element that is topical or in focus—as is implied by the scare quotes used here:

(181) Dadalhin ni Rosa ang   pera kay Juan
        FUT.take by Rosa TOP/FOC   money to John
        ('Rosa took the money to John')

(see on this Schachter 1976: 496–7). Whatever the historical source of this construction, it is relatively denaturalized. The same can be said of subjecthood, which Anderson (1997a: §3.3.2) groups with the 'topic/focus' as a (distinct) **grammatical**, rather than a directly semantically based, relation. Subjects are primarily marked by an affix or a position that has no obvious semantic function, but whose deployment is conventional, whatever might be the (natural) source of such constructions. As in the phonology, signs of the natural source may persist, in the present case in the form of subjecthood being not untypically (but not necessarily) of topic status.

The 'topic/focus' seems to have a natural source in a topicalizer, as does placement of the initial element in the similar phenomenon of 'verb-second' word order in Germanic languages. Thus the initial subordinate clause in (182) is not necessarily topical or in focus:

(182) Als ich in   die Schule ging,   regnete es
        as   I   into the school was.going rained   it

(see further Anderson 2006b: §7.2, and Volume I, §7.3). Similarly, subjects have a plausible source (illustrated by the prehistory of pre-Indo-European that can be reconstructed from the morphology of its descendants) in extension of the grammatical properties of an agentive topic to, crucially, the single participant in intransitive predications.

The analogy with phonology extends, in some cases at least, to the displacement of such phenomena to serve a function distinct from that connected with its original source. In the case of subjects, for instance, they provide, apart from anything else, one way of supplying a determinate candidate for apparent gaps in structure, however we analyse the gaps. Subjects thus play a role in the construction of transclausal dependencies, as in, say, *Blackadder tends/likes to beat Baldrick*. There is obviously something missing in the lower clause, given that *beat* normally involves two participants, and that subject formation is obligatory (in most constructions and in many languages). We can deduce that what is missing is what would otherwise be the subject of *beat*, and the unmarked subject of an agentive verb is the agentive. And a candidate for the 'missing' subject of *beat* appears ectopically, 'displaced', before *tends/likes*.

In terms of the framework assumed here, *Blackadder* can therefore be joined to *beat* by a transclausal dependency (involving a free absolutive, as discussed in §3.7 of Volume I, and pursued in §5.1 below). *Blackadder* is subject of both *tends/likes* and *beat*. Grammatical relations often provide in this way for the recoverability of apparent deletions, and so also aid in syntactic succinctness and integration. We have a displacement of such denaturalized functors as subjects from their role in expressing semantic or pragmatic relations to a role in the construction of complex dependency structures.

We can also discern denaturalization in systems of grammatical gender. And there is displacement in those (not uncommon) systems where grammatical or natural gender is primarily signalled not on the noun but on associated words, such as in German. However, this is a very 'natural' displacement if agreement is indeed basic to the development of systems of morphologically marked gender, as discussed in Chapter 6 of Volume II.

We can also view as a further instance of a common displacement the Basque constructions in (I.149c), referred to above in §4.4.2, or in more complex examples such as (183):

(I.149) c. Paulok   untzia   aurdiki   du
         Paul   vase.the throw.PST.PTCP NPST.(III.SG.ABS)(III.SG.ERG)
         ('Paul threw the vase')

(183) a. Lorea   aitari   eman   diot
           flower.the father.to give.PST.PTCP NPST.(III.SG.ABS)(III.SG.DAT)
                                                                (I.SG.ERG)
        ('I gave the flower to father')
      b. Lorea   aitari   eman   diozu
           flower.the father.to give.PST.PTCP NPST.(III.SG.ABS)(III.SG.DAT)
                                                                (II.SG.ERG)
        ('You gave the flower to father')
      c. Loreak   aitari   eman   diozkat
           flowers.the father.to give.PST.PTCP NPST.(III.PL.ABS)(III.SG.DAT)
                                                                (I.SG.ERG)
        ('I gave the flowers to father')
      d. Emazkiok!
         'Give them to him'

The verb *eman* 'give' takes three participant arguments whose person-number function is agreed with. But agreement with these arguments is displaced onto the clause-final finiteness element rather than being marked on the participle whose valency determines the range of agreement. Compare the 'non-periphrastic' imperative in (183d), where agreement is marked on the *eman* verb itself. But here, on the assumption that the verb in (183d) is complex, with a {P;N} subjoined to a {P}, the agreement could be a property of either component.

In §4.4.2 I contrasted such structures as (I.149c) and (183a-c) with the Greek (I.201a):

(I.201) a. Θa plirosi   o astinomikos
           FUT pay.AORIST.III.SG. the policeman ('The policeman will pay')

Here the agreement appears on the syntactically non-finite form *plirosi*, and the finite does not inflect. In comparison with (I.210a), (I.149c) and (183a-c) show a displacement of the agreement markers away from the verb whose valency they expound.

In languages with agreement only with a grammatical relation like subject we can scarcely talk of 'displacement'. If we assume that the verb form in the Latin of (II.60c) is a complex of {P} and {P;N} and the *est* of (II.60k) is a {P} with an adjoined {P;N}, *monita/monitus*, then the subject argument of the latter is also a dependent of *est* by virtue of being shared by the free absolutive of the {P}:

(II.60) c. *present indicative passive* monitor 's/he is reminded'
         k. *perfect indicative passive* monita/monitus est 's/he was reminded'

This assumes the (simplified) configuration in (184b) for (184a):

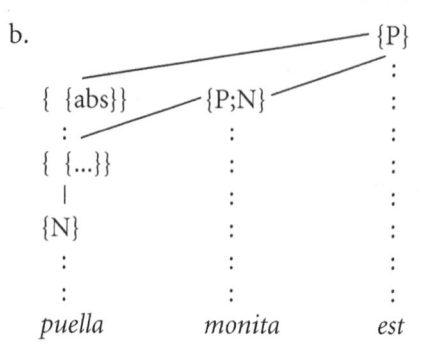

(184) a. Puella monita est ('The girl was warned')

b.
```
                                    ─ {P}
                                   ╱   :
    { {abs}}      ─ {P;N} ─────────    :
       :         ╱    :                :
    { {...}}   ╱      :                :
       |     ╱        :                :
      {N}  ╱          :                :
       :               :                :
       :               :                :
     puella         monita             est
```

This sharing of the argument is manifested morphologically in the person-number agreement on *est* combined with the gender-number-case agreement on *monita/monitus*.

Even the displacement in the Basque of (I.149c) and (183) is a rather different, less drastic kind from that we associated with the development of *i*-umlaut in Old English, which involved morphologization of the conditions determining the occurrence of the umlauted vowels. I shall be suggesting in §5.5 that the occurrence of the particular kind of displacement in the syntax illustrated by (I.149c) and (183) may be related to a distinction between syntax and phonology associated with differences in the demands of the interfaces. But, like the other syntactic displacements we have looked at, it shares with displacement in phonology the notion of movement towards less direct association with the interface, phonetic or semantic, displacement from the position in structure that would be expected by direct reflection of the interface with semantics. The displacement in agreement, moreover, in common with other phenomena, phonological and syntactic, touched on in this chapter, can be seen as promoting integration and succinctness of the finite clause, or of the word, in the case of the (morpho)phonology.

4.6.3 *Morphological grammaticalization*

The complex interface represented by morphology is particularly susceptible to increase in grammaticalization. I mention here only one rather striking example that is also discussed in another context. In §2.3.2 of the second volume in this series, I look at the 'preterite-present' verbs of Old English. These are, roughly, verbs whose finite present sense is signalled by forms that otherwise mark the past of strong verbs. Thus, the forms in (II.18a) belong to 'normal' strong verbs, and express past plural indicative:

(II.18) a. bundon 'bound', numon 'took'
b. gemunon 'remember', unnon 'grant'

But the forms in (II.18b) belong to 'preterite-presents', and are to be interpreted as present. The 'normal' present forms in strong verbs are of the shape *bindaþ* and *nimaþ*. In order to generalize the rules that relate syntactic categories to their expression it was suggested in Volume II that the finite present categories of 'preterite-presents' are 'shifted' as in (II.21a):

(II.21) *realignment of finite preterite-present strong verbs*
    a. {Pp,finite,pres} ⇒ {past}
    b. {Pp,finite,past} ⇒ {weak,past}

('Pp' is 'preterite-present'.) At the same time these verbs are provided in (II.21b) with a past paradigm that conforms to that of the weak verbs, so that the past of *gemunan* is signalled by a -*d*-, as in *gemunde* 's/he remembered'. Compare *lærde* 's/he taught'.

The category introduced on the right of (II.21a) is remote from the substance it expresses. Its presence is motivated by the rules of expression at the expense of semantic transparency. This class has a long history, and its Old English status has resulted from the reinterpretation of an Indo-European perfect form expressing the result of a process as representing simply the resulting present state. At least some of the members of the Old English 'preterite-present' class still betray such a 'resultative state' source: *wat* and *cann* 'know' (see Ono 1975: 33), *ah* 'possess', *deag* 'avail', *þearf* 'need', *sceal* 'shall', *geman* 'remember', *beneah* 'be enough', *mot* 'must', *mæg* 'may'. Overall we have evidence of a striking history of denaturalization and displacement, one that I have merely touched on here.

4.7 Conclusion

In this and the previous chapter I have moved away from the syntax-phonology analogies involving various obviously dependency-associated properties (complement, adjunct, specifier), and have invoked a range of other analogies, involving the relations among features, segmental and extrasegmental, and linearity.

Chapter 3 was concerned with the internal structure of the basic unit, and its relation to hierarchies of relative preponderance and markedness, involving detailed analogies between phonology and syntax. Thereafter, in this chapter, we looked at the well-studied diversity in the relation between particularly secondary features and segments in phonology, and traced something of the extent to which these structural relations are replicated in the syntax. In particular, we looked at various illustrations of the behaviour of extrasegmental (prosodic) elements, including harmony (§4.2), umlaut (§4.4), and the local manifestation of such elements (§4.3); and I tried to identify analogues in the syntax, specifically involving 'sequence of tenses' and agreement in relation to harmony and umlaut, respectively, and 'expletive *there*' and negation with respect to contrastively non-localized elements that are localized derivatively, such as English [h] and the Danish stød. The former is segmental, the latter subsegmental.

Many of the proposed analyses of the phonological phenomena discussed invoked underspecification and polysystemicity, and in §4.5 I focused specifically on analogies between phonology and syntax involving these and contrastivity, particularly in relation to vowel systems and verbal aspect. Whereas the previous sections dealt with syntagmaticity and linearity, in this one we turned to paradigmaticity and linearity—or, more generally, structural position. In trying to show that various notions associated with linearity apply to syntax as well as phonology, all these sections are intended to contribute to 'Syntax and Linearity'.

And the discussion was rounded off (in §4.6) by a brief consideration of the parallel manifestation in the two planes of grammaticalization, involving particularly some of the phenomena looked at in previous sections. Syntax and phonology are themselves grammaticalizations: it therefore seemed appropriate to end the discussion in the present chapter with a glance at such parallels in further grammaticalization.

The various dimensions of componentiality and extrasegmentality were illustrated with a range of data from different languages, in some cases considered in some detail, in order, it is hoped, to render less harmful any superficiality in the interpretation of the putative analogy that might arise from the necessarily brief and partial accounts offered here. Together, these discussions in Chapters 3 and 4 offer a body of evidence, complementing that in Chapters 2 in particular, for a particular kind of limitation on the distinctiveness of modules, a limitation on distinctiveness as a manifestation of autonomy. This limitation arises, in the first place, from the application of the same cognitive apparatus to the various modules that provide the succession of grammatical representations of mental domains that allow cognitive scenes to be expressed phonetically. Secondly, the perception of shared properties between, crucially, the domains grammaticalized by the two planes of language encourages the common cognitive apparatus to arrive at similar analyses for these properties. This results in widespread structural parallelism between the two planes, with morphological structure, such as it is, being parasitic upon the structural properties of the planes.

Analogy itself is limited by perceived differences between the two planes, however. As a consequence of pursuing the above proposed analogies in some detail, we have already encountered in this survey some restrictions on analogies. I have throughout commented on indications that these restrictions in the development of parallels have to do with intrinsic differences between the two modules of syntax and phonology: the differences can be attributed to the differing demands and limitations of the extralinguistic domains with which they interface, and to the architectural relationships between the two planes themselves and with the lexicon. This area is the concern of Part III of this volume, which explores more systematically the bases for limitation of the extent of analogy between syntax and phonology. Thus, given the recognition, particularly (as just described) in §4.6 of this chapter, of all of phonology and syntax as grammaticalization, we can perhaps formulate the primary concern of the following chapter as an examination of the limits that continue to be imposed by the respective basic substances with which they interface on the development of parallel (further) grammaticalizations in the two planes. Substance is significant for the recognition of both analogies and the bases for dis-analogy.

Part III
Why Syntax is Different

5

Categorization

In Part III of this Volume I look more consistently at how the different demands of the interfaces limit the scope for analogy. For it is not difficult to think of apparent discrepancies in the structural properties of the two planes; indeed, we have already encountered some. And this applies to more formal properties as well as to those that very directly reflect (differences in) the interfaced extralinguistic modules. By now in our discussion this situation demands some concerted and systematic attention.

Unsurprisingly, it seems to be the case that, to generalize somewhat prematurely, but on the basis of what we have already encountered, syntax displays possibilities not paralleled in the phonology. As we have seen, on the one hand, the particular substantive basis for phonology restricts possibilities that are more fully exploited in the syntax; and, on the other, the requirements of the more complex cognitive domain inhabited by what the syntax represents leads to developments that are simply unnecessary in phonology. Phonological representation is restricted by association with the physical medium in which it is implemented; syntax is a representational medium that must try to accommodate the intricacies of the large domain to be represented. Restrictions required by the extralinguistic domain also account for the major respect in which phonology is more complex than syntax—namely in its preference for maximization of dependency relations. In Chapter 2 I associated this with the maintenance of timing relations among phonetic properties: §2.5 illustrates the role of dependency and its absence in relation to timing between segments and between parts of segments.

The sign relation mediates between the two linguistic planes of representation and their unequal structural complexities. In what follows I shall focus in the first instance on the operation of the second, semantically based, factor that leads to dis-analogy, though the effects of the two extralinguistic domains are usually intimately intertwined. This means that in considering varying properties we shall find ourselves having to take account of both the **demands of semanticity** and **restrictions by phoneticity**.

Powerful distinctive demands on the syntax are imposed by its semanticity, then; the conceptual complexities of the domain that it is interfaced with demand elaborations that are not required in the phonology. Semanticity requires a more complex articulation of various structural properties, notably the system of categories and the range of manners in which categories can be related. In particular, the representation of perceived 'scenes' requires, in the first place, an elaboration of the notion of transitivity: we need in the syntax to be able to express the possible participation of a range of complements and adjuncts in the 'scene' whose event type is expressed by the predicator. If we are to avoid unnecessary power and abstractness (such as 'light verbs' and other aspects of syntactic decomposition of lexical items), the representation of these requirements can be seen to involve a system of **semantic relations**, 'labelled transitivities', not obviously necessary in the phonology.

We need the syntax to provide, as well, for the representation of 'scenes' within 'scenes'. This involves much more extensive and differential embedding compared with what seems to be necessary within the phonology. We also need to be able to provide for the different modes in which a 'scene' might be viewed: 'scenes' which are elsewhere represented as events may be presented as entities or as qualities that characterize entities. Just as different languages offer us different views of the world, so within any language categorial differences enable users of the language to present their world from different perspectives. This may be provided for by **alternative lexicalizations** (say, *brush*, noun, vs. *sweep*, verb). But also, to varying degrees in different languages, there may be provided, affording greater lexical economy, formally simple devices of **lexical derivation** which mark some items as expressing complex categories wherein one category subsumes another (*sweeper* vs. *sweep*). And, again with varying commonness in languages, there may be deployed devices which allow for **recategorization** without overt marking (*brush*, noun, vs. *brush*, verb), i.e. there may be **conversion**.

'Category change' and the derivation of one category from another are unnecessary synchronically in the phonology; indeed, the notion is incompatible with the fixed (perceptual) phonetic basis for the phonological categories, however much the precise realization of the categories of the phonology may be context- and system-dependent. We saw in §4.5.3 how complex derivational structure complicates application of the notion of contrast to syntactic categorizations; such complications are unthinkable in a system of representation, such as phonology, where contrast correlates directly with perceptual manifestation.

Semanticity also brings along a context. Utterances are located in space and time and tied to a particular speaker and addressee(s). And they make extralinguistic reference. Just as the semantic relations make possible the varyingly complex predications that express the internal structure of 'scenes', so these further aspects of semanticity are articulated by the features of other **functional categories**. Finite elements distinguish the various prototypical locutionary functions of utterances, as discussed in Volume I, Part II. Deixis and reference are associated with the determiner, including the derived determiners based on names and pronouns. There is no replication in phonology of these functions and the corresponding categories. The functional categories {P} and {N} serve to embed syntactic structures in the speech situation they occupy. As we have seen, {P} allows the expression of grammaticalized speech acts and relates utterances to the participants in the particular act and the temporal placement of the utterance. {N} enables reference to be made to participants and non-participants in the act and, via deixis, the local relation of the latter to the participants.

We must now look more carefully at these particular aspects of semanticity—the presence of functional categories in general, but particularly of that which bears the semantic relations, and the role of lexical derivation—before proceeding to others, some of which will emerge naturally in the course of the immediately following discussion, including familiar ones such as what is involved in the phenomenon of **ectopicity**, 'displacement' of an element from its normal position.

However, we should also acknowledge, before doing so, a limitation imposed by semanticity. It is incompatible with semanticity for there to be system-dependent—i.e. cross-linguistically variable—non-specifications among the primary categories. The lexicon is a crucial point of access to semantics. In so far as the basic semantic distinctions ('entity', 'event', 'scene', etc.) that are relevant to primary categorization are universal, this precludes system-dependent non-specification. At most, some lexical systems may be relatively underspecified, make fewer distinctions, compared with others. Adjectives, for instance, may be lacking as a word class in particular language, and the invocation of such a category may not be relevant to the syntax of the language. And, as we have encountered, there may be languages where even nouns and verbs are not lexically distinct—though the lexicon provides means (principally functional categories) whereby the functions associated with the categories noun and verb may be distinguished.

The contrastive phonological representations that are deposited in the lexicon are, on the other hand, not directly accessed by the phonetics; in this case, system-dependent non-specification—language- and even subsystem-specific—is eliminated by the redundancies that 'feed' the interface with phonetics. Indeed, this is the major role of phonology, to fill out the information required by the phonic interface. The difference between the two planes with respect to system dependence follows from the directionality of re-representation and the different orientations of the two planes towards the lexicon. The lexicon has a direct connection with semantics but only indirectly a phonetic orientation.

I present here the schematic representation of the structure of the grammar given finally in §3.1 of Volume I:

A basic grammar III

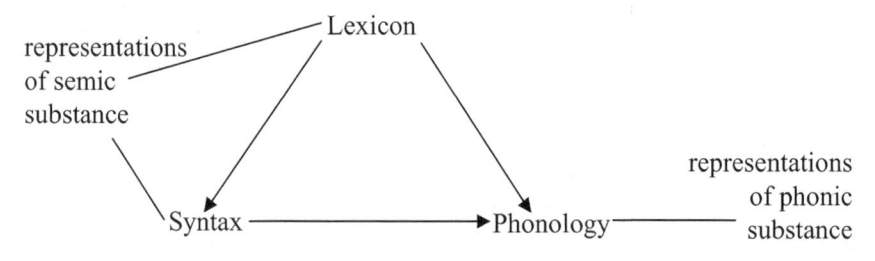

```
                    Lexicon
representations  ╱        ╲
of semic       ╱          ╲
substance    ╱            ╲
           ╱              ╲            representations
          ╱                ╲                of phonic
         Syntax ─────────→ Phonology ─────  substance
```

Let us begin to look now in more detail at the requirements of the 'semic substance' that is grammaticalized as syntax.

In what remains of this chapter we focus on the need for functional categories in the syntax, and their role in fulfilling cognitive demands, before we turn in the following chapter to the role of derivation and other mechanisms of embedding. I highlighted in Chapter 2 some rather obvious similarities between syntactic and phonological structure in the area of transitivity, and I exemplified in §2.3–4 the structures in the syntax and phonology that correspond in displaying distinctions associated with transitivity: transitivity and intransitivity, complementation vs. adjunction, specification. Let us return to and extend that discussion and confront the limitations of the analogy.

5.1 Functional categories

If we consider the representations for the syllable and clause structures in (185), where the former is a simplification of (54) from Chapter 2, the parallels seem to be pervasive:

(185) a.

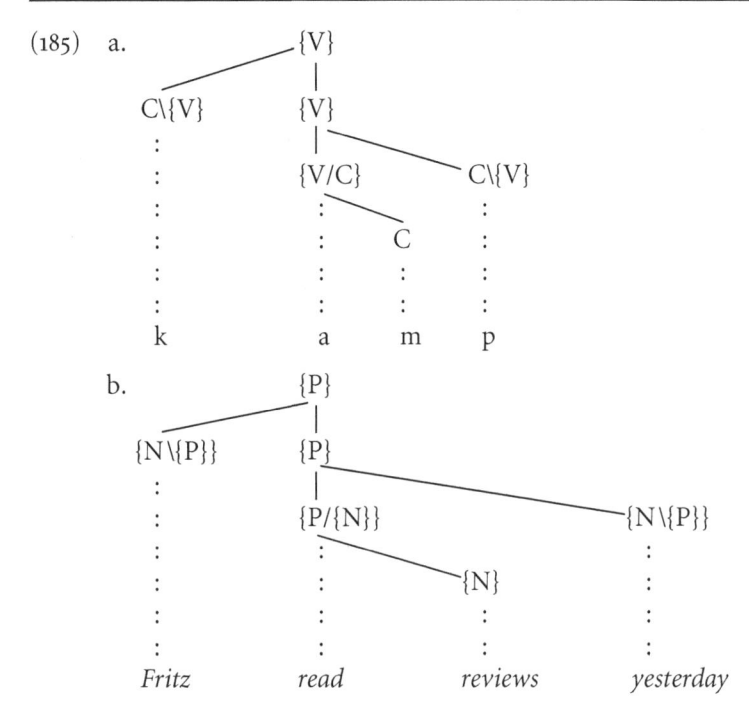

```
           {V}
            |
   C\{V}   {V}
    :       |
    :     {V/C}      C\{V}
    :       :    C    :
    :       :    :    :
    :       :    :    :
    k       a    m    p
```

b.
```
            {P}
             |
   {N\{P}}  {P}
    :        |
    :      {P/{N}}              {N\{P}}
    :        :        {N}         :
    :        :         :          :
    :        :         :          :
    :        :         :          :
   Fritz   read     reviews    yesterday
```

(185a)—and indeed (54)—does not implement the maximization of dependency that is argued for in Part II. And this already disguises a difference from syntax that is motivated by phonetic interfacing—namely, the guarantee of timing. But (185b) represents an even more drastic simplification. The representations in (185) extract a 'skeleton' in common that is in many regards uncharacteristic of either plane.

I have backtracked a little in (185b) from the assumptions concerning syntactic structure made in the discussion of a basic notional grammar in Chapter 3 of Volume I. What is missing is the functional/lexical distinction among syntactic categories. I have operated in relation to (185b) as if the syntactic categories were structured as simply as the phonological ones, with no such (functional/lexical) distinction, and I have represented the subject as an adjunct—as if it were a topic. This representation is meant both to lay out in a more systematic way the motivations for recognizing a parallelism and to hint at the inaccuracies involved in positing it. My intention is that by reviewing the motivations for this clausal representation we shall highlight more exactly where the transitivity analogy breaks down.

5.1.1 The need for functors

What (185) conveys is that, like consonants, nouns may be adjuncts (*yesterday*), as well as complements (*reviews*); and it embodies the traditional syntactic assumption that it is appropriate to distinguish between the more closely bound adjunct exemplified by *yesterday* and the 'predicate-external' *Fritz*. Observation of such parallelism is not new (cf. e.g., in the not too distant past, Pike 1967). More recently, it underlies Carstairs-McCarthy's (1998, 1999) argument that syntactic structure evolved as an 'exaptation' of phonological. However that may be, there are places where the parallelism rather clearly breaks down.[45]

One of these is made plain if we restore the full structure of (54), which was simplified in (185a); this reveals a kind of regularity not found in the syntax, involving the determination of the linearization therein (I have highlighted the linearity of the graphic representation by the concatenation signs ('+')):

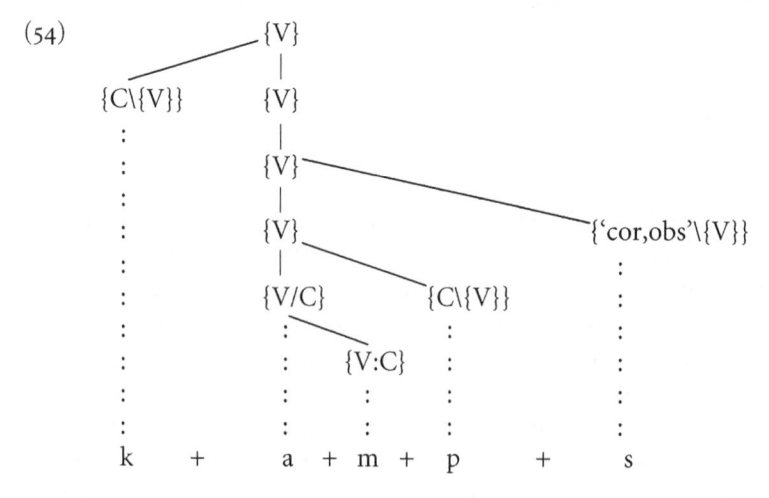

(54)

```
                    {V}
                     |
  {C\{V}}           {V}
    :               |
    :              {V}
    :               |
    :              {V}                        {'cor,obs'\{V}}
    :               |
    :            {V/C}      {C\{V}}
    :             :           :                   :
    :             :  {V:C}    :                   :
    :             :    :      :                   :
    :             :    :      :                   :
    k    +    a   +   m   +   p        +         s
```

The ordering of the consonants with each other is determined by the sonority hierarchy, so that rhymal [m] precedes [p], and by the exceptions to it, such as that affecting 'coronal obstruents'. This reflects the demands of the apparatus that implements phonological structure, particularly syllabicity. There is thus no analogy to these restrictions in syntax. A predicator in different (and sometimes the same) languages, for instance, may precede or follow or

---

[45] As already indicated, I do not pursue here the debate aroused by Carstairs-McCarthy's proposals (cf. note 11). I do not subscribe to the view espoused by (most on) both sides of the main debate that it is desirable or necessary to envisage a formally detailed autonomous linguistic faculty ('universal grammar') whose evolution is the subject of dispute.

come between various complements and adjuncts. It is rather obvious that not all languages share the SVO clause pattern exemplified in (185b): the difference between SVO and the also widely testified SOV and VSO types, to take only the majority types, would then represent syntactic variation that does not seem to be paralleled in the phonology: we have cross-linguistic variation in linearity. Phonology lacks this variation, in accordance with the requirements of the sonority hierarchy, and ultimately physical instantiation.[46]

Phonetic considerations—especially timing—also underlie dependency maximization. Recall such representations as (58):

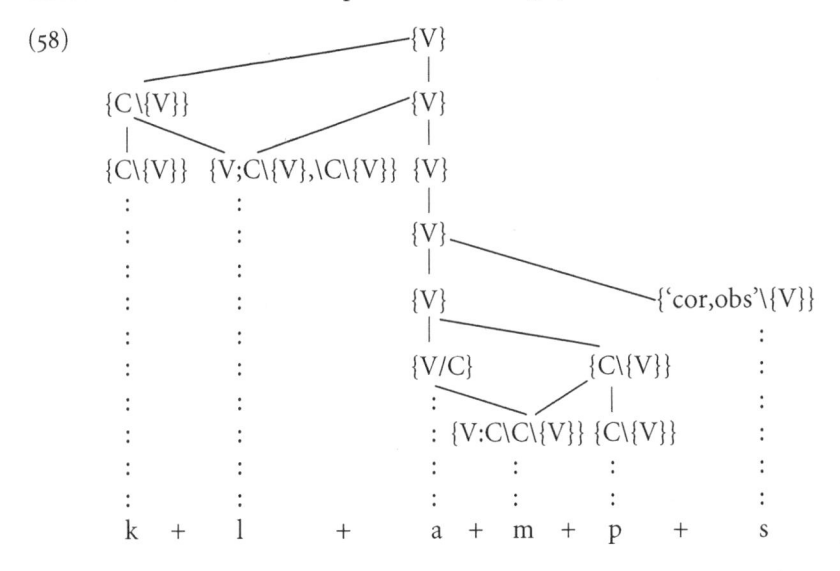

(58)
```
                            {V}
                             |
    {C\{V}}                 {V}
       |                     |
    {C\{V}}  {V;C\{V},\C\{V}}  {V}
       :          :            |
       :          :           {V}
       :          :            |
       :          :           {V}           {'cor,obs'\{V}}
       :          :            |                  :
       :          :          {V/C}      {C\{V}}   :
       :          :           :            |      :
       :          :    : {V:C\C\{V}}  {C\{V}}     :
       :          :           :    :    :         :
       :          :           :    :    :         :
       k    +    l    +     a  +  m  + p    +     s
```

Syntax apparently lacks obvious motivations for maximization, given the simplicity of the timing of syntactic elements.

However, if we abstract away linearity and dependency maximization, we might at least claim that configurationally and in categorial structure, the parallelism with phonology is more widely attested than simply in SVO languages. The attestation is weakened to the extent that there are apparently languages that lack a 'VP' constituent, i.e. the construction headed by the

---

[46] Of course, I do not entertain the proposition that all languages have the same 'basic word order': this would entail massive structural mutilations as part of the description of particular languages, as well as being quite unmotivated, except by theory-internal assumptions that countenance such mutilations. All word orders are equally derivative and invariant once assigned. And languages are more or less monolithic in how consistently a particular order of head and dependent is applied to different construction types, and each is potentially capable of showing various (often functionally motivated) sub regularities.

lowest {P} in (185b) (with the middle {P} allowing optional expansion of that): so-called 'non-configurational' languages (e.g. Hale 1983; Farkas 1986). Even in such cases the (non-)status of 'VP' remains controversial, however. On the other hand, there are languages that lack syllable codas, whereas there seem to be no languages that have only intransitive predicators. But perhaps the greatest problems are associated with the incapacity of something like (185b) to sustain the range of distinctions required by its (extralinguistic) interface domain, as anticipated at the beginning of this chapter.

One obvious discrepancy between the planes, even if we restrict our attention to English, is introduced by the observation that *yesterday* is not a typical adjunct. More often they are prepositional, as in (186); they introduce a category which intervenes between the verb and a nominal, but seems to be part of the argument:

(186) a. Fritz read reviews on Tuesday
b. Fritz left on Wednesday

It is not, clearly, that the absence or presence of this category is criterial for the distinction between complement and adjunct, or that such a preference is necessarily to be attributed to other languages, given that there are some in which both complements and adjuncts (as well as 'subjects') are typically marked uniformly by presence of some 'particle', either a postposition or 'enclitic' or inflection (recall §1.7). Rather, what is of interest here is that we seem to have introduced a distinct category, which is called 'functor' by Anderson (1997a), and whose character is outlined in Chapter 3 of Volume I of this trilogy. This is a type of category that, as a study of its distribution reveals, is not paralleled in the phonology. It is a functional category, a more general notion again introduced in Volume I, Chapter 3. I shall expand on these various functional notions in what follows, in this rather different context from that of the first volume.

Also, as anticipated, questions arise concerning the onset/subject analogy. As recognized by the 'maximal onset principle', whereby onsets are maximized at the expense of codas, and as embodied in (28)*, there is a strong tendency towards the filling of onsets:

(28)*   *unmarked syllable structure*
        {C} + {V}

Certainly, pressure to fill the onset in English connected speech is manifested by the 'capturing' by vowel-initial syllables of consonants from a preceding coda ('liaison') or, as in South African English, by insertion of an 'expletive' glottal stop (e.g. Giegerich 1992: §9.3.1), as is also well attested in German.

Cross-linguistically, some languages lack codas, while languages lacking onsets completely seem to be almost non-existent (though see Breen and Pensalfini 1999, on Arrernte). Filled onsets are certainly unmarked, at least.

However, it is often proposed that 'subject'—traditionally, the position in structure that is manifested as *Fritz* in (185b)—is an absolute universal, not merely preferred, and that, according to one formulation, in a 'full clause' '[Spec,IP] is obligatory' (Chomsky 1995: 55). '[Spec,IP]' is an interpretation of the traditional 'subject' relation, though it indeed may apparently be filled by not just an expletive (*It is raining*) but even by an 'empty' category.[47]

But this alleged universal status of 'subject' depends on affording some latitude to the notion 'subject', as well as the invoking of a battery of otherwise unwarranted 'empty' elements. I assume here a properly restrictive view of syntax which eschews empty elements. Moreover, the absence of a strict analogue to the traditional notion of 'subject' in languages with 'ergative' syntax and in many 'topic-prominent' languages, as well as in the 'topic/focus' type illustrated by Tagalog, is ignored at the expense of misrepresenting the typologically significant syntactic differences between these language types (see Anderson 1977: §3.5, 1997a: §3.1, 2006b: ch. 7). In particular, subjecthood is only one form that the grammaticalization of the topic can take (see again Anderson 2006b: ch. 7). And these various grammaticalized relations offer variant divergences from any direct analogy with phonological onsets.

In respect of pervasiveness, the extent of any analogy, beyond being preferentially filled, between onset and subject (or, better, Anderson's 1997a

---

[47] Chomsky (1981: 209–10) gives a rather different definition of subject. Thus 'the basic structure of S' is given in his (66):

(66)   NP INFL VP, where INFL = [[±Tense], (AGR)]

where 'AGR = PRO is obligatory with [+Tense] and excluded with [−Tense]'. And 'subject' is introduced so:

...let us introduce the term 'SUBJECT' having the following sense: the subject of an infinitive, an NP or a small clause...is a SUBJECT; AGR in (66) is a subject, but NP in (66) is not if INFL contains AGR.... Thus we take the SUBJECT to be the capitalized element in (67):

(67)   (i)   John [$_{INFL}$ past AGR] win
       (ii) he wants (very much) [for JOHN to win]
       (iii) he believes [JOHN to be intelligent]
       (iv) [JOHN's reading the book] surprised me
       (v)   he considers [JOHN intelligent]

Here 'SUBJECT' fails even more signally to refer to simply the prototypical exemplar of the traditional 'subject'. And this disjunctive definition not merely changes the idea of how subjecthood is expressed but also makes its independent content even more mysterious than it has been in the case of the traditional 'subject'—apart from what might be deduced from its alleged role in the formulation of theory-internal putative 'principles'.

'principal grammatical relation', including subjects, topics, absolutives, and 'topic/focus', depending on language type) remains uncertain. If, for instance, the 'topic/focus' of Tagalog is a 'principal grammatical relation', it is not universal in apparently 'full clauses'. Recall the discussion of (150a) in §4.3.1, which lacks the 'topic/focus' marker we find in (150b):

(150) a. May   aksidente Kagabi
         there-was accident   last-night
      b. Dadalhin ni Rosa ang pera   kay Juan
         Will-take by Rosa T/F money to   John

Nevertheless, 'principal grammatical relations' seem to be more insistently present than filled onsets. §2.2 suggested a less grammaticalized analogue to the phonological onset might be the topic, with its typically initial placement and non-universality, in the sentences of most languages at least. This would further undermine the analogy suggested by (185)—but by substituting a more plausible one, perhaps.

What is more problematical about (185b) is that, whether, given its position, one might regard *Fritz* there as specifically a specifier or simply an adjunct, non-expletive occupants of the position are nevertheless semantically essential to a clause containing the particular verb on which it depends, unless the verb takes no semantically required argument (as in *It rains*). Semantically, *Fritz* is as much of a 'complement' as *reviews*: both of them represent **participants** (in Halliday's (1994) 'notional' terminology) in the 'scene' labelled by that verb, rather than a circumstance in the scene. I have already argued that the complement/argument distinction in syntax is semantically based: syntactic criteria cannot be consistently maintained, and their unaided deployment has led to much terminological confusion. **Circumstantial** is (in Hallidayan terms) the role of the adjuncts *yesterday/on Tuesday/on Wednesday* in (185b/186), which are not demanded by the specific semantics of the verb. One problem in according a complement/participant status to subjects, and involving a difference from phonology, obviously, is that *Fritz* doesn't appear in what we have been regarding as a complement position in English. I return to this below, in §5.3. But also, ignoring this for the moment, we are now in the position of associating with a verb more than one complement. And this also differs from the phonology, and necessitates some way of differentiating the complements.

Now, these particular 'complements' can often be distinguished configurationally—though, as we've observed, this differentiation, dependent on the positing of 'VP', is itself problematical. But we also find verbs that take three participants, as in (187):

(187) a. Fritz received reviews from Millie (yesterday/on Tuesday)
 b. Reviews ranged from good to indifferent

Do we then have to allow for clauses with more than one (post-verbal) complement? And why? And how?

The answer to the first question is self-evidently 'yes', I suggest. Even if we choose to (allow ourselves to) 'decompose' such clauses into simpler sub-predications, the arguments still form a unified valency, associated with one particular predicator word. The answer to the second question is that we need to be able to represent and to differentiate among the roles of the participants in the 'scene' whose type is labelled by the verb, and, as we have just conceded, the verb may have more than one complement in order to do this.

The final question asks how these complements are to be differentiated. The two post-verbal participants (complements) in (187a) can be differentiated as non-prepositional vs. prepositional. But those in (187b) are both prepositional (whatever one makes of the categorial status of the items they introduce). Moreover, though the order of the complements is the usual one (perhaps for reasons to do with iconicity), in other cases either is equally possible, depending on the context:

(188) a. They travelled from London to York
 b. They travelled to York from London

However (188a) is again perhaps preferable on iconic grounds in many contexts.

What distinguishes the complements in (188) is the prepositions, and these prepositions reflect the participant types—or semantic relations—that are demanded by the verb. We again encounter the functor category introduced above, and we are beginning to witness the peculiarities of its distribution. For, even where there is no overt role-differentiator (*He gave me her/He gave her me*), and there may be ambiguity, the participants in principle satisfy different participant demands of the predicator, specifically demands that they fulfil some particular semantic relation in the 'scene' represented. But in that case these semantic relations are apparently borne by a functor that is not marked by a preposition. We must show how this is possible within a restrictive framework.

Related is the further observation that we can also rank these notionally differentiated participant types in terms of their eligibility in English (and many other languages) for lacking a preposition and for subject position. So, as concerns choice of subject, the sentient goal ('experiencer/receiver') in (187a) and the source of the action in (188) outrank the other participants for the subject slot. And what might be called the neutral relation, but what, following Volume I, I refer to as the 'absolutive', associated with *reviews*, usually lacks prepositional marking, like the sentient goal; and, even when outranked for subject position, as in (187a), it occurs closer to the verb than another non-subject participant. In (187b), in the absence of an outranking participant type, it occupies subject position. The structure in (185b) that is apparently analogous to the phonological structure of (185a) is determined by the array of participant types associated with particular verbs, and constitutes a 'grammaticalization' of it, in terms of absence of overt representation of some semantic relations, and of the consequent neutralization in expression associated with subjecthood.

The need for more-than-unary complementation reflects interface requirements: specifically, provision of the capacity to represent complex 'scenes' with multiple participants as well as (potentially) multiple circumstantials. But this also involves the explicit articulation of means of differentiating between different participant types as well as circumstance types, i.e. a means of differentiating among semantic relations. As anticipated, the major means is an instance of a category type absent from the phonology.

This is a type that may be realized in various ways, as has already begun to emerge from discussion of (187-8). It may be represented in a 'pure' form, or **analytically**, as in the post-verbals in (189a); or it may be realized along with, **cumulated** with, other syntactic categories, as in (b); or it may be 'absorbed' into another category, and be expressed **morphologically**, as in (c); or it may be reflected only **positionally**, as in (d):

(189)   a. Fritz lives at home/Fritz went to Rome
       b. Fritz lives there/below us
       c. Fredericus Romam iit
          Frederic   to.Rome went
       d. Fritz read reviews

Following still the discussion of Volume I, we can associate (189a) with the configuration in (190a):

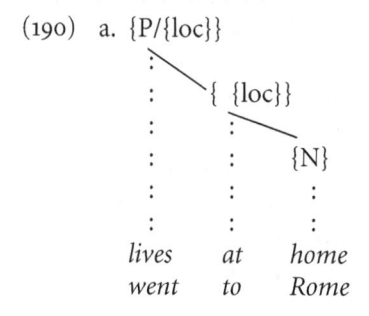

(190)   a. {P/{loc}}

```
         {  {loc}}
                  {N}


    lives    at    home
    went     to    Rome
```

b. {P/{loc}}
　　：
　　：　　{ {loc}}
　　：　　　|
　　：　　 {N}
　　：　　　：
　　：　　　：
　　lives　there

b*. {P/{loc}}
　　：
　　：　　{ {loc}}
　　：　　　|
　　：　　{N/{{loc}}}
　　：　　　：
　　：　　　：　　{ {loc}}
　　：　　　：　　　|
　　：　　　：　　 {N}
　　：　　　：　　　：
　　：　　　：　　　：
　　lives　below　　　us

c.　　　　　　　　{P/{loc}}
　　　　　　　　　：
　{ {loc}}　　　：
　　 |　　　　　：
　　{N}　　　　：
　　　：　　　　：
　　　：　　　　：
　　Romam　　　iit

d. {P/{abs}}
　　：
　　：　　{ {abs}}
　　：　　　|
　　：　　 {N}
　　：　　　：
　　：　　　：
　　read　reviews

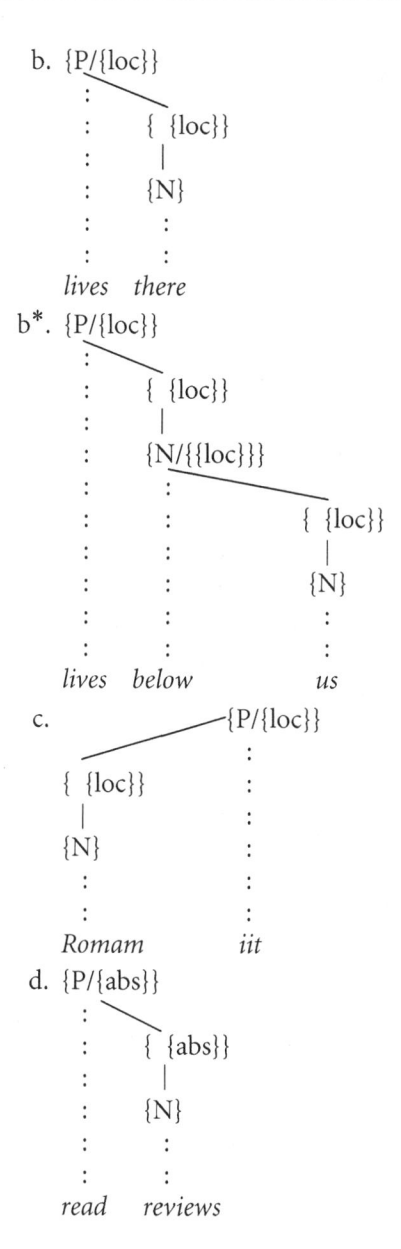

The semantic relation {loc(ative)} is a secondary category of the functional category in question, the **functor**. This primary category itself is left here unspecified; and this is not by oversight, or a temporary measure: functor is the category that is neither predicable nor referentiable, so it lacks both **P** and

N, the predicability and referentiability features. The functor links the predicator to its arguments, and its secondary categories label the relations that hold between predicator and argument, so identifying which of the relations demanded by the predicator the argument satisfies.

The verb in (190a) is subcategorized for at least a locative complement; and this valency is satisfied by the locative functor. Functors in general are subcategorized for a nominal complement, and, since this is redundant, specification of this has been left out of the representations (following the practice of Volume I). The goal relation of *to Rome* is a variant of {loc} associated with directional verbs. In (190b) we have a lexically complex category involving a functor that is absorbed into a simple deictic element (*there*), not specified other than as {N} in this representation; and in (190b)* there is lexical absorption into an orientational element that may itself be complement-taking (*below*)—I have assumed here a (further) locative complement. The former is an adverb, the latter typical of many (complex) prepositions. In (190c) the functor again heads a complex categorization, but in this case it is itself given morphological expression in the form of the inflection on the form of the name subjoined to it: *Romam* is the singular accusative whose citation (nominative) form is *Roma*.

Thus, in (190a) the functor has independent lexical status; in (190b) and (c) it is lexically part of a complex, with a morphological marker in (190c). The functor in (190d), however, is not given any lexical expression: there and in e.g. (187a) the {abs(olutive)} (neutral) required by the valency of the verb is identified by the location of the otherwise unsignalled absolutive immediately to the right of the verb. All of the complex categories in (190b-d) are supplied by the lexicon, just like the simple adposition in (190a); they are not created in the syntax.

The adjuncts of (185b), (186), and (187a), *yesterday* and *on Tuesday/on Wednesday*, are similarly introduced by functors, independent or not, specifically the {loc} functor, which in conjunction with the temporal nominals specifies the temporal location of the scene; these are circumstantial arguments. In this case, of course, their presence is not required by the subcategorization of the verb, but they are themselves characterized as seeking ('\') a verb to modify, as again described in Volume I, Chapter 3, and as illustrated here in (191) (where again I lay aside consideration of the status of the subject):

(191)   {P}
          |
        {P/{abs}}
          :
          :   { {abs}}   { {loc}\{P}}
          : | |
          :   {N}   {N}
          :   :   :
          :   :   :
         read   reviews   yesterday

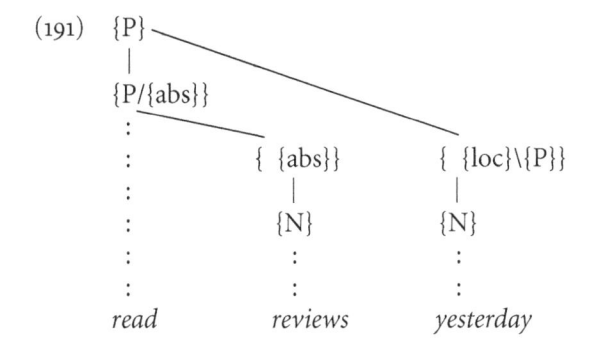

Both complex functor categories in (191) lack a morphological or 'analytic' marker of the functor, but are differentiated by position—and semantic selection.

I am suggesting that (190–1) are more adequate representations than (the relevant part of) (185b). They differ in incorporating the **functional argument structure** (Anderson 2006b: §8.5) of this part of the clause, provided essentially by the functors. This elaboration compared with the phonology is necessitated by the demands of the interface for an adequate representation of conceptual 'scenes'. And these functional argument structures involve crucially a category that universally lacks a substantive primary categorization. This category is of a type absent from the phonology. It is characteristic of it that, as I have just been illustrating, it may be manifested in various ways, as adposition, as inflection, or by the position of the element illustrating whose categorizations it heads. In this latter respect, variability of realization, the functor is the paradigm example of a functional category. Let us now broaden our concern to embrace these in general.

5.1.2 *The role of functional categories*

The presence of a functional/lexical distinction involves a specialization of a set of primary categories which articulate different aspects of the functional structure attributed to the representation of the 'scene' by the syntax. The functors, in particular, enable expression of the varied functions of arguments. But, as anticipated in the initial discussion, there are other sets of functions to be expressed in the syntax. And these too are functions not replicated in the phonology.

In Volume I, §3.4, I introduce, together with functors, the other possible functional categories envisaged by Anderson (1997a):

Functional Categories (Anderson 1997a)
Finiteness   {P}
Determinative   {N}
Comparator   {P.N}
Functor   { }

The functional categories involve only simple combination of the features **P** and **N**, including absence of either or both. The full stop in the representation for the comparator insists on a relationship of simple combination, in contrast with those involving asymmetries (even if mutual, as in the case of adjectives).

The lexical categories thus involve internal dependency relations, with adjectives being the most complex in invoking mutual dependency (rather than co-occurrence—as attributed above to the comparator):

lexical categories
{P;N} {N;P} {P:N}
verb   noun   adjective

With the verb **P** is preponderant, governs; with nouns it is **N**.

As observed in §3.4 of Volume I, Anderson (2007) suggests that the functional categories are also inherently relational, but take only one complement at a time. This complement-taking is central to their functional role. We have necessarily { /}, {P/}, {N/}, {P.N/}, rather than non-valent instances of functional categories. This relationality is crucial in differentiating the functional categories proper from names, which are uncomplemented. In this way names are distinguished specifically from functors: functors = { /}, names = { }. I shall not pursue this. But, in recognition of the distinctiveness of names (and pronouns) from determiners, I shall prefer (in accordance with the usage of Volume I) the term determiner to refer to the functional category {N}: names and pronouns are only derivatively {N}s; they may be subjoined to a determiner. To serve as arguments they must be so subjoined.

§3.4 of Volume I also discusses the **finiteness** category, as presented in (43) of that study; and it is examined in some detail in Part III of the same study. I shall be brief here: my main aim is to illustrate the cognitively required role of the functional categories, rather than to re-explore them in any detail:

(I.43) a. {P}
            ⋮＼
            ⋮ ＼{P;N}
            ⋮   ⋮
            ⋮   ⋮
           may sing
       b. {P}
           |
          {P:N}
            ⋮
            ⋮
          sings

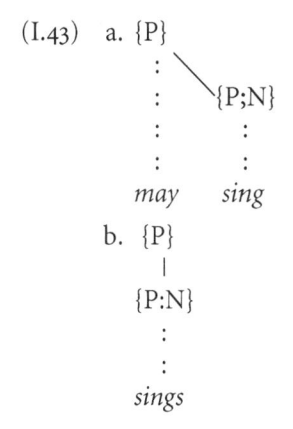

(I.43a) illustrates analytic expression of the finiteness element, by an operative; in (I.43b) it is absorbed lexically in the verb. To the extent that in English morphological tense, and person/number outside nominals, are associated with finiteness, its presence may be said to be expressed—or at least reflected—morphologically in that language. But they are not necessarily associated with finiteness in other languages.

The functional role of (syntactic) finiteness is to license independent predication: the presence of the finiteness element guarantees the independent predicational status of the construction (other things being equal). The different moods of the independent sentence—interrogative, imperative, declarative, etc.—are associated, as secondary features, with the finiteness element. And finiteness in general embeds the sentence in the speech-act situation. Finiteness thus defines the **functional locutionary structure** of a predication that is an independent sentence, or potentially so. Again, its presence as a category is a response to an interface demand to represent, in this case, the communicative function of the sentence. Even when subordinate, the finite clause retains connections with speech-act context (tense etc.), as well as the potential to serve as a complete independent sentence—though this glosses over the kinds of complexity in finite status discussed in Chapter 7 of Volume I.

The role of the **determiner** is to provide a potential referent for the arguments in the functional argument structure. Just as verbs, which label predication types, combine with finiteness to provide independent predications, so nouns (and other 'entitatives' in the terminology of §3.4 of Volume I—names and pronouns, as well as nouns), combine with determiners, in adjunction or subjunction, to constitute a referentiable argument of a participant or circumstantial relation. Nouns themselves are not extralinguistically referential, but label entity types.

This role of determiners is exemplified by the post-verbal nominal phrases in (192):

(192)   a. Fritz read some reviews
       b. Fritz read a review
       c. Fritz read reviews
       d. Fritz read trash

Some and *a* are determiners: they take as a complement a partitive noun, i.e., a noun in a partitive (functor) relation to them. They introduce an analytic expression of determination. I represent this as in (193a), which also includes a partitive functor that is not given distinct expression, but has been absorbed lexically by the noun:

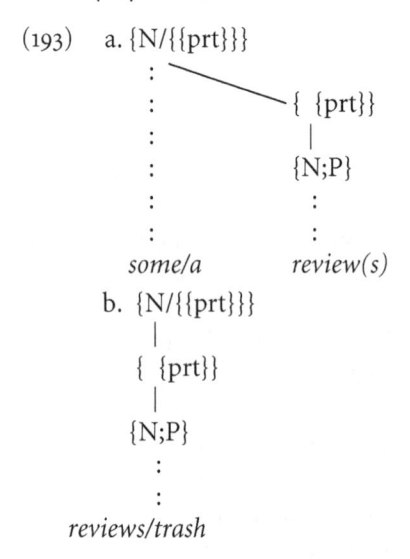

(193)   a. {N/{{prt}}}

$$\begin{array}{cc} & \{\ \{prt\}\} \\ & | \\ & \{N;P\} \end{array}$$

some/a   review(s)

      b. {N/{{prt}}}
           |
        { {prt}}
           |
        {N;P}

    reviews/trash

(I ignore differences due to the presence vs. absence of plurality/singularity.) Elsewhere, the p(a)rt(itive) functor may have overt expression:

(194)   Fritz read one/some of the reviews

The in (194) is another type of determiner, a definite; it is the definite congener of *some/a(n)*. *The* embodies the speaker's assumption that the hearer can identify the referent:

(195) {N{def}/{prt}}
```
         :        ╲
         :         ╲{ {prt}}
         :             |
         :           {N;P}
         :             :
         :             :
        the         review(s)
```

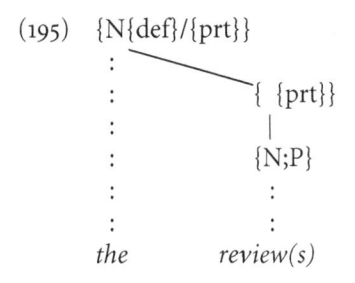

In (192c/d) even the determiner is not expressed by a separate item (periphrastically), but the whole configuration in (193b) is expressed by a single item. This variability in type of realization (independent or not) is again illustrative of a property of functional categories. Determiners define the **functional referential structure** of arguments, again clearly in response to an interface need, in this case the need to locate referential coordinates for arguments.[48]

The **comparator** is the functional category associated with adjectives. Like adjectives (Anderson 1997a: §2.4), the comparator seems to be less prevalent than the other primary categories; it is the most complex functional category, the congener of the most complex lexical category. In English it may be expressed independently (analytically) or morphologically, or possibly in cumulation (and lexicalized), as respectively in (196):

(196) a. Bob is more energetic than John
      b. Bob is stronger than John
      c. Bob is different than John

It appears to differ from the adjective in its specifier, *much* rather than *very*—though its specifier may be specified in turn by the adjectival specifier. This is all illustrated in the examples in (197):

(197) a. Bob is (very) energetic/strong
      b. Bob is ((very) much) more energetic
      c. Bob is ((very) much) stronger

We consider some implications of this in the short excursus that follows this section.

---

[48] Again (cf. the above discussion of finiteness), I have been brief on the character of determiners. A fuller account would provide not just much more detail concerning what I have dealt with here but also some provision for (in particular) generics, deictics, pronouns, and names. Fortunately, once more the reader may consult, as well as Volume I, a compatible fuller treatment in Anderson (2007). There deictics, pronouns, and names are grouped together as derived determiners.

Phonology-Syntax Analogies

At this point what there is to observe, briefly once more, is that the comparator introduces the **functional structure of comparison**. It enables degree of possession of properties to be compared; it allows overt expression of relativity, a capacity once more with obvious interface benefits. Specifically, the comparator exploits the gradient character of core (that is, intensity of quality) adjectives: cf. e.g. Bolinger's view of 'the adjective as the basic intensifiable' (1972: 168–72). It enables them, via the functional structure it brings along, to relate the relative strengths of the properties of entities.

We are now in a position to complete the representation of (191), by virtue of introducing the distinction between {P} and {P;N} and recognizing the role of the free absolutive:

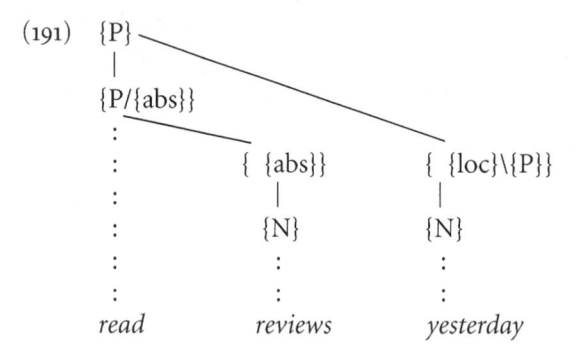

(191)   {P}
          |
        {P/{abs}}
          :
          :   { {abs}}   { {loc}\{P}}
          : | |
          :   {N}   {N}
          :   :   :
          :   :   :
         read   reviews   yesterday

Compare (191) with (191)*:

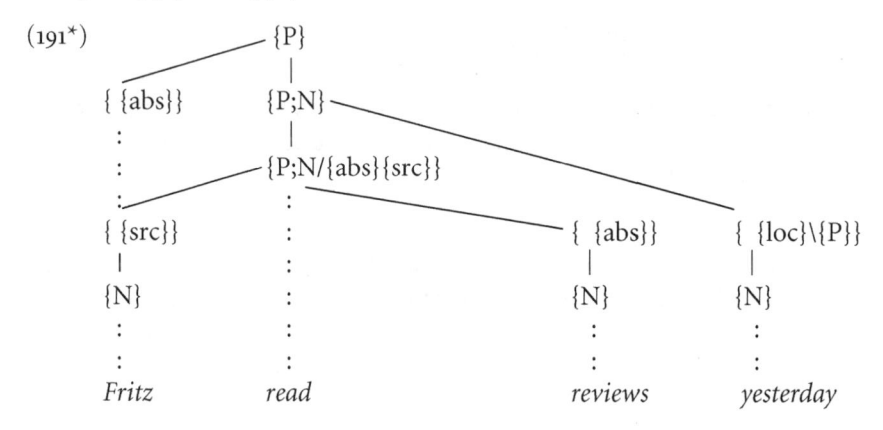

(191*)   {P}
                     |
        { {abs}}   {P;N}
                     |
                  {P;N/{abs}{src}}
                     :
        { {src}}   :   { {abs}}   { {loc}\{P}}
          | : | |
         {N}   :   {N}   {N}
          :   :   :   :
          :   :   :   :
        Fritz   read   reviews   yesterday

This recognizes the distinctiveness of subject as a 'complement'. The subject is that participant in a predication that is highest on the subject-selection hierarchy—here the agentive {{src}}. It is this argument that satisfies the need, as a functor, of the upper, free absolutive for an {N}, and adopts its

Categorization 261

position on linearization, before the verbals. The free absolutive is free by virtue of not figuring as part of the valency of its predicator, but introduced in default of a lexically required absolutive. Other functors are valency satisfiers (participants), or introduce circumstantials. The formation of grammatical relations like subject is another, distinct function of the functor.

The resulting representation may introduce non-projectivity, 'tangling', if the {P} is independent, as in (II.74a), where a dependency arc crosses an association line:

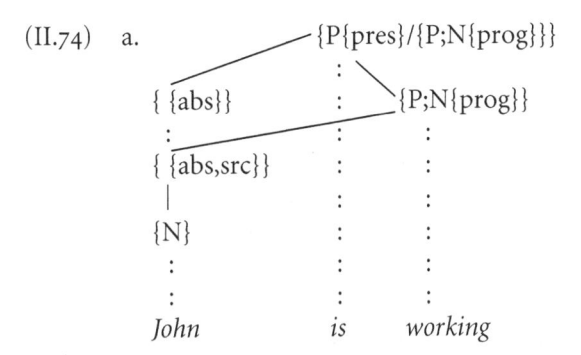

(II.74) a.

```
                    ┌─{P{pres}/{P;N{prog}}}
          {{abs}}   :    ╲{P;N{prog}}
            :       :        :
          {{abs,src}}  :     :
            |       :        :
           {N}      :        :
            :       :        :
            :       :        :
           John    is     working
```

The presence of a free absolutive and the introduction of 'tangling' takes the representation of clauses even further from analogy with phonology—particularly in comparison with such representations as (58), with the dependency maximization and the lack of 'tangling' that are characteristic of phonological representations:

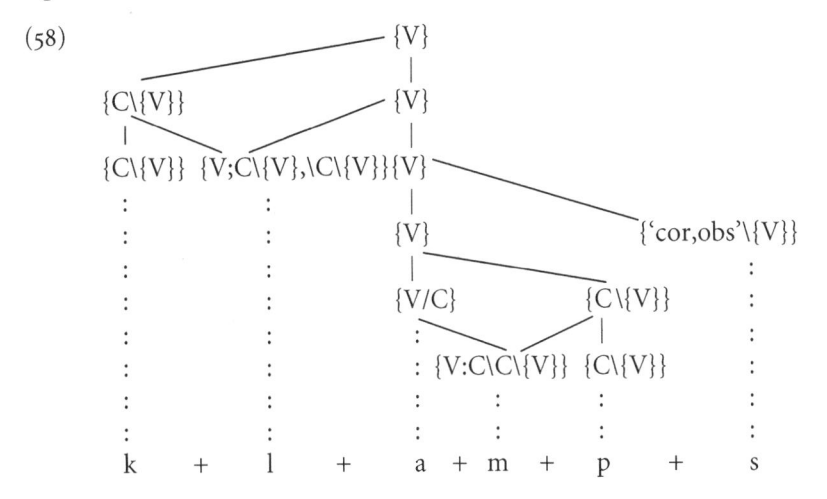

(58)

```
                          ┌─ {V}
                          |
          {C\{V}}       {V}
            |            |
          {C\{V}}  {V;C\{V},\C\{V}}{V}
            :       :        |
            :       :       {V}              {'cor,obs'\{V}}
            :       :        |
            :       :      {V/C}         {C\{V}}
            :       :        :             |
            :       :     : {V:C\C\{V}}  {C\{V}}
            :       :     :    :    :       :
            :       :     :    :    :       :
            k   +   l  +  a  + m  + p   +   s
```

Only a ghost of an overall analogy manifests itself, despite the presence of transparent analogies based on dependency, for instance.

5.1.3 Conclusion

We have seen that similar interface motivations underlie the other functional categories. And the syntactic capacities of these categories are 'co-operative'. The functors articulate the functional argument structure, allowing predicators to be linked to arguments which have referentiability. Finiteness enhances the predicational character of verbs, allowing them to occur in independent predications. A determiner enhances the referential capacity of nouns, enabling them to be associated with referents and constitute arguments. I have gone into a little (but obviously, and as reiterated, far from exhaustive) detail concerning these functional categories because they introduce a functional dimension, and the need for a functional/lexical distinction, that is absent from phonological structure. They perform complex roles in representing and articulating semantic functions, which it has behoved me to give at least an outline account of.

Anderson (1997a: 128) concludes: 'each of the simple, functional classes {N}, {P} and {P.N} is, then, a closed class specialization of the corresponding open class, with members that are denotatively desemanticised, more "abstract", less specific concerning entity/event/quality type'. This specialization is dictated by the needs of the semantic interface. As a consequence, the structure of the syllable is closer to the traditional, but here regarded as incomplete, representation of the clause embodied in (185b) than the structure of the clause on the interpretation offered in this section, which shows complications reflecting perceived differences in the two major extralinguistic domains that interface with language.

However, the basic dependency-based analogies between syntax and phonology—involving complementation and modification—remain apparent within the syntactic elaborations. Syntactic structures introduce categorial elaborations of the elements that can participate in these basic relations. Moreover, ontogenetically, we should rather speak of the lexical categories as specializations of the corresponding functional and naming ones, rather than vice versa. The name, { }, is the most fundamental category, whose first elaboration is the relator category { / } that in turn spawns the various functional categories and their complementation requirement (Anderson 2007: §9.3). The basic syntactic distinction is between a relational category (or 'pivot') and a non-relational (or 'open') category, the latter of which is the preferred locus for lexical innovation. Compare the relational vowel and the non-relational consonant of early phonology. Thus, acquisitionally early syntactic structures have more in common with phonological structure than the adult systems we have been considering here. What comes to make a big difference between categorizations in the two planes are both the distinguishing of functional and lexical categories, with distinctive roles in the syntax, and the explosion of the membership of lexical categories once they are so differentiated.

5.2 Excursus on specifiers and intensification

The present section initially may perhaps strike the reader as constituting what Tobias Smollett describes as 'a Digression which some Readers may think impertinent' (*The Adventures of Ferdinand Count Fathom*, heading of chapter VIII). But it should become clear that it does spring immediately from the concerns of the previous section, as well as contributing to our ongoing concern with the problematical notion of 'specifier'.

The apparent presence, in English at least, of both an adjective specifier, *very* in (197a), and a comparator specifier, *much* in (197b-c), and indeed a specifier of the latter specifier, *very* in (197b-c), and the difficulty of ascertaining many more specifiers elsewhere, raises some questions concerning the distribution of specifiers, and their categorial content, apart from their general modifying and identifying functions:

(197)   a. Bob is (very) energetic/strong
       b. Bob is ((very) much) more energetic
       c. Bob is ((very) much) stronger

The most general question is: are there distinctive specifiers associated with modifying and identifying all combinations of **P** and **N**?

Among the functional categories, we seem to be able to associate specifiers with both comparators and functors. In both cases they may legitimately be described as in some way intensifying, as illustrated in (198a-b):

(198)   a. right at the door
       b. much stronger/more beautiful
       c. that he loves it

It seems too that we can associate subordinate {P} with a specifier, in the shape of a complementizer that identifies it as such, as in (198c): see further §6.2.3. The complementizer is scarcely 'intensifying', though. It is perhaps untypical in this respect, because of its primary function of marking a particular {P} as not independent.

But, though a case can perhaps be made, among functional categories, for specification of functors and comparators, and even dependent-{P}, at least, the only lexical category that has commonly been seen as taking a specifier and that also conforms to the restricted sense (simplex, identifying of a subclass) that has been adopted here is the adjective. Let us therefore reconsider the status of *very*, often taken, as in the preceding, as specifier of the adjective, indeed as a paradigm case of the specifier.

On the assumptions I have been making so far, *very* is both specifier of the adjective, {\{P:N}}, as in (197a), and specifier of the comparator specifier, {\{\{P.N}}}, as in (197b-c). The (relevant subclasses of the) specified categories are both interpretable as 'intensifiable', to use Bolinger's term. This is still a rather curious distribution, however. Say, therefore, we take the hint offered by the other lexical categories—which are resistant to consensual identification of a specifier—and deny adjectival-specifier status to *very*: all lexical categories lack specifiers. And we regard *very* as, rather, always a specifier of a specifier, i.e. schematically {\{\ }}, as it clearly is in (197b-c). Let's look at the consequence of such an interpretation, along with the suggestion concerning specifiers that substantively they are prototypically intensifiers.

Say that gradable adjectives (when simply positive rather than comparative) incorporate a specifier; they are lexically intensified: *Betsy is very strong* means that Betsy has a markedly positive amount of this quality, and *Betsy is strong* means that she merely has a positive amount, but nevertheless relatively intensified. It is above the median on a 'strong-weak' scale. This means that as well as specifying the specifier of a comparator, as in (197b-c), *very* can be regarded as specifying an incorporated specifier in (197a). *Very* always intensifies an intensifier, specifies a specifier. What is being claimed on the basis of this, then, is that there are no 'analytic' specifiers of lexical categories, but that adjectives lexically incorporate one. Indeed, the presence of this intensifier characterizes lexically those 'core' adjectives that are traditionally classed as 'gradable'.

This means that that we might represent the examples in (197a) as in (199a) and (b), where 'itf' is 'intensification', and (197b-c) as (199c-d):

(199) a. {P:N}
            |
           {{itf}\{P:N}}
            ⋮
            ⋮
           energetic/strong

b.
```
                    {P:N}
                      |
              ─── {{itf}\}
                      |
   {{itf}\{itf}\}   {{itf}\{P:N}}
        :                :
        :                :
      very       energetic/strong
```

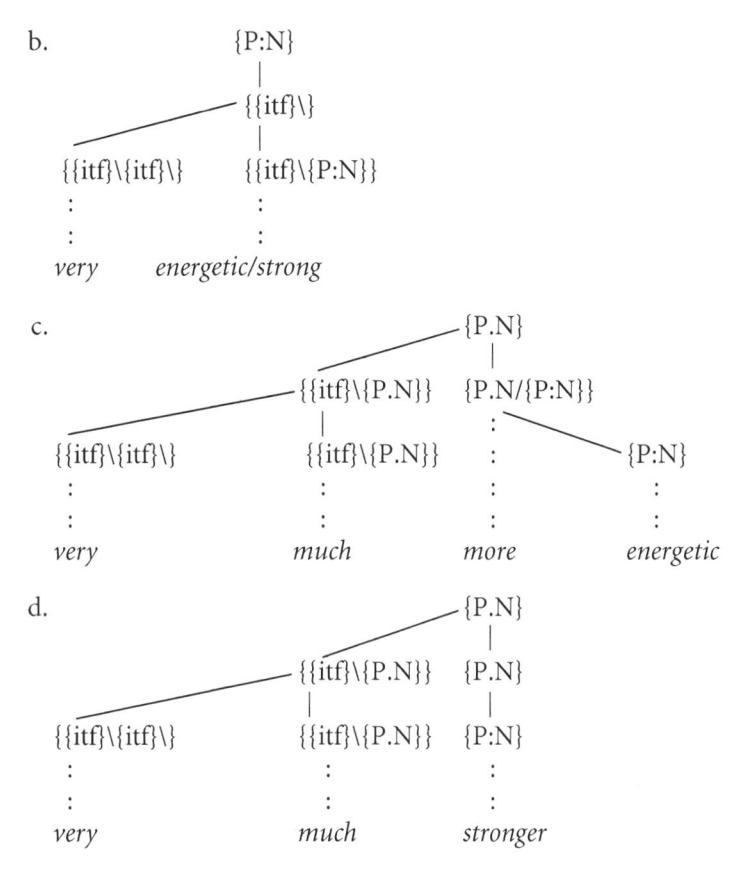

c.
```
                                    ─── {P.N}
                                          |
                        ─── {{itf}\{P.N}}  {P.N/{P:N}}
                              |               :
   {{itf}\{itf}\}          {{itf}\{P.N}}      :         ─── {P:N}
        :                       :             :                :
        :                       :             :                :
      very                    much          more           energetic
```

d.
```
                                    ─── {P.N}
                                          |
                        ─── {{itf}\{P.N}}  {P.N}
                              |               |
   {{itf}\{itf}\}          {{itf}\{P.N}}     {P:N}
        :                       :              :
        :                       :              :
      very                    much          stronger
```

The positive degree of gradable adjectives incorporates a specifier that is the rough equivalent of *much*: to be *energetic/strong* is to have 'much energy/strength'—or, more analytically still: to be *energetic/strong* is to have 'much intensity of energy/strength'. The comparative degree does not incorporate *much*, though it can take it as an independent specifier. This correlates with a familiar difference in interpretation between positive and comparative: saying that 'X is more energetic than Y' does not imply that 'X is energetic' (or that 'Y is not energetic'). The comparative lacks the internal intensifier.

The analysis of *much* as an intensifier/specifier also seems to be appropriate in its role as an adjective converted to a determiner, in such as (200a-b), the first of which, for instance, we can represent as in (201):

(200) a. Much money has been lost
b. Much of the money has been lost
c. Dissenters were few
d. We are many
e. What I need is little
f That isn't much

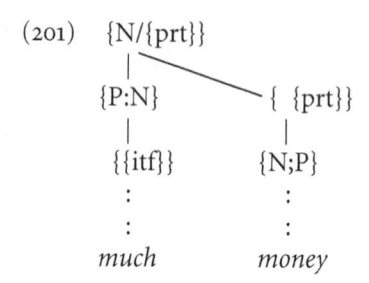

(201) {N/{prt}}
          |
       {P:N} ──────── { {prt}}
          | |
       {{itf}}   {N;P}
          ⋮   ⋮
          ⋮   ⋮
        much   money

Recall the simple determiner in (193a), discussed above:

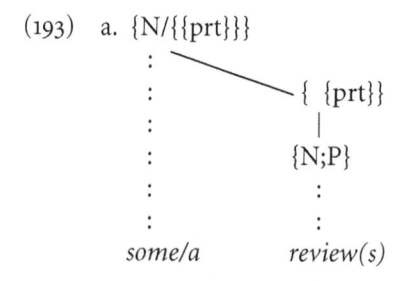

(193) a. {N/{{prt}}}
          ⋮
          ⋮ ──────── { {prt}}
          ⋮ |
          ⋮   {N;P}
          ⋮   ⋮
          ⋮   ⋮
        some/a   review(s)

I associate the distinctiveness, among determiners, of the behaviour of *much, many, little*, and *few*—in, for instance, occurring as predicative, as in (200c-f) (for details see e.g. Carden 1973)—with their being based on internally specified adjectives, as shown in (201).

(202) involves various enrichments of the structure in (201):

(202) a. more money
b. very much money
c. much more money
d. very much more money

(203) represents the last of these, which brings together components from all of the others, and from (199):

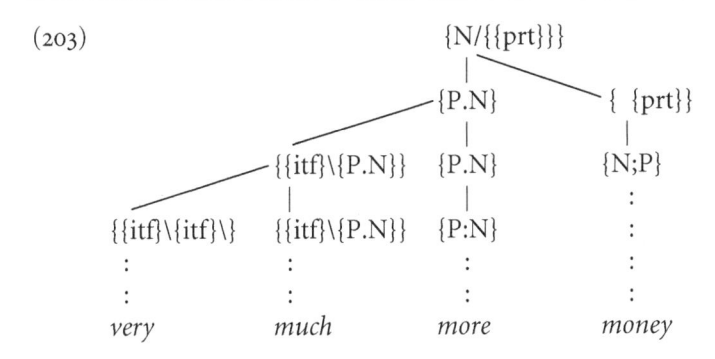

(203)
```
                        {N/{{prt}}}
                         |
                  ─{P.N}        ╲{ {prt}}
                   |              |
           ─{{itf}\{P.N}}  {P.N}  {N;P}
            |               |      :
  {{itf}\{itf}\}  {{itf}\{P.N}}  {P:N}
     :            :              :    :
     :            :              :    :
   very         much           more  money
```

Here there is an attributive comparator, {P.N}, to which the adjective is subjoined, and which is modified by a specifier, which in turn is modified by a specifier of a specifier, i.e. *very*.

If indeed gradable adjectives are represented as in (199a), then there is no independent adjectival specifier as such; we have only, in such constructions, a specifier of the functional category comparator (*much*) or a specifier of a specifier (*very*). In that case, perhaps there are indeed no external specifiers of lexical categories. Such specifiers intensify functional categories, specifically— as well as another specifier. The latter is exemplified by *very* and by *almost* in *almost right at the top*. So far it looks as if they specify, among functional categories, the empty functional category (functor) and the fullest (comparator). This would be another property differentiating lexical and functional categories in the syntax, reinforcing the need to draw such a distinction— crucially in the present context, one that is lacking in the phonology.[49]

On the other hand, if it is the case that only functional categories are specified, the apparent absence of a prototypical specifier of finiteness, despite its status as a functional category, may indicate, whatever else, a further analogy. I remarked in note 13 on the absence of an obvious specifier for vowels; at most there is perhaps a segment-internal one (Anderson 1986a: §7)—if this is indeed an appropriate representation for the [ju] in such as *muse*. It is, then, perhaps significant that it is **P** and **V**, analogical features in terms of their relational centrality, that lack typical specification when these features uniquely define a category. The specifier of {P} is not intensifying and identifies specifically dependent {P}, and {V} at most may have a segment-internal specifier. This observation would be more telling if, on the other hand, there were a specifier for {N}, determiner.

---

[49] Our discussion has focused on comparative and positive gradable adjectives. I have not considered superlatives, since they introduce additional considerations to do with definiteness. However, they do not seem to be problematical for what is being suggested.

Perhaps this is what we find in (204a), despite the apparently aberrant positioning of the putative specifier, again *very*:

(204) a. The very man for the job arrived at that very moment
b. This is the very large bag I was looking for

The putative specifier does seem to fit notionally, in intensifying the definite determiner; and its post-head position marks it as a distinct specifier from the specifier-of-a-specifier *very*—though this does mean that what it specifies may be ambiguous in the written language, as illustrated by (204b).

This last analysis, whereby the absence of a normal specifier with {V} and {P} emerges as a natural analogy, remains even more speculative than the rest of the proposals in this section. But we can at least say that if syntactic specifiers are prototypically intensifiers, then their concentrations in the area of locatives, adjectives, and comparators is a natural one. And their more tenuous manifestation in relation to finites and determiners accords with this. Moreover, the stronger attestation with functors may be significant. With adjectives and comparators, **P** and **N** are of equal prominence, so prominence is neutralized; with functors, **P** and **N** are simply absent.

What is perhaps more central to our present concerns, however, is what the preceding tells us about the specifier analogy that, according to Anderson (2006a), holds between the likes of *very* and the [S] of *st(r)*-type clusters. [S] functions like a syntactic specifier in being one-membered and in signalling the presence of the neutralized obstruent subclass that follows. But can it be said to 'intensify'? Can we, for instance, regard the presence of the sibilant [s] as an 'intensification' of the aspiration that accompanies syllable-initial voiceless plosives in English? If such a scenario is implausible, we have an analogy that does not seem to be based on perception of a similarity in substance, but purely on functional similarities (such as flagging-up a particular subclass). There would then be only a remote connection with the interfaces in the case of this analogy.

5.3 Reduced transitivity in phonology, and minimal syllables: Kabardian

We now turn to further indications of the limitation of the transitivity analogy, beyond that occasioned by the absence in the phonology of functional categories, specifically the restriction to monotransitivity.

In English and elsewhere, it seems that phonology, lacking functors (and a distinct class of functional categories in general) and having only very unspecific valencies, as well as obeying strict linearity requirements, is restricted to at most the simple unary complementation again illustrated schematically in (185a):

(185) a.
```
              {V}
              |
  {C\{V}}    {V}
   :          |
   :         {V/C}         {C\{V}}
   :          :             :
   :          :    {C}      :
   :          :     :       :
   :          :     :       :
   k          a     m       p
```

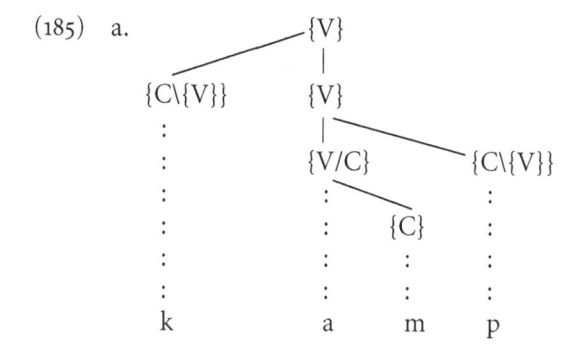

And, of course, there are phonologies in which the transitivity system is much reduced, minimal, or even absent: there are languages in which there are no phonological complements, others (such as Fijian) in which there are not even adjuncts to constitute a coda. Only (28)* need be invoked in relation to syllable sequencing in this last case:

(28)*   unmarked syllable structure
        {C} + {V}

Such systems are 'subtransitive'.

The range of syllable-structure possibilities (from such 'minimal' systems as Fijian to others, such as that of English, involving complements and various different kinds of adjunction) is charted in Blevins (1995: §4). She describes these possibilities as involving 'parametric variation'; but surely what we have here is simply 'variation'. These transparently learnable variations need not be part of 'universal grammar', though, of course, for functional reasons different transitivity possibilities may correlate with other properties of the system they are associated with.

Thus, if, as argued above, the characterization of clause structure requires elaboration of the (admittedly simplified) traditional picture given in (185b), syllable structure, on the other hand, in many languages refers to distinctions in transitivity little or not at all:

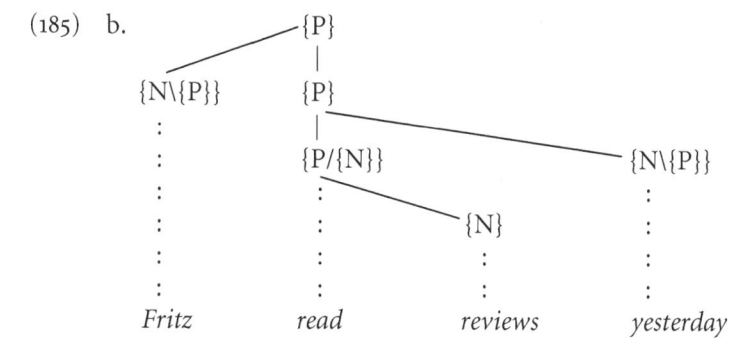

(185) b.
```
                {P}
                 |
  {N\{P}}       {P}
   :             |
   :           {P/{N}}              {N\{P}}
   :             :                   :
   :             :      {N}          :
   :             :       :           :
   :             :       :           :
   Fritz        read   reviews     yesterday
```

Transitivity of some (non-minimal) sort is crucial to syntactic structure; in phonology it may be marginal. Such reveals the strength of requirements to do with semanticity.

An example of a system reduced in a slightly different—and perhaps even more drastic—way is provided by the phonology of Kabardian. It can be argued that Kabardian lacks contrastive vowels; vowels need not be specified as such in the lexicon. The 'transitivity' system is entirely dismantled. This is essentially the position of Kuipers (1960), whose analysis has been reformulated in the sort of terms I have been working with here—and defended from the criticisms of Halle (1970)—by Anderson (1991). Here I offer an interpretation of the proposals made in this last in terms of extrasegmentality, such that vowel segments as such are absent from the lexicon.

The first step in motivating such an analysis of Kabardian is the observation that the quality distinctions in the language that come to be associated with vowels are, with a few exceptions, also associated with their onsets, so can readily be regarded as extrasegmental features of the syllable. Exceptional is the distinction between the vowels in (205a):

(205) a. zə 'one' vs. næ 'eye'
 b. ji 'eight' vs. px´enz 'twisted'
 c. pq'y 'bone' vs. jelirq'ɑs 'crawfish'
 d. wups 'plane!' vs. k'°o 'go'

The vowels in (205b-d), however, can be seen as variants of those in (205a) that are associated with different extrasegmentals. The superscripting in [px´] indicates palatalization, in [pq'] a glottalic/ejective, and in [k'°] a labialized glottalic. Thus the acute/palatal vowels in (205b) are associated with a preceding palatalized consonant or [j]; the vowel symbols in (the final syllables in) (205c) are Kuipers's representation for discoloured, 'back unrounded' vowels, and they appear after uvulars, pharyngals, and laryngals, which all involve a retracted tongue root; the vowels in (205d) are grave after labialized consonants and [w].

Vowels other than in (205a), whose onset-syllabic sequence corresponds simply to (206a), are associated with the extrasegmentals in the schemas of (206b-c):

(206) a. (C(V
 b. (i(C(V
 c. (ə(C(V
 d. (u(C(V

Extrasegmental **i** is manifested as palatalization of the onset or as onset [j], and as acute versions of the vowels otherwise realized as in (205a). The acute versions are [i] and [e] (as in (205b)).

This immediately suggests, as a further step in the analysis, that the first of the vowels of (205a) is unspecified as to secondary category, and that the secondary categorizations of these two vowels are thus lexically { } and {v}. So that the phonetic value of the vowel in the first word in (205a) is filled in as a default. There is no motivation for introducing the complexity of invoking a bilateral substantive contrast in vowel segments; there is merely one between **v** and its absence. We return in a moment to the consequence of this.

[j] is also presumably an unspecified onset, with its colour being due to the extrasegmental, as is that of [w], in its case due to the **u** extrasegmental. The vowels of (205d) again reflect a combination of **u** with the contents of (207), giving [u] and [o] respectively.

ə in (206c) is a cover symbol for no specification; I use this device here in order to distinguish for the reader between extrasegmental and segmental non-specification. Extrasegmental ə involves suppression of vowel qualities, and it combines with { } and {v} to give 'back unrounded' secondary categorizations, after pharyngals, uvulars, and plain laryngals. Kuipers groups [h], [j] (for which he offers the alternative representation [h′]), and [w] (= [h°]) as respectively the plain, palatalized, and labialized laryngals; and he notes that [h] in Kabardian is usually voiced. However, while [ə] is one possible realization for the unspecified vowel following plain laryngals, i.e. of a quality identical to that of the vowel when there is no extrasegmental present, as in (205a), more commonly we find a vowel which is more retracted, and given a distinct symbol by Kuipers, as in (205c): [y] and [ɑ] are back unrounded, [ə] and [æ] are 'central'. And it is these 'back unrounded' vowels that we find after uvulars and pharyngals.

If we associate uvulars and pharyngals with the respective secondary categorizations in (207a) (cf. Anderson (1991: 25) for a somewhat different suggestion), i.e. as having suppressed vowel colour, then the presence of the ə reflects the effect of the extrasegmental:

(207) a. {ə}   {ə,v}
      b. ə(C{ } ə(C{v}
      c. { }   {v}

And the vowels in this environment would also be doubly discoloured—i.e. 'back unrounded' rather than merely 'central', as in (207b). We find a similar pair of vowels after (plain) Pharyngals, but they too also allow the unmarked vowels of (205a), i.e. as represented in (207c). They apparently can be followed by the simple vowels in (207c), without extrasegmental. However that may be, there is no motivation for attributing contrastiveness to the vowel qualities in (205c) qua vowel qualities, any more than those in (205b/d).

The only contrast in vowel quality in Kabardian is apparently between **v** and its absence. This is reminiscent of the situation with English [h], discussed in §4.3.1: it too is in contrast only with its absence. But [h] also, as argued there, is not contrastively positioned, and was thus analysed as an extrasegmental property of the syllable. If, in the same way, the **v** of the {v}-vowel in Kabardian is also extrasegmental, there is nothing to occupy the vowel position in syllables and this need not be indicated lexically. All vowel qualities are extrasegmental or default. **v** is distinctive in combining with all the others. The position of vowels is thus not associated with a substantive contrast, and the vowel category is introduced derivatively in response to (28)*:

(28)* *unmarked syllable structure, as well as, uniquely, derivationality*
{C} + {V}

In Kabardian, only consonants and extrasegmentals (including {v}) contrast.

The lexical phonological representations of items in Kabardian is a string of **minimal syllables**, some of them amplified by extrasegmentals (**i, ə,** or **u** with or without **v**) but all of them lacking vowel segments. We can represent the lexical possibilities as in (208), where no primary **V** element need be included (where the angles include optional elements and the braces alternatives:

(208) $\left< \begin{Bmatrix} i \\ ə \\ u \end{Bmatrix} \right> \text{<v>} (C(C...$

The vowel positions are added derivatively to carry the manifestation of the extrasegmentals, or in default of these the ə that realizes the position occupied by { }. And structures compatible with the phonetic interface are thus created.

Kabardian thus illustrates rather dramatically that lexical representations of the phonology of items can assume a massively reduced character, with all that is redundant left to the phonology to fill in. Such remoteness of the phonological representations of the lexicon from implementation, combined with the fundamental role of lexical marking of 'extended transitivity' (via semantic relations) in projecting syntactic structures, permits this discrepancy in richness between phonological and syntactic 'transitivity' specifications.[50]

Kabardian phonology displays a radical reduction at a lexical level of any indication of clause-like structure; but, as in other languages, a pattern of onsets, nuclei, and codas does emerge, derivatively, redundantly. The lexical syllable structure of Kabardian is nonetheless minimal (onset vs. vowelless rhyme), in contrast with the enrichments of clause structure, particularly in terms of the distinction between functional and lexical categories that I have argued for in this chapter in relation to syntax. Certainly, languages vary in the degree of overt 'decomposition' of potentially complex categories that they show, with one extreme being languages with so-called 'serial verbs' (amply illustrated in e.g. Crowley 2002). And thus the internal complexity of lexical specifications may vary from language to language. But it remains the case that the complexity of argument structures is very much impoverished in the phonology, to the extent in some cases of obliteration. And this reflects a difference in the extralinguistic interfaces entertained by syntax and phonology and the respective relationship of the two planes to the lexicon and to each other.

---

[50] This brief account of the status of vowels in Kabardian, based on Kuipers (1960) and Anderson (1991), ignores various related factors discussed in some detail in these places, some of which are controversial, as I shall indicate in what follows in this note. Other omissions are less important.

I have omitted consideration of the 'half-rounded' vowel variants found after unlabialized but before labialized consonants. Also, as well as there being a set of 'plain' uvulars, such as the voiceless plosive [q] (or the corresponding ejective in (205c)), Kabardian also has a set of labialized congeners, such as [q°], whose role in the pattern of vowel variation is unclear to me. More importantly, I have ignored the third vowel (to those in (207)) that is sometimes argued to be contrastive in Kabardian.

This vowel, [a:], along with other long-vowel manifestations, is argued by both Kuipers (1960) and Halle (1970) to be a manifestation of a vowel (in the notation used here, a { } or a {v}) plus laryngeal. Thus, in the case of these other long vowels we find the alternations in (i):

(i) [i:] ~ [əj], [e:] ~ [aj], [u:] ~ [əw], [o:] ~ [aw]

The long vowel variants manifest mutual contamination by the two elements in the other variant, though in the case of [əj] and [əw] the first element has no content with which to contaminate the other. Kuipers analyses [a:] as, similarly, a variant either of the sequence [ah], parallel to what we find in (i) (except that [h] is neither acute nor grave, and therefore also has no content with which to contaminate the other element) or of [ha] (which occurs as such a sequence only post-accentually). I have presupposed some such analysis here—though the status of this last vowel, in particular, including its 'length', is a matter of dispute (see, on this and related controversies, e.g. Trubetzkoy 1925; Szereményi 1967; Kuipers 1968; Catford 1977; Comrie 1981: 206–7; Wood 1991).

A similar phonological analysis to that proposed here for Kabardian may be appropriate to Turkish, on the basis of the discussion in §4.2.2.

5.4 Reduction in lexical categories in syntax

We also find, however, a different kind of reduction in the lexical differences between categories required by different languages. In particular languages some syntactic categorial distinctions may not be given word-class status. The sets of primary syntactic categories I have talked about here are not necessarily minimum. In describing these I draw again on §3.4 of Volume I:

Primary Syntactic Categories (Anderson 2007)
Functional		Lexical	
Finiteness	{P/}	Verb	{P;N</>}
Comparator	{P.N/}	Adjective	{P:N</>}
Determiner	{N/}	Noun	{N;P</>}
Functor	{ /}	Name	{ }

Adjectives do not seem to be universally attested as a word class (and are lacking in Hixkaryana, for instance—Derbyshire 1979). Moreover, there are apparently languages to which we can attribute a much reduced lexical system like the following, which lacks a word-class distinction between noun and verb:

Primary Syntactic Categories
Functional		Lexical	
Finiteness	{P}	Contentive	{P,N}
Determiner	{N}		
Functor	{ }		

The above set of categories thus characterizes the word classes of languages which not only lack adjectives, but also are alleged to lack a basic verb/noun distinction in word class (for references, see Mithun 1999: §2.3, as well as the rather inconclusive discussion in Anderson 1997b: §2.1.4). Compare already Boas (1911) on Kwakiutl: 'all stems are neutral, neither noun nor verb'. There is a single lexical category given recognition in the lexicon: all non-functional words and non-names belong to it. It can be characterized as a word class in terms of the simple combination of **P** and **N**, {P,N}, where the comma indicates a simple combination not in contrast with ':'—cf. the comparator above, shown as {P.N}, which is in contrast with asymmetrical combinations. The functional categories in such languages differ as a group from this **contentive** lexical category in lacking any binary combination.

The existence of such languages remains controversial, and the issues are delicate (see again Mithun 1999: §2.3, and Jacobsen 1979; Kinkade 1983; van Eijk and Hess 1986; Demirdache and Matthewson 1995, for example). And it is my impression that generally, even in languages for which such a reduced system may be appropriate, one can talk of particular items having a propensity to occur in one function rather than the other, i.e. preferably to occur, via absorption of a functional category, in one categorial role or the other. And this is unsurprising, given the ontological basis for the 'verb/noun' distinction in category. But it may indeed be that these languages illustrate that this ontological distinction can be grammaticalized without being lexicalized. This lexical gap thus does not call into question the ontological status of noun and verb or the generality in languages of presence of the distinction. Such a distinction is basic to syntactic structure, and its syntactic consequences are observable in putative 'contentive-only' languages. Let us look at how the grammatical (as opposed to lexical, or word-class) distinction is drawn. Crucial in this is the role of the appropriate functional categories, {P} and {N}.

{N} in such a language may be realized as a determiner, including particularly, as a derived determiner, a pronoun, or a name, as in Nootka (Swadesh 1936–8): recall that names are grouped with pronouns as derived {N}s by Anderson (2007). And the operative may similarly appear as an independent word, like the 'copula' in Inland Olympic Salish (Kinkade 1976: 19). But functional categories may or may not be given expression as a separate word class. And it is also the determiner and the finiteness category that allow contentives to occur as respectively arguments and predicators, via the derived categories in (209), alternative expansions of {P,N}:

(209) a. {P}
        |
       {P,N}
     b. {N}
        |
       {P,N}

The functional categories, including functors, provide for the variable syntax of contentives; the complex categories in (209) are distinguished by distribution and also usually morphologically.

For we do not wish to say that such languages lack the capacity to differentiate the syntactic categories 'verb' and 'noun', or (more accurately) predicator and argument. What is lacking is a lexical class difference between such (cf. Lyons 1977: §11.2). As Mithun (1999) says of Swadesh's famous examples illustrating the syntactic versatility of Nootka lexical items, two of which are replicated in (210), 'there is no question that the first words... are

functioning syntactically as predicates, and the words that follow as arguments'
(1999: 61):

(210) a. mamo·kma   qo·ʔasʔi
         he.is.working the.man
      b. qo·ʔasma mamo·kʔi
         he.is.man the.working

In such a system, however, despite the variation in derived categorization, basic lexical categories are apparently reduced to one, the only possibility in the system of lexical categories involving combination of the two features.

For our present concerns, the important point that emerges from this brief scrutiny of the syntax of languages with reduced inventories of word classes is that the functional/lexical distinction, characteristic of the syntax and absent from the phonology, is preserved even in such circumstances. It is essential to the semantic expressivity of syntax. In particular, the enhancement of 'transitivity' allowed for by the presence of functors and finiteness is not sacrificed. And the presence of all three obligatory functional categories ensures the articulation of contextually embedded complete predications. Even though, as in the phonology, there may be a reduction in lexical distinctions between syntactic categories, there is no equivalent to the reductions in 'transitivity' and internal categorial structure, involving particularly under- or non-specification of primary categories, that can be associated with the phonology, as was illustrated in §5.3.

5.5 Conclusion

I have argued in this chapter that the enrichments of clause, as opposed to syllable, structure presented here are motivated by the need to represent 'scenes' of a relatively complex character, as well as the kind of act in which the 'scenes' are presented (assertive, questioning, etc.) and the identity of participants and circumstances in the 'scene'. Crucial here is the presence of { }, and of {P} and {N}. There is also a further set of non-parallels which, as well as manifesting interface constraints on phonology, reflects another aspect of contextual interface requirements, the need on the part of syntax to signal the communicative function of particular elements in the utterance, as well as the participant roles they serve (associated with functors). Along with cross-linguistic variation in serialization (SOV vs. VSO etc.), we also find not just intra-linguistic signalling of semantic or grammatical relations by position, as with subject and non-subject in English, but also 'word-order variation' that signals communicative function (topicality and the like). Sonority considerations severely constrain such variation in sequencing in the phonology.

Consideration of thematic structure (embodying communicative function) moves us into referential rather than predicational aspects of functional structure, however; and I pursue this separately in Chapter 6. At the beginning of that chapter I turn to a discussion 'bridging' the areas discussed in the two chapters, concerned with the representation of 'scenes within entities' as well as 'scenes within scenes'.

In the present chapter I have focused on the prominence of the functional/lexical distinction in syntactic structure, and its role in enabling syntax to fulfil the need to represent 'scenes' of varying complexity. Further consideration of one apparent side-issue here—the proposed restriction of overt specifiers to functional categories—illuminates a perplexing aspect of structure. Specifiers in English occupy a marked position vis-à-vis their heads; they typically precede, in accordance with sequencing (a) (repeated from §3.6 of Volume I):

> *Syntactic Sequencing in English*
> a) *marked*: a → b ⇒ b + a
> b) *default*: a → b ⇒ a + b

This positioning is shared by subjects, despite their being untypical as specifiers. Nevertheless, subjects have been defined here as (whatever is associated with) free absolutives of {P}, again a functional category. Moreover, the free absolutive is not a complement of {P}, but a dependent that identifies {P}. Otherwise, it differs from specifier *very* only in being redundantly complement-taking (as a functor), and thus having to share the complement of a lower functor (or take an expletive). It looks as if, despite (subordinate) {P} having a rather more conventional (though still not prototypical) specifier in the form of the complementizer, the free functor of {P} has been drawn into the 'specifier' class, at least as far as positioning is concerned, by such similarities of syntax.

Finally here let me return, as a further illustration of the importance of the functional/lexical distinction in the syntax, which has been the theme of this section, to the kind of displacement illustrated by the Basque verbal forms of (183), which was introduced in another context (in §4.6.2):

(183)   a. Lorea   aitari   eman   diot
           flower.the father.to to give.PST.PTCP NPST.(III.SG.ABS)(III.SG.DAT)
                                                              (I.SG.ERG)

      ('I gave the flower to father')

b. Lorea   aitari   eman   diozu
   flower.the father.to give.PST.PTCP NPST.(III.SG.ABS)(III.SG.DAT)
                                                                        (II.SG.ERG)
   ('You gave the flower to father')
c. Loreak   aitari   eman   diozkat
   flowers.the father.to give. PST.PTCP NPST.(III.PL.ABS)(III.SG.DAT)
                                                                        (I.SG.ERG)
   ('I gave the flowers to father')

Here, as we have seen, the elements in concord with the arguments required by the lexical verb are attached to the operative in final position in each clause. This reflects one effect of the grammaticalization of the functional/lexical distinction. Secondary categories, particularly relational ones, as here, that are associated with lexical categories tend to 'percolate' to a governing functional one, in this case the primary category bearing finiteness, the relational centre of the clause. A distinction analogous to that between lexical verbal and functional verbal is of course absent from the phonology, where the distinctive importance of the specialization of functional categories is neither highlighted nor necessary. Trivially, the mechanism of phonological umlauts, for instance, which are analogous to concord, does not involve the mediation of a functional category.

The upward 'percolation' I have just described is a further illustration of the **Functionality Principle** introduced in §6.6 of Volume I and which is also invoked in the discussion of grammatical periphrases in Volume II, particularly Chapter 3:

Functionality Principle
Seek functional status

Just as lexical categories seek functional status, either by adjunction or subjunction to a functional category, so secondary features seek functional status. In the case of the lexical primary categories functionality ensures integration into the structures of phrases and clauses—in general in the functional structure. In achieving functionality secondary features gain greater salience for themselves and integration of the phrase or clause in which they occur. This integrating function is illustrated by agreement phenomena in general, as well as by harmony—though in that case the integration is imposed 'from above', and is referential rather simply agreement in expression. As we have witnessed, this integration function, at least, we can associate with a phonological analogy.

I have devoted a lot of attention in this chapter to the nature and individual characters of functional categories. This is partly because presence vs. absence of this distinction underlies perhaps some of the most important differences between syntactic and phonological structure. These involve not just the elaborations of clausal and phrasal structure, compared with syllables and clusters, commented on in what immediately precedes. Functional categories also play an important role in the distinctive syntactic phenomena to be looked at in the following chapter, to do with the facilitation of embedding and the prescribing of allowable 'tangling', i.e. legitimate violations of projectivity (involving possibly 'long-distance dependencies'). The functional categories have also received this attention because their role in frustrating syntax-phonology analogies is perhaps less obvious than the other factors involved in the presence in the syntax of extended embedding and of 'tangling' that we shall now be looking at.

6

Structure

This chapter focuses on the two major aspects of syntax which allow for the expression of complex 'entities' and 'scenes', 'entities' that denote 'scenes', 'scenes' involving 'subscenes', etc. One aspect is more obviously lexically based, often dependent on morphological expression of complexity. One primary category may be derived from another by taking that other as a subjoined dependent, by being absorbed by that other: we have **lexical derivationality**. The other facilitator of the expression of complex cognitive structures utilizes the capacity of the syntax for the **recursive embedding** of one structure within another—though this can occur too in response to lexical categorization. Indeed, we shall find that some of the structural properties commonly associated with the elaboration of syntactic representations are replicated in intra-word categorial structure—though not, of course, replication of syntactic serialization.

Both derivation and syntactic embedding can manifest **recursion**, which I understand simply as recurrence of the same primary category as a subordinate in a single linguistic structure. The structure may be lexical or syntactic. Formally, this phenomenon could also be manifested in phonological structure, but we shall find restrictions on such recursive capacities as are, or indeed, could be, paralleled to any great extent in phonology—again for reasons to do with the nature of the interface and its physical implementation. Consideration of these means of elaborating the syntax will lead us into other aspects of discrepancy between syntax and phonology, notably the presence of **ectopicity** in syntax, apparent 'displacement' of an element from its expected position in a structure.

6.1 Lexical derivation

In Volume I of this trilogy in particular I invoke various complex categories which involve the subjunction of categories to other categories, especially subjunction to functional categories. Such internal categorial complexity seems to be typical of the lexical items from which the syntax is projected. In some cases this kind of complexity is formally expressed in the morphology, inflectional or derivational. What is traditionally regarded as **inflectional morphology** reflects the presence of superjoined (absorbing) functional categories (case, finiteness) or of subjoined (incorporated) secondary categories (person, tense) which may very well abbreviate functional-category-based structures. **Derivational morphology**, on the other hand, is principally concerned with relationships between primary lexical categories, but also notional subcategories, which may be more or less transparently expressed, more or less productive. These primarily involve **absorptions**, where the base is the absorbed category (e.g. *sing-er*), rather than **incorporations**, where the governing category is the base (e.g. *sing-s*). However, languages can also show **compounding**, in which we have multiple bases (e.g. *folk-song*).

Anderson (1984) offers an account of English derivations based on roughly the assumptions adopted here. The discussion that follows is less extended, and illustrative only, as well as taking advantage of more recent research, some of it incorporated in other parts of this trilogy.

6.1.1 *Affixation, mutation, and conversion*

Lexical derivation may be expressed morphologically in various ways, principally by affixation, as in *kindness* or *unkind*, or mutation of the base, as in *feed*, based on *food*, or conversion, as in *drive* the noun, based on the verb. Or lexical relationships may not be expressed. For instance, the core meaning of the verb *show* is based on a categorization associated with the verb *see*—as is indeed marked by causative affixation in a number of languages. In what follows I shall mainly illustrate lexical derivation with instances of affixation, particularly since this represents the least controversial expression of lexical relationship. It is also much more productive than mutation. And this focus means that our focus of interest can be elsewhere, on the recategorizations involved rather than the means of expression (or its absence).

In the present study we have already encountered such derivationality as is described above in the discussion in §3.1 of deverbal nouns like that in (115), repeated in that form here:

Structure   283

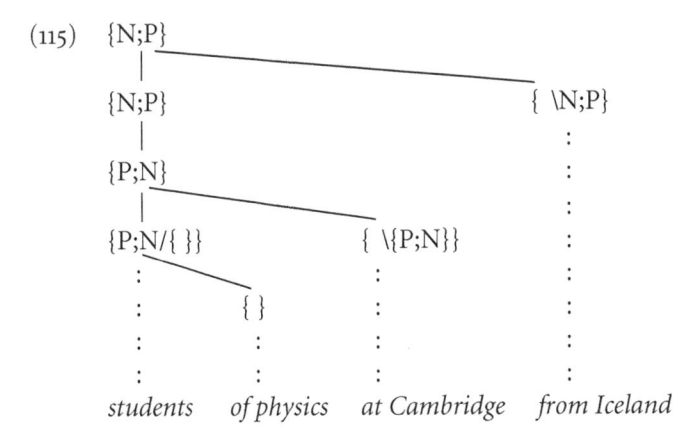

(115)   {N;P}
          |
         {N;P}   { \N;P}
          | :
         {P;N}   :
          | :
         {P;N/{ }}   { \{P;N}}   :
          :   \   :   :
          :   { }   :   :
          :   :   :   :
          :   :   :   :
        students of physics at Cambridge from Iceland

This shows an 'embedding' of {P;N} within {N;P}, but this 'embedding' is simply a reflection of the absorbing subjunctive dependency line relating two distinct categories. And there is no free recursion, despite the replication of both {N;P} and {P;N}. This replication in each case is a result of the copying of a category above itself that accommodates a modifier.

And we can indeed now flesh out the representation in (115) with the appropriate functional categories, most obviously as in (115)*:

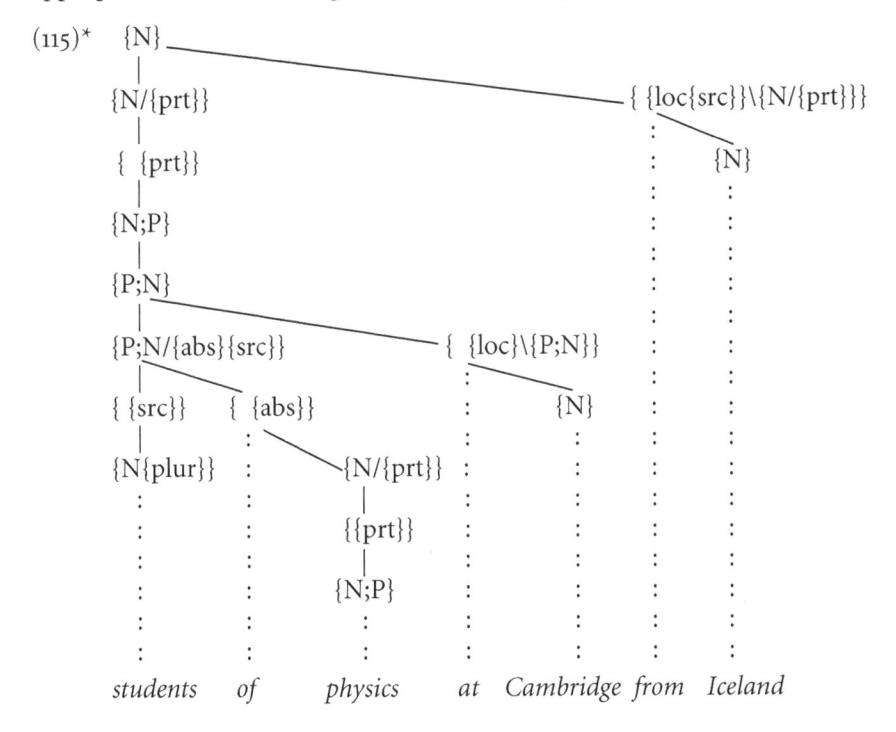

(115)*   {N}
          |
         {N/{prt}}   ─ { {loc{src}}\{N/{prt}}}
          | :
         { {prt}}   :   {N}
          | :   :
         {N;P}   :   :
          | :   :
         {P;N}   :   :
          | :   :
         {P;N/{abs}{src}}   ─ { {loc}\{P;N}}   :   :
          | :   :   :
        { {src}} { {abs}}   {N}   :   :
          | \   :   :   :
        {N{plur}} : {N/{prt}} :   :   :   :
          :   : | :   :   :   :
          :   : {{prt}}   :   :   :   :
          :   : | :   :   :   :
          :   : {N;P}   :   :   :   :
          :   :   :   :   :   :   :
          :   :   :   :   :   :   :
        students of physics   at   Cambridge   from   Iceland

The {loc{src}} feature complex introduces the spatial source; {src} (uncombined with **loc**) is the relation of the argument that is the source of the action; {prt} is another, adnominal, instance of source that for transparency I have distinguished by its own label. On these see particularly §3.7 in Volume I. In (115)* we have an agentive deverbal noun which has inherited much of the argument structure of the verb it is based on. The range of 'modifiers' of the noun and the differences between them (e.g. in placement—as discussed in §3.1) depend on the richness of this internal structure.

(115)* preserves a rather traditional idea of attributives as modifiers. We return to attributivization in §6.2.2, however, where I adopt the analysis of Anderson (2007), whereby attributives are categories converted into determiners, thus removing (restrictive) modification from dependence on the {N} to which the noun (such as *students* in (115)*) is subjoined. At that point we shall look at the modification to the representation in (115)* that this requires. Meanwhile (115)* and the like will serve as an initial illustration that adopts a more traditional view of noun 'modifiers'.

As we have seen, with such complex nouns the equivalents of verbal complements are much more generally omissible than in the case of independent verbs—as well as having their relation consistently expressed by an overt functor when they follow the noun. And pre-nominal circumstantials 'lose' the adverbial *-ly* if they have one when used adverbially, as shown in (211):

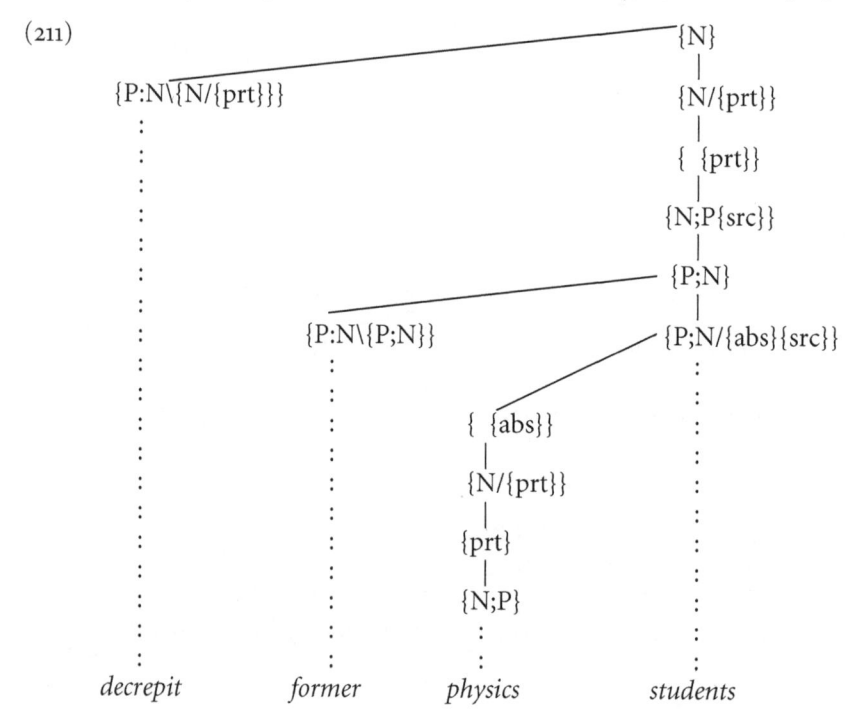

(211)

{P:N\{N/{prt}}}   {N}
                  |
                  {N/{prt}}
                  |
                  { {prt}}
                  |
                  {N;P{src}}
                  |
                  {P;N}
                  |
{P:N\{P;N}}   {P;N/{abs}{src}}

        { {abs}}
        |
        {N/{prt}}
        |
        {prt}
        |
        {N;P}

decrepit   former   physics   students

The circumstantial adjective in (211) corresponds to the adverb in *They were formerly students*.

The morphosyntax of the derived noun again continues to manifest its polycategoriality. As another manifestation of this, we can recall that, as observed above, again in §3.1, the adjective in *a beautiful singer* is ambiguous between an attributive interpretation and a circumstantial/adjunct one. Such derivational relationships thus have important consequences for interpretation and thus for the syntactic differences that determine different interpretations. The internal structure of the noun is reflected in the syntax of the latter.

The example in (115)* does not seem to manifest true recursion—unless we extend the derivation, as in, say, *studentship*. And there are many other examples where we find, say, a noun category recurring in a lexical subjunction-path—as in *victimization*. We can represent the categorization of the latter, schematically, as in (212):

(212) {N;P}
         |
       {P;N}
         |
       {N;P}

Here the noun base is verbalized and the resulting verb nominalized. And there are grounds for regarding *victim* itself as lexically derived (cf. §2.4 in Volume I). Such recursive structures are common in the lexicon.

The categorial complexities involved in these cases are again a response to interface requirements, in this case the need to be able to provide for an entity an economical label, in the form of a lexical item, that is based on a characteristic and relevant activity. This is one kind of recurrent manifestation of the **metonymic** basis for many derivational relationships.

Metonymy is also apparent in the verb-to-noun conversions sampled in (213a) (drawn immediately from Colman and Anderson 2004, ultimately from Clark and Clark 1979):

(213) a. *some verb-to-noun conversions in English*

Type	Examples
agentive	cook, spy
resultative	win, guess
goal	drop, dump
patient	smoke, drink
actional	run, climb, smoke

b. {N;P$_i$}
　　　　|
　　　{P;N/{src$_j$}}

In each of these 'the label for an event is used for an entity which plays one of a set of roles in the event' (Colman and Anderson 2004) or nominalizes the event itself. (213b) illustrates in a crude way the kind of structure associated with the former type, where the head is identical to (in this instance) the agentive argument of the verb.

These examples also illustrate the importance of the functional category of functors for the description of derivational relationships: where they are not based directly on the predicator (actional), the metonymies involve the secondary features of the functor category, in combination with nominal features (agentive nominalization: source + human), or, without such limitation, as in goal, patient, resultative.

We can see the same impulse and the same semantic relations at work in the formation of denominal verbs in (214):

(214)　*some noun-to-verb conversions in English*
　　　　Type　　　　　　　　*Examples*
　　　　locatum-based　　　　newspaper the shelves, rouge the cheeks
　　　　goal-based　　　　　 pot the begonias, table, garage, field, ground, seat, can
　　　　duration-based　　　 winter in California, overnight at the White House
　　　　agent-based　　　　　police the park, clown, soldier, butcher
　　　　translative-based　　cripple the man, crumb the bread; the trail forked
　　　　instrument-based　　 bicycle, nail, knife

In this case, 'the label for an entity is used for an event in which the entity plays one of a set of semantic roles' (Colman and Anderson 2004). Such derivational relationships accommodate concepts to different 'modes of signifying'—to adopt the terminology of the Stoics.

This rich patterning of derivational relationships is thus motivated by the requirements of the semantic interface. We are, despite the work of Levinson (2003b) and others (as in Levinson and Wilkins 2006), at the very beginning of understanding the reciprocal effects of linguistic structure (grammaticalization) and cognitive distinctions, however. But an analogue to this rich patterning of derivation is not manifested in the phonology, where there are no such requirements, and where, as I have reiterated, the invocation of derivational relationships between different phonological categories would indeed make nonsense of the perceptual basis of the categorial features. For the phonology such relationships are both unnecessary and not possible.

Other derivational relationships can be seen as allowing for compact expression of complex scenes, scenes which contain other scenes as part of their structure. This is well illustrated by causative constructions such as that in (215b), from Turkish, which is based derivationally on the intransitive in (a):

(215) a. Hasan öl- dü
   Hasan die-PST ('Hasan died')

   b. Ali Hasan-ı öl- dür- dü
   Ali Hasan-ACC die-CAUS- PST ('Ali killed Hasan')

   c. Kasap et-i kes-ti
   butcher meat-ACC cut-PST ('The butcher cut the meat')

   d. Hasan kasab- a et- i kes-tir- di
   Hasan butcher-DAT meat-ACC cut-CAUS-PST
   ('Hasan had the butcher cut the meat')

   e. Ahmet Hasan-a et- i piş- ir- t- ti
   Ahmet Hasan-DAT meat-ACC cook-CAUS-CAUS-PST
   ('Ahmet made Hasan cook the meat')

   f. {P}
      |
      {P;N/{src}}
      |
      {P;N/{loc{goal/{N{e}}}}}
      |
      {P:N/{src}}
      |
      {P;N/{loc{goal/{N{e}}}}}
      |
      {P;N/...}

(examples from Aissen 1979, Comrie 1985; ACC = accusative, DAT = dative; for further discussion see Anderson 2005b). (215d) shows the causative of a transitive, (c); and (215e) shows a causative of a causative.

The internal structure of the (finite) verb in this last is exhibited in (215f) (on such see again Anderson 2005b). Each causative component expresses that its subject is the immediate agent/source in the coming into existence

({N{e}}) of an event. In the first instance the event is the coming into existence of the inferior causative. The latter brings about the coming into existence of the event denoted by the base verb, here *piş*, whose valency I have left unspecified. Here we have **direct recursion**—as opposed to the indirect recursion of *victimization* and the like. There is specifically a subjunction path of {P;N}s.

Again, no such representational requirements as are served by these derivational structures are associated with the phonology, and no such structures are evident in the phonology. One might certainly want to say that in some specific morphophonological relationship or other, such as that involved in the familiar *ser*e*ne/ser*e*nity* and the like, a particular intransitive vowel, here [iː], 'corresponds to' a particular transitive, here [ɛ]. But it is not obvious why one would want to say that the phonological representation of the one includes that of the other, that they are derivationally related in such a way, i.e. phonologically rather than morphologically. This would introduce undesirable abstractness (but see e.g. Anderson 1994, who derives by redundancy the difference in vowel quality on the basis of a common source).

Relationships of the character of the forms in (215) are of interest here for a further reason. They can be used to illustrate the limits of morphological expression of complex 'scenes', the problems attendant on extension of such structural relationships to accommodate increasing complexity. These limitations are already suggested by what we can observe concerning the forms in (215). The argument in (215b) which corresponds to the subject of (215a) is marked by an oblique case, the accusative; but in order to cater for the causative of the transitive in (215c), which already has an accusative argument, the argument corresponding to the subject of the base transitive is dative in (215d). These observations raise the questions: how many arguments can be 'assimilated' by a single (albeit complex) verb, and how are they to be distinguished consistently?

The ditransitive in (216a) (in which the verb is an irregular causative, though I haven't marked it as such) already contains a dative argument, and here the causative based on it in (b) resorts to marking of the argument corresponding to the subject of (216a) by an adposition otherwise used with 'passive agents':

(216) a. Müdür   Hasan-a   mektub-u   göster-di
          director Hasan-DAT   letter-ACC show-PST
          ('The director showed the letter to Hasan')

       b. Dişçi   Hasan-a   mektub-u   müdür tarafından göster-t-   ti
          dentist Hasan-DAT   letter-   ACC director by   show-CAUS-PST
          ('The dentist made the director show the letter to Hasan')

c. Dişçi   müdür- e   mektub-u   Hasan-a   göster-t-   ti
   dentist director-DAT letter-   ACC Hasan-DAT show-CAUS-PST
   ('The dentist made the director show the letter to Hasan')

d. Ahmet Hasan-a   biz-i   çalış-tır-   t-   tı
   Ahmet Hasan-DAT we-ACC work-CAUS-CAUS-PST
   ('Ahmet made Hasan make us work')

(Comrie 1985: 340). Only some speakers are happy with the alternative possibility for the causative of (216a), the doubling of the dative in (216c) (Zimmer 1976: 409–12). Zimmer observes further that some speakers of Turkish are not just unhappy with sentences like (216c), where we have causativization of a ditransitive (i.e. of the causative of a transitive verb), but they also tend to reject causativization of the causative of intransitive bases whose one argument is an agent. Thus, whereas (215e), involving causativization of the causative of a non-agentive intransitive is quite acceptable, (216d) is for such speakers 'very awkward at best' (Zimmer 1976: 409). Conceptual requirements are straining at the limits of the derivational capacity of the lexicon, and particularly the capacity of a single clause to sustain expression of the multiple argument structures associated with complex lexical items composed of paths of lexical categories.

Of course, categorially complex conceptual structures of a causative type can also be associated with non-derived items. Witness the English gloss to the verb in (215b), which is not morphologically related to the verbal gloss in (215a); or English *show*, which, unlike the verb in (216d), is not even an irregular overt causative. Lexical items can indeed subtend categorial structures associated with very complex and subtle semantic properties. But non-derived forms have the same kind of limitations as derived concerning how much argument structure they can support. Moreover, the signalling by individual lexical items of systematically more complex structures which speakers may have only peripheral use for is uneconomic at best; it is a marginally beneficial expansion of the lexicon—though it must be conceded that the lexicon's tolerance of such is remarkable. Nevertheless, the capacity of predicational constructions to absorb multiple argument structures is strained by some of the possibilities we have been looking at.

Enter syntax at this point, and specifically the facility for constructional embedding, to which we turn in §6.2. However, before that, there is a final aspect of complex lexical structures that I should comment on, involving the phenomenon of compounding, where we have a word with multiple bases.

6.1.2 Compounding

It is helpful, I think, to contrast compounds with the multi-word lexical items, or **idioms**, discussed in §3.1.1 of Volume II. An example of these is (II.57a), where a sequence of words has as a whole a meaning distinct from their expected compositional meaning:

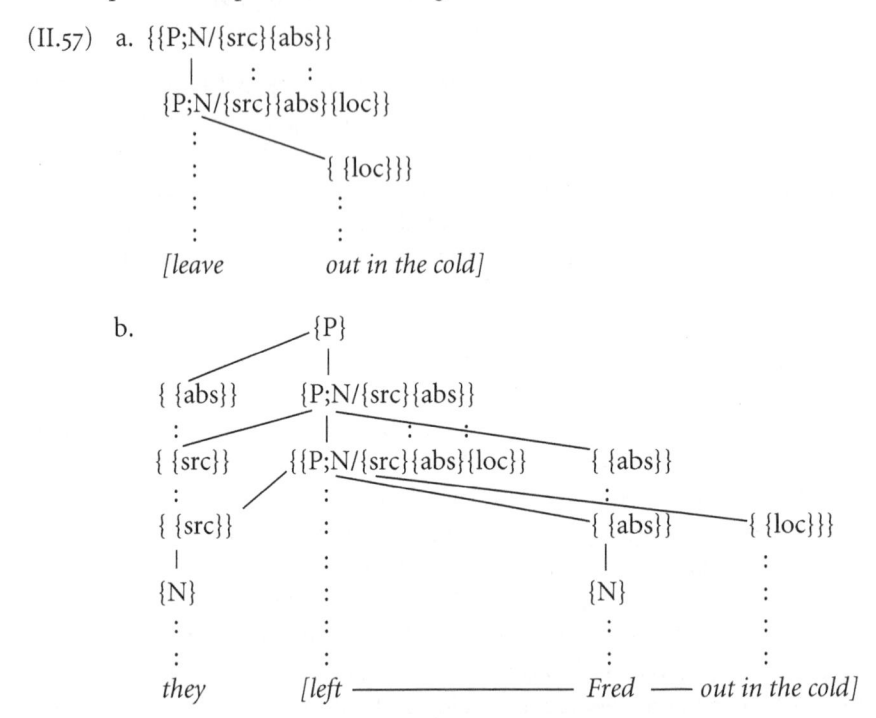

(II.57) a. {{P;N/{src}{abs}}
    | :   :
    {P;N/{src}{abs}{loc}}
    :
    :   { {loc}}}
    :   :
    :   :
    [leave   out in the cold]

b.   {P}
          / |
    { {abs}} {P;N/{src}{abs}}
     : | :   :
    { {src}} {{P;N/{src}{abs}{loc}}}   { {abs}}
     :   :   :
    { {src}}   :   { {abs}}   { {loc}}}
     | : | :
    {N}   :   {N}   :
     :   :   :   :
    they   [left   Fred —— out in the cold]

This sequence is a single lexical item, but it is syntactically complex: its elements are sequenced by the normal rules of syntax, the verb can vary in accordance with the forms allowed to verbs, and in many cases the sequence may be interrupted by an element that is lexically variable—as with *Fred* in (57b). The form of the latter is not determined by the idiom.

Though compounds may develop non-compositionality, their elements do not necessarily follow the sequence associated with their syntactic equivalents. Certainly, what is apparently a verb in *landslide* follows its 'subject', but this is not the case in *popcorn*, say. Moreover, compounds largely lack expression of functional categories. And even with the complex preposition in *outdoors* its dimensional nominal aspect is what is most salient. Syntactically these whole compounds comport themselves as a unitary word, with sequencing of the expounding bases that obeys distinct, morphological principles. This typical kind of compound is not syntactically complex, then, unlike the idioms alluded to above.

I suggest, moreover, that internally compounds lack a distinction between functional and lexical category: in English categorization is reduced to noun ({N}), verb ({P}), and adjective ({P,N}); and their relationships to each other are articulated by the secondary features of the functor category, which lacks all of these primary features and here is not expounded independently. This is illustrated by the representation in (217a):

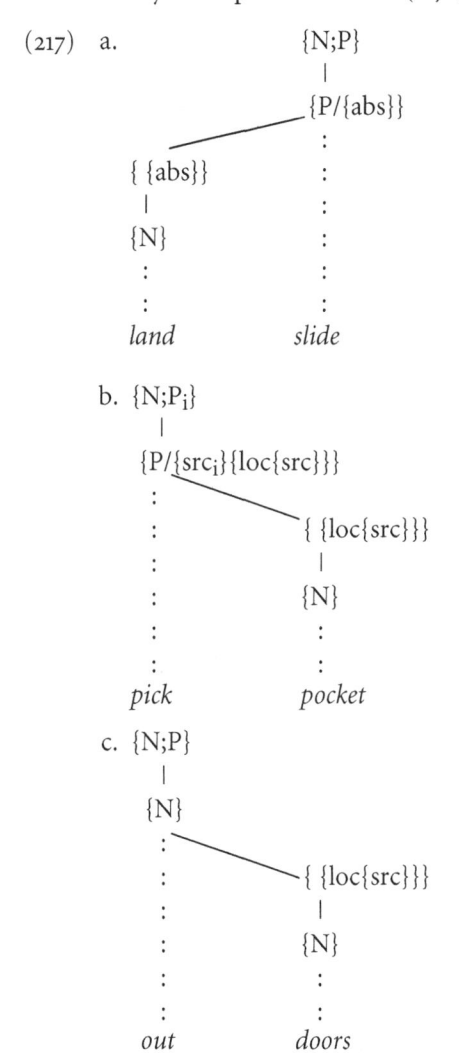

(217) a.
$$\{N;P\}$$
|
$\{P/\{abs\}\}$

{ {abs}}
|
{N}
⋮
⋮
land   slide

b. $\{N;P_i\}$
|
$\{P/\{src_i\}\{loc\{src\}\}\}$

{ {loc{src}}}
|
{N}
⋮
⋮
pick   pocket

c. {N;P}
|
{N}

{ {loc{src}}}
|
{N}
⋮
⋮
out   doors

d.
```
                        {N;P}
                          |
                  ┌───── {N}
                  │       |
       {P,N\{N}}          {N}
           ⋮               ⋮
           ⋮               ⋮
         black           bird
```

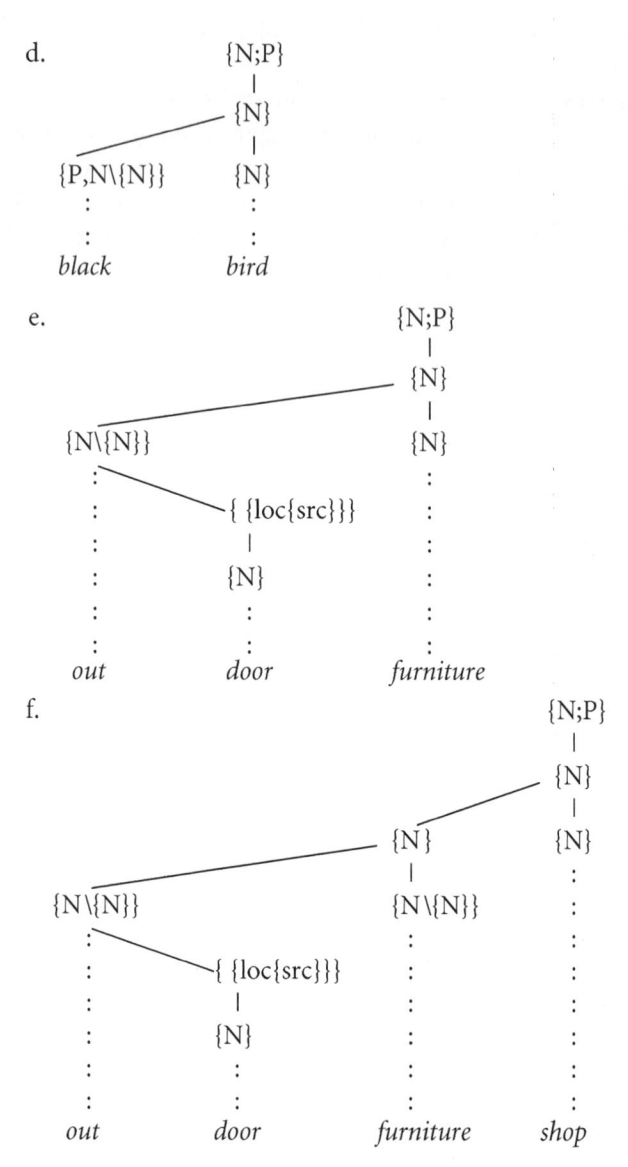

e.
```
                                    {N;P}
                                      |
                          ┌───────── {N}
                          │           |
        {N\{N}}                       {N}
           ⋮                           ⋮
           ⋮  ┌── { {loc{src}}}        ⋮
           ⋮  │         |              ⋮
           ⋮  │        {N}             ⋮
           ⋮  │         ⋮              ⋮
           ⋮  ⋮         ⋮              ⋮
          out         door          furniture
```

f.
```
                                                {N;P}
                                                  |
                                         ┌────── {N}
                                         │        |
                              ┌───────── {N}     {N}
                              │           |       ⋮
        {N\{N}}                         {N\{N}}   ⋮
           ⋮                              ⋮       ⋮
           ⋮  ┌── { {loc{src}}}           ⋮       ⋮
           ⋮  │         |                 ⋮       ⋮
           ⋮  │        {N}                ⋮       ⋮
           ⋮  │         ⋮                 ⋮       ⋮
           ⋮  ⋮         ⋮                 ⋮       ⋮
          out         door           furniture  shop
```

In (217a) the head is a concrete noun converted from verb. Sometimes the head is identical to an argument of the verbal component, as in (217b), where we have an agentive formation. And sometimes the agentive argument is spelled out by a suffix, as in *dressmaker*. In (217c) *out* is treated as an areal noun, and in (217d) we have an idiomatic modifier-noun formation. (217e-f) show further extensions of (217c) of the modifying type of (217d).

Structure 293

(217) illustrates only nominal compounds, where the pattern illustrated by (217d-f) is very characteristic of such, particularly the more extended ones. As modifications they do not manifest recursive subjunctions, but we have direct adjunctive recursions: {N} dependent on {P}. And in (217b) we have indirect recursion of {N}. Such exemplificatory compounds thus confirm that the lexicon contains both direct and indirect recursions. And they also illustrate something of the generative capacity of the lexicon. But this is demonstrated much more generally in Pustejovsky (1995), for instance. And, of course, other languages exhibit more prolific compounding.

I venture no further into the perennially contentious area of lexical compounding. Anderson (1984: 66) remarks that 'the characterisation of compounds, the nature of compound-formation and its status in the grammar remain rather obscure'. It seems to me in this basic respect nothing much has changed. Thus the schematic representations in (217) are even more tentative than those offered elsewhere in these volumes. And they are also vulnerable to the revision of the interpretation of noun modification suggested in §6.2.2 below. But they perhaps have sufficient motivation to illustrate the recursive character of compounding—in so far as such is necessary.

And I cannot leave compounding without considering whether there might be a phonological analogy. Again the motivation for such recursive structural elaboration is minimal in the phonology. But perhaps there is an analogue to compounding itself in the nature of diphthong structures. Such structure is illustrated in the representation in (156c) of the Danish diphthong represented orthographically as *eg*:

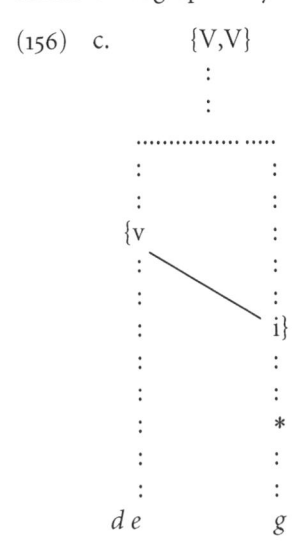

(156) c.   {V,V}
               ⋮
               ⋮
         ....
           ⋮   ⋮
          {v   ⋮
           ⋮\   ⋮
           ⋮ \   ⋮
           ⋮ \   ⋮
           ⋮   \ i}
           ⋮   ⋮
           ⋮   *
           ⋮   ⋮
           ⋮   ⋮
          d e   g

294 *Phonology-Syntax Analogies*

Here we have a 'compound' single segment, with a subsegmental vowel feature that is (redundantly) dependent on another. But perhaps closer, in involving primary categories, is the structure of affricates, such as [tˆs], where we have a single segment composed of two potential segments. The dependency relation in these segment-internal sequences is determined by sonority—or rather anti-sonority in the latter case. What may be in common between morphological and phonological compounding is the relative saliency of the head. However that may be, the compounding capacity is at best minimally implemented in the phonology.

6.2 Recursion

Recursion is often cited as a crucial property of syntax, and it is certainly more evident therein. But, as we have just seen, we must include here some lexical structures involving the derivation of one primary category from another. This represents structural analogy of a more local sort, between the manifestation of syntactic categories in syntax proper and in the lexicon, rather than between the two planes. However, before embarking on recursion in syntax proper, let us firstly look at its role, if any, in phonology—as well as trying to begin to clarify further what might be involved in such a concept.

6.2.1 *Direct recursion, or why phonology is different*

We indeed seem to be able to associate recursive embedding, in a rather trivial sense, with structures such as (61b)*, from Chapter 2, repeated here for convenience, with a slight modification to be commented on below:

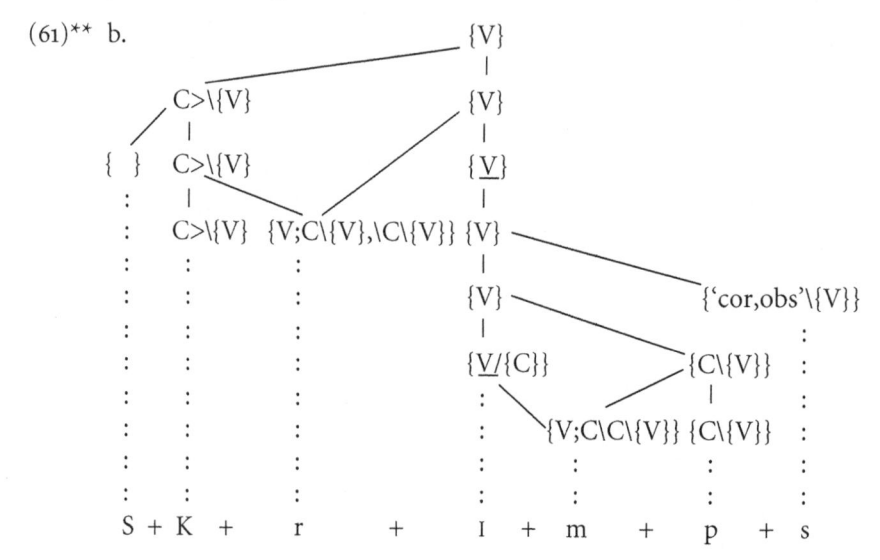

(61)** b.

$$
\begin{array}{c}
\{V\} \\
|
\end{array}
$$

```
            C>\{V}                      {V}
              |                          |
   { }     C>\{V}                       {V}
    :        |                           |
    :     C>\{V}  {V;C\{V},\C\{V}}    {V}
    :        :       :                   |
    :        :       :                  {V}                    {'cor,obs'\{V}}
    :        :       :                   |                         :
    :        :       :                 {V/{C}}                  {C\{V}}
    :        :       :                   :   \                     |
    :        :       :                   :    {V;C\C\{V}}     {C\{V}}    :
    :        :       :                   :       :              :        :
    :        :       :                   :       :              :        :
    S  +  K  +       r       +           l   +   m        +     p    +   s
```

Structure   295

A series of {V}s and a couple of series of {C}s in subjunction are embedded one in another, thus recursively. Most of these examples we can discuss, however, on the same grounds as the recurring {N;P}s and {P;N}s in (115) and (211) discussed in the previous section: namely, in that these recurrences are only the replication of a modified category that is required to accommodate a modifier. However, some of the recurrent {V}s occur independently of modification by a consonant. The rhyme and syllable levels—underlined in (61b)**—are independently recursive.

And we can, indeed, extend the recursively subjoined {V}s as in (61b)***:

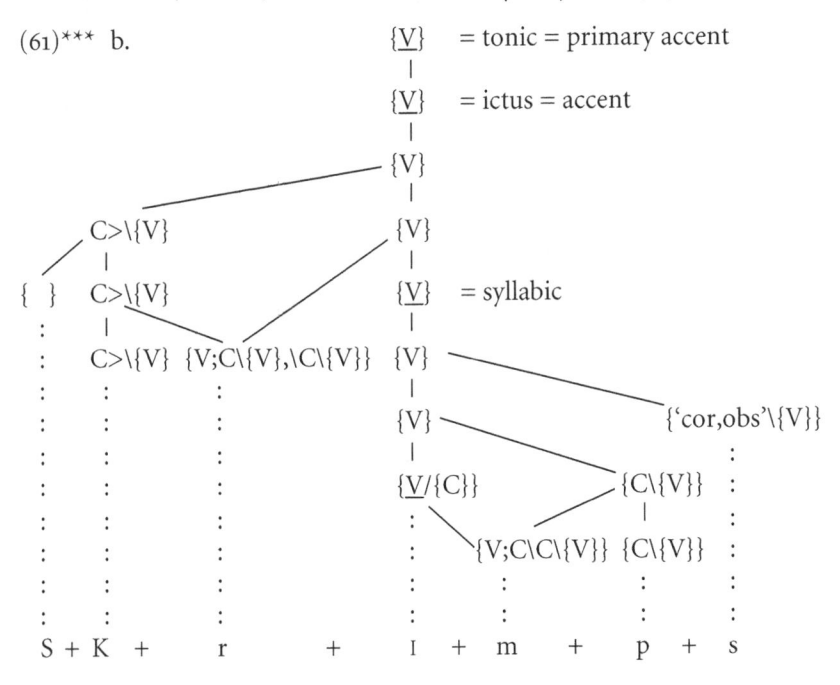

(61)*** b.
$\quad$ {V} = tonic = primary accent
$\quad$ |
$\quad$ {V} = ictus = accent
$\quad$ |
$\quad$ {V}
$\quad$ |
C>\{V}$\quad\quad${V}
|$\quad\quad\quad\quad$|
{ }$\quad$C>\{V}$\quad\quad${V} = syllabic
$\quad$ |$\quad\quad\quad\quad$|
$\quad$ C>\{V} {V;C\{V},\C\{V}} {V}
$\quad\quad\quad\quad\quad\quad\quad$ |
$\quad\quad\quad\quad\quad\quad\quad$ {V}$\quad\quad\quad\quad\quad\quad$ {'cor,obs'\{V}}
$\quad\quad\quad\quad\quad\quad\quad$ |
$\quad\quad\quad\quad\quad\quad\quad$ {V/{C}}$\quad\quad$ {C\{V}}
$\quad\quad\quad\quad\quad\quad\quad\quad\quad$ {V;C\C\{V}} {C\{V}}

S + K +$\quad$ r$\quad$ +$\quad\quad$ I + m$\quad$ +$\quad$ p + s

The phonological representation of the word in (61b)*** is now more complete. It bears an inherent primary accent, which outranks any other accent, one involving only an ictus, the governor of a foot.

This is not illustrated in (61b)***, but is manifested in, for instance, *undertaken*, as represented in (218), which omits replicas introduced by modification, and assumes rhoticity and that the nasal is in this instance not syllabic:

296 *Phonology-Syntax Analogies*

(218)

```
                              *
                              |
    *                 *
    |                 |
    *         *       *         *
    |        /|      /|        /|
    *       * *     * *       * *
     \     /   \   /   \     /   \
      *   *     * *     *   *     *
      :   :     : :     :   :     :
      :   :     : :     :   :     :
      u   n     d e     r   t     a     k     e     n
```

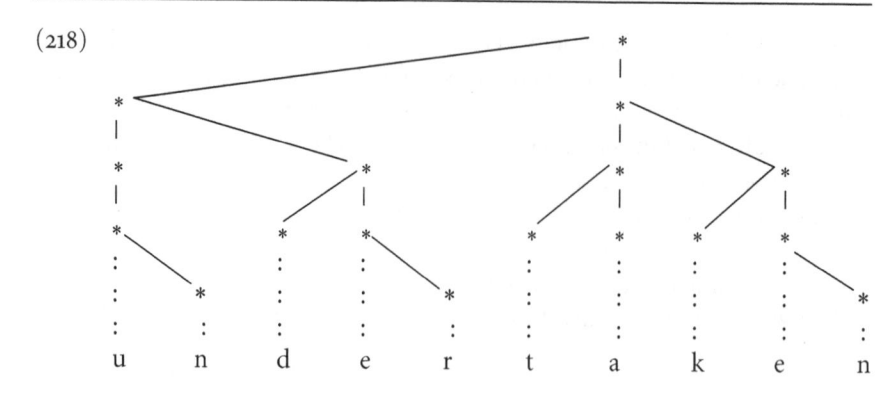

This hierarchization of necessary levels resembles the rank scale of Halliday (1967)—though he doesn't recognize a rhyme level (nor the equivalent of a verb phrase, for that matter). And super-syllabic hierarchization is demanded by the phonetic realization of phonology in terms of different degrees of prominence. Each level is distinguished by a particular (degree of a) phonetic property, except the rhymal head vs. syllabic distinction, whose motivation is distributional, and figurative. However, in accordance with this different status, languages that lack codas (or onsets) will simply lack a syllable-rhyme distinction. So Halliday's reduced hierarchy is general, and rhyme an optional but common extension of it (as perhaps with verb phrase).

Halliday (1961) argues for a similar hierarchy in syntax—an analogous rank scale. But, despite his robust response (1966) to Matthews's (1966) criticisms of the syntactic scale, syntactic structures seem to be rather differently articulated. Hierarchization in syntax is imposed by valency requirements (a property that, as we have seen, is marginal in phonology, being limited at most to simple transitivity of vowels. Thus {P} typically requires {P;N} as an argument, {P;N} typically takes functors as arguments, functors typically require {N}s, and {N}s typically take {N;P} or { }—at which point we come to the end of the road, in the absence of recursion. But these valency requirements are not absolute; there are other possibilities. And this structuring strikes me as rather different from the rigid phonological hierarchy, mostly required by phonetic demands. The syntactic hierarchy, as we have been witnessing, is a response, in the form of different categorizations and their valencies, to the need to express complex scenes. And this may involve, for example, the embedding of a {P} at a much lower level in the rough hierarchization I've enumerated. The 'rank' hierarchy of phonology, interpreted, as here, in terms of dependency relations, involves subjunctional recurrence only of the same category, {V}, with each level above the syllable adding to its prominence. 'Rank' seems to be a dis-analogy, another example of why phonology is different.

Neither the direct subjunctional recurrence of (218) nor the indirect recurrence of the morphosyntactic representations of the previous section represents what syntacticians have in mind when they refer to recursion. Recursion is usually envisaged as involving adjunctive structures. A minimal manifestation of such recursion is any (adjunctive) dependency relation where the tail and the terminal have the same primary categorization. In what we have looked at, adjunction in phonology has involved **unidirectional categorial progression**: thus while consonants depend on vowels, as again illustrated by (61b)**, the converse is not the case; and, in the unmarked case more sonorous consonants depend on less sonorous. In these cases there is no (adjunctive) recursion of categories. These limitations are clearly related to the physical limitations on syllable structure which underlie sonority.

It has been argued, however, that also **recursion** may be exhibited by tone units. Thus, for instance, Anderson (1986a: §17) analyses an utterance like that in (219) as involving the head of a tone group (a tonic) dependent on another such head, as indicated roughly in that representation, where the lowest-level {V}s are syllable heads, the next are governors of feet (ictus), the next tone group heads, and the highest governor is a tonic that takes another adjoined to it to the left:

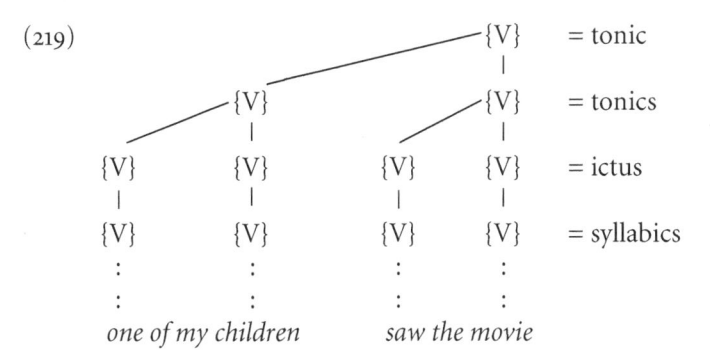

(219)

```
                              ─{V}      = tonic
                               │
         ─{V}            ─{V}            = tonics
          │               │
{V}      {V}    {V}      {V}             = ictus
 │        │      │        │
{V}      {V}    {V}      {V}             = syllabics
 ⋮        ⋮      ⋮        ⋮
one of my children   saw the movie
```

(cf. too e.g. Halliday 1967; Crystal 1969: §5.10.2; Ladd 1986).[51]

Thus, if we want to generalize over recursive embedding in the phonology, the only general limitation on the adjunction of {V} and consonants is that {V} cannot be adjoined to a consonant, but that some {V}-headed constructions can be adjoined one to another. The force of what, on the basis of this,

---

[51] This minor manifestation of recursion in the phonology intrudes exactly where the phonology is directly responsive to the requirements of the semantic interface, in the area of intonation, where the 'double articulation' of language breaks down (recall the discussion in Volume I, particularly Ch. 4). The significance of this clearly deserves further investigation.

we can conclude about recursion in the phonology depends upon the appropriateness of the above kind of analysis of intonation units, however. And even if it is appropriate, it introduces only a very shallow depth of recursion, though the depth of intonational embedding within utterances remains uncertain (as emerges, for instance, from Jun's concluding chapter to the collection in Jun 2005). Moreover, there are other types of recursion in syntax than the **direct** type illustrated by the {V}-to-{V} adjunction we find in (218).

Indeed, direct recursion tends to be avoided in the syntax. And this seems to be largely due to the intervention of functional categories, as well as the absence of interface-determined restrictions parallel to that underlying the failure of consonants to govern vowels. Even such a representation as (138a)* from Chapter 4 involves a {P;N} intervening between the two {P} nodes and a {P} between the two {P;N}s:

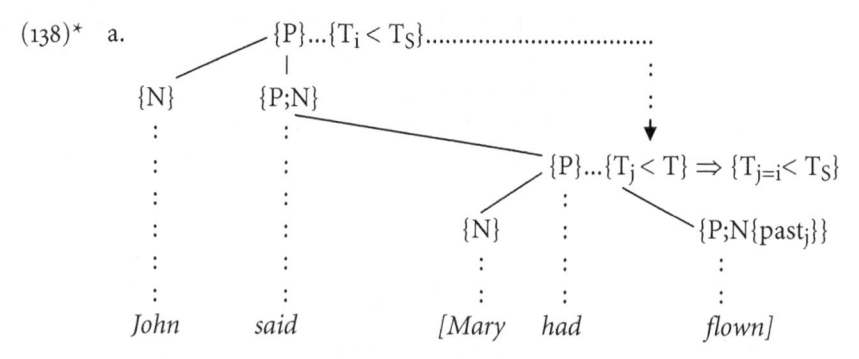

(138)* a.

$\{P\}...\{T_i < T_S\}$...............

{N}   {P;N}

$\{P\}...\{T_j < T\} \Rightarrow \{T_{j=i} < T_S\}$

{N}   {P;N{past$_j$}}

John   said   [Mary   had   flown]

Let us now include in the representation for this sentence the subcategorization of *say* as a predication-taking verb, but not functor nodes (as again not relevant, yet), and omit the tense aspect of the structure, as also not relevant at this point:

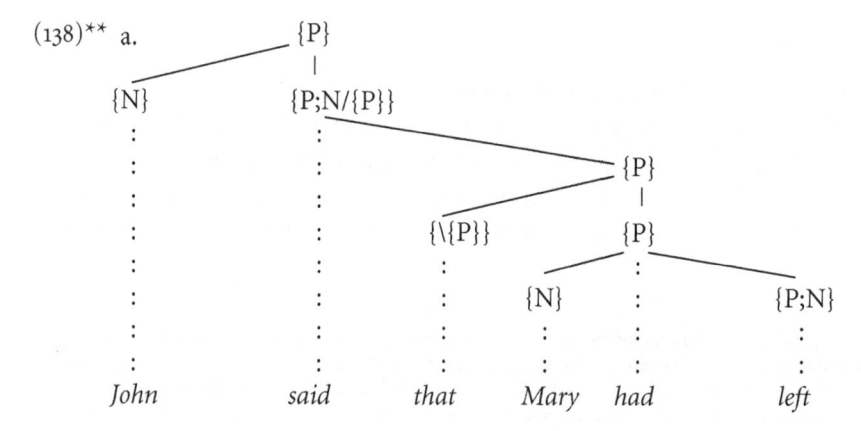

(138)** a.

{P}

{N}   {P;N/{P}}

{P}

{\{P}}   {P}

{N}   {P;N}

John   said   that   Mary   had   left

(138a)** also includes the optional complementizer, here represented as an adjunct, whose status we come to in subsection §6.2.3. (138a)** makes it clear that we do not have direct recursion. But that the *said* {P;N} is both dependent on and complemented by {P} is nevertheless closer to direct recursion than we tend to find elsewhere in the syntax.[52]

However, the most direct recursion is illustrated by those verbal elements that do not occur in finite position. I approach this phenomenon via a brief survey of the role of verbal non-finites in English. I do not pursue here the idea that direct or linear recursion of {P} is manifested by the phenomenon of so-called 'sentential coordination'.

Verbs in English (and many languages) can incorporate lexically a finiteness element; they can thus occur in either kind of configuration that we find in (173), again repeated for ease of reference:

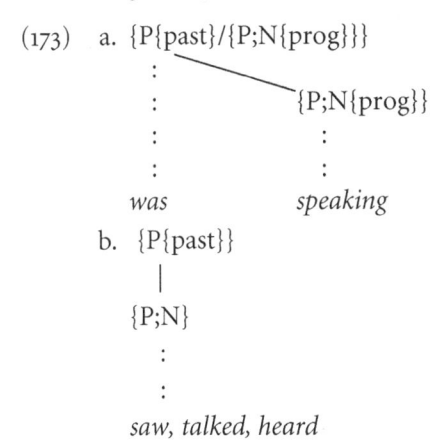

(173) a. {P{past}/{P;N{prog}}}
    :
    :   {P;N{prog}}
    :   :
    :   :
    was   speaking

   b. {P{past}}
       |
      {P;N}
       :
       :
      saw, talked, heard

The configuration in (173b) is made available lexically by a redundancy of the form of (I.44):

(I.44)   {P}
                   |
      {P;N} ⇔ {P;N}

(I.44) enables lexical verbs to occur as finites.

Some verb forms overtly reflect failure of (I.44): these are non-finite forms that are morphologically marked as such. They are forms which are

---

[52] If we analyse the complementizer as a kind of functional category, as has been common of late, then we move even further from direct recursion. However, this does not seem to be an appropriate analysis: again see the excursus devoted to this issue in §6.2.3.

categorized lexically as exceptions to (I.44), i.e. as {P;N{*(I.44)}}; I shall abbreviate this as {P;N{*P}}. Since such forms cannot normally form independent predications, they figure as arguments in the predications headed by other predicators, either via a functor, as in (220) and (221), or directly as dependents of a verbal, as in (222):

(220) a. Betsy is pleased at [John('s) know<u>ing</u> the truth]
b. Betsy is pleased [for John <u>to</u> know the truth]

(221) a. [John('s) know<u>ing</u> the truth] pleased Betsy
b. [For John <u>to</u> know the truth] pleased Betsy

(222) a. John likes [know<u>ing</u> the truth]
b. John likes [<u>to</u> know the truth]

The functor governing the {P;N} is overt in (220a)—though it disappears under subject formation in (221a); the categorial status of *for* in the corresponding (b) examples is more controversial. The elements that signal the status of the {*P} forms are underlined: in one case they are morphological (*-ing*), in the other analytic (*to*).

Given the role of these verbal forms as an argument serving a semantic function, it is not surprising that such forms are typically nominalizations in origin, nominals being the prototypical argument type. And, indeed, as is familiar, the incorporated {*P} form of the (a) examples in (220–2) is still paralleled by nominalizations, as illustrated in (223):

(223) a. John('s) painting the wall was a disaster
b. John's painting of the wall was a disaster

In (223b), which is ambiguous between an 'event' (or action) reading of the *-ing* form and an 'entity' (or concrete) reading, the nominal structure is signalled very overtly, by the obligatory genitive inflection on *John* and the preposition following *painting*. But its nominal basis is still pertinent synchronically in (223a). Recall the discussion of 'nouniness' in §3.1.

Other subordinates have a full clausal structure, as in (224):

(224) a. It seems (that) John knows the truth
b. It surprises me (that) John knows the truth

Now, generally, arguments are introduced by a semantic relation, and necessarily if they are nominal. But Anderson (1997a: §3.6) argues that the finite subordinate in (224a) depends directly on the main verb; their relationship is 'unmediated', as he puts it, by a semantic relation. Thus, the subordinate clause in (224a), lacking a semantic relation, cannot occupy subject position, unlike that in (224b):

(225) a. *That John knows the truth seems
       b. That John knows the truth surprises me
       c. Betsy was pleased by John('s) knowing the truth

Similarly, the subordinates in (221/222), whose relationship to the superordinate predicator is mediated by a functor (bearing a semantic relation) can optionally occupy subject position. And the more 'nouny' (221a) can in turn be passivized, as in (225c).

The clausal argument in (225a) does not have a governing functor to enable it to undergo subject formation. The only (non-incorporated) semantic relation associated with *seem* is a free absolutive, indeed two of them, one associated with its {P} component and one with {P;N}, as in (226), where I have begun to (re)introduce the functor categories into structures, but omitted any representation of *that*, as not relevant at this point, and certainly not obviously functoral:

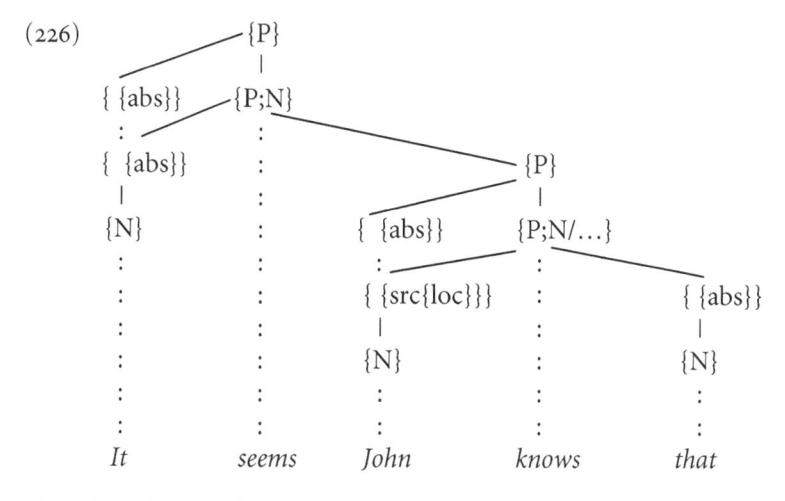

(226)

```
                    {P}
                     |
      {{abs}}      {P;N}
         :           :
      {{abs}}        :                        {P}
         |           :                         |
        {N}          :       {{abs}}        {P;N/...}
         :           :          :
         :           :       {{src{loc}}}    :      {{abs}}
         :           :          |            :         |
         :           :         {N}           :        {N}
         :           :          :            :         :
         :           :          :            :         :
         It        seems      John         knows      that
```

There is no lower subject available to be hosted by the free absolutives of *seem*; *John* is hosted by the free absolutive of the {P} in the subordinate clause. The absolutives of *seem* are satisfied by an 'expletive', as shown in (224a/226). Note finally that (224b) shows that subject formation of the clause is optional even with 'mediated' clausal arguments. The subordinate in (226) lacks a governing functor, but it evinces direct recursion only to the extent that the two verb forms *seems* and *knows* as a whole are directly linked by dependency. We still have an alternation of categories: {P} → {P;N} → {P} → {P;N}. We are now getting closer to an instantiation of direct embedding, however.

Seem in (224) takes an 'unmediated' verbal complement that is a full clause. But *seem* is subcategorized for predicators of various sorts, as illustrated by (227):

(227) a. John seems to know the truth
      b. John seems very nice
      c. John seems a nice man

The subordinates in (227) are also 'unmediated'; like the full clause in (224a) they depend directly on the superordinate verb, and cannot be subjects of *seem*. But in this case the subject of the lower predicator shares the free absolutives of *seem*; otherwise they have no host for subject formation.

If this analysis is appropriate, then (227a) shows direct embedding, as represented in (228), which does not represent the subject-sharing:

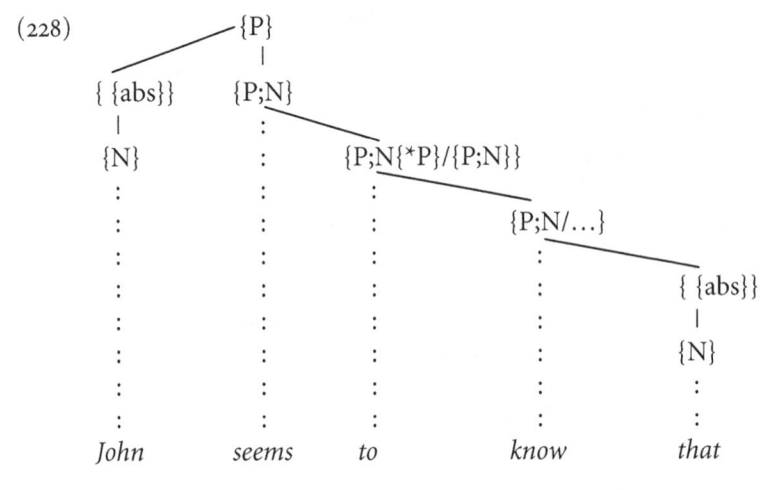

(228)

```
                    {P}
                     |
  {{abs}}          {P;N}
     |               :
    {N}             :        {P;N{*P}/{P;N}}
     :              :              :
     :              :              :         {P;N/...}
     :              :              :              :
     :              :              :              :          {{abs}}
     :              :              :              :             |
     :              :              :              :            {N}
     :              :              :              :             :
     :              :              :              :             :
   John          seems            to            know          that
```

I have represented *to* as an analytic marker of non-finiteness that as a verb takes a non-finite verb as its complement. We thus have a succession of directly dependent {P;N}s in (228). I return to the representation of *to* and other aspects of the syntax of (228) in §6.3. My main aim here is to illustrate direct recursion in the syntax.

The *-ing* form can also be directly embedded, as in (229), as can the {*P} form in (230) whose historical source is a deverbal adjective:

(229)   Betsy saw John painting the wall

(230)   Betsy had John fired

I do not pursue this here. But I recall to our attention that these forms also have a role in forming verbal periphrases, as exemplified in (173a), repeated just above. This latter role is a major concern of Volume II of this trilogy.

The periphrast/operative distinction, discussed in §4.3.5 of Volume II, is significant in our scrutiny of structural analogy: periphrasts, with minimal content and a paradigmatic role, are the result of a grammaticalization, a general phenomenon common to phonology and syntax (as was illustrated in §4.6). But operatives in general introduce a differentiation (functional vs. lexical) not found in phonology. What is perhaps more important in the present context, however, is that English periphrasts allow for rather obvious direct recursion.

English periphrasts *be* and *have* have both an operative and a lexical verb status, as illustrated in (231) and (232), respectively:

(231) a. Fred is dressing
      b. Fred has dressed
      c. Fred is dressed (by his valet)

(232) a. Fred will be dressing
      b. Fred will have dressed
      c. Fred will be dressed (by his valet)

The resulting recursion may be illustrated by (233a), wherein all the verbal forms after the first one are {P;N}:

(233) a. It may have been being repaired
      b. Bill doesn't remember it having been being repaired

These non-finites are distinguished from each other by the category that they subcategorize for: thus *have* requires a {P;N} that is past; the first *be* is subcategorized for {P:N{progressive}}; and the second for {P;N{passive}}. We have, however, despite these differences in valency, a chain of {P;N}s, here and in the non-finite sequence (beginning with *remember*) of (233b).

Similar but potentially more extended chaining is associated with the non-finite periphrast *to*, whose presence is necessary to the occurrence of most infinitival verbs (which lack distinctive morphology in English). Thus we can build up chains of the character of (234):

(234) Bill wants to seem to try to begin to...

Again, all the forms after *wants* are {P;N}. In notional terms, it is clear why it is {P;N}, lexical verbs, that most clearly manifest direct recursion in the syntax. This allows the expression of linked 'scenes' within 'scenes' within a unified structure. The most directly linked lack even the *to* that separates the full verbs expressing the linked 'scenes'. This is illustrated by the 'direct perception' constructions discussed in §2.2 of Volume I—as exemplified in (I.11):

(I.11)   I saw Bill leave, I heard Bill leave, I felt Bill tremble

Volume I describes the expressions in (I.11) as 'iconic', so far as the immediate juxtaposition of the two verbs to the shared argument mirrors the temporal coincidence of the events they represent.

All the periphrases in (233) involve non-finite forms historically based on non-verbal constructions, involving deverbal nouns and adjectives. As observed already, non-finite forms in general tend to be traceable as originating in de-verbalizing constructions. This may reflect the historically secondary character of verbal subordinations. They seem either to be de-paratactic or their origin is based on derivation, involving the reconceptualizations we associate with difference in primary syntactic category. A verb is reintroduced as part of a nominal construction, for instance: 'events' are reintroduced as parts of 'entities'. We have a change in 'mode of signifying'.

This is quite nicely illustrated by the syntax of Turkish (as emerges rather clearly from some work of Jim Miller's, to which I am indebted). Consider the constructions in (235) (exemplified using his notation):

(235)   a. yazdiğim   mektub
           write.NOM.POSS.I.SG   letter
           ('the letter (that) I wrote')

        b. Ankara'ya   geldiğim-   de   yağmur   yağiyordu
           Ankara.DAT   come.NOM.POSS.I.SG-LOC   rain   was.raining
           ('When I arrived in Ankara it was raining')

        c. Ayşenin   mektubu   yazdiğini   söyledik
           Ayşe.GEN   the.letter write.NOM.POSS.III.SG   we.said
           ('We said (that) Ayşe was writing the letter')

        d. Onu   gelecek   diye   bekliyorum
           him   he.will.come   saying   I.am.waiting
           ('I am waiting in the expectation that he will come')

        e. Aliyi gördün-se, neler yaptığını   anlat
           Ali   you.saw-   if   what   do.NOM.POSS.III.SG   tell
           ('If you have seen Ali, tell me what he is doing')

In the construction in (235a) that 'corresponds to' a relative clause in English, the suffix labelled NOM(inalizing) transparently derives nouns. Such a derived form may bear case endings elsewhere; and to it in (235a) is attached a POSS (essive) suffix. We find a similar construction in the 'equivalent' in (235b) of a subordinate clause of time in English, but here the possessed nominalized verb bears the DAT(ive) case inflection. And the same is true of the 'equivalent' of an English complement clause in (235c), which contains a nominal in the GEN(itive) in place of the English subordinate unmarked subject. (235d), on the other hand, retains paratactic elements which involve a subordinating construction in the English translation of them (see Lewis 1978: 109-10). Miller suggests that the only type of finite subordinate clause that Turkish possesses is the conditional of (235e). But even it is not fully finite on the basis of what is assumed in Chapter 6 of Volume I, in that the verb form in (325e) is explicitly marked by the suffix -*se* as subordinate, unable to occur in a main clause, despite signalling tense and concord. Turkish is not exceptional in its lack of subordinate finites; it is characteristic of many languages, though often disguised by descriptive grammars (as e.g. also with Tibetan).

Although it may be the case that, as Noonan claims, 'all languages have some sort of sentence-like complement type' (1985: 49), the elements that introduce even 'sentence-like' complements, conventionally grouped as 'complementizers', 'typically derive historically from pronouns, conjunctions, adpositions or case markers' (Noonan 1985: 47), i.e. elements mostly associated with nominal constructions. Could it be, after all, that the basic template for the independent clause, and indeed even a complex sentence, resembles that for the syllable in at least this respect: the centre of the clause is 'verbal', as the centre of the syllable is vocalic; non-central elements are interpreted as non-verbal, just as non-central elements in the syllable are non-vocalic?

However, what is most relevant to present concerns is that phonology not only differs from syntax in showing only limited recursion, it also manifests only direct recursion as against the vastly preponderant indirect recursion of the syntax, to which we now turn. These differences between the planes follow from interface requirements to do with sonority and syllable formation, on the one hand, and the (non-)presence of complexities in representation that necessitate complex categorization, on the other. Even the extent in phonology of direct adjunctive recursion is at best very limited, whereas there are languages like English where it is extensively manifested in infinitive constructions.

6.2.2 Indirect recursion

Most extended indirect recursion in syntax depends on one or both of two properties, both of which we have looked at in some form already. Derivational morphology has just been discussed in §6.1, indeed. It allows for lexical structures wherein one lexical category is absorbed into another one, as illustrated in (115)* (repeated here for ease of reference), and may lead to recursion in the arguments of the various components:

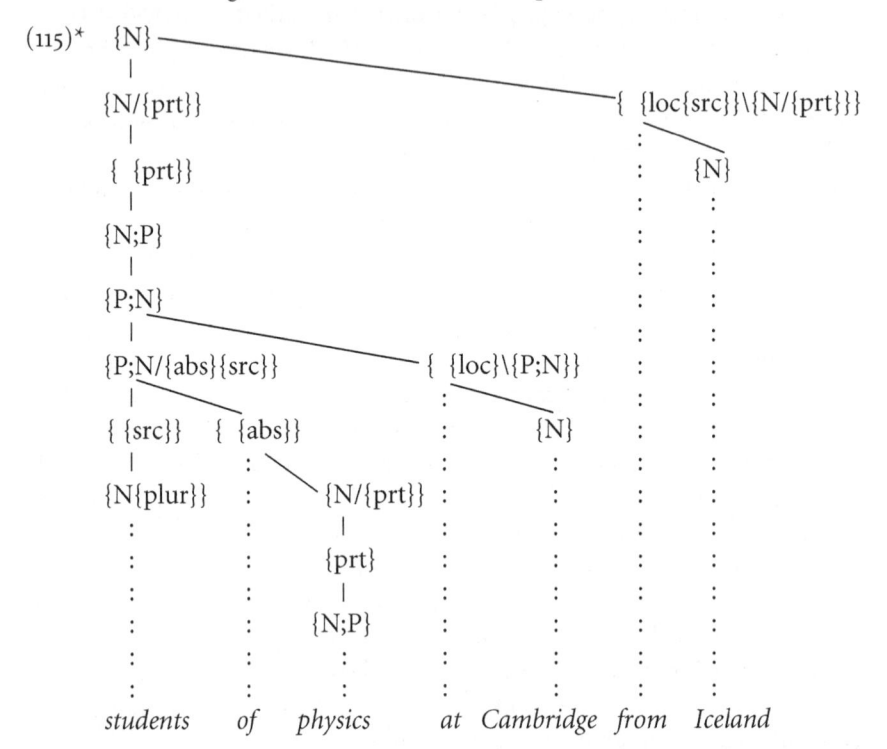

(115)*
```
        {N}
         |
       {N/{prt}}                              { {loc{src}}\{N/{prt}}}
         |                                        :
       { {prt}}                               :   {N}
         |                                    :   :
        {N;P}                                 :   :
         |                                    :   :
        {P;N}                                 :   :
         |                                    :   :
     {P;N/{abs}{src}}      { {loc}\{P;N}}     :   :
         |                      :             :   :
   { {src}}  { {abs}}       :   {N}           :   :
         |      :  \            :             :   :
     {N{plur}}  :   {N/{prt}}  :              :   :
         :      :    |          :             :   :
         :      :   {prt}       :             :   :
         :      :    |          :             :   :
         :      :   {N;P}       :             :   :
         :      :    :          :             :   :
         :      :    :          :             :   :
      students  of physics   at Cambridge  from  Iceland
```

This means, for instance, that, in this case, a nominal structure that can appear as an argument in a predication, as (115)* might be, introduces within itself, as well as the substructure associated with the attributive, which may be extended, the head of a predicational structure with further arguments which can in turn include further predicational and nominal structures. Even within the lexical structure, as we have seen, we have subjunctional recursion in examples such as (212):

(212) {N;P}
|
{P;N}
|
{N;P}

But the syntactic structures introduced by complex lexical structures show even more facility for the development of recursion, via adjunction.

And this depends on the second property of syntactic categorization that facilitates indirect adjunctional recursion. Instrumental here are (combination of) the complement, or '/', relation and the modification, or '\', relation. In the syntax, unlike in phonology, these relations allow for widespread adjunctional recursions. In this respect, there are again interface-imposed limitations on recursion in the phonology, primarily to do with the restriction of vowels to dependence on (if anything) other vowels, and the limited deployment of transitivity, as well as other physically based limitations. There are no such restrictions on e.g. verbals; and transitivity in syntax is much more varied.

The structure of participation and circumstantialization, was illustrated by the functor phrase in (191), where for the moment I preserve the category assignments that were assigned at the point in the discussion from which (191) is drawn (which ignored the functional/lexical distinction among categories):

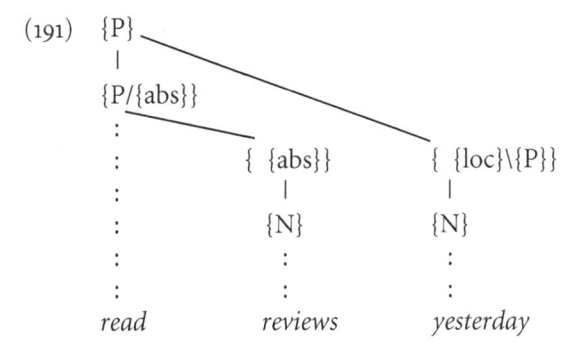

(191) {P}
       |
     {P/{abs}}
       :
       :   { {abs}}   { {loc}\{P}}
       : | |
       :   {N}   {N}
       :   :   :
       :   :   :
      read   reviews   yesterday

Functor phrases may be extended in various ways utilizing these two relations. (236) reminds us of a small sample of circumstantial types from English, all permitting further extension:

(236) a. on the day before his birthday
      b. on leaving for his villa in Spain
      c. when he left for his villa in Spain
      d. as frequently as possible
      e. on (\ /) leaving (/) for (/) his (\) villa in (\ /) Spain

All of (236a-d) but the last are rather obviously based on functor phrases, but even (236d) is interpretable as involving a functor-deriving suffix *-ly*. The initial form in (236c) is a cumulation of functor and *wh*-form (the character of which we return to in the following section). And all of (236a-d) to varying degrees and in various ways allow for further embedding involving '/' and '\', as is illustrated in (236e). This last attaches to each word in (236b) an indication of the modification and/or complement-taking relations it contracts; so that, for instance, *on* both heads a circumstantial phrase and also governs the following deverbal nominal phrase.

In Spain in (236e) is marked as a 'modifier' of the noun *villa*. It is now time to confront whether such a status is appropriate for noun 'modifiers'. Despite the view whereby the like of *in Spain* represents 'noun modification', I now want to pursue a suggestion that nouns do not take modifiers, and that these 'modifiers' involve a distinct variety of recursion. Let us look back over our treatment of noun 'modifiers' thus far.

I introduced in §2.4 of Volume I of the trilogy a distinct manifestation of 'modification' from circumstantial, which was labelled attributive; and this was elaborated upon a little in §6.2.1 in the present chapter. And attributive is illustrated by *in Spain* and by *from Iceland* in (115)*, repeated at the beginning of this subsection. In the case of attributivization, both adjectives and verbs, and finite clauses, for instance, may have this function, along with functors like *in* of *in Spain* or (237d) and the locative source phrase in (237e) as well as that in (115)*:

(237) a. students who(m) they taught/matriculated students
 b. students living in college/visiting students
 c. students aware of the possibilities/(very) serious students
 d. students who live in college
 e. students from the working class/working-class students

These are traditionally regarded as 'modifiers', indeed 'the modifiers par excellence', and this is how I have presented them so far. I shall now, however, suggest, following Anderson (2007) and (2008), that these forms functioning as attributives are all converted into '{N/{prt}}', whatever their basic primary category. The various post-nominal categories in (237) are subjoined to a determiner that introduces a subset of the set of entities denoted by the dependent of the { {prt}} that the determiner is subcategorized for. Attributives illustrate not modification but the recursive role in the syntax of partitive determiners. Let us look at what this involves.

Anderson (2007: e.g. §9.1.6) suggests the following kind of representation for attributives:

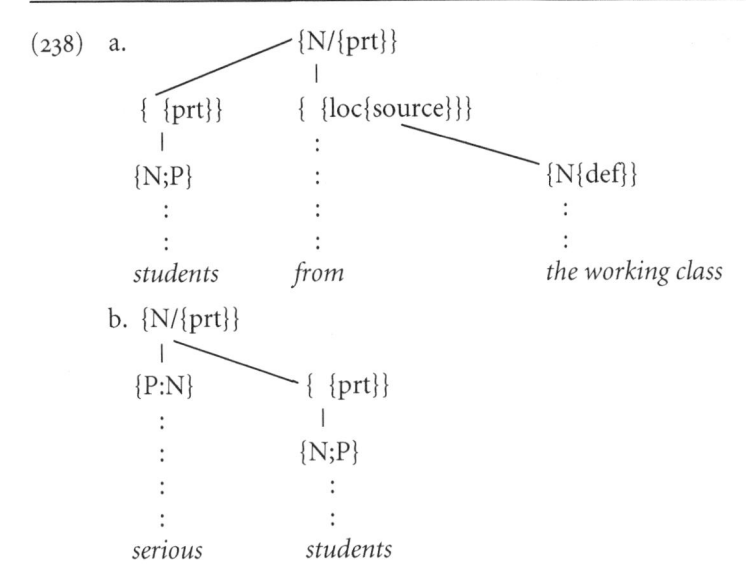

(238) a.
```
                ┌─{N/{prt}}
                │
  { {prt}}    { {loc{source}}}
     │           :
   {N;P}         :              {N{def}}
     :           :                 :
     :           :                 :
  students      from        the working class
```
b. {N/{prt}}
```
   │
 {P:N}        { {prt}}
   :            │
   :          {N;P}
   :            :
   :            :
 serious     students
```

Any post-nominal phrase in each of (237) contains an attributive element that is overtly complemented, and appears to the right of the modified noun, as in (238a), with attributive locative. Such is regular in English with attributives whose bases are accompanied by complements or adjuncts. Pre-nominal attributives such as that in *(very) serious students* (237c), where the adjective is not overtly complemented but may have a specifier or adjunct, are typically also partitive determiner phrases; the pre-nominal attributive is represented in (238b).[53]

Attributivization is another manifestation of the '/' relation rather than constituting, with adjuncts, a 'modifier', or '\', and it crucially involves a partitive determiner. An interesting consequence of this analysis is that prototypical nouns as such show neither complementation nor modification. They are in this respect even more inert than non-vowels, which cannot govern vowels but at least can be modified by other non-vowels. This governing

---

[53] This difference in position in English of complemented and uncomplemented attributives is consistent with the subject also being a complement of its verb, in that even when no (other) complement or adjunct is present, the attributive finite clause is postposed, because it is complemented by the subject, as in (237d)—or as more simply exemplified in (i):

(i) students who work

It is unnecessary to invoke finiteness here, for instance, as a separate factor determining 'modifier', or rather attributive, position. The full-clause attributive is complemented, so follows the noun.

function within nominals is taken over by a functional category, the determiner. In what follows, I shall adopt the spirit of the proposal concerning attributives adopted in Anderson (2007)—and in Chapter 6 of Volume II of the present trilogy.

We must modify the illustrative representation of the structure projected by derived nouns that was repeated at the beginning of this subsection, which as it stands does not recognize the role of the partitive determiner. To remedy this, we must substitute for (115)* the revised representation in (115)**:

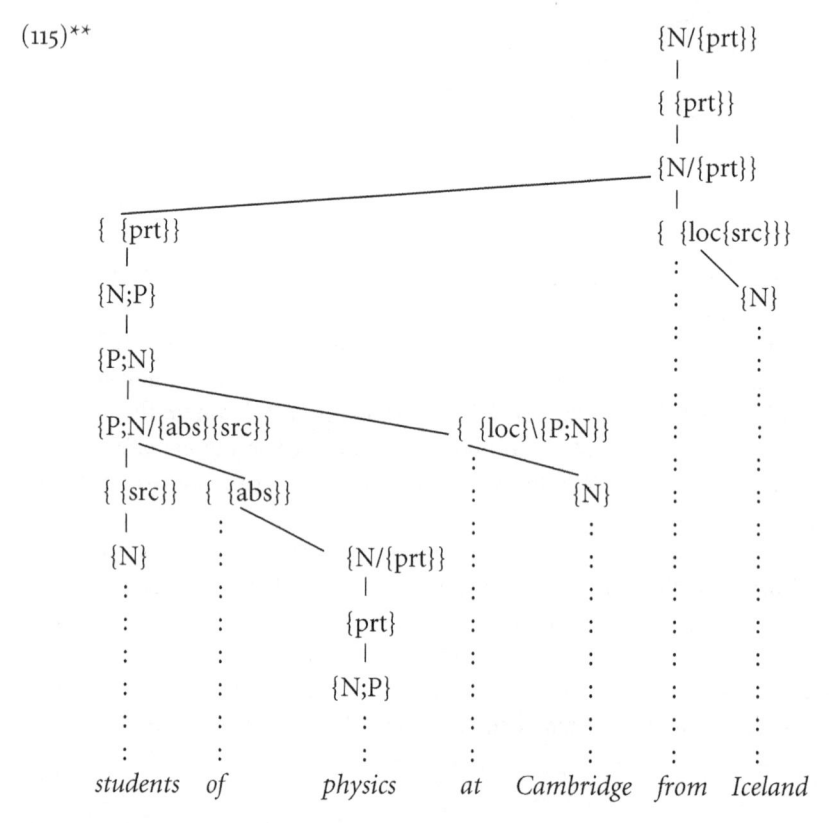

(115)**

```
                                                              {N/{prt}}
                                                                 |
                                                              { {prt}}
                                                                 |
                                          _____{N/{prt}}
                                         |                       |
        { {prt}}                         |                    { {loc{src}}}
           |                             :                        \
        {N;P}                            :                         {N}
           |                             :                          :
        {P;N}                            :                          :
           |                             :                          :
        {P;N/{abs}{src}} ——————— { {loc}\{P;N}}                     :
           |                      :                                 :
        { {src}}  { {abs}}        :          {N}                    :
           |        :             :           :                     :
        {N}         :        {N/{prt}}  :     :      :      :       :
           :        :           |       :     :      :      :       :
           :        :        {prt}      :     :      :      :       :
           :        :           |       :     :      :      :       :
           :        :        {N;P}      :     :      :      :       :
           :        :           :       :     :      :      :       :
           :        :           :       :     :      :      :       :
        students    of       physics    at  Cambridge  from  Iceland
```

Here attribution is interpreted as involving the conversion of the functor phrase, *from Iceland*, into a partitive {N} that takes as a complement, via a partitive, the noun realized as *student*. Such a converted functor phrase is but one variety of complemented attributive. The attributive may be a verb, finite or non-finite, a noun, an adjective, a functor phrase, etc., a set which seems to be inclusive of all primary categorizations except that post-nominal determiners (as in *our friend the burglar*) involve instead apposition to the first determiner phrase.

Similarly, instead of (211), we have ((211)*:

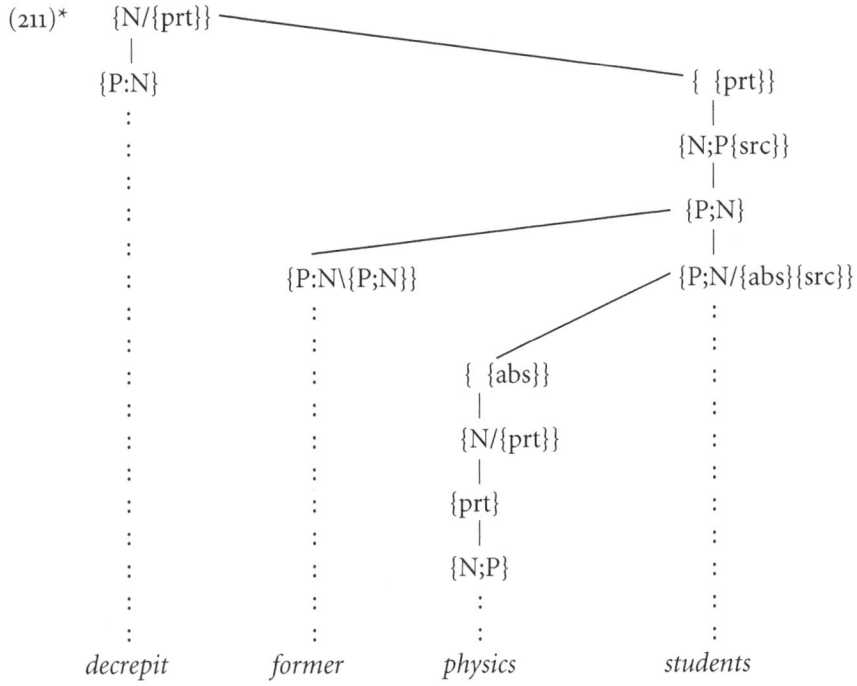

(211)*
```
        {N/{prt}}
           |
         {P:N}                                        { {prt}}
           :                                             |
           :                                         {N;P{src}}
           :                                             |
           :                                           {P;N}
           :                                             |
           :          {P:N\{P;N}}                   {P;N/{abs}{src}}
           :               :                             :
           :               :      { {abs}}               :
           :               :         |                   :
           :               :      {N/{prt}}              :
           :               :         |                   :
           :               :       {prt}                 :
           :               :         |                   :
           :               :       {N;P}                 :
           :               :         :                   :
           :               :         :                   :
        decrepit        former    physics            students
```

Here the attributive is an uncomplemented adjective, and so precedes the subjunction path terminating in the noun. Any non-attributive determiner takes the head of such paths as its dependent. The upward extension of nouns as attributive paths and finally a determiner is analogous to the extension of verbs by a succession of {P}s, as described in Part III of Volume I.

As before, this representation makes explicit the interaction between internal categorial structure and syntax, but it also illustrates all of the embedding devices discussed in this subsection: as we ascend in the tree, verb complementation, involving the lower {P;N}; modification, as in the relation between the adjunct and this {P;N}; and again complementation, but in this case of partitive determiners, on the present interpretation of attributivization. The noun that has often been regarded as the 'head' of such constructions is not as such a head. It is subordinate not just to simple determiners like *the* but also to attributives. In the tree in (115)** the noun is the most remote leaf from the root. (115)** exhibits recursion of {N/{prt}}, which is a prolific source of indirect recursive extensions of nominal structure. Such a characterization of attributives provides a natural account of linearity restrictions on adjacent attributives. Thus, a 'size' attributive like *large* does not normally complement a 'colour' attributive like *blue*: *large blue eyes*, **blue large eyes*.

Example (237a), involving an attributive full clause, introduces another respect in which the semantically driven syntax requires formal properties that do not seem to be characteristic of the phonology. (237a) contains a structure in which we have an **ectopic** element (as described in Chapter 4 of Volume I), namely *who(m)*: this element appears to be a non-subject complement of *taught*, as well as being co-referential with *students*, but it does not occur in a position we otherwise expect of a non-subject complement of a verb in English. This is another circumstance, other than subjecthood, in which we find a 'misplaced' complement, so that (237a) contains two ectopic elements, the subject and another complement of the verb. In the next section I look at the characterization of such elements and at the motivations for ectopicity. This begins to move us away from just the predicational aspect of the semantics of syntax towards the referential.

Firstly, however, I make a brief excursus on those markers of embedding, the complementizers, whose analysis I shall suggest throws some further light on the nature of functional categories. This excursus follows directly from the preceding, in a negative way, in so far as what has emerged latterly, particularly in the analysis of attributives, is a reinforcement of the importance of functional categories in syntax, particularly functors and determiners; whereas I shall now spend a little time confirming that another putative functional category, the complementizer, is not necessarily one.

6.2.3 *Excursus on complementizers*

In many recent accounts, complementizers are analysed as a kind of functional category (compare the discussion of §7.3 of Volume I). A complementizer's status as such might be represented (in present terms) in (239), again omitting (other) functors, for simplicity:

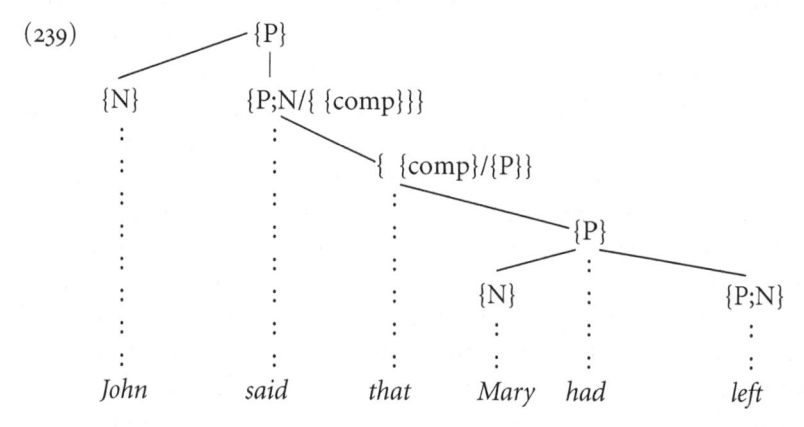

(239)

{N}   {P;N/{ {comp}}}
            {P}
       { {comp}/{P}}
                {P}
            {N}   {P;N}

John   said   that   Mary   had   left

In (239) the complementizer is analysed as a kind of functor that takes a predicational argument. However, though a functoral analysis of subordinating conjunctions, such as that in (236c), seems to me to be entirely appropriate, as is evident from what follows, such sentential complementizers in English conform much more readily to the pattern of specifiers.

Unlike conjunctions, including interrogatives, *that* does not participate in the argument structure of the clause it initiates. Consider the behaviour of the *when* in (240)—and (236c):

(240) a. I don't know when he arrived
b. When he arrived is a secret

(236) c. when he left for his villa in Spain

In (240) *when* bears a circumstantial relation to the verb it precedes, the verb of the subordinate clause; and in (236c) it simultaneously indicates the function of the circumstantial subordinate in the main clause. Neither of these close relationships is to be attributed to the complementizer in (241):

(241) a. I don't know (that) he arrived
b. That he arrived is a secret

That neither determines the function of an element within the clause it initiates nor specifies the function for that clause itself in the main clause. The 'objecthood' and subjecthood of *he arrived* is indicated positionally; neither is the semantic relation of *he arrived* signalled by *that*. In not signalling the function of its putative 'complement' (except indeed that it is subordinate), the complementizer is crucially unlike (other) functional categories.

Functional categories license the occurrence of their complements: determiners license nouns as arguments; functors license arguments to perform particular semantic roles; the finiteness element licenses a clause as an independent predication. *That* doesn't seem to license the following clause for anything. Rather it serves to mark a clause as not fulfilling the function of an independent predication; and it often does that optionally. Thus the *that* in (241a) may simply be omitted.

Other factors may supervene, of course: for instance, the initial *that* in (241b) must be present for reasons of transparency of parsing: in the absence of *that* in (241b) *he arrived* could lead us down a 'garden path'. This cognitively based requirement has apparently been denaturalized or routinized (grammaticalized further). It applies for some speakers also to finite clauses apposed to the subject, exemplified by (242a), where the likelihood of 'garden-pathing' is perhaps less:

(242) a. The idea ?*(that) Bill should resign is unappealing
b. Who made the suggestion ?(that) Bill should resign

(242b) seems to be a little more generally acceptable, even though, like (241b), in the absence of *that*, it also could perhaps involve 'garden-pathing'. Here too the subordinate clause is in apposition with *the suggestion*.[54]

In earlier English, conjunctions and complementizers could co-occur (*when that...*, etc.—see e.g. Onions 1904: §47; Fischer 1992: §4.6.3). And a few fossils remain in present-day English (*so that, in order that*—Poutsma 1926: ch. LXI, §6; and Radford 1988: §9.10, for instance, notes a few recent examples of *wh*-forms preceding *that*). But in general *that* is now used to mark a subordinate finite only in the absence of other markers, and often not even then (except in the interests of parsing efficiency). It is, appropriately (given its name), associated with specifying sentential complements—but also appositions, as in (242).

The existence of such earlier constructions has made it tempting, particularly in an abstract 'derivational' framework, to put forward diachronically inspired suggestions concerning conjunctions and complementizers. Thus, for instance, along the lines of the familiar tradition described in e.g. Radford 1997; Haegeman and Guéron 1999: ch. 2, §1.1.2, it is proposed that (at least some) such subordinating conjunctions specify a functional category, complementizer (or 'C'), if complementizer is indeed interpreted as such. These conjunctions would constitute curious specifiers, however: they are not closed-class (consider *whatever time of day* in *Whatever time of day he arrived, they were out*, etc.), and they now for the most part only specify the complementizer when it is 'empty'.

These objections apply to such a treatment of *wh*-forms in general; and the first of them also applies to the treatment of subjects as specifiers: see further §6.3. The proposal emanating from Chomsky (1986: §2) that

---

[54] As concerns omission or not of the complementizer, recall that in German, presence of the 'specifier' is accompanied by non-finite (i.e. verb-final) word order, as in (ia):

(i) a. Er sagte, daß er dich gesehen hätte
he said that he you seen had
b. Er sagte, er hätte dich gesehen
he said he had you seen

Compare the unspecified complement in (ib). *Daß* thus seems to have basically the same status as French *que*, as a marker of a subordinate clause, but it is present only if the full clause is non-finite. The clause is morphosyntactically finite but the presence of the complementizer signals its syntactically non-finite status, associated with 'verb-final': cf. §6.4.3 of Volume I. *Daß* is an obligatory marker of non-finite full clauses. I suggest further in §2.3.3 of the present study that 'specifiers' in general are associated with neutralizations in the category they specify.

wh-phrases move to 'specifier-of-comp' position destroys any coherence the notion specifier might have. And this objection extends to any analysis involving movement, and thus syntactic recategorization (compare the discussion in Chapter 5 of Volume I). Such proposals represent the desperation of a framework based on 'movement' that therefore has to locate 'landing sites' somewhere or other. I shall outline in §6.3 an analysis which is more in line with the earlier notion in generative studies that interrogative *wh*-forms occupy a position in a projection of {P} ('S-bar', or rather 'V-bar')—and see again Volume I, in this case Chapter 4.

Advocates of the complementizer-as-functional-category approach make great play with the mutual incompatibility, or complementarity, in apparently prepredicational or predication-initial position, of the complementizer-specifier and the auxiliary in interrogative sentences and the like, as illustrated by (243a) vs. (b):

(243) a. Will Bill meet George?
b. She asked whether Bill will meet George
c. May says that Bill will meet George
d. Bill will meet George
e. May says Bill will meet George

The 'auxiliary' in (243a) is said to occupy an empty comp position corresponding to the position of *that* in (c). But the complementizer position is also empty in both of (243d-e). Why can't or doesn't the 'auxiliary' occupy the empty position here? The answer, according to Chomsky (1995: 289), lies in some mysterious property of 'strength of features' (involving again—compare §2.1 in Volume I—the 'Q' feature):

For English, Q [the feature associated with the comp of interrogative clauses - *JMA*] is strong. Therefore, when Q is introduced into the derivation, its strong feature must be eliminated by insertion of F_Q in its checking domain before Q is embedded in any distinct configuration... F_Q may enter the checking domain by Merge or Move, by substitution or adjunction.

The exposition initiated by this quotation is continued throughout a section and beyond, without there emerging any clarification of the nature of 'strong' beyond its alleged relevance to placement. A rather less arcane scenario presents itself, however, based on the same distributional observations.

That and 'inversion' are mutually exclusive because *that* is a specifier of subordinate finites, or full clauses—and so, of course, doesn't occur in main clauses. And 'inversion' in subordinate questions is unnecessary because the interrogative clause is governed by a predicator of interrogation or, more generally, of incertitude, as well as by an initial interrogative form in all cases, so that signalling its status by 'inversion' is unnecessary (but recall Volume I, Chapter 4 for a more complete account). Radford virtually concedes the first part of this when he admits that 'complementizers can't be used to fill COMP in main clauses' (1997: 219): this is because complementizers are specifiers of subordinate finites (prototypically complements)—and there is indeed no 'COMP' in main clauses. More accurately, in terms of §6.7.2 of Volume I, *that* specifies subject-taking subordinate clauses. Observe too that it is surely bizarre to label a 'position' in main clauses by a category label associated with a class that cannot occupy that 'position' in main clauses. Whatever their origin (often as determiners), complementizers signal the presence of a complement or appositional (thus, not main) clause: hence their name.[55]

[55] This is not the place to pursue further problems raised by (interpretations of) Chomsky's proposal, or the variant which invokes (possibly null) interrogative operators. I note elsewhere (e.g. in §4.6 of Volume I) Radford's (1997: 295) citation, in support of such an analysis, of the existence of familiar Shakespearean examples such as that in (i), with initial *whether* in a main-clause question:

(i) Whether had you rather lead mine eyes or eye your master's heels?

(*Merry Wives of Windsor*, III.ii)

He goes on to suggest that 'given the null-operator analysis, we could posit that root yes-no have essentially the same syntax as in Early Modern English, save that they could be introduced by the overt operator *whether* in Early Modern English, but are introduced by a covert operator *Op* in present-day English'. This rather underlines the fact that, given the equivalence of *Op* and *whether*, we apparently have the same set of initial operator elements in both main and subordinate questions (except that in subordinates we can have the 'complementizer' *if*, as an alternative to *whether* + comp). If both main and subordinate questions can be introduced by operator specifier + empty comp, why is there, after all, 'inversion' only in main clauses (though not in *Bill will meet George?* etc., which otherwise have the properties of interrogatives)?

Invocation of earlier uses of *whether* also introduces a range of questions and wishes concerning its status and development, and those of 'inversion', none of which seem to have obvious answers within, or motivations for, a framework that posits these abstract devices. Particularly, as again noted in §4.6 of Volume I, though we do find examples like (iia) in Old English, with initial *hwæðer* and 'inversion', parallel, apparently, to later (i), this is exceptional, and normally there is no 'inversion' and the verb is subjunctive, as in (iib):

(ii) a. Hwæðer geleornodest þu,   þe   myd þam eagum, þe mid þam
       Whether learned   you either with the eyes   or with the
       ingeþance?
       mind

   (Did you learn with your eyes or with your mind?)

   (*Soliloquies of Augustine*, 22.3)

   b. Hwæðer ic mote   lybban oðþæt ic hine geseo?
      Whether I am-allowed-SUBJ to-live until I him see

   (May I remain alive until I see him?)

   (Ælfric's *Homilies*, i.136.30)

(See Mitchell 1985: §§1873, 1656, for these and other examples.) The 'inverted' word order and declarativeness that we find with *hwæðer* in (iia), on the other hand, are usually associated with

Similarly, the obsolete *when that...* construction, alluded to above, can be interpreted as a containing a complex functor including a temporal element (*when*), with apposed clause, where the complex temporal is immediately followed by a specifier (*that*) of that clause. Without any further foraying into the earlier history of *that*, it seems clear that what has changed in the case of clausal *that* is its restriction, as such a specifier, in more recent English, to clauses not introduced by a conjunction.

The discussion in Chapter 7 of Volume I makes it clear that the preceding conclusion concerning complementizers in English does not necessarily extend in that form to some other languages. Compare the analysis of French subordinator *que* offered in (I.205a):

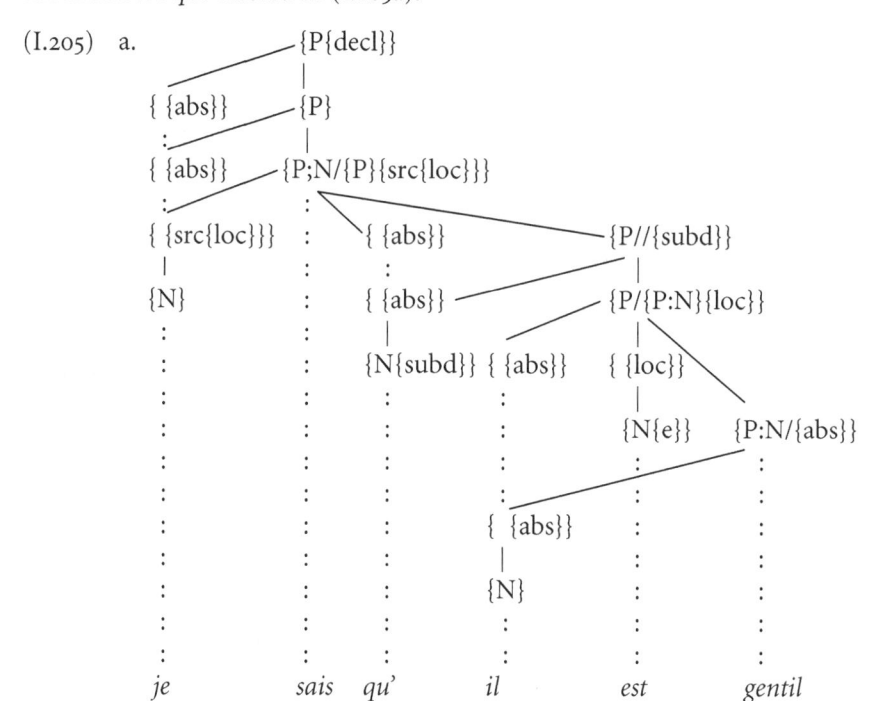

(I.205) a.

```
                        {P{decl}}
                           |
        {{abs}}         {P}
                           |
        {{abs}}        {P;N/{P}{src{loc}}}
                           
    {{src{loc}}}  :    {{abs}}              {P//{subd}}
        |         :       :                     |
       {N}        :    {{abs}}            {P/{P:N}{loc}}
        :         :       |                     |
        :         :    {N{subd}} {{abs}}    {{loc}}
        :         :       :        :            |
        :         :       :        :         {N{e}}    {P:N/{abs}}
        :         :       :        :            :            :
        :         :       :     {{abs}}         :            :
        :         :       :        |            :            :
        :         :       :       {N}           :            :
        :         :       :        :            :            :
        :         :       :        :            :            :
        je        sais   qu'       il          est         gentil
```

questioning of an argument rather than the clause, as further illustrated in (iii):

(iii) Hwæðer ðincð   þe þonne betre, þe   ðæt soð þe seo soðfestnes?
      Which think-DECL you then   better either the truth or the sincerity

  (Which do you think better, truth or sincerity?)

(Mitchell 1985: §1662). The subjunctive in (iia) is a marker of the openness (irrealis status) of the predicator in propositional questions. Presence of *hwæðer* is not necessarily associated with 'inversion'.

Que here is an expletive subordinator that fills the empty absolutive of a subordinating {P}. Nevertheless, this subordinator does not display the verb-governing properties of (239). And, like *that*, it indicates the presence of a subordinate {P}.

That is also uncharacteristic as a specifier in not signalling 'intensification' (cf. *very*). But in another respect it is analogous to the phonological specifier [S] of [sp-]-type clusters. [S] signals the presence of what is otherwise the prototypical syllable, {C} + {V}, but complicates this by its presence. *That* signals the presence of a potentially independent predication, but marks it as subordinate.

6.2.4 Conclusion

In this and the preceding section there have been examined the roles of the categorial complexity expressed in potentially recursive derivational morphology (§6.1) and of recursive embedding, direct (§6.2.1) and indirect (§6.2.2), in enhancing the expressive potential of the syntax. Again, the presence of these is in response to the need for articulation of the demands of the interface, in particular for the representation of 'scenes within scenes' and 'scenes within entities', where the representation of these 'scenes' and 'entities' themselves may have quite complex internal structure. These are, in the case of derivation and indirect embedding at least, extensions that are unnecessary to the phonology, and whose application there would anyway be inhibited by its phoneticity.

Derivationality is incompatible with the direct phonetic manifestation of phonological categorization; lexical derivation is foreign to phonology. And recursion in phonology is restrained by its physical implementation, whereby the implementation of syllables, for example, renders non-viable the dependency of vowels on consonants—thus eliminating the possibility of indirect adjunctional recursion. Syntax has only the less stringent and varyingly applicable restraint of attention-span and short-term memory. On the other hand, there may be languages (such as Pirahã—see e.g. Everett 2010 on the controversy surrounding its analysis) where recursive adjunctional embedding is absent from the syntax, and complex 'scenes' are depicted paratactically by ordered juxtaposition of sentences. Nevertheless, we can directly relate what dis-analogies we find between the planes to the differing demands of the substantive domains with which they interface. Deployment of any kind of recursion in language in limited by non-linguistic capacities—or incapacities—particularly of memory and of implementation. In the case of phonology limitation also flows from a linguistic factor, in the shape of its interpretative status in relation to lexicon and syntax. The work reported on in Everett (2010) suggests that in syntax an intralinguistic, intrinsic limit on adjunctive recursion can be also imposed—indeed an absolute limit. How absolute, however, will depend on the theory of categorization invoked in describing the structure of languages. In any case, this would amount to saying that there can be categorical grammaticalization of non-linguistic limitations on deployment of the general cognitive capacity for recursion.

I have not considered here the further extensions of syntactic structure involved in apposition and parataxis (though there is some illustration of the former in §5.3 of the first volume of the trilogy), which further increase the discrepancy in elaboration of structure between syntax and phonology, once more on the basis of substantive demands.

Certainly such 'functional' accounts of structural differences as I am offering here must remain speculative. But we shall make little progress in understanding the how of language if we do not dare also to ask why. And our speculations can be rationally justified by the scope of their proposed explanatory coverage and by whatever further insights in the how and the why that they might lead to.

Finally in this section, there was appended (in §6.2.3) an excursus on the categorial status of complementizers. Consideration of this permitted further clarification of what is and what is not a functional category. This is directly related to our ongoing concerns at this point, in so far as functional categories have a fundamental status in the elaboration of syntactic structure. It is therefore important to try to develop a more exact idea of their character. We turn now to another, related discrepancy between phonology and syntax, associated with the variability in placement of particular syntactic units. And here again functional categories are centrally involved.

6.3 Ambidependency, projectivity, and ectopicity

A further striking difference between syntax and phonology is the prevalence of 'displacements' of elements from their accustomed positions—what I have been referring to as ectopicity. It is not just that, as observed above, syntactic elements may vary in their relative positions both cross-linguistically (SVO, VSO, etc.) and intralinguistically (as, in a minor way, with the adverb positions in English); but in certain circumstances particular elements may be 'displaced' to positions which reflect neither their immediate dependency nor their usual or expected positioning. I do not interpret such ectopicities as involving 'movement'. Rather, syntactic positions are established directly on the basis of categories (derived from the lexicon or discourse, and inherently unordered with respect to each other) and the dependencies based on these. These orderings, once established, are invariant. The ectopicities manifest the result of requirements on syntax for certain elements to be multi-functional. These are again requirements not imposed in phonology and, again, at odds with phoneticity. The only phonological analogue of such multi-functionality is the maximization of dependency that I have associated with the maintenance of timing relations.

320 *Phonology-Syntax Analogies*

The results of these requirements in the syntax are multiple attachments, **ambi-dependencies**, designed to satisfy all valency requirements: an element may depend on two different heads. And these attachments in turn may introduce conflicts in positioning. The latter are resolved in favour of linearizing in accord with signalling discourse function ('topicalization'), or, in a more grammaticalized form, in favour of adopting the position of grammaticalized topics such as the free absolutive of {P}. And this results in ectopicity: an argument appears in a position that is not the unmarked one for such an argument. Maximization of dependency in phonology and the ambi-dependency it may introduce do not countenance ectopicity.

Let us begin to examine further these various aspects of ectopicity, and why this departure from projectivity is necessary in syntax. Our examination must include specification of the limitations that can be imposed on the potential power of the multiple-attachment structural property—and on resulting 'tangling' in some graphic representations. There are, and there have to be, strict limits on the conditions under which ectopicities occur. Otherwise we are plunged into an analogue to the kind of dilemmas associated with the introduction of 'transformations'. What follows builds on what is discussed concerning such matters in another context in Volume I.

6.3.1 *Raising and subjects*

One of the most generally recognized manifestations of ectopicity is that exemplified by (224) above. What is involved there is clarified if we now include, in the first place, those of the excluded valencies and dependencies missing from the representation of the structure of (224) that were given in (228):

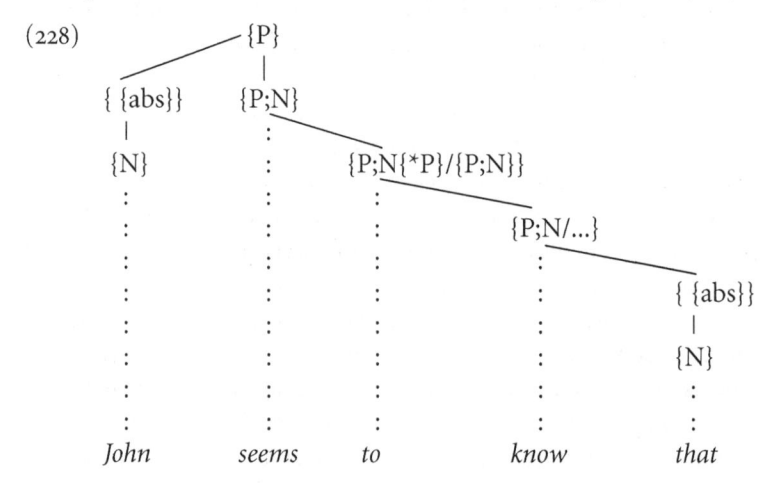

(228)

```
                    {P}
                     |
   {{abs}}         {P;N}
      |              :
     {N}             :         {P;N{*P}/{P;N}}
      :              :              :
      :              :              :        {P;N/...}
      :              :              :           :
      :              :              :           :        {{abs}}
      :              :              :           :           |
      :              :              :           :          {N}
      :              :              :           :           :
      :              :              :           :           :
     John         seems            to         know         that
```

The verb *know* has two arguments, the absolutive *that* and the {src{loc}} *John*. The latter, complex relation is that of the 'experiencer', the location of the experience—but its relational identity is not important here. More relevantly, both *to* and *know* can be treated as verbs, with the former being a non-finite that takes a non-finite complement but does not undergo finiteness formation (indicated by *P—recall §6.2.1); infinitival *to* has no finite (or indeed non-infinitival) congeners.

This representation should be completed (as concerns our present focus of interest) as in (228)*, in accordance with the framework outlined in §3.5 of Volume I:

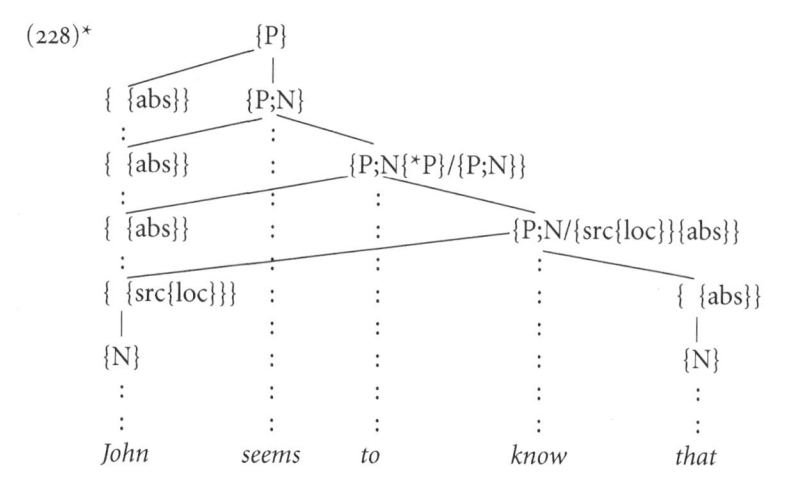

(228)*
```
                    {P}
                     |
      { {abs}}     {P;N}
                  
      { {abs}}    :    {P;N{*P}/{P;N}}
                  
      { {abs}}    :    :    {P;N/{src{loc}}{abs}}
                  
     { {src{loc}}} :    :    :         { {abs}}
          |                                 |
         {N}      :    :    :              {N}
          :       :    :    :               :
         John   seems  to  know            that
```

John is an argument of the lowest verbal in (228)*, as failed to be indicated in (228); and this is indicated in (228)* by the dependency arc which links the 'experiencer' with the *know* verb. It is also the argument that we would expect to be the subject of *know*, but 'non-mediated' infinitives cannot sustain a full set of complements (recall §6.2.1), and the potential subject is 'squeezed out'. In this case it is available for **argument-sharing**, as discussed pervasively in Volume I. This occurs when the upper predication contains an absolutive that is not subcategorized-for, that is not part of the valency of the predicator, and thus lacks an argument of its own.

We have already briefly encountered argument-sharing in this volume in §4.3.1 in discussing subject formation and the absence of the usual selection of subject. Subject formation corresponds to one manifestation of the 'raising' illustrated by (228)*. Recall (151) from §4.3.1:

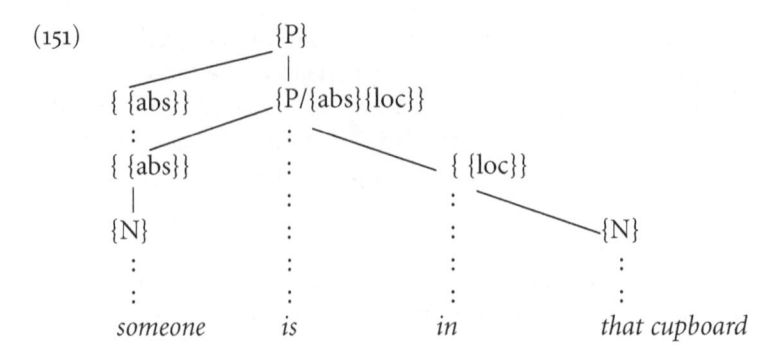

(151)
```
                    {P}
                     |
      {{abs}}    {P/{abs}{loc}}
        ⋮            ⋮
      {{abs}}        ⋮         {{loc}}
        |            ⋮           ⋮
       {N}           ⋮           ⋮        {N}
        ⋮            ⋮           ⋮         ⋮
        ⋮            ⋮           ⋮         ⋮
      someone        is          in     that cupboard
```

In (151) the *someone* {N} is shared by the subcategorized absolutive of the lower {P} and the absolutive of the upper {P}, which is not part of its valency.

In the present case, both *to* and *seem* lack {abs} in their subcategorization. Therefore an unsubcategorized-for {abs}—what in Volume I is called a **free absolutive**—is introduced. This is to satisfy the general requirement that every predication must contain an { {abs}} (recall again Anderson 1997a: 166–7). This is one manifestation of the special status of absolutive among the semantic relations: it is the non-specific relation whose content depends on the kind of predicator whose argument it introduces (which in turn largely depends on the other semantic relations involved); and, uniquely, absolutive may occur twice in a predication unaccompanied by another relation (i.e. uncompounded), to form equatives, such as *James is the one with red hair/The one with red hair is James*. Likewise, if a predication lacks a subcategorized-for { {abs}}, then it is a free absolutive that is introduced in default; this is the basic minimum for predications (see particularly §3.6 in Volume I).

The free absolutive, like any other functor, needs to take an {N} as a complement. This requirement may be satisfied by an expletive, as in (226):

(226)   It seems that John knows the truth

Or it may be satisfied by argument-sharing, specifically with the argument of a predicator dependent on the *seem* verb that would be the subject of that predicator in a main clause. In (228)* the latter is what happens, successively, with the free absolutive in both the *to* and the *seem* predications. The position of the shared argument is determined by the uppermost predicator, here the finiteness element associated with *seems*, to whose left the shared argument is placed. Limitation of multiple attachment to such highly specific circumstances allows for 'tangling' to be strictly licensed.

Thus, in the structure in (228)* the topmost { {abs}} is the free absolutive associated with the finiteness element which has all the rest of the sentence subordinate to it, and though it is not an intrinsic specifier, the free absolutive is serialized in 'specifier position', unlike regular (subcategorized-for) arguments.

This reflects its origin as a grammaticalized topic. The position of *John* in (228)* is determined by the normal positioning of the highest functor in the chain of associated functors, the unspecified-for { {abs}} of {P}. Linearity, as elsewhere, is derivative of the categorial configuration, created in accordance with lexical selection, satisfaction of valency requirements, and of the dependency relations projected from these categories. The manifestation of the valency of *know* in (224) cannot be entirely satisfied within the clause, which as an 'unmediated' non-finite has no provision for subject realization. The mediated non-finite of *For Bobby to live there is unwise* at least has a marked overt subject. So the valency of *know* must be accommodated partly outwith it, at the same time fulfilling the requirements of the free absolutives of *seem* and so adopting the position of the free absolutive (i.e. the subject) of *seem*.

The preceding illustrates how in general the ectopicity of subjects in English is provided for. Free {abs} has a crucial role to play in ectopicities in general, in overriding, via argument-sharing, the normal positioning of the elements which share with the free absolutive. Firstly in illustrating argument-sharing further, let me say a little more about the character of subject formation, again following the proposals outlined in Volume I. (224) introduces other considerations than simple subject formation in so far as it is a structure including an unmediated non-finite as well as a main clause.

The behaviour of subjects can perhaps be exemplified more transparently if we substitute for (228)* a monoclausal example without the other instances of free absolutive than that of {P}. We can do this by now completing, along the lines of (151), the representation in (191), wherein we left the status of subjects aside, by omitting the agentive argument of *read*:

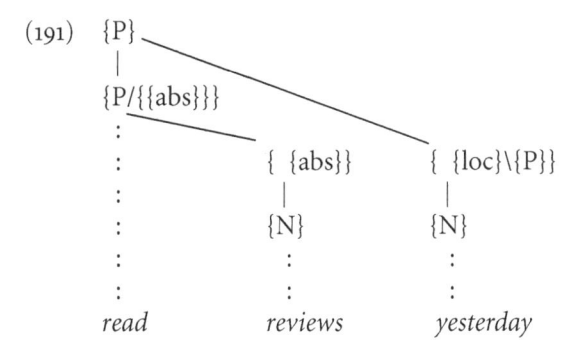

(191)   {P}
         |
        {P/{{abs}}}
         :
         :   { {abs}}   { {loc}\{P}}
         : | |
         :   {N}   {N}
         :   :   :
         :   :   :
        read   reviews   yesterday

(244) gives a more complete picture of the whole sentence:

324 *Phonology-Syntax Analogies*

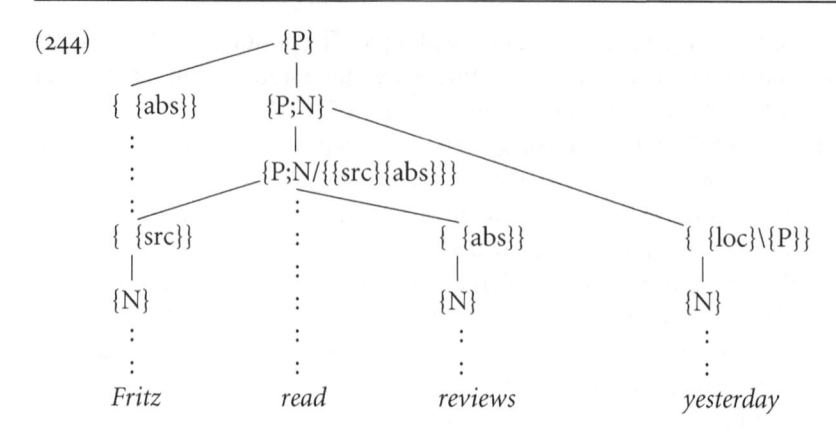

(244)

```
                    {P}
                     |
   { {abs}}        {P;N}
     ⋮              |
     ⋮           {P;N/{{src}{abs}}}
     ⋮              ⋮
   { {src}}         ⋮        { {abs}}         { {loc}\{P}}
     |              ⋮          |                |
    {N}             ⋮         {N}              {N}
     ⋮              ⋮          ⋮                ⋮
     ⋮              ⋮          ⋮                ⋮
    Fritz          read      reviews          yesterday
```

(244) differentiates between '{P;N}' and the finiteness element '{P}', and completes the subcategorization of *read*, whose {P;N} component involves two participants, one of them the prospective subject. But again this 'unmediated' non-finite cannot itself accommodate a subject. And the subject ({ {src}}) argument is shared with the free absolutive associated with the finiteness element {P}. The {P;N} introduced by the adjunct, as usual, does not receive a free absolutive. We see from (228)* and (244) that in these cases formation of the subject structure involves 'raising' to {P}. But (228)* involves two 'raisings', one of them to {P;N}.

In (245), the finiteness element is given independent expression as an operative, here a form of *have*, but the syntax is otherwise the same:

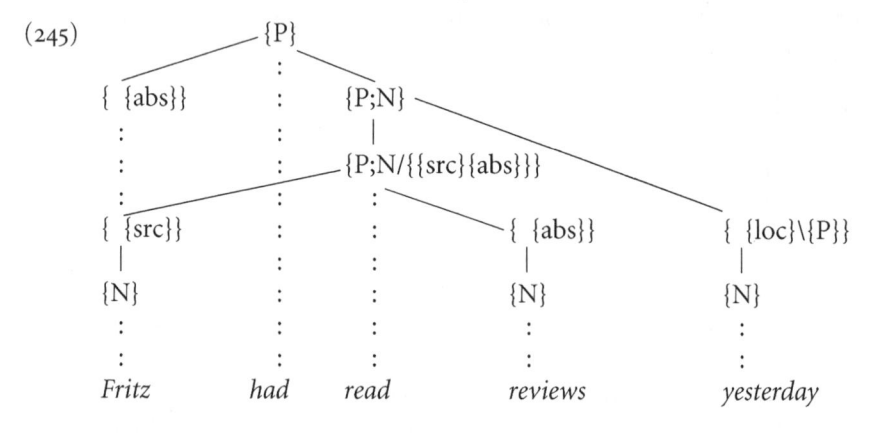

(245)

```
                    {P}
                     ⋮
   { {abs}}         ⋮        {P;N}
     ⋮              ⋮          |
     ⋮              ⋮       {P;N/{{src}{abs}}}
     ⋮              ⋮          ⋮
   { {src}}         ⋮          ⋮      { {abs}}      { {loc}\{P}}
     |              ⋮          ⋮        |              |
    {N}             ⋮          ⋮       {N}            {N}
     ⋮              ⋮          ⋮        ⋮              ⋮
     ⋮              ⋮          ⋮        ⋮              ⋮
    Fritz          had        read    reviews         yesterday
```

In all these cases, argument-sharing with the free absolutive of {P} in effect collapses 'raising' and 'subject formation'. And in (228)* there is also 'raising' to the free absolutive of {P;N} and further sharing.

In (246), however, the free { {abs}} of the {P;N} component of *expect*, whose valency includes a {P;N} and an 'experiencer', is outranked as potential subject by this subcategorized-for { {src{loc}}} ('experiencer') argument, which shares its argument with the free absolutive of {P}:

(246)

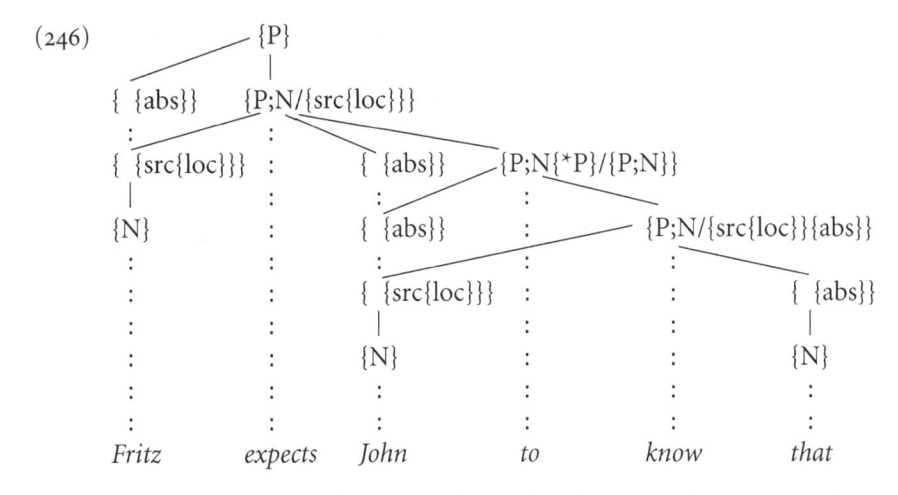

```
                    {P}
                     |
    { {abs}}    {P;N/{src{loc}}}
       :              :
    { {src{loc}}}  :    { {abs}}   {P;N{*P}/{P;N}}
       |           :      :
      {N}          :    { {abs}}    :    {P;N/{src{loc}}{abs}}
       :           :      :         :         :
       :           :    { {src{loc}}}  :     :    { {abs}}
       :           :      |         :    :         |
       :           :     {N}        :    :        {N}
       :           :      :         :    :         :
       :           :      :         :    :         :
      Fritz     expects  John       to  know      that
```

And we have so-called 'subject-to-object raising'. But again manifestation of the valency requirements of the lower verb is partly satisfied outside the {P;N} clause.

As I've observed, these instances of argument-sharing, or **ambi-dependency**, all introduce not just 'multi-motherhood', i.e. items that depend on more than one head, as with *John* in (246), but also 'tangling', crossing of dependency and association lines. The 'tangling' in (246), however, is minimal, in involving only the head of the infinitival 'periphrasis'. That in (228)* is rather more substantial, and obviously can increase as further such subordinates are embedded within the lower clause.

We also find further intra-clausal manifestations of these properties in such clauses as those in (247):

(247) a. Never had Eric eaten such a meal
      b. What had Eric eaten?

(247) both involve 'tangling', due to the ectopicity of (respectively) *never* and *what* and the 'inversion' induced by intra-clausal argument-sharing. We look more carefully at the representations of these clauses in §6.3.2, which are also discussed more fully (in the case of interrogatives) in Chapter 4 of the first volume of the trilogy. But already we can observe that (247) involve less grammaticalization than in the case of subjects—let alone the 'object' of (246). With subjects the conflict of positioning is resolved in favour of the heavily grammaticalized free absolutive of the {P} introduced by finiteness formation, while in (247) what is preferred is an 'actual' topical position. The highest grammaticalization, in (246), involves no conflict of positioning, if we count the 'periphrastic' infinitive as a unit; and this correlates with the

preference of 'subject-to-object raising' for SVO languages, where conflict is minimalized.

The interest of ectopicity for questions of analogy is that there is no analogue of these more salient violations of restrictions on tree structure in phonology. One role of these argument-sharings is to integrate the structure in a compact fashion. This is not so pressing in the case of phonology, given that embeddings are less complex and shallower, and there is no need to allow for the integration of 'long-distance' dependencies. Thus, in Chapter 2 only simple ambi-dependency, or 'double motherhood', without 'tangling', was envisaged internally to the syllable, as exemplified in (58), repeated here from §2.3.3:

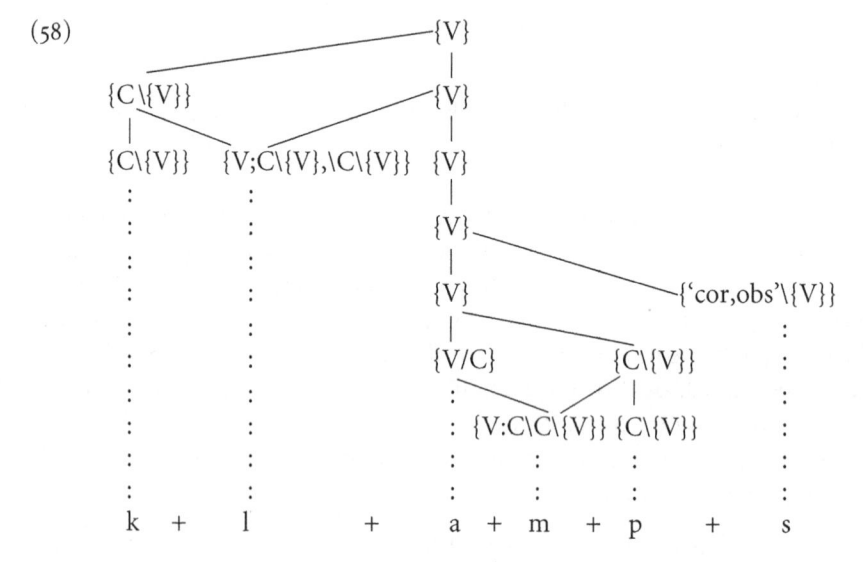

(58)

```
                              {V}
                               |
   {C\{V}}               {V}
      |                   |
   {C\{V}}  {V;C\{V},\C\{V}} {V}
    :         :             |
    :         :           {V}
    :         :             |
    :         :           {V}                {'cor,obs'\{V}}
    :         :             |                      :
    :         :          {V/C}        {C\{V}}      :
    :         :             :           |          :
    :         :       {V:C\C\{V}} {C\{V}}          :
    :         :             :     :     :          :
    k    +    l    +    a  +  m  +  p    +    s
```

And intersyllabic 'sharing', or **ambisyllabicity**, is also limited in this way, as well as being a foot-internal phenomenon.

The consequences of ambisyllabicity are manifested, for example, in the familiar phonetically Janus-like character of the medial stop in *petrol* and the like. This is succinctly illustrated by Giegerich (1992: 221), who cites the following examples and transcriptions, among others:

(248) a. matron   b. petrol   c. Butlin
          [metɹən]   [pʰeʔtɹə̥ɫ]   [bʌʔtlɪn]

In (248a) the medial stop, following an intransitive vowel, belongs entirely to the following syllable, and its status as syllable-initial is associated with aspiration; in (248c) the medial stop, since [tl-] is not a viable initial cluster, belongs only to the initial syllable, whose transitivity it satisfies, and its status as syllable-final is associated with glottal reinforcement; but the medial stop in (248b), which both satisfies the transitivity requirement of the preceding vowel and can form a cluster with the following consonant, and so does, consistent with onset maximization, belongs to both syllables. The stop is thus both syllable-final and syllable-initial. It is shared; and the sharing is driven by the transitivity requirement of the first vowel and its reconciliation with the onset maximization appropriate to the second. As a consequence the shared segment is both glottally reinforced and aspirated.

Blevins, among others, cites arguments that 'ambisyllabic representations are unnecessary when rules of resyllabification are invoked' (1995: 232), and she claims that 'a theory without access to ambisyllabic representations is to be preferred on grounds of restrictiveness' (ibid). Blevins comments further:

> Extending syllable theory to incorporate ambisyllabicity allows for systems in which a minimal three-way phonological distinction in intervocalic consonants is possible: these segments may belong exclusively to the second syllable (the typical output of the CV-rule); exclusively to the first syllable...; or to both syllables...

And she concludes: 'until such minimal three-way contrasts are demonstrated, a theory without access to ambisyllabic representations is to be preferred on grounds of restrictiveness'.

However, in the first place, a theory without recourse to resyllabification is more restrictive still than one without ambisyllabicity. Appeal to a representational property such as ambisyllabicity is far less damaging to a restrictive view of phonology than appeal to resyllabification, which introduces unwarranted abstractness. Moreover, if ambisyllabicity is conditioned by coincidence of transitivity of the preceding vowel and the satisfaction of onset maximization, and lacking otherwise, no three-way contrast, as opposed to conditioned alternative syllabifications, is predicted—contrary to what is claimed by Blevins to be a consequence of ambisyllabicity. And we have independent motivation for the transitivity dependence of ambisyllabicity in English from the failure of transitive vowels to occur in unreduced monosyllables (*[bʌ] etc. vs. *bee* etc.). Ambisyllabicity in phonology and interclausal ambidependency in syntax are both motivated by subcategorizational requirements, the transitivity both of some vowels and of functors.

Of course, it is important to recognize the possibility of 'mismatches' between phonetics and phonology, as Blevins (1995: §6.5) observes; phonetic ambisyllabicity need not be 'matched' by phonological ambisyllabicity. But demonstration of the existence of particular instances of 'mismatch' demands more evidence than Blevins provides in this case. Alleged 'mismatches' must be shown to be such; lack of a 'mismatch' is the default expectation. Postulation of phonological ambisyllabicity recognizes a property of phonology that has a 'natural' basis in phonetics.

Moreover, Blevins implies an analogy between phonetic ambisyllabicity and the difficulty of defining 'phonetic boundaries between segments' (1995: 244: n. 68): this analogy is defective. Ambisyllability does not involve 'blurred syllable boundaries' but a segment shared between syllables. As concerns 'blurring', it is a quite other issue, also, whether, anyway, the expectations of many phonologists are 'over-segmentalized', over-concerned with attributing segmentality in the phonology. This is perhaps again a reflex of an alphabetized culture.

It is thus plausible to associate ambidependency with both syntax and phonology; and in both it serves an integrative function. Importantly, however, ambidependencies in the phonology respect 'no-tangling', and other restrictions; integration does not demand further departure from proper-tree structure. Ambidependency in syntax is not limited in this way: the integration of 'long-distance' dependencies motivates further relaxations, and thus 'tangling'—in strictly specified situations.

Both the kind of more radical argument-sharing that we find in the syntax and its limitation are allowed for by the development of functional categories, particularly functors, and among them particularly free absolutive and their argument-sharing capacity. We have already established that functional categories, with their variant modes of realization—as separate word, as affix, as lexically incorporated—are inimical in this respect to the interface properties of the phonology. But they are also responsible for allowing 'tangling', which would be phonetically implausible. We find once more that the presence vs. absence of the functional/lexical distinction is fundamental to the explication of structural differences between syntax and phonology.

6.3.2 *Free absolutives and thematic structure*

The present subsection moves further still from the area where the 'double-motherhood' analogy is found in both phonology and syntax. Its aim is to illustrate something more of the role of argument-sharing in syntax, and thus of the widespread relevance of the concept when—and only when—the right conditions are met.

In the cases we've been looking at, argument-sharing is firmly routinized, despite having a rationale in satisfying the relationality of verbals via introduction of a free absolutive. But as with other routinizations it has also acquired functional motivations: it facilitates integration of the clausal structure, as observed. As part of this the role of the subject-selection hierarchy makes the identification of the apparently 'missing' argument in types of lower clause identifiable. However, such argument-sharing, involving free absolutive, has retained elsewhere another more obviously interface-serving function.

Within a single clause, typically a main clause, the ectopicity associated with argument-sharing identifies a slot, iconically earlier than any position its contents would otherwise occupy, that is the unmarked location for **thematically significant referential material**. Here we might expect to find topical or empathetic material, as in (249):

(249) John I may abandon

The position and the argument-sharing are again associated with a free absolutive. The 'thematic structure' under discussion here, which is associated with topicality and focus, is not to be confused with the malapropism 'thematic role'.

Again in such a case we have 'tangling', as typically elsewhere with free absolutives. We might interpret the syntax of (249) as represented in (250a):

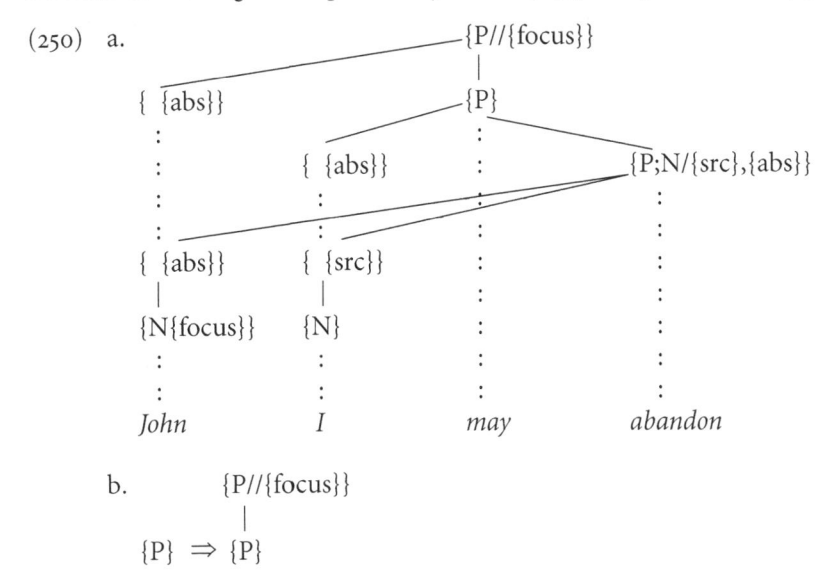

(250) a.

{ {abs}}   {P//{focus}}
              |
              {P}
  :   { {abs}}   :   {P;N/{src},{abs}}
  :   :   :   :
{ {abs}} { {src}} :   :
  | |
{N{focus}} {N}
  :   :   :   :
  :   :   :   :
 John   I   may   abandon

b.   {P//{focus}}
             |
         {P} ⇒ {P}

The basic finiteness element, as with the interrogatives described in Chapter 4 of Volume I, and returned to below, may be extended, in the lexicon, with a superjoined {P}, in this case a focus {P}, as in (250b). This superjoined {P} is a variant of the locutionary {P} discussed in Volume I, Chapter 6, in particular. The free absolutive of the focus predicator need not be filled by the subject of the sentence, but can be shared with other arguments, or indeed other elements; the subcategorization ('//') of the focus {P} 'instructs' its free absolutive to seek an element bearing the focus feature. The effect of (250) is to allow *John* to 'displace to itself' the thematically most significant slot, otherwise residually associated with the subject (by default), despite routinization. It may be that the natural basis of argument-sharing with free absolutive lies in such a thematic function, associated with sharing of arguments with the free absolutive of a topic/focus-introducing predication. In some languages the topic/focus may be independently chosen, and not identified with an element in the rest of the sentence.

Given its foundation in pragmatic interface requirements, this is not a function shared with the phonology. And, indeed, as observed, such ectopicity would be incompatible with the nature of the phonological interface. It is the semanticity of syntax that enables us as users to reconcile the dislocation with the other structural properties of the displaced item, such as its satisfaction of the subcategorization requirements of some relatively distant predicator. This is not only lacking in phonology, but also the determination of linearity in phonology is associated with largely invariable interface properties to do with sonority, and also sign consistency. For instance, simplex formatives do not vary (non-inter-dialectally) in the order of their component syllables; such variation within a lexical item is a feature of morphological 'operations'.

In (250) the subject of *abandon* shares its argument with the free absolutive of the modal, but it does not share with the { {abs}} of the focus predicator. Nevertheless, the subject occurs on the left of its head, which is also a {P}. This contrasts with the situation in interrogatives, where it is only the uppermost {P} that takes its free absolutive to the left (recall §§4.3, 6.4 of Volume I). This restriction reflects the continuance in interrogatives and some other constructions of a 'V-2' constraint ('verb-second'—referring to the required position of the finite verb).

In this way, a rather more drastic 'usurpation' of the privileged pre-verbal subject position is associated with some of those constructions in English which represent residues of the 'V-2' syntax which at least partially (or as an option) characterized main clause in Old English (as it does more consistently in Modern German):

(251) a. Þa astah se Hælend up on ane dune
      then went the lord   up on a   mountain
    b. Þa eodon hie ut
      Then went   they out

(examples from Fischer et al. 2000: ch. 4, who provide a guide to the complexities of the situation in Old English). Like subjecthood itself, 'V-2' structures appear to be thematic in origin. But in German the pre-verbal initial element is not necessarily topical; the construction is routinized (cf. again Anderson 2006b: 151–2). In Old English there is variation in conformity to 'V-2'. In a 'V-2' construction it is only the highest {P} in the clause that takes its free absolutive to the left. In the absence of 'V-2' all {P}s takes their free absolutives to the left (in subject-initial languages). Let us now look at the present-day English situation.

There is in general in present-day English no conformity to 'V-2', so that (249) illustrates a pattern violating 'V-2'; but there are four main 'V-2 residuals' in English, exemplified in (252):

(252) a. What had Eric eaten?
       b. Never had Eric eaten such a meal
       c. There were bugs in the soup
       d. Here comes Charley

(a)–(c) in (252) involve operative verbals, and the first pair are associated with 'tangling'. The second pair does not involve 'tangling', and they are more restricted in various ways. (252d) is the only one in which figures (a restricted set of) ordinary finite lexical verbs (as more generally in Old English and German). And (252c) is distinguished from all the rest by clear evidence of the acquisition of syntactic-subject status by the initial element; this is shown by its undergoing 'inversion' in questions (i.e. in combination with (252a)-type structures), such as *Were there bugs in the soup? Where were there bugs?* (recall again §4.3.1).

What in (252a) is not a subject, but *Eric* is, despite its post-operative position. Thus we can find the latter 'raised' with respect to *seem*, associated with subjecthood, whereas *what* satisfies the interrogative {P} that heads the whole sentence:

(253)   What does Eric seem to have eaten?

Thus, as argued in Chapter 4 of Volume I, a nominal such as *Eric* does not occupy uppermost-free-absolutive position with respect to the finite verb in (252a) or (253); this has been 'usurped' by *what*. I suggest for (252a) the (simplified) representation in (254) (based on the discussion in trilogy Volume I):

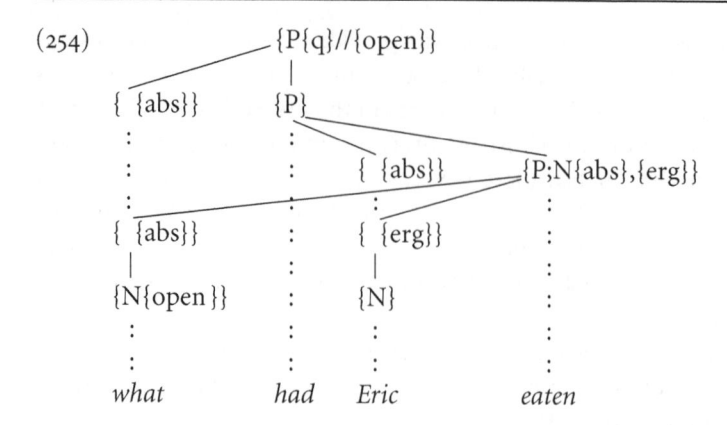

(254)
```
                    ┌─ {P{q}//{open}}
                    │
    { {abs}}      {P}
      ⋮            ⋮
      ⋮            ⋮       { {abs}}  ──  {P;N{abs},{erg}}
      ⋮            ⋮          ⋮              ⋮
    { {abs}}       ⋮       { {erg}}          ⋮
       │           ⋮          │              ⋮
    {N{open}}      ⋮         {N}             ⋮
       ⋮           ⋮          ⋮              ⋮
       ⋮           ⋮          ⋮              ⋮
      what        had        Eric          eaten
```

In this case, *Eric* is shared, as any subject would be, with the free absolutive of the basic finiteness element realized as *had*. But it fails to be realized in the initial, pre-verbal position usual with subjects. This position is instead occupied by the { {abs}} of {P{q}} which, as required by the subcategorization of {P{q}} shares its argument with the {open}-form. The {open}-form is required indirectly ('//') by this predicator, to satisfy its valency. The word order is a residue of the 'V-2' constraint, in that, unlike in (249), the presence of the {open}-form 'displaces' the subject from pre-finite position. The *Eric* argument is, like any other dependents of the lower {P}, serialized to the right of its head. It continues to control concord via its dependence on the free absolutive of this {P}, and there is no other candidate for subjecthood.

The upper {P} in (254) is introduced by the redundancy (62b) of Volume I, interrogative-formation:

(I.62) b.   {P{q}//{open}}
                              │
             {P}   ⇔   {P}

However, if it is the unmarked situation in English that all free absolutives of a {P} occur to the left of that {P}, then the interrogative redundancy of (I.62b) should be qualified as in (I.62)*:

(I.62)*   {P{q}//{open}}
                              │
             {P}   ⇔   {P{*SS(a)}}

{*SS(a)} marks this lower {P} as an exception to the syntactic sequencing rule (a) in English, to which {P} normally conforms, unlike other heads:

Syntactic Sequencing in English
a) *marked:* a → b ⇒ b + a
b) *default:* a → b ⇒ a + b

It will thus conform to the default (b). This exceptional status with respect to sequencing (a) is what characterizes 'V-2'. If 'V-2' is general in the language, then only the uppermost {P} will conform to (a) in general.

Eric in (252b) also qualifies as a subject, in determining concord, as in (255a), and to the extent that (255b) is acceptable, given the recessive status of the construction:

(255) a. Never has Eric eaten such a meal
       b. ?Never does Eric seem to have eaten such a meal

These and (252b) involve a focus construction like that in (249):

(249) John I may abandon

But in this case the negative focused adjunct 'displaces' the subject from pre-finite position, and the subject follows its head, as in questions; again we have the 'V-2' effect:

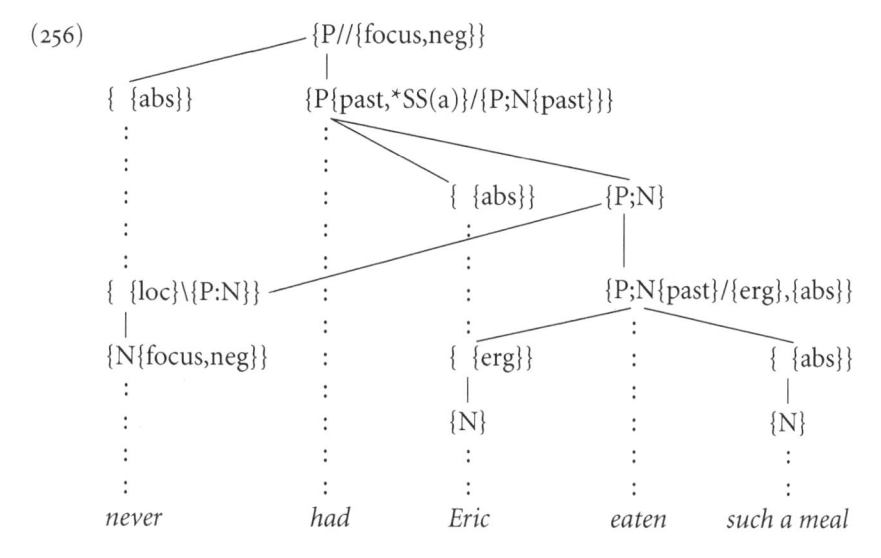

(256)
```
                    ─{P//{focus,neg}}
                      │
  { {abs}}          {P{past,*SS(a)}/{P;N{past}}}
    :                 :
    :                 :
    :                 :
    :                 :        { {abs}}      _{P;N}
    :                 :          :            │
    :                 :          :            │
  { {loc}\{P:N}}      :          :          {P;N{past}/{erg},{abs}}
    │                 :          :            :
  {N{focus,neg}}      :        { {erg}}     : { {abs}}
    :                 :          │            :  │
    :                 :         {N}           : {N}
    :                 :          :            :  :
    :                 :          :            :  :
  never              had         Eric       eaten such a meal
```

(255) also differs from (249) in being restricted to negative focused elements. To this extent it is 'idiomatic'.

Both (252a) and (b) display a considerably diluted form of 'V-2', in that only operatives are involved, while Old English 'V-2' involved all (finite) verbals. And they also diverge from classic 'V-2' structures (like those in

German), if both (253) and (255b) are acceptable, in so far as the 'displaced' subjects in these constructions may be associated with a subordinate predicator of which they are also the syntactic subjects (Anderson 1997a: 288–91) and have undergone 'raising'. The morphosyntactic properties usually associated with subjects are obviously not matched by such evidence of syntactic subjecthood in German indicative main clauses.

(252c) also is very restricted, indeed to sentences with a *be* subcategorized for an indefinite absolutive and a (non-directional) locative:

(252) c. There were bugs in the soup

And, as already observed in (§4.3.1), in sentences such as (252c) the pre-finite position seems again to have been 'usurped', but in this case by an element that has taken on the role of subject. Subject position is filled by an 'expletive' rather than the argument expected by the subject-selection hierarchy. We have further grammaticalization of 'V-2'. The subcategorized-for and putative subject post-verbal { {abs}} argument *bugs* retains the **morphosyntactic subject** property of controlling concord (cf. *There was a bug in the soup*), but the **syntactic subject** is *there*.

This *there*, as well as showing 'inversion', undergoes 'raising', for instance, as shown in (257a):

(257) a. There seem to have been bugs in the soup
       b. Bugs were in the soup
       c. Fred was in the water
       d. Fred has a lifejacket

Concord in (257a) appears on the finite most immediately superordinate to the absolutive 'displaced' from syntactic subjecthood. The potential subject *bugs* that has failed to occupy subject position in (252c) and (257a), does so in the less common structure in (257b). The motivation for the preference of (252c) over (257b) is clearly thematic: indefinites are disfavoured as utterance-introducers. The definite absolutive in (257c) occupies subject position, however. In analysing the structure of (252c) it is useful to look at its syntax in the context of the other aspect-voice operative, which also seems to be capable of taking solely non-verbal arguments, illustrated in (257d).

As we have seen, *be* and *have* are operatives that, unlike the English modals, have overtly non-finite forms: both are non-finite in *He may have been sleeping*. They can be both {P} and {P;N}. However, they can also apparently violate the requirement of an unmarked operator to be subcategorized for a {P;N} (and typically nothing else). Like lexical verbals they can take purely nominal arguments, as in (257) (or with equative *be*). Nevertheless in these

Structure 335

circumstances, like operatives elsewhere they 'invert' and take a following negation, though this is variable in the case of have (*Does Fred have a lifejacket?* etc. are often preferred). On the other hand, in questions their subject follows them; and we have associated this position with dependence of the free absolutive on {P;N}, or on a {P} that is not the highest in the case of interrogatives and focused negatives.

I suggest that the latter property is associated, in the first place, with the fact that operatives that do not subcategorize for {P;N} undergo an analogue to the (44) redundancy of Volume I, Chapter 3, the redundancy that allows finiteness to lexical verbs:

(I.44)   {P}
                           |
        {P;N}   ⇒   {P;N}

That is, operatives that are subcategorized for non-predicative participants can be subjoined to another operator that lacks such a valency. We have the option in (254), available to {P}s that can also be {P;N}, thus not to modals:

(258)   {P}
                                |
        {P/{X}{Y}}   ⇒   {P/{X}{Y}}
        where 'X' and 'Y' are each any semantic relation

The formulation in (258) excludes modals, since the {P} involved only has two non-predicative participants. It does apply to (252c) (and the sentences in (257)), however, where (258) provides a {P} above the 'original' semantic-relation-bearing non-modal {P}.

Now, what differentiates between (257a) and (257b-c) is not just the failure of the indefinite lower absolutive to undergo subject formation and 'raise' to be hosted by the upper absolutive, but also whether the lower {P} also comes to be marked as {*SS(a)}, which blocks it from preceding its head. Thus, in the case of (257a), (258) could be formulated, more fully, as in (258a)*:

(258)* a.   {P}
                                     |
            {P/{X}{Y}}   ⇒   {P{*SS(a)}/{X}{Y}}
            where 'X' and 'Y' are each any semantic relation

        b.   {P}
                                     |
            {P/{X}{Y}}   ⇒   {P<{*SS(a)}>/{X}{Y}}
            where 'X' and 'Y' are each any semantic relation

We can amalgamate the two variants as (258b)*. The fuller version is favoured by sentences containing indefinite absolutives, such as (257a). In this case, the finiteness element introduced by (258)* has its free absolutive satisfied by an 'expletive', and the lower absolutive follows its {P}, in accordance with the *{SS(a)} requirement.

We thus have for (252c) the structure outlined in (259a) rather than (259b), suitable for (257c):

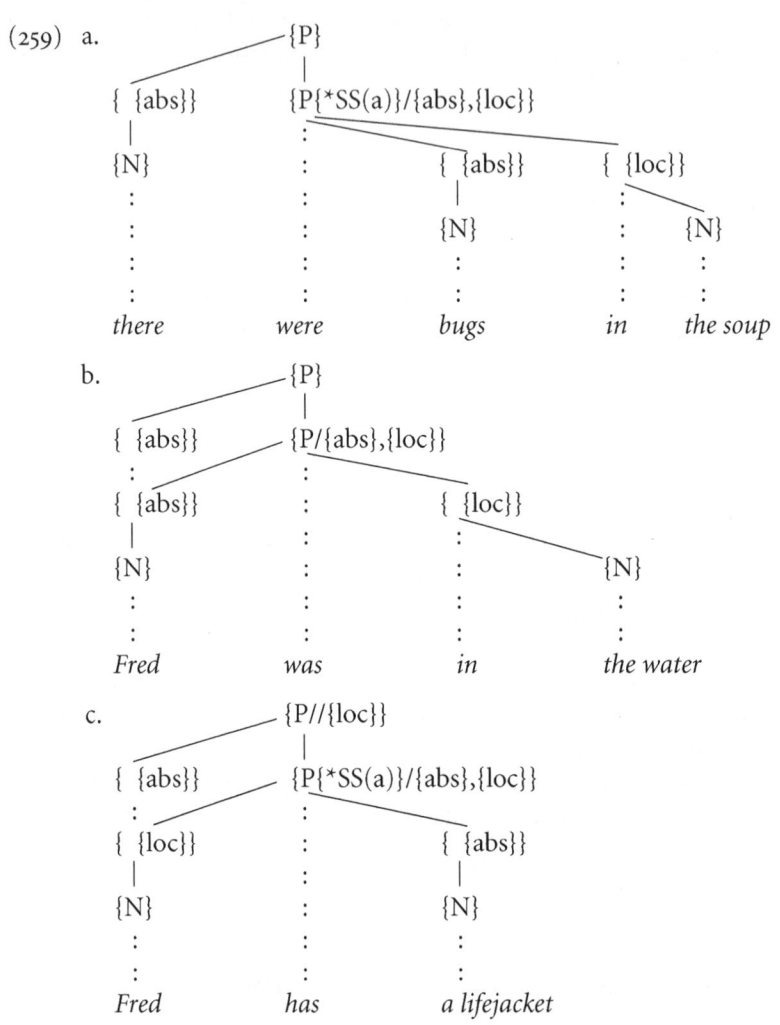

(259) a.
```
                    {P}
                     |
   { {abs}}      {P{*SS(a)}/{abs},{loc}}
      |               :
     {N}           { {abs}}        { {loc}}
      :               |               :
      :              {N}          :    {N}
      :               :           :     :
      :               :           :     :
      :               :           :     :
    there           were        bugs   in   the soup
```

b.
```
                    {P}
                     |
   { {abs}}      {P/{abs},{loc}}
      :               :
   { {abs}}        { {loc}}
      |               :
     {N}             :          {N}
      :              :           :
      :              :           :
     Fred          was          in      the water
```

c.
```
                 {P//{loc}}
                     |
   { {abs}}      {P{*SS(a)}/{abs},{loc}}
      :               :
   { {loc}}        { {abs}}
      |               |
     {N}             {N}
      :              :
      :              :
     Fred          has         a lifejacket
```

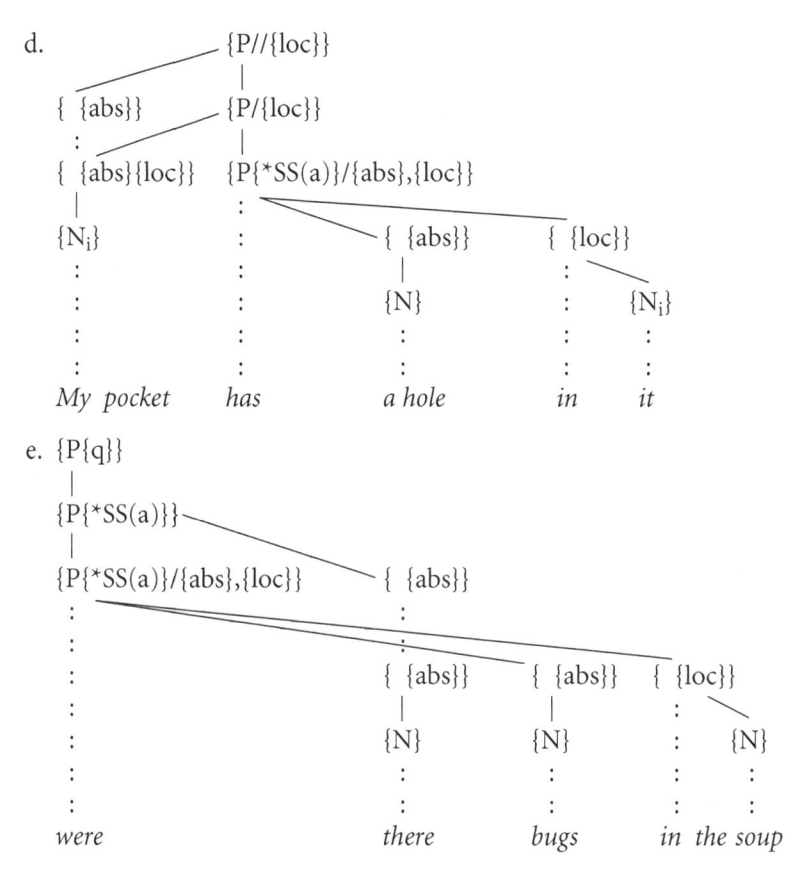

d.
```
              {P//{loc}}
                 |
{ {abs}}      {P/{loc}}
  :              |
{ {abs}{loc}}  {P{*SS(a)}/{abs},{loc}}
    |             :
   {Nᵢ}           :        { {abs}}      { {loc}}
    :             :            |            :
    :             :           {N}           :    {Nᵢ}
    :             :            :            :     :
    :             :            :            :     :
My pocket       has          a hole        in    it
```

e. {P{q}}
```
   |
  {P{*SS(a)}}
   |
  {P{*SS(a)}/{abs},{loc}}        { {abs}}
      :                              :
      :                              :
      :                           { {abs}}    { {abs}}   { {loc}}
      :                              |            |         :
      :                             {N}          {N}        :    {N}
      :                              :            :         :     :
      :                              :            :         :     :
    were                           there        bugs     in the soup
```

The expletive *there* of (259a) is dedicated to syntactic subjecthood in a predication with just such a configuration as we have here (recall again §4.3.1). And the 'displaced' lower absolutive in (259a) attaches to the right of {P;N}, as expected. The *have* of (257d) has a similar categorial complexity to that shown in (259a), but with the added complication shown in (259c). The upper {P} in (259c) also requires that its absolutive is ultimately satisfied by a locative, as shown in this representation. I shall not deal with the details of the *have*-construction of (259d), which involves a further topic-derived categorial component in the lexical categorization of *have*.

The {P}–{P} complexes in (259) involving *be* and *have* can be subjoined to an interrogative {P}, unlike the {P}–{P;N} complexes created by (I.44). Recall (I.63)*:

(I.63)* *{P{q}//{open}}
          |
         {P}
          |
        {P;N}

unless the free absolutive of {P{q}} hosts the subject

Thus, we have (I.81), rather than *Left Bert on Tuesday?* from §4.3.2 of Volume I:

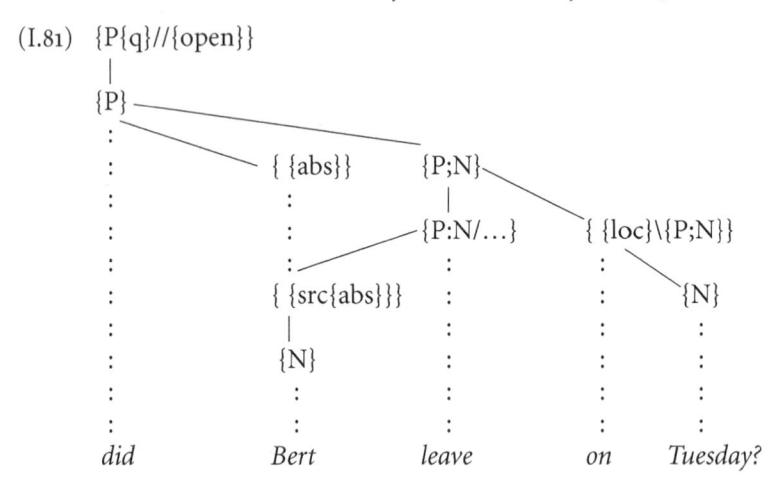

(I.81) {P{q}//{open}}
          |
         {P} ─────────────────────
          ⋮   ╲
          ⋮   { {abs}}   {P;N}╲
          ⋮   ⋮ |
          ⋮   ⋮   {P:N/...}   { {loc}\{P;N}}
          ⋮   ⋮   ⋮   ⋮ ╲
          ⋮   { {src{abs}}}   ⋮   ⋮   {N}
          ⋮ | ⋮   ⋮   ⋮
          ⋮   {N}   ⋮   ⋮   ⋮
          ⋮   ⋮   ⋮   ⋮   ⋮
          ⋮   ⋮   ⋮   ⋮   ⋮
         did   Bert   leave   on   Tuesday?

And compare (259e), with inversion of the whole complex. We can perhaps associate this difference with the substantive lightness of the lowest {P} in (259e), compared with the {P;N} of (I.63)*.

The presence of 'inversion' etc. with the *have* of (259c) is variable, however. Presumably, the *have* of *Does Fred have a lifejacket?*, as opposed to *Has Fred a lifejacket?*, contains a {P;N} as the lowest component in its lexical categorization, given that the aspect-voice verbals can undergo de-finitization, though in other circumstances, usually (cf. §I.6.6). This configuration would thus violate (I.63)*; and specification as {*SS(a)} would be unnecessary. These items are in this way 'intermediate' between lexical verbs and regular operatives—unsurprisingly, given their subcategorization pattern, with some valencies including only semantic relations. *Have*, as the more complex of the aspect-voice operatives, as shown in (259), is the one that assimilates to a regular verb most readily—no doubt assisted by the existence of other verbal *have*'s of long standing. The prehistory of operative *have* is intertwined with that of causative *have*, for instance (Kilpiö 2010).

(252c) is to some extent an 'idiomatic' construction, then; and (252d), another locative construction, is also 'idiomatic':

(252) c. There were bugs in the soup
 d. Here comes Charley

The construction in (252c) is indeed interpretable as a specialization of the structure of (252d). However, in some respects (252d) is a more faithful reflection of 'V-2' than the others we have been looking at. It involves 'inversion' of lexical verbs—and its dynamic and immediate presentational character is indeed interpretable as inimical to the use of 'analytic' expression. And the displaced 'subject', though retaining its morphosyntactic properties, does not seem to be a syntactic subject. This is, as noted, characteristic of 'full-blown V-2', such as we find in German main clauses. However, this manifestation of 'V-2' is as 'residual', or 'idiomatic', as some of the others we have been looking at, in that the sentence-initial item in the present expressions is restricted in current English to a small set of pronominal (spatial and temporal) locatives and suitable (locative-taking) verbs.

We can perhaps associate the structure given in (260) with such a sentence as (252d):

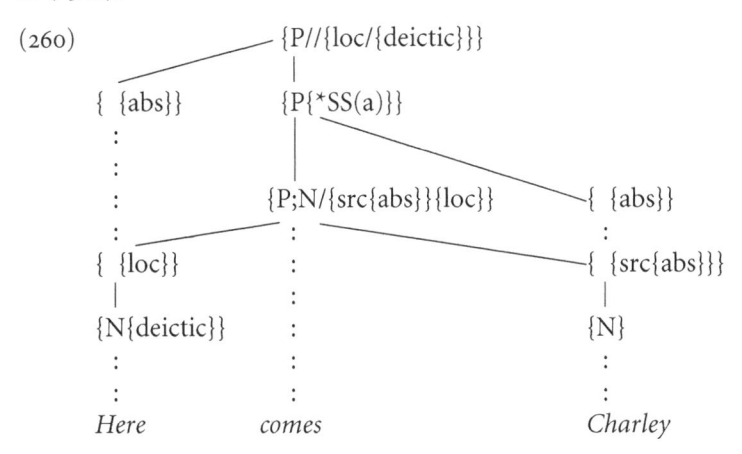

(260)

{P//{loc/{deictic}}}
|
{ {abs}}   {P{*SS(a)}}
 :
 :   {P;N/{src{abs}}{loc}}   { {abs}}
 :   :   :
{ {loc}}   :   { {src{abs}}}
 | : |
{N{deictic}}   :   {N}
 :   :   :
 :   :   :
Here   comes   Charley

As in interrogatives, {*SS(a)} is added to the lower {P} when it is subjoined to the {P//{loc/{deictic}}}. But the subjoined configuration of predicators in (260) is not disallowed; this it shares with the operative-only configuration in (259d). There is no analogue in these cases to (I.63)*, which requires 'inversion' with an operative in interrogatives involving lexical verbs. The result is that the locative of the {P;N} satisfies the free absolutive of the upper. And the intransitive agent of {P;N} satisfies the free absolutive of the lower {P}, in accordance with the subject-selection hierarchy; and this is reflected in agreement.

6.3.3 Conclusion

The relevance of these various ectopic constructions to our ongoing discussion is that, in the first place, they all illustrate the role of thematic factors—topicality, contrast, focus, empathy—in accounting for ectopicity, even where the construction has been grammaticalized and/or lexicalized. But the lack of phonological analogies to such ectopicities follows not just from their semantic motivation, i.e. interface requirements on the syntax which are putatively absent from phonology, but also from the problems that ectopicity would present for interface requirements on the phonology. Phonology reflects what thematic distinctions it does in terms of intonation rather than variation in linearity of segments.

Linearity within the syllable is almost entirely invariant, and determined largely by sonority plus possibly primitive distinctions between complement, adjunct, and specifier. Dependency relations in the phonology are reflected in relative timing, and there thus can be no argument-sharing between elements in different syllables, except at the boundary (ambisyllabicity), and then only within the foot. As observed, it seems that consequently we can require projectivity ('no-tangling') of phonological representations. This is ensured if ambidependency which is not syllable-internal occurs only where syllables meet and not otherwise across boundaries, i.e. if it is limited to ambisyllabicity. The latter is moreover, as a foot-internal phenomenon, an integrator of foot structure.

In §6.3.1 we were concerned with the role of free absolutives in the ectopicities associated with 'raising' and subject formation, and with the relation between 'raising' and subjecthood. The discussion in §6.3.2 pursued this theme of the role of free absolutive in ectopicities, but it also enabled us to characterize what is involved in 'V-2' structures, both 'full V-2' constructions and the 'residues' to be found in English. 'V-2' follows from a restriction on the normal (pre-head) positioning of the free absolutives of {P}, such that in a path of {P}s a lower {P} subject to 'V-2' takes its free absolutive to the right.

This section has confirmed that functional categories are perhaps the most important factor in the flexibility of syntactic structure, including the introduction of non-projective structures. But, at the same time, functional categories also constitute one element in the constraining of projectivity violations. In all the cases we have looked at the violation is associated with argument-sharing by functional categories. Such argument-sharing need not, indeed, involve 'tangling', as can be seen in several of the structures we have been discussing. Thus, in (246) not all of the sharing of arguments involves violation of projectivity:

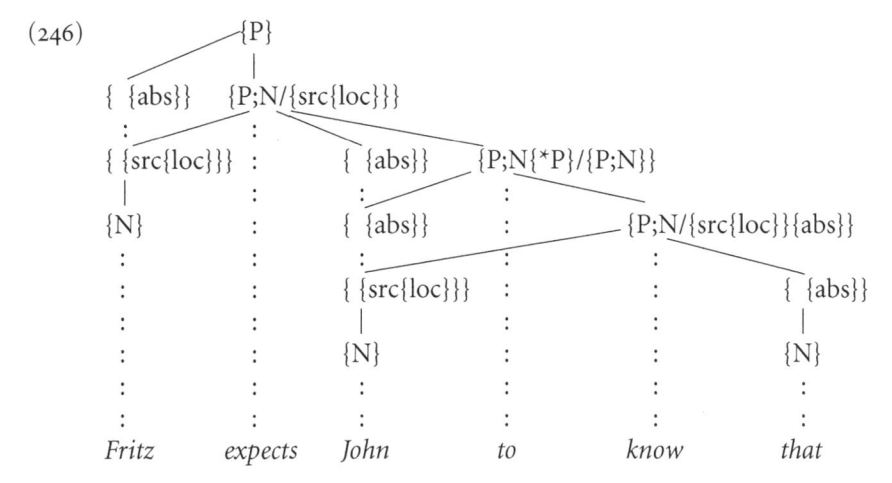

(246)

```
                    {P}
                    |
   { {abs}}    {P;N/{src{loc}}}
     :              :
{ {src{loc}}}  :    { {abs}}    {P;N{*P}/{P;N}}
     |         :      :              :
    {N}        :    { {abs}}    :    {P;N/{src{loc}}{abs}}
     :         :      :         :         :
     :         :  { {src{loc}}} :         :      { {abs}}
     :         :      |         :         :         |
     :         :     {N}        :         :        {N}
     :         :      :         :         :         :
     :         :      :         :         :         :
    Fritz    expects John       to       know      that
```

Indeed, only the arc linking the *know* verb with *John* introduces 'tangling', and this involves the association line linking a node to the lexically 'empty' *to*. In particular, 'tangling' is restricted in all the cases we have looked at to circumstances where the upper one of the sharing functors is a free absolutive, an { {abs}} not included in the subcategorization of the predicator it is dependent on but introduced by a general requirement that every predicator contain an absolutive functor. This seems to be the result of an analogue to the phonological preference for 'CV' syllables, and specifically {C} + {V} syllables. The unmarked predication is { {abs}} + P, whatever else may be present in a particular instance.

7

Analogy, dis-analogy, and secondary categories

Part III concludes with a look at some recent developments in ideas of representation, the effect of which is to highlight the configurational similarities between syntactic and phonological representations at the expense of their distinctive substantive alphabets. These remind us, if of nothing else, of the pervasive presence of the impulse to analogy, as a counter to the discrepancies surveyed in the preceding chapters in Part III of the present volume—though even there analogies have persisted in popping up.

I discuss here some suggestions that might appear at first to increase the discrepancy in the respective elaborations of phonological and syntactic categorization so far envisaged in our discussion. I turn firstly, in §7.1, to evidence for the internal complexity of at least some occurrences of secondary features in the syntax, but without necessarily eliminating the features from the alphabet of syntax. These comprise features expressed by inflectional morphology. Then, in §7.2, we look at some proposals that do involve reduction in the alphabet of features in phonology in favour of greater configurationality and a greater contribution from a small number of features, notably **V** and **C**. The ultimate effect in both cases turns out to be more complex than simply increasing the discrepancy between the two planes, however. Instead, we are confronted with a reassertion of the strength of the impulse towards structural analogy within language—which returns us to the initial theme of the present study, the role of analogy in reducing the autonomous character of the planes of language. It seems to me that this might form a fitting counter-conclusion to that part of this volume devoted to dis-analogies.

7.1 The complexity of secondary features in syntax

There is an aspect of lexical structure the complexity of which my presentation so far has left hidden, or at least underdeveloped in any consistent way.

Many at least of the secondary syntactic features that I have appealed to in the syntax do not seem to be atomic: they can be decomposed categorially. We have associated the secondary features of functors with a hierarchy (Volume I, §3.5): secondary, tertiary, ... But yet more serious categorial complexity can be discerned. The categorial structure provided by the lexicon is more complex than is implied by labelling verbals as {past}, for instance—as has already emerged in §§4.2–3. There are indeed cogent reasons for supposing that many of the labels I have given to secondary features conceal categorial structures. This is another aspect of the complexity of the syntactic categorization that interprets our perceptions.

Throughout these volumes there have been indications of the need to think of many secondary features as labels for more complex categorizations. Already in Volume I it was found necessary to de-compose 'negative' into a negatively oriented locative predication where the locative is an existential {N}. As in §3.5 of Volume II, we shall find the presence of {N} in accommodating such complexities to be pervasive.

Another area where this complexity has already made itself apparent is that of agreement on verbals—verb concord. Recall the examples from Basque in (183):

(183)   a. Lorea   aitari   eman   diot
            flower.the father.to give.PST.PTCP NPST.(III.SG.ABS)(III.SG.DAT)
                                                                          (I.SG.ERG)
            ('I gave the flower to father')

         b. Lorea   aitari   eman   diozu
            flower.the father.to give.PST.PTCP NPST.(III.SG.ABS)(III.SG.DAT)
                                                                          (II.SG.ERG)
            ('You gave the flower to father')

         c. Loreak   aitari   eman   diozkat
            flowers.the father.to give.PST.PTCP NPST.(III.PL.ABS)(III.SG.DAT)
                                                                          (I.SG.ERG)
            ('I gave the flowers to father')

In each case in (183) the final operative signals the presence of three arguments, a source (morphologically ergative), a 'recipient' (dative), and an absolutive (sometimes called 'nominative' in Basque studies); and each of these is differentiated for person and number. These secondary categories, semantic relations, speech-act-participant status (person), and number, can otherwise be associated more intimately with different categories than the verbal in language: semantic relations are associated with the functor, person with pronouns, and number with pronouns and determiners.

Functors commonly appear as adpositions or (case) inflections on nominals. Compare the gloss to (183a), i.e. (261a), with adposition, and the original of the 'to father' part of it, i.e. (261b):

(261)   a. I gave the flower to father
         b. *Basque* aitari—*cf. absolutive* aita

Number is marked on determiners, either simple (pronouns) or determiners with an adjoined noun (262a), or with a subjoined lexical nominal (262b) or adjectival (262c):

(262)   a. this/these (street/streets)
         b. (the) street/streets
         c. *Basque* aker   okerrak
             billy-goat one-eyed.DEF.PL
             ('the one-eyed billy goats')

Thus, the number marking in (262) and person are associated with {N} and the semantic relations in (261) with functors. These are their natural attachments, involving respectively extralinguistic reference (which includes deixis and enumeration) and mode of participation in the predication. This suggests that the signalling of these on verbals is lexically derived, by incorporation; and that the incorporation consists of functor and nominal specifications.

On this assumption, we can represent the internal structure of the operative in (183c) as in (263):

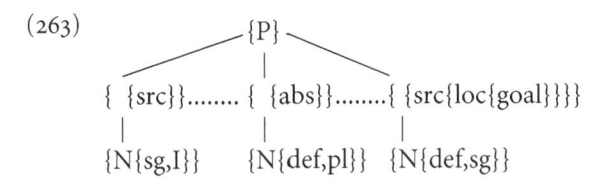

(263)   {P}
                      |
      { {src}}........{ {abs}}........{ {src{loc{goal}}}}
         | | |
     {N{sg,I}} {N{def,pl}} {N{def,sg}}

Compare the representation of the functoral distinctions suggested in Volume I for the 'synthetic' Basque verb in (I.85), where, as in (263), the dotted horizontal indicates absence in the categorial representation of linearization, which is performed by the morphology with respect to the exponents of these combinations of categories:

(I.85)   a. dakartza
            III,SG.carry.III,PL ('He carries them')

b.
```
            {P;N}
         /        \
  { {src}}..........{ {abs}}
      |                 |
     {N}               {N}
```

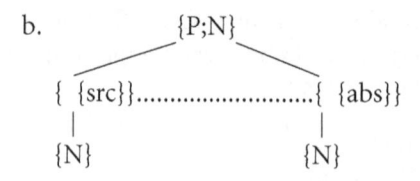

The {P;N} in (I.85b) is also finite, but otherwise no further elements need be present for this expression to constitute a complete sentence. Independent nominal arguments corresponding to the source and absolutive substructures in (I.85b) are apposed to the latter (I.5.4).

The source (agentive) argument in (183c/263) is marked as a speech-act participant, in this instance the source of the utterance ('I'). It is thus redundantly definite, since deictic. The first-person source is not distinctively represented as such in (263), except on the operative. The other two arguments are marked for definiteness (as indicated in the glosses), and are redundantly non-partakers in the speech act. They are in apposition to the verbal participants. The concord-markers are incorporated functors which are themselves complex and incorporate pronouns. And verb concord does not necessarily involve agreement, given the optionality of the apposing elements.

We find similar configurations, again associated with concord, also expressed morphologically only on the verb in, say, the following Selayarese examples also from Volume I (§5.4.2):

(I.148) a. máŋŋaŋ-i   hásaŋ aló-nni
            tired-III.ABS Hasan day-this   ('Hasan is tired today')
        b. la-   pállu-i   berasá-ñjo i- hásaŋ
           III.ERG-cook-III.ABS rice-   the Mr-Hasan
           ('Hasan cooked the rice')

(ABS = absolutive, ERG = ergative). In both these cases, the optional full nominal arguments are co-referential with the incorporated functor configurations, which contain the {N}s that bear co-referentiality. These are again not directly verbal features but indications of incorporation of non-verbal categories.

In §I.5.4.2 again, I suggest that the lexical structure of *seem* is as in (144a):

(I.144) a. {P;N/{src{loc}}{P;N}}
                    |
              { {src{loc}}}
                    |
                  {N_i}

Again the functor phrase is incorporated, in this case non-overtly. However, a circumstantial may be apposed to this incorporated 'experiencer', as in (I.145):

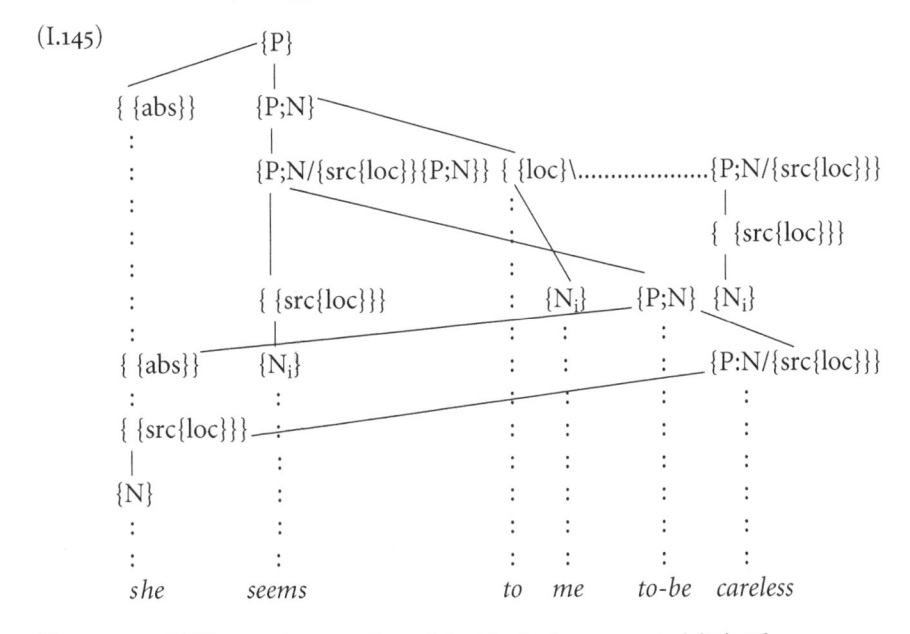

(I.145)

```
              {P}
              |
{{abs}}     {P;N}
  :           |
  :         {P;N/{src{loc}}{P;N}}  { {loc}\...................{P;N/{src{loc}}}
  :           |                        :\                        |
  :           |                        : \                   { {src{loc}}}
  :           |                        :  \                      |
  :         { {src{loc}}}              : {Nᵢ}  {P;N} {Nᵢ}
  :           |                        :  :     :
{{abs}}     {Nᵢ}                       :  :     :    {P:N/{src{loc}}}
  :           :                        :  :     :       :
{{src{loc}}}─┤                         :  :     :       :
  |           :                        :  :     :       :
 {N}          :                        :  :     :       :
  :           :                        :  :     :       :
  :           :                        :  :     :       :
 she        seems                      to  me  to-be careless
```

The apposed {N} must be co-referential with the incorporated {N}. Thus, agreement again involves marking for potential co-referentiality. And in this case the verbal agreement is not merely optional but also not morphologically signalled.

Similarly, verbal tense, involving temporal reference, is otherwise, and appropriately, associated with temporal nominals, as in *last week, in the past, the week after next*, etc. The features of the category of tense were discussed in another context in §3.3.1, 3.3.3 of Volume I. There I distinguished absolute, or deictic tenses, characterized as being 'identified directly with respect to the moment of speaking', from relative tense, identified in relation to another tense. And their characterization was explored further in §4.2.3. But we should now confront the fact that, as a localizing and referential function, the identification of temporal location is particularly associated with locative phrases (*on a Monday*), and deictic reference is associated with determiners (*this* etc.), including pronouns, the same primary categories as are deployed in verb concord—but here associated with temporal nominality, expressed as name, noun, or pronoun.

We can observe such combinations in deictic locative phrases like *on next Tuesday, at this time*. An adverb such as *now* is a single-lexeme deictic locative phrase (typically functioning as a circumstantial), of the minimal dimensionality of (264a), and *then* might be represented as in (b):

(264) a. { {loc}}
         |
       {N{T$_i$ ⊃ T$_S$}}
         ⋮
       now

   b. { {loc}}
         |
       {N{T$_S$ ⊄ T$_i$}}
         ⋮
       then

   c. { {loc}}
         |
       {N{T$_i$ < T$_S$}}
         ⋮
       formerly

   d. { {loc}}
         |
       {N{T$_i$}}
         |
       { {loc}}
         |
       {N{*front*}}
         |
       { {loc}}
         |
       {N{T}}
         ⋮
       formerly

These employ the system of representation of §4.2.3. Recall the formulation of tense reference, as concerns past and present:

the structure of tense reference
Let T$_S$ be the time of speaking, and let T$_i$ be the time referred to.
Then deictic {past$_i$} = T$_i$ < (precedes) T$_S$, and {pres$_i$} = T$_i$ ⊃ (includes) T$_S$.

Now includes the time of speaking, and *then* is indifferent to the past/future distinction; it is merely not present. But the adverb of (264c) is marked as past. Such representations are still no doubt abbreviatory, and need some such expansion as in (264d), for *formerly*. The lower 'T' is unspecified: depending on the situation it could be either '{T_S}' or '{T_j}' that follows '{T_i}'. The feature *front* is a fudge for the representation of the dimensional {N}. It also ignores the orientational ambivalence of time metaphors: is the past or the future 'in front of' us? Or, rather, it assumes the former interpretation in this case. But (264d) displays more fully the combination of functors and nominals involved in the articulation of the reference of temporals.

There is a natural association between tense and location and reference; and these latter are primarily properties of functors and {N}s. So, it is appropriate to suggest again that verbal tense also involves morphologically expressed incorporated functor phrases which again enter into relations of deixis and co-reference. Verbal tense is thus another lexicalized configuration of the character of (264d), but realized entirely morphologically rather than as an independent item. So that we might represent a deictic past as in (265), indicating this aspect of *was*:

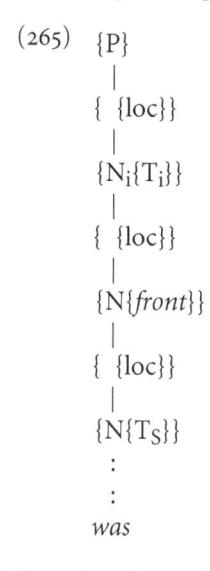

(265) {P}
        |
       { {loc}}
        |
       {N_i{T_j}}
        |
       { {loc}}
        |
       {N{*front*}}
        |
       { {loc}}
        |
       {N{T_S}}
        ⋮
        ⋮
       was

The subscript on the {N{T_i}} reminds us that this {N} enters into relationships of co-reference with other items containing such an {N}—nominal, adverbial, verbal, mediated by clausal status of tense in terms of the discussion in §4.2.3.

In §4.2.3, I suggested that past tense reference was a feature of the clause that involves spread of the tense reference of the governing {P} to accessible elements and agreement between that {P} and those elements which are specified for tense. Recall (138)*:

(138)* a.

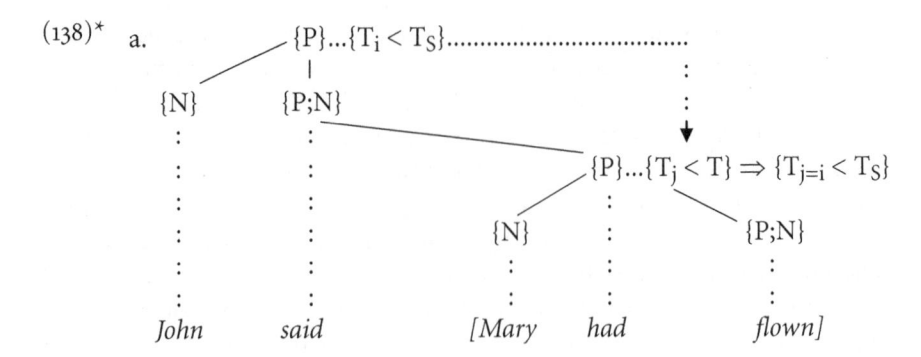

$$\{P\}...\{T_i < T_S\}$$

{N} {P;N}

{P}...{T_j < T} $\Rightarrow$ {T_{j=i} < T_S}

{N} {P;N}

John said [Mary had flown]

Other eligible elements for tense harmony include the circumstantial in (142), for instance, where (142a) also involves agreement:

(142) a. She left last Tuesday
b. She left on Tuesday

By recognizing the determiner, or {N}, affiliation of tense, as in (265), we can achieve homogeneity and naturalness of representation if {P} in (138)* incorporates a temporal locative. 'Tense harmony' involves agreement in the locative temporal {N}s.

We might thus envisage, instead of (138)*, the representation in (266), where for transparency I abbreviate the representation for tense, and for ease of comparison with (138)* I maintain the absence of the functor specifications of the participants in the predications, as well as argument-sharing:

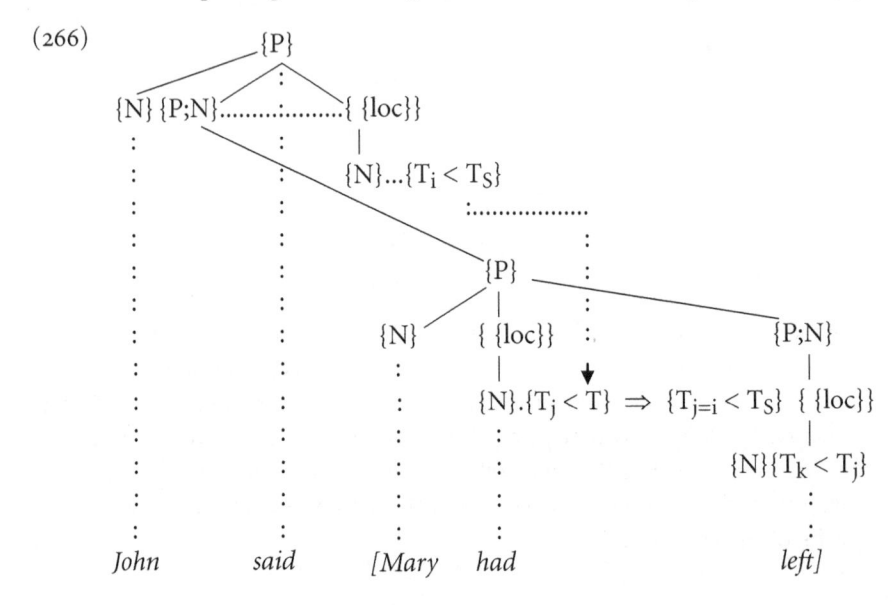

(266)

{P}

{N} {P;N}......{ {loc}}

{N}...{T_i < T_S}

{P}

{N} { {loc}} {P;N}

{N}.{T_j < T} $\Rightarrow$ {T_{j=i} < T_S} { {loc}}

{N}{T_k < T_j}

John said [Mary had left]

In accordance with the formulation of pastness harmony in §4.2.3, the clausal past, attached to the head of the construction, {P}, is associated by harmony with the lower incorporated locative temporal in (266), and fills out its specification with 'T$_S$'. The structures immediately subjoined to {P} (joined by a horizontal association line) are in both cases built in the lexicon. The *left* form in (266) is also formed in the lexicon, as past; it is relatively past with respect to the time reference of the governing {P}.

In the case of the two {P}s in (266) 'tense harmony' is a matter of matching, and 'spreading' of the tense reference. So too in (142a) (from §4.2.3) there is agreement between the locative {N}s realized by the two forms—verbal and nominal—that are assigned deictic past in the lexicon:

(142) a. She left last Tuesday
b. She left on Tuesday

But in (142b) the whole past reference is 'spread' from the {P} to an item whose {N} is unmarked for tense. It is the spread of reference that is analogous to the phonic 'spreading' of vowel harmony.

This again leaves much unexplored in this area, in relation to agreement phenomena in general, but particularly as concerns tense harmony. The extent and the details of 'tense harmony' await much further study. And this must pay attention to, for instance, the observation that a {P;N} subjoined to a deictic {P} cannot itself be tensed. This is why the *have* periphrasis is necessary in the lower finite clause in (266), as outlined in §6.2.2, and as is explored more fully, though from a different perspective, in Volume II.

I look there at the differences between such periphrases and, for instance, the 'displacement' of the agreement in the 'analytic' verb forms in Basque sentences of (183) from the verb to the operative. Also in Volume II (Chapter 6) there is exploration of agreement in gender, which like other cases of agreement, crucially involves {N}. This, and agreement of number, and, as we have seen, the expression of reference and deixis are consistently associated with this single category.

A further instance of lexical categorial decomposition is provided in §3.5 of Volume II, where it is suggested that such verbal secondary features as {prog(ressive)} are categorially complex. The progressive involves at least the structure in (95), from §II.3.5, with participation of a locative existential {N}:

(II.95)

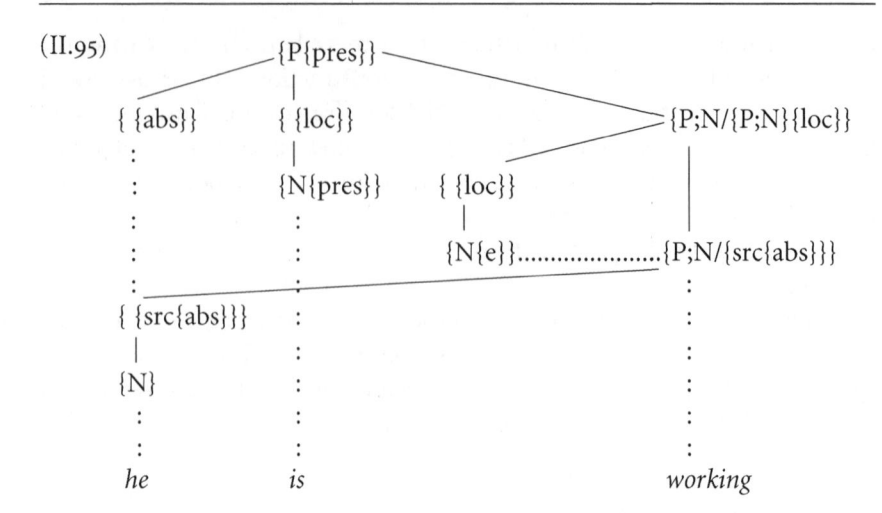

```
                    {P{pres}}
                        |
    { {abs}}        { {loc}}                         {P;N/{P;N}{loc}}
      :                 |                                   |
      :              {N{pres}}       { {loc}}               |
      :                 :               |                   |
      :                 :            {N{e}}............{P;N/{src{abs}}}
      :_____ :                                   :
    { {src{abs}}}       :                                   :
      |                 :                                   :
     {N}                :                                   :
      :                 :                                   :
      :                 :                                   :
      he                is                              working
```

The elaboration of the perfect is also suggested in §II.3.5, again with participation of functors and {N}:

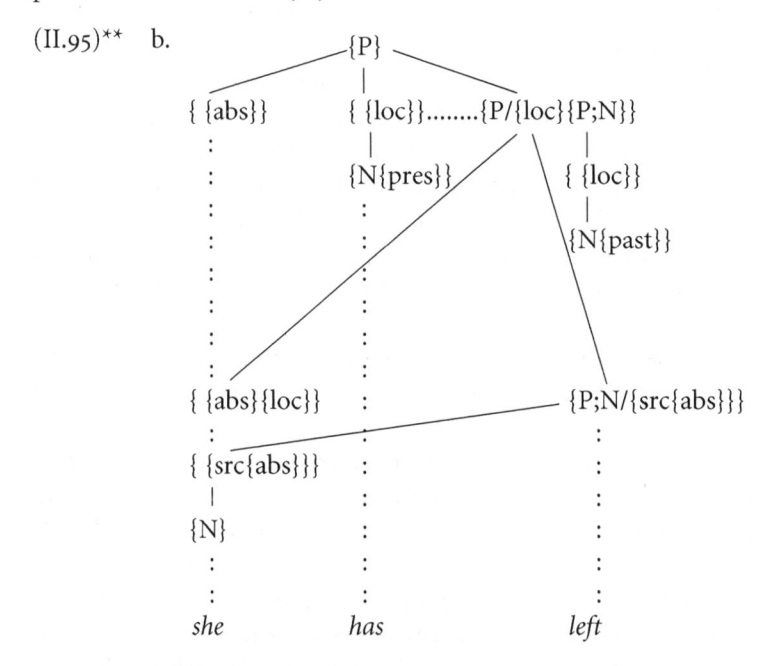

(II.95)** b.

```
                       {P}
                        |
    { {abs}}        { {loc}}........{P/{loc}{P;N}}
      :                 |                   |
      :              {N{pres}}           { {loc}}
      :                 :                   |
      :                 :                {N{past}}
      :                 :                   :
      :                 :                   :
      :                 :                   :
    { {abs}{loc}}       :           {P;N/{src{abs}}}
      :                                     :
    { {src{abs}}}       :                   :
      |                 :                   :
     {N}                :                   :
      :                 :                   :
      :                 :                   :
      she              has                 left
```

Passives similarly emerge as (II.92b)*:

(II.92)*b.

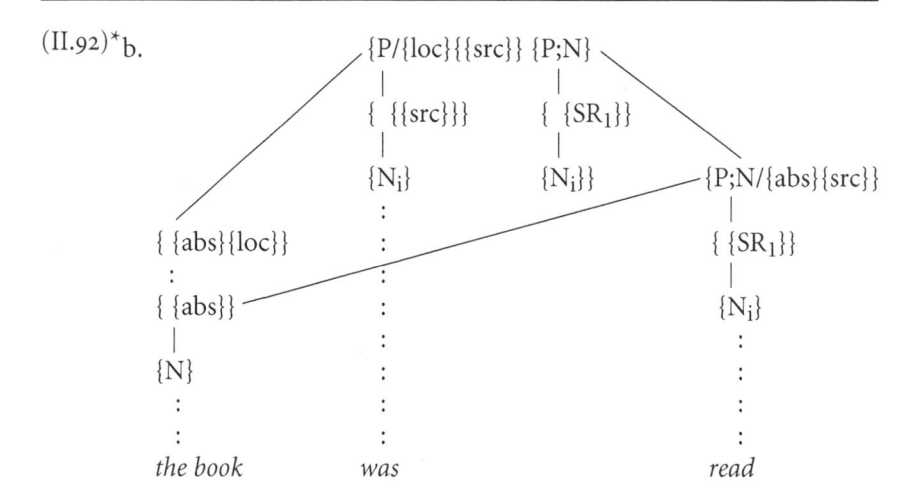

```
              {P/{loc}{{src}} {P;N}
                |              |
             { {{src}} }    { {SR₁} }
                |              |
               {Nᵢ}          {Nᵢ}           {P;N/{abs}{src}}
                                               |
   { {abs}{loc} }                           { {SR₁} }
        ⋮                                      |
   { {abs} }                                  {Nᵢ}
        |          ⋮                            ⋮
       {N}         ⋮                            ⋮
        ⋮          ⋮                            ⋮
    the book      was                         read
```

The introduction of these representations here is intended merely to illustrate still more the extent of deconstruction of this kind that seems to be appropriate.

All of these remarks are only suggestive of the categorial complexity associated with what might be taken to be simply secondary syntactic features. I have merely touched on a vast domain in introducing such complex lexical structures. Nevertheless, the description of these phenomena points to a lexical complication with extensive syntactic consequences that again is not paralleled in the phonology. Phenomena that were earlier in this work attributed to simple secondary features have been progressively reinterpreted as involving internal structure and categorial complexity. And again this reflects the different extralinguistic interfaces involved: such categorial complexity is neither appropriate nor feasible in a phonically based system of representation; and they reflect with respect to the syntax the need for compact representation and orientation of the 'scenes' that the syntax seeks to convey. The inadequacy of direct phonetic expression of cognitive 'scenes' is accommodated by the 'double articulation' of language, whereby complex categorial relationships are packaged in 'bite-sized' chunks that can be realized as phonological forms based on a small number of contrasts.

As confessed, I do not pursue these elaborations of syntactic categorization here. I want to compare the examples of this given above of the non-atomic character of the syntactic secondary categories that were appealed to in previous sections with the consequences of proposals concerning the secondary features of the phonology. These deconstructions of syntactic features like verbal concord and tense involve at most only a minimal reduction or reinterpretation in the alphabet of secondary syntactic features. Mostly what is involved is a more restrictive realignment of secondary and primary categories, with a clustering of particularly inflectionally expressed secondary features on {N}. The overall consequence is a more detailed articulation of the alignment of such secondary features with primaries.

What I turn to now are suggestions that in the phonology categorial structure is even less diverse in terms of membership of the set of features than we have been assuming. Combined with what we have just been looking at, involving elaboration in syntax of the secondary categorization, these proposals might appear to suggest that the contrast between syntax and phonology in terms of categorial elaboration is even more marked than argued here so far. But, as I have said, things are not that simple. Reduction in alphabet in the phonology is also achieved via the elaboration of categorial structure. And there are also signs of alphabet economy in syntax.

7.2 Minimalizing the alphabet of phonology

As I have observed, Anderson and Ewen (1987: §6.1.2) suggest that their compactness/lowness component {a} be interpreted as {v}, i.e. it is the V that appears in the set of secondary features. And this proposal has been adopted here. There is a natural relationship between {V} and {a}: {V} + {a} is maximal vocalicness. Anderson and Ewen point out that this identification also appropriately distinguishes {a} from the other two basic secondary features associated with vowels in their system, {i} and {u}; {i} and {u} are the 'vowel colours', and they both have reduced harmonic energy compared with {a}. Thus, {a} very commonly in vowel systems combines with one of the other two features, and there seem to be indeed systems where {a} and the other feature are involved in asymmetrical combinations, such as {a;i} vs. {i;a}. But combination of {i} and {u} is very much rarer, and asymmetrical combinations vanishingly instantiated.[56]

Such a proposal as Anderson and Ewen's reduces variety in the components of categorial representation in the phonology. In the course of the present volume I have added a secondary {c} to {v}, as deployed in distinguishing between the sonorants in (79), of §2.4.3:

(79)   a. {V;C{c}}   b. {V;C}   c. {V;C{v}}
            nasal   lateral   rhotic

---

[56] Compare with the 'vowel colours'—an appropriate synaesthetic term, I suggest—what Donegan (1978) distinguishes as 'chromatic' properties, and Schane (1984) as 'tonality particles'. The latter, unlike the equivalent of {a} (or rather {v}, on the view adopted here), cannot be duplicated in the representation of a single vowel in Schane's system of representation.

However, a much more radical proposal concerning cross-gestural presence of the same feature, with striking implications for the vocabulary of phonology, has been developed over a number of years by Harry van der Hulst—beginning, as far as I am aware with van der Hulst (1988a,b): see van der Hulst (2005) for a more recent statement. Let me try to sketch the kind of system proposed.

Rightly is the framework he advocates dubbed 'radical CV phonology', in so far as the number of basic elements of the phonological system is reduced to two, 'C' and 'V'. They recur through three distinct **gestures** which together are taken to characterize the structure of the segment: the three gestures are Manner, Place, and Laryngeal, organized as in (267):

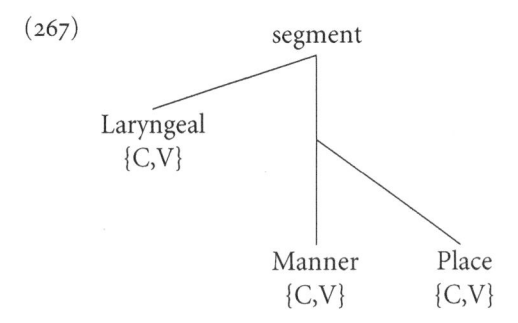

(267)

```
                    segment
               ╱       │
         Laryngeal     │
          {C,V}        │
                       │  ╲
                       │    ╲
                    Manner   Place
                    {C,V}    {C,V}
```

(van der Hulst 2005: 195). The 'outer' subordinate, Laryngeal, is, in accordance with this 'more peripheral' status, 'more optional'. 'Manner' comprises, roughly, the primary categories of the preceding discussion, 'Place' the secondary—though, as we shall see, van der Hulst includes some secondary categories in Manner. Laryngeal categories have not been a focus of attention here, but have been assumed to belong among the secondary categories.

The nature of the above and other of van der Hulst's trees is unclear; they seem to be some sort of amalgam of dependency and constituency representations. But, for comparison with the kind of framework adopted here, the above intra segmental relationships can be represented in present terms as a path of subjunctions, as in (268):

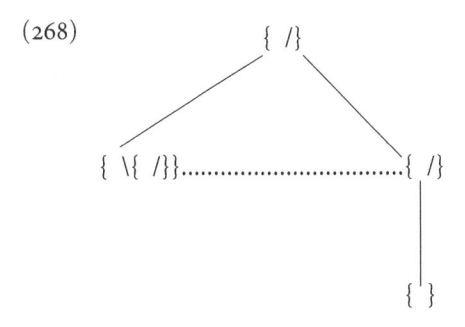

(268)

```
                { /}
              ╱      ╲
       { \{ /}}........{ /}
                        │
                       { }
```

Here { /} = 'Manner', { \{ /}} = 'Laryngeal', { } = 'Place'; i.e. the gestures are defined in terms of their valency. This representation assumes the universality of Place, even if non-contrasting and though its content is not independent of its head ('Manner'); whereas Laryngeal is optional. But see further below.

If appeal is made in this way to valency, which is independently necessary, the gestural labels of (267)—both 'laryngeal' etc. and 'C' and 'V'—are redundant. The representation in (268) can be seen as amplifying and structuring the simple division into primary and secondary categories that I have deployed in what precedes, but without increasing the phonological categorial vocabulary—or, indeed, having recourse to 'C' and 'V'. This does not argue against interpreting features as involving uniformly 'C' and 'V', merely that differentiating the gestures in these terms is unnecessary, since this can be done configurationally, without substantive labelling. 'C' and 'V' need have no place in gestural labelling.

But there are other proposed 'extensions' of 'C' and 'V' to consider. In terms of van der Hulst's proposals, within each gesture there is a primary and a secondary distinction between 'C' and 'V', as shown in (269) (= van der Hulst's 2005: (2a)):

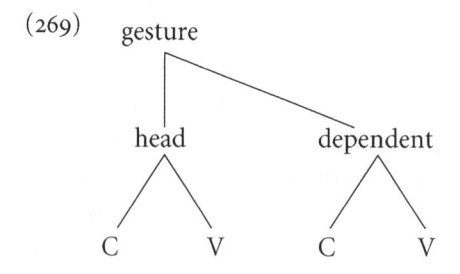

(269)   gesture
        /   \
     head   dependent
     / \   / \
    C   V   C   V

In terms, again, of the notation used in this book, (269) is equivalent to the possibilities allowed by (270a), or rather (270b), on the assumption that head and dependent cannot be identical:

(270)   a. V;V V;C C;V C;C
        b. V   V;C C;V C

Recall that the semicolon notation is merely a notation for dependency equivalent to tree structure, with the head preceding the dependent. Again the node labels, 'head' and 'dependent' in (269) are redundant. There is even less need to appeal to such 'substance', or at least 'alphabetic elements', as van der Hulst proposes.

Van der Hulst (2005: §1.3) also applies the CV distinction to syllable structure, with results that accord well with the configurations assumed in the present work, except that he advocates a much more restrictive structure for the syllable, as in (271), his (6b):

(271)
```
           ┌─── syllable
           │
     C (onset)    V (rhyme)
      ⋮     ╲      ⋮    ╲
      ⋮      V     ⋮     C
      ⋮      ⋮     ⋮     ⋮
      ⋮      ⋮     ⋮     ⋮
      X      X     X     X
```

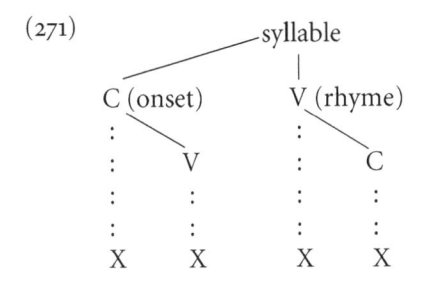

But once more, in terms of the framework assumed here, what is involved in syllable structure is primarily a question of dependency relations rather than 'C' vs. 'V', as shown in (272):

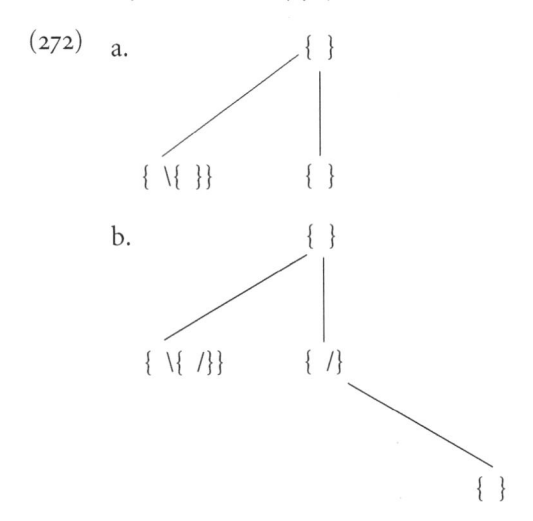

(272) a.
```
              { }
            ╱  │
     { \{ }}   { }
```

b.
```
              { }
            ╱  │
    { \{ /}}   { /}
                  ╲
                   { }
```

In terms of (272) there are two types of rhyme, intransitive and transitive, and languages may incline more to one than the other. In terms of what is discussed in this study, the onsets and codas may be expanded as indicated in (273):

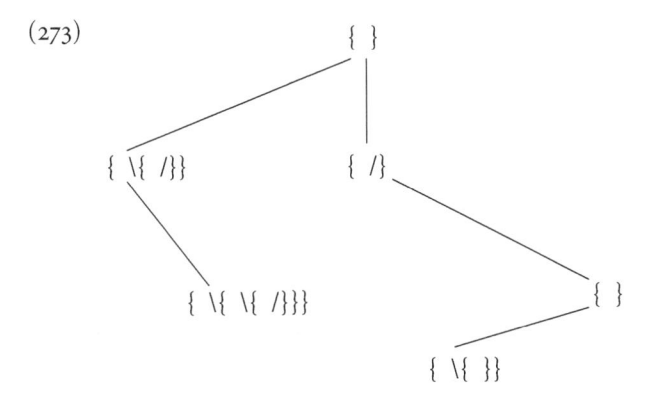

(273)
```
                    { }
                 ╱   │
        { \{ /}}     { /}
             ╲           ╲
              { \{ \{ /}}}    { }
                               ╲
                                { \{ }}
```

And to ensure timing these new segments are also adjoined to the head of the syllable, as in (58) (which also includes the coda adjunct and 'extrametrical' coronal obstruent), from §2.3.3:

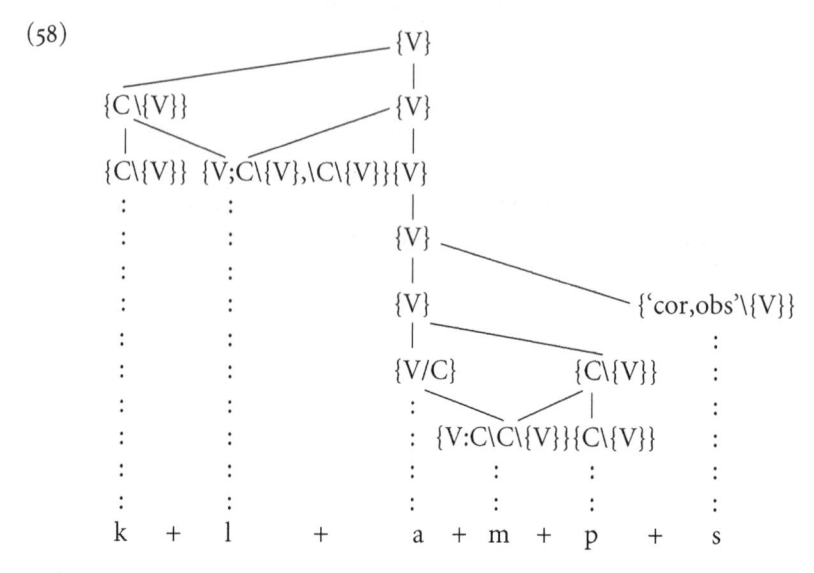

(58)

```
                              {V}
                               |
   {C\{V}}                    {V}
      |                        |
   {C\{V}}  {V;C\{V},\C\{V}}{V}
     ⋮        ⋮                |
     ⋮        ⋮               {V}
     ⋮        ⋮                |
     ⋮        ⋮               {V}                    {'cor,obs'\{V}}
     ⋮        ⋮                |                          ⋮
     ⋮        ⋮              {V/C}         {C\{V}}        ⋮
     ⋮        ⋮                ⋮             |            ⋮
     ⋮        ⋮                ⋮  {V:C\C\{V}}{C\{V}}      ⋮
     ⋮        ⋮                ⋮   ⋮     ⋮     ⋮          ⋮
     ⋮        ⋮                ⋮   ⋮     ⋮     ⋮          ⋮
     k   +   l    +           a  + m  + p  +  s
```

The pattern of primary categorization by **V** and **C** is built on the skeleton of dependencies and valencies of (273). Further addition gives (61)*:

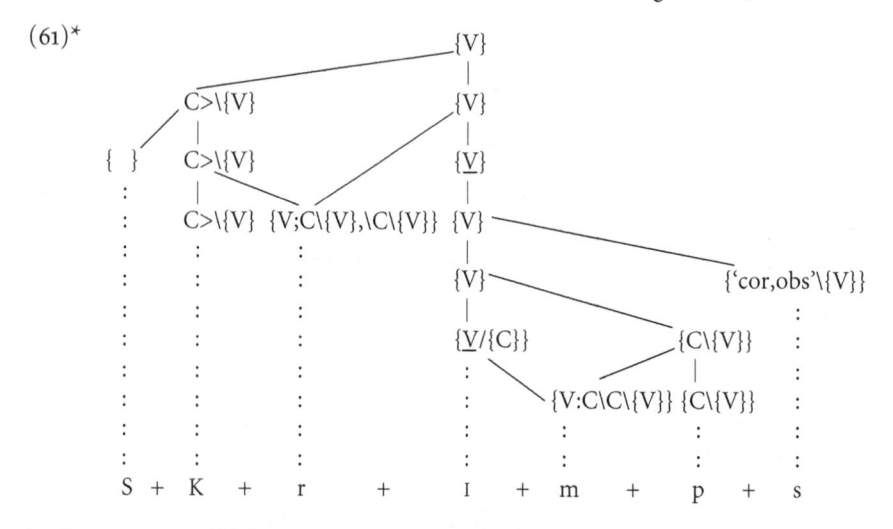

(61)*

```
                                    {V}
                                     |
           C>\{V}                   {V}
              |                      |
    { }   C>\{V}                    {V}
     ⋮        |                      |
     ⋮    C>\{V}  {V;C\{V},\C\{V}} {V}
     ⋮      ⋮        ⋮               |
     ⋮      ⋮        ⋮              {V}                    {'cor,obs'\{V}}
     ⋮      ⋮        ⋮               |                          ⋮
     ⋮      ⋮        ⋮            {V/{C}}         {C\{V}}       ⋮
     ⋮      ⋮        ⋮               ⋮              |           ⋮
     ⋮      ⋮        ⋮               ⋮    {V:C\C\{V}} {C\{V}}   ⋮
     ⋮      ⋮        ⋮               ⋮      ⋮          ⋮        ⋮
     ⋮      ⋮        ⋮               ⋮      ⋮          ⋮        ⋮
     S  +   K   +    r    +          l  +  m    +     p    +    s
```

In these terms, syllable structure can extend to certain physically and perceptually determined limits. If (271) does not have a similar status and capacity for extended expression, then recourse will have to be had to 'empty categories' to allow for phonetically more complex syllables. As with 'government phonology' and its descendants, this perpetuates, in a different plane, and even more unnecessarily, the errors of transformational syntax.

My main point concerning these 'organizational extensions' of the domain of 'C' and 'V', however, is that it is simply unnecessary to label the gestures and syllables as such; the gestures are defined configurationally, the syllable is a skeleton for primary categories. Their only content is that of the basic-level features that realize these configurations, as in our discussions here. But this is only one, somewhat negative aspect of the interest of van der Hulst's proposals, though it has involved us in reaffirming the importance of phonological configurationality.

Also relevant here in these proposals is the extension of 'C' and 'V' into the representation of the non-Manner gestures themselves. And the most striking innovation is perhaps in the interpretation of Place features—though, as always, van der Hulst is careful to acknowledge antecedents (2005: §3.4), extending back to Jacobson, Fant, and Halle (1952), at least. Van der Hulst (2005: §3) advocates that vowels ('syllable heads') and obstruents (sonorant consonants, which are not 'onset heads', are assumed to be 'phonologically placeless') are distinguished in terms of 'V' and 'C'.

He tabulates the correspondences in (274), his (33):

(274) onset   rhyme
       C(c) lingual *lingual*   ⇒ coronal: /t/   C(c) front *front*: /i/
       Cv   lingual *peripheral*   ⇒ coronal: /T/   Cv   front *round*: /y/
       Vc   peripheral *lingual*   ⇒ dorsal: /k/   Vc   back *front*: /ɯ/
       V(v) peripheral *peripheral* ⇒ labial: /p/   V(v) back *round*: /u/

/T/ stands for 'some kind of "posterior" coronal' (van der Hulst 2005: 214), including palatals and retroflexes. The dependent element is in lower case, and it is italicized in the 'phonetic glosses'. Van der Hulst provides cross-linguistic motivations for the distribution of 'V' and 'C' in these representations. However, some of the problems he notes in relation to (274) are resolved if we interpret this extension of 'C' and 'V' into Place in terms of the framework I have been deploying here (basically a reduced version of Anderson and Ewen's 1987 suggested system), in particular the provision for simple combination and the recognition of the system relativity of representations.

If we utilize the possibility of simple combination, then we can have instead of (274) something like (275), where I preserve, except where commented on, van der Hulst's labels ('lingual', 'front', etc.), for ease of comparison, but without necessarily subscribing to these:

(275) onset   rhyme
       C   lingual   ⇒ coronal: /t/   C   front: /i/
       V,C   lingual & peripheral   ⇒ dorsal: /k/   V,C front & round: /y/
       V   peripheral   ⇒ labial: /p/   V   round: /u/

Van der Hulst's (2005) notes as one problem with his proposals that /ɯ/ is ranked above /y/ in terms of unmarkedness—which is unfortunate, given the acknowledged existence of languages with the latter and not the former, and perhaps not vice versa. In terms of (275) a system without /ɯ/ and with /y/ is to be expected; similarly, a system with /k/ and without /T/ (the latter again being marked) is to be expected. These distinctions are simply not allowed for by (275); the unmarked realizations of 'V,C' are /k/ and /y/.

However, (275) can presumably be expanded in languages which show the less common oppositions represented in (276):

(276) onset   rhyme
       C   lingual   ⇒ coronal: /t/   C   front: /i/
       C;V   lingual over peripheral ⇒ coronal: /T/   C;V front over round: /y/
       V;C   peripheral over lingual ⇒ dorsal: /k/   V;C back over front: /ɯ/
       V   peripheral   ⇒ labial: /p/   V   round: /u/

This treatment assumes that representations are system-relative: a [k] will differ in its representation depending on the nature of the system in which it appears.

However, the treatment of /ɯ/ in (274) and (276) is still problematical. And I have emphasized this by showing in (275) and (276) that it is only that particular vowel that necessitates the swapping between 'round' and 'back' in (276)—and (274). I'm not sure that /ɯ/ is not better described as simply lacking a Place 'C' and 'V', on the understanding that this non-combination is more marked than any simple combination: such a segment 'withdraws' from this subsystem of combinations. This last suggestion correlates with Anderson and Durand's proposal that the vowel that renders a system asymmetrical is marked as exceptional by virtue of having no specification for Place (in van der Hulst's terms), and is filled in by default; such a vowel displays local markedness.

Nor is it obvious that palatal consonants should be treated as in (276), rather than by, say, additional subjoined categorization (van der Hulst's 'adjunction'), as van der Hulst suggests for palatalization (and labialization (2005: §3.2); alternatively, in the terms used above, they involve a tertiary feature. In other words, I am not convinced that the expansions for the *onset* and *rhyme* systems in (276) are necessary. On the other hand, the vowel height dimension does seem to require at least such expansion.

Van der Hulst (§2.2) presents vowel height, involving relative stricture, as manifestation of rhyme-head Manner, as in (277), his (27a):

(277)   Rhyme head
      V(v)   low *low*: /a/
      Vc   low *high*: /ɛ,ɔ/
      Cv   high *low*: /e,o/
      C(c)   high *high*: /i,u/

Again, utilizing the simple-combination possibility, we can translate this as in (278):

(278)   Rhyme head
      V   low: /a/
      V,C   high & low: /e,o/
      C   high: /i,u/

But in some languages this is expanded to (279):

(279)   Rhyme head
      V   low: /a/
      V;C   low over high: /ɛ,ɔ/
      C;V   high over low: /e,o/
      C   high: /i,u/

These possibilities confirm my doubts about treating [ɯ] as belonging in the hierarchy of (276), or (274). In (278) {V,C}, despite the translation as /e,o/, is a genuine neutralization of /ɛ,ɔ/ and /e,o/, and may be realized as either the higher or lower or neither and usually, indeed, variably (depending on context). This is not the case with {V,C} in the *rhyme* set of (275), which cannot appear as either [y] or [ɯ]: {i,u}, in the notation used generally in this book, is not a neutralization of {i;u} and {u;i}; in a system without the alleged opposition between {i;u} and {u;i} {i,u} = [y].

To seek for parallelism—viz. replication of 'C(c)' vs. 'Cv' vs. 'Vc' vs. 'V (v)'—in all these different areas is perhaps to repeat the error of X-bar syntax: the substance of different areas may not require the completely homogeneous solutions that abstract symmetry demands. The preceding brief description does not at all do justice to van der Hulst's richly detailed comprehensive system and the arguments he adduces in its favour, and many fundamental questions remain untouched by it. I do not pursue, for instance, whether it is appropriate to offer description of the various manifestations of 'C' and 'V' only in articulatory terms, which are not necessarily directly relevant to perception; nor do I consider the consequences of an apparent neglect of the distinction between (what in the present work are called) primary and secondary categories, based on their relevance to distribution in the syllable.

While in some ways sympathetic to the motivations for extension of the **C** and **V** distinction to areas beyond primary categorial representations (as I trust I have made clear), I am uneasy about the imposition of such an inflexible schema as he proposes throughout these substantively different areas of phonology. And it also seems to me, as I have tried to illustrate, that much more of phonological representation is purely configurational rather than having recourse to labelling as 'C' and 'V'. Further, if representations are reduced to sets of asymmetrical relations between **C** and **V**, at least one of these symbols can be dispensed with in favour of a truly privative relation: representations are constructed out of configurations involving simply **V** (which, as rhyme head, provides the phonetic syllable, the basis for speech) and its absence. Phonology contains a single substantive category. It is not clear that this is a desirable conclusion.

7.3 Conclusion: Configuration vs. alphabet proliferation

Without pursuing the 'CV hypothesis' any further, important as the repercussions may be, if it is generally viable in some form, we can see already that the reduction of the inventory of the phonological alphabet involved in its implementation has to be balanced by more extensive recourse to configurational distinctions.

In the context of this Part, what is significant is that in either case—whether there is preferred a more extensive alphabet or more extensive recourse to configuration and more diversification of the phonetic realizations of the elements of the alphabet—the structural and alphabetical elaboration of the phonology is much more limited than in the syntax, on account of familiar demands by the respective interfaces. But the content of the present section also throws a different light on analogy, one which highlights the pervasiveness of analogical structuring of linguistic representations.

What unites the suggestions about the different planes that we have looked at in the preceding two subsections is the elaboration in both instances of the (subjunctional) configurational structure of basic elements. This strategy seems to capture some important generalizations, and deserves further exploration. Could this strategy be the basis for another analogy, limited, of course, by the different scopes of the two interface domains? Namely, a preference for exploitation of internal configurations, rather than proliferation of substantive features? This would also involve a preference for 'analogy' in something like the sense associated with the traditional 'analogy' vs. 'anomaly' debate alluded to at the very beginning of the Introduction to Chapter 1. Within certain limits recurrent relational configurations are preferred to both feature proliferation and attachment of features to disparate hosts, as with tenses. And could this preference have a basis in the interfaces, in reflecting the perceived structure of the interface domains?

Within the present chapter, economy of alphabet in both planes is mainly manifested in the deployment of primary features as also secondary—partly because more recourse is had to configurational distinctions than in what is proposed by van der Hulst. As recalled initially in the preceding subsection, I suggested in §2.4 that both **V** and **C** had secondary equivalents, **v** and **c**, as deployed in (78) and (79):

(78) a {V;C{v}} [r] {V;C} [l]
 b. {C;V{v}} [v] {C;V} [f]
 c. {C{v}} [d] {C} [t]
 d. {V{v}} [a] {V{i/u/ }} [i],[u],[ə]

(79) a. {V;C{c}} b. {V;C} c. {V;C{v}}
 nasal lateral rhotic

In these terms, various distinctions are marked by the presence or lack of {v} in (78), and the different types of sonorant consonants in (79) are differentiated by the presence of either {v} or {c} or the absence of both. (78) and (79) lack instances of obstruents and vowels with secondary {c}: there are no {C;V {c}} or {C{c}} or {V{c}}. This is not something I pursue here, except to speculate that this may be how alternative airstream mechanisms and voiceless vowels are introduced into the system.

The relevant point in the present context is that, analogously, in the syntax various less or more prototypical categories can be seen as involving **p** or **n**. Whether presence of secondary **p** or **n** marks the subcategory as prototypical or marked depends on the character of the primary categorization. Thus 'relational' nouns and adjectives, which are marked, are interpreted as having a secondary {p}, as in (80a-b), and stative verbs similarly have an {n}, as in (80e), while declaratives, prototypical finites, have both {P} and {p}, and definites both {N} and {n}, as in (80c-d):

(80) a. {N;P{p}}
 b. {P:N{p}}

c. {P{p}}
   d. {N{n}}
   e. {P;N{n}}

In this way it may be that the impulse to exploit configurationality associated with both planes is accompanied by such economy of alphabets as I have just illustrated. And this economy depends on another kind of perceived analogy, involving similarities between the domains of primary and secondary categorization in both planes; we have intra-alphabetic analogies. For all the strength of the factors favouring non-analogy, the common logic of the building of linguistic representations again emerges strongly in the two planes.

Conclusion

I have sought in this volume to identify various formal properties that are shared by phonology and syntax. Their existence is consistent with the structural analogy assumption, which leads us to expect such sharing of structural properties, except when this is frustrated by the different interface requirements on syntax and phonology, including the relationship between the two planes, i.e. their own interface, involving crucially the lexicon. These analogies arise both from perceived analogues in the substances of the respective interfaces and from deployment of the same logical apparatus in the construction of syntactic and phonological representations.

The main detailed discussion in the study was preceded by a prelude (Chapter 1) in which some of the main issues raised by this assumption are given an airing, and where it is put into some kind of historical perspective. In particular I discuss there the incompatibility of the structural analogy assumption with an 'austere' view of 'universal grammar' that has been advocated recently, one which excludes phonology from universal grammar; and I offer there too a preliminary defence of the proposition that there are shared formal cross-planar properties not all of which are based on very obvious similarities in substance. Thus, analogies involving 'headhood' are based on perceptible distributional analogies between the two substances, analogies derivative of cognitive salience of some kind. But, perhaps less obvious is a substantial basis for the 'transitivity' analogy discussed more fully in Chapter 2. However, any distinction between substantive vs. formal basis for a particular analogy is, indeed, difficult to draw, given the current state of knowledge. For instance, how purely formal is the relationality that underlies the transitivity analogy?

Some of these analogical properties are associated with the distinction 'head' vs. 'dependent': crucially there are the distinctions among dependents between complement, adjunct, and specifier. In Chapter 2 I try to show that these varieties of the dependency relation of adjunction are fundamental to the phonology in being potentially contrastive, and that they can determine other properties of phonological representation, such as linearity, vowel weight, and aperture, and timing, which are more intimately related to the phonetic interface. It seems plausible to say that it is among properties that are not narrowly particular to the characterization or to the limitations of a particular interface that we can expect to find the most fully developed analogies, though we are far from demonstrating this empirically. The syntactic application of the head-based notions discussed in relation to the phonology in Chapter 2 are familiar, so that that chapter is mainly devoted to their application in phonology—though some clarification of my interpretation of the syntactic manifestations is given in the present context.

Chapter 3, moving away from the 'adjunctional' analogies of the previous chapter, turns to the analogical composition of minimal units and their categories on the two planes. These discussions are followed in the succeeding chapter by further analogies, partly based on the analogy in categorial structure. These further analogies are perhaps in this case more familiar in their phonological guise, involving, in particular, extrasegmental/clausal elements, analogies to do with 'harmony' and 'umlaut', as well as 'underspecification' and 'polysystemicity'. These very terms summon up what have been thought of as traditional phonological concerns. But a range of phenomena in a range of languages testifies to the appropriateness of such analogous analyses in the two planes. The characterizations of the analogies all involve relatively formal notions, but at least 'harmony' and 'umlaut' have a clear substantive basis in their phonetic application, and arguably in their semantic; and in both planes they serve to bind constructions together.

However, the nature of the respective interfaces to syntax and phonology limit the extent of analogical patterning even among more formal properties. Crucially, the semanticity of syntax demands structural distinctions not required in the phonology. These elaborations are also often incompatible with the restrictions imposed by the nature of the physical medium of transmission with which the perceptual elements of phonology ultimately interface. Chapter 5 attempts to illustrate both these aspects in relation to the development, uniquely in the syntax, of functional categories, and Chapter 6 continues the illustrations in relation to the role of lexical derivation and extended recursive embedding as responses to the need for the syntax to express complex cognitive 'scenes', including entities seen as 'scenes', and vice versa, and 'scenes' within 'scenes'. The representation of 'scenes' and integration of their expression often involve the kind of 'displacements' that we can associate with e.g. *wh*-forms in English, what I have called 'ectopicities', as illustrated in §6.3. Such 'displacements' are again not to be reconciled with phoneticity. §6.3.2 discusses how ectopicities are also associated with the referential aspect of syntactic representations and specifically with the expression of their thematic, or discoursal, structure. And Chapter 6 as a whole serves to confirm the centrality to the syntax of the distinction between functional and lexical category. Crucial is the role of free absolutives, functors that are not sanctioned by a valency nor seek to modify.

In all the cases discussed in Chapters 5 and 6 the demands of complex semanticity, including referentiality, are not paralleled in the phonology; and, indeed, incorporation of these properties responding to the demands of semanticity would be incompatible with phoneticity, given the physical basis of the expression of phonological constructions. Nevertheless, we can generalize that syntax as well as phonology lacks any appeal to structural mutations ('movements' and the like) and 'empty' categories (see too on this Volume I of the trilogy): rich substance-grounded categorizations and internal configurations derived from the lexicon obviate the need for them even in the syntax.

Chapter 7 offers a discussion of some recent developments that both illustrate discrepancies between the planes, thus supplementing Chapter 5 and Chapter 6, and also introduce possible further analogies. Thus, in the first place, the alphabet of phonology may be even more limited, in comparison with that of syntax, than suggested by the dimensions assumed in these studies on modularity. This arises from the use of the same elements as both primary and secondary features and from more distinctions being ascribed to configuration rather than the substantive alphabet. The use of a single feature as both primary and secondary is also characteristic of the syntax, but the impact of this on the much larger alphabet of syntactic features is not as significant as in the phonology. Secondly, the reinterpretation of syntactic categories as well as phonological as involving more configurationality suggests that maximum exploitation of the latter may be shared by the planes. In this way potential dis-analogy (the extent of the alphabets) is associated with possible analogies (the impulse to configurationality and features with alternative statuses)—a fitting ending to the volume, it might be thought.

The situation described here overall, involving analogies, and limitations on these by the interfaces—a picture in accord with the structural analogy assumption, including its provisos—is also compatible with the view that syntax and phonology are created by language learners on the basis of exposure to language phenomena and using common cognitive capacities which are constrained by cognitive needs and limitations, limitations which in particular cases may be more and less relevant to the respective interfaces of the two planes. It is a truism that the two planes interface with two quite different cognitive domains, whose linking by linguistic representations depends on a 'double articulation'. And the orientation of the two planes is very different, with syntax providing a representation for our cognition and phonology providing perception-based representations that are amenable to articulatory and perceptual implementation. And language allows for a series of re-representations to mediate between these two mental domains. But the process of re-representation requires no appeal to content-free categories or structural mutations. And these are not analogical properties.

The pervasively analogical situation described and motivated here is—to put it no more strongly—rather unexpected on the 'austere' view of 'universal grammar' addressed in the initial chapter of this study, a consequence of which was to exclude phonology from universal grammar—a situation which discourages any expectation of inter planar analogies. On the present view, to the extent that there are such analogies between planes, they are based on perceived similarities in the different mental substances being represented, but also on application of the same general mental apparatus to constructs in both phonology and syntax. I have offered motivations for adopting a view of language that is compatible with supposing that the learning of language can take place on the basis of these non-linguistic capacities and their interaction with experience. Thus, it is not necessary to assume that analogies are based on shared properties of a 'universal grammar', one that (in this case) assumes that phonology after all is 'austerely autonomous', as some researchers have recently argued. Such a concept of universal grammar is superfluous.

Volume I in this trilogy was concerned with the fundamental permeability of the linguistic module of syntax. It is, on the one hand, a projection of notionally based categories, categories that grammaticalize perceived cognitive distinctions: it is a response to extralinguistic content. On the other hand, one of the direct means of expression that constitute the essential content of syntax is phonological (intonational, in particular), and even another expressive device, linearity ('word order'), is based on the 'substance' of time, ultimately the linearity of time associated with transmission by phonic means (as well as graphic substitutes). Re-representation using additional, auxiliary substantively based alphabets (phonological, concatenative, as well as hierarchizing) defines the submodules of syntax. Moreover, linearity and intonation are also directly at the service of communicative needs of the immediate context, in the form of indicating thematic structure, the structuring of information appropriate to that context. This modular permeability, extralinguistic and intralinguistic, is one kind of limitation on the autonomy of language and its modules.

In the present volume we have looked in the first place, on the other hand, at limitations on distinctiveness in the structures exhibited by the two linguistic modules of phonology and syntax. These limitations follow from the structural analogy assumption. These analogies are putatively based, as we have seen, on shared cognitive capacities and the sharing of structural properties by the extralinguistic modules that are interfaced with. Evidence for structural analogy is evidence against the structural autonomy of phonology and syntax. It can be argued that indeed sufficient evidence has been presented here for us to claim that any structural distinctiveness attributable to a linguistic module as such is itself severely limited, and substance-dependent.

Certainly, as I have stressed, the demands of analogy are in turn constrained by the different extralinguistic domains with which the two planes interface and by the asymmetrical relation between the two planes themselves. As a means of (re)expression, phonology pre-supposes syntax as well as lexicon. What is to be expressed is much more complex than can be given direct phonetic expression: hence the 'double articulation' of language. Phoneticity rejects certain of the structure types evident in the syntax. But even this encouragement to plane particularity reflects the permeability of both linguistic modules to their respective interfacing extralinguistic domains.

The study that immediately precedes this one in this series of three illustrates interaction between modules within the language system, between the lexicon and the two planes. It looks in particular at the role of the lexicon, not merely as a repository of pairings of categorizations in the alphabets of the planes, but rather as a 'filter' between them. The phenomena involved correspond to what one might want to call 'interactions at the interface'; but the articulation of these interactions involves fundamental properties of each plane. Even relationships among the linguistic modules that are localized at the interface can be scarcely said to be 'marginal' in their effects on fundamental categorizations. Even 'interactions at the interface' compromise the autonomy of modules. But they do so without damaging the basis for modularity, which is the distinctive basic alphabet of each module. The possession by both the planes of language of a distinctive basic substantive alphabet is a fundamental analogy. And modularity is based on this analogy. One should not confuse modularity with autonomy or innateness, however. Modularity can be acquired developmentally, as a result of learning and construction, as is evident from studies of reading and writing. The more interesting hypothesis is that such is also the case with the language module. And analogy is a crucial component in this construction.

General Epilogue

Not much is served either by simply repeating here the individual conclusions to the other studies or, on the other hand, by failing at the end of the trilogy to relate the present volume to those that precede. I want to draw out something of what these studies contribute as a whole, and particularly the common purpose it is my intention that they should be seen to have. This purpose starts from the notion of the substantivity of language, including of its modularization. The purpose is to examine from different aspects of linguistic study the consequences of assuming substantivity. Important here is the establishment of motivations for modularizing; and a further issue has been the extent to which modules are autonomous. The idea of grammar that emerges from these volumes or is confirmed by them is of a set of modules defined by the re-representation that introduces their particular substantive alphabets. In general re-representation is asymmetrical; the exponent does not impinge on what is expressed. We have one-way 'separation'. Modularity is a product of substantive re-representation. A view of language as such a system of substance-driven re-representations—as a complex system of successive expressions—is inimical to the notion of an autonomous universal grammar, as expanded on in Volume I, in particular. Let me try to summarize what I think we can conclude on the basis of the research embodied in this trilogy of volumes.

The basic source of modularization is the lexicon, where there occurs the radical re-representation of exponence—re-representation of content by expression. This is not only asymmetrical but is also in the majority of instances minimally representational, or iconic: only in onomatopoeia and the like does the expression reflect aspects of content. In the lexicon there is grammaticalization of concepts as syntactic categorizations and sounds as phonological categories, and association of instances of the two category types as the poles of linguistic signs. The poles of a sign may be categorially relatively simple or relatively complex. Syntactic categories are usually expounded by more than one phonological segment; the flexibility in range of exponents that this allows is the major benefit of the 'double articulations' established in the lexicon. But it is syntactic elements that most extensively display complexity of internal categorial structure.

In particular, the syntactic pole may be structured by non-linearized dependencies (subjunctions) to show relatedness between lexical items. Further, the primary (distribution-determining) categories are associated with features of secondary categories, either inherently (e.g. a particular gender feature) or facultatively, electively (e.g. choice of tense or aspect). And the secondary categories are notionally appropriate to the primary categories that are their fundamental, natural locus. Thus, inherent, classificatory features are particularly appropriate to entitatives (nouns, pronouns, names), while elective features relate to the dynamic or modal character of prototypical verbs. A further part of categorization is the marking of valency (required complement types) and (facultatively) the potential for modification of another category. And this is particularly characteristic of verbs, whereas prototypical nouns are syntactically inert; and the structures they project are united by agreement rather than the valencies that projected verbal structures. Entitatives and verbals occupy the poles of the categorial dimension of relative referentiality vs. predicativity.

The syntactic categorizations, including these relational indications, are the grammaticalization of the basic substance of syntax; they are the basic alphabet. And they are projected as the structures of the module of syntax. Syntax is driven by (combinations of) categories with a notional substance. And the distributions of the categories are determined by their notionally prototypical members. Non-prototypical members—say nouns based on verbs, whether this relationship is expressed morphologically or not—show distributions contaminated by the presence of an alien category in their make-up. They thus muddy the basic distinctiveness of the behaviour of the different primary categories. Distributions reflect the structures projected by the categories, and these structures themselves introduce distinctive substantively based auxiliary representations—hierarchization, linearity, intonation.

This projection of representations of structure from the categorizations provided by the lexicon is characteristic of both the planes of phonology and syntax—a basic analogy. Thus, dependency relations are introduced in accordance with the categorizations. Substantively, the dependency relations are based on a particular kind of cognitive saliency, a relational saliency. If there is satisfaction of the valencies and modificational potentials of a group of items selected from the lexicon, then they can constitute a predication that is well formed in its dependency configuration (in a fashion familiar from the various implementations of 'categorial grammar'); it is well formed with respect to this submodule of syntax or phonology. The further expression of syntactic and phonological categories is also performed by further substantive-based submodules that interpret categories and their dependency relations in terms of a new auxiliary alphabet.

Some syntactic categorizations are expressed phonologically, particularly by intonation, based on various phonetic parameters. And there is a further submodule that linearizes the exponents of syntax and phonology; this submodule grammaticalizes the perception of ordering in time (or some substitute substance). This submodule interprets the dependency structures, as well as categorization; and the phonological submodule in syntax interprets all of these. As concerns the identification of modularities, the modules of syntax and phonology and their submodules are defined by their distinct substantive alphabets of re-representation. These re-representations cumulatively construct syntactic relationships.

Syntactic categorizations have as lexical exponents—the other poles of the signs—sets of phonological categories. Some complex syntactic categorizations within the lexicon may also be expounded overtly by morphological structure, as illustrated for inflectional distinctions in Volume II of the trilogy. This 'inter plane' of morphology is not associated with a substantive alphabet of its own but introduces bracketings (marking the presence of affixes) or its presence is signalled by 'mutational' phonological differences in the base of the complex form (e.g. by the reflex of '*i*-umlaut'—*foot/feet* etc.). Morphological structure may have other phonological consequences for phonological exponence, such as contributing to the determination of the dependency relations among accents, their location, and their secondary features. We can define the morphological module—and the lexicon in general—as a complex interface. The lexicon contains minimal signs, and it is the poles of only these signs that are extrapolated into the syntax and phonology; it does not contain 'non-signs', alleged linguistic elements with one or both poles missing ('empty' categories).

Likewise, phonology and syntax share structure-building restrictions, such that categories 'don't move', nor does an element change category within these planes. Like the syntax, the phonological module displays submodules that establish dependency structures and linearity, and it too involves phonological distinctions. But the submodules are not necessarily hierarchized in the same way. In this case categories based on perception of phonic substance (rather than cognitive distinctions) form the basic alphabet of the module itself. And the role of the module is to fill out the phonological contrasts supplied by the lexicon and by the syntax, and reconciling the inputs from these two sources, i.e. the contrasts of lexical and sentential phonology.

The substances that syntax and phonology share, such as those that are grammaticalized as dependency and linearity, together with a shared cognitive capacity for structuring, underpin analogies between the two planes, as illustrated in this final study. But the limited, redundancy-filling role of the phonology underlies some of the structural discrepancies that we have found between the two planes, despite these shared submodularities and parallel structural restrictions. This limited role is determined by the directness and specialization of the relation between phonological representations and the perceptions of sound that they grammaticalize.

The individual volumes of the trilogy illustrate and elaborate crucial aspects of this general scheme and the limitations it places on the nature and independence of modules defined in this substance-based way. Thus, Volume I illustrates the fundamental role of categories based on cognitive distinctions in the organization of syntax. It is not just that the characterization and distribution of syntactic categories themselves are based on the cognitive nature of the individual categories—which immediately frustrates homologizing proposals like 'X-bar syntax'—but also that the erection of dependency structures, including 'long-distance' dependencies, is mediated directly by these categories rather than 'movements' and non-signs ('empty' categories). The latter have no substantive basis, and are thus predictably unnecessary. Syntax, like language as a whole, is an expressional system of facilitatory substantive re-representation, not autonomous manipulation—and despite routinizations, de-naturalizations, that are a function of usage.

Crucial in the erection of complex and possibly discontinuous syntactic structures is the role of the free absolutive, whose presence is a grammaticalized response to logical requirements on the predicational representation of cognitive 'scenes' as minimally bipartite ('predicate'–'argument'). Associated with the free absolutive is both the acknowledgement of ectopicities, 'displacements', and the unification of the expression of complex 'scenes' with interrelated components. The role of free absolutives provides an insight into the nature and the limitations on the 'tangling' associated with ectopicities—why they are necessary and what the restrictions on them are, as well as, indeed, the need for restrictiveness.

The free absolutive is one manifestation of the importance for the syntax of the distinction between lexical and functional categories. The latter provide the essential links in the building of structures appropriate to referentiality (determinatives), argument status (functors), and independent sentencehood (operatives). Operatives also bear the secondary features that grammaticalize moods, whose realization has a fundamental effect on sentence structure. Chapter 6 of the first volume illustrates how the realization of finiteness can involve a range of expression types based on different substances—thus, position, intonation, inflection, items dedicated to particular moods. And Volume II displays the interaction in English between the ecphrastic expression of the secondary mood features of finiteness (such as 'question') and the periphrastic expression of other secondary categories (such as aspect).

As discussed in Chapter 5 of the present volume, the functional/lexical distinction among categories—and its absence from phonology—is another factor in restricting the scope for the analogies that are the concern of the volume. It has been illustrated in detail in Volume III as a whole, that the existence of both analogies between syntax and phonology and limitations on analogy are substantively based, not autonomous with respect to extralinguistic mental properties. Analogy is motivated not just by the parallel in submodularization but also by the application to these of the same battery of pattern-seeking and pattern-constructing mental capacities. But, as we have seen, the discrepancy between the respective extralinguistic mental domains that access the phonology and the syntax (in the first place, merely in magnitude alone) and the status of phonology as the bridge, via exponence, to manifestation of linguistic structure as articulation and perception both frustrate some of the potential parallelism in structure between the two planes. Phonology does not need nor can it sustain some of the structural elaboration required by the syntax in the latter's role as representing cognitive 'scenes'. And exponence imposes a one-way 'separation' from syntax, and represents its only access to the latter.

Differentiation of access to extralinguistic domains and to the categories that grammaticalize them is made principally in the lexicon. The set of individual minimal (non-phrasal) lexical items, or minimal signs, embodies the most pervasive manifestation of the asymmetrical exponence relation. Thus, phonological expression does not determine syntactic category, while the syntactic categories that form the functional and expressive morphosyntactic systems of Volume II determine aspects of phonological representation. But the difference between these two systems motivates recognition of the need to accommodate the configurations of syntactic categories to how they are expressed morphologically—as signally in the case of the Old English preterite-present verbs, whose syntactic categorization needs to be 'manipulated' to ensure consistent morphophonological exponence. However, at most, phonological considerations (such as conjugational classes that have a phonological basis—as with the Old English strong verb) are relevant to the rules of expression that interpret these categories in morphological terms, not to the syntactic behaviour of the categories.

But there is at least one way in which even this exponential asymmetry is partially countered, as it were by default. We find in the syntax verbals with valencies whose main or only role (as defined by their categorization) is to compensate for the failure of certain combinations of secondary syntactic features to be given expression in synthetic finites: these verbals are periphrasts. I recall here the characterization of 'progressive *be*' in English, which is dedicated to remedying a gap in the system of morphological representation, namely that progressive is not available to finite lexical verbs:

(II.82)   b. {P/{P;N{prog}}}

A failure in lexical representation is accommodated by the availability of expression in an extralexical domain not otherwise accessible to the morphophonological output of lexical exponence.

Moreover, there is a tendency among 'formal' grammarians to underestimate the role of iconicity in the formation of linguistic structure. It is not just that there are minimal signs where the relationship between the poles of the sign is not completely arbitrary—i.e. the exponence shows the grammaticalization of the natural relationship that we call 'onomatopoeia'. But also it has been variously observed that syntactic structure may grammaticalize an iconic relationship. We looked at a minor instance of this in §2.2 of Volume I in discussing the absence in (I.11) of the infinitival *to* that is otherwise regular with infinitives dependent on a lexical verb:

(I.11)   I saw Bill leave, I heard Bill leave, I felt Bill tremble

There I suggested that the absence of *to* with these verbs of direct perception, and thus the juxtaposition of perception verb, perceived entity, and perceived event, highlights the simultaneity of the perception of Bill and the perceived event involving Bill.

But perhaps the most striking 'leak back' running counter to the exponence relation is the temporal one whereby the linguistic structures that grammaticalize our cognition provide templates for the interpretation of new experience. The most salient manifestation of this is in the coining of metaphors. It seems that some kind of tempered 'Sapir-Whorf' view can be maintained, such that on our understanding of experience a 'linguistic grid' is imposed, and reimposed, 'figuratively', in other domains, to varying extents. Language is not a 'passive' re-representation. A range of recent work on the interaction between cognition and language is adding weight to such view. In individual cases of figurative extension, how enlightening rather than simply distorting or distortion-preserving is such redeployment of linguistic structure in a new domain depends on the accuracy of the perception and the success of the imagination that gives rise to it. Other communicative and social motivations underlie the prevalence of reliance on routinization, on formulae, that counter balances attempts at innovation.

This takes us into another well-trodden but poorly understood kind of interfacing, that involving speakers' negotiations concerning their individual representations of what they think they perceive. A deeper understanding of this interfacing will eventually enable us to gain insight into language as a figurative device, a device that enables the activation, de-activation (routinization), and reactivation of the figures that drive linguistic structure. Such a figurative capacity is not adequately simulated as or by the kind of computational device that grammar is commonly conceived to be. Pursuit of the latter in an effort to understand figurativeness would be to compound the errors of the past.

For something went drastically wrong with the scholarly study of language in the course of the twentieth century. A prominent aspect of the project that runs through these volumes is the attempt to recover what the twentieth century deprived us of, with the help of tools that the twentieth century has provided, including the notions of 'structure' and 'structuralism'—as long as we recognize the basis of structure in substance. This is the kernel of what we have lost, and is what needs re-recognition. The sterility of much of modern linguistics derives in large part from a 'wrong turning' that deprived it of an awareness as students of language of where we come from—which engendered an unhealthy diachronic parochialism that has continued to repeat itself in microcosm into the present century. In evaluating the present, an important, I would say essential, perspective is afforded by a knowledge of the past.

A major factor in this 'wrong turning' was the insistence on autonomy of various sorts by the early structuralists and, increasingly, by their successors. This general insistence on the autonomy of language and its study was understandable early in the twentieth century, at a period when the study of language was still pervaded by pseudo-logical and pseudo-psychological terminology masquerading as description of language. But it resulted, again increasingly, in the rejection, as relevant to the understanding and characterizing of the structure of language, of general cognitive and perceptual capacities that it is now, increasingly, being discovered are highly pertinent.

The autonomy of the study of language, however, does not depend on this rejection. The structure of language grammaticalizes the substances that it represents, as a result of the nature of representation itself, which reflects the needs of a complex system principally devoted to the expression of our conception of complex situations in a form that can be accommodated to perceptual capacities and their temporal implementation. Nor does the study of syntax require its isolation from other aspects of language; indeed, it is impossible to construct a credible theory of syntax based on such a premise.

The present volumes do not argue for some post-structuralist approach to language. Nor, I hope, do they reveal an underestimation of the manifold insights that emerged in the course of the last century—despite, rather than because (as is often assumed), the climate of strict separation of syntax and semantics that prevailed. Rather, the volumes are intended to direct our attention to what we can learn from pre-structural attitudes to language—to what we largely lost in the course of the twentieth century, as a result of the discrediting of pre-twentieth-century linguistics. Our ignorance of the past is great—despite the fine, but often ignored, historiographic work that has been done. And it is not enlightened by misguided uncontextualized attempts to discover precursors among a few scholars of the past, attempts which result in misrepresentation of the history of our discipline and our relationship to it.

Apart from an understanding of what to eschew, there is much of positive value that we have learnt from the twentieth century—in terms of, for instance, better understanding of the formal properties of the representational structures that characterize language, and improvements in fieldwork and corpus techniques for investigation. It is my view that, taken together with this, and in the context of deepening knowledge of language diversity, the combination of a proper diffidence towards present understanding and an awareness of the past and what it came to understand about language offers an exciting future to the present-day student of language and languages.

The present volumes are an attempt to give some substance to that view. Whether this attempt has succeeded in this and also fulfilled the common and complementary aims set out initially in each prologue is for the reader to judge, of course. For my part, what we have looked at suggests that, given certain pre-disposing physiological developments, the evolution of language itself is a cultural rather than a biological phenomenon.

One thing that does seem clear is that adoption of the view of language as a cultural artefact means that talk of the 'language faculty' or 'linguistic competence' vs. 'performance' does not make much sense—as opposed to acknowledging the varying strengths in learners of the impulse to acquire language and their varying competency in the use of language, and indeed in its acquisition. When we use the internalized cultural entity that is language, we deploy, or perform with, a bundle of capacities that are not specifically linguistic, and whose composition can vary in accordance with what aspects of language are being used, and for what purpose. Thus, in assembling a sentence from a selected set of lexical entries, we can, on the basis of notional categories, call upon such general cognitive capacities as memory and the ability both to build structure and to conceptualize recursion and discontinuity therein. And clearly individuals internalize the cultural entity to varying extents and vary not just in the skill with which they deploy it but also in the version they have internalized. These are further aspects of the language variability whose investigation is the main concern of linguistics, along with the extent of the correlation with substance of language structure and its variation.

References

Ackema, P., Brandt, P., Schoorlemmer, M., and Weerman, F. (2006). *Arguments and Agreement*. Oxford: Oxford University Press.

Adger, D., Pintzuk, S., Plunkett, B., and Tsoulas, G. (eds.) (1999). *Specifiers: Minimalist Approaches*. Oxford: Oxford University Press.

Agutter, A. J. L. (1988a). 'The not-so-Scottish vowel length rule', in Anderson and Macleod (eds.), 120–32.

——(1988b). 'The dangers of dialect parochialism: The Scottish vowel length rule', in J. Fisiak (ed.), *Historical Dialectology*, 1–21. Berlin: Mouton de Gruyter.

Aissen, J. (1979). *The Syntax of Causative Constructions*. New York: Garland.

Aitken, A. J. (1981). 'The Scottish vowel-length rule', in M. Benskin and M. L. Samuels (eds.), *So Meny People Longages and Tonges*, 131–57. Edinburgh: Benskin & Samuels.

Anderson, J. M. (1972). 'Remarks on the hierarchy of quasi-predications', *Revue roumaine de linguistique* 17: 23–44, 121–40, 193–202, 319–35.

——(1973a). 'The ghost of times past', *Foundations of Language* 9: 481–91.

——(1973b). 'On existence and the perfect', *Foundations of Language* 10: 333–7.

——(1976a). *On Serialisation in English Syntax*. Ludwigsburg: Ludwigsburg Studies in Language and Linguistics, 1.

——(1976b). 'Perfect possibilities and existential constraints', *Studia Anglica Posnaniensia* 7: 3–6.

——(1977). *On Case Grammar: Prolegomena to a Theory of Grammatical Relations*. London: Croom Helm.

——(1984). *Case Grammar and the Lexicon*. University of Ulster Occasional Papers in Linguistics and Language Learning, no. 10.

——(1985). 'Structural analogy and dependency phonology', *Acta Linguistica Hafniensia* 19: 5–44. (Revised version in Anderson, J. and Durand, J. (1986). *Explorations in Dependency Phonology*, 55–133. Dordrecht: Foris.)

——(1986a). 'Suprasegmental dependencies', in J. Durand (ed.), *Dependency and Non-linear Phonology*, 55–133. London: Croom Helm.

——(1986b). 'The English prosody /h/', in D. Kastovsky and A. Szwedek (eds.), *Linguistics across Historical and Geographical Boundaries*, 799–809. Berlin: Mouton de Gruyter.

——(1986c). 'Structural analogy and case grammar', *Lingua* 70: 79–129.

——(1987a). 'The limits of linearity', in Anderson and Durand (eds.), 169–90.

——(1987b). 'The tradition of structural analogy', in R. Steele and T. Threadgold (eds.), *Language Topics: Essays in Honour of Michael Halliday*, 33–43. Amsterdam: John Benjamins.

——(1988a). 'System geometry and segment structure: A question of Scots economy', *NELS* 18, 22–37.

——(1988b). 'More on slips and syllable structure', *Phonology* 5: 157–9.

Anderson, J. M. (1988c). 'The type of Old English impersonals', in Anderson and Macleod (eds.), 1–32.

——(1988d). 'Old English ablaut again: The essentially concrete character of dependency phonology', in C. Duncan-Rose and T. Vennemann (eds.), *On Language: Rhetorica, Phonologica, Syntactica—A Festschrift for Robert P. Stockwell from his Friends and Colleagues*, 161–82. London: Routledge.

——(1990). 'On the status of auxiliaries in notional grammar', *Journal of Linguistics* 26: 341–62.

——(1991). 'Kabardian disemvowelled, again', *Studia Linguistica* 45: 18–48.

——(1992). *Linguistic Representation: Structural Analogy and Stratification*. Berlin: Mouton de Gruyter.

——(1993). 'Morphology, phonology and the Scottish vowel-length rule', *Journal of Linguistics* 29: 419–30.

——(1994). 'Contrastivity and non-specification in a dependency phonology of English', *Studia Anglica Posnaniensia* 28: 3–35.

——(1997a). *A Notional Theory of Syntactic Categories*. Cambridge: Cambridge University Press.

——(1997b). 'English phonology: Theoretical, clinical and medieval', in J. L. Chamoza and T. Guzmán (eds.), *Studies in Middle English Language and Literature*, 9–29. Oviedo: University of Oviedo.

——(2000). 'Markedness and the ontogenesis of syntax', *Folia Linguistica* 34: 147–83.

——(2001a). 'A major restructuring in the English consonant system: The de-linearization of [h] and the de-consonantization of [w] and [j]', *English Language and Linguistics* 5: 199–212.

——(2001b). 'Modals, subjunctives and (non-)finiteness', *English Language and Linguistics* 5, 159–66.

——(2001c). 'Finiteness, in Greek, and elsewhere', *Poznań Studies in Contemporary Linguistics* 37: 5–33.

——(2004a). 'Contrast in phonology, structural analogy, and the interfaces', *Studia Linguistica* 58: 269–97.

——(2004b). 'Syntactic categories and syntactic change: The development of subjunctive periphrases in English', in B. Crespo and I. Moskowich (eds.), *New Trends in Historical Linguistics: An Atlantic View*, 31–73. Universidade da Coruña.

——(2005a). 'Structuralism and autonomy: From Saussure to Chomsky', *Historiographia Linguistica* 32: 117–48.

——(2005b). 'The argument structure of morphological causatives', *Poznań Studies in Contemporary Linguistics* 40: 27–89.

——(2005c). 'Old English *I*-umlaut (for the umpteenth time)', *English Language and Linguistics* 9: 195–227.

——(2006a). 'Structural analogy and universal grammar', *Lingua* 116: 601–33.

——(2006b). *Modern Grammars of Case: A Retrospective*. Oxford: Oxford University Press.

——(2007). *The Grammar of Names*. Oxford: Oxford University Press.

―― (2008). 'A case of functional equivalence' in J. Andor, B. Hollósy, T. Laczkó, and P. Pelyvás (eds.), *When Grammar Minds Language and Literature: Festschrift for Prof. Béla Korponay on the Occasion of his 80th Birthday*, 45–63. Debrecen: Institute of English and American Studies, University of Debrecen.

―― and Durand, J. (1986). Introduction to Anderson and Durand (eds.), 1–13.

――――(eds.) (1986). *Explorations in Dependency Phonology*. Dordrecht: Foris.

――――(1988a). 'Underspecification and dependency phonology', in P. M. Bertinetto and M. Loporcaro (eds.), *Certamen Phonologicum: Papers from the 1987 Cortona Phonology Meeting*, 3–36. Turin: Rosenberg & Sellier.

――――(1988b). 'Vowel harmony and non-specification in Nez Perce', in H. G. van der Hulst and N. S. H. Smith (eds.), *Features, Segmental Structure and Harmony Processes, II*, 1–17. Dordrecht: Foris.

――――(1993). 'Segments non-spécifiés et sous-spécifiés en phonologie de dépendance: le yawelmani et les autres dialectes de yokuts', in B. Laks and A. Rialland (eds.), *Architecture et géométrie des représentations phonologiques*, 233–53. Paris: Editions du CNRS.

――and Ewen, C. J. (1987). *Principles of Dependency Phonology*. Cambridge: Cambridge University Press.

――――and Staun, J. (1985). 'Phonological structure: Segmental, suprasegmental and extrasegmental', *Phonology Yearbook* 2: 203–24.

――and Jones, C. (1974). 'Three theses concerning phonological representations', *Journal of Linguistics* 10: 1–26.

――――(eds.) (1974). *Historical Linguistics II: Theory and Description in Phonology*, 311–52. Amsterdam: North-Holland.

――and Macleod, N. (eds.) (1988). *Edinburgh Studies in the English Language*. Edinburgh: John Donald.

Anderson, L. B. (1975). 'Phonetic and psychological explanation for vowel harmony, especially in Finnish'. Ph.D. dissertation, University of Chicago.

――(1980). 'Using asymmetrical and gradient data in the study of vowel harmony', in Vago (ed.), 271–340.

Anderson, S.R. (1980). 'Problems and perspectives in the description of vowel harmony', in R. Vago (ed.) *Issues in Vowel Harmony*, 1–48. Amsterdam: Benjamins.

Anderson, S.R. (1985). 'Inflectional morphology', in T. Shopen (ed.) (1985b), 150–201.

Archangeli, D. and Langendoen, D. T. (eds.) (1997). *Optimality Theory: An Overview*. Oxford & Malden, MA: Blackwell.

Aronoff, M. (1992). 'Segmentalism in linguistics: The alphabetic basis of phonological theory', in P. Downing, S. D. Lima, and M. Noonan (eds.), *The Linguistics of Literacy*, 71–82. Amsterdam: John Benjamins.

Arrivé, M. and Ablali, D. (2000). 'Hjelmslev et Martinet: Correspondance, traduction, problèmes théoriques', *Bulletin de la Société de Linguistique de Paris* 37: 33–57.

Aurnague, M. and Durand, J. (2003). 'Quelques aspects de la phonologie du français au Pays Basque', *La tribune internationale des langues vivantes* 33: 110–16.

Aurnague, M. and Durand, J. and Eychenne, J. (2004). 'La phonologie du français contemporain au Pays basque et son contexte sociolinguistique', in M. P. Perea (ed.), *Dialectologia i recursos informatics*, 155–98. Barcelona: Promociones y Publicaciones Universitarias.

Austin, F. (1984). 'Double negatives and the eighteenth century', in N. F. Blake and C. Jones (eds.), *English Historical Linguistics: Studies in Development*, 138–48. Sheffield: The Centre for English Cultural Tradition and Language, University of Sheffield.

Bache, C. (1978). *The Order of Pre-modifying Adjectives in Present-day English*. Odense: Odense University Press.

Basbøll. H. (2005). *The Phonology of Danish*. Oxford: Oxford University Press.

Bauer, L. (1994). 'Structural analogy: An examination of some recent claims', *Studies in Language* 18: 1–22.

Bazell, C. E. (1949a). 'On the neutralisation of syntactic oppositions', in C. A. Bodelsen, P. Diderichsen, E. Fischer-Jørgensen, and J. Holt (eds.), *Recherches structurales* 1949, 77–86. (Travaux du cercle linguistique de Copenhague, V.) [Reprinted in Hamp, Householder, and Austerlitz (eds.), 208–15.]

——(1949b). 'On the problem of the morpheme', *Archivum Linguisticum* 1: 1–15. [Reprinted in Hamp, Householder and Austerlitz (eds.), 216–26.]

——(1954). 'The sememe', *Litera* (Istanbul) 1: 17–31. [Reprinted in Hamp, Householder, and Austerlitz, (eds.), 329–40.]

——(1956). 'The grapheme', *Litera* (Istanbul) 3: 43–6. [Reprinted in Hamp, Householder, and Austerlitz, (eds.), 359–61.]

Bermúdez-Otero, R. and Börjars, K. (2006). 'Markedness in phonology and syntax: the problem of grounding', *Lingua* 116: 710–56.

Bickerton, D. (2000). 'Calls aren't words, syllables aren't syntax': Review of Carstairs McCarthy 1999. *Psycholoquy* 11, 114, 2.

Bird, S. and Klein, E. (1990). 'Phonological events', *Journal of Linguistics* 26: 33–56.

Blevins, J. (1995). 'The syllable in phonological theory', in Goldsmith (ed.), 206–44.

Bloch, B. (1941). 'Phonemic overlapping', *American Speech* 16: 278–84. [Reprinted in Joos (ed.), 93–6.]

Boas, F. (1911). *Introduction to the Handbook of American Indian Languages*. Washington, DC.

Böhm, R. (1993). 'Predicate-argument structure, relational typology and (anti) passives: Towards an integrated localist case grammar account'. Duisburg: LAUD, Series A. No. 336.

——(1994). 'Deriving derived intransitivity: Structural analogy and mutation vs. mutilation of lexical argument structure', presented 16/06/94 at the Institute for Functional Language Research, University of Amsterdam.

Bolinger, D. L. (1967). 'Adjectives in English: Attribution and predication', *Lingua* 18: 1–34.

——(1972). *Degree Words*. The Hague: Mouton.

Borgstrøm, C. H. (1940). *The Dialects of the Outer Hebrides*. (= A Linguistic Survey of the Gaelic Dialects of Scotland, vol. 1.) [= Supplementary volume, *Norsk Tidskrift för Sprogvidenskap*.] Oslo: H. Aschehoug.

Breen, G. and Pensalfini, R. (1999). 'Arrernte: A language with no syllable onsets', *Linguistic Inquiry* 30: 1–25.

Bresnan, J. (2000). 'Optional syntax', in J. Dekkers, F. van der Leeuw, and J. van de Weijer (eds.), *Optimality Theory: phonology. Syntax, and Acquisition*, 334–85. Oxford: Oxford University Press.

Bromberger, S. and Halle, M. (1989). 'Why phonology is different', *Linguistic Inquiry* 20: 51–70.

——(2000). 'The ontology of phonology', in N. Burton-Roberts, P. Carr, and G. Docherty (eds.), 19–37. [Revised version of ch. 9 of Sylvain Bromberger, *On What We Know We Don't Know*. CSLI Publications, Stanford University, Stanford, CA, 1992.]

Browman, C. P. and Goldstein, L. (1986). 'Towards an articulatory phonology', *Phonology Yearbook* 3: 219–52.

——(1988). 'Some notes on syllable structure in articulatory phonology', *Phonetica* 45: 140–55.

——(1992). 'Articulatory phonology: An overview', *Phonetica* 45: 155–80.

Brunner, K. (1965). *Altenglische Grammatik, nach der angelsächsische Grammatik von Eduard Sievers*, 3rd edn. Tübingen: Niemeyer.

Burton-Roberts, N. (2000). 'Where and what is Phonology? A representational perspective', in Burton-Roberts, Carr, and Docherty (eds.), 39–66.

——Carr, P., and Docherty, G. (eds.) (2000). *Phonological Knowledge: Conceptual and Empirical Issues*. Oxford: Oxford University Press.

Cairns, C. E. and Feinstein, M. (1982). 'Markedness and the theory of syllable structure', *Linguistic Inquiry* 13, 193–255.

Campbell, A. (1959). *Old English Grammar*. London: Oxford University Press.

Carden, G. (1973). *English Quantifiers: Logical Structure and Linguistic Variation*. Tokyo: Taishukan.

Carr, P. (1990). *Linguistic Realities*. Cambridge: Cambridge University Press.

——(1992). 'Strict cyclicity, structure preservation and the Scottish vowel-length rule', *Journal of Linguistics* 28: 91–114.

——(1993). *Phonology*. London: Macmillan.

——(2000). 'Scientific realism, sociophonetic variation, and innate endowments in phonology', in Burton-Roberts, Carr, and Docherty (eds.), 67–104.

——(2005). 'Salience, headhood and analogies', in Carr, Durand, and Ewen (eds.), 15–30.

——(2006). 'Universal grammar and syntax/phonology parallelisms', *Lingua* 116: 634–56.

——Durand, J., and Ewen, C. J. (eds.) (2005). *Headhood, Elements, Specification, and Contrast*. Amsterdam & Philadelphia: John Benjamins.

Carstairs-McCarthy, A. (1998). 'Synonymy avoidance, phonology and the origin of syntax', in J. Hurford, M. Studdert-Kennedy, and C. Knight (eds.), *Approaches to the Evolution of Language: Social and Cognitive Bases*, 279–96. Cambridge: Cambridge University Press.

——(1999). *The Origins of Complex Language: An Inquiry into the Evolutionary Beginnings of Sentences, Syllables, and Truth*. Oxford: Oxford University Press.

Catford, J. C. (1977). 'Mountain tongues: The languages of the Caucasus', *Annual Review of Anthropology* 6: 283–314.

Chadwick, N. (1975). *A Descriptive Study of the Djingili Language*. Canberra: Australian Institute of Aboriginal Studies.

Chatman, S. (1960). 'Pre-adjectivals in the English nominal phrase', *American Speech* 35: 83–99.

Chomsky, N. (1957). *Syntactic Structures*. The Hague: Mouton.

——(1965). *Aspects of the Theory of Syntax*. Cambridge, MA: MIT Press.

——(1970). 'Remarks on nominalization', in R. A. Jacobs and P. S. Rosenbaum (eds.), *Readings in English Transformational Grammar*, 184–221. Waltham, MA: Ginn.

——(1973). 'Conditions on transformations', in S. R. Anderson and P. Kiparsky (eds.), *A Festschrift for Morris Halle*, 232–86. New York: Holt, Rinehart & Winston.

——(1981). *Lectures on Government and Binding: The Pisa Lectures*. Dordrecht: Foris.

——(1986). *Barriers*. Cambridge, MA: MIT Press.

——(1993). *Language and Thought*. Rhode Island: Moyer Bell.

——(1995). *The Minimalist Program*. Cambridge, MA: MIT Press.

——and Halle, M. (1968). *The Sound Pattern of English*. New York: Harper & Row.

————and Lukoff, F. (1956). 'On accent and juncture in English', in M. Halle et al. (eds.), *For Roman Jakobson*, 65–80. The Hague: Mouton.

——and Lasnik, H. (1977). 'Filters and control', *Linguistic Inquiry* 8: 425–504.

Chung, S. and Timberlake, A. (1985). 'Tense, aspect, and mood', in Shopen (ed.) (1985b), 202–58.

Clark, E. and Clark, H. (1979). 'When nouns surface as verbs', *Language* 55: 767–811.

Clements, G. N. (1981). 'The hierarchical representation of tone features', in I. R. Dihoff (ed.), *Current Approaches to African Linguistics*, vol. 1, 145–76. Dordrecht: Foris.

——and Hume, E. V. (1995). 'The internal organization of speech sounds', in Goldsmith (ed.), 245–306.

——and Keyser, S. J. (1983). *CV Phonology: A Generative Theory of the Syllable*. Cambridge, MA: MIT Press.

——and Sezer, E. (1982). 'Vowel and consonant disharmony in Turkish', in H. G. van der Hulst and N. S. H. Smith (eds.), *The Structure of Phonological Representations, II*, 213–55. Dordrecht: Foris.

Coleman, J. (1992). 'The phonetic interpretation of headed phonological structures containing overlapping constituents', *Phonology* 9: 1–44.

——(1995). 'Declarative lexical phonology', in J. Durand and F. Katamba (eds.), *Frontiers of Phonology: Atoms, Structures, Derivations*, 333–82. London: Longman.

Colman, F. (1983). 'Old English /a/ ≠ /æ/ or [a] ~ [æ]?', *Folia Linguistica Historica* 4: 265–85.

——(2005). 'Old English *I*-umlaut: Dependency, contrast and non-specification', in Carr, Durand, and Ewen (eds.), 31–62.

——and Anderson, J. M. (2004). 'On metonymy as word-formation: With special reference to Old English', *English Studies* 85: 547–65.

Comrie, B. (1976). *Aspect*. Cambridge: Cambridge University Press.
——(1981). *The Languages of the Soviet Union*. Cambridge: Cambridge University Press.
——(1985). 'Causative verb formation and other verb-deriving morphology', in Shopen (ed.) (1985b), 309–48.
——(1986). 'Tense in indirect speech', *Folia Linguistica* 20: 265–96.
Corbett, G. G. (2000). *Number*. Cambridge: Cambridge University Press.
Croft, W. (2001). *Radical Construction Grammar: Syntactic Theory in Typological Perspective*. Oxford: Oxford University Press.
Crowley, T. (2002). *Serial Verbs in Oceanic: A Descriptive Typology*. Oxford: Oxford University Press.
Crystal, D. (1969). *Prosodic Systems and Intonation in English*. Cambridge: Cambridge University Press.
Culicover, P. W., Wasow, T., and Akmajian, A. (eds.) (1977). *Formal Syntax*. New York: Academic Press.
Dahl, Ö. (1985). *Tense and Aspect Systems*. Oxford: Blackwell.
Declerck, R. (1988). 'Sequence of tenses in English', Faculteit Letteren en Wijsbegeerte K. U. Leuven Campus Kortrijk, preprint no. 53.
Demirdache, H. and Matthewson, L. (1995). 'On the universality of syntactic categories', *NELS* 25, 79–94.
Denton, J. M., Chan, G. P., and Canakis, C. P. (eds.) (1992). *Papers from the 28th Regional Meeting of the Chicago Linguistic Society, 2: The Cycle in Linguistic Theory*. Chicago Linguistic Society.
Derbyshire, D. C. (1979). *Hixkaryana*. Amsterdam: North-Holland.
Dinnsen, D. A., Chin, S. B., Elbert, M., and Powell, T. W. (1990). 'Some constraints on functionally disordered phonologies: Phonetic inventories and phonotactics', *Journal of Speech and Hearing Research* 33: 28–37.
Dixon, R. M. W. (1982). *Where have All the Adjectives Gone?* Berlin: de Gruyter.
Donegan, P. (1978). 'On the natural phonology of vowels'. Ph.D. dissertation, Ohio State University.
Durand, J. (1976). 'Generative phonology, dependency phonology and Southern French', *Lingua e stile* 11: 3–23.
——(1990). *Generative and Non-linear phonology*. London: Longman.
——(1995). 'Universalism in phonology: Atoms, structures and derivations', in Durand and Katamba (eds.), 267–88.
——(2009). 'Essai de panorama critique des accents du midi', in L. Baronian and F. Martineau (eds.), *Le français, d'un continent à l'autre : Mélanges offerts à Yves Charles Morin*, 123–70. (Collection Les Voies du français.) Québec: Presses de l'Université Laval.
——and Katamba, F. (eds.) (1995). *Frontiers of Phonology: Atoms, Structures, Derivations*, 34–79. London: Longman.
van Eijk, J. and Hess, T. (1986). 'Noun and verb in Salish', *Lingua* 69: 319–31.

Eimas, P. D., Siqueland, E. R., Jusczyk, P., and Vigorito, J. (1971). 'Speech perception in infants', *Science* 171: 303–18.
Emonds, J. (1976). *A Transformational Approach to English Syntax: Root, Structure-Preserving and Local Transformations*. New York: Academic Press.
——(1987). 'Parts of speech in generative grammar', *Linguistic Analysis* 17: 3–41.
Everett, D. (2010). 'The shrinking Chomskyan corner: A reply to Nevins, Pesetsky, Rodrigues', available at: <http://llc.illinoisstate.edu/dlevere/research/Recursion.shtml>.
Ewen, C. J. (1977). 'Aitken's Law and the phonatory gesture in dependency phonology', *Lingua* 41: 307–29.
Eychenne, J. (2006). 'Aspects de la phonologie du schwa dans le français contemporain: Optimalité, visibilité prosodique, gradience'. Ph.D. thesis, University of Toulouse-le-Mirail.
Faber, A. (1992). 'Phonemic segmentation as epiphenomenal: Evidence from the history of alphabetic writing', in P. Downing, S. D. Lima, and M. Noonan (eds.), *The Linguistics of Literacy*, 111–34. Amsterdam: John Benjamins.
Fanselow, G., Fery, C., Schesewsky, M., and Fogel, R. (eds.) (2006). *Gradience in Grammar: Generative Perspectives*. Oxford: Oxford University Press.
Farkas, D. (1986). 'On the syntactic position of focus in Hungarian', *Natural Language and Linguistic Theory* 4: 77–96.
Firth, J. R. (1948). 'Sounds and prosodies', *Transactions of the Philological Society*, 127–52. [Reprinted in J. R. Firth, *Papers in Linguistics 1934–1951*, 121–38. London: Oxford University Press, 1957.]
Fischer, O. (1992). 'Syntax', in N. F. Blake (ed.), *The Cambridge History of the English Language, II: 1066–1476*, 207–408. Cambridge: Cambridge University Press.
——Kemenade, A. van, Koopman, W., and Wurff, W. van der (2000). *The Syntax of Early English*. Cambridge: Cambridge University Press.
Fischer-Jørgensen, E. (1952). 'Glossematics'. Lecture given to the Washington Linguistics Club.
Fitch, W. T., Hauser, M. D., and Chomsky, N. (2005). 'The evolution of the language faculty: Clarifications and implications', *Cognition* 97: 179–210.
Gazdar, G., Klein, E., Pullum, G. K., and Sag, I. A. (1985). *Generalized Phrase Structure Grammar*. Oxford: Basil Blackwell.
Giegerich, H. J. (1992). *English Phonology: An Introduction*. Cambridge: Cambridge University Press.
——(1999). *Lexical Strata in English: Morphological Causes, Phonological Effects*. Cambridge: Cambridge University Press.
Gil, D. and Radzinsky, D. (1984). 'Georgian syllable onsets: Some arguments for unordered hierarchic phonological structures', presented at the Fifth International Phonology Meeting, Eisenstadt.
Goldsmith, J. A. (1990). *Autosegmental and Metrical Phonology*. Oxford: Blackwell.
——(ed.) (1995). *The Handbook of Phonological Theory*. Oxford: Blackwell.

Golston, C. (1995). 'Syntax outranks phonology: Evidence from Ancient Greek', *Phonology* 12: 343–68.
Goyvaerts, D. L. (1968). 'An introductory study on the ordering of a string of adjectives in present-day English', *Philologica Pragensia* 1: 12–28.
Haegeman, L. (1991). *Introduction to Government and Binding Theory*, 1st edn. Oxford: Blackwell.
—— and Guéron, J. (1999). *English Grammar: A Generative Perspective*. Oxford: Blackwell.
Hale, K. (1983). 'Warlpiri and the grammar of non-configurational languages', *Natural Language and Linguistic Theory* 1: 5–47.
—— and Keyser, S. J. (2002). *Prolegomena to a Theory of Argument Structure*. Cambridge, MA: MIT Press.
—— and White Eagle, J. (1980). 'A preliminary metrical account of Winnebago accent', *International Journal of American Linguistics* 46: 117–32.
Hale, M. and Reiss, C. (2000a). 'Phonology as cognition', in Burton-Roberts, Carr, and Docherty (eds.), 161–84.
————(2000b). 'Substance abuse and dysfunctionalism: Current trends in phonology', *Linguistic Inquiry* 31: 157–69.
Hall, T. A. (2001). 'The distribution of superheavy syllables in Modern English', *Folia Linguistica* 35: 399–442.
Halle, M. (1964). 'On the bases of phonology', in J. A. Fodor and J. J. Katz (eds.), *The Structure of Language: Readings in the Philosophy of Language*, 324–33. Englewood Cliffs, NJ: Prentice-Hall.
——(1970). 'Is Kabardian a vowel-less language?' *Foundations of Language* 6: 95–103.
—— and Idsardi, W. (1995). 'General properties of stress and metrical structures', in Goldsmith (ed.), 403–43.
—— and Vergnaud, J.-R. (1981). 'Harmony Processes', in W. Klein and W. Levelt (eds.), *Crossing the Boundaries in Linguistics*. Dordrecht: Reidel.
————(1987). *An Essay on Stress*. Cambridge, MA: MIT Press.
Halliday, M. A. K. (1961). 'Categories of the theory of grammar', *Word* 17: 241–92.
——(1966). 'The concept of rank: A reply', *Journal of Linguistics* 2: 110–18.
——(1967). *Intonation and Grammar in British English*. The Hague: Mouton.
——(1994). *An Introduction to Functional Grammar*, 2nd edn. London: Arnold.
Hamp, E., Householder, F. W., and Austerlitz, R. (eds.) (1966). *Readings in Linguistics II*. Chicago: University of Chicago Press.
Harms, R. T. (1968). *Introduction to Phonological Theory*. Englewood Cliffs, NJ: Prentice-Hall.
Harris, J. and Lindsay, G. (1995). 'The elements of phonological representation', in Durand and Katamba (eds.), 34–79.
Hauser, M. D., Chomsky, N., and Fitch, W. T. (2002). 'The faculty of language: What is it, who has it and how did it evolve?', *Science* 298: 1569–79.
Heijkoop, A. C. (1997). 'Underspecification and contrast: Consonant harmony in early language acquisition', in A. Sorace, C. Heycock, and R. Shillcock (eds.), *Proceedings of the GALA '97 Conference on Language Acquisition*, 23–9. Edinburgh: HCRC, University of Edinburgh.

Heijkoop, A. C. (1998). 'The early acquisition of segment specification: The evolution of the child's phonological system, in particular the development of the articulatory and categorial gesture, with special reference to English and Dutch'. Ph.D. thesis, University of Edinburgh.

Hind, K. (1997). 'Phonologising articulatory phonology'. Ph.D. thesis, University of Edinburgh.

Hjelmslev, L. (1937). 'La syllabation en slave', in *Mélanges Aleksander Belic*, 315–24. Belgrade.

——(1938). 'Essai d'une théorie des morphèmes', in K. Barr et al. (eds.), *Actes du quatrième Congrès International de Linguistes*, 140–51. Copenhagen: Munksgaard. [Reprinted in L. Hjelmslev (1959), 152–64.]

——(1939). 'The syllable as a structural unit', in *Proceedings of the Third International Congress of Phonetic Sciences*, 266–72. Ghent.

——(1953). *Prolegomena to a Theory of Language*. Madison: University of Wisconsin Press. [Translated by Francis J. Whitfield from *Omkring sprogteoriens grundlæggelse*, Ejnar Munksgaard, Copenhagen, 1943.]

——(1954). 'La stratification du langage', *Word* 10: 163–88. [Reprinted in Hjelmslev (1959), 36–68.]

——(1959). *Essais linguistiques*. (= *Travaux du cercle linguistique de Copenhague* XII.) Copenhagen: Naturmetodens Sproginstitut, Nordisk Sprog- og Kulturforlag.

Hogg, R. M. (1992). *Old English Grammar*. Oxford: Oxford University Press.

Holton, D., Mackridge, P., and Philippaki-Warburton, I. (1997). *Greek: A Comprehensive Grammar of the Modern Language*. London: Routledge.

Hopper, P. J. and Traugott, E. (1993). *Grammaticalization*. Cambridge: Cambridge University Press.

Huddleston, R. D. (1969). 'Some observations on tense and deixis in English', *Language* 45: 777–806.

Hulst, H. G. van der (1988a). 'The dual interpretation of |i|, |u| and |a|', in J. Blevins and J. Carter (eds.), *Proceedings from NELS 18*, vol. 1. Amherst: GLSA.

——(1988b). 'The geometry of vocalic features', in H. van der Hulst and N. S. H. Smith (eds.), *Features, Segmental Structure and Harmony Processes*, part II, 77–125. Dordrecht: Foris.

——(1989). 'Atoms of segmental structure: Components, gestures and dependency', *Phonology* 6: 253–84.

——(1994). 'Radical CV phonology: The locational gesture', *UCL Working Papers in Linguistics* 6: 439–77.

——(1995). 'Radical CV phonology: The categorial gesture', in Durand and Katamba (eds.), 80–116.

——(2000). 'Modularity and modality in phonology', in Burton-Roberts, Carr, and Docherty (eds.), 207–43.

——(2005). 'The molecular structure of phonological segments', in Carr, Durand, and Ewen (eds.), 193–234.

——and Ritter, R. (1999). 'Head-driven phonology', in H. G. van der Hulst and N. Ritter (eds.), *The Syllable: Views and Facts*, 113–68. Berlin: Mouton de Gruyter.

——and Smith, N. S. H. (1985). 'Vowel features and umlaut in Djingili, Nyangumarda and Warlpiri', *Phonology Yearbook* 2: 277–303.

——and van de Weijer, J. (1990). 'Topics in Turkish phonology', in H. E. Boeschoten and L. T. Verhoeven (eds.), *Structure and Use of Turkish*. Leiden: E. J. Brill.

————(1995). 'Vowel harmony', in Goldsmith (ed.), 495–534.

Jackendoff, R. S. (1977a). 'Constraints on phrase structure rules', in Culicover, Wasow, and Akmajian (eds.), 249–83.

——(1977b). *X′ Syntax: A Study of Phrase Structure*. Cambridge, MA: MIT Press.

——(1990). *Semantic Structures*. Cambridge, MA: MIT Press.

——and Pinker, S. (2005). 'The nature of the language faculty and its implications for evolution of language', *Cognition* 97: 211–25.

Jacobsen, W. (1979). 'Noun and verb in Nootkan', in B. Efrat (ed.), *The Victoria Conference on Northwestern Languages, 1976*, 83–155. British Columbia Provincial Museum, Heritage Record no. 4.

Jakobson, R., Fant, G., and Halle, M. (1952). *Preliminaries to Speech Analysis*. Cambridge, MA: MIT Press.

——and Halle, M. (1956). *Fundamentals of Language*. The Hague: Mouton.

Jenkins, L. (1975). *The English Existential*. Tübingen: Max Niemeyer.

Jensen, J. T. (2000). 'Against ambisyllabicity', *Phonology* 17: 187–235.

Jespersen, O. (1917). *Negation in English and Other Languages*. Copenhagen: Ejnar Munksgaard.

——(1931). *A Modern English Grammar on Historical Principles, IV: Syntax, III*. London and Copenhagen: George Allen & Unwin and Ejnar Munksgaard.

Jones, C. (1989). *A History of English Phonology*. London: Longman.

Joos, M. (ed.) (1958). *Readings in Linguistics: The Development of Descriptive Linguistics in America since 1925*, 55–80. New York: American Council of Learned Societies.

Jun, S.-A. (ed.) (2005). *Prosodic Typology: The Phonology of Intonation and Phrasing*. Oxford: Oxford University Press.

Juul, A. (1975). *On Concord of Number in Modern English*. Copenhagen: Nova.

Kamp, J. A. W. (1975). 'Two theories about adjectives', in Keenan (ed.), 123–55.

Kaye, J. (1990). '"Coda" licensing', *Phonology* 7: 301–30.

——(1995). 'Derivations and interfaces', in Durand and Katamba (eds.), 290–332.

——Lowenstamm, J., and Vergnaud, J.-R. (1985). 'The internal structure of phonological elements: A theory of charm and government', *Phonology Yearbook* 2: 305–28.

————(1990). 'Constituent structure and government in phonology', *Phonology* 7: 193–231.

Keenan, E. L. (ed.), *Formal Semantics of Natural Language*. Cambridge: Cambridge University Press.

Kilpiö, M. (2010). 'Causative *habban* in Old English', presented at the 16th International Conference on English Historical Linguistics, Pécs, 27th August.

Kingston, J. and Beckman, M. E. (eds.) (1990). *Papers in Laboratory Phonology 1: The Grammar and Physics of Speech*. Cambridge: Cambridge University Press.

Kinkade, M. D. (1976). 'The copula and negatives in Inland Olympic Salish', *International Journal of American Linguistics* 42: 17–23.

——(1983). 'Salish evidence against the universality of "noun" and "verb"', *Lingua* 60: 25–39.

Koutsoudas, A. (ed.) (1975). *The Application and Ordering of Grammatical Rules*. The Hague: Mouton.

——Sanders, G., and Noll, C. (1974). 'On the application of phonological rules', *Language* 50: 1–28.

Kuhl, P. and Miller, J. D. (1975). 'Speech perception by the chinchilla: Voiced-voiceless distinction in alveolar plosive consonants', *Science* 190: 69–72.

Kuipers, A. H. (1960). *Phoneme and Morpheme in Kabardian (Eastern Adyghe)*. The Hague: Mouton.

——(1968). 'Unique types and typological universals', in J. C. Heestermann, G. H. Schokker, and V. I. Subramoniam (eds.), *Pratidānam: Indian, Iranian and Indo-European Studies presented to Franciscus Bernardus Jacobus Kuiper on his Sixtieth Birthday*, 68–88. The Hague: Mouton.

Kuryłowicz, J. (1949). 'La notion de l'isomorphisme', in C. A. Bodelsen, P. Diderichsen, E. Fischer-Jørgensen, and J. Holt (eds.), *Recherches structurales*, 48–60. (= Travaux du cercle linguistique de Copenhague, V.)

Ladd, D. R. (1986). 'Intonational phrasing: The case for recursive prosodic structure', *Phonology Yearbook* 3: 311–40.

——(1990). 'Metrical representation of pitch register', in Kingston and Beckman (eds.), 35–57.

Langacker, R.W. (2003). 'Constructions in cognitive grammar', *English Linguistics* 20: 41–83.

Lappin, S. (2005). 'Machine learning and the cognitive basis of natural language', in *Proceedings of Computational Linguistics in the Netherlands 2004*, 1–11. Leiden.

——and Shieber, S. M. (2007). 'Machine learning theory and practice as a source of insight into universal grammar', *Journal of Linguistics* 43: 393–427.

Lasnik, H. (1999). *Minimalist Analysis*. Oxford: Blackwell.

Lass, R. (1974). 'Linguistic orthogenesis? Scots vowel quantity and the English length conspiracy', in Anderson and Jones (eds.), 311–52.

——(1976). *English Phonology and Phonological Theory: Synchronic and Diachronic Studies*. Cambridge: Cambridge University Press.

——(1984). *Phonology: An Introduction to Basic Concepts*. Cambridge: Cambridge University Press.

——(1987). 'Intradiphthongal dependencies', in Anderson and Durand (eds.), 109–31.

——(1994). *Old English: A Historical Linguistic Companion*. Cambridge: Cambridge University Press.

——and Anderson, J. M. (1975). *Old English Phonology.* Cambridge: Cambridge University Press.

Levinson, S. C. (2003a). 'Language and mind: Let's get the issues straight!', in D. Gentner and S. Goldin-Meadow (eds.), *Language and Mind: Advances in the Study of Language and Thought,* 26–46. Cambridge, MA: MIT Press.

——(2003b). *Space in Language and Cognition.* Cambridge: Cambridge University Press.

——and Wilkins, D. (eds.) (2006). *Grammars of Space.* Cambridge: Cambridge University Press.

Lewis, G. L. (1978). *Turkish Grammar.* Oxford: Oxford University Press.

Lightfoot, D. (1999). *The Development of Language: Acquisition, Change, and Evolution.* Oxford: Blackwell.

Lindsey, G. and Scancarelli, J. (1985). 'Where have all the adjectives come from? The case of Cherokee', *Proceedings of the Annual Meeting of the Berkeley Linguistics Society* 11: 207–15.

Locke, J. L. (1983). *Phonological Acquisition and Change.* New York: Academic Press.

Lodge, K. R. (1984). *Studies in the Phonology of Colloquial English.* London: Croom Helm.

Lyons, J. (1962). 'Phonemic and non-phonemic phonology: Some typological reflections', *International Journal of American Linguistics* 28: 127–33.

——(1975). 'Deixis as the source of reference', in Keenan (ed.), 61–83.

——(1977). *Semantics.* Cambridge: Cambridge University Press.

McCawley, J. D. (1971). 'Tense and time reference in English', in C. J. Fillmore and D. T. Langendoen (eds.), *Studies in Linguistic Semantics,* 97–113. New York: Holt, Rinehart & Winston.

McMahon, A. M. S. (1989). 'Constraining lexical phonology: Evidence from English vowels'. Ph.D. thesis, University of Edinburgh.

——(1991). 'Lexical phonology and sound change: The case of the Scottish vowel length rule', *Journal of Linguistics* 27: 29–53.

Martinet, A. (1957). 'Arbitraire linguistique et double articulation', *Cahiers Ferdinand de Saussure* 15: 105–16. [Reprinted in Hamp, Householder, and Austerlitz, 371–8.]

Mascaró, J. (1976). 'Catalan phonology and the phonological cycle'. Ph.D. dissertation, MIT.

Matthews, P. H. (1966). 'The concept of rank in "Neo-Firthian" grammar', *Journal of Linguistics* 2: 101–10.

——(2001). *A Short History of Structural Linguistics.* Cambridge: Cambridge University Press.

——(2007). *Syntactic Relations: A Critical Survey.* Cambridge: Cambridge University Press.

Menn, L. and Stoel-Gammon, C. (1995). 'Phonological development', in P. Fletcher and B. MacWhinney (eds.), *The Handbook of Child Language,* 335–59. Oxford: Blackwell.

Miner, K. L. (1979). 'Dorsey's Law in Winnebago-Chiwere and Winnebago accent', *International Journal of American Linguistics* 45: 25–33.
Mitchell, B. (1985). *Old English Syntax, I*. Oxford: Oxford University Press.
Mithun, M. (1999). *The Languages of Native North America*. Cambridge: Cambridge University Press.
Montreuil, J.-P. (2004). 'Fragmenting weight in Scottish English', *La Tribune Internationale des Langues Vivantes* 36: 114–22.
Mulder, Jan W. F. (2000). 'Beyond realism', *Folia Linguistica* 34: 285–305.
Nartey, J. N. A. (1979). *A Study in Phonemic Universals*. Los Angeles, CA: UCLA Working Papers in Phonetics 46.
Newmeyer, F. J. (1990). Review of J. A. Hawkins (ed.), *Explaining Language Universals*, Oxford: Blackwell, 1988, *Journal of Linguistics* 26: 203–22.
——(1991). 'Functional explanation in linguistics and the origins of language', *Language and Communication* 11: 3–28.
——(2000). 'Three book-length studies of language evolution', *Journal of Linguistics* 36: 383–95.
Noonan, M. (1985). 'Complementation', in Shopen (ed.) (1985a), 42–140.
Noske, R. G., Schinkel, J., and Smith, N. S. H. (1982). 'The question of rule-ordering: Some counter fallacies', *Journal of Linguistics* 18: 389–408.
Obendorfer, R. (1998). *Weak Forms in Present-day English*. Oslo: Novus Press.
Oftedal, M. (1956). *The Gaelic of Leurbost, Isle of Lewis*. (= *A Linguistic Survey of the Gaelic Dialects of Scotland, vol. 3.*) Supplementary volume, *Norsk Tidskrift för Sprogvidenskap*. Oslo: H. Aschehoug.
Ogura, S. (1932). *Sendai hogen onin ko*. Tokyo: Toko Shoin.
Ohala, J. and Kawasaki, H. (1984). 'Prosodic phonology and phonetics', *Phonology Yearbook* 1: 113–27.
Onions, C. F. (1904). *An Advanced English Syntax*. London: Swan, Sonnenschein & Co.
Ono, S. (1975). 'The Old English verbs of knowing', *Studies in English Literature* 1975: 33–60.
Palmer, F. R. (ed.) (1970). *Prosodic Analysis*. Oxford: Oxford University Press.
Paradis, C. and Prunet, J.-F. (eds.) (1991). *The Special Status of Coronals: Internal and External Influence*. San Diego, CA: Academic Press.
Peng, F. C. C. (1985). 'On the possible clusters of mb, nd and [ŋ]g in Proto-Japanese', in J. Fisiak (ed.), *Papers from the 6th International Conference on Historical Linguistics*, 409–625. Amsterdam: John Benjamins.
Pike, K. L. (1947). *Phonemics: A Technique for Reducing Languages to Writing*. Ann Arbor: University of Michigan Press.
——(1967). *Language in Relation to a Unified Theory of the Structure of Human Behaviour*, 2nd edn. The Hague: Mouton.
Pollard, C. and Sag, I. A. (1994). *Head-driven Phrase Structure Grammar*. Chicago: University of Chicago Press.
Poser, W. (1984). 'The phonetics and phonology of tone and intonation in Japanese'. Ph.D. dissertation, MIT.

Poutsma, H. (1926). *A Grammar of Late Modern English, II: The Parts of Speech, §II: The Verb and the Particles*. Groningen: P. Noordhoff.

Pullum, G. K. (1992). 'The origins of the cyclic principle', in J. Marshall Denton, G. P. Chan, and C. P. Canakis, (eds.), *Papers from the 28th Regional Meeting of the Chicago Linguistic Society, 2: The Cycle in Linguistic Theory*, 209–35. Chicago Linguistic Society.

Pustejovsky, J. (1995). *The Generative Lexicon*. Cambridge, MA: MIT Press.

Radford, A. (1988). *Transformational Grammar: A First Course*. Cambridge: Cambridge University Press.

——(1997). *Syntactic Theory and the Structure of English: A Minimalist Approach*. Cambridge: Cambridge University Press.

Reiss, C. (2007). 'Modularity in the sound domain: implications for the purview of universal grammar', in G. Ramchand and C. Reiss (eds.), *The Oxford Handbook of Linguistic Interfaces*, 53–79. Oxford: Oxford University Press.

Rialland, A. and Djamouri, R. (1984). 'Harmonie vocalique, consonantique et structures de dépendance dans le mot en mongol khalkha', *Bulletin de la Société de Linguistique de Paris* 74: 333–83.

Riemsdijk, H. van (1992). 'Complements, adjuncts and adjacency in phrase structure', in L. Tasmowski and A. Zribi-Hertz (eds.), *De la musique à la linguistique: Festschrift for Nicolas Ruwet*, 498–512. Ghent: Communication & Cognition.

——(1998). 'Categorial feature magnetism: The endocentricity and distribution of projections', *Journal of Comparative Germanic Linguistics* 2: 1–48.

Rijkhoff, J. (2002). *The Noun Phrase*. Oxford Studies in Typology and Linguistic Theory. Oxford: Oxford University Press.

Ringen, C. (1975). 'Vowel harmony: Theoretical implications'. Ph.D. dissertation, Indiana University.

Robinson, L. W. (1972). *An Iowa/Otoe-English Dictionary*. Unpublished.

Roey, J. van (1969). 'The order of post-nominal modifiers in present-day English', *English Studies* 50: 20–31.

Ross, J. R. (1973). 'Nouniness', in O. Fujimura (ed.), *Three Dimensions of Linguistic Theory*, 137–257. Tokyo: TEC.

Sampson, G. (1997). *Educating Eve: The 'Language Instinct' Debate*. London: Cassell. (Revised edition: *The Language Instinct Debate*, London & New York: Continuum, 2005.)

——(2002). *Empirical Linguistics*. London & New York: Continuum.

Sapir, E. (1933). 'La réalité psychologique des phonèmes', *Journal de psychologie normale et pathologique*, 30: 247–65. [Reprinted as: 'The psychological reality of phonemes', in D. G. Mandelbaum (ed.), *Selected Writings of Edward Sapir in Language Culture and Personality*, 46–60. Berkeley & Los Angeles, CA: University of California Press, 1963.]

Schachter, P. (1976). 'The subject in Philippine languages: Topic, actor, actor-topic, or none of the above', in C. N. Li (ed.), *Subject and Topic*, 491–518. New York: Academic Press.

Schane, S. A. (1971). 'The phoneme revisited', *Language* 47: 503–21.

——(1984). 'The fundamentals of particle phonology', *Phonology Yearbook* 1: 129–55.

Scobbie, J. M., Hewlett, N., and Turk, A. E. (2001). 'Standard English in Edinburgh and Glasgow: The Scottish vowel length rule revealed', ch.13 in P. Foulkes and G. Docherty (eds.), *Urban Voices*, London: Arnold.

Selkirk, E. (1977). 'Some remarks on noun phrase structure', in Culicover, Wasow, and Akmajian (eds.), 285–316.

Shieber, S. M. (1986). *An Introduction to Unification-Based Approaches to Grammar*. Stanford, California: CSLI.

Shopen, T. (ed.) (1985a). *Language Typology and Syntactic Description, II: Complex Constructions.* Cambridge: Cambridge University Press.

——(ed.) (1985b). *Language Typology and Syntactic Description, III: Grammatical Categories and the Lexicon.* Cambridge: Cambridge University Press.

Siegel, M. E. A. (1980). *Capturing the Adjective.* New York: Garland.

Siertsema, B. (1965). *A Study of Glossematics*, 2nd edn. The Hague: Martinus Nijhoff.

Silverman, D. (2006). *A Critical Introduction to Phonology: of Sound, Mind, and Body.* London and New York: Continuum.

Skousen, R. (1973). 'Finnish vowel harmony: Rules and conditions', in M. Kenstowicz and C. W. Kisseberth (eds.), *Issues in Phonological Theory*, 118–29. The Hague: Mouton.

Sommerstein, A. H. (1977). *Modern Phonology.* London: Edward Arnold.

Sportiche, D. (1988). 'A theory of floating quantifiers and its corollaries for constituent structure', *Linguistic Inquiry* 19: 425–49.

Staun, J. (1987). 'On the representation of stød', in Anderson and Durand (eds.), 169–98.

——(1996). 'On structural analogy', *Word* 47: 193–205.

Steriade, D. (1982). 'Greek prosodies and the nature of syllabification'. Ph.D. dissertation, MIT.

——(1990). 'Gestures and autosegments: Comments on Browman and Goldstein's paper ['Gestures in articulatory phonology']', in Kingston and Beckman (eds.), 382–97.

——(1995). 'Underspecification and markedness', in Goldsmith (ed.), 114–74.

Stowell, T. (1982). 'The tense of infinitives', *Linguistic Inquiry* 13: 560–70.

Swadesh, M. (1936–8). 'Nootka internal syntax', *International Journal of American Linguistics* 9: 77–102.

Szemerényi, O. (1967). 'The new look of Indo-European: Reconstruction and typology', *Phonetica* 17: 65–99.

Tallerman, M. (2006). 'Challenging the syllabic model of "syntax-as-it-is"', *Lingua* 116: 689–709.

Taylor, M. V. (1974). 'The great Southern Scots conspiracy: Patterns in the development of Northern English', in Anderson and Jones (eds.), 403–26.

Trubetzkoy, N. S. (1925). Review of N. Yakovlev (1923) *Tablitsky fonetiki kabardinskogo iazika, Bulletin de la Société de Linguistique de Paris* 26: 277–86.

Twaddell, W. F. (1935). *On Defining the Phoneme.* Language Monograph 16. [Reprinted in Joos (ed.), 55–80.]

Vago, R. (ed.) (1980). *Issues in Vowel Harmony.* Amsterdam: John Benjamins.

Vendler, Z. (1968). *Adjectives and Nominalizations.* Papers in Formal Linguistics 5. The Hague: Mouton.

Wells, J. C. (1982). *Accents of English, II: The British Isles.* Cambridge: Cambridge University Press.

Welmers, W. E. (1973). *African Language Structures.* Berkeley, CA: University of California Press.

Wettstein, P. (1942). *The Phonology of a Berwickshire Dialect.* Zurich: Schuler s.a.

Wood, S. A. J. (1991). 'Vertical, monovocalic and other "impossible" vowel systems: A review of the articulation of the Kabardian vowels', *Studia Linguistica* 45: 49–70.

Zai, R. (1942). *The Phonology of the Morebattle Dialect (E. Roxburghshire).* Lucerne: Raeber.

Zimmer, K. (1976). 'Some constraints on Turkish causativisation', in M. Shibatani (ed.), *Syntax and Semantics 6: The Grammar of Causative Constructions,* 339–412. New York: Academic Press.

Index of Authors Cited

Ablali, D. 21
Ackema, P. 215
Adger, D. 62, 63
Agutter, A. J. L. 107
Aissen, J. 287
Aitken, A. J. 106
Anderson, J. M. 5, 19, 20, 21, 22, 24, 27, 30, 32, 34, 35, 36, 38, 39, 40, 42, 43, 44, 46, 48, 49, 51, 52, 53, 55, 57, 60, 61, 62, 63, 64, 65, 66, 71, 75, 79, 80, 81, 86, 87, 89, 90, 93, 94, 95, 98, 105, 107, 111, 112, 114, 126, 143, 151, 153, 155, 156, 157, 158, 159, 167, 170, 177, 181, 183, 187, 188, 189, 191, 193, 194, 195, 196, 199, 202, 204, 205, 208, 209, 211, 214, 215, 223, 225, 226, 231, 232, 248, 249, 255, 256, 259, 262, 267, 268, 270, 271, 273, 274, 275, 282, 284, 285, 286, 287, 288, 293, 297, 300, 308, 310, 322, 331, 334, 354, 359
Anderson, L. B. 166
Anderson, S. R. 48, 173, 174, 191, 211
Archangeli, D. 23
Aronoff, M. 74
Arrivé, M. 21
Aurnague, M. 107, 108
Austin, F. 199

Bache, C. 47
Basbøll. H. 200, 202
Bauer, L. 21, 61
Bazell, C. E. 21, 22
Bermúdez-Otero, R. 33
Bickerton, D. 61
Bird, S. 83, 116
Blevins, J. 79, 269, 327–8
Bloch, B. 73
Boas, F. 274
Böhm, R. 151
Bolinger, D. L. 46, 260, 264
Borgström, C. H. 131
Börjars, K. 33
Brandt, P. 215
Breen, G. 249
Bresnan, J. 62

Bromberger, S. 31, 32, 53
Browman, C. P. 116, 192
Brunner, K. 204
Burton-Roberts, N. 28, 32, 40

Cairns, C. E. 95
Campbell, A. 204, 205, 206
Carden, G. 266
Carr, P. 22, 32, 34, 35, 52, 53, 55, 59, 60, 61, 64, 65, 66, 107, 159, 160, 173, 229
Carstairs-McCarthy, A. 61, 246
Catford, J. C. 273
Chadwick, N. 203
Chatman, S. 47
Chin, S. B. 157, 158
Chomsky, N. 23, 24, 26, 27, 28, 29, 31, 32, 33, 36–8, 38, 39, 47, 249, 314, 315, 316
Chung, S. 178, 223
Clark, E. 285
Clark, H. 285
Clements, G. N. 30, 61, 174, 175, 202
Coleman, J. 32, 126
Colman, F. 206, 207, 208, 285, 286
Comrie, B. 179, 221, 222, 223, 273, 287, 289
Corbett, G. G. 217
Croft, W. 160, 211
Crowley, T. 273
Crystal, D. 61, 297

Dahl, Ö 223
Declerck, R. 179, 190
Demirdache, H. 274
Derbyshire, D. C. 274
Dinnsen, D. A. 157, 158
Dixon, R. M. W. 157
Djamouri, R. 193
Donegan, P. 354
Durand, J. 22, 32, 107, 108, 110, 167, 208, 360

van Eijk, J. 274
Eimas, P. D. 159
Elbert, M. 157, 158
Emonds, J. 38, 62

Everett, D. 33, 318
Ewen, C. J. 22, 52, 64, 79, 80, 81, 86, 87, 89, 95, 105, 107, 112, 151, 156, 167, 189, 202, 354, 359
Eychenne, J. 107, 108, 110

Faber, A. 74
Fanselow, G. 145
Fant, G. 189
Farkas, D. 248
Feinstein, M. 95
Fery, C. 145
Firth, J. R. 74, 119, 166, 192
Fischer, O. 314, 331
Fischer-Jørgensen, E. 51
Fitch, W. T., 33
Fogel, R. 145

Gazdar, G. 39
Giegerich, H. J. 74, 122, 248, 326
Gil, D. 81
Goldsmith, J. A. 30, 173
Goldstein, L. 116, 192
Golston, C. 142
Goyvaerts, D. L. 47
Guéron, J. 25, 62, 63, 314

Haegeman, L. 25, 62, 63, 314
Hale, K. 30, 122, 127–30, 248
Hale, M. 28
Hall, T. A. 90
Halle, M. 23, 24, 25, 26, 30, 31, 32, 53, 122, 127–9, 129, 176, 189, 204, 270, 273, 359
Halliday, M. A. K. 21, 47, 250, 296, 297
Harms, R. T. 26
Harris, J. 32
Hauser, M. D. 33
Heijkoop, A. C. 157, 158, 219
Hess, T. 274
Hewlett, N. 106, 107
Hind, K. 122, 124, 131
Hjelmslev, L. 5, 21, 39, 51, 60
Hogg, R. M. 204, 206, 208, 226
Holton, D. 101, 220
Huddleston, R. D. 183
Hulst, H. G. van der 30, 31, 48, 166, 166, 173, 189, 203, 204, 218, 355, 356, 359–61, 363
Hume, E. V. 30

Idsardi, W. 30, 129

Jackendoff, R. S. 23, 24, 30, 33, 55, 62
Jacobsen, W. 274
Jakobson, R. 24, 167, 189
Jenkins, L. 195
Jensen, J. T. 136
Jespersen, O. 183, 191, 199
Jones, C. 22, 131
Jun, S.-A. 298
Jusczyk, P. 159
Juul, A. 47

Kager, R. 30
Kamp, J. A. W. 46
Kawasaki, H. 64, 83
Kaye, J. 29, 31, 32
Keyser, S. J. 30, 202
Kilpiö, M. 338.
Kinkade, M. D. 274, 275
Klein, E. 39, 83, 116
Koutsoudas, A. 93
Kuhl, P. 159
Kuipers, A. H. 270, 271, 273
Kuryłowicz, J. 21, 51

Ladd, D. R. 61, 297
Langacker, R. W. 46
Langendoen, D. T. 23
Lappin, S. 34
Lasnik, H. 26, 28
Lass, R. 105, 106, 204, 219, 225
Levinson, S. C. 159–60, 286
Lewis, G. L. 305
Lightfoot, D. 34
Lindsay, G. 32
Lindsey, G. 157
Locke, J. L. 158
Lodge, K. R. 107
Lowenstamm, J. 31
Lukoff, F. 23
Lyons, J. 74, 159, 275

Mackridge, P. 101, 220
McMahon, A. M. S. 197
Martinet, A. 21, 58
Mascaró, J. 24
Matthews, P. H. 32, 51, 296
Matthewson, L. 274

Index of Authors Cited

Menn, L. 157
Miller, J. D. 159
Miller, J. E. 304–5
Miner, K. L. 110, 122–3, 127–8, 129, 131
Mitchell, B. 316, 317
Mithun, M. 274, 275
Montreuil, J.-P. 107
Mulder, J. W. F. 21

Nartey, J. N. A. 157
Newmeyer, F. J. 33, 61
Noll, C. 93
Noonan, M. 305
Noske, R. G. 107

Obendorfer, R. 57
Odden, D. 30
Oftedal, M. 131
Ogura, S. 120.
Ohala, J. 64, 83
Onions, C. F. 314
Ono, S. 235

Palmer, F. R. 192
Paradis, C. 91, 219
Peng, F. C. C. 119, 120
Pensalfini, R. 249
Philippaki-Warburton, I. 101, 220
Pike, K. L. 21, 74, 246
Pinker, S. 33
Pintzuk, S. 62, 63
Plunkett, B. 62, 63
Pollard, C. 39, 63
Poser, W. 176
Poutsma, H. 150, 183, 314
Powell, T. W. 157, 158
Prunet, J.-F. 91, 219
Pullum, G. K. 23, 39
Pustejovsky, J. 293

Radford, A. 24–7, 44, 63, 314, 316
Radzinsky, D. 81
Reiss, C. 14, 28
Rialland, A. 193
Riemsdijk, H. van 27, 59
Rijkhoff, J. 27, 47
Ringen, C. 166
Ritter, R. 31
Robinson, L. W. 122

Roey, J. van 47
Ross, J. R. 144–6, 151

Sag, I. A. 39, 63
Sampson, G. 34, 145
Sanders, G. 93
Sapir, E. 75, 376
Scancarelli, J. 157
Schachter, P. 231
Schane, S. A. 74, 354
Schesewsky, M. 145
Schinkel, J. 107
Schoorlemmer, M. 215
Scobbie, J. M. 106, 107
Selkirk, E. 30, 46
Sezer, E. 174, 175
Shieber, S. M. 34, 135
Siegel, M. E. A. 46
Siertsema, B. 21
Silverman, D. 75
Siqueland, E. R. 159
Skousen, R. 166
Smith, N. S. H. 107, 203, 204, 218
Sommerstein, A. H. 66, 74
Sportiche, D. 63
Staun, J. 22, 81, 202
Steriade, D. 78, 86, 122, 124, 131, 191
Stoel-Gammon, C. 157
Stowell, T. 27
Swadesh, M. 275
Szemerényi, O. 273

Tallerman, M. 60, 61
Taylor, M. V. 106
Timberlake, A. 178, 223
Trubetzkoy, N. S. 273
Tsoulas, G. 62, 63
Turk, A. E. 106, 107
Twaddell, W. F. 73, 75

Vendler, Z. 47
Vergnaud, J.-R. 31, 53, 122, 127–9, 176, 204
Vigorito, J. 159

Weerman, F. 215
Weijer, J. van de 166, 173
Wells, J. C. 107
Welmers, W. E. 222

Wettstein, P. 106
White Eagle, J. 122, 127–30
Wilkins, D. 286
Wood, S. A. J. 273

Yip, M. 30

Zai, R. 106
Zimmer, K. 289

Subject index

absolute tense: see tense
absorption (lexical) 132, 252, 254, 257, 258, 275, 281–3, 289, 306; see too conversion
acute (phonological feature) 105, 107, 123, 167–8, 170–2, 173–8, 209, 270–1, 273
 non- 167–8
adjective 24–5, 42–4, 46, 63, 89, 134, 143, 144, 156–8, 227, 256, 259–60, 263–4, 274, 291
 attributive 211, 213, 227, 265, 308–11
 circumstantial 285
 complemented see relational
 denominal 157
 deverbal 152, 157, 302, 304
 gradable/gradient 66, 100, 134, 135, 260, 265–8
 intersective vs. non- 285
 non-universality of 157, 243, 274
 predicative 46, 155
 relational 115, 152, 158, 227, 311, 363
 strong and weak, in Old English 224–5, 235, 375
adjunct vs. complement 12–4
adjunction, definition of 14
adposition 60, 63, 151, 254–5, 268, 305, 345; see too functor, postposition, preposition
adverb 43, 186, 188, 254, 284–5, 319, 347, 348–9
'adverbial' 220
AGR 249
agreement (in syntax) 27, 62, 121, 180, 188, 200, 210–8, 232–4, 236, 278, 340, 344, 346–7, 349–51, 372; see too concord
 and 'specifier' 62
 and umlaut 203
 as a property of determiner 188, 212, 344–54
 as integrative 278, 372
 grammatical vs. lexical 212, 213
 in phonology 97, 112, 121

integrative function of 234, 278, 326
 of definiteness 210, 213
 of gender 211, 212, 213, 218, 232, 351
 of person-number 188, 213, 234
 of number 213, 217–8
 of tense 181, 187, 192, 210, 211
 referential 213
'Aitken's Law' 106
alphabet (of (sub)module) 5–14
 and analogy 8, 11, 343–64, 365
 of phonology 143
 of syntax 7, 14, 143
alternative lexicalizations 242
ambidependency 133–8, 318–20, 327–8, 340
 integrative function of 328, 340
ambisyllabicity 108, 135–6, 224, 326–8, 340
aperture (phonological) 72, 104–10, 138, 366
'appendix' (phonological) 89–92
apposition 59, 187, 216, 218, 310, 314, 316, 319, 346
 and co-indexing 216
argument-sharing 321–30, 340, 350; see too free absolutive
argument structure 139, 157, 197, 255, 273, 284, 289, 313
 functional 255, 257, 262
Arrernte 249
aspect 7, 8, 48, 62, 236, 298, 372, 375; see too habitual, imperfective, perfect, perfective, progressive
 in English and Greek 219–24
 -voice operative 334, 338
association (line) 13–4, 62, 75, 93, 154, 169–72, 176–8, 180, 183–4, 188, 190–1, 193–202, 203–5, 210–6, 224, 261, 270, 322–5, 341, 351, 371
attributive 45–6, 153–5, 211, 227, 267, 284, 285, 306, 308–12
 and word classes 227, 308
 post-nominal 154, 283–4, 306, 308, 309, 310, 312

attributive (*cont.*)
  pre-nominal 47, 155, 284, 309, 311
attributivization 48, 153, 284, 308–9, 311
autonomy 34, 40, 46, 49–52, 236, 368–9, 377;
  see too exponence
auxiliary alphabet 373
auxiliary verb 315, 368, 372

basic units 116, 137, 141–163, 166
Basque, verb concord in 214, 215, 232, 234,
  277, 344–5, 351

case 27, 214, 234, 249, 305, 345; see too functor
checked vowel 56–8, 104–8, 230
  as transitive 56
circumstantials 152–5, 186–8, 197, 250, 252, 254,
  258, 261, 284–5, 307–8, 313, 347, 350
co-reference 180, 312, 346–9
coda 58, 61, 65, 81–2, 88–90, 94, 112, 121, 138,
  152, 224, 247–9, 269, 273, 296, 357–8
  -less languages 85
cognitive adjacency 2
cognitive basis for syntax 1, 14, 26, 34–5, 48,
  49, 50, 76, 137, 152, 159, 256, 281,
  368, 373
cognitive salience 2, 12, 35, 40, 48–9, 52, 58, 71,
  84, 95, 138, 211, 365, 372
cognitive scene: see scene (cognitive)
compact (phonological feature) 105, 107, 156,
  167, 173–4, 225, 354
comparator 256, 259–60, 263–4, 267–8, 274
complement characterized 12–4
complementizer 102, 263, 277, 299, 305, 312–9
compounding 129, 282, 289–94
  in phonology 294
concord (verbal) 121, 132, 195, 210, 213–8, 231,
  278, 305, 332–4, 344, 346–7, 353
  of tense: see agreement of tense, and tense,
    sequence of
conditionals 305
configuration 59, 63, 87, 97, 102, 120, 136, 138,
  141, 149–50, 156, 172, 188, 195, 221,
  234, 247–8, 250, 252, 259, 299, 315,
  323, 337–9, 367, 372, 375
  and alphabet size 343–63
conjugation 210, 214, 224–5, 375
  and declension 8

and periphrasis 15
consonant cluster 86–90, 93, 96, 100–1, 108,
  112, 119, 121, 123, 124, 125, 131, 142, 152,
  178, 193, 268, 279, 318, 326–7
  and headship 64–5, 97–8, 101, 118–9
  and sequencing 85, 98
  obstruent voicing in 97
constituency 53, 63–4, 202, 247, 355
  and conceptual grouping 2, 64
contrafactive feature as harmonic 191
contrastivity 7, 12, 66, 71, 72, 79, 80–3, 98,
  100–1, 104–10, 122, 131, 138, 142, 155,
  160, 165–71, 195, 202, 207, 227, 236,
  243, 270, 272–3, 365
  and neutralization 73–9
  maximization of 78–80, 167, 227
  paradigmatic vs. syntagmatic 75–6
conventionality: see grammaticalization,
  routinization
conversion (lexical) 7, 43, 156, 242, 265, 282,
  284–6, 292, 308, 310; see too
  absorption
copula 198, 275
'coronal obstruents' 88–9, 91–3, 97, 246, 358
coronals and underspecification 219
creaky voice 200
cumulation 251, 259, 308
cyclicity 23–4, 61

D-structure vs. S-structure 39
Danish and stød 200–2, 236, 293
declarative 125, 129, 223, 257, 316, 363
declension 213; see too conjugation
definite 115, 159, 199, 212, 258, 267, 268, 334,
  346, 365
  agreement 199, 214, 216
  article 258, 268
  non-
    past reference 190
    past reference 189–90
demoted finites 102
dependency, definition of 2; see too
  adjunction, cognitive salience,
  subjunction
  maximization of 97, 117, 126, 132, 137, 139,
    241, 245, 247, 261, 319–20, 327;
    see too timing

derivational morphology 5, 7, 121, 228, 231, 282, 287–9, 306, 318
determinative: see determiner
determiner 27, 44, 152, 153, 181, 188, 190, 200, 210, 211, 213, 214, 216, 217, 243, 256–9, 262, 265–8, 274, 275, 284, 308–13, 316, 344–5, 347, 350; see too definite, indefinite
  'existentially uncommitted' 200
  partitive 308–11
  phrase 210–3, 216–7
determinerization 211
diphthong 104–5, 107, 122, 128, 293
  in Danish 201–2, 293
  in Old English 206–7
discourse 2, 41, 50, 136, 198, 319–20
  phonology 142
distributive 218
diversification in expression 76–7, 362
Djingili 203–4, 218
Dorsey's Law in Winnebago-Chiwere 73, 122–4, 127, 131, 192
double articulation 12, 33, 156, 181, 188, 228, 297, 353, 368–9, 372
double-motherhood 97; see too ambidependency
dual (primary/secondary) feature 98, 113–5, 117–21, 122, 144, 157–8, 167–79, 184, 186, 189–90, 194, 200, 204, 206–8, 225–6, 230, 271–3, 354, 363
Dutch 219

E-language vs. I-language 29
earlierEnglish 314
ectopicity 197, 232, 243, 280, 312, 319, 320, 323, 325–6, 329, 330, 340, 366, 374
elective vs. inherent features: see secondary features
-eme 21
'empty' category 8, 29, 34, 39, 49–50, 98, 215, 249, 314, 358, 367, 373, 374
encapsulation 10
entitative 159, 212, 257, 372
entity 258, 285
  vs. event 3, 7, 48, 96, 243, 262, 286, 300, 376
equative 134, 322

event 187, 189, 190, 242, 288; see too entity vs. event
event structure (phonological) 83
existential 187, 191, 344, 351; see too negatives, progressive
existental *there* 193, 195–8, 200
expletive 102, 195–6, 198, 236, 248–50, 277, 301, 318, 322, 334, 336, 337
  in phonology 248
exponence, definition of 3, 8–9, 11, 15, 22, 41, 78, 83, 93, 126, 219, 229, 345, 371, 373, 375–6
  and separation 8, 371, 375
expression, definition of 3–8
extrasegmentals 116, 165, 166–218, 230, 235–6, 270–2, 366
  monosegmental realization of 192–8
  'fast sequences': see Winnebago

feature: see dual feature, primary feature, secondary feature
figurativeness 59–60, 100–1, 296, 376–7
finiteness 95, 180–1, 197, 215, 233, 256–7, 259, 262, 267, 274–8, 282, 299, 302, 309, 313, 321–5, 329, 332, 335–4, 374–5
  -formation 197, 322, 335–6
Finnish 110, 166–72, 178, 179, 185, 188–9, 194, 205, 209
flat (phonological feature) 167
focus 329–30, 333, 340; see too topic/focus
foot 108, 136, 224, 295, 326, 340
formative 5, 107, 132, 166, 168, 193–4, 330
free absolutive 196, 198, 214, 232–3, 260–1, 277, 301–2, 320, 322–5, 328–32, 335–6, 338–41, 367, 374
  and thematic structure 328–40
  definition of 197
French 59, 108, 132, 211–3, 314, 317
  of the Midi 107–10
fricatives 86–7, 89, 101, 106, 111–4, 143, 155, 157–8, 231
functional argument structure 255–7, 262
functional category 25, 27, 44, 61, 63, 65, 132, 157, 159–62, 181, 188, 190, 197, 210–4, 218, 229, 243–4, 248, 253, 255–6, 259, 262–4, 267–8, 274–9, 282–2, 286, 290, 298–9, 310, 312–5, 319, 328, 340, 366, 374

functional locutionary structure 257
functional referential structure 259
functional structure of comparison 260
functionality 278
  principle 278
functor 44, 60, 100, 113, 135, 151, 160, 162, 188, 197, 214, 216, 232, 246–56, 258, 260–2, 263–4, 267–8, 274–7, 284, 286, 291, 296, 298, 300–1, 308, 312–3, 317, 322–3, 327–8, 341, 344–7, 349–50, 352, 367, 374
  and incorporation 345–52
  and specification 263–8, 277
  and subject selection 197
  as attributive 308–10
  phrase 60, 307–8, 310

gender 7, 25, 48, 143, 211–3, 218, 232, 234, 351, 372, 377
  grammatical and natural 212–3, 232
  referential 213
German 101, 232, 248, 314, 334
  and 'V-2' 330–1, 339
Germanic 203–4, 207, 231
gerund 150
glottal stop 195, 248
government phonology 29, 31–2, 53, 124, 359
grammatical relation 196, 231–5, 250, 261, 276
  principal 250
grammaticalization 1–3, 5, 8, 12, 15, 22, 26, 29, 40, 61, 64–5, 71–2, 75, 77, 101, 106, 137–8, 165, 196, 203, 228–37, 244, 249–50, 252, 275, 278, 286, 303, 313, 319–30, 323, 325, 334, 340, 368, 371–7
  by denaturalization 229–35, 313
  by displacement 229–35
  morphological 234
grave (phonological feature) 118, 129, 167, 173–5, 208–9, 270, 273
Greek 100–1, 214
  agreement in 215, 233
  aspect in 219–23
  gender in 113
groundedness 1–2, 7, 10, 23, 26, 28–9, 49–50, 64, 67, 367
Guaraní 78

[h] in English 94, 193–9, 200, 236, 271
  h-sequencing 193–5, 199
[h] in Kabardian 271, 273
habitual 185, 220–3
harmony (of vowels) 117, 165, 166–92, 193, 199, 203, 204–5, 209, 211, 213, 216–7, 236, 366
  integrative function of 172, 278
  of number 217
  of tense 178–91, 211, 216–7, 350–1
head 2, 12–4, 31, 34–5, 40, 43, 45–6, 48, 50–1, 141, 151–2, 154, 160, 164, 170, 177, 180–1, 191, 193, 200, 205, 210–2, 247, 254–5, 263, 268, 277, 286, 292, 294, 296–7, 300, 306, 308, 311, 320, 325, 330–1, 333, 335, 340, 351, 356, 358–9, 361–2, 365–6; see too dependency
  accentual 200, 205
  -based analogies 51, 52–139, 141
  convention 89–90
  morphological 177, 205
head-driven phonology 31
Hixkaryana 274
Hungarian, agreement in 210, 212, 216

'I-to-C movement' 315
iconicity 3, 251, 304, 329, 371, 376
ictus 295, 297
idioms 44, 160, 180–1, 333, 339
  and compounds 290–2
imperative 159, 233, 257
imperfective 190, 220–3
incorporation (lexical) 43, 188, 215, 282, 305, 345–6
indefinite 53, 61, 198, 199, 334–6
  past reference 192
indicative 233, 235, 334
Indo-European 232, 235
infinitive 249, 305, 321, 325, 376
  bare 376
  periphrastic (*to-*) 325
INFL 249
inter-plane 5, 50, 77
interface 3–4, 6–7, 14, 22, 36–7, 39, 41, 49, 50–1, 72, 77–8, 83–5, 91, 103–4, 110, 131, 136, 138, 143, 155, 159, 161, 165–6, 172, 188, 192, 195, 197, 222, 228–9,

234, 237, 241–2, 252, 262, 268, 273, 298, 318, 330, 353, 362–3, 365–9, 373
lexical 6, 77, 181, 197
of morphology 8, 234
with phonetics 72, 98, 116, 138–9, 155, 188, 234, 244, 272, 276, 281, 298, 305, 307, 318, 330, 340, 366
with pragmatics 47, 139, 229, 232, 330
with semantics 136, 143, 155, 172, 188, 234, 248, 255, 257, 259, 260, 262, 276, 285–7, 318, 329
interpretation, definition of 3
interrogative 257, 313, 315–6, 325, 329–32, 335, 337, 339
intonation 9–10, 14, 30, 74, 227, 297–8, 340, 368, 372–3, 375
intrinsic ordering 208
inversion of 'verb' and subject 195, 199, 315–7, 325, 331, 334–5, 338–9
irrealis 76, 191, 223, 317

Japanese 60, 119–21

Kabardian 268–73
Kalenjin 204
Korean 155
and spatial distinctions 159–60
Kwakiutl 274
Kwakw'ala 191

language acquisition 33–4, 60, 156–60, 219, 263, 331, 378
holistic phase in 160
language and perception of spatial distinctions: see Korean
language as a computational system 14, 28, 377
'language faculty' 33, 378
'in a narrow sense' 33
Latin:
agreement in 121
tense and aspect in 182, 219, 233
level (of language) 36–41, 66, 74, 82, 273
lexical category 41, 132, 258, 264, 274, 291, 306, 367
lexical causatives:
morphological 282, 289

non-morphological 289
lexical derivation 7, 147, 154, 228, 242–4, 281–2, 285–7, 289, 318, 366; see too absorption, conversion, derivational morphology
lexical redundancy:
phonological 81, 90, 98, 105, 109, 135, 193, 202, 219, 288
syntactic 14, 299, 332, 335, 374
lexicon, definition of 3, 5–6
linearity 11, 27, 40, 51, 55, 67, 72, 75, 78, 79–103, 110, 116, 132, 137–9, 142, 246–7, 268, 311, 313, 330, 340, 365, 368, 371, 373–4
non- 165–237
linearization 2–4, 9, 13–4, 30, 72, 75, 77, 70, 79–104, 104, 139, 151, 165, 181, 193, 198, 246, 261, 320, 345, 373; see too sequencing, serialization, word order
and time 2, 11, 41, 85, 137–9, 368, 373
liquids 111–2, 114, 158
localism 60

markedness 81–3, 135, 150, 156–61, 219, 222–4, 235, 277, 323, 333, 360, 363
of aspect and tense 220, 223–4
mediated and unmediated verbal complements 300–2, 321, 323–4, 349
metaphor 57, 349, 376
metonymy 285–6
Middle English 117, 131
modal verbal 330, 334–5, 372
modifier 13–4, 43, 87, 103, 153–5, 295, 309
'nominal' 47, 155, 284, 292, 308–9
modularity 2, 4–6, 10–1, 36–7, 41, 367, 369, 371
strict: see encapsulation
module, definition of 2–6
Mongolian 193
mood 101, 211, 257, 374–5; see too declarative, imperative, interrogative
morphophoneme 75
morphosyntactic systems 48, 226, 285, 297, 334, 339, 375
mutation in structure 8, 11, 40, 41, 72, 78, 95, 128, 367–8, 373

name 96, 134, 143, 159, 212, 243, 254, 256–9, 262, 274, 275, 295, 347, 372

nasal 89–9, 98, 106, 111–21, 130, 144, 157–8,
    205–6, 224–6, 230, 295, 354, 363
nasal vowel 121
nasality 78, 114, 119, 120, 151
naturalness 25, 26, 156, 160–1, 192, 218, 232,
    268, 311, 350, 372, 376
  phonetic 25, 231, 195, 226, 230–1, 328, 354
  semantic 25–7, 50, 212–3, 221, 231, 268, 345,
    349–50
nature vs. nurture 19
negatives 5, 145, 344
  and inversion 333, 335
  multiple 199
  placement 199–200, 203
neutralization 27, 65–6, 73–7, 98–104, 122, 135,
    226, 361
  and subjecthood 252
  class 64–5, 268
  in syntactic category 268, 314
nominals 212, 254, 257, 300, 310, 345, 347, 349
non-compositionality 290
non-configurational 248
non-definite: see definite
non-factive: see irrealis
non-finites 102, 143, 148–50, 190–1, 200, 223,
    227, 233, 299, 302–4, 310, 314, 321,
    323–4, 334; see too demoted finites
  and word order 314
  mediated and unmediated 323
  morphological 299
  recursion of 302–3
  types of 303–4
non-projectivity 340; see too tangling
non-rhotic 122
non-specification 167, 206–8, 218–9, 222,
    271, 276
  extrasegmental 271
  in syntax 221–2, 276
  irreducible 219
  system-dependent 218–9, 221, 243–4
  system-independent 219, 222
Nootka 275
notionalism 6–7, 11, 14, 23, 25–8, 30, 33, 34, 37,
    48, 55, 64, 76, 95, 100, 103, 134, 147,
    152, 157, 211–2, 220, 245, 250–1, 268,
    282, 303, 368, 372, 378

noun 24–7, 42, 44–7, 65, 134, 143, 147–8, 151,
    152, 153, 155, 157, 181, 227, 242–3, 246,
    256–9, 262, 274–5, 285, 291, 293, 308,
    313, 347
  and gender agreement 211–3, 232
  and number 217–8, 345
  as leaf 27, 46–7, 96, 212, 308–11, 372
  compounds 291–3
  derived 27, 30–1, 44–6, 148–9, 150–1, 152,
    153, 155, 228, 282, 284–5, 292, 304–5,
    310, 372
  notional basis for 1, 3, 7, 27, 35, 48–9,
    152, 159
  relational 45–6, 125, 152, 158, 363
  specifier of 44
  syntactic inertness of: see as leaf
  tensed 191
noun phrase 60, 199
'nouniness' 95, 115, 142, 144–51, 156, 300–1
NP 25, 50, 65, 211, 213, 249
number 27, 211, 217, 217, 344–5, 351
  agreement 188, 213–4, 216–8, 233–4, 257
  dual 217

'object' 38, 150, 210, 217, 325
Old English 131, 199, 316, 375
  and 'V-2' 330–4
  i-umlaut in 203–9
    and grammaticalization 229–31, 334
    and neutralization 224–5
  preterite-present verbs in 234–5, 375
  strong and weak adjectives in 224–5,
    235, 375
  strong verbs in 224–5, 375
onomatopoeia 3, 371, 376
onset 64, 65, 73, 81, 88, 93–104, 125–7, 134–5,
    138, 152, 159, 193–5, 205, 218, 222, 224,
    248–50, 270–3, 296, 357, 359–60
  and subject 58, 61, 63–4, 248
  and topic 61, 64
  maximization of 90, 135, 248, 327
  short-lag vs. long-lag 159
opacity 166
  in 'sequence of tenses' 179
  in vowel harmony 173–8
openness of truth value 332, 338

operative 27, 187, 214–6, 227, 257, 262, 275, 278, 324, 331, 333, 335, 338, 339, 344–6, 351, 374
  aspect-voice 334–5, 338
  vs. periphrast 303
optative 217
optimality 23

palatal: see acute
paradigmaticity 7–8, 33, 75–7, 150, 224, 227–8, 230–1, 235–6, 303
passive 8, 233, 288, 303, 352
past participle:
  and tense 188–91
  in Basque 233
perceptual basis for phonology 1–3, 10–2, 25, 77, 187, 371, 374
perfect 183, 190, 352
  in Indo-European 235
  in Latin 233
perfective 220–4
periphrasis (grammatical) 7–8, 15, 151, 183–4, 191, 220–1, 233, 259, 278, 303–4, 325, 351, 375–6
person 188, 211, 213–4, 217, 233–4, 257, 282, 344–6
phoneme 36, 51, 73–5, 108, 216
  and orthography 66, 74, 226
phoneticity, restrictions by: see interface with phonetics
phonological categories 1, 3, 7, 9–10, 26, 76–7, 91, 101, 144, 188, 222, 227–8, 242, 287, 318, 336, 371, 373
phonology as interpretative 37
  and syntax as non-derivational 22, 40–1, 72, 78, 128, 286–8, 314, 318
Pirahã 33, 318
plane, definition of 3, 5; see too inter-plane
pluralia tantum 217
polysystemicity 74, 80, 110, 165, 218, 222–6, 236, 366
postposition 60, 248
pragmatics: see interface with pragmatics
predicativity 42, 46, 155, 266, 372
  non- 134, 315, 335
preposition 24–5, 42–4, 153, 248, 251–4, 290, 300; see too functor

specifier of 63, 100, 135
primary category 7, 28, 31, 44, 80, 83, 92, 108, 114–5, 118, 134, 143, 152, 155, 162, 170, 180, 199, 222, 227, 243, 253, 255, 259, 276, 278, 281, 294, 297, 308, 310, 347, 355, 358–63, 372
  cross-classes of 24–6
primary feature 28, 86, 107, 113–7, 151, 157, 160–2, 291, 363
progressive 150, 174, 220–3, 303, 351, 353, 376
projection 3, 6, 40–1, 44, 48, 50, 62, 89, 180–1, 198, 212, 315, 368, 372
  definition of 3
pronoun 91, 132, 134, 212, 143, 256–9, 275, 305, 344–7, 372
prosody 1, 9–10
prototypical category member 7, 27, 43, 45–8, 105, 152–3, 155, 221, 227, 267–8, 277, 309, 363, 372
prototypicality 27, 43, 45–8, 79, 84, 96, 105, 115, 151–2, 215, 221, 243, 249, 264, 300, 316, 318, 363

quantifier 199
  de-adjectival 265–7

radical CV phonology 355–62
raising 197, 334, 340
  and subject formation 197, 320–4
  'to-object' 324–6
re-representation 3–4, 6, 8–9, 12, 15, 41, 72, 156, 228, 368, 371, 373–4, 376
  definition of 3
recursion 33, 55, 62, 281, 294–319, 366, 378
  and cognition 33, 318–9, 378
  direct 288
  in phonology 61, 92, 293, 294–8, 318
  and unidirectional categorial progression 297
  in syntax 281, 293, 294, 298–305, 318
  indefinite 61
  indirect (in syntax) 293, 306–12, 318
  lexical 281–93, 310–2
reference 43, 96, 157, 159, 181, 183, 213, 216; see too co-reference
  speech-act 181
tense 76, 180–91; see too tense

reference (cont.)
    with nouns 191
relative tense: see tense
representation, definition of 1–15
resyllabification 127, 327
rhoticity 295
rhotics 112–4, 122, 354, 363
routinization 328, 330, 374, 376–7; see too grammaticalization

[S-] 64–6, 73–4, 97–101, 103, 113, 134–5, 218, 268, 318
Salish, Inland Olympic 275
scene (cognitive) 151–2, 161, 181, 236, 242–3, 250–5, 276–7, 281, 287–8, 296, 303–6, 318, 353, 366, 374–5
Scottish Gaelic 131
Scottish vowel length rule 106–7, 111, 115
secondary categories 7–8, 10, 30, 104–5, 107, 110, 121, 134, 143, 151, 167, 178, 180–1, 188, 218–9, 222, 254, 271, 278, 282, 364, 372, 375
    deconstruction of 345–62, 364
secondary feature 86, 98, 105, 108, 112–22, 138, 142–3, 151, 157, 162, 165–8, 170, 178, 180, 182, 188–9, 194, 199, 202, 204–5, 209, 211, 214, 236, 257, 278, 286, 291, 343–4, 351, 353–4, 367, 373–4
    elective vs. inherent 48, 190–1, 212, 218, 372
Selayarese 215, 218, 346
semantic relation 195, 242–3, 251–3, 272, 286, 300–1, 313, 322, 335, 338, 344–5
semanticity, demands of: see interface with semantics
sequencing 47, 75, 78, 80, 116; see too linearization, serialization, word order
    intrasyllabic 71–2, 80–101, 103, 113, 126, 144, 195, 269, 277
        partial non- 81
        total non- 82
    of [h]: see h-sequencing
    syntactic, in English 82–3, 277, 332–3
    in idioms 290
'serial verbs' 273
serialization 80; see too linearization, sequencing, word order
    phonological 93–4, 98, 165–6, 194

syntactic 53, 80, 276, 281, 322, 332;
sign 3–8, 39–41, 76, 181, 231, 241, 246, 330, 371–6
    non- 8, 39, 373–4; see too 'empty' category
sonorant consonants 27, 75, 79–81, 86–7, 108, 114, 117–8, 123, 143–4, 155, 158, 161, 354, 359, 363
    in Danish 201–2
    in Winnebago 123–7, 131
sonority hierarchy 79, 85–9, 95, 115, 142, 144, 152, 161, 246–7
    and sequencing: see sequencing, intrasyllabic
South African English 248
specifier 35, 43–4, 62–6, 100–4, 133–5, 137, 141, 235, 259, 277, 309, 365
    and intensification 263–8
    and subject 63, 250, 322
    archetypical 63–4, 100, 135
    in German 101–3
    in phonology 63, 65–6, 71, 98–101, 104, 133–5, 137, 141, 235, 318, 340, 365
    of determiner 268
    of finiteness 100, 267, 313
speech act 76, 160, 243, 257
    participants 159, 344, 346
stød(-basis): see Danish 200–3
stops 66, 89, 96, 98, 101, 106, 111, 114, 121, 115, 118–9, 121, 157–8, 160, 326–7
    glottal 158, 195, 248
    as secondary features 118–9, 158
structural integration 92, 95, 97, 136, 232–4, 278, 326–8, 366
subject 44, 55, 62, 145, 163, 195–8, 214–5, 232–3, 245, 251–4, 260–1, 276, 287–8, 290, 302, 309, 312–3, 316, 321–5, 329–34, 338–9
    and onset 58, 61, 64, 245, 248–9
    as non-universal 196, 249
    expletive 195–6
    formation 55, 195–8, 232, 300–2, 321, 323–4, 335, 340
    marked vs. unmarked 102, 150, 232, 305
    morphosyntactic 195, 198
    -selection hierarchy 197–8, 329, 334, 340
    -verb agreement 210, 214–5; see too verb concord

subjunction 14, 30, 43, 55, 116–7, 122, 132, 180, 184, 197, 213–4, 233, 254, 256–7, 267, 278, 281–2, 283–5, 288, 295, 308, 311, 335, 337, 339, 345, 351, 360
subjunctive 228, 316–7
submodule 2–4, 9, 11, 40–1, 51, 85, 139, 368, 373
subordinate clause 101–2, 190, 212, 231, 301, 305, 313–4, 316
subordinating conjunctions 43, 305, 313–4, 317
syllabic consonants 113, 119
syllabic prominence: see sonority
syllable 60–5, 75–6, 79–83, 88–90, 93, 95–7, 104, 112, 114–5, 117, 119–20, 123–9, 134–6, 138, 151–2, 160–1, 168, 173–4, 184, 193–5, 200, 205, 214, 224, 244, 248, 261, 268, 276, 279, 295–8, 305, 318, 326–8, 330, 340–1, 356–9, 362
  unmarked 81, 96, 135, 195, 248, 318
  minimal ('vowelless') 268–73
  sequencing in: see sequencing, intrasyllabic
  transitive vs. intransitive 89, 104–10
  weight 82, 104–10
syntactic sequencing: see sequencing
system-dependency 80, 158, 219, 221–2, 242–4
  sub- 80, 218

Tagalog 196, 231, 249–50
tangling 55–6, 59, 93, 261, 279, 320, 322, 325–6, 329, 331, 341, 374; see too non-projectivity
  and phonology 261, 328, 340
  licensing of 279, 320, 322, 328–9, 341, 374
tense 7, 48, 183–92, 210, 249, 257, 282, 298, 305, 347–53, 372; see too reference
  absolute 183, 347
  and aspect redundancies 219–224
  and finiteness 257, 305
  deconstruction of 347–53
  default 185
  deictic 183, 185, 347
  domain 190
  future 185
  harmony: see sequence of
  nominal: see tensed noun
  non-past 222

past 181, 184, 189, 190, 223, 348
  non-specific 189
  predictive 185; see too future
  present 189, 224, 348
  reference 181–5, 187, 188, 189, 190, 347, 349, 351
    and location 349–50, 353
    the structure of 182–3, 185, 188, 348
  relative 183–4, 185, 189, 347
  sequence of 178–92, 199, 210–1, 213, 216–7, 236, 350–1
  and temporal circumstantials 186–8, 349
tensed adjective 46
tensed noun 191
thematic structure 277, 328–40, 367–8
Tibetan 305
tier 23, 30, 124, 192
timing 72, 111–37, 138, 139, 158, 241, 319
  and ambidependency 135–7, 138, 340
  in phonology 72–3, 74, 97, 114–7, 137–9, 162, 245, 247, 319, 340, 358, 366
  and loss of dependency 97, 118–21, 122–31, 132, 138, 192
  in syntax 121, 131–3, 136–7, 138–9, 162, 247, 366
tone group 297
tonic 295, 297
topic 41, 61, 64, 196, 231–2, 245, 249, 250, 277, 320, 323, 325, 329, 331, 337, 340
  /focus (grammatical relation) 196, 231, 249, 250, 330
  formation 196
  prominence 249
  vs. comment 82
transitivity 40, 42–4, 53, 133–6, 138–9, 141–2, 162, 232, 242, 244–5, 248, 269–70, 287–9, 307, 339, 365
  in phonology 41, 49, 51, 56–60, 64–5, 72, 83–5, 87–92, 104–110, 111, 116, 122, 133–6, 138–9, 141–2, 152, 200–2, 205–6, 224, 230, 244–5, 288, 296, 307, 326–7, 357, 365
  reduced 268–76
Turkish 305
  morphological causatives in 287–9, 304

Turkish (cont.)
  vowel harmony 172, 173–8, 179, 184–5, 205, 273

umlaut 165, 191, 203–4, 210–3, 215–8, 236, 278, 366
  in Old English 203–9, 224–6, 229–31, 234, 373
underspecification 78, 165, 166–72, 207–8, 218–9, 227, 236, 243, 266
unidirectional categorial progression in phonology 297
'universal grammar' 20–9, 32–6, 47–53, 60, 63, 229, 246, 269, 365, 368, 371

'V-2': see verb second
valency 57, 135–6, 197–8, 233, 251, 254, 261, 288, 296, 303, 320–5, 332, 335, 356, 367, 372
verb 13, 24–7, 42–9, 53, 55, 59, 62, 85, 89, 102, 115, 132, 134, 136, 141, 153, 155, 157, 159–60, 162, 186–91, 199–200, 219–23, 228, 242, 243, 248, 250–2, 254, 256, 262, 274–5, 281, 286, 313, 314–5, 331, 335, 339, 351, 372, 376
  agentive 232
  and argument-sharing 320–5, 341
  and nouniness 143–52
  and recursion 298, 302–7, 308, 310–2
  causative 282, 287–9
  complementless 250
  concord 210–8, 232, 277–8, 344–7, 351, 353
  denominal 286
  in compounds 291–2
  in idioms 290
  in Old English:
    preterite-present 234–5, 375
    strong 224–5, 375
  'light' 242

of direct perception 376
of saying 180–5, 189–91
notional basis for 1, 3, 7, 27, 35, 42, 48–9, 62, 152, 275
stative 115, 363
verb phrase 53, 296; see too VP
verb-initial 102
verb-second 102, 231, 330–4, 339–40
verbal noun 259
verbals 53, 65, 84, 95–6, 102, 153, 160, 187, 188, 199, 203, 214, 218, 261, 328, 333, 344–5, 375–6
voice 334, 338; see too passive
voiced 87–8, 100, 106, 112–3, 120–1, 157, 159, 271
voiceless 64, 87, 89, 92, 95–6, 101, 106, 111–2, 120, 123, 127, 157, 160, 268, 273
vowels 363
VP 50, 55, 58, 65, 249–50
  -less 247–8

weight in phonology 40, 56, 57, 59, 72, 82, 104–13, 138–9, 366
  and stød-basis 201
weight in syntax 57, 59
  constructional 59
wh-word 308, 314–5, 366
Winnebago 110, 122–31, 139; see too Dorsey's Law
word order 4, 13, 47, 101–3, 132, 197, 231, 276, 314, 316, 332, 368; see too linearization, sequencing, serialization
  'basic' 247

X-bar hypothesis 26–7, 29, 35, 42–4, 47–50, 66, 152, 361, 374

Yoruba 222
Yup'ik 217